TRANSLINGUAL PRACTICE

*Literature, National Culture, and Translated
Modernity—China, 1900-1937*

TRANSLINGUAL PRACTICE

Literature, National Culture, and Translated Modernity—China, 1900-1937

LYDIA H. LIU

STANFORD UNIVERSITY PRESS

Stanford, California

To my mother and the memory of my father
LIU GUANGLIAN *(1932–94)*

you are nothing but
a pictograph that's lost its sound.

—Bei Dao, "Panni zhe" (Rebel)

你僅僅是一個
失去聲音的象形文字

Acknowledgments

Major portions of Chapter 3 were published under the title "Translingual Practice: The Discourse of Individualism Between China and the West" by Duke University Press in *Positions* 1 (Spring 1993). A revised version of the second half of Chapter 7 appeared in Inderpal Grewal and Caren Kaplan, eds., *Scattered Hegemonies* (Minneapolis: Minnesota University Press, Copyright © 1994 by the Regents of the University of Minnesota) as well as in Angela Zito and Tani Barlow, eds., *Body, Subject, Power in China* (Chicago: University of Chicago Press, 1994). Somewhat altered versions of parts of Chapters 5 and 6 were published under the title "Narratives of Modern Selfhood" in Liu Kang and Xiaobing Tang, eds., *Politics, Ideology, and Literary Discourse in Modern China* (Durham, N.C.: Duke University Press, 1993).

A year of teaching relief and substantial research was made possible by a fellowship from the Townsend Center for the Humanities and a Career Development grant from the Chancellor's office at the University of California, Berkeley in 1991–92. I finished the final revisions on sabbatical leave in the spring semester of 1995 supplemented by a Humanities Research grant at Berkeley. Over the years, I also received faculty research grants from the Committee on Research and research assistantships from the Center for Chinese Studies that made a huge difference in the progress of my research and writing. I am grateful to all these sources for kindly supporting my work.

Most of my scholarly indebtedness is detailed in the Notes. I owe my intellectual development to many friends, teachers, and colleagues; without them this book could not have been written. The stimulating conversations I had with the Chinese writer and critic Li Tuo in the spring of 1992 when he lectured at Berkeley convinced me of the importance of focusing on this project and leaving my dissertation behind. To his relentless style of questioning and warm encouragement, I owe the initial conception of this book as well as its subsequent metamorphoses. Many thanks go to Patrick Hanan, Leo Ou-fan Lee, and Yi-tsi Mei Feuerwerker, whose guidance and generosity have sustained me through years of hard work since graduate school. I have learned a great deal from their criticisms and comments on this as well as on my earlier work, including my Ph.D. dissertation. I am grateful to Cyril Birch, Edward Gunn, Wen-hsin Yeh, Jon Kowallis, Ellen Widmer, Shu-mei Shih, and James Hevia for their stimulating written comments on the individual chapters. Scholarly suggestions were also provided by Frederic Wakeman, Samuel Cheung, Jeanne Tai, Tani Barlow, Inderpal Grewal, Eric Naiman, Meng Yue, and Chen Xiaomei. My colleagues in the Comparative Literature and English Departments Timothy Hampton, Leslie Kurk, Michael Lucey, and Celeste Langen gave me friendly support and careful criticisms of several draft chapters, for which I am very grateful. I also thank Milan Hejtmanek and Stephen West for kindly offering their knowledge and time to help format the camera-ready version of the Appendixes on a Chinese software. Andrew Jones, Qian Jun, Marcella Gregory, and Christopher Laughrun have contributed to this project as my research assistants, and they have my deep gratitude. Andrew's preparation of the Appendixes, Selected Bibliography, and Character List was imaginative and meticulous, more so than I had any right to expect. My friend Meng Yue, besides being supportive in numerous other ways, also gave me a hand in the tedious process of proofreading the Appendixes. The writing of this manuscript benefited from the graduate seminars I taught in the Departments of Comparative Literature and East Asian Languages at Berkeley between 1990 and 1994. To the graduate students who read and commented on parts of my work in those classes, I am more than thankful. I presented the results of this research to Leo Lee's Cultural Studies Colloquium at the Fairbank Center, Harvard University, in winter 1994 and was able to incorporate some of the criticisms in my final revisions. I thank the organizer and the participants of that seminar for providing me with this opportunity. John Ziemer of Stanford University Press is an exemplary editor who navigated me through the process of manuscript revision and preparation with great expertise and patience. His knowledgeable and meticulous editing, the reputation of which had first drawn me to this press, made the present book much more polished and readable than its earlier form. My deepest debt is to my parents, Liu Guanglian and Sun Chengxiu, who always believed in daughters and supported my work in diaspora. My father passed away before he could see the actual publication of this book. I dedicate this book to his memory with love and gratitude.

L.H.L.

Contents

Appendixes

Preface

Are languages incommensurate? If so, how do people establish and maintain *hypothetical equivalences* between words and their meanings? What does it mean to translate one culture into the language of another on the basis of commonly perceived equivalences? For instance, can we talk, or stop talking, about "modernity" across the East–West divide without subjecting the experience of the one to representations, translations, or interpretations by the other? Who fixes and polices the borders between the two? Are the borders easily crossed? Is it possible to have reliable comparative categories on universal or transhistorical grounds?

I propose the idea of "translingual practice" in this book to raise the possibility of rethinking cross-cultural interpretation and forms of linguistic mediation between East and West. Over the past two decades or so, there has been no lack of sophisticated discussions of postcoloniality, cultures, identities, self and other, and so on, but these discussions have reached the point where it becomes unthinkable to continue treating the concrete language issue in cross-cultural scholarship as a superfluity or merely part of a critique of the effects of colonialism and imperialism. I find the work of postcolonial theorists very stimulating and am indebted to the interesting new ways of thinking their scholarship has opened up. At the same time, my research in modern Chinese history and literature has led me to confront phenomena and problems that cannot easily be brought under the postcolonial paradigm of Western domination and native resistance. I am struck by the irony that, in the very act of criticizing Western domination, one often ends up reifying the power of the dominator to a degree that the agency of non-Western cultures is reduced to a single possibility: resistance.

Are there ways of reconceptualizing this problematic? Homi Bhabha's elaboration of hybridity in *The Location of Culture* tries to add corrective nuances to the postcolonial approach by eliminating the opposition of Self and Other. He draws attention to diasporic situations in which metropolitan European languages disseminate a hybridity of local dialects that return to caricature the presumed integrity of the language of the colonizer. Salman Rushdie's stammering S. S. Sisodia, whom Bhabha loves to quote, articulates this condition of postcolonial caricature very well: "The trouble with the Engenglish is that their hiss hiss history happened overseas, so they dodo don't know what it means" (Rushdie, p. 343). But we must not forget that there are vast areas in this world where metropolitan European languages are not spoken or have not succeeded in competing with native languages and acquiring the status of a national language or dialect. What does the experience of those people and those places tell us about history, agency, hegemony, modernity, and subjectivity?

This book provides me an opportunity to look into language practice as a site of manifested historical relationships where the meanings of Western domination and the anti-imperialist struggle may be reopened and interrogated in a new light. As someone who grew up speaking and writing Chinese in mainland China and did not adopt English as a foreign language until after the Cultural Revolution, I am fascinated by what has happened to the modern Chinese language, especially the written form, since its early exposure to English, modern Japanese, and other foreign languages. In this study, I intend to explore the wide-ranging Chinese contact/collision with European languages and literatures (often mediated through Japan), focusing special attention on the period from the turn of the century to the beginning of the Anti-Japanese War (1937), which encompasses the rise of modern Chinese literature and its early canonization. My emphasis on language and literature, however, does not presuppose a metaphysical divide between representation and reality. What I try to do here is to place language and literary practices at the heart of China's experience of the modern and of its much troubled relationship with the West. If modern Chinese literature stands out as an important event in this period, it is not so much because fiction, poetry, and other literary forms are transparent vehicles of self-expression that register the heartbeat of history in a mimetic fashion as because reading, writing, and other literary practices are perceived as potent agents in China's nation building and its imaginary/imaginative construction of "modern" men and women.

I took care to put the word "modernity" in quotation marks in the opening paragraph. My intention was to point to earlier quotations whose origins are lost in numerous repetitions, evocations, translations, and reproductions. Indeed, what do we mean when we say that the Chinese equivalent of "modernity" or "modern" is *xiandai xing* or *xiandai*? At which moment and in what context does that equivalence or translation become meaningful? From a poststructuralist point of view, performative/constative narratives such as repeated evocations of an idea through situated writing and speech are the materials that make up what intellectual historians perceive as the "continuity" of that idea. The act of translation, for example, cannot but participate in the performativity of a language that circumscribes and is circumscribed by the historical contingency of that act. Any attempt to historicize above and beyond the circumstances of such performative/constative acts of speech and writing (evocation, translation, citation in and out of context, and so on) is bound to lead to the reification of the idea, concept, or theory being analyzed and, consequently, to the impoverishment of our understanding of historical practice. My use or critique of "modernity," therefore, relies on a citational/translational approach that takes account of both the earlier evocations of that notion and my own present engagement with it; this remains true even when I eschew the use of quotation marks in this book. Briefly put, I bring up this much cited, translated, citable(?), and translatable(?) notion to talk about the *discursive construct of the Chinese modern.*

The central questions I ask myself in this regard are How do people imagine and talk about the Chinese *xiandai* condition? and its corollary: What happens when certain types of discourses are preferred and legitimized over and above others? I am less concerned, though, with the question of the nature of the local character of the Chinese modern. This last question cannot reasonably be approached or contested without substantial engagement with the discursive practice of twentieth-century Chinese intellectuals. Of course, I do not claim that this discussion of the discursive notion of the modern exhausts the kinds of questions that may be posed about Chinese modernity. In the context of this study, however, it helps me avoid playing into the old oppositional paradigm that predefines what is modern and what is traditional, which persists in many contemporary historical writings on East–West relations.

The binary of East and West has been much contested and rightly so. But is it enough to dismiss the binary on the grounds of fictitious invention or construction? My own view is that a more effective way of deconstructing the East–West binary would be to pinpoint, whenever possible, those historical moments in which the usage of this idea becomes contextually meaningful and acquires legitimacy in a given language. If I continue to evoke East and West in this study, it is because I wish to call attention to their translated performance in modern Chinese as *dongfang* and *xifang*. This manner of engagement with modern translations puts me in a position to question the *self-evidence of the commonsense world* (in Pierre Bourdieu's words) in which twentieth-century Chinese writers *name* their difference from whatever contingent identities they perceive as existing before their own time or being imposed from the outside. In other words, I am concerned with the rhetorical strategies, translations, discursive formations, naming practices, legitimizing processes, tropes, and narrative modes that bear upon the historical conditions of the Chinese experience of the modern since the latter half of the nineteenth century.

It should be clear by now that this book is not about translation in the ordinary sense of the word, much less the so-called sinification of foreign terms and discourses. To talk comfortably about sinification, one would have to assume a good deal about China's confidence in the absolute centrality of its own civilization vis-à-vis the rest of the world, whereas that confidence was almost completely shattered by the presence of the West in the period I examine, so much so that China could no longer maintain a separate identity for itself without making explicit or implicit references to the rest of the world, which is often represented by the West. Nor am I particularly concerned with neutral-sounding, universalizing projects such as the domestication of foreign words in any language contexts—a frequent concern of historical linguistics. The true object of my theoretical interest is the *legitimation of the "modern" and the "West"* in Chinese literary discourse as well as the *ambivalence of Chinese agency* in these mediated processes of legitimation. Hence, much of the introductory chapter is devoted to rethinking, critically, the condition of contemporary theoretical discourses about East and West, language and power, history and change. Needless to say, I rely on the idea of translingual practice to tackle afresh some of the major methodological concerns in comparative literature, historical scholarship, and cultural studies.

Chapters 2 through 9 are subsumed under three broad headings, each of which centers on a distinct aspect of translated modernity from the perspective of translingual practice. Part I is an attempt to explore the discursive terrain as mapped out by the dominant concerns of "nation" and "individual" in modern Chinese literary discourse. I devote my attention to two outstanding discourses in that regard: the theory of *guomin xing* (national character) and *geren zhuyi* (individualism); each is a neologistic loanword translation of an earlier Japanese translation of a European concept and theory. I argue that it is within and against the boundaries of these translated theories and discourses that May Fourth writers stake some of their central claims to modernity.

Lest my work be misunderstood as a keyword study in the manner of Raymond Williams, I emphasize that my concerns lie beyond establishing the changing meanings of words, concepts, and discourses that are thought to bear witness to larger historical processes. Given my focus on the legitimation of the modern in Chinese literary practice, it is inevitable that I should also consider the issue of translingual modes of representation. My reading of Lu Xun's "The True Story of Ah Q," for example, seeks to understand the story's appropriation of the discourse of national character in terms of a mediated construction of narratorial subjectivity. This approach is further emphasized in Part II as I raise the question of how the experience of the Chinese modern is worked out in such concrete figures of literary representation as narrative modes, novelistic realism, stylistic innovations, the deixis of writing in the first person, gendered tropes of modernity, representations of the inner world, and transpositions of psychoanalytical symbolism. Although many of these features were unmistakably new to Chinese literature and often came with self-proclaimed affinities with European languages and literatures, there were many others that cannot be safely traced to the effects of foreign influence. For instance, what are some of the surplus meanings that cannot be accounted for by the notion of influence? A seemingly plausible interpretation offered by some scholars is that these are traditional sensibilities transformed into modern forms of expression. An immediate difficulty is, however, in deciding where to draw the line between the traditional and the modern.

In my analysis of these mediated forms of representation between Chinese and foreign literatures, I have resisted the temptation of explaining *change* in terms of either foreign impact or indigenous evolution, the choice of which would bring the issue to a premature closure when one ought to be opening it up to further inquiry. The notion of *translated modernity* is useful because it allows me to identify and interpret those contingent moments and processes that are reducible neither to foreign impact nor to the self-explanatory logic of the indigenous tradition. Readers will notice that my choice and reading of concrete literary texts are prompted by this central problematic of cross-cultural interpretation rather than by the coherence of the modern Chinese literary canon itself.

Indeed, the canon itself needs to be called into question. Part III, "Nation Building and Culture Building," continues to ponder the meaning of agency, mediation, and translated knowledge, but it does so by taking up the question of legitimation in the areas of canon making, literary criticism, and other culture-building projects. Specifically, I interrogate the function of modern literary criticism in the Republican period and look into the circumstances of canon making, such as the compilation of the authoritative *Compendium of Modern Chinese Literature* in 1935–36. I am particularly interested in the ways in which modern Chinese culture *interprets its own moment and mode of unfolding* and the ways in which literary projects lend themselves to the diverse political aspirations of individual writers and critics who see themselves engaged, nonetheless, in collectively working out the very contradiction of their existence. That is, what it means to be *Zhongguo ren* (men and women of the Middle Kingdom) in terms of what is not of the Middle Kingdom. This contradiction endorses as well as undermines their unprecedented move of positing Chinese literature and culture as one among many national literatures and cultures in the world. I conclude this book by rethinking the debates on national essence as a culture-building discourse. The changing dynamics of this discourse between the late Qing and the Republican periods brings out the full range of competing narratives and counter-discourses that will inevitably complicate our understanding of the meaning of national culture and translated modernity in China.

TRANSLINGUAL PRACTICE

*Literature, National Culture, and Translated
Modernity—China, 1900-1937*

CHAPTER I

Introduction:
The Problem of Language in
Cross-Cultural Studies

Strictly speaking, comparative scholarship that aims to *cross* cultures can do nothing but translate. As a trope of epistemological crossing, translation always says one thing in terms of another, although it must pretend to speak the truth for the sake of fidelity (or sanity, to be more exact). But leaving aside the marital trope of fidelity and the logocentric notion of truth—concepts that readily lend themselves to deconstructionist criticism—what else do we know or can we say about translation and its implications for cross-cultural understanding? And indeed, what does it mean for a contemporary scholar to cross the "language barrier" between two or more cultures and linguistic communities?

Admittedly, much more is involved here than what is commonly known as an interlingual transaction between a source language and a target language.[1] Even before I take up the subject of this book, I find myself facing larger problems, such as certain entrenched ways of thinking about cultural difference in the Western academy. For example, disciplinary boundaries and familiar modes of intellectual inquiry often generate difficult interpretive problems regarding cultures and languages other than one's own.[2] In whose terms, for which linguistic constituency, and in the name of what kinds of knowledge or intellectual authority does one perform acts of translation between cultures? The question becomes doubly acute when one crosses from the West to the East, or vice versa. Of course, the difficulty is compounded when the object of the inquiry itself, such as modern Chinese literature, does not constitute a pristine territory of native knowledge "uncontaminated" by earlier historical forces that have coerced and conditioned similar crossings in the recent past, namely, the translation of the West and the invention of the modern Chinese language. Although I do not presume to have an answer to these questions, I will venture these multilayered crossings in this book, an undertaking fated to describe as well as to enact the predicament of its subject.[3]

Perhaps, I would do better by reframing my problematic in a slightly different context. Let me evoke briefly a running debate among anthropologists on the notion of cultural translation, a debate I believe has important ramifications for literary studies, history, and other disciplines in the humanities. For many years, British social anthropologists have used the concept of cultural translation at its various stages of theoretical elaboration to develop a notion of interpretation that, ideally, will account for the difference between their own culture and the non-European societies they study. Edmund Leach, for example, describes the typical ethnographic moment as follows:

> Let me recapitulate. We started by emphasizing how different are "the others" —and made them not only different but remote and inferior. Sentimentally, we then took the opposite track and argued that all human beings are alike; we can understand Trobrianders or the Barotse because their motivations are just the same as our own; but that didn't work either, "the others" remained obstinately other. But now we have come to see that the essential problem is one of translation. The linguists have shown us that all translation is difficult, and that perfect translation is usually impossible. And yet we know that for *practical purposes* a tolerably satisfactory translation is always possible even when the original "text" is highly abstruse. Languages are different but not so different as all that. Looked at in this way social anthropologists are engaged in establishing a methodology for the translation of cultural language. (Italics added)[4]

One would like to have as much faith in the power of cultural translation as Leach, but the phrase "practical purposes" lets the cat out of the bag. To me, the crucial thing here is not whether translation between cultures is possible (people do it anyway), or whether the "other" is knowable, or even whether an abstruse "text" is decipherable, but what practical purpose or needs (which sustain one's methodological paraphernalia) bring an ethnographer to pursue cultural translation. This is precisely the point at which the question I raised earlier should intervene: In whose terms, for which linguistic constituency, and in the name of what kinds of knowledge or intellectual authority does an ethnographer perform acts of translation between cultures?

In a pointed criticism of the British ethnographic tradition, Talal Asad sites the concept of cultural translation in power relations and urges us to

consider the problematic of cross-cultural interpretation with close attention to the actual historical environment in which both the ethnographer
and his native informant live, yet do not speak the same language:

> To put it crudely, because the languages of the Third World societies—in-
> cluding, of course, the societies that social anthropologists have traditionally
> studied—are "weaker" in relation to Western languages (and today, espe-
> cially to English), they are more likely to submit to forcible transformation
> in the translation process than the other way around. The reason for this is,
> first, that in their political-economic relations with Third World countries,
> Western nations have the greater ability to manipulate the latter. And, sec-
> ond, Western languages produce and deploy *desired* knowledge more readily
> than Third World languages do.[5]

Asad's critique of the notion of cultural translation has major implications for comparative scholarship and for cross-cultural studies such as
this one.[6] It warns us that the business of translating a culture into another
language has little, if anything, to do with individual free choice or linguistic competence. If we have learned anything useful from Foucault, it
should be clear that we must confront forms of institutional practices and
the knowledge/power relationships that authorize certain ways of knowing while discouraging others. One familiar way of producing knowledge
about other people and other cultures is to construct the terms of comparison on the ground of perceived linguistic equivalence. Yet that ground
of equivalence itself often goes unexamined.

Tropes of Equivalence, East and West

> The dictionary is based on the hypothesis—obviously an
> unproven one—that languages are made up of equivalent
> synonyms.
>
> —Jorge Luis Borges

The idea that languages are commensurate and equivalents exist naturally between them is, of course, a common illusion that philosophers,
linguists, and theorists of translation have tried in vain to dispel. Nietzsche, for example, attacked the illusion by showing that the equating of
the unequal is simply a metaphorical function of language that lays claim
to truth. "What therefore is truth? A mobile army of metaphors, met-
onymies, anthropomorphisms: in short a sum of human relations which
became poetically and rhetorically intensified, metamorphosed, adorned,
and after long usage seem to a nation fixed, canonic and binding; truths

are illusions of which one has forgotten that they *are* illusions."[7] Gayatri Spivak explicates that Nietzsche's definition of metaphor points to the construction of an identity between dissimilar things, as the original phrase used in his essay is *Gleich machen* (make equal), "calling to mind the German word 'Gleichnis'—image, simile, similitude, comparison, allegory, parable—an unmistakable pointer to figurative practice in general."[8] Ironically, the philosopher himself has not been able to escape the fate of being translated and turned into another kind of illusion through the metaphorical equation of German and other languages. The thriving industry of bilingual dictionaries depends on the tenacity of this illusion— its will to power. It is the business of this industry to make sure that one understand "that languages are made up of equivalent synonyms."[9] The implication for cross-cultural comparison is that one relies on a conceptual model derived from the bilingual dictionary—that is, a word in language A must equal a word or a phrase in language B; otherwise one of the languages is lacking—to form opinions about other peoples or to lay philosophical grounds for discourses about other cultures and, conversely, about one's own totalized identity.

Let me illustrate the problem by reflecting on a famous passage from Heidegger's "Aus einen Gespräch von der Sprache" (Dialogue on language) between a European philosopher (Heidegger) and a Japanese interlocutor (Tezuka). The following excerpt is taken from the latter half of their dialogue (J refers to the Japanese and F [I in English] to the Fragenden or Inquirer):

J: Da Sie mir, oder besser den vermutenden Andeutungen, die ich vorbringe, zuhören, erwacht in mir ein Zutrauen, mein Zögern zu lassen, das mich bislang davor zurückhielt, Ihnen auf Ihre Frage zu antworten.

F: Sie meinen die Frage, welches Wort Ihre Sprache spricht für das, was wir Europäer "Sprache" nennen.

J: Dieses Wort scheute ich mich bis zu diesem Augenblick zu sagen, weil ich eine Übersetzung geben muß, durch die sich unser Wort für Sprache wie eine bloße Bilderschrift ausnimmt, nämlich im Vorstellungsbezirk von Begriffen; denn nur durch sie sucht die europäische Wissenschaft und ihre Philosophie das Wesen der Sprache zu fassen.

F: Wie heißt das japanische Wort für "Sprache"?

J: (nach weiterem Zögern) Es heißt "*Koto ba*".

F: Und was sagt dies?

J: *ba* nennt die Blätter, auch und zumal die Blütenblätter. Denken Sie an die Kirschblüte und an die Pflaumenblüte.

F: Und was sagt *Koto*?

J: Diese Frage is am schwersten zu beantworten. Indessen wird ein Versuch dadurch erleichtert, daß wir das *Iki* zu erläutern wagten: das reine Entzücken der rufenden Stille. Das Wehen der Stille, die dies rufende Entzücken ereignet, ist das Waltende, das jenes Entzücken kommen läßt. *Koto* nennt aber immer zugleich das jeweils Entzückende selbst, das einzig je im unwiederholbaren Augenblick mit der Fülle seines Anmutens zum Scheinen kommt.

F: *Koto* wäre dann das Ereignis der lichtenden Botschaft der Anmut.

J: Herrlich gesagt; nur führt das Wort "Anmut" das heutige Vorstellen zu leicht in die Irre. . . .

J: The fact that you give ear to me, or better, to the probing intimations I propose, awakens in me the confidence to drop my hesitations which have so far kept me from answering your question.

I: You mean the question which word in your language speaks for what we Europeans call "language."

J: Up to this moment I have shied away from that word, because I must give a translation which makes our word for language look like a mere pictograph, to wit, something that belongs within the precincts of conceptual ideas; for European science and its philosophy try to grasp the nature of language only by way of concepts.

I: What is the Japanese word for "language"?

J: (*after further hesitation*) It is "*Koto ba*."

I: And what does that say?

J: *ba* means leaves, including and especially the leaves of a blossom—petals. Think of cherry blossoms or plum blossoms.

I: And what does *Koto* say?

J: This is the question most difficult to answer. But it is easier now to attempt an answer because we have ventured to explain *Iki*: the pure delight of the beckoning stillness. The breath of stillness that makes this beckoning delight come into its own is the reign under which that delight is made to come. But *Koto* always also names that which in the event gives delight, itself, that which uniquely in each unrepeatable moment comes to radiance in the fullness of its grace.

I: *Koto*, then, would be the appropriating occurrence of the lightening message of grace.

J: Beautifully said! Only the word "grace" easily misleads the modern mind. . . .[10]

This exchange is illuminating in a number of ways. First, it enacts in a single dramatic performance the impossibility and yet the necessity of translation between East and West. The European Inquirer, who is undoubtedly aware of the pitfalls of translation, nonetheless insists on having a Japanese equivalent of the European concept of language. Second, before the Japanese interlocutor is compelled to answer the Inquirer's question "What is the Japanese word for 'language' "—the type of syntax that makes the nonexistence of an equivalent unthinkable without its being interpreted as a "lack"—he explains his reasons for hesitation (this hesitation, reintroduced by the parenthesized italics a few lines later, effectively disrupts the flow of the conversation). The fear that his translation would make the Japanese "equivalent" for language look like a mere pictograph is not entirely groundless because his subsequent description of *koto ba* probably succeeds in doing just that in German. Third, the Inquirer's summary of the meaning of *koto* after the lengthy description given by his interlocutor points to something other than the translation of a Japanese word. As an appropriating gesture, it leads to Heidegger's own theory of Saying or *Sage*, which the Inquirer describes a moment later: "Denn es müßte sich etwas ereignen, wodurch sich dem Botengang jene Weite öffnete und *zu*leuchtete, in der das Wesen der Sage zum Scheinen kommt" (For something would have to come about by which that vast distance in which the nature of Saying assumes its radiance, opened itself to the messenger's course and shone upon it).[11] The words "die Sage," "der Botengang," and "*zu*leuchten" seem to echo his free translation of the Japanese *koto ba*, namely, "das *Ereignis* der *lichtenden Botschaft* der Anmut" (the appropriating occurrence of the lightening message of grace; italics added), but they speak more pertinently to some of the central tropes the philosopher uses in his own meditations on *Ereignis* (appropriation), *Eigenen* (owning), *Lichtung* (clearing), and so on.[12] In a remarkable moment of *mise en abyme*, Heidegger's language acts out the appropriation that it speaks about, by illustrating the predicament of translation in the very act of translation.

"A Dialogue on Language" was a central component of Heidegger's discourse on language in his later career when the philosopher developed his important notion of language as the "House of Being." It is worth speculating, though, what the conversation would have become if the philosopher had learned Japanese and conducted and transcribed this dialogue in that language. Most likely, the questions would not have been raised or would have had to be formulated differently. This dialogue highlights a number of problematic areas in the so-called exchange between East and West in modern history, not the least of which is the language of theory that expresses or implies a universal concern but in fact bears witness to its own limitations as a European language. To me, it seems sheer folly to wield an analytical concept or category indifferently anywhere as if that which makes sense in one place must necessarily obtain elsewhere.

The implications of such language interaction between East and West are manifold. At a certain point, the crossing of language boundaries stops being a linguistic issue, for words are easily translated into analytical (often universal) categories in the hands of scholars who need conceptual models for cross-cultural studies. This happens almost daily in the scholarly realm of "pseudo-universals" criticized by Eugene Eoyang in a recent study. The subtle or not so subtle bias that informs certain comparative questions—Why is there no epic in Chinese? Is there a civil society in China? etc.—often says more about the inquirer than the object of inquiry. As Eoyang puts it well, "The obverse questions are rarely, if ever, asked. Why are there no dynastic histories in the West? Why has the West produced no counterpart to *Shijing*? Are there equivalents to the *lüshi* and *zaju* forms in the West? If these challenges to lacunae in the West strike one as slightly absurd, then we must consider the possibility that the original questions might be equally pointless."[13] Eoyang attributes the problem of pseudo-universals to the fundamental confusion of premise and methodology in comparative scholarship. But are there even more firmly entrenched beliefs in what a language can or cannot do that compel such confusion? We must face the question of translation that Heidegger's dialogue raises. Are analytical categories translated less frequently into the other language than they are used in one's own? What happens in such instances of translation? What is gained or lost? Perhaps, the crux of the matter is not so much that analytical categories cannot be applied across the board because they fail to have universal relevance—the impulse to translate is in fact unstoppable—but that the crossing of analytical categories over language boundaries, like any other crossing or transgression, is bound to entail confrontations charged with contentious claims to power. To be sure, universality is neither true nor false, but any intellectual claim to it should be rigorously examined in the light of its own linguistic specificity and sources of authority.

Consider some of the words frequently used and abused in this capacity across the disciplines of the humanities and social sciences: "the self," "person," and "individual." What is the Chinese, Japanese, or Arabic equivalent(s) of the word "self"? This troublesome question rests on the assumption that equivalence of meaning can readily be established between different languages. Does not the existence of bilingual dictionaries attest to this fact? I hear people ask—Isn't it true that the category of the "self" has existed all along in the Chinese philosophical tradition? What about the Confucian notion of *ji*, etc.? I find the questions themselves rather dubious because they overlook the fact that the "trope of equivalence" between the English word "self" and the Chinese *ji*, *wo*, *ziwo* and other words has been established only recently in the process of translation and fixed by means of modern bilingual dictionaries.[14] Thus any linkages that exist derive from historical coincidences whose meanings are contingent on the politics of translingual practice. Once such linkages are established, a text becomes "translatable" in the ordinary sense of the word. The point I want to stress here, and it cannot be stressed enough, is that serious methodological problems arise when a cross-cultural comparative theory is built upon the basis of an essential category, such as "self" or "individual," whose linguistic identity transcends the history of translation and imposes its own discursive priority on a different culture.[15] The assumed homogeneity between *ji*, *wo*, or *ziwo* and "self" inevitably blots out the history of each word and the history of translation of "self" in modern Chinese, inasmuch as difference cannot be conceived at the ontological level without first presenting itself at the constitutive level where the question of linguistic transaction must be brought in.[16] In a recent commentary on Leibniz's "Letter on the Natural Theology of the Chinese," Haun Saussy points out that mutual translatability between two languages can be assured "only after the little word 'is' has been stripped of its meaning. Once the thing has been taken out of being, there is not much left for ontologists to disagree about."[17]

In the past decade or so, philosophers, anthropologists, and sociologists have discussed whether the notions of the self, person, and individual, however defined and however unstable, should continue to be used as analytical categories in the face of poststructuralist critiques. Charles Taylor, for example, has devoted several studies to the problems of self, identity, and language in Western philosophy, and his notions of agency, human significance, and public space of disclosure have attracted much attention in the West lately.[18] His *Sources of the Self*, in particular, attempts to challenge the deconstructive critique of the Western notions of subjectivity by seeking a multilayered historical understanding of the self in the West. Taylor's approach to the genesis of modern identity and his broad vision and integrative thinking have been eagerly embraced by scholars across a wide array of fields and disciplines. But, what seems to be a promising sign of intervention into deconstruction at one level turns out to reaffirm Judaeo-Christian values at another. This comes out strongly in Taylor's ethical thinking, when he allows the Judaeo-Christian tradition to lay exclusive claim to the ideals of the good. Although the author never loses sight of the historical meanings of these ideals per se, he tends to de-emphasize certain levels of historical practice being associated with or performed in the name of these ideals.[19] One senses a strongly evangelical move as the book closes with a moralistic telos: the hope of man's moral redemption, we are told, resides "in Judaeo-Christian theism (however terrible the record of its adherents in history), and in its central promise of a divine affirmation of the human, more total than humans can ever attain unaided" (p. 521). If the violence of history can be thus contained and suppressed by parentheses, one wonders if the very ground for critical thinking does not drop from sight altogether.[20]

Why should the self be an analytical category in the first place? "It is quite possible to be human, to think in a human manner without any particular 'notions' of the person." British scholar Steven Collins's critique of the philosophical category of the self opens a new horizon for the possibility of grounding the notion of the person and self in the practice of modern academic disciplines. In a re-evaluation of the Année sociologique school, he points out that although Durkheim and Marcel Mauss, who emphasize an empirical or sociological approach, speak of categories developing and changing, both rely on Kantian philosophical categories to begin with. Thus, even as empirical science compels Mauss to formulate a non-essentialist notion of the person, he nonetheless allows the *sense* of the self to stand as an overriding, philosophical category. "If the category is necessary and universal, and so in a sense a priori," Collins observes, "then in just this sense it cannot have a history."[21]

This concern is shared by a number of other British and French anthropologists who participate in rethinking the legacy of the Année sociologique school, especially the impact of Mauss's famous 1938 essay, "A Category of the Human Mind: The Notion of the Person; the Notion of Self."[22] These scholars criticize Mauss's Eurocentrism and problematic use of philosophical categories for their universalist pretensions and try to grapple with the double bind of what Martin Hollis calls "the historical and analytic category" of the person in their own scholarship.[23] In doing so, they effectively highlight the historical conditions under which the self, person, and individual have come to be established and naturalized as analytical categories in the Western academy.

For many reasons, this kind of self-reflexive critique has done little to change the disciplinary practice of mainstream scholarship; people continue to rely on the categories of the self, person, and individual to access knowledge about the "authentic" identity of another culture as opposed to their own totalized self-perception. The knowledge obtained this way cannot but be tautological: either non-Western cultures are deficient in concepts of the self, person, and individual; or their concepts essentially differ from their Western counterparts. My question is whether the precondition for this kind of knowledge exists before the categories themselves are applied. Or does it really matter? The reason I wish to draw attention to this situation is not because I think cultural relativism is more desirable than transdiscursive approaches—no one wishes to trivialize the issue on that ground—but because the situation relates to the conditioning of knowledge that predicates any attempted crossings between languages and cultures. This condition must itself be explained rather than assumed; hence the question: What induces scholars in the West to look for a singular cultural conception of the self in other cultures? Besides the inevitable exercise of power through specialized knowledge, I believe the phenomenon also has something to do with certain time-honored assumptions about translation and difference in the Western philosophical discourse on language.

Translating Difference—An Oxymoron?

> We are digging the pit of Babel.
>
> —Kafka

Tradutore, traditore. This Italian aphorism has long been a cliché in English: "The translator is a betrayer." However, as soon as one starts to take the English translation too literally, one stumbles into the epistemological trap of paying homage to the translator(s) of the aphorism who necessarily betrays the original. Apropos of this classic example of the difficulty of translation, Roman Jakobson remarked in his essay "On Linguistic Aspects of Translation" that the English translation of the Italian aphorism "would deprive the Italian rhyming epigram of all its paronomastic value. Hence a cognitive attitude would compel us to change this aphorism into a more explicit statement and to answer the questions: translator of what messages? betrayer of what values?"[24] Here Jakobson was exclusively concerned with the untranslatability of poetry where phonemic similarity and differentiation participate in semantic relationships and therefore contribute to the making of overall textual meanings. As a structural linguist who contributed much to the study of poetics, Jakobson pointed out that the aphorism *tradutore, traditore* makes sense in Italian primarily because the two words are confronted and juxtaposed in a contiguous relation within the phonemic code of that language, which cannot be reproduced in English. Consequently, the loss of the paronomastic or poetic aspect of signification in the English translation gives a prosaic turn to the aphorism, converting it into a flat indicative statement that makes a truth claim: the translator is a betrayer.

The question I want to raise in conjunction with Jakobson's example, however, is not about the metaphor of betrayal or fidelity, for this is something that Derrida and others have effectively deconstructed in their critique of the notion of originary and teleologic presence in the logocentric tradition of Western metaphysics.[25] Nor am I particularly interested in the untranslatability of the phonemic code or the paronomastic aspect of a verbal code into which Jakobson and other comparative linguists have offered much insight.[26] To my mind, Jakobson's example evokes a central problematic in theories of translation that has for centuries preoccupied translators, linguists, and philosophers of language in the West. My concern with that problematic can be summarized as follows: apart from technical linguistic reasons, what theoretical assumptions about *difference* between languages prompt theorists to raise the issue of translatability and untranslatability over and over again?

The tower of Babel is often invoked by theorists of translation to symbolize the chaos of human communication. As if prefiguring the long history of Bible translation, the Babel story itself (Gen 11:6) derives in part from earlier Sumerian legend and made its way into the Hebrew Bible through adaptation and translation.[27] Babel not only figures the impossibility of translating among the irreducible multiplicity of tongues but institutes a desire for completion and for the original Logos. As George Steiner has pointed out, theologians and metaphysicians of language who strive to attenuate this second banishment from the universal grammar of Adam generally believe that "a single primal language, an *Ur-Sprache*, lies behind our present discord, behind the abrupt warring tongues which followed on the collapse of Nimrod's ziggurat."[28] However, the faith in the original Word does not help resolve the contradiction of a common language when it comes to translating the Bible into vernacular tongues. The history of Bible translation and the politics of Christianity are fraught with ambivalent practices. As Willis Barnstone puts it, "On the one hand, there is the sacred view that holds to the process of entropy, the idea that any passage between languages implies waste, corruption, and fundamental loss. On the other, there is the constant didactic and messianic need to spread the word of God to potential converts, for which Bible translation is an indispensable tool."[29]

Steiner perceives a decisive link between this earlier kabbalistic understanding of translation and modern, rational theory of language or linguistic study, in that the latter continues to debate the question whether translation is possible. In his erudite book *After Babel*, he divides the history of translation theory in the West into four periods. The first period, characterized by an immediate empirical focus, extends from Cicero's *Libellus de optimo genere oratorum* of 46 B.C. and Horace's reiteration of this formula in the *Ars poetica* some twenty years later all the way to Hölderlin's commentary on his own translations of Sophocles in 1804. The second stage is one of theory and hermeneutic inquiry initiated by Friedrich Schleiermacher's decisive essay *Über die verschiedenen Methoden des Übersetzens* (1813) and taken up by A. W. Schlegel, Humboldt, Goethe, Schopenhauer, Ezra Pound, Walter Benjamin, and others. After this age of philosophic-poetic theory, Russian and Czech scholars, heirs to the Formalist movement, introduced the third period of translation theory by applying structural linguistics and information theory to the discussion of interlingual exchange. Andrei Fedorov's *Introduction to the Theory of Translation* (*Vvedenie v teoriiu perevoda*; Moscow, 1953) is representative of this collaborative scientific effort. Somewhat overlapping with the scientific stage—a necessary contradiction in Steiner's attempt to periodize—the fourth period begins in the early 1960's when the rediscovery of Walter Benjamin's paper "Die Aufgabe des Übersetzers" (The task of the translator), originally published in 1923, together with the influence of Heidegger and Hans-Georg Gadamer, caused a reversion to hermeneutic inquiries into translation and interpretation.[30] Although Steiner's periodization may well be disputed, his critical survey provides remarkable insights into some of the major concerns with the theories of translation examined by his book.[31] For instance, he argues that

> all theories of translation—formal, pragmatic, chronological—are only variants of a single, inescapable question. In what ways can or ought fidelity to be achieved? What is the optimal correlation between the A text in the source-language and the B text in the receptor-language? The issue has been debated for over two thousand years. But is there anything of substance to add to Saint Jerome's statement of the alternatives: *verbum e verbo*, word by word in the case of the mysteries, but meaning by meaning, *sed sensum exprimere de sensus*, everywhere else?   (pp. 261–62)

Steiner's observation runs the risk of oversimplifying the situation of translation theory, but it is a risk worth taking because it raises issues that more than compensate for its reductive approach. Focusing on the ways in which the perennial question of translatability has been asked in translation theories, Steiner offers a historical critique of the metaphysical foundation of Western philosophical tradition and, in particular, its universalist notion of language. His criticism brings a widely held assumption into question, namely, that the underlying structure of language is universal and common to all men. Dissimilarities between human tongues are essentially of the surface. Translation is realizable precisely because those deep-seated universals, genetic, historical, social, from which all grammars derive can be located and recognized as operative in every human idiom, however singular or bizarre its superficial forms. To translate is to descend beneath the exterior disparities of two languages in order to bring into vital play their analogous and, at the final depths, common principles of being. (p. 73)

Is Steiner overstating his case? Readers might object that Sapir and Whorf's cultural relativism can hardly fit into this totalizing picture; in fact, Sapir and Whorf were bent on undermining a universalist understanding of language and reality. According to their familiar theses, no two languages are sufficiently similar to be considered as representing the same social reality, and different societies live in distinct, linguistically determined worlds, not the same world that happens to have different labels attached to it. This metalinguistics of "thought worlds" or cultural relativism, which aspires to a universal condition in its own way, has come under attack on various intellectual fronts, empirical and philosophical, from ethnographers and linguists. What interests me here is not the validity of the Sapir-Whorf hypothesis about the linguistic worldview of a given community, but an undisputed area of intellectual thinking inhabited by both universalists and cultural relativists, one that predicates a mode of knowledge on translation while ostensibly contesting the possibility of translation. This contradiction simply brings in the old question of translatability and untranslatability through the back door, as the following passage from Whorf illustrates very well:

> In translating into English, the Hopi will say that these entities in process of causation "will come" or that they—the Hopi—"will come to" them, but in their own language, there are no verbs corresponding to our "come" and "go" that mean simple and abstract motion, our purely kinematic concept. The words in this case translated "come" refer to the process of eventuating without calling it motion—they are "eventuates to here" (*pew'i*) or "eventuates from it" (*angqö*) or "arrived" (*pitu*, pl. *öki*) which refers only to the terminal manifestation, the actual arrival at a given point, not to any motion preceding it.[32]

By performing a literal translation between English and Hopi on the spot, the author inadvertently undermines his own theory of well-defined boundaries of ethno-linguistic communities. One might want to ask, following Steiner, "if languages were monads with essentially discordant mappings of reality, how then could we communicate interlingually?

How could we acquire a second tongue or traverse into another language-world by means of translation?"[33] To push these questions further in the direction of a politics of interlingual transaction, it seems that the very theoretical language that helped Whorf arrive at his conclusion that Hopi could not be understood except on its own terms somehow also entitled him to a free translation of this "exotic" language to an English-speaking audience.

Perhaps, it would be useful to turn to Walter Benjamin's essay "The Task of the Translator" at this point, for not only is Benjamin self-reflexive about his role as a practicing translator but his formulation of cross-linguistic communication follows a new mode of inquiry that promises to take us outside the familiar terrain of universalism and cultural relativism. The essay in question, which prefaces Benjamin's translation of Baudelaire's *Tableaux parisiens*, is an attempt to rethink the question of translatability beyond the problematic of the original and translated text. "The question of whether a work is translatable has a dual meaning," said Benjamin, "Either: Will an adequate translator ever be found among the totality of its readers? Or, more pertinently: Does its nature lend itself to translation and, therefore, in view of the significance of the mode, call for it?"[34] He dismissed the factor of readers' reception or the "ideal" receiver as a useful approach to the theoretical issues under question. In his view, the original in the source language and its translation in the receptor language must yield to a third concept, *die reine Sprache*, or pure language, which "no longer means or expresses anything but is, as expressionless and creative Word, that which is meant in all languages."[35] This conceptualization may be said to anticipate French deconstructive theory in its displacement of the notions of fidelity, originality, presence, and authenticity, which explains Benjamin's popularity among poststructuralists in our own time.[36] But there are tensions in his thought that seem to point away from deconstructionist concerns toward something else. For instance, Benjamin stated that the telos of translation is the possibility of God's messianic return.[37] The messianic troping Benjamin used throughout his essay must be taken seriously because it suggests important linkages between his thinking and the earlier theoretical/theological concerns that Steiner describes. What is pure language? It binds both the original and translation to Holy Writ and belongs to the realm of God's remembrance where the original and translation co-exist in a complementary relationship (Derrida later picks up the idea of complementarity). It is in this sense that "the translatability of linguistic creations ought to be considered even if men should prove unable to translate them."[38]

Not surprisingly, Bible translation serves as "the prototype or the ideal of all translation."[39] In his desire to rid translation of its indebtedness to the original text, Benjamin reveals, wittingly or not, his own profound indebtedness to the story of Babel.

But can the Babel story not be questioned on its own ground? Has the story itself not been translated into and read in numerous tongues and, therefore, always already contradicted the myth of the origin? Derrida raises this question in his essay "Des Tours de Babel." Through a "complementary" re-reading of Maurice de Gandillac's French translation of Benjamin, he offers a deconstructionist approach to the problematic of translation theory. He reminds us that the irony surrounding the story of Babel is that "one pays little attention to this fact: it is in translation that we most often read this narrative" and yet one continues to reiterate the impossibility of translation.[40] Here we have come full circle from the double bind of Jakobson's example of *tradutore, traditore*, with the vital exception that the structural linguist's concern with the original and its untranslatability is now replaced by a fundamental questioning of the metaphysical status of the original and originary text.

Benjamin's notion of complementarity thus acquires a fresh importance in Derrida's reconsideration of the concepts of origin, intention, and the relations between the languages involved in translation processes. That is to say, translation is no longer a matter of transferring meaning between languages "within the horizon of an absolutely pure, transparent, and unequivocal translatability."[41] The original and translation complement each other to produce meanings larger than mere copies or reproduction: "These languages relate to one another in translation according to an unheard-of-mode. They complete each other, says Benjamin; but no other completeness in the world can represent this one, or that symbolic complementarity."[42] In this sense, the question of translatability/untranslatability that earlier theorists and structural linguists have raised becomes a moot point. The irreducible multiplicity of languages cannot be reduced to anything other than itself, and yet, like proper names, these languages are bound to call for interpretation, translation, and complementarity. Babel and God are examples of such names that simultaneously command and forbid one to translate.

Derrida's reading of Benjamin leads to a radical rethinking of the problematic of translation theory in the manner of what Steiner would call the mode of philosophic-poetic inquiry in the contemporary West. Here translation becomes an oxymoron: inasmuch as nothing can be reduced to anything else and translation cannot but say one thing in terms of another, the epistemic violence is committed out of necessity—a condition that circumscribes cognitive understanding itself and must, therefore, be grasped in its proper context. Through Benjamin, Derrida is able to contribute new insights to an old problematic in his powerful critique of Western metaphysics. But precisely because his attention is fixed on Western metaphysics, his critique cannot break away from the hold of the object of his critique to allow him to ask such mundane questions as How does hypothetical equivalence get established and maintained between concrete languages? What needs are served by such acts of equation historically? These are not just technical or linguistic issues that one may hope to resolve in a case-by-case study; rather, they point to forms of practice and power that deserve our foremost attention in cross-cultural and translingual inquiries.

Perhaps the thing to do is go beyond the deconstructionist stage of trying to prove that equivalents do not exist and look, instead, into their *manner of becoming*. For it is the making of hypothetical equivalences that enables the modus operandi of translation and its politics. For instance, historically when and how do equivalents or tropes of equivalence get established between languages? Is it possible that at certain levels of practice some equivalents might cease to be mere illusions? What enables such changes? Under what conditions does difference, which is the perceived ground for the inscription of equivalence, become translatable in "other words"? When we are confronted with languages that are radically different from Indo-European languages, such as classical and modern vernacular Chinese, in what terms should that difference be conceptualized for the purpose of understanding translation and translingual practice?

Steiner, for example, gives an interesting description of the Chinese language (a language he did not know) in order to illustrate what he takes to be the radical difference of a non-European language. "Chinese is composed mainly of monosyllabic units with a wide range of diverse meanings. The grammar lacks clear tense distinctions. The characters are logographic but many contain pictorial rudiments or suggestions. The relations between propositions are paratactic rather than syntactic and punctuation marks represent breathing pauses far more than they do logical or grammatical segmentations."[43] Somewhat curious about the sources of information Steiner uses here, I checked the article he cites, which was written by Achilles Fang, a renowned sinologist in the 1950's and 1960's. A quick comparison of the two texts reveals that Fang's discussion, which addresses the difficulty of translating classical Chinese *shi* and *wen*, is taken out of its immediate context and used by Steiner to generalize about the Chinese language. To be sure, Fang would probably have never used the verb "lack" to characterize classical Chinese vis-à-vis European languages or describe Chinese as composed of monosyllabic units any more than he would say Indo-European languages were full of redundant grammatical units. In the context of his outdated essay, entitled "Some Reflections on the Difficulty of Translation," Fang stressed the need for a translator of classical Chinese texts to attend to the elements of rhetoric, quotation and allusion, sentiment, punctuation, parataxis, particles, context, and so on. He brought up the question of grammar in criticizing sinologists "who still think Chinese (classical Chinese) is a 'language' in the conventional sense."[44] Interestingly, Steiner overlooks the implied critique of the Western notion of "language," which might have proved useful in strengthening his own critique of the Western philosophy of language. Of course, in order to create a genuine confrontation between these languages, one not only needs a firsthand knowledge of the languages involved, but must guard vigilantly against easily assuming an equivalence between any pair of words, idioms, or languages.

But a question lingers: Can we talk about an "uncontaminated" Chinese notion of language *in English*? And can we do so even in Chinese in the wake of all that has happened in the past one and a half centuries? Languages change, and Chinese is no exception. Since the latter half of the nineteenth century, massive (unidirectional) interactions between Chinese, Japanese, and modern European languages have taken place. If Chinese remains one of the most difficult languages to translate, the chances are that the difficulty lies in the growing number of hypothetical equivalents between Chinese and other languages, rather than the lack thereof. Modern Chinese words and concepts as well as those from the classical language, which are increasingly mediated through modern Chinese, often present hidden snares, even though on the surface they seem relatively transparent. Edward Gunn's recent *Rewriting Chinese* offers some brilliant insights in this respect by documenting the major innovations in modern Chinese prose style since the turn of the twentieth century. His detailed stylistic analysis reveals, for example, that as many as 21 out of the 44 major types of innovations that he categorizes according to the criteria of grammatical construction, rhetorical invention, and sentence cohesion result from exposure to European languages and Japanese through translation.[45]

In the area of loanword studies, mainland Chinese linguists Gao

Mingkai and Liu Zhengtan have identified 1,266 onetime neologisms that are now part of the mainstream vocabulary of modern Chinese; of these 459 compounds were borrowed from Japanese *kanji* (Chinese character) translations of European words, mainly English.[46] This pioneering work was published in 1958; in the same year, a linguist named Wang Lida came up with a list of 588 loanwords from *kanji* translation independently.[47] Based on the findings of these linguists, Japanese sinologist Sanetō Kei-shū pinpointed 830 loanwords from Japanese *kanji* translations, of which 98 percent are nouns (note, however, that a Chinese word may often belong to two or more parts of speech; many of the words Sanetō classifies as nouns can also function as verbs).[48] Yue-him Tam's research in late Qing and early Republican publications has added 233 more to Sanetō's list, which brings the neologisms from Japanese *kanji* translation to the grand total of 1,063.[49] Even then, as Tam reminds us, the list is far from exhaustive, but it serves to illustrate the extent to which the infusion of loanword neologisms has changed the Chinese language since the nineteenth century. Moreover, many of these terms also entered the Korean and Vietnamese languages—which heretofore had been dominated by the Chinese writing system—at the turn of the century. A more recent study done by Italian linguist Federico Masini further complicates this picture by showing that up to a quarter of the total number of what were previously considered Japanese loans in modern Chinese had actually been invented in Chinese first by nineteenth-century Protestant missionaries and their native collaborators in the process of translating secular texts (mainly English) and that it was not until the second half of the nineteenth century that the Japanese began to adopt those neologisms in their own second-hand translations of the same texts and to create their own calques (loan-translations) and semantic loans.[50]

Needless to say, lexical borrowing or loan translation is unique neither to China nor to modern times. The Japanese had long borrowed from classical Chinese before the two-way and reverse process began in the late nineteenth century.[51] Calques, semantic, and other loans from Central Asian, Arabic, and Northern Asian sources found their way into Chinese as early as the Han dynasty, and translations of Buddhist texts in the Six Dynasties period introduced a fairly large number of Sanskrit terms.[52] But the massive influx of neologisms in the late nineteenth century and the first quarter of the twentieth century was unprecedented in terms of scale and influence. It fundamentally transformed the Chinese language at almost every level of linguistic experience, rendering classical Chinese nearly obsolete. The situation reminds one of Bakhtin's description of vernacular translations in sixteenth-century Europe: "An intense interorientation, interaction, and mutual clarification of languages took place during that period. The two languages frankly and intensely peered into each other's faces, and each became more aware of itself, its potentialities and limitations, in the light of the other. This line drawn between the languages was seen in relation to each object, each concept, and each point of view."[53] Perhaps the analogy with sixteenth-century Europe is not so appropriate after all, because the interactions among Chinese, modern Japanese, and European languages have predominantly been unidirectional rather than mutual.[54] The need to account for the cause and manner of this imbalance cries out for a radically different approach, one that Bakhtin's otherwise excellent study of hybrid linguistic interactions in the European context cannot provide.

Earlier in this chapter, I criticized transhistorical uses of concepts of the individual and self in certain areas of contemporary scholarship. What I would like to do now is explore alternative avenues for cross-cultural and cross-linguistic inquiry, since the rejection of universal categories on linguistic grounds does not preclude the possibility of talking about cross-cultural issues on those same grounds. Once again, to evoke the archetypal question, what is the Chinese equivalent(s) of the English word X or Y? If questions like this seem inevitable, as indeed they are in comparative studies, can we pose them in a way that will help open up, rather than assume, the hypothetical equivalence of meanings between the languages—an assumption so jealously guarded by bilingual dictionaries? As I argue above, analytical categories cannot operate fruitfully in a transhistorical and transdiscursive mode. But neither do I think that cultural relativism provides a viable solution in this fast shrinking world of ours, in which geopolitical boundaries are constantly being redrawn and crossed, and in which the need for translation and interaction is literally thrust on people who had little contact before. It seems to me that, to eschew the transhistorical/transdiscursive approach on the one hand and cultural relativism on the other, one must turn to the occurrences of historical contact, interaction, translation, and the travel of words and ideas between languages.

Take, for example, the term *geren zhuyi* in modern Chinese, which is a neologistic equivalent, via the Japanese *kanji* translation *kojin shugi*, of English "individualism." The trajectory of the discourse of *geren zhuyi* in China, which I discuss at length in Chapter 3, offers a good example of the complex ways in which ideas operate through translation and translingual practice. In this case, one can talk about linkages between "individualism" and *geren zhuyi* meaningfully in a historical/translingual context without using the one or the other as an absolute category of analysis. My point can be stated simply: a cross-cultural study must examine its own condition of possibility. Constituted as a translingual act itself, it enters, rather than sits above, the dynamic history of the relationship between words, concepts, categories, and discourse. One way of unraveling that relationship is to engage rigorously with those words, concepts, categories, and discourses beyond the realm of common sense, dictionary definition, and even historical linguistics.

Traveling Theory and the Postcolonial Critique

What happens when a word, category, or discourse "travels" from one language to another? In nineteenth-century colonial and imperialist discourse, the travel of ideas and theories from Europe to the rest of the world usually evoked notions of expansion, enlightenment, progress, and teleological history. In recent years, the move to historicize and decolonize knowledge in various academic disciplines has led to a growing number of studies that scrutinize these notions. The word "travel" is no longer seen as innocent and is often put in quotation marks. Edward Said's notion of "traveling theory" has gained wide circulation in the past decade and is worth critical reflection here. This notion registers a tendency to push contemporary Marxian theory beyond some of its dominant models, such as the mode of production, consumption, and the like, to arrive at a more fluid sense of literary practice. With the help of what he terms "critical consciousness"—a notion ill-defined but daring enough to evoke a space beyond (not outside) theory—Said introduces a concept of literary practice that emphasizes creative borrowing, appropriation, and the movement of ideas and theories from place to place in an international environment.[55] Apropos of the manner in which theories and ideas travel, Said sees four main stages:

> First, there is the point of origin, or what seems like one, a set of initial
> circumstances in which the idea came to birth or entered discourse. Second,
> there is a distance transversed, a passage through the pressure of various con-
> texts as the idea moves from an earlier point to another time and place where
> it will come into a new prominence. Third, there is a set of conditions—
> call them conditions of acceptance or, as an inevitable part of acceptance,
> resistances—which then confronts the transplanted theory or idea, making
> possible its introduction or toleration, however alien it might appear to be.
> Fourth, the now full (or partly) accommodated (or incorporated) idea is to
> some extent transformed by its new uses, its new position in a new time and
> place.[56]

Having introduced his general framework, Said then examines the intellectual development of three major Marxian literary critics, Georg Lukács, Lucien Goldmann, and Raymond Williams, with Foucault thrown in toward the end, and measures the career of each critic against his historical environment. For some inexplicable reason, however, his discussion does not go beyond the usual argument that theory is always a response to changing social and historical circumstances, and the traveling aspect of his theory is abandoned along the way. As I tried to figure out an explanation for this, it occurred to me that perhaps the notion itself lacked the kind of intellectual rigor needed for its own fulfillment. Indeed, who does the traveling? Does theory travel? If so, how? Granting theory such subjectivity leads to a further question: What is the means of transportation? Is it the aircraft, automobile, rickshaw, train, man-of-war, or space shuttle? Commenting on Said's oversight, James Clifford suggests that "Lukácsian Marxism in his essay seems to travel by immigrant boat; theory nowadays takes the plane, sometimes with round-trip tickets."[57] I would take this point a step further: not only does the concept of traveling theory tend to affirm the primacy of theory (or Western theory in the context of Said's book) by endowing the latter with full-fledged, mobile subjectivity, but it fails to account for the vehicle of translation. With the suppression of that vehicle, travel becomes such an abstract idea that it makes no difference in which direction theory travels (from West to East or vice versa) and for what purpose (cultural exchange, imperialism, or colonization?), or in which language and for what audience.

It is not as if Said has paid little attention to the question of translation elsewhere. In fact, his widely influential *Orientalism* and later writings all tackle the representation and translation of cultural difference in the Orientalist textual tradition of the West, and Said himself has become a leading contemporary critic of the history of colonialism, imperialism, and ethnocentrism in the West.[58] It is ironic, therefore, that his notion of traveling theory is generally interpreted as if theory (read Western theory) were a hero from a European picaresque narrative who initiates the trip, encounters obstacles en route, and always ends up being accommodated one way or another by the host country.[59] Inasmuch as language transaction is always a contested territory in national and international struggles, one must rethink one's priorities in theorizing the migration of ideas and theory and ask what role translation and related practices play in the construction of relations of power between the so-called First and Third worlds. Indeed, what happens when languages meet during the East–West encounter? Are the relations of power between the two always

reducible to patterns of domination and resistance? Is the cultural critic
not risking too much for granting too little to the agency of non-Western
languages in these transactions?

Recent work in poststructuralist and postcolonial studies has initiated
an important rethinking of the problem of language and translation in
historical terms. The idea of historicity used in this body of scholarship is
pitted against teleological History written with a capital H. It emphasizes,
instead, "effective history," an idea borrowed from Nietzsche (*wirkliche
Historie*) and Gadamer (*Wirkungsgeschichte*) that refers to the part of the past
that is still operative and meaningful in the present.[60] This understanding of historicity enables postcolonial critics to raise questions about the
"effective history" of the text: "Who uses/interprets the text? How is it
used, and for what?"[61] In putting their questions this way, these critics are
not trying to reduce history to texts, but are emphasizing texts as social
facts like any other facts, capable of being deployed for political or ideological purposes. As Mary Louise Pratt puts it in a recent study of travel
writing and European colonialism:

> How has travel and exploration writing *produced* "the rest of the world" for
> European readerships at particular points in Europe's expansionist trajec-
> tory? How has it produced Europe's differentiated conceptions of itself in
> relation to something it became possible to call "the rest of the world"?
> How do such signifying practices encode and legitimate the aspirations of
> economic expansion and empire? How do they betray them?[62]

The study of language has acquired a fresh urgency in these various
historical projects. Words, texts, discourse, and vocabulary enter one's
scholarship as veritable historical accounts per se, not just as sources of
historical information about something more important than themselves.
Obviously, Foucault's work has greatly influenced this line of thinking
among those who study former European colonies in Asia, America, and
Africa. For example, in research on the relationship between colonial control and the use of Swahili as a lingua franca in the former Belgian Congo,
anthropologist Johannes Fabian expounds the relevance of the Foucaultian
notion of discourse to his own work:

> Here the notion of discourse is of methodological value. The assumption
> is that ideas and ideologies expressing as well as informing colonial praxis
> are formulated and perpetuated (and occasionally changed) in ways of talk-
> ing and writing about the *oeuvre civilisatrice*. In interpreting this sort of talk
> as discourse one is less interested in the truth value of specific statements,
> in the question, for instance, whether a certain author really expressed his

convictions, gave an accurate report of facts, and so on. Instead one seeks to appreciate the documentary value of a "style" by discerning key notions, rules of combining these and theoretical devices used to build arguments. In short, one concentrates on elements which determined the shape and content of colonial thought irrespective of individual intentions.[63]

Fabian's analysis of Swahili language manuals and other colonial documents relating to Katanga demonstrates that promotion of this language was a vital part of the promotion of the symbolic power of the colonial administration.[64] One might object that there is nothing new about languages being used to serve political and ideological goals.[65] But Fabian raises an important question by placing language practice at the heart of colonial history while linking that "effective history" with a series of genealogies of imperialist expansion and of the development of modern linguistics and anthropology as scientific disciplines.[66] For instance, he reminds us that one of the earliest linguistic undertakings to include African and Asian languages for comparative research in Europe was an ambitious collection of vocabularies called *Linguarum totius orbis vocabularia comparativa* . . . , a project conceived and initiated by Catherine the Great, Empress of Russia, and completed by Peter Simon Pallas (Moscow, 1787 and 1789). Vocabulary lists were sent to the governors of the Russian empire to be forwarded to official interpreters and translators and, through Russian ambassadors in Madrid, London, and the Hague, they reached Spanish, English, and Dutch colonies, and even China. George Washington took a personal interest and asked the governors of the United States to participate in the collection of material.[67] Thus "translations were regarded as official business and the wordlists became documents of state, witnessed to with stamps and signatures."[68]

In a recent study of colonial India and postcoloniality, Tejaswini Niranjana raises a similar point about translation and sees it as "part of the colonial discourse of Orientalism" and "British efforts to obtain information about the people ruled by the merchants of the East India Company." She defines colonial discourse as "the body of knowledge, modes of representation, strategies of power, law, discipline, and so on, that are employed in the construction and domination of 'colonial subjects.'" Based on an interesting re-reading of Benjamin, de Man, and Derrida, she proposes a postcolonial concept of translation and history and stresses the linkage between the two in the desire to "re-translate" and to "re-write history." "To read existing translations against the grain," she says, "is also to read colonial historiography from a post-colonial perspective, and a critic alert to the ruses of colonial discourse can help uncover what Walter Benjamin calls 'the second tradition,' the history of resistance."[69] Niranjana's re-reading of colonial discourse is enabled by what she calls "a post-colonial perspective." But in the course of doing so, she unwittingly privileges European languages as a host language (or target language) where meanings are decided. If the postcolonial critic continues to emphasize European languages in these accounts of East–West linguistic transactions and to leave the unspoken part of that history/story unaddressed, how far can she go toward fulfilling her own promise of rewriting history? The irony is that one often remembers only to forget. By refreshing our memories of the past crimes committed by imperialism, the postcolonial critic inadvertently erases traces of the previous histories of anti-imperialist struggle to which he or she rightly belongs.[70] Why are Mao and Gandhi often forgotten as Derrida or Benjamin is evoked as the oppositional voice to the hegemony of the West? If poststructuralism is the driving force that gives a new impetus and new meaning to the contemporary criticism of colonialism and imperialism, then one must take account of the fact that the critique of "cultural imperialism" has its own genealogies and has long been part of the anti-imperialist legacies of non-Western peoples.

What happens when a European text gets translated into a non-European language? Can the power relationship between East and West be reinvented (if not reversed) in that case? If so, how? These are the questions that Vicente Rafael has tried to address in his study of Spanish evangelization and the emergence of Tagalog colonial society in the Philippines. He compares the different modes of translation in Tagalog and Castilian and shows that this difference greatly complicated the process of native conversion and often confounded the missionaries' expectations. Something interesting happens when two languages are brought into confrontation in these moments:

> For in setting languages in motion, translation tended to cast intentions adrift, now laying, now subverting the ideological grounds of colonial hegemony. The necessity of employing the native vernaculars in spreading the Word of God constrained the universalizing assumptions and totalizing impulses of a colonial-Christian order. It is this contradiction precipitated by translation that we see played out in the history of Tagalog conversion.[71]

Rafael's insight is important. His acute understanding of the complexities of linguistic transaction between East and West is not without some relevance to the concept of translingual practice I discuss here.[72] However, the idea of resistance and subversion that runs throughout his book and prevails in current postcolonial theory in general needs a critical re-examination. To the extent that the postcolonial critic wishes to de-colonize certain kinds of knowledge that have dominated the world for the past few hundred years, resistance describes his or her own condition of being just as much as it does that of the colonial world s/he describes. But the same idea also runs the risk of reducing the power relationship between East and West to that of native resistance and Western domina-tion, as I point out above.[73] There is a certain amount of danger in reifying the patterns of resistance and domination, however complicated they are, along the East/West divide, since the boundaries between the two are frequently permeable and subject to changing conditions. As Lisa Lowe puts it well in her critique of the notions of Occident and Orient, "When we maintain a static dualism of identity and difference, and uphold the logic of the dualism as the means of explaining how a discourse expresses domination and subordination, we fail to account for the differences in-herent in each term."[74] In my own study of translingual practice, I argue that a non-European language does not automatically constitute a site of resistance to European languages. Rather, I see it as a much neglected area where complex processes of domination, resistance, and appropriation can be observed and interpreted from within the discursive context of that language as well as in connection with other linguistic environments.

Host Language and Guest Language

In the following pages I propose the notion of translingual practice to ground my study of an earlier moment of historical transaction between China and the West in language practices. Since the modern intellectual tradition in China began with translation, adaptation, appropriation, and other interlingual practices related to the West, it is inevitable that this inquiry should take translation as its point of departure. Yan Fu's inter-pretive translation of Thomas Huxley's *Evolution and Ethics* (1898) and other Western texts had an enormous impact on China and helped fash-ion an entire generation of Chinese intelligentsia.[75] In literature, Lin Shu's immensely popular renderings of over a hundred foreign works into lit-erary Chinese predated publication of Lu Xun's first modern short story (1918) by many years.[76] Literary historian A Ying (Qian Xingcun) esti-mates that of the at least 1,500 published works of fiction in the last decade of the Qing, two-thirds are translations of foreign literature and many are English and French works.[77] (The word "translation" should be understood here as a shorthand for adaptation, appropriation, and other related translingual practices.) As several studies have pointed out, the rise of modern journalism and major publishing businesses such as the Commercial Press in China's metropolitan centers had a direct bearing on the growing popularity of translated literature.[78] The majority of modern Chinese writers first tried their hand at translation and then moved on to other literary activities.[79] Lu Xun translated numerous Russian and Japanese works into Chinese, and one of his first books, a collaboration with his brother Zhou Zuoren during their student days in Japan, was a collection of translations called *Yuwai xiaoshuo ji* (Anthology of foreign fiction; 1909).[80] Throughout his life, he translated and encouraged translation of foreign works and continued to do so after he stopped writing fiction. Among other well-known figures in May Fourth literature, Yu Dafu translated Rousseau, and Guo Moruo's rendering of Goethe's *Die Leiden des jungen Werther* into the modern vernacular became a bestseller among urban youths.

However, I must hasten to add that the point of translingual practice is not to study the history of translation, much less the technical aspects of translation, although one could benefit from excursions into the one or the other.[81] I am interested in theoretical problems that lead up to an investigation of the *condition of translation* and of discursive practices that ensue from initial interlingual contacts between languages. Broadly defined, the study of translingual practice examines the process by which new words, meanings, discourses, and modes of representation arise, circulate, and acquire legitimacy within the host language due to, or in spite of, the latter's contact/collision with the guest language. Meanings, therefore, are not so much "transformed" when concepts pass from the guest language to the host language as invented within the local environment of the latter. In that sense, translation is no longer a neutral event untouched by the contending interests of political and ideological struggles. Instead, it becomes the very site of such struggles where the guest language is forced to encounter the host language, where the irreducible differences between them are fought out, authorities invoked or challenged, ambiguities dissolved or created, and so forth, until new words and meanings emerge in the host language itself. I hope the notion of translingual practice will eventually lead to a theoretical vocabulary that helps account for the process of adaptation, translation, introduction, and domestication of words, categories, discourses, and modes of representation from one language to another and, furthermore, helps explain the modes of transmission, manipulation, deployment, and domination within the power structure of the host language. My goal is to reconceptualize the problematic of "language" in a new set of relationships that is not predicated on some of the familiar premises of contemporary theories of language, which tend to take metropolitan European tongues as a point of departure.

A word of explanation about some of the terms I use here. If it is true that the translator or some other agent in the host language always initiates the linguistic transaction by inviting, selecting, combining, and reinventing words and texts from the guest language and, moreover, if the needs of the translator and his/her audience together determine and negotiate the meaning (i.e., usefulness) of the text taken from the guest language, then the terms traditional theorists of translation use to designate the languages involved in translation, such as "source" and "target/receptor," are not only inappropriate but misleading. The idea of source language often relies on concepts of authenticity, origin, influence, and so on, and has the disadvantage of re-introducing the age-old problematic of translatability/untranslatability into the discussion. On the other hand, the notion of target language implies a teleological goal, a distance to be crossed in order to reach the plenitude of meaning; it thus misrepresents the ways in which the trope of equivalence is conceived in the host language, relegating its agency to secondary importance. Instead of continuing to subscribe to such metaphysical concerns perpetuated by the naming of a source and a target, I adopt the notions "host language" and "guest language" in this book (the Chinese equivalents, *zhufang yuyan* and *kefang yuyan*, would even more radically alter the relationship between the original and translation), which should allow me to place more emphasis on the host language than it has heretofore received. In this light, the knowledge/power dyad that Talal Asad so lucidly describes in the passage quoted at the beginning of this chapter should be re-examined, for his description overlooks the possibility that a non-European host language may violate, displace, and usurp the authority of the guest language in the process of translation as well as be transformed by it or be in complicity with it. These complex forms of mediations during the historical contact between China and the West are the main concerns of the individual chapters in this book.

Theory of Change, Neologisms, and Discursive Histories

It is my contention that the study of modern Chinese history must take the history of translingual practice into account. The prominence of the problem of language in the Chinese imagination of modernity can hardly be disputed. "What is so 'modern' about modern Chinese history and literature?" asks Leo Ou-fan Lee in a recent article. "In what ways did the May Fourth generation, and their predecessors, attempt to define their difference from the past and articulate a new range of sensibilities which they would consider 'modern'?"[82] Indeed, the quoted status of the word "modern" highlighted here by Lee alerts one to the question of "translated" modernity in the history of translingual practice between China and the West. Rather than continuing to argue about tradition and modernity as essential categories, one is compelled to ask How do twentieth-century Chinese *name* the condition of their existence? What kind of language do they use in talking about their differences from whatever contingent identities they perceive as existing before their own time or being imposed from the outside? What rhetorical strategies, discursive formations, naming practices, legitimizing processes, tropes, and narrative modes impinge upon the historical conditions of the Chinese experience of the modern?

The problem of methodology in Chinese historical studies has not gone unexamined in the past decades. For example, in a critique of American historical writings about China since John Fairbank and Joseph Levenson, Paul Cohen urges historians to rethink their priorities in explaining the recent changes in Chinese history. He focuses on three dominant conceptual paradigms in his book *Discovering History in China* and suggests an alternative he terms the "China-centered approach." To summarize his poignant criticism in a somewhat reductive fashion, the impact-response theory, the first of the three paradigms he discusses, emphasizes China's response to the Western challenge and often "prompts historians to define aspects of recent Chinese history that had no obvious connections with the Western presence as unimportant—or, alternatively, as important *only* insofar as they shed light on China's response to the West." The second of these approaches—the tradition-modernity model—has deep roots in nineteenth-century ethnocentrism and imposes on Chinese history an external—"parochially Western—definition of what change is and what kinds of change are important." The third, or the imperialism, approach falls into "the ahistorical trap of *assuming* for Chinese history a 'natural' or 'normal' course of development with which Western (and later Japanese) imperialism interfered."[83] As a corrective to the above, Cohen draws attention to the work of a younger generation of China historians who have turned to a *China-centered* approach. In his view, this approach has the advantage of avoiding imported criteria by beginning with Chinese problems set in a Chinese context, whether these problems are generated by the West or have no Western connection at all.

This new approach, which effectively challenges the established way of writing Chinese history, has important implications for literary studies as well. Instead of continuing to do so-called influence studies in the time-honored sense of comparative literature, one could stress the agency of the host language (modern Chinese in this case) in the meaning-making process of translation so that the guest language need not carry a signature of authenticity around in order to make sense in the new context. On the other hand, at least in sinological studies, one can afford to be China-centered without ceasing to adopt the Western-centered perception of what is important or unimportant for scholarship. I am reminded of a criticism Rey Chow made some time ago: "In sinology and Chinese studies, where the emphases on 'heritage' are clearly immovable, the homage to the West has long been paid in the form of what seems to be its opposite—in the idealist insistence on a separate, self-sufficient 'Chinese tradition' that should be lined up against the Western one because it is as great if not greater. The 'rejection' of the West in this instance is solemnly respectful; by upholding 'China,' it repeats the hegemonic overtones of that which is rejected."[84]

Indeed, to draw a clear line between the indigenous Chinese and the exogenous Western in the late twentieth century is almost an epistemological impossibility. The fact that one writes about China for an English-speaking academic audience further complicates the situation. Interestingly, the theoretical impulse for the China-centered approach does not originate in China but draws its inspiration from the works of objectivist sociologists and anthropologists in the contemporary West who emphasize the "regional approach" as a more valid one than those they have discredited. As Pierre Bourdieu aptly puts it, "What is at stake here is the power of imposing a vision of the social world through principles of di-vision which, when they are imposed on a whole group, establish meaning and a consensus about meaning, and in particular about the identity and unity of the group, which creates the reality of the unity and the identity of the group."[85] In other words, regionalist discourse is a performative discourse that seeks to legitimate a new definition of the frontiers whereby the *region*, a reality thus named, becomes the site of the struggle to *define* reality, rather than simply the "reality" itself. It is not difficult to see that the theoretical frontiers in this case are, once again, set and framed by contemporary Western academic discourses.[86]

Consider, on the other hand, the situation in which one does historiography strictly for a Chinese academic audience in the Chinese language. Would one not be using a language already thoroughly "contaminated" by the influx of neologisms and theories from China's earlier and current contact with the West? Paradoxically, contemporary Chinese scholars in China can assume "China-centeredness" in their own work even as they speak and write an *ouhua* or Europeanized Chinese language.[87] There, as much as here, the "indigenous Chinese" can no longer be so easily separated out from the "exogenous Western." Given these difficulties and constraints, my question is whether one can still talk about change and transaction between East and West in twentieth-century China without privileging the West, modernity, progress, or other post-Enlightenment notions on the one hand and without holding on to a reified idea of indigenous China on the other.

Since the death of Levenson in 1969, as Theodore Huters has recently pointed out, there has been "a curious and very marked silence concerning the traumatic choices that the coming of the West presented to China. This silence is striking in that modern Chinese literature has traditionally dated itself as beginning in a movement to discard the native literary language in favor of a literary language explicitly based on Western models."[88] Indeed, Levenson's totalizing statements about Confucian China and its modern fate may no longer obtain, but the question of how to explain the "traumatic choices" made by the Chinese since their violent encounters with Western imperialism does not easily go away. This is a historical question as well as a theoretical challenge to contemporary scholarship. Recently, Gayatri Spivak has brought attention to a theory of change developed by contemporary South Asian historians that I find interesting and not without relevance to what I am trying to talk about here.

> The work of the Subaltern Studies group offers a theory of change. The insertion of India into colonialism is generally defined as a change from semi-feudalism into capitalist subjection. Such a definition theorizes the change within the great narrative of the modes of production and, by uneasy implication, within the narrative of the transition from feudalism to capitalism. Concurrently, this change is seen as the inauguration of politicization for the colonized. The colonial subject is seen as emerging from those parts of the indigenous élite which come to be loosely described as "bourgeois nationalist." The Subaltern Studies group seems to be revising this general definition and its theorization by proposing at least two things: first, that the moment(s) of change be pluralized and plotted as *confrontations* rather than *transition* (they would thus be seen in relation to histories of domination and exploitation rather than within a great modes-of-production narrative) and, secondly, that such changes are signalled or marked by a functional change in sign-systems.[89]

The theoretical model advanced by the South Asian historians is thought-provoking in that they eschew the idea of "transition," at least in Spivak's interpretation of it—whether from East to West, from tradition to modernity, or from feudalism to capitalism—and turn, instead, to the notion of "confrontation," which provides a new perspective for understanding the kinds of changes that have occurred since the encounter of East and West. Their approach renders the old problematic of tradition and modernity uninteresting and opens modern history to alternative avenues of interpretation.[90]

One could object that this theory does not apply to the Chinese situation on the grounds that India was a British colony and China was not. I wonder, however, if the real issue here is one of compatibility at the level of "experience." Behind the obvious truthfulness of this objection, is there an anxiety or intellectual bias that gravitates toward European theory as a universal bearer of meaning and value? Objections to the use of European theory in the China field are, however, seldom raised on the same ground—namely, that Western theory fails to apply to China because the former has linkages with a colonial/imperialist past whereas the latter has had an opposite "experience." On the contrary, the terms of difference are almost always constructed along the line of Western theory versus Chinese reality.[91] In that sense, the work of the Subaltern historians is inspiring, for they do not assume a hegemonic divide between Western theory and someone else's reality. To them, the realities of the West, India, and other places are to be equally subjected to theoretical critique and interrogated in light of the history of their mutual involvement and contention. Needless to say, the terms of such critique need to be constantly negotiated between these different localities.

I emphasize historical *linkages*—rather than commonalities—between these localities, the kind of linkages that Lu Xun, for example, discerned in writing "Moluo shili shuo" (On the power of Mara poetry) in 1907. Commenting on how his compatriots treated their less fortunate neighbors or nations that had been colonized by the imperialist forces, he said:

> One need only step out into the streets of any major Chinese city, to meet with soldiers sauntering about the marketplace, serenading us with martial airs that rebuke the servility of India and Poland; these have become so widespread as to practically constitute a national anthem for us. This is due to the fact that China, in spite of her present situation, is always anxious to jump at any chance to cite at length her past glories, yet now she feels deprived of the capacity to do so, and can only resort to comparisons of herself with

captive neighbors that have either fallen under the yoke of servitude or ceased to exist, hoping thereby to show off her own superiority.[92]

Lu Xun is alluding to two popular songs allegedly composed by the reformer Zhang Zhidong entitled *Xuetang ge* (Song for the new-style school) and *Jun ge* (Army song). The first contains the lines: "Poland lies shattered, India is done, / The last of the Jews to the four winds is flung!" and the second: "Prithee look toward India vast, / As slaves enchained, they'll never last!"[93] Lu Xun's critique of the self-perception of the Chinese in the larger context of colonialism and imperialism is a useful reminder of the dangers of exaggerating China's uniqueness at the expense of erasing the traces of its involvement (and collusion) with other localities and histories. At issue, therefore, is not who was colonized and who was not, but how to interpret the interconnected moments of confrontation between those who sought to conquer the world and those who struggled to survive under such enormous pressures.

This new emphasis inevitably turns our concern with abstract questions of continuity or transition in modern history to contingencies, struggles, and surprising twists and turns of events at each moment of confrontation between nations or different groups of people. In my study of translingual practice, I am interested in conditions under which "confrontations" occur between China, Japan, and the West at the site of translation or wherever the languages happen to meet, for this is where the irreducible differences between the host language and the guest language are fought out, authorities invoked or challenged, and ambiguities dissolved or created. In short, the confrontations register a meaning-making history that cuts across different national languages and histories.

The trope for change in the context of translingual practice is neologism or neologistic construction. This metaphorical projection of linguistic mediations will be better understood after we take a close look at the actual routes by which modern neologisms, especially Sino-Japanese-European ones, traveled and took residence in modern Chinese.[94] According to Gao Mingkai and Liu Zhengtan, the influx of calques, semantic, and other loans into late nineteenth-century and early twentieth-century literary and vernacular Chinese followed a typical pattern; that is, the Japanese used *kanji* (Chinese characters) to translate European terms, and the neologisms were then imported back into the Chinese language. The majority of these borrowings fall under three headings: (1) two-character compounds made up of Chinese characters that are found only in premodern Japanese and do not appear in classical Chinese. Examples are *renli che* (rickshaw; *jinrikisha*), *changhe* (occasion; *baii*), and *zongjiao* (religion; *shūkyō*);[95] (2) classical Chinese expressions used by the Japanese to translate Western terms that were then imported back into Chinese with a radical change in meaning, such as *geming* (revolution; *kakumei*), *wenhua* (culture; *bunka*), *jingji* (economy; *keizai*); and *kexue* (science; *kagaku*).[96] (3) modern Japanese compounds that have no equivalent in classical Chinese, such as *zhongzu* (race; *shūzoku*), *meishu* (art; *bijutsu*), *meixue* (aesthetics; *bigaku*), and *guoji* (international; *kokusai*).[97] Chapter 2 of this book is devoted to the trajectory of one such loanword translation: the Japanese *kanji* rendering of "national character," *kokuminsei*, which became the Chinese *guomin xing* through loanword translation. This translation is one of several discursive occurrences that have profoundly transformed the sensibilities of generations of the Chinese in the twentieth century. I evoke the word "occurrences" here in the sense that Paul de Man uses it in discussing Benjamin's essay on translation: "When Luther translated, translated the Bible, something occurred—at that moment, something happened—not in the immediate sense that from then on there were wars and then the course of history was changed—that is a by-product. What really occurred was that . . . translation. Then there are, in the history of texts, texts which are occurrences."[98] As Chapter 2 demonstrates, the loanword translation of "national character" into Chinese is an example of just such an event that catalyzes another important event, which, in Lu Xun's view, is no less than the invention of modern Chinese literature itself.

Of the three types of loanwords identified by Gao and Liu, the second is the most deceptively transparent, because these "return graphic loans" are easily mistaken as direct derivatives from classical Chinese.[99] Gao and Liu warn that one should be careful about equating these loanwords with their classical counterparts. For example, the modern meaning of *wenhua* (culture) derives from the Japanese *kanji* compound *bunka*, and it is through borrowing that an equivalence was established between the Chinese *wenhua* and the English "culture" (French *culture*; German *die Kultur*). In classical Chinese, *wenhua* denoted the state of refinement or artistic cultivation as opposed to *wu* or military prowess, carrying none of the ethnographic connotations of "culture" commonly associated with the two-character compound in today's usage.[100] Chapter 9 of this book pursues the ways in which this translingual notion of *wenhua* or culture—an omnipotent cliché that has generated some of the most vibrant and contentious debates in the modern world—evolved into a central bearer of meaning and difference between countries and peoples in the intellectual discourse of late Qing and Republican China.

The massive influx of semantic translations and "return graphic loans" *interrupt* the classical etymons in ways that profoundly change their meanings and status. Because of this historical interruption, one can no longer bypass the Japanese *bunka* to explicate the meaning of *wenhua* as if the existence of a classical Chinese term written with the same characters would automatically account for the meaning of its modern counterpart. Of course, the etymological routes taken by these Sino-Japanese-English semantic and loan translations were by no means limited to the three as proposed above by Gao and Liu. A newly published study by Federico Masini shows that the Japanese had borrowed nineteenth-century neologisms, calques, and semantic translations from Chinese before the reverse process began in China some years later. These new terms were invented by Protestant missionaries and their Chinese assistants in the collaborative rendering of secular texts from the West around the early and mid-nineteenth century. The Japanese adopted some of these terms in their *kanji* translations and began to coin their own neologisms in Chinese characters in a similar fashion. To complicate the picture further, many of these early Chinese translations of European terms had had relatively limited impact within China, and the Japanese borrowing was often instrumental to their widespread influence at home. In fact, the Japanese role was so crucial in the "round-trip" dissemination of these autochthonous neologisms that some of them came to be regarded as Japanese loanwords by the Chinese themselves.[101]

This round-trip dissemination of autochthonous neologisms, which is often hard to distinguish from the etymological route taken by return graphic loans from Japan, accounts for linguists' difficulty in trying to determine the origins of some of the modern Chinese lexicon. For example, scholars since Gao and Liu have long considered the compound *wenxue* in its present usage a return graphic loan from the Japanese *bungaku*, that is, a *kanji* translation of the English term "literature."[102] According to Masini, however, *wenxue* with this new meaning dates at least as early as American missionary Elijah C. Bridgman's *Meiligeguo zhilüe* (Short history of America; 1831), a Chinese-language history of America that included neologisms such as *wenxue* (literature), *maoyi* (trade), *falü* (law), *huolunchuan* (paddleboat powered by steam), *huolunche* (steam-powered train), *huoche* (train), *gongsi* (United East India Company).[103] These and a host of other Chinese neologisms traveled to Japan in the 1860's and 1870's when the Japanese started translating Wei Yuan's *Haiguo tuzhi* (Maps and documents on maritime countries; 1844), a multivolume anthology that contained excerpts from Bridgman's book and other missionary works. "These works and the neologisms would have probably remained confined to a very narrow circle had the texts not been included in the *Haiguo tuzhi*. Their fate is therefore linked to the diffusion of Wei Yuan's work first in China and then in Japan." [104] Indeed, the etymology of these neologisms is so inextricably bound up with their patterns of diffusion in China, Japan, and back again in China that, in reflecting on their history, one cannot afford to dwell on a single point of origin as the exclusive locus of meaning but must, instead, allow for a fluid sense of etymology. In other words, the patterns of diffusion sometimes prove to be just as decisive as the moment of invention. It is possible that if Yan Fu had coined his neologisms before the 1860's and had been translated into Japanese, some of his creations might have survived and, through the Japanese mediation, found their way back into the modern Chinese lexicon.

Wenxue, a direct neologistic translation of the English term "literature" by an American missionary, may not qualify as a return loan from Japanese but, through a process of round-trip diffusion via Japan, this term became widespread and evolved into a standard translation of "literature" in China. [105] For want of a better word, one might want to call it a round-trip neologism to underscore this interesting connection with the Japanese *bungaku*. Chapter 8 is devoted to discussing this translingual concept of literature in the making of a modern canon known as *The Compendium of Modern Chinese Literature*. Published in 1935–36, the famous anthology took fiction, poetry, drama, and familiar prose to be "proper" *wenxue* forms while relegating all other forms of writing to the status of non-*wenxue*. This is certainly a far cry from the classical concept of *wenxue*, although nowadays not even classical works can escape contamination by this translingual notion of literature. Witness the numerous histories and anthologies of classical Chinese *wenxue* published in the twentieth century where poetry, fiction, drama, and, to a lesser degree, familiar prose are similarly designated as *wenxue*, whereas the rest of the classical genres are redistributed along the lines of *lishi* (history), *zongjiao* (religion), *zhexue* (philosophy), and other spheres of knowledge that are themselves created on the basis of neologistic translations of Western concepts. In short, classical Chinese "literature" is subjected to radical reinvention in terms of modern literature even as the latter invents itself at the same time.

European-Japanese loanwords that take up residence in modern Chinese sometimes start out by competing with transliterations. As Appendixes F and G illustrate, some neologisms began as a Chinese transliteration of a foreign word or, at least, ran parallel to the European-Japanese semantic and loan translation of the same word. Before long the translation took over and rendered the transliteration obsolete. This is attributable to the ideographic character of Chinese writing, which favors semantic or loan translation over phonemic transliteration.[106] The translation of the word "democracy" is a case in point. For a period of time, the transliteration *demokelaxi* and its loan translation *minzhu* (*minshu*) coexisted, but the loan translation soon replaced the awkward sounding transliteration to become the only acceptable equivalent of "democracy" in use today. To complicate the situation further, the loan translation *minzhu* happens to coincide with one of the oldest expressions in classical Chinese (see Appendix A). But it would be a serious mistake to equate the classical *minzhu* with the loan translation on the basis of their identical written forms. Classical *minzhu* has a genitive structure (roughly, "ruler of the people"), which cannot be further removed from the subject-predicate semantic structure of the modern compound ("people rule").[107]

Needless to say, not all neologisms were semantic or loan translations. In fact, one of the most fascinating neologisms invented in this period was the gendering of the third-person pronoun in written Chinese, which occurred directly between European languages and Chinese.[108] The original form of the Chinese character for the pronoun *ta* contains an ungendered *ren* radical (denoting the human species), and the gendering of this pronoun arose from circumstances of translation. For thousands of years, the Chinese had lived comfortably with the ungendered form of *ta* and other ungendered deictic forms. Suddenly they discovered that Chinese had no equivalent for the third-person feminine pronoun in English, French, and other European languages.[109] Some Chinese perceived the absence of an equivalent as an essential lack in the Chinese language itself, and efforts were made to design neologisms to fill this lack. (It seems to me that this anxiety reflects a historical situation of perceived inequality between languages rather than a failing in the language itself. For instance, one does not experience much inconvenience when translating the French feminine plural *elles* into the ungendered English "they.") After a few years of experiments with regional forms, such as *yi* from the Wu dialect, writers and linguists finally settled on writing the feminine *ta* with a *nü* (woman) radical.[110] For instance, Lu Xun's use of the third-person pronoun in his fiction reflects this interesting period of experimentation. As one study has pointed out, he started out by using *ta* written with its usual ungendered radical *ren* interchangeably with the Wu dialect word *yi* when he referred to his female characters in some of the early stories, such as

"Tomorrow" (1920).[111] The feminine pronoun written with a *nü* radical did not appear in his works until "New Year's Sacrifice," which was written in 1924. A year later, Lu Xun began to adopt another neologism, *ta* with a *niu* (cattle) radical, to refer to animals, as in "Regret for the Past" (1925).

The appearance of the feminine and animal/neuter pronouns succeeded in converting the ungendered *ta* into a masculine pronoun, even though the ungendered written form underwent not the slightest morphological change. In other words, the invention of the gendered neologisms forced the original *ta* to assume a masculine character, which is, nonetheless, contradicted by its ungendered radical *ren*. This is a perfect illustration of the Saussurian principle of differentiation whereby meanings become possible only when elements of a language enter a relation of similarity and differentiation. In the case of *ta* and related neologisms, the morphology of written Chinese characters rather than pronunciation serves to differentiate the different meanings. As far as pronunciation is concerned, the feminine *ta* and the animal/neuter *ta* are indistinguishable from the masculine *ta*.

Liu Fu (Liu Bannong), who is credited with the invention of the feminine *ta*, once attempted to introduce an element of differentiation at the phonemic level as well.[112] In a 1920 essay "Ta zi wenti" (The problem of feminine *ta*), he argued:

> The most difficult task facing us is how to pronounce this sign. Mr. Zhou Zuoren prefers *yi* to the feminine *ta* mainly because the latter is indistinguishable from the masculine *ta* to the ear, as Mr. Han Bing has rightly pointed out, even though the difference seems clear enough visually. Admittedly, *yi* is pronounced differently from the masculine *ta*, but it has the following disadvantages that seem to make the feminine *ta* a better choice in the final analysis. First, when it comes to colloquial speech, *yi* cannot have popular appeal because its usage as a third-person pronoun is restricted to a small local area. Second, the word is not marked by a female radical as in the case of the feminine *ta*. Third, *yi* smacks of the classical language and sounds awkward when used in the vernacular. I suggest that we adopt the feminine *ta* and make some slight changes to the way it is pronounced. Originally the masculine *ta* had two pronunciations in Mandarin: /t'a/ in colloquial speech and /t'uo/ in literary reading. What we can do is to keep the first pronunciation for the masculine *ta* and use the second one for the feminine pronoun.[113]

For the reasons Liu Fu mentioned, *yi* as a feminine third-person pronoun soon dropped out of written vernacular Chinese to be replaced by *ta* as the acceptable feminine pronoun, although the alternative pronunciation /t'uo/ proposed by Liu has never materialized. Here, one can probably glimpse how *guoyu* (national language), or *putongyu* (Standard Mandarin) as Liu terms it, achieved its hegemonic status over regional dialects.[114] On the other hand, one must also keep the ideographic nature of written Chinese characters in mind; that is, written modern Chinese overlaps, but cannot be simply equated, with spoken Mandarin syllables, unlike romanized characters that are supposed to represent sound. For instance, the character *ta* written with a feminine radical is now widely recognized as a third-person feminine pronoun in written Chinese by Mandarin speakers as well as by other dialect groups, although no one, as far as I know, can produce a pronunciation that separates it from its masculine and animal/neuter counterparts either in Mandarin or in regional dialects.

The gendering of the third-person pronoun in the written language has important implications for the study of translingual representations of gender in modern Chinese literature. The splitting of a formerly ungendered Chinese *ta* into feminine and masculine forms introduced a level of symbolic reality that had never existed in written Chinese. It is not as if women and men have not been perceived or spoken of as sexual beings or *yin/yang* categories prior to the twentieth century, but the deictic relationship—in the manner of man speaking to and about woman, or woman speaking to and about man, and the like—that is enabled by such a split at the symbolic level of the pronoun allows gender to shape social relations of power in a new language. For instance, the Shen Congwen story I analyze in Chapter 6 contains a narrative of class that is consistently played out in terms of deictic construction of gender and desire. In it, an anonymous gentrywoman designated by the feminine pronoun *ta* is admired by three aspiring lower-class men who are addressed by the narrator in the first-person plural, *women* (we/us), constructed specifically as masculine and lower class in the story. These men cannot hope to enter "her" world because the deictic impasse between "her" class and "our" class is insurmountable.[115] Or consider Lu Xun's "New Year's Sacrifice" where a deictic narrative about class and gender captures a reverse situation—the upper-class narrator "I" speaks to and about a lower-class woman *ta*. In a broader sense, deictic constructions of gender reflect and participate in a larger gendering process under way since the turn of the twentieth century, as Chinese men, women, and the state discover separately for themselves and in terms of one another that they all have a stake in deciding how gender difference should be constructed and what kind of political investment that difference should or could represent in

China's pursuit of modernity.[116] The tensions generated between some of these constructed positions in literary criticism are discussed at length in Chapters 5, 6, and 7.

Neologisms in modern Chinese do more than bear physical witness to historical change. I am reminded of a statement Adorno once made in a different context: "Every foreign word contains the explosive material of enlightenment, contains in its controlled use the knowledge that what is immediate cannot be said in unmediated form but only expressed in and through reflection and mediation."[117] Catapulted into existence through translingual interaction with foreign words, neologisms and neologistic constructions occupy an intermediary position of past and present that demands a different reading of historical change. For one thing, change can hardly be a transition from an intact past to the present, for there exist multiple mediations that do not substantiate the claims of a reified past.[118] For another thing, the transformation of a native language cannot be explained simply in terms of impact from the outside as, for example, Levenson would have argued, because foreign terms are subjected to the same logic of translingual reading as is the native classical language through the mediation of translation. In *Confucian China and Its Modern Fate*, Levenson asserts that "what the West has probably done to China is to change the latter's language—what China has done to the West is to enlarge the latter's vocabulary."[119] Although this observation accurately captures the power relationship between China and the West, Levenson's underlying assumptions about what change is and how it occurs prevent him from taking the processes of linguistic mediation seriously or literally (for he is using "language" and "vocabulary" as metaphors) and from re-examining the meaning of Chinese agency. The round-trip words and other neologisms in modern Chinese embody an idea of change that renders the question of historical continuity and discontinuity less than meaningful. Rather than continuing to debate how modernized (read Westernized) China is or how traditional it still remains—these being two contradictory positions frequently articulated among scholars of differing intellectual persuasion[120]—one might do well to focus on the ways in which intellectual resources from the West and from China's past are cited, translated, appropriated, or claimed in moments of perceived historical contingency so that something called *change* may be produced. In my view, this change is always already different from China's own past and from the West, but have profound linkages with both.

Arif Dirlik provides a useful insight into this problematic of change in his recent study of Chinese anarchism.[121] He shows, for example, that nationalism in modern Chinese intellectual discourse pointed to "a new kind of universalism that pushed against the boundaries imposed by a national reorganization of society." At issue is not the collapse of a Confucian order in the Levensonian sense, but the emergence of a new dialectical view of the nation and global society that enabled the "redefinition of China as a nation in a world of nations" while eliciting "as its dialectical counterpoint a new vision of a world in which nations would once again disappear and humankind would discover a world of unity." The utopian goal of such universalism is always already embedded in something more than the ancient Chinese ideal of *datong* (great unity), a term often appropriated by Chinese intellectuals in writing about China's future. Rather, as Dirlik describes so well in his discussion of Kang Youwei's *Datong shu* (The book of great unity):

> Kang's society of Great Unity represented the final stage of human progress, following stages of familism and nationalism, in that order. The utopia drew its name and virtues from a native Chinese utopian tradition, but already its inspiration came from the future—a future, moreover, that transcended China's own world and took as its scope the global society of which China had just become an integral part.[122]

Indeed, Confucianism was reinterpreted and appropriated by Kang to solve the crisis of China's positioning in the modern world. His disciple Tan Sitong did something similar by establishing a hypothetical equivalence between "the ideal of 'great unity' (*datong*) in the *Book of Rites* and what would appear to be a reference to Edward Bellamy's *Looking Backward*" (pp. 56–57). These acts of *equating* ideas from the Chinese classics and concepts imported from the West are significant in that they introduced a level of mediated reality or change that came into existence only after the act of equating had been initiated.

Neologism or neologistic construction is an excellent trope for change, because it has been invented simultaneously to represent and to replace foreign words, and in so doing, it identifies itself as Chinese and foreign locked in linguistic tension. One does not translate between equivalents; rather, one creates tropes of equivalence in the middle zone of interlinear translation between the host and the guest languages. This middle zone of hypothetical equivalence, which is occupied by neologistic imagination, becomes the very ground for change, a change that cannot be reduced to an essentialist understanding of modernity, for that which is untraditional is not necessarily Western and that which is called modern is not necessarily un-Chinese. A question may be asked: What do we make of those words and symbolic constructions that are exclusively of indigenous origin and have not been touched by neologistic loanwords? To answer this question, I would like to recall an example I gave earlier of the engendering of the masculine pronoun *ta*. Morphologically speaking, this character has not changed a bit, yet because of the differential intervention of the feminine *ta* and the animal/neuter *ta* in the overall system of modern Chinese, the word no longer means what it used to mean and has been made to stand for the masculine third-person singular. This *relational* transformation behind the appearance of an unchanging construction applies, I think, to other aspects of modern vernacular written Chinese as well. The presence of neologisms points to a much more widely based and deep-seated revolutionary process that has fundamentally changed the linguistic landscape of China.

It is commonplace in speech-act theory that words exist not simply to reflect external reality but to make things happen. My emphasis on translingual practice by no means reduces historical events to linguistic practices; rather, it aims to expand the notion of history by treating language, discourse, text (including historical writing itself), as genuine historical events, not the least of which is the power of discursive acts to produce the terms of legitimation in shaping the historical real.[123] To conclude this discussion, I anticipate Chapter 3 by offering a few remarks on the power of words to shape what is often termed reality. That chapter discusses the changing meaning of the translingual notion of *geren zhuyi* (individualism) in the Chinese theory of modern nation-state in the early Republican period. The point I would make here in light of that analysis is that, after 1949, the discursive struggle surrounding the meaning of individualism begins to play a remarkable role in China's reinvention of the relationship both between East and West and between the state and its intelligentsia. The state has a political stake in presenting the idea of individualism to its people as *un-Chinese*, with the consequence that the idea becomes a synecdoche for a negative West. Paradoxically, the anti-Western rhetoric of the state is most effective when it causes its opponents to rally around individualism in the predictable gesture of pro-Western defiance. What tends to be neglected, forgotten, or suppressed in these endless contentions for or against the West is precisely the potent history surrounding the discourse of individualism within China, a century-long history of translingual practice fraught with political exigencies. As late as the mid-1980's, there was a major controversy over critic Liu Zaifu's theory of literary subjectivity in mainland China.[124] In many ways, that controversy carried over some familiar overtones from earlier debates on individualism, but it also took on a character of violence reminiscent of the Cultural Revolution.[125] Yet, there is another kind of violence not so acutely felt but all the more damaging, which is amnesia, a forgetting of the discursive history of the past. I myself feel deeply connected with that history, not only because I grew up during the Cultural Revolution but, more important, because I have a utopian desire to resist that amnesia. So let this book be an embodiment of that desire.

PART I

*Between the Nation and
the Individual*

CHAPTER 2

Translating National Character:
Lu Xun and Arthur Smith

Shortly before I left China, an eminent Chinese writer pressed
me to say what I considered the chief defects of the Chinese.
With some reluctance, I mentioned three: avarice, cowardice,
and callousness. Strange to say, my interlocutor, instead of getting angry, admitted the justice of my criticism, and proceeded
to discuss possible remedies. This is a sample of the intellectual
integrity which is one of China's greatest virtues.[1]

Thus Bertrand Russell on one of his many conversations with the
Chinese writers and academics who hosted his trip to China in the winter
of 1920. During his visit, the philosopher gave numerous lectures, con-
versed with the urban elite, made friends, and toured Chinese cities and
the countryside with great enthusiasm. When he returned to England in
the following year, he did what he had always done after a trip abroad: he
wrote about his experiences in minute detail. The essays he wrote eventually crystallized into a book entitled *The Problem of China* (1922), which
has a lengthy chapter on the subject of "Chinese character." Russell began
by dismissing the common myth of the "subtle Oriental," arguing that
"in a game of mutual deception an Englishman or an American can beat
a Chinese nine times out of ten."[2] One might suspect that the author was
targeting a popular Orientalist myth about Chinamen that had dominated
the writings of European and American missionaries for well over a century, but the passage quoted above seems to contradict that speculation.

This passage demonstrates an interesting twist on what ethnographers call the relationship between the knower (Russell) and his native
informant (the Chinese interlocutor), for the latter is shown as soliciting
self-knowledge from the Western philosopher and ends up being neither a
native informant nor much of a knower. What does Russell's narrative tell
us about the Chinese and about himself as an author? Should it be read

as just another case of the Orientalism that Said criticizes in a somewhat different context? In other words, has Russell invented a factitious China for the gaze of Westerners? It seems to me that the dramatic encounter between Russell and his Chinese interlocutor, which is not without resemblances to the dialogue between Heidegger and his Japanese interlocutor discussed in Chapter 1, points to something far more complicated than Orientalist maneuvers. Among other things, it suggests that the making of the myth of national character involves a large measure of coauthorship; furthermore, since the chapter was promptly rendered into Chinese and published in a respectable journal in China, the myth was, in fact, coauthored twice and differently: once in the English original and again in Chinese translation.

The coauthorship of Chinese character in the English original, symbolized here by the exchange between the two interlocutors in that conversation, has the effect of consolidating the author's own knowledge about the other even as the subjectivity of the anonymous other is consumed in the process of appropriation. Like missionaries before him, Russell took something to be an essential Chinese virtue that, in fact, bears eloquent witness to the circumstances of modern history within which are embedded his own language and that of his Chinese interlocutor. Avarice, cowardice, and callousness are staple categories of a long-standing missionary discourse about Chinese character that need not surprise the reader. Inasmuch as Russell himself was deeply entrenched in the nineteenth-century European theory of national character, he remained impervious to the historical contingency of his own discourse. By the same token, the "eminent" Chinese writer whose identity was suppressed by Russell's narrative belonged to a generation of Chinese caught in the traumatic circumstances of their time. In their desire to resolve the crisis of national identity in the age of Western imperialism, the majority of China's elite would have asked a similar question.

Having said that, however, I must emphasize that the relationship between Russell's book and its intended English-speaking audience by no means authorizes a single reading, for rupture takes place as soon as translation begins. I am referring to the second stage of coauthorship—when a Chinese translator began introducing Russell's chapter on Chinese character to an *unintended*, Chinese-speaking audience. This translation was brought out by *Dongfang zazhi* (Eastern miscellany) in 1922 directly following the first publication of the essay in the *Atlantic Monthly*. As a matter of fact, the chapter on Chinese character was the only one of Russell's fifteen-odd chapters rendered into Chinese at that time. This chapter was chosen because, as the translator Yuzhi put it in an appended note, "the question of the Chinese *guomin xing* [national character] is one that fascinates us more than anything else."[3] Like many of his predecessors, Russell was being reframed by the Chinese debate on national character through the mediation of translingual practice.[4]

This preamble on Russell is intended to raise a number of questions, theoretical as well as historical, concerning the discursive relationship between East and West in the modern era. What happened when translation and translingual practice subjected the European theory of national character to the interpretation of an "unintended" audience of Chinese speakers? Is there an intellectually more challenging way to account for the historical transaction between East and West than Orientalism, since the latter often reduced the exchange to a matter of specularity between the gazer and the object of the gaze? What kind of light, one might ask, mediated that gaze? What were the terms of the Chinese debate on national character? How did May Fourth writers and critics articulate their agenda concerning the transformation of Chinese national character through literary efforts?

I begin by taking a brief look at the debate on national character before the rise of modern Chinese literature and then focus on the specific role that Western missionaries such as Arthur Smith played in the invention of the myth of Chinese character. I examine the ambivalent reinvention of that myth by the Chinese themselves, especially in May Fourth literary discourse, whose climactic event is Lu Xun's "True Story of Ah Q" (1921). By unraveling the circumstances of Lu Xun's contact with Smith's book, *Chinese Characteristics*, as well as his lifelong obsession with the question of national character, I try to illustrate the central predicament of modern Chinese intellectuals, who sought self-knowledge under the heavy burden of modernity.[5]

The Myth of National Character

The Chinese compound *guomin xing* (or variants *minzu xing*, *guomin de pingge*, etc.) is a Meiji neologism (*kokuminsei*), or one of several neologisms, that the Japanese used to translate the modern European notion of national character often associated with intellectual movements between the eighteenth and nineteenth century. Fueled by the idea of *Volksgeist* (folk spirit), which dominated nationalist discourse in German Romanticism, national character stressed the organic differences between nations and, more often than not, the great depth of the German mind and

German uniqueness. Among the leading French and German thinkers of the time, Herder (1744–1803) exercised the most profound impact on the development of this essentialist notion of national individuality and consciousness.[6] His theory attained an enormous popularity in the nineteenth and early twentieth centuries and still prevails in our post–Cold War era in some mediated forms.[7] The idea of national character subsumes human differences under the totalizing category of national identity and has proved tremendously useful in legitimizing Western imperialist expansion and domination of the world.[8] Its rhetoric of racial superiority, in particular, has been deployed to explain away the violence of the East–West encounter in terms of cultural essentialism and evolutionary progress, thus depriving the conquered race or nation of the ground of authority from which alternative views of difference, cultural or historical, could be articulated. (As is shown in Chapter 9, Zhang Binglin was probably one of the few to recognize the gravity of this situation and to fight in the desperate attempt to reclaim discursive authority for the Chinese.)[9]

The concept of national character, like the majority of Japanese neologisms brought into China at the turn of the twentieth century and afterward, was first used by late Qing intellectuals to develop their own theory of the modern nation-state. In a 1902 essay entitled "Xinmin yi" (Discourse on the new citizen), Liang Qichao expressed a keen interest in identifying the cause of the evils responsible for the deplorable state of the Chinese *guomin* (citizen).[10] Among other things, he attributed the evils to flaws or weaknesses in Chinese national character. In "Lun Zhongguo guomin zhi pinge" (On the character of the Chinese citizen; 1903), he pinpointed these flaws as a lack of nationalism, a lack of the will for independence and autonomy, and the absence of public spirit.[11] Between the years 1899 and 1903, Liang wrote numerous essays elaborating this idea from various angles. Examples include "Zhongguo jiruo suyuan lun" (China's weaknesses and their historical origins), "Shi zhong dexing xiangfan xiangcheng yi" (Ten moral characteristics and their positive or negative implications), "Lun Zhongguo renzhong zhi jianglai" (On the future of the Chinese race), "Guomin shida yuanqi lun" (On the ten essential spirits of the citizen), and, most important, his *Xinmin shuo* (The new citizen).[12] No matter what its contemporary political purpose in the aftermath of the Hundred Days Reform, Liang's theory exerted a profound influence on Chinese intellectuals that by far exceeded the exigencies of any particular political agenda in the years that followed. Sun Yat-sen, for instance, found it necessary to speak of China's problems in these terms. The Chinese, he said, are a peace-loving people, but they are servile, ignorant, self-centered, and lacking in the ideal of freedom.[13] The fact that Liang Qichao and Sun Yat-sen were the foremost critics of Western imperialism of their time and yet still had to subscribe to a discourse that European nations first used to stake their claim to racial superiority points to the central predicament of the Chinese intellectual. This predicament, as my analysis shows, characterizes all subsequent attempts either to claim or to reject Chinese national identity.[14]

In February 1917, *Xin qingnian* (New youth) published an article by Guang Sheng entitled "Zhongguo guomin xing jiqi ruodian" (The national character of the Chinese and its weaknesses). This essay deserves special attention because it crystallizes all the seminal arguments surrounding the notion of national character prior to the May Fourth movement. The author defined national character as an aggregate of *zhong xing* (racial character), *guo xing* (state character), and *zongjiao xing* (religious character), and on this basis he compared the Chinese with other races and nations. In short, he conceptualized the major differences between the Europeans and the Chinese according to their different attitudes toward foreign nations and religions. The Europeans are xenophobic and exclusionist; the Chinese, tolerant. Guang Sheng's point was that the Chinese capacity for tolerance had led to a disregard for independent thinking and individual freedom, which he saw as going hand in hand with the lack of a judiciary and a democratic tradition. He concluded by emphasizing the need for a radical transformation of the flawed national character, because it was no longer capable of meeting the historical demands of the modern world.[15]

If a Darwinian view compelled Guang Sheng to explain the weaknesses of Chinese character in terms of historical expediency,[16] the antitraditionalist Chen Duxiu dispensed with all of this as he tried to give the concept an essentialist turn in his "Dong xi minzu genben sixiang zhi chayi" (The fundamental difference between the thought of Eastern and Western peoples) and "Wo zhi aiguo zhuyi" (My kind of patriotism). To this leader of the New Culture movement, the Chinese national character was criticizable simply on the grounds that it was Chinese and that it was traditional. Chen Duxiu's position was more or less shared by Li Dazhao in "Dong xi wenming genben zhi yidian" (The fundamental differences between the civilizations of the East and West; 1918) and Meng Zhen in "Xinqi boruo de guoren" (The feeble spirit of the Chinese).[17] The question of national character was thus effectively incorporated into the campaign against traditional culture and cast in predominantly negative terms during the New Culture movement and the May Fourth period, whence it turned practically into a near equivalent of *guomin liegen xing* (flawed national character), as we now know it.[18] As *gaizao guomin xing* (transforming the national character) became the dominant theme in the meta-narrative of Chinese modernity, many began to accept modern literature as the best means to remedy China's problems. Over the years, literature and literary criticism proved remarkably successful in rendering the discourse of national character transparent and inimical to historical analysis—so much so that very few studies, except for Marxist criticism, have escaped the grip of its self-evident rhetoric.[19]

What is wrong with the Chinese national character? Who is responsible for its flaws? How can we change it for the better? These are the kinds of questions that profoundly disturbed the May Fourth generation who both inherited the intellectual burden of their late Qing predecessors and faced many historical crises in their own time. But the same questions also inspired those who had lost faith in the majority of the popular theories that professed to explain the cause of China's weakness. Lu Xun is a case in point. Becoming disenchanted with the study of medical science in his youth, he raised doubts about the potency of science, asking what medicine could really do for a nation weak in spirit. He seized upon the theory of *guomin xing* as an alternative and believed that he had found a diagnostic method to cure the sick Chinese people. At this embryonic stage of May Fourth literature, the theory of national character equipped Lu Xun and his generation of writers with a powerful language of self-criticism, one that would ultimately target Confucianism as the chief evil of Chinese tradition. More significantly, the theory of national character led them to justify Chinese literary modernity as a national project whose importance to China's nation-building efforts fundamentally outstripped that of state wealth, military power, science and technology, and the like. Modern literature was thus entrusted with the clinical task of "dissecting" (Lu Xun's favorite verb) the sick mind of the nation in order to restore life to its weakened body. It became for Lu Xun "a way to find out about his people—about what constitutes, or is lacking in, the 'Chinese national character'—now that he had realized that root of their illness did not at all lie with their bodies."[20] The medical and anatomical tropes that dominated the debate on literary modernity effected a subtle homology between the literary and the clinical, and this "metaphorical" analogy helped arrogate the healing power of medical science to May Fourth literature while elevating the status of literature above that of science on the basis of a mind-body opposition.

Lu Xun became acquainted with the theory by reading Liang Qichao and other late Qing reformers, but not until he went to Japan and especially after reading Arthur Smith's *Chinese Characteristics* (in a Japanese translation) did he seriously begin to contemplate the possibility of transforming the Chinese character by means of literature.[21] Through the power of his charismatic influence, the subject of national character has gained a firm hold on the imagination of Chinese intellectuals for nearly a century in the form of a collective obsession. Since they are preoccupied with defining, identifying, criticizing, and transforming the Chinese character, many of them stop short of problematizing the discourse of national character itself or reflecting on the contingency of its own historical validity. As recently as the 1980's, post-Mao intellectuals once again asked the century-old question: "What is wrong with Chinese character?" as if one could, indeed, come up with a genuine answer.[22] Of course, until that question itself is subjected to interrogation, one can hardly raise alternative questions concerning modern Chinese history and literature.

Lu Xun and Arthur Smith

The theory of Chinese character was imported to Asia by Westerners, mainly Western missionaries, long before Chinese enlightenment thinkers used it to promote modern literature. The circumstances of Lu Xun's encounter with this theory through the works of Arthur Smith provide rich grounds for a focused look at the meaning of Chinese literary modernity in the early twentieth century. Smith (known to the Chinese as Ming Enpu) was a missionary from North America who spent many years in China during the latter part of the nineteenth century.[23] He wrote a number of books on the subject of Chinese people while a missionary in rural North China. *Chinese Characteristics* was first published as a series of essays in the *North-China Daily News* of Shanghai in 1889; like most missionary travel narratives, it enjoyed great popularity among Westerners in Asia, as well as in Britain, the United States, and Canada and reached a wide audience, religious and secular alike. It was the most widely read and influential American work on China of its time and as late as 1920 was still among the five most read books on China among foreigners living in China.[24] As evidence of its continued influence on the American understanding of the Chinese, a contemporary critic of Smith's views observes that "Smith builds up a complex view of some basic Chinese characteristics. If some of them seem familiar today, we should remind ourselves that earlier writers, from Marco Polo to S. Wells Williams, left out a great many things that are just those that we think most interesting."[25]

Although Smith's book was but one of many channels through which the theory of national character became known and disseminated among the Chinese, it happened to be the primary source for Lu Xun's conception of national character.[26] *Chinese Characteristics* first captured Lu Xun's attention through the industrious efforts of a Japanese translator named Shibue Tamotsu who rendered the 1894 edition of Smith's book into Japanese and brought it out in 1896. According to Zhang Mengyang, Lu Xun came into contact with this translation during his student days in Japan (1902–9) when the theory of national character was being passionately discussed by Japanese nationalists.[27] On more than one occasion, Lu Xun alluded to this book as well as to the Japanese translation in his letters, diary, and familiar prose (*zawen*). In the entry for July 2, 1926, of the "Mashang zhi riji" installments (Subchapter of the instant journal; 1926), for instance, he mentioned a book written in Japanese whose title he translated as *Cong xiaoshuo kanlai de Zhina minzu xing* (Chinese characteristics perceived from their fictional works), which he had bought in Beijing.[28] (A passionate bibliophile, Lu Xun filled his diaries, real and fictional, with such details.) He pointed out the heavy debt of the author of the book, Yasuoka Hideo, to Smith's *Chinese Characteristics*.[29] "As early as twenty years ago [*sic*]," Lu Xun recalled, "the Japanese had already published a translation under the title of *Shinajin kishitsu*. We Chinese, however, barely took notice of the existence of that book."[30] Apparently, he had Shibue Tamotsu's 1896 translation in mind. It is interesting to note that Lu Xun disagreed with Yasuoka on a number of issues and even made fun of some of his mistakes on occasion. For instance, in the entry for July 4, 1926, of "Mashang zhi riji," he ridiculed Yasuoka for taking Chinese cuisine as indicative of a collective erotic obsession. On the other hand, Lu Xun strove to show that his quarrel with the Japanese author by no means canceled out the need for the Chinese to criticize their own national character. "It is no easy task to determine the true nature [of Chinese character]," said Lu Xun in the same entry. "Alas, the Chinese prefer not to think about themselves that way."[31]

Seven years later, Lu Xun again alluded to the Smith book in connection with the question of national character in a letter to Tao Kangde dated October 27, 1933.

> Nowadays, there is no lack of so-called *Shinatō* [China experts] in Japan but very few who truly know China. Most of the attacks on the weaknesses of the Chinese in that country have been based on a master text—Smith's *Chinese Characteristics*. The original work, which was rendered into Japanese nearly forty years ago, surpasses the similar line of work done by the Japanese them-

selves. It would be a good idea to have the book translated and introduced to the Chinese audience (although I realize that it contains miscellaneous errors). I wonder if the English original is still in print.[32]

Lu Xun's desire to see Smith's book in Chinese translation remained strong throughout his life. Shortly before his death, in "'Li ci cunzhao,' no. 3" (Memorandum, no. 3), he wrote: "I still have hopes that someone will eventually start translating Smith's *Chinese Characteristics*, because this book offers insights that would lead us to analyze, question, improve, and transform ourselves. Rather than clamoring for recognition and praise from others, we must struggle with ourselves and find out what it means to be Chinese."[33] Scholars such as Zhang Mengyang complained in the 1980's that Lu Xun's deathbed wish remained unfulfilled after all these years.[34] In fact, two Chinese translations exist. The first one, entitled *Zhinaren zhi qizhi* after the Japanese *Shinajin kishitsu—kishitsu* being an alternative semantic translation of "character"—is a close rendering of Shibue's 1896 version of Smith's book in classical Chinese including the Japanese translator's notes and commentaries. It was translated and published by Zuoxin she in Shanghai in 1903.[35] Lu Xun did not see this version because it came out the year after he left for Japan. The second version is a free adaptation of Smith's work, not from a Japanese translation but directly from the English original, published in 1937, the year after Lu Xun's death. The translator Pan Guangdan, a returned student from North America and a leading eugenist and Freudian literary critic of his time, rendered fifteen chapters of Smith's book into vernacular Chinese and included them in his *Minzu texing yu minzu weisheng* (National character and national hygiene), which was part of a series of popular writings on eugenics, culture, and biological science organized by Wang Yunwu of the Commercial Press[36] (see Figs. 1a–c). Interestingly, neither Lu Xun nor Pan Guangdan seemed aware of the existence of the 1903 version.

What sort of a book is *Chinese Characteristics*? Smith's critic, Charles W. Hayford, notes that the book is flawed by "immaturity of theory and by Smith's failure to examine his own middle-class American culture in such a way as to understand its relativity." Although I agree with much of what Hayford says about Smith's limitations, he seems to imply that a self-reflexive, properly trained ethnographic approach would have helped eliminate its ethnocentrism.[37] In my view, it was perhaps not Smith's theoretical immaturity but his profound intellectual indebtedness to the nineteenth-century European theory of national character that led him to take the positions he did.[38] Smith proposed 26 main categories as the theoretical ground for his definition of Chinese character and devoted

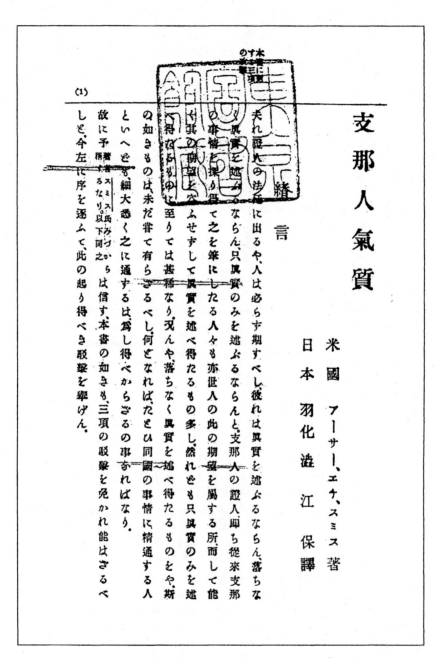

支那人氣質

米國　アーサー、エナ、スミス　著

日本　羽化遊江　保譯

(1)

緒言

夫れ證人の法廷に出るや、人は必らず期すべし彼れは眞實を逃ぶるならん、落ちな
らん、只眞實のみを逃ぶるならんと、支那人の證人即ち從來支那
の事情と操り得て之を筆にしたる人々も亦世人の此の期望を屬する所而して能
ふせずして眞實を逃べ得たるもの多し、然れども只眞實のみを逃
べ得たるものは甚稀なり、况んや落ちなく眞實を逃べ得たるものをや、斯
の如きものは未だ嘗て有らざるべし、何となれば、たとひ同國の事情に精通する人
といへども細大悉く之に通するは爲し得べからざるの事あればなり、
故に予輩スミス氏みづから(以下同之)は信す、本書の如きも三項の敗撃を免かれ能はざるべ
しと、今左に序を逐ふて、此の起り得べき敗撃を舉げん、

FIG. IA. First page of Preface of Shibue Tamotsu's Japanese translation of Arthur Smith's *Chinese Characteristics* (1896)

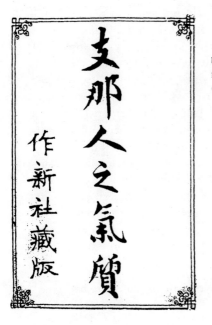

支那人之氣質

作新社藏版

FIG. IB. Title page of the 1903 Chinese rendering of the Japanese version of *Chinese Characteristics*

FIG. IC. Sample page from Pan Guangdan's 1937 vernacular Chinese translation of *Chinese Characteristics*

一七　愛臉皮的中國人

　　我說臉皮是中國人特性之一。臉皮是一種大家有的東西，如今說是中國人特性之一，似乎是太不合情理了。但我不妨解釋一下我這裏所稱的臉皮也就是中國人心目中的臉皮，並不指頭部前面的那一薄層，却是一個綜合的名詞，中間包括許多的意思，不要說我們西洋人描寫不來，恐怕根本就懷它不得。

　　我們真要明白這臉皮的意義於萬一的話，我們先得了解，中國民族是富有戲劇的本能的一個民族。戲劇可以說是中國獨一無二的公共娛樂戲劇之於中國人好比運動之於英國人，或鬥牛之於西班牙人。一個中國人遇到了甚麼事故，他就立刻把自己常作一折戲裏的一門脚色。他就唱諾連聲或磕頭如搗蒜在一個西洋人看來似乎是絕對不必的，並且除了引人發笑以外絲毫不能有甚麼功用。中國人的思想也不脫戲臺上的意味。假使他受了人家的欺侮或奚落以

一七　愛臉皮的中國人

一四九

a chapter to each: face, economy, industry, politeness, a disregard for time, a disregard for accuracy, a talent for misunderstanding, a talent for indirection, flexible inflexibility, intellectual turbidity, an absence of nerves, contempt for foreigners, an absence of public spirit, conservatism, indifference to comfort and convenience, physical vitality, patience and perseverance, contentment and cheerfulness, filial piety, benevolence, an absence of sympathy, social typhoons [sic], mutual responsibility and respect for law, mutual suspicion, an absence of sincerity, polytheism-pantheism-atheism.[39] Within each chapter, Smith elaborated on the category by telling anecdotes and making generalized (and relentlessly comparative) statements about the Chinese race as a whole.[40]

Take the chapter on "the absence of nerves." Smith describes the Chinese as being oblivious to levels of pain, noise, or life's other inconveniences that Occidentals (often equated with the Anglo-Saxon race in his writings) find unacceptable or offensive. Commenting on what he calls the Chinese habits of sleep, he wrote:

> In the item of sleep, the Chinese establishes the same difference between himself and the Occidental as in the directions already specified. Generally speaking, he is able to sleep anywhere. None of the trifling disturbances which drive us to despair annoy him. With a brick for a pillow, he can lie down on his bed of stalks or mud bricks or rattan and sleep the sleep of the just, with no reference to the rest of the creation. He does not want his room darkened, nor does he require others to be still. The "infant crying in the night" may continue to cry for all he cares, for it does not disturb him. In some regions the entire population seem to fall asleep, as by a common instinct (like that of the hibernating bear), during the first two hours of summer afternoons, and they do this with regularity, no matter where they may be. At two hours after noon the universe at such seasons is as still as at two hours after midnight. In the case of most working-people, at least, and also in that of many others, position in sleep is of no sort of consequence. It would be easy to raise in China an army of a million men—nay, of ten millions— tested by competitive examination as to their capacity to go to sleep across three wheelbarrows, with head downwards, like a spider, their mouths wide open and a fly inside.[41]

This passage vividly captures Smith's style of presentation. The use of the present tense and of the totalizing phrase "the Chinese" provided him with a powerful grammar of truth, and he devoted this grammar to the singular task of spelling out the essential difference between the Chinese and the Occidental. Sleep, as a common physiological marker, serves to delineate a field of cultural difference whose meanings are predetermined by reference to the indisputable superiority of the Occidental. At

issue is not a question of misrepresentation, but one of discursive power
that reduces the object of its description to a less than human animal
through rhetorical and figurative uses of language. One cannot help but
be struck by the contemptuous metaphors meant to be humorous such as
the "hibernating bear" and "spiders." This contempt no doubt reflects the
author's racist attitude toward the Chinese, but something else in it seems
to circumscribe his racism in class terms; that is, Smith's relationship with
his native servants. Given that the closest tie that could be formed between a foreign missionary and a Chinese in those early years was that between master and servant—the local gentry openly showed their hostility
to the missionary presence—it is not surprising that Smith, who complained constantly about his native servants, cited many anecdotes that
derive either from his own unhappy experience with the Chinese working class or from others' accounts of similar experiences. This class-based
relationship between the foreigner and his native servant was invariably
exploited in the service of the familiar discourse of Chinese national character and, at the same time, remained itself unseen and unarticulated as
the fundamental condition of that discourse.

When this relationship gets played out at the level of international
politics, the rhetorical question Smith asked in his concluding chapter
seems inevitable: "Can China be reformed from within herself?"[42] His
answer is that China stands in need of foreign interventions so the evangelical message of Christian civilization may spread and improve the character of its people. "In order to reform China, the springs of character
must be *reached* and *purified*, conscience must be practically *enthroned*, and
no longer imprisoned in its own palace like the long line of Japanese Mika-
dos"[43] (italics added). How would a Chinese respond to such missionary
rhetoric? The novelist Lao She, who had extensive contact with Christian
missionaries in his early youth, left a scathing caricature of missionaries
in his novel, *Er Ma* (Mr. Ma and son). The following passage from the
novel may shed some useful light on the unspoken message of Smith's
statement.

> The Reverend Evans was a man who had spent over 20 years in China as
> a missionary. He knew everything about China—from the mythical days
> when Fu Xi invented the Eight Trigrams, all the way up to the time Yuan
> Shikai proclaimed himself emperor (that was an event which particularly
> delighted him). He was so knowledgeable about China that aside from the
> fact that his spoken Chinese was poor, he could literally pass for a walking
> encyclopedia of China. And he genuinely loved the Chinese people. Some-
> times in the middle of the night when he couldn't get to sleep, he prayed to

God that China would someday by colonized by the British; with burning tears in his eyes, he beseeched the Lord: if the Chinese don't let the British take over, then all those masses of yellow-faced, black-haired souls will *never* make it to heaven![44]

If Reverend Evans is a mere fictional character brought to life by the genius of Lao She, he is no more so than the Chinese characters portrayed by Smith. The points of resemblance between Evans and Smith are startling, although in Smith's case the reader does not have a detached narrator directing attention to the irony of the situation or to Smith's violent verbs. The fact is that those verbs translate extremely well into imperialist action: invasion (reaching), conquer (purifying), and the seizure of sovereignty (enthroning).[45]

"Missionary discursive practices were intended to, and in fact did, shape reality rather than merely passively reflect or mirror it," as James Hevia points out in a recent study.[46] His analysis of the missionary accounts (including Smith's *China in Convulsion*) of the atrocities committed by the Allies in retaliation for the Boxer Rebellion lends a great deal of insight into the ways in which those early *representations*—such as the implicit and explicit comparison with biblical events, the portrayal of deceased missionaries as martyrs, and pronouncements on Chinese character—shaped the historical "real" and the ways in which future generations perceived it.[47] Missionary discourse and the imperialist actions of the Eight Powers in the aftermath of the Boxer movement implicate each other in more ways than the metaphorical linkages suggested above. (Incidentally, Lao She's father, who was a Manchu guard at the Forbidden City in Beijing, was killed during the Allied assault on the city.)[48]

Indeed, the same can be said of the missionary discourses on the Chinese national character that should not be taken as mere false representations of the Chinese but, rather, as genuine historical events that have shaped the course of modern history and the relation between China and the West. Smith's book belongs to a special genre of missionary and imperialist writings that made a huge difference in modern Western perceptions of China and the Chinese, as well as the self-perception of the Chinese and the Westerners themselves. Some of the earliest efforts to theorize about Chinese character were written by American missionary S. W. Williams, who published *The Middle Kingdom* in 1848; British missionary Henry Charles Sirr, whose *China and the Chinese* came out in 1849; French missionary Evariste-Regis Huc, who brought out *The Chinese Empire* in 1854; and Thomas Taylor Meadows, who wrote *The Chinese and Their Rebellions* in 1856 and is quoted by Smith in *Chinese Characteristics.*

Others include Sir Walter Henry Medhurst, the famous author of *The Foreigner in Far Cathay* (1872), and British journalist George Wingrove Cooke, who served as the China correspondent for the *London Times* between 1857 and 1858. Smith quotes from the preface to Cooke's published collection of letters in his own introduction to *Chinese Characteristics*. His quote is particularly illuminating for understanding the myth of national character in the nineteenth century. The intertextual relationship thus established between Smith and Cooke betrays the status of Western knowledge regarding Chinese character that is thoroughly embedded in the theoretical discourse of its time and has little to do with the transparent or objective truths it claims. In fact, Cooke himself expressed a certain degree of ambivalence regarding the knowledge claims of this discourse. To illustrate my point, I quote a lengthy passage from Cooke's preface:

> I have, in these letters, introduced no elaborate essay upon Chinese character. It is a great omission. No theme could be more tempting, no subject could afford wider scope for ingenious hypothesis, profound generalization, and triumphant dogmatism. Every small critic will, probably, utterly despise me for not having made something out of such opportunities. The truth is, that I have written several very fine characters for the whole Chinese race, but having the misfortune to have the people under my eye at the same time with my essay, they were always saying something or doing something which rubbed so rudely against my hypothesis, that in the interest of truth I burnt several successive letters. I may add that I have often talked over this matter with the most eminent and candid sinologues, and have always found them ready to agree with me as to the impossibility of *a Western mind forming* a conception of Chinese character as a whole. These difficulties, however, occur only to those who know the Chinese practically: a smart writer, entirely ignorant of the subject, might readily strike off a brilliant and antithetical analysis, which should leave nothing to be desired but *Truth*.
>
> Some day, perhaps, we may acquire the necessary knowledge to give to each of the glaring inconsistencies of a Chinaman's mind its proper weight and influence in the general mass. At present, I at least must be content to avoid strict definitions, and to describe a Chinaman by his most prominent qualities.[49] (Italics added)

Apart from dropping or changing the words italicized above, Smith's quotation from Cooke's preface misses the subtle irony of the latter's apology by construing it as a failed attempt to describe Chinese character. Using Cooke's ambivalent rhetoric to his own advantage, he argues that, after several hundred years of acquaintance with China, Westerners are now ready to form some kind of integrated knowledge about the Chinese just as they have done with other complex natural phenomena.[50] His own work would typify such knowledge.

Did Smith invent a China for the Orientalist gaze of the West? True, Smith played an important part in introducing the resources of a totalizing discourse about the Chinese to the elite Chinese such as Lu Xun, and the affinities between his text and the phenomenon Said discusses in *Orientalism* seem obvious. Such an explanation cannot, however, bring out the full complexity of the picture, particularly when one is also dealing with the translation and translingual practice surrounding the theory of Chinese national character within China. What happens when the same missionary discourse is put to an "unintended" use by an "unintended" audience? What kind of reality does it shape? These questions must be asked in the context of Chinese translingual practice, for as soon as the host language is brought into the picture (and it must be), the situation becomes far more blurred than the often-assumed specular relationship between the subject and object in contemporary East–West cultural criticism. Unlike some of the earlier Orientalist philosophers and philologists who had written stories about the Far East, Smith and some of his predecessors such as Henry Charles Sirr and the others mentioned above were also translated into Chinese (although many of these translations were excerpts rather than whole texts). And the majority of these translations came via Japan, having either been introduced by the Japanese first or simply reworked from Japanese translations.[51] The fact that these texts were translated and read by the Chinese and participated in the Chinese debate on national character presents us with a different set of problems from the Orientalist problematic that Said treats so well in another context.

Translating National Character

When knowledge passes from the guest language to the host language, it inevitably takes on new meanings in its new historico-linguistic environment; the translation remains connected with the original idea as no more and, perhaps no less, than a *trope of equivalence*. Everything else must be determined by the users of the host language. In the course of translingual practice, the assumed meanings of Smith's text were thus intercepted by the unintended audiences (first Japanese and then Chinese) who subjected them to unexpected readings and appropriation in the context of the host language. Lu Xun was among the first generation of this unintended Chinese audience, but he was no ordinary reader or translator. On the basis of an earlier Japanese translation of the Smith book, he "translated" the missionary theory of Chinese character into his own literary practice and became the foremost architect of modern Chinese fiction.

From early on, Lu Xun's struggle with the question of national identity was fraught with conflicts, doubts, and ambivalences. On the one hand, he was attracted to the discourse of national character as a theory that would enable him and others to explain the traumatic experience of the Chinese since the Opium War of 1839–42; on the other hand, his subscription to that theory was simultaneously thwarted by his situated subjectivity as a Chinese, which had nothing in common with the condescending view of missionaries like Smith. In *Wang you Lu Xun yinxiang ji* (Reminiscences of my late friend Lu Xun), Xu Shoushang, a lifelong friend of Lu Xun, recalled Lu Xun's early contact with the discourse of national character in Japan.

> During the time the two of us were together at the Kōbun Institute, Lu Xun would often bring up three major questions for discussion, and these were all interconnected questions: First, what was the best ideal of human nature? Second, what was most lacking in Chinese national character? Third, what were the roots of its sickness? His decision to give up medicine in order to throw himself wholeheartedly into literary movements was driven by the desire to solve those problems, and he grappled with them throughout his life. He knew that even though such problems would not disappear overnight it was still worth the effort, and he was willing to make personal contributions to a possible solution. With that goal in mind, he started creating journals and translating fiction and wrote the several million words that he did in the subsequent years.[52]

Xu's view is supported by Lu Xun's confession in the much-quoted preface to his first collection of short stories, *Nahan* (Call to arms). Recalling the circumstances of his conversion from medical studies to modern literature at the Sendai Medical School, Lu Xun wrote:

> I do not know what advanced methods are now used to teach microbiology, but at that time lantern slides were used to show the microbes; and if the lecture ended early, the instructor might show slides of national scenery or news to fill up the time. This was during the Russo-Japanese War, so there were many war films, and I had to join in the clapping and cheering in the lecture hall along with the other students. It was a long time since I had seen any compatriots, but one day I saw a film showing some Chinese, one of whom was bound, while many others stood around him. They were all strong fellows but appeared completely apathetic. According to the commentary, the one with his hands bound was a spy working for the Russians, who was to have his head cut off by the Japanese military as a warning to others, while the Chinese beside him had come to enjoy the spectacle.
>
> Before the term was over I had left for Tokyo, because after this film I felt that medical science was not so crucial after all. When the people of a nation

FIG. 2. The execution of an alleged Chinese spy in Manchuria by Japanese soldiers during the Russo-Japanese War (1905)

were ignorant and weak *guomin* [citizens], it mattered little whether or not they were physically strong if in the end they amounted to little more than the object of a futile spectacle or the audience for such a spectacle. Physical illness, by comparison, seemed not such a terrible thing after all, although it too cost lives. I came to the conclusion that the important thing to do was to transform people's spirit and that literature was the best suitable means to that end. Hence my decision to promote a literary movement.[53]

This passage tends to be quoted and analyzed by critics who wish to establish a straightforward biographical reading of the author's fictional works. For many years, scholars have labored to identify the slide in question, but with little success; and it has been suggested that the famous incident may have been fabricated by the author out of events he had witnessed or heard about.[54] In 1983, Japanese scholar Ōta Susumu brought to light an obscure photo carrying the date 1905 (see Fig. 2). The small print on the side reads "Execution of a Russian spy. Among the audience were also soldiers laughing (shot outside the town of Kaiyuan, Manchuria, on March 20, 1905)." The date coincides with the period of the Russo-Japanese War described in Lu Xun's narrative and, moreover, the content of the photo bears a striking resemblance to that of the slide he claims to have seen. For all these similarities, however, scholars have not been able to establish the exact relationship between the two.[55]

However, the recovery of the slide and the factual ground for Lu Xun's narrative would not automatically account for the power of Lu Xun's narrative. One would be still interpreting Lu Xun in the scholarly mode of the *free indirect style*, that is, a paraphrasing, albeit in scholarly narrative prose, of his enlightenment ideas in his own terms.[56] My reading intends to focus on the rhetoric of representation in this haunting narrative of violence: Who represents and who gets represented? Who views the representation?

Lu Xun's strikingly poignant description of his traumatic experience calls for a reading that must account for the violence of representation, and not just the representation of violence, inflicted by a cinematic spectacle upon an unintended audience—Lu Xun the narrator.[57] The spectacle, the viewers framed by the spectacle, the viewers outside that frame, the unintended Chinese viewer among the audience, who in turn becomes the narrator that recounts the story one reads, and, finally, the reader who is made to go through the mediated viewing experience—all these must be taken into account as part of our complex experience of Lu Xun's representation of horror. In a later and less discussed essay that evokes the same incident, Lu Xun tried to grapple with the contradiction of his position as a Chinese viewer in that soul-wrenching moment. In this 1926 essay—entitled "Tengye xiansheng" (Professor Fujino) and devoted to the fond recollection of Fujino Gonkyurō, a teacher at the Sendai Medical School—Lu Xun reframed his story about the news slide:

> During my second year, bacteriology was added to the curriculum and the configuration of bacteria was taught exclusively through film slides. Whenever the lecture ended early, the instructor would show slides of news to fill up the time, much of which had to do with the Japanese military triumph over the Russians. Unfortunately, some Chinese were depicted in one of those shows who had been caught by the Japanese for allegedly spying for the Russians and were about to be executed. *There was a group of Chinese men witnessing the execution within the film but, in the lecture hall, there was another Chinese watching. It was I myself.*
>
> "*Banzai!*" They clapped hands and cheered loudly.
>
> As a rule, the clapping of hands and cheering would follow each of the shows. But this time I found them particularly jarring to the ear. Years later after I returned to China, I was to witness similar scenes of execution that people would watch with relish and cheer as if they were all intoxicated. Oh, what imbecility! It was there and then that my thinking underwent a transformation.[58] (Italics added)

The transformation alluded to here is Lu Xun's decision to abandon his medical studies. More explicitly than in the preface quoted earlier, Lu Xun drew a sharp distinction between himself and the cheering Japanese viewers in the lecture hall—he cannot join in their cheering and clapping. With equal vehemence, he refused to identify with the Chinese onlookers he saw in the film or in real life. His subjectivity coincided with, but refused to be, either the object or audience of such representation. The coincidence and the refusal duly translated into numerous spectacles of violence in stories such as "Medicine," "A Warning to the Public," and "The True Story of Ah Q," as well as in some of his "Wild Grass" poems in which an unfeeling crowd watches the execution or plight of their countrymen with great relish. Staged as a representation of Chinese national character, the drama of violence in these texts also unfolds at the level of reading where the reader is shocked to discover that she or he is implicated in the violence of representation by being induced to play the role of a witness to the same spectacle of horror enacted over and over again in Lu Xun's texts. Indeed, the multiple coincidences and noncoincidences between the reader, the narrator, the spectator within the text, and those outside it raise important questions for our understanding of Lu Xun's subject position in the matter of Chinese national character.

Scholars are divided on Lu Xun's view of national character. To some, Lu Xun's concept of *guomin xing* refers to the negative aspect of national character (*guomin liegen xing*), which they locate specifically in the context of national struggles against imperialism and feudalism during the Republican period.[59] Others see this concept as an equivalent of *minzu xing* defined as a totality of homogeneous ideas, mood, will, and emotion conditioned by social norms and by national history and economy.[60] Whatever their personal agenda, most critics share the assumption that national character is an essential, unproblematic category of analysis in the study of Lu Xun.[61] Rather than viewing Lu Xun as a participant in the making of a historical discourse, they generally credit him with the discovery of Chinese national character per se. "The True Story of Ah Q" readily plays into this picture.

"Ah Q" stands for a twentieth-century legacy in Chinese literature and culture. As contemporary critic Li Tuo sums up so well: "The word 'Ah Q' never used to exist in the Chinese language. It was the pure invention of Lu Xun. However, once the idea escaped from under the pen of its creator, it took on a life of its own and traveled among hundreds of thousands of people whose repeated evocations and citations helped generate further topics and discourses."[62] Of those topics and discourses, the theory of national character has claimed the attention of the majority of Chinese readers and critics. Drawing mainly on Lu Xun's own desire to transform the national character of the Chinese, critics hail "The True Story of Ah Q" as a quintessential text about the Chinese national character.[63] They cite much evidence from Lu Xun's own works in support of that view, and their evidence generally affirms the character of Ah Q as an embodiment of Chinese national character.[64] But little attention has been paid to the equal contribution to the myth of national character made by the body of literary criticism that aims to legitimize the reading of national character. The criticism is inescapably contaminated by the same intellectual predicaments with which Lu Xun himself had to struggle. The latter's nightmare of having to bear witness to the cinematic scene of horror is replayed in a literary criticism that insists on testifying to the execution of the flawed national character in Lu Xun's fiction. Such is the power of Lu Xun's representation of fragmented subjectivity that the cinematic scene always comes back to haunt the critics in various forms of violence.

In textual analyses, Ah Q's obsession with face is often cited as a central argument for Chinese national character. Ah Q's tendency to rationalize defeat has inspired some of the most entertaining episodes in the story. The most poignant is the moment when Ah Q, who has never held a writing brush in his life, is asked to draw a circle (in place of a signature) on a court document that probably contains his own death sentence. Embarrassed that he cannot make the circle round, Ah Q thinks that "in this world it was the fate of everybody at some time to be dragged in and out of prison, and to have to draw circles on paper; it was only because his circle had not been round that he felt there was a stain on his reputation. Presently, however, he regained composure by thinking, 'Only idiots can make perfect circles.' And with this thought he fell asleep."[65] This depiction no doubt reflects the essence of Ah Q-ism, but what does it tell us about Chinese national character in general? One thing at least is certain: before the arrival of the missionary discourse, face had not been a meaningful category in the comparative study of cultures, much less the unique property of the Chinese. The first chapter of *Chinese Characteristics*, for example, is devoted to face.[66] We are told that "once rightly apprehended, 'face' will be found to be in itself a key to the combination lock of many of the most important characteristics of the Chinese. . . . To save one's face and lose one's life would not seem to us very attractive, but we have heard of a Chinese District Magistrate who, as a special favour, was allowed to be beheaded in his robes of office in order to save his face!"

Smith attributed the cult of face to the strong Chinese instinct for drama: "Upon very slight provocation, any Chinese regards himself in the light of an actor in a drama. He throws himself into theatrical attitudes, performs the salaam, falls upon his knees, prostrates himself and strikes his head upon the earth, under circumstances which to an Occidental seem to make such actions superfluous, not to say ridiculous. A Chinese thinks in theatrical terms."[67]

James Hevia makes an illuminating observation about Smith's category of face in his discussion of the Allies' brutality against the city of Beijing during their crackdown on the Boxer Rebellion.

> Smith presented this "Chinese characteristic" as an accurate representation of Chinese social behavior, and it has come down to us largely unquestioned in that form. The point is not whether face is actually an organizing category in Chinese practices but rather the place that it holds in a Western discourse of ritualized destruction and lesson teaching. We must consider, in other words, the role of face in authorizing the destruction of walls, towers, and temples. The China lore of missionaries such as Brown and Smith constituted "face" as a singular attribute of the colonized, while denying that representatives of the allied powers were concerned themselves with appearances or that their discursive practices might actually produce "face." Constructing their Chinese in these terms (making their object, as it were, responsible for the illusions of face), the Powers could then in good conscience act with impunity against symbols they took as significant to a Chinese mind that could mistakenly ascribe magical powers to walls and confuse the apparent and the real.[68]

But what happens when this missionary story about face is put to an unintended use by the Chinese? One must account for the complexities of the trajectory of a discourse when translingual practice is involved. Thirty years after Smith made those pronouncements about face in Chinese culture, his script was enacted almost verbatim by a theatrical Ah Q. In the scene preceding his execution, Ah Q is put on a convict's cart and paraded through the streets. When he realizes that he is heading for the execution ground, he regrets that he has not sung any lines from an opera and searches his memory for a suitable song: "His thoughts revolved like a whirlwind: *The Young Widow and Her Husband's Grave* was not heroic enough. The words of 'I regret to have killed' in *The Battle of Dragon and Tiger* were too poor. *I'll thrash you with a steel mace* was still the best. But when he wanted to raise his hands, he remembered that they were bound together; so he did not sing *I'll thrash you* either."[69] Vain, pathetic, ridiculous, and, worst of all, theatrical, Ah Q's performance seems to confirm

Smith's description of Chinese character except for some significant details. First, Lu Xun was already acquainted with Smith's theory of Chinese
character before he conceived the idea of "Ah Q," which suggests that his
story might be connected with the earlier text in more ways than just con-
firming Smith's point. Second, Smith's magistrate wore a dignified robe,
whereas Lu Xun's narrator informs us that Ah Q is forced into a "white
[mourning] vest of foreign cloth." Are there points of allusion between
the two texts? Does the Ah Q who wears a "white vest of foreign cloth"
represent Chinese character, or something else? One further question: Is
the theory of Chinese character fabricated with the same foreign material
as the mourning vest?

In 1926, five years after the publication of "Ah Q," Lu Xun mentioned
Smith's chapter on face in an essay and made the following tongue-in-
cheek comment:

> I know quite a number of foreigners who devote themselves to the study of
> so-called Chinese *ti mian* or *mianzi* [face]. They are either influenced by Smith
> or have discovered the topic through their own experiments. But I suspect
> that those foreigners are long seasoned in this kind of knowledge and have
> even put it to standard practice. I am sure that, if they continue to improve
> on their knowledge, they will not only be invincible in diplomatic trans-
> actions, but win the good faith of those upper-class *Shinajin* [here Lu Xun
> uses a derogatory Japanese term for the Chinese] as well. They will then have
> to say *hua ren* [a Chinese term for the Chinese] instead of *Shinajin*, for this
> form of address, too, has to do with the face of the "Chinese."[70]

Lu Xun's satiric barb is directed at those whose knowledge of Chinese
character is far from disinterested. The study of face, as he observed with
acute insight, has something to do with transactions between imperialists
and the upper-class Chinese, and the theory is useful to them not so much
because it provides a credible explanation for the Chinese race as because
their mutual interests are served by it. If class figures as an important
factor in Lu Xun's understanding of Chinese character, how does Ah Q
fit into this picture? Does not an illiterate, homeless lumpen like Ah Q
precisely call the theory into question? Did Lu Xun contradict himself?
Where exactly did he stand in relation to Smith?

Patrick Hanan's study of the literary prototype for Ah Q sheds impor-
tant light on these questions. Taking up Zhou Zuoren's suggestion that
Lu Xun's technique of irony in "Ah Q" was mainly modeled on that of
Gogol, the Polish novelist Henryk Sienkiewicz, and the Japanese novelist
Natsume Sōseki, he pursues at greater lengths the textual linkages be-

tween "Ah Q" and two stories written by Lu Xun's favorite Polish writer, Sienkiewicz. His analysis reveals striking similarities between "Ah Q" and Sienkiewicz's "Bartek the Victor" and "Charcoal Sketches," both of which are characterized by the use of a "high irony on the narrator's part to treat the meanest figures in village life."[71] The protagonist in "Bartek the Victor" is a Polish peasant whose talent for self-deception anticipates Ah Q's philosophy of so-called spiritual victory. Bartek is a perennial loser in the games of life, and Zolzik, the hero of the other story, is a pathetic figure whose romantic longings or lust for the wife of the peasant Repa prefigures Ah Q's absurd romance. In fact, the connections between "Ah Q" and the Sienkiewicz stories established by Patrick Hanan extend well beyond those parallels to certain broad features. The disquisition on Ah Q's name, for example, echoes a passage at the beginning of "Bartek the Victor," and according to Hanan, the word *zhengzhuan* in the title of Lu Xun's story may have been inspired by the ironic term "proper biographies" found in "Charcoal Sketches," although Lu Xun's narrator chooses to give us a different explanation within the context of the story.[72] Hanan's investigation by no means suggests that Lu Xun's story is derivative of Sienkiewicz's works, but it does indicate that the character of Ah Q exceeds national boundaries by a large measure and that the problem of class as transposed from the Polish literary prototype may be the relevant factor here.

Class-informed readings do from time to time pose a challenge to the interpretation of Ah Q as an embodiment of national character, but that challenge seldom proceeds from a concern with the interplay of textual sources as Hanan has analyzed. It is represented by orthodox Chinese Marxist critics who, since Qian Xingcun in the 1930's, have interpreted the story of Ah Q on a basis of class struggle.[73] According to this line of criticism, Lu Xun's story does not reflect the Chinese national character but rather the deplorable situation of the lower-class Chinese peasant who had to live through the hard times of the Republican revolution. In arguing for a class-informed reading, these critics base their claim on Lu Xun's works. The complexity of Lu Xun's thinking allows the Marxist critics to find powerful evidence from his voluminous prose writings to discredit a reading based entirely on the theory of national character.[74] They demonstrate that Lu Xun draws a line between the upper class (*shangdeng ren*) and the downtrodden (*xiadeng ren*) when discoursing on Chinese national character.[75] The key evidence they cite is an essay called "Deng xia manbi" (Writing under the lamplight) in which Lu Xun commented on Bertrand Russell's remarks about Chinese character and criticized him for mistaking the smiles on the faces of the Chinese coolies as a quintessential Chinese virtue. Russell wrote:

> I remember one hot day when a party of us were crossing the hills in chairs—the way was rough and very steep, the work for the coolies very severe. At the highest point of our journey, we stopped for ten minutes to let the men rest. Instantly, they all sat in a row, brought out their pipes, and began to laugh among themselves as if they had not a care in the world. In any country that had learned the virtue of forethought, they would have devoted the moments to complaining of the heat, in order to increase their tip.[76]

Lu Xun observed sarcastically: "If the coolies did not smile to their patron, China would stop being the kind of country it is now."[77]

Marxist criticism is illuminating in its attention to the manifold layers of Lu Xun's thinking about China as a hierarchical society, but it has tended to dismiss Lu Xun's concern with national character as a limitation in the evolution of his thought and to take his later interest in class as a sign of his surmounting of that limitation.[78] To my mind, this argument is not convincing, because it cannot explain the dynamic of a discursive struggle where no ideas, certainly not Lu Xun's, could uniformly follow a single tendency. To impose a judgment of historical limitation on Lu Xun from a teleological point of view is to blot out the extraordinary complexity of Lu Xun's mind, one that has confounded critics with such contradictory evidence.[79] A more fruitful critique of the concept of national character, it seems to me, lies not in the homology between Lu Xun and a theory imported from the West (the usual assumption of Marxist critics when they fault Lu Xun for his early limitations), but rather in the tensions between the two, including those moments when Lu Xun appears to endorse the theory without reservation. My own reading of "Ah Q" will explore these tensions by focusing on the rupture of the imported theory caused by the narrator's insertion of a different subjectivity in the narrative.

Subjectivity in Cross-Writing: The Narrator in "The True Story of Ah Q"

On more than a few occasions, Lu Xun confessed that "The True Story of Ah Q" was intended to be a portrayal of the national soul of the Chinese. For example, his preface to the Russian edition of the story contains the following statement: "I tried my best to paint the soul of our countrymen in modern times, but I am not so certain whether my endeavor has been successful or not."[80] This remark is repeatedly invoked by critics who try to restrict the story to a single privileged reading. Here, I call attention to another essay, entitled "Zaitan baoliu" (My further views on reservation), in which Lu Xun gives this reading an unexpected twist. Writing in the third person, which brings the familiar voice of the narrator of "Ah Q" immediately to the reader's mind, he says: "Twelve years ago, Lu Xun wrote a story called 'The True Story of Ah Q' with the intention of exposing the weakness of his fellow citizens, although he did not specify whether he himself was included therein or not. This year, a number of individuals have come out to identify themselves as 'Ah Q.' That must have been part of the unfortunate karma of the modern age."[81] At one level, this quote is a sardonic reflection on some contemporary interpretations of the story as a roman à clef; at another level, however, the author inadvertently raises a question relating to the relationship among the author, text, and the reader, as well as to the problem of interpretation. What intrigues me here is not whether Lu Xun was capable of including himself in the criticism or to what degree he shares the national weaknesses that he attributed to Ah Q and to the people of Weizhuang. There is ample evidence in Lu Xun's works for his belief that critics are no more exempt from criticism than anybody else. "It is true that I dissect other people all the time," wrote Lu Xun, using one of his favorite anatomical tropes, "but I dissect myself much more often and much more savagely."[82] The narrator of his earlier story "The Diary of a Madman," confesses that he might be just as guilty of the crime of cannibalism as the people he accuses. It is not as if one needs to interrogate again the relationship between the critic and the object of criticism, which has been pointed out by most Lu Xun scholars.

The unexpected twist that Lu Xun gave to the reading of "Ah Q" in the essay "Zaitan baoliu" is, to my mind, the linkages he perceived between the text and the act of interpretation. This perception led to a profound distrust of the author–reader continuum, a distrust that, on the one hand, exposes the author to the same critique (should he himself be included?) as he has meted out to others and, on the other hand, obstructs the reader's identification with the object of criticism (roman à clef). What this means for interpretation of the story is that it brings the question of narratorial mediation to the fore. That is, if the identity of Ah Q or the question of who should be included in the Ah Q category (author or reader?) need not guide the direction of one's reading, then the question becomes What is there in the narrative itself that makes the critique of Ah Q and national character possible in the first place? This question places the mediation of the narrator and the construction of his subjectivity at the heart of the problem of interpretation. Lu Xun's account of the classroom scene in his preface to *Nahan* finds interesting resonances here. The staging of the spectacle of horror that is watched by Chinese spectators within the frame of the photograph is in turn watched by an unintended audience, Lu Xun, who becomes the retrospective narrator of the refracted viewing experience. This convoluted relationship between a spectacle and its several relays of audiences as well as the voice that recounts the story is mirrored by an equally complicated relationship between the text of "Ah Q" and its implied readership as well as the mediatory voice of the narrator.

Criticisms that emphasize ideology in "The True Story of Ah Q" have tended to overlook the facts that Lu Xun went to great lengths to tease his hero and that the reader cannot but be entertained by Ah Q's monumental stupidity, although s/he may feel slightly guilty afterward. And why not, since the implied reader is induced to join the cannibalistic mob watching the execution of the "tragic" hero in the final scene? Killing two birds with one stone? Precisely. Lu Xun seemed to take as much delight in compromising the implied reader as he did in poking fun at his characters. How did he accomplish all this in a deceptively straightforward narrative?

Hanan's analysis of Lu Xun's technique pinpoints irony as the chief rhetorical figure in the story. "Ah Q" falls into what Hanan calls the "category of presentational irony" in that the narrator is given a distinct persona, referring to himself in the first person and speaking in a tone "in violent contrast to the events described; one is lofty, the other squalid, and the contrast makes the latter ridiculous."[83] In other words, Lu Xun's narrator is responsible for the "raising" and "lowering" effect of irony as, for example, in his treatment of Ah Q as a candidate for a biography and his simultaneous debasement of a time-honored genre of historiography by linking it with the life of an illiterate, depraved peasant. This use of irony may legitimately be grasped in terms of Bakhtin's perceptive analysis of comic style in novelistic discourse, particularly, his concept of "parodic stylization." This term describes a typical aspect of heteroglossia or hybrid construction where the "act of authorial unmasking, which is openly accomplished within the boundaries of a single simple sentence, merges with the unmasking of another's speech." Bakhtin mentions Gogol, one of Lu Xun's favorite Russian writers, in this context and sees his writing as an example of grotesque pseudo-objective motivation, that is, a highly mediated representation or hybridization of another's language or "general opinion" by the narrator *as if* it were his own language or opinion.[84] I find this understanding of narratorial mediation very useful and, by extending it to the reading below, try to bring out the manner in which the knowledge of national character in "Ah Q" is mediated through the opaque presence of the narrator. Specifically, I argue that the narrator is the key factor in the construction of the multilayered meanings within the story and that those meanings are embedded in the structured relationships that bind the narrator (dramatized "author"), Ah Q, the residents of Weizhuang, and the implied reader together.

Like Ah Q, the narrator is a fictional character invented by Lu Xun, but unlike the "realistic" peasant, this "I" inhabits two fictional/stylistic worlds simultaneously (or two diegeses, in Genette's terminology) and shuttles between them with the imputed invisibility of an omniscient narrator. Chapter 1 opens with the first of these worlds when the first-person narrator introduces himself as the "author" of a work that bears the title of "The True Story of Ah Q," a work that has not yet been written. The fact the narrator speaks from within the narrative about writing a story that has already been written (as far as the reader is concerned) draws a fine line between the extradiegetic level (i.e., narrator speaking from outside the fictional world he is recounting) and the autodiegetic level (narrator being the subject and object of narration simultaneously) within the narrative itself.[85] Indeed, the two levels quickly collapse into one as the story unfolds, which leads to the difficulty of reading between the lines, or rather between the levels. Yet these levels are absolutely crucial to an understanding of the relationship between the narrator and the fictional world he depicts.

The second of the fictional worlds is much easier to grasp than the first since it more or less conforms to the ordinary expectation of what a good story should consist of: time, place, events, character, and so forth. In this case, the privileged time is the period before and after the 1911 Revolution, and the setting is a village in southern China called Weizhuang, where a series of events will change the lives of the villagers and end the wretched life of Ah Q. The formal boundary of this world is marked by Chapter 2, where the narrator ceases to speak in the first person and begins to assume the third-person omniscient voice. Since the first-person narrative in Chapter 1 frames the third-person narrative in the following chapters (one may in fact treat the introductory chapter as a narrative frame), it cannot but affect the meanings that subsequent episodes generate in the story. What I am trying to suggest is that the reading of Ah Q's story cannot but take full account of the presence or erased presence of the narrator.

As a dramatized "author," the narrator in Chapter 1 reveals himself to be an old-fashioned Chinese literatus caught in a period of transition.

His several allusions to the journal *New Youth* suggest that the time of his writing, which was that of the May Fourth period, is separated from the time of the story by almost a decade. The narrator's knowledge of the old learning is obvious as he deliberates the pros and cons of the various biographical genres; moreover, he has some knowledge of Western literature as well. But he is uncomfortable with the old learning, which he mocks and parodies relentlessly; nor does he particularly fancy the idea of the new. For instance, his exaggerated concern with Ah Q's name and family genealogy parodies the pretentiousness of traditional Confucian values, but the adoption of the Western alphabet does not necessarily relegate him to the camp of the New Culturalists either. The following is extracted from his elaborate disquisition on Ah Q's name:

> Since I am afraid the new system of phonetics has not yet come into common use, there is nothing for it but to use the Western alphabet, writing the name according to the English spelling as Ah Quei and abbreviating it to Ah Q. This approximates to blindly following the *New Youth* magazine, and I am thoroughly ashamed of myself; but since even such a learned man as Mr. Chao's son could not solve my problem, what else can I do?[86]

Ah Q is a product of translingual practice after all! Recall that the making of this story itself involves as many as four different languages directly or indirectly: English (Arthur Smith), Japanese (Shibue Tamotsu et al.), Polish (Sienkiewicz), and modern vernacular Chinese. The protagonist Ah Q's name, as the narrator tells us, is an English transliteration and abbreviation of an ambiguous Chinese folk name, although in the story proper Ah Q himself detests all that the Imitation Foreign Devil symbolizes. But if there is the least likelihood that the narrator or the stylistic voice might be mistaken for Lu Xun himself, one can hardly miss the marked difference in the above quote. Whereas Lu Xun was a regular contributor to the *New Youth* magazine and a leader of the New Culture movement, this narrator here adopts the views of a Mr. Chao while putting them down at the same time. The subtle stylistic device, which explores the ambiguous space between "tradition" (read Chinese) and "modernity" (read Western), builds up an extremely complex narrative structure in which the voice of the narrator shifts back and forth, creating the "raising" and "lowering" effects of irony within a broad range of stylistic possibilities. The shifting voice, which switches to the third person in the subsequent chapter, provides the key to the interpretation of the story.

My question in this reading is not To what extent is Ah Q a symbol of national character? or To what extent may he be viewed as a specimen of the lower-class peasant? Rather, I ask What are the relationships between the narrator and Ah Q and between the narrator and the people of Weizhuang? Where does the question of national identity figure in this scenario? Even in the chapters dominated by the third-person omniscient narrator, these questions cannot be ignored, because the omniscient point of view is clearly restricted by a selected narrative focus on the village of Weizhuang. In other words, the invisible narrator never leaves the village, even as Ah Q is forced to go to town after a series of blunders involving women, theft, and punishments by the Zhao family. This is rather unusual for a self-proclaimed biographer who ought to be following his hero wherever he goes. But Lu Xun's narrator is a most peculiar biographer. What he does is, instead, to skip the gap between Ah Q's departure and his next arrival and move on to tell what happened after Ah Q returns to the village. The opening passage of Chapter 6 marks one of those returns that may provide a clue to the nature of this narrative strategy: "Weizhuang did not see Ah Q again till just after the Moon Festival that year. Everybody was surprised to hear of his return, and this made them think back and wonder where he had been all that time" (pp. 93, *89*). At this point, the narrator sees *with* the collective eyes of the people of Weizhuang, and throughout Chapter 6 his knowledge of Ah Q is carefully restricted to what the village folks know, although he also manages to maintain an ironic distance from them at the same time. When Ah Q lies about his adventure in town, the narrator observes in a detached manner: "According to Ah Q, he had been a servant in the house of a successful provincial candidate. This part of the story filled all who heard it with awe" (pp. 95, *90*).

Elsewhere, the narrative point of view does not always coincide with that of the villagers. In the majority of the chapters, the narrator weaves in and out of Ah Q's mind, using psycho-narration, thought language, free indirect style, and the like to bring out the contrast between harsh reality and Ah Q's delusions. But it is always within Weizhuang or within the transactions between Ah Q and the villagers that the narrator locates his story. Should Weizhuang be interpreted as a microcosmic image of China? If so, the people in it must represent the national character, as Lu Xun himself once suggested in the preface to the Russian edition of "Ah Q." But what about the narrator, who also inhabits the microcosm of Weizhuang? If he is contained by that world, what enables his sarcasm at the stupidities of Ah Q and at the pettiness and cruelty of the village people?

Here we can note the role of writing, for writing empowers the narrator in the same way that illiteracy disempowers Ah Q.[87] The story begins with the narrator's disquisition on historical writing and Ah Q's name, and it practically ends with an almost symmetrical episode in which Ah Q not only is incapable of signing his name on a piece of court paper that probably contains his own death sentence but, when asked to draw a circle instead of his signature, fails to accomplish that task as well. The scene is unforgettable.

> Then a man in a long coat brought a sheet of paper and held a brush in front of Ah Q, which he wanted to thrust into his hand. Ah Q was now nearly frightened out of his wits, because this was the first time in his life that his hand had ever come into contact with a writing brush. He was just wondering how to hold it when the man pointed out a place on the paper, and told him to sign his name.
> "I—I—can't write," said Ah Q, shamefaced, nervously holding the brush.
> "In that case, to make it easy for you, draw a circle!"
> Ah Q tried to draw a circle, but the hand with which he grasped the brush trembled, so the man spread the paper on the ground for him. Ah Q bent down and, as painstakingly as if his life depended on it, drew a circle. Afraid people would laugh at him, he determined to make the circle round; however, not only was that wretched brush very heavy, but it would not do his bidding. Instead it wobbled from side to side; and just as the line was about to close it swerved out again, making a shape like a melon seed.   (pp. 111, 108-9)

If Ah Q had drawn a perfect circle, it would have resembled the English letter O, not far in the alphabet from the letter Q. But since the power of naming and writing is in the hands of the narrator, Ah Q's failure to draw the miraculous circle is not surprising. All he can do is tremble before the enormous symbolic authority attached to writing in Chinese culture and later rationalize his failure into victory as is his wont. By contrast, the narrator's ability to write entitles him to certain kinds of subjectivities denied to Ah Q even as it frees him from the latter's vices. In fact, the presentation of the narrator as Ah Q's opposite signals the vast chasm existing between them as members of two different classes known as *shangdeng ren* and *xiadeng ren*. The narrator's criticisms of Ah Q and condescension, sympathy, and even ambivalence toward him are conditioned by his elevated status as a writer and by his exclusive access to knowledge. This includes not only the knowledge of Chinese history and Western literature exhibited in the course of the story but also knowledge obtained through an omniscient narrative point of view that penetrates the mind of Ah Q as well as the minds of the public in Weizhuang.

Being a dramatized author/narrator also means cutting out a subject-position in the fabric of the story. The subject-position in "Ah Q" significantly ruptures one's knowledge of Chinese national character. It is not as if the myth of Chinese character were not there; after all, Smith's treatise on the Chinese obsession with face was hardly lost on Lu Xun or Ah Q. My point is that Lu Xun's story creates not only an Ah Q but also a Chinese narrator capable of analyzing and criticizing the protagonist. The introjection of such narratorial subjectivity profoundly supersedes Smith's totalizing theory of Chinese character and leads to a radical rewriting of the missionary discourse in terms of Chinese literary modernity. This rewriting sought to redefine the role of the Chinese literary elite vis-à-vis the lower class represented by ignorant underdogs like Ah Q, as May Fourth literature appointed itself the voice of enlightenment speaking to and about the masses. May Fourth writers such as Lu Xun deployed the theory of Chinese character to justify this endeavor by pointing an accusing finger at the indigenous tradition, culture, and the classical heritage and, in so doing, hoped to emerge as the subject and agent of their own history.

Was their enlightenment project largely successful? Did these intellectuals become advocates of wholesale Westernization and liberal ideologies? How did they negotiate the changing relationship between themselves as cultural critics on the one hand and the state and the rest of the nation on the other hand? These and related questions are the subject of the next chapter.

CHAPTER 3

The Discourse of Individualism

The meaning of a word is its use in speech.
—Wittgenstein

"There can be no question that subjectivism and individualism, joined with pessimism and a feeling for the tragedy of life, along with an inclination to revolt and even the tendency to self-destruction, are the most characteristic qualities of Chinese literature from the May Fourth Movement of 1919 to the outbreak of war with Japan."[1] Jaroslav Průšek's statement has exerted a decisive impact on the study of modern Chinese literature in Europe and the United States and, to a lesser degree, in China. Nowadays, one cannot talk about modern Chinese literature without recognizing some of the broad features highlighted by Průšek. Although his viewpoint is constantly invoked and discussed, it is seldom noticed, however, that the text Průšek cites to substantiate his statement happens to be one of the most interesting examples of translingual practice in modern fiction. The passage in question comes from Mao Dun's novel *Ziye* (Midnight), which contains an intimate exchange between Captain Lei and his onetime sweetheart Mrs. Wu, now the wife of a powerful Shanghai industrialist. Captain Lei takes a well-worn copy of Goethe's *Die Leiden des jungen Werthers* in Chinese (*Shaonian Weite zhi fannao*; trans. Guo Moruo, 1922) from his pocket and presents it to Mrs. Wu to impress her with his selfless devotion. Commenting on this famous scene (Captain Lei's self-conscious replication of Werther's part in translation never fails to amuse the Chinese reader), Průšek remarks: "The passage is extremely interesting for the way it shows how the greatest product of European Romanticism found a kindred spirit and mood among Chinese revolutionary youth. It testifies to how the moods in China were reminiscent in many aspects of the moods of European Romanticism and its exaggerated individualism, tragic coloring and feeling of 'Weltschmerz.' "[2] Although Průšek may have missed the subtle irony of the scene he so interprets—after all, the narrator's careful manipulation of the situation merits some attention—he raises an important point about the linkages between individualism, European literature, intertextuality, and Chinese literary modernity.[3] But what precisely do these linkages tell us about individualism, European literature, intertextuality, Chinese literary modernity, or their imputed relationships? Can these be adequately explained in terms of "kindred spirit," "moods," "*Weltschmerz*," or even "influence"?

To a literary historian, the trajectory of individualism in twentieth-century China is both fascinating and puzzling.[4] Fascinating because *geren* (Japanese *kojin*), or the individual, is said to have ushered in the dawn of Chinese enlightenment when s/he first appeared on the literary horizon in the figure of a modern protagonist. What is so puzzling is that those who lived through the period have told vastly different stories about the meaning of individualism to themselves and to one another. Reading between the lines of the conflicting representations and interpretations of their experiences, one perceives traces of unspoken desires, frustrated ambitions and hopes, and struggles. To be sure, making sense of what people said, wrote, or thought about in the past is never easy, but that need not deter one from pursuing the possibility of some degree of understanding. Rather than asking the same questions that Chinese intellectuals put to themselves decades ago, I want to raise issues in this chapter that help unpack precisely the kinds of questions that those people once deemed worthwhile to bring up or fight over in the context of their own struggles.[5] That means I need to look into the translingual practices surrounding the notion of individualism and Chinese literary modernity and to interrogate the linkages between the two in a mutually critical light. Put more accurately, I situate my analysis of the discourse of individualism within the problematic of Chinese literary modernity, as I did with the theory of national character in the preceding chapter.

Hu Shi's "General Introduction" to the *Compendium of Modern Chinese Literature* offers an interesting perspective on this issue, because he placed the question of individualism at the heart of literary reform.[6] According to him, two essays from the New Culture movement deserve special attention because they exerted a decisive impact on the literary theory of this period. The first is his own article entitled "Yibusheng zhuyi" (Ibsenism), published in *New Youth* (1918), and the other is Zhou Zuoren's "Ren de wenxue" (A humane literature), which appeared six months later in the same journal. Speaking of the circumstances surrounding the composition of his own essay, Hu Shi recalled:

> After *New Youth* was resurrected in January 1918, we were determined to make two moves. The first was to reject the classical writing and write exclusively in vernacular Chinese; the second was to devote ourselves to translating modern literary works from the West. In June of the same year, *New Youth* was able to bring out a "Special Issue on Ibsen," which included a full translation of the play *Nora* [*A Doll's House*] that I had done in collaboration with Mr. Luo Jialun, as well as Mr. Tao Lugong's translation of another play entitled *Public Enemy*. As it was the first time that such a formidable writer from the contemporary West was being introduced to China, I decided to write an essay called "Ibsenism," in which I borrowed the words of Ibsen to articulate the conviction shared by all members of the *New Youth* Society, that is, our commitment to "fully developed individualism." As Ibsen put it, "What I would like most to see happen to you is a true and pure form of egocentrism, one that can sometimes give you the feeling that your own needs are the most important thing of all and that nothing else matters. . . . If you wish to serve society, the best way to do it would be to put some effort into yourself and become somebody. . . . Sometimes I have the feeling that the whole world is like a wrecked ship on the ocean and that the first thing one should do under those circumstances is to save one's own self."[7]

Hu then discussed Zhou Zuoren's essay, calling it the most important manifesto in literary reform. Zhou Zuoren's individualism revolves around the concept of humanism and induces a radical transvaluation of the concept of *ren* (human) from its traditional meaning in classical Chinese philosophy. To him, *ren* is a biological animal whose telos of evolution is marked by the perfect union of body and soul. In order to achieve that union, *ren* must be liberated from the shackles of tradition and ritual; hence the need for humanism. In a passage quoted by Hu Shi, Zhou Zuoren says: "By humanism I do not mean that which is commonly understood as philanthropism, which extends sympathy and material comfort to others, but rather *geren zhuyi* [individualism] which is a subject-centered human philosophy."[8]

To what extent does Hu Shi's assertion or his enlistment of Zhou Zuoren's support confirm the idea that individualism played a vital role in the genesis of modern Chinese literature? Perhaps the question itself is not very well put, although the idea is certainly the mainstay of Průšek's argument (which derives from, and is framed by, the views of people like Hu Shi) when he maintains that individualism and subjectivism are the prominent characteristics of May Fourth literature in comparison with previous literary traditions. One could object that traditional Chinese lyrical poetry and a variety of genres in the general category of familiar prose indulged in lyricism and excessive subjectivism. Průšek himself is not unaware of this problem, for he immediately returns to the tradition of the Manchu literati to seek evidence of continuity between traditional and modern literature. Once again, we are reading a familiar narrative of continuity and discontinuity. Perhaps, in the case of such implied either/ or questions (tradition or modernity), one can easily marshal textual evidence in support of an idea or, if one wishes, use the same evidence to contradict the idea, depending on how one reads the evidence or defines the idea (which opens up another can of worms).[9]

In looking at the trajectory of the discourse of individualism, for instance, the evidence clearly points to the existence of neologisms such as *ziwo, geren,* and *geren zhuyi* (self, individual, individualism) that carved a special niche for themselves in public discourse as early as the late Qing period and that achieved enormous popularity in the New Culture movement and literary reform, as is shown by the essays of Hu Shi and Zhou Zuoren.[10] But is the evidence self-evident? How should we interpret this massive amount of evidence? If the popularized concepts of Westernization, iconoclasm, and anti-traditionalism do not take us very far beyond reifying the claims of May Fourth writers, what kind of knowledge does that evidence bring to light? Is it possible to pose the question of individualism as a theoretical problem in the context of translingual practice and Chinese modernity rather than to foreclose it as an established fact or as one of those timeless motifs?

In this chapter, I analyze the rhetoric of individualism as well as the epistemic/linguistic conditions under which the concept itself may be legitimately grasped in the Chinese context. I am interested in the etymological relationship between Chinese, Japanese, and English in the translation of individualism with particular emphasis on the host language or modern Chinese as a source of meaning. Through a critique of the "influence" model, including its ancillary propositions of authenticity and invocations of authority, I offer some reflections on the putative status of knowledge and the implied power relationship between host and guest languages surrounding the discussion of individualism.

The Host Language as a Source of Meaning

The inaugural issue of the journal *Xin chao* (Renaissance, or New tide), published by students at Beijing University at the peak of the New Culture movement, carried a polemical piece by Chen Jia'ai, entitled "Xin"

(New). This article spelled out the rhetoric of modernity in a series of tropes. "The new is singular, and the old is plural," said the author. "The former is singular for being absolutely unique, whereas the latter is plural for being open to infinite multiplication." Armed with the figure of inflective grammar, the author then proceeded to elaborate his point about old and new using the metaphor of genealogy: "It takes two, man and wife, to make a single son at a time (even twins come one after the other). Conversely, parents that give birth to the son were in turn brought into the world by the grandparents, who owed their lives to the great-grand parents *ad infinitum*." [11] Far from being a treatise preaching filial piety, the essay tried to make the point that "old" ideas, like the older generation, were bound to be replaced by "new" ones, which the author defined in the rest of the essay as singular, unique, modern, and therefore superior.

As Leo Lee has pointed out, "This intellectual posture of newness does not by itself represent anything new, for in traditional China there were indeed recurrent debates between 'new' and 'old'—or between 'moderns' or 'ancients'—in matters related to scholarly texts as well as government policy. What makes for the qualitative difference in the May Fourth formulation lies rather in its implicit equation of newness with a new temporal continuum from the present to the future." [12] The equation of newness with a teleological conception of history seems to suggest a Chinese counterpart to—or, more exactly, its accommodation of—the kind of historicism that Hans Blumenberg, for example, talks about in his discussion of European modernity. According to him, the modern view of temporality "removes the dubiousness from what is new and so *terra incognita*, or the *mundas novas*, becomes possible and effective as a *stimulus* to human activity; if one might phrase the process as a paradox, surprise is something to be expected." [13] Opposed to the ancient and medieval belief in a closed cosmos, the modern Enlightenment notion of temporality always looks forward to a future that might contain elements that could render previous "realities" unreal. In that sense, the new must be constantly renewed and relegitimized.

The legitimation of the "new" in the May Fourth Chinese context clearly has other dimensions than the temporal one, for it also points to a major spatial and cultural reorientation in China's forced awareness of its own place in the modern world. Since the West sought expansion of its territory in the name of the future and progress, China had to endure the violence of imperialism in order to come to terms with its future and its "modernity." [14] The equation of the modern and a powerful West, therefore, provides the primary condition for the equation of "new" and a desirable future in the May Fourth discourse. As we have seen in Chen Jia'ai's essay, the argument for the new and the unique is couched, not surprisingly, in the trope of Indo-European grammatical number—*danshu* (the singular) versus *zhongshu* (the plural)—not available in the Chinese language. Inasmuch as the figure of speech in this passage draws on the resources of the inflective Indo-European languages, the allegorical thrust of the text may, therefore, be read as privileging the categories of the modern, Western, and individual (symbolized by the son), as opposed to those of the traditional, Chinese, and familial (represented by the older generation). Such rhetoric became a driving force behind most of the radical discourses of selfhood, nationhood, and modernity in the May Fourth era.

Since the inflective grammar of the modern self is embedded from the first moment in a history of contested meanings within which the idea of nationhood looms large, it is difficult, if not impossible, to treat the self as an isolated site of unique personal identity. The sources of this difficulty, as I see it, lie not so much in the ontological, psychoanalytical (such as Lacanian theory), or linguistic considerations that usually enable our academic deconstruction of the unitary subject or from the so-called unbroken tradition of holism in Chinese culture as in the particular kind of history that China and the Chinese were forced to go through since the mid-nineteenth century. In other words, the violence of China's encounter with the West forces modern nationhood upon selfhood, and vice versa, under unique circumstances. Yet the modern self is never quite reducible to national identity. On the contrary, it is the incongruities, tensions, and struggles between the two as well as their mutual implication and complicity that give full meaning to the lived experience of Chinese modernity.

When the English word "self" first entered modern Chinese discourse, a number of Chinese characters were used to translate it, including *ziwo, wo, ji,* and *xiaoji. Ziwo,* like many other two-character nouns in modern Chinese, is probably a returned graphic loanword imported from Meiji Japan.[15] The rest of the translations of "self" were appropriated from classical Chinese philosophy, Neo-Confucianism in particular, although with a radical and important shift in meaning. To complicate the situation further, there is also a family of words *geren, gewei, geti* in modern Chinese—translations of the English word "individual"—that are sometimes used interchangeably with the *ziwo* family. The slippage of *ziwo, wo, geren, gewei, geti,* and *ji* not only inherits the slippage of meaning between "self" and "individual" in the English original but reflects the complex scenario of translingual practices and its politics in the Chinese context. Just as the concepts themselves defy fixing, the attempt to pin down the notion of the individual or individualism in modern Chinese to one or two definitions will prove counterproductive. The important thing to do here is probe into the translingual practice between East and West that has tried to give such a concept a name, an essence, or reality in modern Chinese.

Geren zhuyi (individualism) happened to be one of those concepts that held out great promise for resolving the problematic of the modern self and nation but, as I demonstrate below, it instead complicated the situation. This neologism, like many others, was invented by Meiji intellectuals in Japan to translate Western liberal and nationalist theories of "individualism" (*kojin shugi*). Following its introduction into China at the turn of the twentieth century, it soon grew to be a chief signpost on the discursive terrain of the self in modern China. In order to tease out the meaning of individualism in the Chinese context, I begin by making a brief comparison between two antithetical views about individualism and its relevance to China. The first view was expressed in an article entitled "Gewei zhuyi" (Individualism) published in the *Eastern Miscellany* in 1916. Jia Yi, who signed this essay, said: "Individualism is utterly alien to the Chinese mind. Inasmuch as the clan, local district, state, and society hold absolute dominance, there is no chance for the individual to emerge."[16] A contrary view appears in Bertrand Russell's *Problem of China*: "Individualism has perished in the West, but in China it survives, for good as well as for evil."[17] Both authors seem to have subscribed to a notion of individualism that predicates a core of fixed values, yet their views were mediated by a profound sense of crisis about the state of their respective nations— Jia Yi's poverty-stricken China and Russell's post–World War I Europe— and by a desire for the other (although for both that desire seems embedded *a priori* in the economy of Western Enlightenment ideology). The contrast in their individual positions has major methodological implications for me, because it renders any potential quest for an essential and fixed meaning of the individual and individualism futile and misguided. What really matters here is the discursive practice surrounding the notion of individual, self, individualism, and similar terms, as well as the politics of such practice.

This point, however, is not as self-evident as it appears. On the contrary, much of the existing historiography on the theme of the Chinese enlightenment in the New Culture movement treats the concept of individualism as a given value. For instance, both Li Zehou and Vera Schwarcz hold May Fourth nationalism chiefly responsible for bringing the New

Culture movement to an untimely end and consequently jeopardizing the project of enlightenment, of which individualism formed an integral part.[18] Both scholars seem to take the grand narrative of the European Enlightenment as a fixed, unproblematic site of meaning against which the success (or failure) of the Chinese enlightenment is to be measured. I would argue, however, that the dynamic history of Chinese enlightenment is in every sense capable of generating its own meanings and terms of interpretation.[19] The subtleties, complexities, and contingencies of given meanings and situations that emerged from the twists and turns of events become visible only if one avoids reading history according to these master codes.

Among the mainland Chinese scholars currently engaged in revisionary historiography, there is a general tendency to dub the May Fourth conception of the individual "inauthentic" on the grounds of its incommensurability with the original, Western notion. They argue that Li Zehou has mistakenly granted a role—however short-lived—to the New Culturalists in the dissemination of the idea of individual freedom. Supporters of this view argue that the tragedy of Chinese intellectuals in the twentieth century has been that they tend to place the highest premium on society, nation, people, and the state but never on the individual, and that "it is absurd to believe that the 'May Fourth' conception of the 'liberation of individuality' came anywhere close to sending the true message of 'individual freedom.'"[20] Although I agree that the May Fourth notion of the individual is always tied up with those of the nation, state, and society, I find it difficult to conceive that the "original" Western notion of the individual is exempted from those external considerations. Nor do I see the Chinese notion as simply a distorted image of the Western idea. As Anthony J. Cascardi points out in *The Subject of Modernity*, the Enlightenment notion of subjectivity in the West is part of the legitimation question in the theory of modernity and that "the culture of modernity is given shape as a divided whole that can only be unified through the powers of an abstract subject, or its political analogue, the autonomous State. Indeed, it can be said that the State gains power and scope precisely insofar as it provides a means through which the divided subjects of modernity can be made whole."[21] In light of Cascardi's analysis of the political theory of Hobbes, Hegel, Heidegger, Weber, and others, one can hardly maintain an essentialist and ahistorical understanding of the individual without upholding a myth of the West. Therefore, the critique of the Chinese concept of the individual as inauthentic is but a recuperation of the reductive rhetoric of Chinese collectivism versus Western individualism and fails to explain why the Western notion of the individual or individualism, authentic or otherwise, was introduced into China in the first place.

In an early essay, "Wenhua pianzhi lun" (Concerning imbalanced cultural development; 1907), Lu Xun offered an explanation that at least situates the problem of the individual and individualism in the context of the late Qing reforms.

> The term *geren* [or "individual"] entered China only within the last few years, but has already fast become the butt of ridicule and debasement by those among our scholars who are purported to understand the world and keep abreast of the times. Anyone identified by them [as a spokesman for the cause of the individual] is most inevitably labeled with an epithet like public enemy. Have not the critics been misled by their own hasty conclusions and fundamental failure to come to a real understanding of the concept of the individual into misconstruing it as some sort of attempt at glorifying the search for personal gain at the expense of innocent victims? A dispassionate examination will most certainly lead to conclusions of an entirely different nature.[22]

To redeem the authentic meaning of the individual and individualism, Lu Xun drew on diverse European intellectual traditions of the eighteenth and nineteenth centuries. He invoked Rousseau, Kierkegaard, Hegel, Schopenhauer, and Ibsen as the voices of dignified individuals, ignoring the frictions or incongruities among those thinkers. This extremely reductive treatment of post-Enlightenment European thought demands a historical explanation. In the context of this essay and elsewhere, such as in "Moluo shili shuo" (The power of Mara poetry; 1907), Lu Xun deployed this rhetoric of (in)authenticity with regard to individualism to criticize the constitutionalists for their worship of wealth and military power. In so doing, he challenged their hold on intellectual authority on its own ground (i.e., knowledge of the West). He seized on individualism as a potential antidote to what he saw as the prevailing vice of rampant materialism. For example, he argued that those Chinese who pursue power, fame, and wealth in the name of progress had consistently misrepresented Western civilization. In his opinion, the true spirit of the West lay beneath the surface of its nineteenth-century materialism, its essence being the noble ideals of the French revolution—egalitarianism, freedom, political rights of the individual. To capture that spirit, one must say "no to materialism" and "yes to the individual."[23] This view of the individual is interesting less for its anticipation of the New Culture movement by many years than for the contextual basis it provides for the study of the discourse of individualism and, particularly, its subsequent metamorphoses.

In a study of the intellectual legacy of Meiji Japan to which theorists of Chinese modernity including Lu Xun were heavily indebted, Andrew E. Barshay points out the importance of grasping the meaning of individual and individualism with due regard for the rise of modern Japanese nationhood. "We cannot treat individual and state as mutually opposed," he argues. "We are not dealing with alienated personalities." Barshay's discussion demonstrates that even in the case of spiritual quest "religion did not form an 'exit option' from earthly—read national and organizational—duties. The nation was to be the object of religious action transmuted into expertise."[24] Likewise, James Fujii's recent study of Sōseki and other modern Japanese writers (some of whom Lu Xun read and liked) shows that the strategies of narrativizing subjects in the works of these writers reveal "resistance and capitulation to, uneasiness and complicity with, the discourses of national consolidation and modernity, which discourses mediated the relationship of writer to state in early twentieth-century Japanese literature."[25] In other words, the performative texts of the *kindai shōsetsu* (modern fiction) are the very site on which the individuated subject, nationhood, textual production, and modernity enter into a meaningful relationship at the moment of their occurrence and interaction.

Indeed, the historical contingency of meanings requires that the notion of the individual be studied as a historical category rather than assumed as a superior, transcendental value. Instead of taking up a position that valorizes the ideology of individualism on behalf of a localized narrative of progress, my study tries to situate the claims of individualism, as postulated by the theory of Chinese modernity, within their specific historical contexts and subject them to critical examination. My argument is that, contrary to common belief, the discourse of individualism stood in a rather ambivalent relation to the master narrative of the nation-state in the early Republican period. Like all other influential discourses of the time, it invested in the major process of power reconfiguration in ways that defy simplistic closure (e.g., authentic vs. inauthentic individualism). As my analysis will show, individualism did not always constitute itself as the counterdiscourse of nationalism nor did the enlightenment see itself as the other of national salvation. Tensions between the two discourses seem to have derived from the instability of their historical meanings just as much as from their mutual implication and complicity.

To give a focused examination of the manner in which the Chinese intellectuals deployed the "Western" discourse of individualism in theories of the modern nation-state during the early decades of the twentieth century, I turn in the next section to the debates on individualism in three of the most influential journals of the time: the *Eastern Miscellany*, *New Youth*, and *Renaissance*. My discussion falls within the period between the mid-1910's and the early 1920's, a relatively short but crucial time that encompassed the New Culture movement, the May Fourth movement, the rise of modern literature, and the founding of the Chinese Communist party. I choose to focus on the *agency* of journalistic debates partly because those journals are seminal historical documents and partly because I wish to avoid treating the concept of individualism as a keyword. I conceive of my study as an investigation of the *rhetorical practice* of journalistic writing rather than a straightforward account of what was said or argued in those journals. This approach, I hope, will allow me to disengage my study of translingual practice from what is generally known as the history of ideas. To be sure, these three journals were not alone in bringing to public awareness the problem of the individual and his/her relationship with the modern nation-state. Nevertheless, they represent some of the most influential voices of the time, and by unraveling the kinds of rhetoric in them, I hope to bring out what was at stake in the discourse of individualism for the nation-building process in early modern China.

The Debate on Individualism in the Early Republican Period

The *Eastern Miscellany*, founded in 1904, was one of the oldest and most influential journals published by the Commercial Press. It started as an open forum for the discussion of politics, national economy, foreign policy, education, and other public issues. After Du Yaquan became its editor-in-chief in 1911, he began to introduce drastic changes in format and content, placing increased emphasis on issues of self, gender, and psychology. Although the question of the individual long preceded the existence of the *Eastern Miscellany* as part of the theory of the nation-state in the writings of Huang Zunxian, Yan Fu, Liang Qichao, and others,[26] Du Yaquan's article "Geren zhi gaige" (Reforming the individual), published in the June 1914 number of the *Eastern Miscellany*, represented one of the first major journalistic efforts to bring this question to the attention of the new republic in the aftermath of the 1911 Revolution.[27] In this essay, Du pointed out that the types of social reform implemented in the preceding few decades had focused exclusively on macro-level politics, the educational system, and the economy, whereas more attention should have been devoted to the reform of *geren*, or the individual (a subtle displacement of Liang Qichao's *xinmin*, or new citizen). As a result, even though the new

republic had replaced the old imperial order, the reform did not fundamentally change the old bureaucracy, which continued to do business as
usual. Moreover, the reformers themselves had become bureaucrats who
went by the name "civil servants of the Republic." Genuine reform, he
emphasized, must originate at the level of the individual, including those
self-appointed reformers. Until the individual begins to face the reality of
"his own frail and unhealthy body, his impotent and weak spirit, his shal-
low and incapable mind, and his disordered and purposeless life, social
reform will be no more than a remote dream."[28] The mere fact that Du
Yaquan stressed the centrality of the individual in the reform program
does not imply that he endorsed the Enlightenment notion of individualism. On the contrary, it is the limits of the individual that he saw and
addressed here.

The concept of individualism had not yet acquired the kind of ideological and emotional baggage that it would accumulate a few years later
when the New Culture movement got under way. For Du Yaquan, the
meaning of individualism was ambivalent and needed redefinition: "We
are not individualists," he said, "but socialism must be imagined on the
basis of individualism. Confucius meant precisely that when he said that
a scholar should study for self-improvement; so did Mencius when he ad-
jured us to cultivate our inner being."[29] What strikes me most about Du's
use of individualism is that he saw it as fully compatible with socialism
and Confucianism. That brings out two points. First, the concept of individualism was undergoing a semantic conversion that aimed to redeem
it from the negative image in which it had been cast by Liang Qichao's
theory of the nation-state. In his *New Citizen* and *On Liberty*, for example,
Liang Qichao allowed the nation-state to take absolute precedence over
the individual and tried to maintain a careful distinction between the liberty of a people and individual freedom by opposing the former to the
latter.[30] What Du Yaquan attempts to do in this essay is to reconcile the
two. Second, individualism was not yet radicalized at this particular junc-
ture of history *either* as the polar opposite of Confucianism or as the other
of socialism. The first such polarization, as I explain below, occurred
around the New Culture movement (1917) and continued through the
May Fourth movement, where individualism came to invest heavily in
the political indictment of traditional Chinese culture. The next wave of
polarization set in during the Communist revolution in the 1920's when
individualism acquired the negative status of bourgeois ideology and was
opposed to socialism.

In Du Yaquan's view, however, individualism is but a modern version of Confucianism that emphasizes the need for self-reform and at the same time articulates a version of socialism that predicates the interest of the average members of society. This peculiar (re)interpretation of Confucianism, socialism, and individualism helps throw light on the reform agenda of Du's time. Since his text and context were thoroughly embedded in the historical circumstances under which he wrote, it is beside the point to argue whether his particular interpretation of any of these ideas is authentic or not. As far as the condition and production of knowledge are concerned, both interpretation and misinterpretation (if there is any such thing) obtain and participate in the making of real historical events. As Edward Said points out, calling one work a misreading of another or relating that misreading to a general theory of interpretation as misinterpretation is "to pay no critical attention to history and to situation."[31] The question that interests me, therefore, is why the author interpreted the way he did and what new meanings were produced in the process.

Du Yaquan's article attempts to generate a public discussion of *geren* (individual) after the founding of the Republic. But the essay does not go beyond constituting the individual as a privileged site of reform, a point of affinity between Du and Liang Qichao. In Min Zhi's article, "Wo" (I or Self), which appeared in the same journal in 1916, the individual began to evolve into something of an absolute value. The author preached self-reliance with an acute "modern" historical consciousness, although much of what he said was couched in the language of ancient Chinese philosophy. Min Zhi situated his argument in the total bankruptcy of the ancient world, pointing out that, at a time when the country disintegrates and poverty, unrest, and catastrophe reign everywhere, the individual is left with no resources. Whereas in the imperial age a man would take consolation in the thought that he could read the sorrows of the people and bring them to the attention of the emperor, nowadays one can do absolutely nothing. The best thing one can do is to fall back on one's own self. Self-reliance thus becomes a necessary means of survival in the modern world. In order to justify his claim that the self is the raison d'être of existence, Min Zhi drew a distinction between *siwo* (private self) and *gongwo* (public self) and elaborated the dialectic of the two on the basis of a worn metaphor. Just as a candle illuminates every corner of the room when it gives out light, he argued, so the pursuit of self-interest will also benefit others. *Gongwo* and *siwo* are thus interconnected and mutually reinforced; the former is set apart from the latter by a sense of moral commitment in its relentless crusade for individual *quanli* (rights). But when he claimed that *gongwo* "must fight those who block its way until the desired objective is achieved and thrive in *jingzheng* [competition]," this public self sounds more like a social Darwinist than a beneficial candle light.[32]

The next issue of the *Eastern Miscellany* (1916) carried the article "Gewei zhuyi" (Individualism) by Jia Yi, who openly championed the Western Enlightenment notion of the individual. Individualism, he argued, is the single most effective medicine to cure China's illness, the root of which lies in its weakness for totalistic thinking. The modern world abhors *longtong* (totality), and everything must be subjected to the scientific law of specification, division, and subdivision. To him, the master trope of modernity is *fen* (to divide, separate, classify, differentiate): "What is modern civilization? By way of illustration, there are branches in science, division of labor in society, liberated individuals, independent personalities, and whatnot." The case of individualism is borne out, moreover, by established modern disciplines such as psychology, sociology, and ethics, all of which are designed, in his view, to assist in "the development of the individual" and his "self-realization."[33] The modern individual and state collectives are now opposed. State, society, community, and family are all supposed to provide for the individual and not to hinder the individual's growth. This kind of oppositional rhetoric would soon help unleash a tremendous amount of political energy during the New Culture movement and the May Fourth period.[34] But the paradox is that, throughout the essay, the author himself remained oblivious to his own totalistic impulse to prescribe individualism as *the* cure for China's illness.

In the next year, Du Yaquan published a new article entitled "Geren yu guojia zhi jieshuo" (The boundary between the individual and the state) in the *Eastern Miscellany* in which he set out to specify the relationship between the individual and the state. Du insisted that the line between the individual and the state be scrupulously drawn so that neither would encroach upon the rights or interests of the other. The oppositional rhetoric noted in Jia Yi's article is now expressed in an unequivocally conflictual framework. "It is commonly believed that the state represents totality, whereas the individual belongs to this totality as a member, who may thus be submerged in the totality." The author then proceeded to criticize such subordination of the individual to the state. In fact, throughout the article one senses a good deal of anxiety about the increasing hold of the state and nationalist discourse on the individual. "Who represents the state?" Du asked, "Perhaps it is just a handful of administrators who decide to sacrifice the interest of the majority to their own will."[35] In a less cynical moment, he pointed out that the architecture of the state is founded on the building blocks of the individual. Without due respect for the integrity of the latter, there can be no reliable support for the former.

On the surface, this sounds like an idea taken directly from German Romantic thinkers, such as Wilhelm von Humboldt, who opposed state action on behalf of the welfare of the citizens because such action, in his view, misunderstands the dignity of man.[36] But, on deeper levels, there is something more interesting going on here than the mere assertion of the *Humanitätsideal*, for Du Yaquan's argument clearly assumes that modernity is quite capable of placing the average individual in an unmediated relation to the nation-state, as opposed to the earlier forms of social organization. The author may well have criticized the oppression of the individual by the state, but his critique cannot disrupt the state–individual continuum that he described so lucidly. The very act of elaborating a dialectic between the two reproduces that continuum. In order for the nation-state to claim the individual in some "unmediated" fashion, the individual must be "liberated" in the first place from the family, clan, or other traditional ties that claim his or her loyalty. The discourse of individualism performed precisely that liberatory role in the early history of modern China. As Tse-tsung Chow points out in a slightly different context, "While the disintegration of the old ethics probably emancipated the individual somewhat from the bond with his family and clan, it also cleared the way for placing the individual in bondage to state, party, or other social and economic organizations."[37] I would also argue that the discourse of individualism has probably accomplished something more than liberating the individual from family only to subject the individual to the state. It contributed to the process of inventing *geren* for the goals of liberation and national revolution. In that sense, despite its apparent clash with the nation-state, the discourse of individualism found itself in complicity with nationalism. As a discursive formation of modernity, the unmediated continuum of the individual and the nation-state seeks to contain the conflicts it generated, which explains why the critique of the state's subordination of the individual can so readily be recuperated by the object of that critique.

Gao Yihan's 1915 essay "Guojia fei rensheng zhi guisu lun" (The state is not the ultimate goal of human life) in *Youth Magazine* (forerunner of *New Youth*) criticizes the modern state in a similar vein, but also introduces the notion of *renmin* (the people), an aggregate of individuals, and treats it as a potential opposite of the state. Like most journalistic writings of the time, this essay contains numerous references to European philosophy and political science, sometimes via the work of Japanese scholars.

Since the enlightenment theory of the nation-state dictates the terms of his critique, the author remained blind to the fact that *renmin* (the people) is just as much a product of the modern nation-state as the individual. What I find most peculiar about his argument, however, is not so much the concept of *renmin* as his translation of "individual" as *xiaoji* instead of the usual word *geren*. *Xiaoji* evokes *daji* (the Greater Self), which serves as a trope for *guojia* (nation-state) and occasionally for *shehui* (society). The author elucidated the relationship of *xiaoji* and the state in the words of a Japanese scholar: " 'The development of *xiaoji* [individual] is the concern of the state. Without the proper development of the individual there can be no proper development of the state.' "[38] This is reminiscent of the earlier dialectic examined above, but here I also see a subtle slippage of meanings and categories. The word *xiao* (small) opens the thinking of the individual to the metaphoric realm of substitution, displacement, and analogy in which the word *da* (big or greater) reigns. In other words, *xiao* is related to *da* not only as its antithetical other but as its hierarchical other, or the lesser of the two. The implication of this linguistic mechanism for our understanding of the problematic of the individual versus the state is manifold, particularly since essays published in *New Youth* during this period were chiefly responsible for disseminating the modern idea of *xiaoji* and *daji*.[39] Inasmuch as the individual is named *xiao* and the state *da*, the critique of the state on behalf of the individual cannot transcend the hierarchical order of a language that names and determines such a relationship. Furthermore, since the concept of the greater *self* seems to project full-fledged subjectivity onto the state, it displaces the individual as agency and a site of power on the discursive level. Indeed, never has the individual been so inextricably bound to the nation-state and so ineluctably claimed by it as when *xiaoji* and *daji* began their dialectical career.

With the advent of *New Youth* on the eve of the New Culture movement, the discourse of individualism began to turn in a new direction. In "Rensheng weiyi zhi mudi" (The sole purpose of life), for example, Li Yishi accused traditional Chinese philosophy of sacrificing individual happiness and self-interest to ritual and social morality. By way of contrast, he extolled the virtues of individualism exhibited by the Anglo-Saxon race and admired their power and wealth, which he attributed to the focus of Western philosophy on the individual. This is a far cry from Du Yaquan's understanding of Confucianism. The radical polarization of individualism (as a privileged signifier of the West) and Confucianism (as the equivalent of Chinese tradition) that subsequently prevailed in the New Culture movement was anticipated in this 1915 essay. To the author,

Confucianism encourages a slave mentality because it ritualizes the dependency of the subject on the ruler, of son on father, and of wife on husband: "Like slaves and beasts of burden, these tragic creatures could not aspire to self-autonomy, to say nothing of self-development. The true law of the universe is *weiwo* [egoism], and it must be maintained at all cost."[40] Li then cited science, sociology, psychology, and nineteenth-century European ethics in support of his theory of self-aggrandizement. But if Li's argument is to be taken seriously at all, it is not difficult to see that his rhetoric derived its power from contradictory sources. Individualism is perceived not only as thoroughly homogeneous with nationalism by virtue of its association with the superior Anglo-Saxon nations, but as anticipating and nurturing it. This observation is not intended as a critique of the author's lack of sophistication, although that is certainly true if we compare him with Gao Yihan. Rather, it serves as a reminder that the discourse of individualism, which never had a stable center of meanings, was undergoing a dramatic process of transformation around the New Culture movement, out of which new configurations of power would emerge.

Chen Duxiu, editor of this iconoclastic journal, seized on the idea of individualism as a powerful weapon to launch his wholesale attack on Chinese tradition. Among the numerous essays he wrote at this stage, the one published in the December 1915 number of *New Youth* entitled "Dong xi minzu genben sixiang zhi chayi" (The fundamental difference between the intellectual traditions of Eastern and Western peoples) probably best represents his early views. Chen assessed the relative strengths or weaknesses of the East and the West by the importance they attach to individualism.

> Western nations give priority to individualism, whereas Eastern nations value family and clan. From the past to the present, Westerners have always been nations of thoroughgoing individualism, including the British and Americans, as well as the French and Germans. The same can be said of Nietzsche and Kant. Their state and society place ethics, morality, politics, and law before everything else and uphold the free rights of the individual and his happiness. The freedom of speech precisely guarantees the development of individuality. Before the law, all individuals are equal. Since the free rights of the individual, called human rights, are protected by the Constitution, the state cannot take them away.[41]

Although Chen Duxiu's rhetoric would undergo an interesting reversal after the May Fourth movement several years later, the view quoted here illustrates the changing rhetoric of this ongoing debate on individualism in which tradition is becoming the chief enemy.

Indeed, it is in this context that the New Culture movement, literary revolution, and their shared antagonism toward tradition should be grasped. In 1916, Li Dazhao published an article in *Chenzhong bao* (Morning bell) entitled "Qingchun Zhonghua zhi chuangzao" (Creating a youthful China), in which he maintained that the creation of a new culture falls upon the shoulders of iconoclastic thinkers who have the courage to challenge tradition with original thinking, to assert the authority of their *ziwo* (self), and to advocate self-awakening.[42] When Hu Shi envisioned literary reform in his two seminal essays "Wenxue gailiang zhuyi" (Suggestions for literary reform; 1917) and "Jianshe de wenxue geming lun" (Toward a constructive theory of literary revolution; 1918), he called on the genuine voice of the individual to replace the ancient classical canon.[43] Likewise, in Zhou Zuoren's essay "Ren de wenxue" (A humane literature) individualism and humanism are proposed as the guiding spirit for modern Chinese literature; his underlying argument is that classical Chinese literature has failed to live up to humanistic goals and must, therefore, be discarded.[44] Indeed, if one were to summarize the remarkable role of the New Culture movement in modern history, one might say that this movement successfully constituted Chinese tradition and its classics as the polar opposite of individualism and humanism, whereas the nation–state, which used to occupy that antithetical position, was now largely taken for granted.

The discussion of individualism during the New Culture movement was by no means confined to theoretical debates, since such considerations lay at the very heart of literary reform. A significant event took place in the stylistics of fiction when May Fourth writers began to translate and introduce modes of psycho-narration, free indirect style, lengthy interior monologue, and other narrative strategies from European fiction into their own works. The impact of this stylistic change has yet to be fully grasped in detailed analysis of individual texts, as my reading of *Camel Xiangzi* attempts to show in the next chapter, and in light of comparative stylistics. By way of suggestion, let me point out that the new stylistics of fiction allowed Chinese writers to locate the protagonist in a new symbolic context, one in which the protagonist no longer serves as a mere element within the nexus of patriarchal kinship and/or in a transcendental, divine scheme as in most premodern Chinese fiction but dominates the text, instead, as the locus of meaning and reality in possession of psychological and moral "truth." Not surprisingly, the May Fourth period was also a time when huge quantities of first-person fiction and autobiography written in a "Western" form appeared.[45] The modern autobiographical subject—one that takes itself seriously, asserts its autonomy against traditional society, and possesses an interiority representable in narrative—made its entry into Chinese literature exactly at the time the individual and tradition were being constructed as polar opposites.[46] To modern writers, this individual self could be immensely empowering, because it enabled him or her to devise a dialogic language with which to attack the status quo, as, for example, Lu Xun did in "The Diary of a Madman." But it could also be problematic, because the individual often turned out to be a misfit in the hostile environment of a rapidly disintegrating society. The Russian "superfluous man," who figured so prominently in Yu Dafu's works, thus became a perfect embodiment of the typical dilemma of modernity.[47]

Yet, to conclude that subjectivism and individualism characterize May Fourth literature is to miss the point. What I am trying to suggest is that the discourse of individualism enabled May Fourth intellectuals to open a new battlefront in their struggle to claim "modernity" and to reject "tradition." It is not as if the individual were valorized at the expense of society or nation. Even as Chinese tradition came under attack, nationalism and social collectivism were never abandoned. On the contrary, collectivism now inhabited the same homogeneous space of modernity as individualism. One need only recall Yu Dafu's protagonist in "Chenlun" (Sinking), who experiences the crisis as one of selfhood, manhood, and nationhood simultaneously. Hu Shi's 1919 essay "Bu xiu" (Immortality) in *New Youth* bears further witness to the May Fourth conception of the individual, nation and society. In it Hu Shi named the individual "I" as *xiaowo*, whose extension or multiplication in society is called *dawo* (greater self).[48] *Xiaowo* is mortal and incomplete; in contrast, *dawo* is immortal and capable of renewing itself. Hu Shi's dialectic of the two selves echoes that of Gao Yihan's *xiaoji* and *daji*, except that in the anti-imperialist context of the May Fourth movement the nation-state is no longer perceived as antithetical to the individual. *Dawo* here stands for modern organic society with which the individual must come to terms under the aegis of the nation-state. Hu Shi's subordination of *xiaowo* (individual) to *dawo* (society) does not, however, indicate a retreat from individualism or enlightenment on the part of the New Culturalists. His position was a logical expression of the theory of modernity, which did not seek so much to liberate individuals as to constitute them as citizens of the nation-state and members of a modern society.

It should come as no surprise that the first essay in the initial issue of *Renaissance* (1919) was devoted to the question of the place of the individual in modern society. Fu Sinian, author of this article, began by establishing the superiority of Western scientific and humanist knowledge against several indigenous intellectual traditions, Daoism, Buddhism, Confucianism. According to him, none of these embodies the truth of human life. One must look, he says, for the truth in biology, psychology, sociology, and so forth, because modern scientific knowledge is subject-centered and humanistic. Finally, Fu brought out his favorite slogan in both Chinese and English: "The free development of the individuals for the Common Welfare." [49] In a footnote, he confessed that because the Chinese language is inimical to his modern way of thinking, he is compelled to use English. To a post–May Fourth ear, this sounds almost like a burlesque of language reform. If the author were to follow this logic all the way through, would he end up finding the free development of the individual inimical to the common welfare of the nation as well? This is precisely the point at which leftist and Marxist intellectuals entered and staked their claims in the aftermath of the May Fourth movement.

Fu Sinian's liberal-humanist ideal was soon displaced by a leftist ideology that cast grave doubts on individualism and capitalized on the conflictual relationship between individual and society. In 1921, *Renaissance* published an article entitled "Wu he wo" (Matter and self) by Wang Xinggong, who tried to bring the autonomy of the individual into question. Wang began by rejecting the notions of "physical self" and "spiritual self," maintaining that this autonomous "I" we call self does not really exist: "If the self at the age of twenty were to encounter the self at the age of forty on the street, they would probably not recognize each other. Nor would anyone else imagine that they were one and the same person. If the identity of the 'I' changes constantly as time goes on and is utterly heterogeneous with itself, can we still maintain that it is a fixed, permanent, and unchanging essence?" [50] The upshot of his argument is that self is a form of experience, forever changing and forever adapting, whose meaning is determined solely by the material world. Therefore, to emphasize the importance of the individual is to misplace one's priority. It is interesting that the author used Confucianism as a scapegoat for misplaced priorities. In his view, the idea of self-cultivation in Confucianism means placing exclusive emphasis on the improvement of the individual, with the implication that a perfect personality would bring about a perfect society. Wang dismissed that idea as sheer illusion. In his opinion, no fundamental change in society will occur until the sociopolitical system is tackled. Therefore, the question of society must take absolute precedence over that of the individual. It is beyond the scope of this book to decide which social theory is more desirable for China, Confucianism or socialism; I am interested only in the ways in which the terms of the debate are set or the uses to which either of those theories is put. To interpret individualism in terms of Confucianism in the anti-traditionalist context of the May Fourth period is to incriminate it and turn it into a negative idea. We have come full circle from Du Yaquan's reconciliation of the two terms where the opposite effect was intended.

Chen Duxiu's about-face on individualism in 1920 is even more illuminating in that respect. In "Xuwu de geren zhuyi ji ren ziran zhuyi" (Nihilistic individualism and laissez-faire theory), he attacked individualism as a socially irresponsible, nihilist idea. Instead of aligning it with Confucianism as Wang Xinggong did, he saw it as originating in Daoism: "The evils that have hindered the development of culture and scholarship in China can be traced back to the nihilist individualism and laissez-faire philosophy of Laozi and Zhuangzi."[51] To be sure, this accusation is anachronistic in the extreme. However, my purpose is not to defend Daoism against ludicrous charges but to call attention to the changing scenario of the discourse of individualism between 1920 and 1921. When one connects individualism with traditional Chinese culture in the May Fourth context, be it Confucianism (Wang Xinggong) or Daoism (Chen Duxiu), one is in fact naming it as the roadblock to social progress and the opposite of socialism or Communism. Of course, what we are witnessing here is not the suppression of the discourse of individualism but the reinvention of it so that the discourse could serve the desired political end in a changing historical context.

One of the earliest sophisticated critiques of individualism as bourgeois ideology, in my view, was offered by Deng Feihuang in an essay entitled "Geren zhuyi de youlai jiqi yingxiang" (The origin and impact of individualism), which appeared in the *Eastern Miscellany* in 1922.[52] In this lengthy article, Deng traced the development of individualism through the rise of the free market and capitalism in the West, and through the Industrial Revolution and the European Enlightenment. He concluded that, as a bourgeois ideology, individualism is passé and should be replaced by socialism. This familiar Marxist critique at least shows some respect for the etymology and historicity of individualism. Since, however, knowledge and power are inextricably linked together, it is not enough to grasp what a discourse says. One must be attentive to what the discourse does as well. In the context of the national politics of the early 1920's, the Marxist evolutionary view of history was used to open up a political future whereby new power configurations involving the Communist party, the Nationalist party, warlords, and imperialist powers began to surface and engage in intense local struggles.[53] By the same token, the

critique of bourgeois individualism introduces a rhetoric of social collectivism that can be used to advance the politics of the left, in much the
same way as did the earlier liberatory discourse of individualism that had
first established the individual–state continuum.

From the mid-1920's through the early 1930's, the discussion of *puluo
wenxue* (proletarian literature) among writers and critics on the left led
to a major rethinking of the earlier iconoclastic literature.[54] Once again,
the notion of individualism came under fire as the new rhetoric began
to stress the importance of class-consciousness in literary production.[55]
Leftist critics and writers tried to promote what they called *geming wenxue*
(revolutionary literature), *dazhong wenyi* (art for the masses), and proletarian literature. Cheng Fangwu, the leading theoretician of the Creation
Society, called for the "revolutionary intelligentsia" to negate themselves
and acquire class consciousness.[56] In order to depict the life of the working class and to produce a non-elite literature, writers must abandon
bourgeois individualism and familiarize themselves with the language of
workers and peasants. Similarly, Lu Xun had renounced his earlier position on individualism by this time and begun to question the idea of
pingmin wenxue (plebeian literature), a humanist notion promoted earlier
by his brother Zhou Zuoren. Lu Xun held that *pingmin wenxue* was self-
contradictory, for literary production had always been the sole prerogative of the upper class. "Until workers and peasants themselves are liberated from the dominant ideology of the elite class, there can be no
literature for ordinary people in the real sense of the word."[57] Lu Xun
was sympathetic to revolutionary literature, although he himself never intended to write proletarian fiction. Yet it is profound irony that his earlier
fiction came under attack from the radical left, especially by the Taiyang
she (The sun society), for more or less the same reasons he outlined in the
passage quoted above. In 1928 Qian Xingcun, a leading member of the
Sun Society, proclaimed the death of individualism and of the liberal ideas
of petty-bourgeois intellectuals.[58] He contended that Lu Xun's cynical,
elitist, negative portrayal of the Chinese peasant class in "The True Story
of Ah Q" and other stories had to be replaced by a revolutionary literature
that anticipates and encourages the coming of class consciousness. The
Sun Society singled out Jiang Guangci's short novel *Shaonian piaobo zhe*
(The youthful tramp; 1926) as the earliest example of proletarian fiction.[59]

The changing rhetoric surrounding the individual, class, state, and
social collectivity tells us much about the historical situatedness of Chinese modernity during the ten-year period examined here. It says very

little, however, except at highly abstract levels, about the ways in which the problem of literary representation entered the discussion of individualism and how that would complicate our understanding of translated modernity. One must turn to literary texts for enlightenment, because meanings in a literary text surface primarily at the level of figural representation and are governed by a set of literary conventions that dictate what is representable and what is not. One of the hallmarks of modern Chinese fiction, as Theodore Huters has rightly pointed out, is its faith in "representationalism."[60] The notion of realism, for example, has changed the imaginary and imaginable relationship between language and reality so profoundly that the burden of representation has become a paramount concern in modern stylistics. In Part II, I turn to translingual modes of representation in modern Chinese fiction to explore further the ways in which the imagining of the individual is played out at the level of literary texts.

PART II

*Translingual Modes of
Representation*

CHAPTER 4

'Homo Economicus' and the
Question of Novelistic Realism

In the three chapters that follow, I take a focused look at translingual modes of representation that constitute the stylistic domain of modern Chinese fiction. By stylistics, I refer to forms of narration and figurative writing that include, but are not limited to, aspects of novelistic realism, narrative remapping of the inner world, the first-person voice, free indirect style, deixis, gendered textual strategies, and so on. When confronted with such instances of novelistic realism and imported stylistic forms of narration, one's first impulse is to see them as obvious examples of European influence or even cultural imperialism. But in a closer look at what actually goes on within those Chinese texts, the linkages between modern Chinese literature and its European counterpart do not appear so self-evident. Nor does the idea of influence provide a sound explanation as to why certain imported modes of representation are preferred over others. In order to make sense of the complexities surrounding translingual modes of representation in modern Chinese fiction, I pursue a reading that takes the traces of "productive distortion" very seriously, that sees them as instances of parodic imitation that bear eloquent witness to the contradictory condition of Chinese modernity.

The individual writers discussed in these chapters are generally known for their self-conscious experimentation with borrowed literary modes, ranging from innovative uses of narrative techniques to broader issues of representation and interpretation. My analysis does not aim to be exhaustive in the sense that I cover every instance of stylistic innovation in modern Chinese literature. Rather, I attempt to interrogate the kinds of historical linkages to be found between Chinese stylistic innovations and imported literary models. Since my main purpose is to raise questions about the legitimation of the modern in Chinese literature, my stylistic approach cannot but depart from the narrowly defined methodology known as "parallel comparison" in my field (i.e., taking two or more texts from each literature and pinpointing their similarities and differences). In general, I find the concept of historical linkage much more productive than either parallel comparison or influence studies.

To illustrate what I mean by historical linkage in the matter of literary style and modes of representation, let me begin with a contemporary example of Sino-English translation. In his rendering of the eighteenth-century Chinese novel *The Story of the Stone*, David Hawkes makes a number of interesting stylistic incursions into Cao Xueqin's novel. For instance, he is given to using *style indirect libre*, or the free indirect style, a narrative device foreign to eighteenth-century Chinese narratives, to translate the narrator's quotation of the character's thought-language.[1] Take the passage in which Cao Xueqin's narrator describes Daiyu's first encounter with Baoyu. Hawkes translates: "Dai-yu looked at him with astonishment. *How strange! How very strange! It was as though she had seen him somewhere before, he was so extraordinarily familiar*"(italics added).[2] To modern literary sensibilities, Hawkes's translation is an enviable example of polished English prose in which the observation of the omniscient narrator glides smoothly into the character's thought-language without leaving obvious marks of stylistic transition. This effect is attributable to the translator's use of free indirect style (the italicized portions), whose function is precisely to mediate between the narrator's report of what he or she observes (omniscience) and the interior monologue of the character. Free indirect style allows the narrator to quote the unspoken thought of the character *indirectly* without being interrupted by verbal marks of quoted speech, such as "she thought," or other such related devices like a verbal shift in the address from "she" or "he" to "I."[3] This stylistic feature is not to be found in Cao Xueqin's original work; there the narrator relies on direct quotation to give us access to Daiyu's inner world. A cursory comparison with the earlier translation by Franz Kuhn illustrates the stylistic transformation Hawkes's translation made in the original.

> Blaujuwel war von seinem Anblick aufs höchste betroffen. "Seltsam, wie bekannt mir seine Züge vorkommen. Als müßte ich ihm schon einmal begegnet sein," *ging es ihr durch den Sinne.* (Black Jade was taken completely by surprise at his appearance. "It is strange how familiar his features seem to me, just as if I had met him before," *she thought to herself.*)[4]

The italicized phrase, omitted by Hawkes in the English translation, is a formulaic expression (*xinxia xiangdao*) that signals the presence of quoted thought in premodern vernacular Chinese fiction and was one of the most commonly used narrative devices for presenting characters' thought-language before the rise of modern narrative techniques and the punctuation system.[5] Whereas Kuhn's translation succeeds in reproducing the *mode of narration* in the Chinese original, Hawkes's version recasts that mode in the language of free indirect style to create a stylistic effect that is smoother and closer to the taste of modern English readers than a rendering more faithful to the original would have been. In so doing, he necessarily "rewrites" the eighteenth-century Chinese novel within the stylistic purview of modern English literary conventions.

Is it not true, however, that all translations rewrite the original? My preamble on Hawkes is intended not to criticize his translation, which I admire greatly, but to present my central argument for this chapter through an example. Briefly, Hawkes's stylistic transformation of *The Story of the Stone* in modern English can be taken to symbolize what has happened to the stylistics of Chinese fiction in the early twentieth century. In both cases, one confronts translingual modes of representation between literary conventions of very different novelistic traditions. Sometime in the late 1910's or even earlier, Chinese writers began to deploy imported (translated) narrative modes in their own works and to write as if they were speaking a Chinese version of Hawkes's *ouhua* or Europeanized Chinese. However, as soon as one makes a generalization like that, one must also confront the following questions: Were these writers simply imitating foreign works? If not, to what extent did the translingual mode of representation define their own experience? What is Chinese? What is non-Chinese?

The introduction of the free indirect style into modern Chinese novelistic writing is but one instance of many such stylistic innovations. This and other modern modes of narration to be discussed in this chapter and the next two have profoundly changed the written vernacular Chinese language. The immensity of these changes is just beginning to be grasped in its proper relation to other historical events. In that sense, the analogy I made above with Hawkes's translation of the *Honglou meng* must admit its own limitation. Except for making a Chinese classic available to English readers and to the sinological establishment, Hawkes's translation can do little to change the English language, whereas the Chinese language and its literary conventions have undergone a convulsive transformation since the recent contact with English and other foreign literatures.[6]

The huge influx of translated European literature into China in the first few decades of the twentieth century so radically transformed the nature of written vernacular Chinese that subsequent translations between modern Chinese and English assume a whole different character. Chinese writers borrowed profusely from English, French, Russian, German, Japanese, Polish, and other literatures in the hope that these borrowings would reinvigorate their own language and invent a new vernacular Chinese suitable for serious purposes in place of the classical language. How successful were they in these efforts? What kind of problems did they encounter as they tried to negotiate a subject position for themselves through cross-writing between Chinese and foreign languages? To approach these questions, it is necessary to conduct a detailed analysis of the modus operandi of translingual modes of representation within individual texts. My discussion begins with Lao She's *Luotuo Xiangzi* (*Camel Xiangzi*), focusing on its representation of *homo economicus* in the translingual mode of novelistic realism.

'Camel Xiangzi'

One hardly needs to "update" Lao She's novelistic style when translating *Camel Xiangzi* into English, simply because the novel operates in translingual modes of narration and is susceptible to translation to begin with. Take a typical moment from Jean M. James's rendering. The passage quoted below describes what happens after the protagonist Xiangzi escapes from the soldiers who kidnapped him: "He stopped worrying and walked on slowly. *He had nothing to fear as long as Heaven protected him. Where was he going?* He didn't think to ask any of the men and women who were already coming out to the fields. *Keep going. It didn't seem to matter much if he didn't sell the camels right away. Get to the city first and then take care of it.* He longed to see the city again"[7] (italics added).

Unlike Hawkes, who must invent free indirect speech where there is none, Jean M. James is translating a text that contains this stylistic feature (the italicized sentences). Third-person narration is characteristic of Lao She's novelistic language, which relies heavily on the use of free indirect style and other such "imported" narrative techniques. The presence of such translingual modes of narration means that one is dealing with a text that is easier to translate more accurately than an eighteenth-century novel like the *Honglou meng*, because the modern text already presumes a hypothetical equivalence between the stylistics of English and Chinese fiction.

Lao She makes abundant uses of psycho-narration, free indirect style, and other novelistic techniques that decades of translations of European realist fiction into vernacular Chinese have made familiar to the Chinese readers. However, the changing stylistics of modern Chinese fiction involves more than the introduction of a cluster of novelistic techniques. It also invests the meaning of a literary text in the person of its protagonist, male or female, who dominates the fictional world as the locus of reality in possession of certain psychological and moral "truths." That is to say, whatever transpires in the novel must be viewed and judged by the reader with reference to the well-being of its main character. This is the kind of epistemological universe into which Lao She's narrator introduces his *homo economicus*, Xiangzi.

Camel Xiangzi showcases the rise and fall of a solitary protagonist on the broad canvas of the Chinese urban society. Published in 1936–37, it is perhaps the only full-length novel in modern Chinese literature to tackle individualism in such detail.[8] Like Ah Q, the protagonist Xiangzi comes from the lowest rank of Chinese society, but, unlike him, Lao She's lower-class protagonist is portrayed with a degree of loving attention and emotional intensity that has no parallel in Chinese fiction. The fact that this novel explicitly addresses the problem of individualism and collectivism suggests an obvious linkage with the earlier debate on proletarian literature discussed in the preceding chapter. But Lao She's ambivalent response to the concerns of leftist writers takes us, at the same time, beyond the political discourse of his time to arrive at a formal solution. An epitome of the modern protagonist, Xiangzi is portrayed in this novel as a supreme individualist who destroys himself simply by being himself. The novel goes on, however, to suggest that the converse is also true: as soon as Xiangzi relinquishes his ambition, his independence, and his individualism, he degenerates to the level of the despicable crowd. At the close of the novel, the narrator diagnoses the physical and moral state of Xiangzi; "Handsome, ambitious, dreamer of fine dreams, selfish, individualistic, sturdy, great Xiangzi. No one knows how many funerals he marched in, and no one knows when or where he was able to get himself buried, that degenerate, selfish, unlucky offspring of society's diseased womb, a ghost caught in Individualism's blind alley" (pp. 308, *249*).

At a certain level, one might interpret this passage in familiar naturalist terms, attributing the downfall of the protagonist to a social environment that "nullifies all his efforts towards independent and honest living."[9] But as David Wang has pointed out, critics who concentrate on Lao She's humanitarian concerns for social underdogs and on his naturalist portrayal of the oppressed often end up paying scant attention to the formal aspects of this novel. In his recent study of Chinese fictional realism, Wang emphasizes the melodramatic and farcical elements, shedding important light on the formal aspects of Lao She's novel.[10] My own reading will press the formal approach further by raising the following questions: How does the novel structure the symbolic relationship between the protagonist and his material world? What defines Xiangzi as *homo economicus* or economic individualist? Does the novel's representation of the body, money, the rickshaw, capital, investment, and other business transactions supply the mere content of the story or, as I suggest below, are they part of an elaborate formal strategy that generates the meaning of Lao She's fictional world? Finally, what is the rhetorical status of the narrator's language and how does it affect interpretation of the novel?

Take the passage quoted above. The narrator's excessive use of contradictory adjectival clauses (great, degenerate, etc.) seems to prevent a single deterministic interpretation, such as naturalism, since some of the clauses clearly undermine the meanings of the others.[11] The language of the novel thus reveals its own rhetorical status as an oxymoron, a site of contradiction that, nonetheless, produces a wealth of meanings. Taking this tension as a cue, my own reading of the novel's representation of *homo economicus* tries to situate itself in the rhetorical space opened up by the narrator's language.

Xiangzi acquires the nickname Camel Xiangzi after a series of adventures that culminate in his stealing three camels and selling them for 35 silver dollars. In his single-minded ambition to own a rickshaw and become an independent man, he needs this money to replace the rickshaw he has lost to the soldiers who kidnapped him. "Camel," therefore, names Xiangzi's symbolic relationship to money, capital, investment, and ownership. This symbolic relationship finds a perfect symbolic locale in Beiping (Beijing), a city that lures the protagonist with an infinite promise of individual success. Infatuated with everything that the city represents—anonymity, independence, opportunity, money, wealth, sensuality—Xiangzi wants very much to be part of that world.

> Xiangzi wanted to kiss it, kiss that gray stinking dirt, adorable dirt, dirt that grew silver dollars! He had no father or mother, brother or sister, and no relatives. The only friend he had was this ancient city. This city gave him everything. Even starving here was better than starving in the country. There were things to look at, sounds to listen to, color and voices everywhere. All you needed was to be willing to sell your strength. There was so much

money here it couldn't be counted. There were ten thousand kinds of grand things here that would never be eaten up or worn out.   (pp. 39, *31*)

In a sense, this passage wonderfully captures the changing socioeconomic relations in early Republican China that David Strand describes in *Rickshaw Beijing*. The migration of the poverty-stricken rural population to the city in search of livelihood brings profound changes in the lives of both urban and rural people. Xiangzi is completely on his own, penniless, rootless, friendless, and without family ties. He seems exactly the type of proletarian laborer who would win the heart of the writers and intellectuals in the 1920's and 1930's and be depicted by them as a symbol of the oppressed. However, is Xiangzi a symbol of the oppressed in Lao She's fiction?

David Strand, who draws heavily on Lao She's novel in his well-documented study of rickshaw men in Beijing, is critical of the literary representations of the social underdogs in the Republican period: "The rickshaw represented poverty and social dislocation, qualities best conveyed by depicting as a victim the man who pulled it. However, this image reflects only part of the reality of being a puller. To stereotype rickshaw men as paupers or beasts of burden ignored the flair for the dramatic they exhibited in the public performance of their job." [12] In view of the fact that a great many modern writers (Lu Xun, Hu Shi, Yu Dafu, and others) seized on the image of the rickshaw puller to protest social injustice or to reflect critically on their own moral position as intellectuals, Strand's point is well taken. However, a literary text does not exist simply to reflect social reality, whether it be a partial truth or the whole truth that one demands from it. It has its own complex conditions of being, not the least of which is its "performative" representation of multifarious interpretations of symbolic reality. Long before the advent of poststructuralism, literary critics disputed and criticized the idea that the novel reflects an unmediated reality as a mimetic fallacy, and historians and social scientists who use literary texts as evidence in their own scholarship might find their insights useful. [13] Strand's interpretive strategy, which fails to constitute itself as a problematic in his account of Lao She's novelistic representation of the rickshaw man, inevitably reveals the status of his own priorities as a labor historian who emphasizes organized labor, collective action, public performance, and the like.

Although there is nothing wrong about choosing an emphasis in one's historical research, the theoretical assumptions underlying Strand's approach should alert the reader to some typical blind spots. Here I will not go into the debate on his application of the notion of civil society to China, which others have criticized. For me, the crux of the matter is the question of realist orthodoxy as a dominant interpretative practice in social sciences. By "realist orthodoxy," I do not mean simply a focusing of attention on the realm of the real, be it civil society or the public sphere; rather, in the words of Justine Rosenberg, it is "a determinate construction of political reality which entails a series of hidden propositions and symptomatic silences." [14] Realism performs its ideological script most effectively when that which is being legitimized through an appeal to the "real" de-legitimizes that which it calls "unreal." Needless to say, this performative function of realism has a huge stake in maintaining the commonsensical, mimetic understanding of how language and literature work; namely, that language and literature reflect reality and never constitute it or act on it in a major way.

In his study of modern Chinese fiction, the late critic Marston Anderson left an important reminder.

> All realist fiction gives itself authority by asserting a privileged relationship with reality. Yet the claim is not simply a passive, a priori assumption but also a formal determinant whose operation is discernible in all examples of the mode. Each new work must reproduce the claim in its own right, thereby affirming its singular command over reality. It should therefore be possible, while suspending intractable epistemological questions, to examine the act of representation as a kind of intellectual labor (or, in linguistic terms, as a motivated speech-act) whose characteristic traces may be discovered in the text. The real may, at least provisionally, be viewed simply as an effect of the fiction. [15]

Beyond the questioning of the real, a literary historian is bound to read a novelist like Lao She differently, because s/he reads historical evidence differently, and that evidence is often borne out by the materiality of the literary text itself. The materiality of Lao She's novel includes an interesting history of textual editions that continually revise, rewrite, and reframe the problem of the real in the novel. [16] Here I draw attention to a remarkable piece of self-criticism by Lao She in a preface to a revised edition of *Camel Xiangzi*; the circumstances make for a revealing comparison with Strand's criticism. Writing for the 1951 publication of *Lao She xuanji* (Selected works of Lao She) by Kaiming shudian, Lao She spoke in a revisionary vein about his earlier novel. "I called him 'a ghost caught in Individualism's blind alley,' " says he, referring to the passage quoted earlier, "but I was actually blaming myself for not having the guts to state explicitly why he failed to rebel. After *Xiangzi* was published, I was reproached by a worker who asked: 'If Xiangzi has to die that way, what hope is there for us people?' His question rendered me speechless."[17] It is not difficult to understand why after 1949 Lao She decided to take a revisionary position with regard to the ending of his novel. After all, the novel itself went through several revisions in the 1950's as the author recanted his earlier emphasis on Xiangzi's individual fate in favor of a more optimistic outlook based on collective action. One scholar treats the several revisions published by the Renmin wenxue publishing house since 1955 as *xinban* (new editions) and calls all the previous editions *jiuban* (old editions).[18] The new editions introduce numerous changes into the text, notably the elimination of a large portion of Chapter 23 and all of Chapter 24.[19]

The deleted chapters and passages depict the horrors of the protagonist's moral and physical deterioration in such a negative light as to suggest a certain degree of self-inflicted suffering. Lao She made a point of deleting the part that portrays the sordid deals Xiangzi makes with Ruan Ming regarding the labor organization, as well as the scene of Ruan's execution. As a result, the revised text emphasizes the destructive forces of the old society and calls for collective action.[20] By eliminating those chapters, Lao She and some of his critics apparently believe that they are offering a "more realistic presentation of life."[21] But this so-called reality had to be "revised" retroactively before it could bear witness to the imputed inevitability of the Communist revolution.[22] Coming from an opposite direction, Strand's reading of Lao She operates, nonetheless, on a similar principle of realism, demanding 'a reality story from a literary text that must be revised retroactively to offer it. In so doing, it obscures both the performative aspect of the novel itself—which I call the strategy of "figural reading" below—and of his own interpretative stance.[23]

Rather than continue to debate the accuracy of the novelistic representation of the experience of rickshaw men in Beijing, we would do well to focus on the questions of representation and interpretation raised by the work itself. What does the figure of Xiangzi represent? Surely, with his ambition, self-love, and dignified sense of labor, this young man is much more than a symbol of the oppressed. The sheer energy of Xiangzi's dream turns rickshaw pulling into an extraordinary human drama whose meanings exceed, by far, the dimension of his adopted profession. Thus the narrator observes at the beginning of the novel:

> His thoughts were fixed on that distant rickshaw, the rickshaw that would make him free and independent, *the rickshaw that would be like his own hands and*

feet. He would no longer have to put up with the bad temper of rickshaw agency owners or be hypocritically polite to others when he had his own rickshaw. With his own strength and his own rickshaw, he would have something to eat when he opened his eyes in the morning.   (pp. 4, 4; italics added)

This passage captures the remarkable quality of Xiangzi's inner life, a feat that could not have been accomplished without the narrator's innovative use of psycho-narration and free indirect style. In fact, much of the pathos and the irony of the story, I believe, has to do with the narrator's manipulation of the modes of narration in recounting Xiangzi's life, particularly, free indirect style (the italicized passages in the preceding quotation). Lao She adapted this technique from European fiction and reinvented it in modern Chinese colored by his Beiping dialect, which imitates the character's language without actually speaking in his or her own voice. In the passage quoted above, the narrator opens by describing the state of Xiangzi's mind as if observed from the outside (psycho-narration). Somewhere with the third mention of the "rickshaw," he switches to free indirect style that closely imitates the character's language.[24] The transition is signaled by the repetition of the word "rickshaw" as well as the emphatic incantation of "his own" as if mirroring the colloquial rhythm of Xiangzi's thought-language. Although the actual words are spoken by the narrator in the third person, the point of view is exclusively Xiangzi's (as will be seen later, the narrator is critical of this view). It is almost as if the narrator, while speaking in his own voice (in the third person), temporarily suspends his point of view in order to adopt that of the character.[25]

Unlike psycho-narration, which describes the mental state of the character exclusively from the narrator's point of view, or quoted monologues (soliloquy), which adopt the character's own voice, free indirect style breaks down the boundary between the narrating voice and the character's interior monologue. This narrative style frees novelistic discourse from rigidly reporting what the narrator sees (omniscience) and what the character says or thinks (marked by quotation marks and other devices, such as a switch in address from the third person to the first, or both) and allows free access to the character's thoughts. In Indo-European languages, these moments are usually accompanied by a change in deictic reference and in the grammatical instance of tense, person, and mood, much in the same way as a direct quotation is converted to indirect quotation, except that the free indirect style often omits verbal marks of stylistic transition, such as "he thought" or "he believed."

Thanks to the absence of tense, person, and other related grammatical markers, modern vernacular Chinese is able to switch narrative modes easily without recourse to the grammatical conversions necessary in Indo-European languages, except for deictic references. As a result, in Chinese, free indirect style retains more ambiguity in its relationship to both omniscient psycho-narration and quoted interior monologue than does its counterpart in other languages. The stylistic effect is that of an uninterrupted flow of narration, somewhat like a free direct discourse, leading to the perfect illusion of a transparent mind. If one were to recast the quoted passage as a straightforward narration and direct quotation without using the free indirect style, it would roughly read:

> His thoughts were fixed on that distant rickshaw, the rickshaw that would make him free and independent, the rickshaw, he said to himself, "like my own hands and feet. So I won't have to put up with the bad temper of rickshaw agency owners, or be humble to others when I have my own rickshaw. With my own strength and my own rickshaw, I'll have something to eat when I open my eyes in the morning."

The stylistic effect of this passage is much weaker when a conventional quoted monologue is substituted for free indirect style. Relying on this and other narrative modes, Lao She's narrator is able to probe the extraordinary depths of Xiangzi's inner world. And it is the presence of this inner world that sets Xiangzi apart from the rest of the rickshaw men; more important, it is the quality of this inner world that endows the humble life of a rickshaw man with larger symbolic meanings of a tragedy.[26]

What is it in the inner world of this rickshaw man that has gripped the hearts of so many readers? Xiangzi's dream of owning a rickshaw is humble compared to that which a more fortunate entrepreneur would probably envision; nonetheless, it is the dream of a *homo economicus* who imagines gaining his independence, self-control, personal dignity, and a livelihood through hard work and private ownership. Lacking other material means of investment, he must sell his strength and convert his muscles ("feet and hands") to capital, which leads to the contradiction of his narcissistic attachment to his body and his profound sense of alienation from it. The rickshaw is not only a means of production, but an image of his alter ego or the impossible plenitude of self-fulfillment. When he buys his first rickshaw at the age of 22, he pulls it to a quiet corner and examines it closely, trying to capture "a reflection of his face in the lacquered panels" (pp. 11, *10*) in a strikingly narcissistic moment. He then decides to celebrate the occasion by naming the day a common birthday for himself and his mirror-image. Free indirect style penetrates his thought as the narrator remarks: "All right, today he had bought a new rickshaw. Let today be his birthday, his and the rickshaw's. It would be easy to remember. Besides, the rickshaw was his heart's blood. There was simply no reason to separate man from rickshaw" (pp. 12, *10*).

If Xiangzi sees the rickshaw as his own double, the bond between them goes deeper than the emotional tie suggested by "his heart's blood." The verb Lao She used for the word translated "separate" in the last sentence is *fenkai suan*, literally "to calculate/count separately." The word *suan* (to calculate or count) is particularly important. Throughout the novel, the narrator draws attention to the degree to which Xiangzi counts and calculates his way through life. Like a thrifty *homo economicus*, he counts his silver dollars and belongings and calculates what amount he should spend on food and clothes and what should be put aside as savings.[27] For instance, after he loses his first rickshaw and sells the camels for 35 silver dollars, Xiangzi makes his way back to the city and figures: "It took a total of *two dollars and twenty cents* to get properly turned out. A jacket and trousers of fine-looking unbleached rough cloth cost *one dollar*, black cloth shoes were *eighty cents*, cotton socks were *fifteen cents*, and a straw hat cost *twenty-five cents*" (pp. 38, *30*; italics added).

Lest one read the above as a simple, realistic description of Xiangzi's poverty, Chapters 7 and 8 provide a focused look at this important aspect of his character. After his unfortunate seduction by Hu Niu, Xiangzi has an opportunity to work for Mr. Cao as his private chauffeur, which greatly improves his circumstances. With renewed hopes, he once again dreams about owning his rickshaw:

> Xiangzi's eyes sparkled when he sat alone in his room figuring out ways to economize and buy a rickshaw. His lips wouldn't stop muttering; it was as if he had some mental illness. He didn't know much about arithmetic and his mind and mouth kept on repeating "six times six is thirty-six." The calculation had little relation to how much money he actually had, but the repetition filled his mind. It was just as if he already had an account balance. (pp. 87, *68*)[28]

Xiangzi never stops counting or calculating, but somehow he falls short of being a fully rational *homo economicus*. Does he miscalculate or is he too much of a dreamer to keep his balance straight? As if an evil star reigned over his life, Xiangzi's art of calculation seems no match for the calculated calamity of his fate (the narrator's plot against him), wherein lies the irony of his situation. By comparison, Gao Ma, the housemaid at Mr. Cao's home, is a better capitalist. A self-taught female version of *homo economicus*, this woman loans the surplus cash from her monthly income out at interest. We are told she is capable of handling her finances in the manner of a "bank manager," and she even advises Xiangzi on how to raise money for his rickshaw. As the story unfolds, the narrator's language increasingly derives tremendous pleasure from adding, counting, detailing, calculating, and speculating. This language catches Xiangzi the miser in a revealing moment: "He took out the few dollars he'd saved during the last few months; all his money was in silver and he turned the coins over quietly one by one, afraid they'd clink. The silver was so white and gleaming, so thick and real and eye-catching, that he felt even more he could not let go of it except to buy a rickshaw" (pp. 90, 70). The sensuality of this description is striking, and it redeems Xiangzi's love of money by aestheticizing it, giving it a human face, a meaning in excess of financial gains, and a pre-capitalist sensibility opposed to Gao Ma's rational world of business management. Xiangzi refuses to open a postal savings account to earn interest on his silver dollars as Gao Ma has advised him to do, because, in his view, "you put in beautiful silver and all they give you for proof is some marks in a book and that ends the whole business" (pp. 90, 71).

This distrust of modern contractual relationships reveals the fundamental contradiction in Xiangzi's chosen way of living: the symbolic world of the rural economy is pitted against the rationality of urban capitalism. The silver dollar represents real value, in the eyes of Xiangzi, by assuming an unalienated relationship between him and his labor. Physical contact with the money (hoarding in a pot), therefore, is of paramount importance since it seems to guarantee a sense of control over his life. Are not self-control and self-determination Xiangzi's ultimate goals? The illusion, however, is soon shattered by the calculated villainy of Detective Sun, who robs Xiangzi of all his life savings. This is the second time, after the soldiers' robbery, that a "chance" catastrophe so brutally overturns Xiangzi's plans.

Xiangzi's precapitalist frame of mind comes into conflict with the circumstances of his life; the means of production are no longer the same as those of rural economy, and the meanings of value, ownership, and independence are being radically redefined. The capitalist system represented in this novel by modern banking suggests a relation of production built on contractual relationships that presuppose individual free choice. Xiangzi rejects these contractual relationships but insists, nonetheless, on cashing in on the capitalist system's promise of independence and individual freedom. This inherent contradiction, as I demonstrate below, sheds important light on Xiangzi's problematic identity as *homo economicus*.

Why does Lao She take such pains to detail monetary transactions and bookkeeping? What, indeed, does the novelistic form have to do with economic individualism? Are there any substantial linkages, over and above superficial resemblances, between Xiangzi and the figure of *homo economicus* that once dominated the English and European novels? Bakhtin observes with acute insight that business life, high finance, and money, that "supreme power of life's new king," play a prominent role in the world of major French novels.[29] Stendhal and Balzac are obvious examples. Likewise, Ian Watt points out in his study of economic individualism in Defoe's works: "All Defoe's heroes pursue money, which he characteristically called 'the general denominating article in the world'; and they pursue it very methodically according to the profit and loss book-keeping which Max Weber considered to be the distinctive technical feature of modern capitalism."[30] In *Moll Flanders*, for example, there is much linen, gold, and jewelry to be counted. Robinson Crusoe is notorious for his meticulous bookkeeping on that little island where one finds memorable pieces of clothing and hardware. To add a further example, Dickens's novels are filled with descriptions of banknotes, bonds, contracts, wills, and other property documents that figure significantly in the structuring of the plot and other symbolic realities in his fiction. Does Lao She's familiarity with these authors suggest some degree of intertextual linkage between *Camel Xiangzi* and European literature, in particular, English fiction? What exactly is the meaning of *homo economicus* in the Chinese context vis-à-vis his European counterparts from the point of view of translingual practice?

Lao She repeatedly mentioned that he had learned his novelistic craft through reading English and European novels. His first novel, *Lao Zhang de zhexue* (The philosophy of Lao Zhang), was written at a library desk at the University of London and inspired by Dickens's *Pickwick Papers* and *Nicholas Nickelby*. During his five years in London, he drew up an ambitious reading list and browsed through all the major authors from the Greek classics to modern English and European novels; the latter were his favorite.[31] In a reminiscence, Lao She confessed his onetime admiration for the English Bible, Shakespeare, Dickens, Swift, Conrad, and Defoe. "Having studied some major English writers," he recalled in 1941, "I got a better idea of what gives a literary style its strength and beauty. Simplicity and naturalness are infinitely preferable to flowery and ornate languages. One finds the soul of simplicity and the cream of the English language in the English Bible and the works of Defoe and Swift."[32]

Studies of literary prototypes, sources, and intertextuality cannot by themselves explain all that goes on in a text; as in the case of Ah Q discussed in Chapter 2, the problem of literary representation involves more complex mediating factors than the often-assumed one-to-one relationship between text and reality. What can we make of Lao She's indebtedness to English literature besides the simplicity of style pointed out by the author himself? One could argue that *Camel Xiangzi* has much in common with Defoe's *Robinson Crusoe* in its unprecedented emphasis on money, economic individualism, independence, the dignity of labor, and the like. One could even go so far as to suggest that Lao She's protagonist is also prefigured by Shakespeare's Hamlet, which would significantly cancel out the utilitarian image of Defoe's hero. My evocation of *Hamlet* here is by no means a free association. Lao She exhibited what David Wang calls his "Hamlet syndrome" in a number of works.[33] As far as *Camel Xiangzi* is concerned, one could cite as evidence the narrator's emphasis on the giant stature of an exceptional hero who outshines everybody else. Xiangzi has handsome limbs, a beautiful body, a noble character, completed with a tragic flaw (honesty to a fault) that brings him down at every turn of life. Witness the elevated theatrical style in which the narrator "soliloquizes" Xiangzi's tragic fate after Hu Niu's death in childbirth: "A rickshaw, a rickshaw, a rickshaw that was his rice bowl. Bought, lost; bought again, sold. Two rises and two falls. It was like the shadow of a ghost; you can never catch it. He'd suffered all those hardships and wrongs in vain. Gone, everything was gone, even his old woman was gone!" (pp. 245, *196*). The reader will readily recognize the free indirect style used by the narrator, a style that translates Xiangzi's interior monologue into his words.[34] The passage is also, however, reminiscent of a Shakespearean soliloquy—including the curious simile of ghost used here—where human life is grasped in terms of rises and falls, where the hero cannot control his own fate, where chance catastrophes abound, and where the tragedy of the hero derives its moving power from stylized soliloquies, and so on. Of course, Lao She's novel converts the stylized soliloquy of tragedy to free indirect speech in the Beijing dialect.[35]

Although Lao She's indebtedness to English literature is indisputable, this interpretation must move beyond the initial level of establishing intertextual linkages in order to avoid becoming an uncontested narrative of literary influence. Xiangzi, a Chinese *homo economicus*, is neither Hamlet nor Robinson Crusoe. Just as a Renaissance hero has little in common with an economic individualist living under industrial capitalism whose utilitarian rationality, optimistic spirit of adventure, and Calvinist sense of salvation preclude the possibility of a tragic outcome, so Xiangzi must also be interpreted on his own ground. But how? In recalling the circumstances surrounding the novel, Lao She once made a remark that may throw some light on this problem.

> What I wanted to find out most about the rickshaw men was not superficial triviality like the way they dress, talk, or carry themselves, but to descend into their inner world through which I might be able catch a glimpse of what hell is like. Whatever is associated with the appearance of a rickshaw puller must be explored in terms of his life experience. I wanted to search for the roots of that experience before I could do justice to poor laborers and their society.[36]

Eschewing a sociological approach, such as that adopted by his contemporary Li Jinghan, who took the rickshaw puller as an object of scientific observation, Lao She wanted to present a novelist's interpretation of (the interior mode of) these men's lives.[37] Rather than claiming to be a transparent representation of social facts, this kind of interpretation calls attention to its own epistemological makeup as such and to its own textual strategy *as an interpretative act.* Thus the word "rickshaw" consistently appears in the text as *yangche* (foreign vehicle), an alternative coinage substituted for the Japanese loanword *renliche* (*jinrikisha*). Whereas the latter assumes neutrality in its representation of the object, the word *yang* (literally, from the ocean or overseas) carries an emotional value—an interpretative surplus value, so to speak—that openly declares the subject-position of a Chinese speaker (ranging from hostility to admiration) toward the imported product labeled as such. The anti-imperialist struggle in the early decades of the twentieth century gave rise to numerous such coinages—a foreigner was called a *yangren* (now *laowai*) instead of *waiguo ren*, imported cloth was *yangbu*, a handgun *yangqiang*, and artillery *yangpao*, and so on.

The rickshaw, a foreign import from Japan, first appeared on the streets of Beijing in 1886 and, almost immediately, became a controversial object. As David Strand notes, on the one hand, rickshaw pulling represented technological progress over a sedan chair, and on the other, "the sight of one human being pulling another also became a symbol of backwardness and exploitation."[38] The degradation of humans to the level of animal was quickly registered by mule-cart drivers, competitors in the profession, who "threw the horrid foreign things, which degraded men to the level of animals, into a canal."[39] This description opens up an interesting avenue to understanding Lao She's novel, not in terms of its accuracy in portraying rickshaw Beijing, as Strand has contended, but in terms of a problem, or several problems, having to do with literary representation, meaning, and interpretation.

In what ways does *yangche* define the meaning of Xiangzi's life as a Chinese *homo economicus*? The rickshaw is a foreign import brought into China together with modern urban culture, semi-colonialism, and capitalism. As an imported symbol of slavery and exploitation, it contradicts the local/peasant symbolism that Xiangzi confers on it when he dreams of gaining control over his destiny through owning a rickshaw. This contradiction dooms all his efforts to transcend the circumstances of poverty, insecurity, homelessness, and dependency in which he finds himself, and he ends up worse off than when he started. The dramatic unfolding of the novel hinges on Xiangzi's fundamental *misrecognition* of the symbol of slavery for a promise of liberation. Capitalism, like all effective ideologies, depends on such misrecognitions on the part of the individual of himself or herself as a free subject capable of choosing one's own form of bondage. "No matter how much the capital," says the narrator when he describes the theory of financial management in connection with Gao Ma's capitalist behavior:

> the theory is the same. Ours is a capitalistic society and for this reason it sifts coins bit by bit like an enormous fine sieve. As the money sifts from top to bottom, only the smallest coins pass through. The theory is also sifted at the same time but there is just as much of it below as above because a theory, unlike coins, doesn't care how small the holes are. It is something disembodied and can flow through the tiniest of holes it pleases. (pp. 89, 69)

This Marxist view drives home the paradox of Xiangzi's life. As a poor peasant at the bottom of the social hierarchy, he gets the smallest coins, if any, that are sifted from the enormous capitalist sieve, and yet his ambition, fueled by the desire to achieve economic independence, is just as strong as that of any capitalist entrepreneur. This paradox is one explanation why Xiangzi can never hope to become a successful *homo economicus* like Robinson Crusoe. Whereas Xiangzi is doomed to toil and selling his physical labor, Crusoe relies on his spirit of adventure to expand the territory of capitalism and conquer the rest of the world precisely by asserting his cultural authority over the native (including his power of naming the other, Friday).[40]

Indeed, *Camel Xiangzi* is as much about the uses and abuses of a young man's body in the changing relations of production caused by the invasion of semi-colonial capitalism as it is about rickshaw pulling. Doomed to a fate of rickshaw pulling, Xiangzi has no means of investment other than his own body, which he finds necessary to convert to capital. The convertible body is thus alienated from its owner, who invests it in order to buy a means of production that only further subjects it to exploitation.

Xiangzi starts out as a bright-eyed peasant lad with supreme confidence in his body. "Looking at his youthful muscles," the narrator remarks in an ironic tone, "it seemed to him it was only a question of time until he achieved his ambition and reached his goal. It was no dream at all" (pp. 5, 5). Whenever Xiangzi sees his fellow top-notch rickshaw men displaying their handsome torsos, he thinks of showing off his own "iron-fan" chest and hard, straight back. His pride and narcissism are wonderfully captured by the narrator through a combined use of straight third-person narration and free indirect style (the italicized part below):

> He'd turn his head to look at his shoulders; *how very broad they were and how very impressive! Once he had his waist bound tightly, he'd put on wide white pants and fasten them down at the cuffs with rubber bands to show off that pair of great big feet! Yes, there was no doubt he could become a most outstanding rickshaw man.* He grinned at himself like a simpleton.   (pp. 6, 5; italics added)

Xiangzi the *homo economicus* knows how to take good care of his body and how to invest it in his dream. He refuses to ruin it either by indulging in liquor or visiting the white houses (brothels). Unlike the rickshaw, this body belongs to him by birthright and seems inalienable. Xiangzi at first believes he can exert absolute control over it. But the novel soon proves him wrong.

His own sexuality is the first to shake this confidence and, despite the revulsion he feels for the tigress daughter of Old Liu, he is seduced by her. It seems to me that sexuality matters in this novel less because Hu Niu matters, which she does in her own way, than because it significantly changes Xiangzi's self-perception by dint of transforming his body into something he can no longer contemplate with full self-assurance. The seduction forces him to confront the unknown and the uncontrollable in himself.

> Not only was it as if something had been glued onto his body. His heart also seemed to have been soiled by black smudges and they could never be washed away. No matter how much he hated her, how much he despised her, she seemed to have gotten hold of his mind. The more unwilling he was to think about it again, the more she kept popping up in his thoughts, naked and offering everything ugly and fine to him all at the same time. It is like buying junk; in the midst of all the rusty iron and bits of copper are some gleaming and colorful little things you cannot resist.   (pp. 69–70, 54)

This equation of female sexuality and soil and junk is probably the most misogynist thing that Lao She ever wrote. One must not overlook the fact, however, that the passage also lets us glimpse Xiangzi's profound sense of uncertainty and ambiguity regarding his own sexuality. He cannot decide whether he is attracted to Hu Niu's nakedness or repelled by it, nor can he tell his body what to do or guide his own thoughts in the direction he wants. Confronted with the power of sexuality in himself, Xiangzi simply loses control: "He became vaguely conscious of an urge much more powerful than himself that was squeezing him into a ball and throwing him into a fire. There was nothing he could do to stop this forward motion" (pp. 71, 55).

Xiangzi's loss of virginity leads to a succession of defeats in his struggle to retain control over his body, mind, masculinity, and integrity. First, he is swindled into marriage by Hu Niu, who pretends to be pregnant and who, after the wedding, forbids him to think about returning to his old profession. When he tries to argue with her, she announces: "You have your plans and I have mine. We'll just see who can drive who to the limit. You got a wife but I was the one who spent the money. You didn't put in a penny of your own. Think it over. Between the two of us, who should listen to who?" (pp. 189, 149). In a male-dominated society where both money and sexual desire are defined in terms of masculinity, Hu Niu's possession of them simultaneously translates into her loss of femininity and Xiangzi's loss of manhood. The gendered character of their domestic quarrels over money, power, and control does not escape Xiangzi, who is, after all, worried about his own manhood. The narrator quotes his interior monologue:

> Now you can accept money when someone gives it to you but there's absolutely no way you can regard yourself as a man afterward. Your courage and your strength don't matter and you have to go and be someone else's slave. You have to be your wife's toy and your father-in-law's lackey. It was as if a man were, in fact, nothing at all, only a bird which goes out by itself to find food and falls into a net. It eats someone else's grain and then behaves itself inside a cage and sings for others and is sold when they feel like it! (pp. 188, 149)

The metaphor of a desexualized bird and its cage echoes a similar metaphor used in Lu Xun's "Regret for the Past," to be discussed in Chapter 6, where Juansheng, the narrator, also regrets his loss of freedom after moving in with Zijun. Interestingly, the male protagonist in each case sees himself as being trapped by the conjugal relationship, although it is the woman who pays the ultimate price of death. After the wedding, arranged single-handedly by Hu Niu, Xiangzi laments his loss of manhood under the dual oppression of money and woman and intuits how much one's gender identity is tied up with power and economic status. In that sense,

Hu Niu's androgyny is not at all mystifying, for it can be explained in terms of her relationship to her father, who exploits her labor for his own selfish ends, as well as in terms of her shrewd grasp of the importance of money and of her own disadvantages as a woman in the society. Being a product of that society, she manipulates, lies, schemes, harasses, threatens, and does everything within her power to obtain the object of her desire, which she could not have gotten otherwise. This woman may outshine men like Xiangzi in certain situations, but, fundamentally, she is a distorted mirror-image of masculinity (money, status, sexual desire) produced by the same forces that condemn her for deviating from the ideal of femininity. Her death in childbirth—a very feminine death—is perhaps an ironic punishment for violating the gender codes of her society.

Xiangzi, of course, does not fare any better. After Hu Niu's death, he sells the rickshaw and takes to drinking, smoking, gambling, cheating, whoring, and abusing his body. The last straw is the loss of his sweetheart, Xiao Fuzi, who hangs herself in despair after being sold to a brothel. Surprisingly or not, it is in the brothel where Xiangzi goes looking for Xiao Fuzi that he is brought face to face with the horrible reality of his own life as *homo economicus*, reflected in the macabre image of a worn-out lower-class prostitute nicknamed "White Flour Sack." Much like Xiangzi who used to take pride in selling his muscles, this woman of forty has sold her body of her own free will and enjoys her way of making a living. A prostitute by choice, White Flour Sack is regarded in the brothel as the only *free individual* and yet, when Xiangzi finds her, she lives in a condition of extreme poverty and filth, having no furniture in her room except for a small *kang* and an old quilt on it. Does this mean that Xiangzi the free individual would end up in a similar state of destitution after years of hope, striving, and hard work? During his bizarre encounter with that woman, Xiangzi begins to have serious doubts about the meaning of his struggle, which soon lead to a total renunciation of all that previously mattered to him. The narrator at this point also seems willing to give him up: "Xiangzi, that very handsome Xiangzi, became a scrawny and filthy low-class rickshaw man. He never washed his face, his body, or his clothes. His head hadn't been shaved in more than a month. He wasn't particular about a rickshaw either" (pp. 291, *234*).

What are we supposed to make of a novel that is calculated to destroy this honest, ambitious, and hardworking *homo economicus*? Why did Lao She refuse to make Xiangzi a successful hero like his prototype Robinson Crusoe? What, indeed, goes wrong here? These questions seem inevitable, although the reader should not think that he or she is the first to ask them. Throughout the novel, the protagonist himself grapples with similar questions in an attempt to comprehend his situation. Like Hamlet who never acts but interprets, Xiangzi is driven by an existential urge to ask Why as he acts out his role as a *homo economicus*, although his interpretation is almost always relayed through the narrator's use of psycho-narration and free indirect style.

But how does the novel's inclusion of the acts of interpretation affect the reader's interpretation? Instead of searching for a definitive reading of Lao She's novel, I argue that the novel poses *interpretation* as a problem of literary representation. Here, I draw attention to a specific moment in the novel where the question of how one might interpret Xiangzi's misfortune is pushed to the foreground. Mr. Cao prompts Xiangzi to tell him the story of his life since their last meeting. Xiangzi properly registers this request as an invitation to reconstruct his life in a verbal form:

> Xiangzi wanted to cry. He didn't know how to tell anyone about his troubles because *his tale was written entirely in blood and lodged in the deepest part of his heart.* He was silent for some time. He longed to *take those words of blood and let them flow out.* They were all there in his memory and, when he thought about them, would come flowing back, so he had to *get them into the right order and arranged well.* He wanted to *tell the history of his life.* While he did not know what it all meant, that string of injustices was plain and clear. (pp. 275, *221*; italics added)

In my opinion, this passage, together with one I will quote shortly, forms the crux of the entire novel. Evoking the metaphor of verbal composition (highlighted here in italics), it reflects critically on the language of the novel itself and does so by focusing on the modes of speech and narration whereby Xiangzi's relationship to his own story must be grasped and whereby the narrator's language and the authority of his interpretation are necessarily brought into question. I first concentrate on Xiangzi's interpretation and then address the status of the narrator's voice.

Xiangzi is encouraged to talk in the presence of Mr. Cao, one of the few people to cross Xiangzi's path who does not take a self-motivated interest in his life and is capable of lending an ear to his story.[41] All of a sudden, the young man seems to discover the power of speech in himself and begins to talk like a madman, hoping to convert his previously silent experience into a coherent account, an autobiographical narrative, so to speak. What, then, does Xiangzi's own narrative say? Does it coincide with the narrator's account? How does the one relate to the other?

Xiangzi's narrative, as the narrator summarizes here for us, starts with his arrival in the city, the beginnings of his career as a rickshaw puller, his tale of how he hoarded money to buy a rickshaw and how he lost it, all the way up to his present situation in a chronological order. On the surface, this appears to confirm the story line provided so far by the narrator himself, but the narrator goes on to report:

> Even he was aware that this was all very strange. How could he talk for so long and so openly and rapidly? Events and all his thoughts came leaping out of his heart one after another. The events themselves seem to find the right words. One sentence pressed after another. Every sentence was a true one, this one to be cherished, that one to be lamented over. His mind could not keep anything back nor could he stop himself from talking. He seemed determined, without any hesitation or confusion, to get out all that was in his heart in one breath. The more he talked the happier he became. He forgot himself because he was already *wrapped up inside the story. He, himself, was in the heart of every sentence, that ambitious, wronged, suffering, and downfallen self.* His head was sweaty when he had finished and his heart was empty. It was a comforting emptiness, like the emptiness you feel when breaking out in a cold sweat after you have fainted.   (pp. 276, 222; italics added)

If Xiangzi's autobiographical impulse to *tell his own story* is poised to challenge the authority of a third-person narrator who claims unlimited access to his inner world on the strength of psycho-narration and free indirect style, this passage draws attention to the fact that an autobiographical narrator can get wrapped up inside his own story and, therefore, should be taken with a grain of salt. Indeed, the novel registers a striking disparity between Xiangzi's self-narration, which is always already mediated through the narrator's psycho-narration and free indirect style, and alternative ways of looking at his situation, including the narrator's own critical judgment from a lofty omniscient third-person point of view. Xiangzi regards his misfortune as totally undeserving: he has been wronged, mistreated, and ill-favored by society or by something he cannot name but is perhaps best described as fate. At the same time, however, the novel offers an interpretation that profoundly undercuts this view. I am referring to an interesting conversation at the beginning of Chapter 23 between Xiangzi and Xiao Ma's grandfather, a retired rickshaw puller and now a street beggar. After the old man hears Xiangzi's recount of his troubles, he offers his own life story as a commentary on Xiangzi's situation:

> "My body and bones were sound and my character good when I started out, and I came straight on down the road to where I am now and ended up like this! Sound body? Even men of iron can't get out of this snare of a world we're in. So you have a good character. What good is that? 'The good are requited with good, the evil with evil.' There never was any such thing! When I was young they called me a zealous fellow. I took everyone else's problems

for my own and did it do me any good? None at all. I've even saved lives. People who jumped in the river, people who'd hanged themselves, I saved them all. And did I get anything for it? Nothing at all! I'm telling you, I'm not the one who decides what day I'll freeze to death. I figure it's perfectly understandable that any poor guy who thinks he can succeed by himself will find it harder than going to heaven." (pp. 284–85, *228–29*)

The old man then proceeds to use the parable of the grasshopper to demonstrate to Xiangzi that a single grasshopper like himself cannot hop a long way by itself and that it takes a whole army of grasshoppers acting together to make a difference.

The old man's wisdom comes very close to the narrator's own judgment of Xiangzi at the close of Chapter 23. Speaking in his own voice, the narrator concludes that Xiangzi's life "might well be ruined by his own hands but he wasn't about to sacrifice anything for anybody. He who works for himself knows how to destroy himself. These are the two starting points of Individualism" (pp. 295, *237*). The narrator's judgment, along with the old man's view, is often evoked as the author's own conclusive pronouncement on the evils of individualism and the need for collective action on a class basis. This seemingly obvious interpretation is reinforced by the authoritative status of the narrative voice in the novel—after all, the narrator is the one who commands the whole novelistic space—and by his omniscient stance with regard to Xiangzi's limited inner world.

Does the novel support the narrator's view that Xiangzi is destroyed by his own individualism, and, as the old man puts it, do the roots of all his misfortunes lie in Xiangzi's lack of class consciousness and in his indifference to the collective cause? As if intended to thwart this interpretation, the novel includes a few important details that cast the opposite of individualism—collective action—in an extremely negative light, particularly the events that unfold around the character Ruan Ming. This young man, who once denounced his teacher Mr. Cao to the authorities for a passing grade, is a political activist who organizes rickshaw pullers for revolutionary struggles. He embraces the left-wing causes of collective action and knows how to cash in on ideas by informing on other people. Xiangzi is also drawn into the demonstrations Ruan organizes and becomes an old hand at flag waving and shouting on those occasions. But, as the narrator puts it in a cynical moment, "Ruan Ming sold his ideas for money. Xiangzi accepted ideas for money. Ruan Ming knew that when the moment of need came he could sacrifice Xiangzi to save his own skin. Xiangzi had certainly never figured things that way, but when the time came he simply did the same thing: he informed on Ruan Ming" (pp. 304,

246). If this is not enough to deflate the grandiose images attached to collective action, the mob scene on the streets of Beijing on the day Ruan Ming is brought to the execution ground casts the worst possible light on what it means to mobilize a crowd. This scene of violence clearly echoes Ah Q's execution in Lu Xun's story, as the narrator reports: "The shouts of the people were like waves on the ocean; those in front rushed back to meet those behind. Everybody turned their mouths down and complained to each other. They were all disappointed. He [Ruan Ming] was only a little monkey like that after all! And he was so floppy and blah! He didn't look up, his face was deathly pale, and he wasn't even making a sound!" (pp. 301, *243*).

What are we to do with such contradictory evidence in a novel that seems to endorse neither individualism nor political action on a collective basis? The narrator sees Xiangzi as a supreme individualist who destroys himself by pursuing his solipsistic dream as *homo economicus*. But, as soon as Xiangzi gives up his ambition, independence, and individualism, he degenerates to the level of the cannibalistic crowd. It seems one cannot take the narrator's judgment too literally without falling into the elaborate interpretive trap set up by the novel itself. Is the reader not incited to ask the big existential questions of Why and Either/Or? Perhaps the point of the novel is precisely to demand and resist interpretation in the very act of interpretation, and to represent conflicting interpretations that compete with one another as truth claims. In short, the problem of literary representation in this novel is ultimately inseparable from that of interpretation.

The multiple interpretive possibilities represented in *Camel Xiangzi* may seem to evoke what Bakhtin calls heteroglossia in his stylistics of the novel, but I see a much more interesting situation than the notion of heteroglossia can explain. Generally speaking, Bakhtin's notion refers to the *hybrid construction* of a language stratified into "social dialects, characteristic group behavior, professional jargons, generic languages, languages of generations and age groups, tendentious languages, languages of the authorities, of various circles and of passing fashions, languages that serve the specific sociopolitical purposes of the day, even of the hour." In novelistic discourse, heteroglossia manifests itself in the hybrid construction of an utterance that "belongs, by its grammatical (syntactic) and compositional markers, to a single speaker, but that actually contains mixed within it two utterances, two speech manners, two styles, two 'languages,' two semantic and axiological belief systems."[42] In the first sense of heteroglossia, Bakhtin is describing a general linguistic situation for a sociologically defined theory of the novel, whereas, in the second sense quoted here, he is speaking of narrative modes like "indirect discourse" and "free indirect style," as narratologists variously term it. Although the idea of heteroglossia may shed useful light on Lao She's novel, the novel itself presents a very different problem for the reader. This is what I call *figural reading*, a kind of coded reading bodied forth or *represented* within the text itself. By engaging with the conflicting *figural readings* provided by the narrator, by Xiangzi himself, as well as by the other characters within the textual economy of the novel, the reader necessarily inserts herself or himself—and, perhaps, can do no more—in the never-ending process of interpretation.

Postscript

I visited Beijing in the winter of 1992, my first trip home in eight and a half years. The city of Beijing had changed beyond recognition, especially in the area of the Haidian district where Xiangzi was supposedly robbed and kidnapped by soldiers when he risked his life taking a client to Qinghua University in his new rickshaw. In December 1992 when I was there, the most eye-catching sight on the streets of Beijing was the endless stream of brightly painted yellow minivans called *miandi* (Beijing slang for minivan taxi; for the transliteration of "taxi," see Appendix F). I was told that those who could not afford a regular cab found these minivans most attractive, since the fare was only ten *yuan* for any distance up to ten kilometers and then one *yuan* for each additional kilometer. I became a regular rider and, besides, enjoyed the opportunity to chat with the drivers. On one occasion, a driver complained to me about his long working hours and the lack of medical insurance for his family since he had lost his job at a state-owned factory that had gone bankrupt. He said that his dream was to buy a taxicab and become his own boss so he would not have to pay a high monthly rent to the leasing company. As if this was not enough to conjure up the image of the rickshaw man in my mind, he turned around and asked me: "Do you know Lao She's novel *Camel Xiangzi*? We are a new generation of Xiangzi. That's what we are."[43] It was not difficult for me to grasp the similarities there, but what really struck me was the way he made the connection. The cab driver was a good reader of literature, for he read Xiangzi as a trope, something that stands for something else, whose meanings are not fixed where they originated but are capable of being deployed to make sense of a totally different situation.

CHAPTER 5

Narratives of Desire:
Negotiating the Real and the Fantastic

The penetrative act of Lao She's narrator toward Xiangzi's consciousness points to something far more thought-provoking and revolutionary than the degree or kind of psychological realism achieved by a modern Chinese novel. In fact, one of the first fruits of Chinese literary cross-breeding with European and Japanese fiction is the objectification of the inner world through the act of storytelling. What could be more striking than the popular metaphor of dissection, a trope mentioned briefly in Chapter 2? The surgical knife used to dissect the human body for scientific research translates in the hands of Lu Xun and his fellow writers into a powerful metaphor for the function of writing. Yu Dafu once remarked, citing examples from European autobiographical writing (particularly Henri Amiel's diary), that first-person narrative is best suited for the task of "dissecting the self."[1] The scientific trope of dissection thus renders the useful service of turning narrative inward in order to penetrate the psychological depths of the mind. As Erich Kahler points out in his study of the internalization of narrative and the rise of individual psychology in early modern Europe, "One's fellow men as well as one's own inner life become objects of conscious observation. In other words, they are objectified."[2] This process of objectification points to the historical unfolding of an important relationship linking the scientific, the social, and the literary that bears directly on the invention of a distinct set of narrative modes for the representation of the inner world.

However, a more interesting phenomenon, one that does not fit neatly into the symbiosis of the scientific and the literary, is happening in the literature of this period. Lu Xun's first published story, the path-breaking

"Kuangren riji" (Diary of a madman), introduced an intensely schizo-phrenic introspective voice into Chinese literature via the Russian writer Gogol. But almost immediately, it cast grave doubts on a narrative frame that seeks to contain the madman's writing in the name of medical science. In a much-quoted frame narrative written in respectable classical Chinese, the fictional editor informs us:

> I took the diary away, read it through, and found that he had suffered from a form of persecution complex. The writing was most confused and inco-herent, and he had made many wild statements; moreover he had omitted to give any dates, so that only by the colour of the ink and the differences in the writing could one tell that it was not written at one time. Certain sections, however, were not altogether disconnected, and I have copied out a part to serve as a subject for medical research.[3]

This conventional frame has the effect of putting the madman's writ-ing in perspective for us.[4] But, what kind of perspective? If the wild statements that immediately follow the editorial passage provided noth-ing more than pathological evidence of a mental disease, we might well be convinced of the truth of the editor's "normal" perspective. The mad-man's diary insists, however, on a symbolic diagnosis of the pathology of Chinese history—with implicit reference to the normality of the West—that exceeds by far any literal interpretations of the individual psyche. This symbolic function of reading and writing is at odds with the positivistic optimism implied by the scientific trope of dissection and turns the latter on its head. What we witness here is an interesting case of intellectual rivalry between scientific discourse and literary discourse at the dawn of Chinese literary modernity, as each lays claim to knowledge of the real and unreal of the human mind.

Remapping the Real and the Unreal

In my discussion of Lao She's stylistics of fiction in Chapter 4, I focused on how Lao She borrowed narrative techniques from European realist fiction to construct the inner world of his inarticulate protagonist Xiangzi. This chapter looks at the problem from a somewhat different angle; it considers narratives of desire in the larger context of the legitima-tion of (pseudo-scientific) psychological and psychoanalytical discourse and the implications of this process for Chinese writing and literary criti-cism in the early twentieth century. What concerns me here is not so much the reception history of Freud, Havelock Ellis, or psychoanalytical theory in general as the problem of the narrative of desire as a translingual mode of representation in Chinese fiction.

Psychoanalytical theory was translated and introduced to Chinese audiences as early as 1907 and commanded the attention of a good number of writers and critics.[5] Several scholars have remarked on Lu Xun's interest, for example, in Freudianism and his experimentation with some of its ideas in *Yecao* (Wild grass) and *Gushi xinbian* (Old stories retold).[6] Other examples are Yu Dafu's autobiographical fiction, Pan Guangdan's well-known case study of Feng Xiaoqing, Zhang Jingsheng's popular writings on biology and sexuality, and Shi Zhecun's fiction, notably "Jiangjun de tou" (The general's head) and "Shi Xiu."[7] These texts tell a fascinating story about how Chinese writers employed a psychoanalytical vocabulary in their works, but, as my discussion below of Shi Zhecun's work will show, the use of Freudianism accounts for only a fraction of the larger problematic of the changing status of literary writings about desire in the 1920's and 1930's. To interrogate the meaning of *yuwang* (desire) adequately in this modern context, one is compelled to broaden one's scope of inquiry considerably both to include and to question the familiar terms of psychoanalytical theory. In other words, desire is not synonymous with sexuality. A fruitful line of inquiry in this case should, at least, involve a concentrated study in the twentieth-century context of the remapping of the real and the unreal, the new sense of lack or fulfillment with reference to the West, and the sensibilities and forms of experience that emerge from translingual modes of storytelling.

In 1922, Guo Moruo published a short story called "Can chun" (Late spring) in the second issue of *Chuangzao jikan* (Creation quarterly). The protagonist of this story is a Chinese medical student named Aimu living in Japan. One day, Aimu takes the train to a nearby town to visit an old friend who attempted suicide after the loss of a parent and is now in a hospital. While there, Aimu encounters a Japanese nurse called S and is greatly taken with her beauty. That night, he finds himself transported to a dream world where he and the Japanese woman have a secret rendezvous atop a mountain. In the course of a heart-to-heart talk, the woman says that she is suffering from tuberculosis and asks Aimu to diagnose her. She then takes off her clothes, revealing her bosom to his admiring gaze. At this critical moment, a friend named Bai Yang suddenly appears, bringing the shocking news that Aimu's wife has murdered their two sons. Aimu rushes back to the scene of horror only to find the mangled limbs of his infant sons lying across the blood-soaked floor and his wife brandishing a dagger like a madwoman. Without putting up the least resistance, he lets her run the dagger through his sorrow-stricken heart and dies holding the dead bodies of his children in his arms. The dream ends abruptly. Aimu wakes up and wonders about its ominous symbolism.[8]

Within a year of the story's publication, Guo Moruo published an article entitled "Piping yu meng" (Criticism and dreams) in the same journal (vol. 2, no. 1), instructing his readers how to interpret the dream symbolism of his story. Responding to charges made by critics about the mediocre quality of his work,[9] Guo pointed out that it was a mistake to read his story as a straightforward narrative with a beginning, a climax, and an ending, because what he was trying to present was the human libido, sexual drive, repression, and the unconscious in the form of a dream symbolism. His reading favors a modern theory of interpretation founded on Freudian psychoanalysis. Since the protagonist is a married man and cannot live out his fantasy about another woman, the story suggests that he unconsciously suppresses that desire until his dream brings out the unconscious in symbolic tropes. Guo went on to explain:

> In his dream, Aimu's rendezvous with S on top of Mt. Fudetate is something that he has desired but could not bring to pass during the day. The sudden arrival of Bai Yang at the critical moment of intimate physical contact between the two suggests that Aimu has sensed that Bai Yang might be a potential obstacle between them, which is bodied forth by the latter's appearance in his dream. The madness of his wife and her murder of their sons point further to the fact that he unconsciously thinks of his wife as the biggest obstacle to the object of his desire, which ultimately finds expression in the dream.[10]

It is not unusual for a writer to defend his or her work, but why did Guo Moruo take such pains to legitimize his story by invoking Freud? (One could have interpreted it in terms of a Chinese man desiring a Japanese woman, a nation-bound desire that exceeds the domain of the merely sexual.) What causes the subordination of *yu* and *qing* (indigenous philosophical notions of desire/lust, feeling/passion/emotion) to a vocabulary of neologisms that Guo employed in his essay with such ease—a vocabulary that readily presupposes a foreign equivalent as its signified: *yuwang* (desire), *qianzai yishi* (the subconscious), *jingshen fenxi* (psychoanalysis)? On the surface, the criticism surrounding "Late Spring" seems to evoke the quarrel between the Creation Society and the Literary Association about the relevance of Western realism, romanticism, expressionism, or even symbolism to modern Chinese literature. Guo Moruo's use of Freud, however, seems to move the quarrel beyond its obvious terms to the changing status of interpretive authority in Chinese literary circles, where the relationship among text, reading, and criticism is undergoing a major transformation. For instance, when in the same essay Guo extended the psychoanalytical approach to the ancient Chinese philosopher Zhuangzi and the traditional drama *The Romance of Western Chamber*, his reading inevitably "modernizes" the meaning of the traditional texts and subjects their dream symbolisms to radical reinterpretation. Here one senses a profound change in the intellectual discourse of the time in which interpretation becomes the very site on which competing theories and discourses wage their struggle for legitimacy and authority.

I am not suggesting that classical Chinese was lacking in the ability to represent the inner world. As a matter of fact, early May Fourth writers were steeped in old learning and often expressed themselves in classical genres, such as *shi* and *ci*. One must, however, take care not to project the twentieth-century psychological understanding of the human mind onto an earlier period. Our sensibilities with regard to what constitutes the inner world have undergone changes of such magnitude in the past hundred years—changes that result precisely from the earlier radicalization of tradition in the name of modern psychology—that the ground for comparing classical and modern literatures in this respect is not readily available. How do we know, for example, that *qing* is the same as "emotion" or "feeling"? How could we prove that the classical *yu* is equivalent to the neologistic use of *yuwang*, or the classical *xin* (heart/mind) to the round-trip loanword *xinli* (psyche)? The point I wish to highlight here is historical rather than comparative. When I say that May Fourth literature puts itself at the service of a humane knowledge that specializes in probing the psychological depths of the mind, I mean precisely what the words themselves suggest. The mind becomes analyzable when terms like *xinli* and *yuwang* become translatable and when translingual modes of narration begin to reconfigure what is real and what is unreal about the human mind.

My observations on Guo Moruo are intended to help frame the question of psychological realism in terms of translingual modes of representation whereby theory, criticism, and creative writing mutually determine what to represent and how to represent it in modern literature. Since literary texts are inextricably bound up with interpretation, one can hardly talk about the representation of the inner world without looking into the linkages between such a representation in a given text and the interpretative mechanisms to be found within and outside the text itself that strive to stimulate and sustain one's desire to read in an "intelligent" (acceptable?) fashion. This is the strategy I adopted in reading Lao She's novel in the preceding chapter, and in my analysis of Shi Zhecun and Yu Dafu in this chapter, I continue to rely on this strategy to probe the meanings of the real and unreal in psychological narratives.

Psychologizing the Fantastic

Yan Jiayan has noted Shi Zhecun's early fascination with Freud and attributes it in part to the influence of psychoanalytical works of European writers such as Arthur Schnitzler and the Japanese Neo-perceptionists.[11] Leo Lee also remarks on Shi's interest in Poe, Barbey d'Aurevilly, James Frazer, Andrew Lang, Fiona Mcleod, and Le Fanu as well as his "obvious Freudian inclination, in pointing to irrational and subconscious forces beyond the ego's control."[12] Indeed, Shi's stories display a strong tendency to indulge in hallucinations, dreams, violence, sorcery, witchcraft, necromancy, black magic, and the like, and they almost certainly invite a psychoanalytical reading. To the extent that concepts such as split identity, displacement, the unconscious, and sexual repression make sense when applied to the small number of experimental works Shi published in the late 1920's and the 1930's, the psychoanalytical approach works very well indeed, and the same approach may be used on other modern writers with varying degrees of success. The reason for this is not because Freud's interpretation of the human psyche is a universally applicable key to the truth of the human mind, capable of explaining all representations of dreams past and present—in fact, classical Chinese fiction offers numerous counterexamples that would render the Freudian vocabulary not so inevitable—but because there are Chinese writers and critics who have made self-conscious attempts to establish a translingual relationship between Chinese fiction and Freudianism. In that sense, their reconfiguration of desire in Freudian terms may very well compel a psychoanalytical reading. Guo Moruo's interpretation of his own story "Late Spring" is an excellent example of the ways in which Freudianism has been utilized by Chinese writers to rethink the nature of desire and how to represent it in modern literary language.

Dream symbolism, which enriched so much of previous Chinese fantastic literature, underwent a significant psychologizing process in the twentieth century, as self-styled enlightened thinkers attacked earlier cosmological and associative interpretations of dreaming as superstition and ignorance. For example, Zhou Zuoren, whose essay "Ren de wenxue" was a main source of inspiration for modern literature in its early days, listed ten types of "inhuman" literature that he would like to see banished from the language. Topping the list are "obscene and erotic fiction," "superstitious books on ghosts and gods," and "books about demons and devils." The reason he gives is that "these books impede the proper development of human nature and create havoc among mankind."[13] The interpretation of dreams in realist fiction thus begins to assume the burden of explaining the human interior in "scientific" terms and renders itself accountable to the psychological real.

Shi's psychoanalytical fiction is certainly a product of those changing circumstances. But, precisely where it seems to accept psychoanalysis wholeheartedly and where Freud's influence is indisputable, something interesting happens and demands an explanation that will complicate our understanding of such influence. My own reading of his fiction tries to confront a paradox in Shi's curious taste for the unusual and the fantastic. On the one hand, his frequent play with Freudian symbolism lays unmistakable claim to psychological realism, but on the other hand this play is often calculated to bring the fantastic and other classical topoi—supposedly exorcised by May Fourth realism—back into Chinese literature, leading to a relegitimation of the fantastic as a symbolic resource.[14]

As the chief editor of the journal *Xiandai* (Les contemporains), Shi Zhicun was instrumental in the promotion of modernist literature associated with the names of James Joyce, Ezra Pound, William Faulkner, Guillaume Apollinaire, André Breton, Paul Eluard, Louis Aragon, and the Japanese Neo-perceptionists in the 1930's.[15] However, by what intellectual route did he arrive at his peculiar Freudian interpretation of the fantastic? An important, but often overlooked, factor is his brief infatuation with French Surrealism. As a student of French literature and a graduate of the French Catholic Aurora University in Shanghai, Shi was familiar with the work of André Breton and other Surrealists, which provided theoretical justifications for his own experiments with fantastic literature. In one of his stories, he even inserted the word "surrealist" in the text.[16]

Breton himself declared uncompromising opposition to the modern rationalizing tendency of Western capitalist society in Freudian terms. As he put it in the first *Manifesto of Surrealism*:

> We all know, in fact, that the insane owe their incarceration to a tiny number of legally reprehensible acts and that, were it not for these acts, their freedom (or what we see as their freedom) would not be threatened. I am willing to admit that they are, to some degree, victims of their imagination, in that it induces them not to pay attention to certain rules—outside of which the

species feels itself threatened—which we are all supposed to know and re-spect. But their profound indifference to the way in which we judge them, allows us to suppose that they derive a great deal of comfort and consola-tion from their imagination, that they enjoy their madness sufficiently to endure the thought that its validity does not extend beyond themselves. And, indeed, hallucinations, illusions, etc., are not a source of trifling pleasure.[17]

Breton was fascinated by the human psyche and its potential for trans-gression and madness. The nonconforming heroine of his novel *Nadja*, for example, is deemed insane by society and locked up in an asylum. Breton accused modern civilization of banishing fantasy and superstition from the mind and tried to reinstate the repressed aspect of mental life in his own writing. Themes of death, the libido, mystery, madness, the unconscious, fantastic imagery, free association of thoughts, and so on dominate his work and that of his fellow Surrealists. We know that Breton once thought of becoming a doctor, had studied with Babinsky, and spent several months as an apprentice doctor in a psychiatric hospital during the war. Although he directed the famous diatribe against asylums and French psychiatrists in *Nadja*, the model of the psychiatric encounter, as analyzed, for example, by Susan Suleiman in *Subversive Intent*, went through an in-ternalizing process in his writing to a degree that the author was probably not aware of. That model, consisting of the analyst's looking at, pointing to, and interrogating the patient, is evoked by Breton's own encounter with Nadja and his own narrative recounting of that encounter. Breton thus is able to " 'play doctor' with the madwoman, to know her carnally and otherwise, without ever forgetting *who* one is ('*qui* je suis'). Without becoming entangled with her, without 'ceasing to be oneself,' without 'haunting' her." [18]

One could argue that Shi Zhecun's works exhibit some of the famil-iar motifs and impulses as to be found in Breton's writing, especially in stories such as "Shi Xiu," "Yecha" (The yaksha), and "Modao" (Sorcery) discussed below, in which woman is a perennial figure of fascination, seduction, mystery, and death. The famous story "Shi Xiu," for example, is a rewriting of an episode from *The Water Margin* with a strong psycho-analytic emphasis. The horrible crime that Shi Xiu commits against Pan Qiaoyun, wife of his sworn brother, is narrated in terms of sexual repres-sion, which is given outlet in the butchering and disemboweling of the desired object by the male protagonist. The violence in the original story is thus psychologized and given a psychoanalytical interpretation.[19]

Writing in Chinese, however, Shi used psychoanalysis in innovative ways that inevitably set him apart from French Surrealism. One important innovation is the symbiotic relationship he introduced between the surrealist uncanny and the classical Chinese genre of the fantastic. I argue that Freudianism provided Shi with a vocabulary that enabled him to translate the classical *zhiguai* tale into a type of Chinese surrealist fiction.[20]

Freud himself once assigned the role of translation to psychoanalytical theory. In *The Interpretation of Dreams*, he stated: "The dream-thoughts and the dream-content are presented to us like two versions of the same subject-matter in two different *languages*. Or more properly, the dream-content seems like a *transcript* of the dream-thoughts into another *mode of expression*, whose *characters and syntactic laws* it is our business to discover by comparing *the original and the translation*"[21] (italics added). Freud conceived of dream symbolism as a problem of representation and interpretation with its own syntax, logic, and coherence to obey. Yet for his system of symbolic interpretation of dreams to be capable of extracting coherent meanings from the chaos of the unconscious mind, Freud had to decide *a priori* that the story of the unconscious is grammatical and syntactical to the extent it is susceptible to decoding by a psychoanalyst equipped with the professional tools of interpretation. That explains why the problem of language or the representability of the unconscious was so central in his thinking on the human mind. In *Interpretation of Dreams* and other works, he was bent on inventing a symbolic language that would allow the psychoanalyst to tell an "intelligent, consistent, unbroken" story of the mind.[22]

This myth of narrative coherence has not gone uncontested. Steven Marcus, for instance, criticizes Freud's manner of storytelling: "No larger tribute has ever been paid to a culture . . . which had produced as one of its chief climaxes the bourgeois novels of the 19th century than this faith of Freud in the healing capacity of coherent story-telling."[23] Indeed, has Freud done anything more than approach the human mind under its narrative impulse? Perhaps the theorist belongs more to the profession of storyteller than medicine. Or, perhaps, the two are linked in some fundamental way that Freud had the insight to draw out.[24]

To the extent that Shi Zhecun's story "Sorcery" (1931) constitutes the fantastic as a figurative language to represent the unrepresentable—the human unconscious—it operates under a similar narrative impulse. But one must also notice the changing meaning of Freudianism in this translingual process: the language of Freudian psychoanalysis allowed Shi to reinstitute the classical topoi of fear, desire, fate, and the supernatural in modern Chinese fiction and to reclaim the classical *zhiguai* tale by psychologizing the fantastic. The rivalry between the scientific and the literary I noted earlier with regard to Lu Xun's story is here worked into a narrative of suspense in which the very notion of the real hangs indecisively between psychological truth and literary truth.

However, in saying that Shi Zhecun psychologizes the fantastic in his fiction, I do not mean to suggest that earlier fantastic fiction did not possess psychological depth. The issue that concerns me here has little to do with the *adequatio* of literary representation to the reality of the human mind, the formulation of which cannot but rely on a metaphysical understanding of how language works. Rather, my approach is intended to bring the language of representation into question so as to reach a historically grounded understanding of the changing conditions of Shi Zhecun's literary discourse. Fantastic literature need not lay claim to psychological depth to be valuable and interesting. However, when it does, as in the case under discussion, it may say something important about the changing perception of what constitutes the fantastic and why it matters for the author to engage in this kind of writing.

"Sorcery" parodies the classical *zhiguai* tale by evoking one of its formulaic storylines—an erotic adventure. To use a typical example, the protagonist, often a talented student, undertakes an innocent excursion or a career-oriented journey to the imperial capital. He encounters an extraordinarily beautiful woman with whom he falls in love instantly. He is invited to stay with her overnight and sometimes longer, enjoys a poetic conversation with her, and makes love to her. In the end, the young man bids farewell to the enchantress and resumes his journey. The moment of revelation comes much later when the protagonist discovers that he has made love to a fox spirit (or the ghost of a long deceased woman) and has stayed in the illusion of a mansion conjured up by her in a graveyard.[25] There have been numerous variations on this archetypal narrative since the early beginnings of the *zhiguai* tale.[26]

Shi Zhecun's protagonist in "Sorcery," which is told in the first person, embarks on a similar erotic adventure, although the setting of the story is decidedly the twentieth century. The narrator lives in metropolitan Shanghai, reads foreign books, goes to cafes and movies, and takes the train whenever he feels like traveling. The journey in question is a weekend excursion to his friends in their Western-style home in suburban Shanghai. During the train ride, he begins to have hallucinations about an old woman sitting in the opposite seat. Who is this strange-looking woman?

> I felt apprehensive about the mysterious old lady sitting all by herself in the
> corner of her seat. She refused the tea brought to her by the waiter and in-

sisted on having plain water instead. How strange! Of course, a sorceress
would not want to touch tea, because it would have invalidated her magic
power. What was the name of that ancient book that mentioned this sort of
thing? I searched my memory for a clue. I recalled the old witches people
talked about in the West who flew on a broomstick to kidnap young children.
I also remembered reading about a yellow-faced old woman in *The Strange
Tales from Pu Songling's Studio* whose spews water from her mouth under the
moonlight. I was convinced that the old woman sitting in the opposite seat
was one of those demons.   (p. 88)

The references to Pu Songling's ghost stories and to the uncanny
figure of the witch in Western folklore are significant. They fabricate a
common literary genealogy out of two different traditions and lay claim
to each in an attempt to relegitimize the fantastic for modern Chinese literature. The figure of the sorceress in this story is *literary* in the exact sense
of the word, for it enters into a relationship with previous literary texts by
evoking them in the title and reflecting on its own intertextual status. The
mention of book titles, therefore, should be taken seriously by the reader,
because they serve as a kind of literary index to the presence of figural
reading in the text.[27] As I suggested earlier, a critic's reading must engage
with or, at least, respond in some degree to the act of reading presented
or performed within the text. What are the books the narrator packs into
his briefcase and reads in his boredom on the train? The first title he mentions is *The Romance of Sorcery*, which he reads in English. There is also a
list of foreign works in Chinese translation, including Le Fanu's fantastic
fiction, *Persian Religious Poetry*, *Cases of Sex Crime*, and *Treasures of English
Poetry*. In addition to these five books, he also has an issue of the *Journal of
Psychology*. Sorcery, poetry, sex, and psychology thus serve as prominent
signposts in the territory of meaning across which Shi Zhecun reinscribes
the fantastic tale.

An early scene illustrates the inter-penetration of the fantastic and the
psychological in this story. Shortly after the narrator arrives at his friend's
house, he is invited to dinner. His hostess, Mrs. Chen, happens to wear a
white silk dress with a low-cut neckline, which makes her look extremely
sensual. The narrator's reaction to her sensuality is captured in remarkable
Freudian language of sublimation and displacement:

The red slice of tomato in my mouth feels like Mrs. Chen's red lips. As I
bite into it, I find myself tasting the bitterness of secret love. I close my eyes
halfway, and, with the half that is open, I watch the smiles and acts of the real
Mrs. Chen; and, with the half that is partially closed, I enjoy the company of
an illusory Mrs. Chen. I see her coming toward me from her side of the table,

hands holding on to the edge of the table and the bottom of her long dress streaming behind. I also see Mr. Chen stepping out of the dining room. Now her right hand is caressing my brow—actually, she is probably touching her own brow. Putting down my knife and fork, I pull out a handkerchief from my pocket to wipe my mouth. At this moment, I see an enormous face, that of Mrs. Chen, coming close to mine. It is so pale! I have never seen a face so deadly white, not even in Japanese women. And she is smiling. Seduction! She then closes her eyes. My goodness, are we kissing each other? Am I committing a crime? Mr. Chen had better not come in at this moment, otherwise I'd be in trouble. (pp. 61–63)

Experiencing Mrs. Chen's lips in the form of a slice of red tomato, the narrator is able to sublimate his desire in the act of suppressing it. The tomato slice turns into a sensual object, as the act of biting becomes a sexual performance. The reader is allowed to witness a multiple process of displacement in which the woman's sex is sublimated into her lips, which in turn get displaced onto the tomato slice. The process of the dream-work that Freud formulates in his analysis of the dream-thought is echoed by this description of repressed desire, which draws on the psychoanalytical symbolism of sublimation, displacement, reversal, and the like.[28]

The same woman metamorphoses into a sorceress in the eyes of the narrator next morning when he sees her holding a black cat in her arms. The shocking revelation explodes like a surrealist epiphany: Mrs. Chen is none other than the old sorceress who has been chasing him from place to place. In this state of mind, the narrator hurriedly takes leave of his host and flees back to Shanghai. Back in the city, he runs into an old acquaintance who is a barmaid and gets himself invited to a café. However, her dress strangely reminds him of Mrs. Chen's, and when he offers to kiss her, she turns into a sorceress instantly. Twenty minutes after this event, he receives a telegram from home announcing that his three-year-old daughter has died. Looking down from the balcony of his apartment, he is greeted with the horrible sight of an old sorceress in black, presumably the same one that pops up everywhere, who hobbles slowly into a nearby alley.

Unlike classical *zhiguai* tales, Shi Zhecun's story does not reveal the true identity of the sorceress to the protagonist, although he is more and more convinced of her reality as the story unfolds. The reader, on the other hand, is forced to confront an interpretive enigma: Is the sorceress a supernatural being or merely a hallucination? If she is nothing but a hallucination caused by the narrator's paranoia, why does the story contain an "inevitable" death, as in most cases of traditional fantastic tales? If, however, the sorceress is meant to be taken as a fantastic creature, why does the narrator make repeated references to his experience of hallucination and nervous breakdown caused by reading too much literature? The ambiguity between the fantastic and the psychological calls into question the divide that separates the two. Just as the psychoanalytical language seeks to explain the human unconscious in symbolic terms of the uncanny, so the fantastic in Shi's story constitutes itself as a surrealistic language that tries to speak the unspeakable, that is, to go beyond "realist" explanations of human experience. The two inter-penetrate at the level of surrealistic representation.

I am suggesting that the reader need not take the narrator's problem with the fantastic as a point of departure. Whereas the narrator demands to know the identity of the ubiquitous sorceress, the reader is free to posit the question of interpretation in heterodiegetic relation to the narrator's world.[29] In other words, he or she can turn the narrator's figural reading around and place the problematic of the fantastic at the source of the enigma: the narrator himself.

The link between the narrator's dread of the sorceress and his obsession with women is striking. As many as eight women are mentioned in this short narrative, not including those he reads about on the train. Interestingly, the majority of them metamorphose into the old sorceress at one point or the other, and the narrator's representation of these metamorphoses provides a useful clue as to how the fantastic might be grasped as an interpretive problem. Below is the narrator's description of Mrs. Chen's metamorphosis:

> The forgotten terror once again froze my heart. How could I have imagined kissing her yesterday? She was a sorceress, perhaps the very metamorphosis of the old sorceress I saw yesterday.—That's why she was able to change her true form into a black stain on the glass of the window to delude my eyes, for I had not seen any stain on the window before she pointed it out to me. Oh, the horror!   (p. 65)

In proportion to the narrator's sense of guilt for the imaginary kiss and his experience of repressed desire the night before, he now perceives Mrs. Chen as a real terror, totally out of control and beyond comprehension. This reversal leads to an extraordinary psychical displacement: it turns him into a victim of harassment rather than a potential transgressor. The image of the old sorceress, who appeared on the train earlier, is now attached to the person of Mrs. Chen. This kind of fantastic metamorphosis works like *modao* or sorcery throughout the story, transforming the young and beautiful into the old and ugly, and the desirable into repulsive creatures.

The narrator's paranoia turns into true victimhood toward the close of the story, as the news of his daughter's death arrives. Such a turn of events seems oddly out of place in the overall scheme of this story, since previously there was no hint that he had a daughter. On the other hand, the bad news seems to be foreshadowed in a surrealist way, because, throughout the narrative, the narrator is pursued by an ominous sense of disaster, as things happen to him mysteriously and almost miraculously. The narrator describes the news of his daughter's death in almost a fatalistic tone:

> My servant handed me a telegram.
> My three-year old daughter had died.
> I dropped the telegram on the floor, stood up, and made for the balcony. It was midnight. The street had a desolate look. Then I caught the sound of footsteps from underneath, advancing slowly and steadily. I bent over the rail and, to my horror, I saw under the dim, greenish light of the gas lamp across the street a solitary old woman dressed in black hobbling into a back alley. (p. 72)

The narrator's reaction to the news of his daughter is minimized to a few words, and there is no elaborate description of his emotions. Instead, by focusing on what he sees afterward, the story brings the two events together forcibly. The perceived linkage between the sorceress and the death of his daughter enables the story to join the fantastic and the psychological at a higher level of surrealistic symbolism. The hallucination must be confirmed by the fantastic event: the sorceress is a messenger of death.

But what does this tragic event have to do with the narrator's repressed sexual desire, which is always somewhat connected with the appearance of the sorceress in this story? The following passage, which tells of his fantasy about the mummy of an imperial concubine, might throw some light on this question. The narrator is looking out the train window.

> There was a huge mound rising up from the ground. If it had been located in China's Central Plains, the archeologist would have thought that the site held the tomb of an imperial concubine of some remote dynasty and would have sent teams to excavate it. And then what? They would have discovered that there was a huge chamber built of stone with a huge stone altar in it, on which a lamp burning human fat was lit. Behind the altar, they'd have found a huge coffin painted in vermilion red lacquer and, of course, dangling from gold chains. And they would then have split the coffin open; yes, they'd have literally performed "coffin splitting" as the saying goes, although no legendary Zhuang Zhou would have jumped out. They'd have found lying

in the coffin a mummy wrapped up tightly in white silk. Oh, the mummy of a beautiful imperial concubine from ancient times with her long, white silk dress streaming behind her. What a marvel it'd have been if she had walked right in our midst! . . . A marvel? No, more than that. She'd have made everybody fall madly in love with her. She'd have been loved with a passion far exceeding the love for a living, present-day woman. If she had allowed herself to be kissed once on her cold lips perfumed with musk, I am positive that whoever had kissed her would have forever lost the desire to touch any living beings. Oh, have I not already seen her: the horizontal white surrounded by vermilion red; the vertical gold—what a magic of dazzling splendor!

But why should I dream like that? Perhaps the stone chamber would be pitch-dark. From the seven-door entrance that they had cut through would have emerged a mysterious, hideous-looking, and deformed old woman. Yes, sorceresses used to inhabit the ancient catacomb ["catacomb" in English in the original]. . . . But, what if the beautiful imperial concubine happened to be the metamorphosis of this sorceress? . . . That would have been dangerous. Whoever kissed her lips would have been stricken by her sorcery, transformed into a chicken, a duck, or a white goose. If one were to be changed into a goose, one's lot would not be too bad. I thought of the sculpture I had seen before. Didn't it represent the Swan pressing on Leda's knees with his powerful wings, while thrusting his head between her legs? Oh, a surrealist erotica!   (pp. 47–49)

The fantasy of necrophilia captures the narrator's libidinous desire in a powerful symbolism in which the dialectic of black and white, death and life, monster and beauty, is fully elaborated. The black, dead, and monstrous woman is the flip side of the white, living, and beautiful woman. They are capable of transmuting into one another, as when the beautiful Mrs. Chen, whose long, white silk dress is reminiscent of that of the imperial concubine, metamorphoses into a sorceress in the narrator's imagination. Perhaps for all his fantasies, the real object of his desire is this unattainable Mrs. Chen who makes him suffer because of his deeply felt guilt over her husband.[30] The allusion to Zeus' rape of Leda suggests the narrator's desire for a similar transgression or adultery. But for a mortal, to sin is to court death. Just as the beautiful Helen of Troy, who is the fruit of Zeus' violent transgression, destroys a whole nation, so woman and death, or sin and death, come to be united as the eternal couple. It is in response to such a mythic view of woman that death becomes all the more significant to the narrator. To him, woman is a paradox: she gives and takes away life; she is both pure and tainted, tainted because of her sexuality.

The narrator's view of death is greatly complicated by his erotic imagination. Death is both a fear and a desire, paralleling and interacting with his fear and desire for the female body. Both his imaginary kissing of Mrs. Chen and his actual kissing of the prostitute in Shanghai are described as if he has kissed the dead lips of the mummy, for they give him a "cold," "eerie" feeling on contact (pp. 66, 71). The repeated references to "catacomb" and the "mummy of the imperial concubine" paint an erotic picture of death, at once disastrous, mysterious, and sensual. Death and Woman. Death as Woman. In this narrative of male desire, the true uncanny emerges as Woman written with a boldface *nü*, who represents the ultimate limits of the unknown to the male narrator. As she unifies the fantastic and the psychological in a surrealistic moment of metamorphosis, her body becomes mummified, whereupon the eroticism of male writing plays out its ritual of necrophilia. If Shi Zhecun deserves a special place in modern Chinese literature for having relegitimated the classical *zhiguai* tale, he must also be credited for exposing some of the allegorical affinities between traditional fantastic literature and psychoanalytical discourse. Indeed, as the fox spirit returns in the guise of the repressed unconscious, the reader should be alerted to the fact that it is the constructed male voice that does the fantasizing, eroticizing, and psychologizing. That brings us to the work of Yu Dafu, whose reputation as a writer of male sexuality deserves an extended comment.

Phantasmagoria of the Real

Yu Dafu's preoccupation with the psychological workings of the mind is well known. His first published story, "Chenlun" (Sinking), was widely criticized for its candid descriptions of masturbation, voyeurism, impotence, and "morbid" sensibilities.[31] Here, I analyze a story that has not received as much critical attention as some of his other works due to its ambiguous generic character. "Huanxiang ji" (Reminiscences on a homebound trip) is a rambling narrative consisting of ten short chapters with a five-chapter sequel. Is it a work of fiction or familiar prose?[32] This ambiguity raises interesting questions about the act of writing itself, although one need not go into the intentionality of the author to ponder the meanings of such an act. Like some of his other works, very little happens in this story; it is by and large an account of the narrator's disjointed flow of thoughts as he embarks on a homecoming journey from Shanghai to his native place, Fuyang. These thoughts are intensely psychologized and gendered through an act of writing that tries to negotiate the real and unreal in the narrator's quest for the self. Unlike Shi Zhecun's traveler who encounters an evil sorceress at every turn, Yu Dafu's narrator seems to reside exclusively in the realm of the real. At least, the fantastic does not present itself to his consciousness in the same manner as it does to that of Shi Zhecun's narrator. If Shi Zhecun successfully transforms a psychological narrative into a modern *zhiguai* tale, Yu Dafu does something very different with the imported psychological understanding of the mind. I will argue that the story turns the very condition of being modern and real into a tale of fantasy and thwarts the superfluous attempt of the critic to establish a generic distinction between fiction and familiar prose.

If the psychological is demarcated as the real in the unfolding of the narrator's uneventful journey, where is the boundary between the real and the unreal? Is first-person narrative adequate to the narrator's experience of self-consciousness? These questions arise as soon as we pause to take a close look at how Yu Dafu's narrator handles metaphorical language. The following passage, for example, throws some interesting light on this problem. As the narrator arrives at the railway station in Hangzhou, he is deeply moved by the familiar sight of the city he loves. The narrating self tries to capture a moment from the past but cannot find the right words to describe it.

There is no way that this sense of loss and disillusionment could be put down in words. But if I must write, I shall have to do so in an extended metaphor. Imagine me in my first bloom of youth when chance threw me into the arms of a paragon of beauty. I was her first love and she had my virgin devotion. We lived together day and night, sleeping and walking hand in hand for months, until I used up my money and she fell in love with someone else, forsaking my arms for his, like the girl Fansu. Since then, poverty, shame, sorrow, and loneliness never for a moment left my side no matter where I would go. As I wandered from place to place, I become older, my body deteriorated, and I wore shabby, torn clothes on my back. After years of vagabond life, I returned one day to the rendezvous where we used to hold hands. The mountain, the river, the plants, the trees, the stars, the moon, and the clouds—all remained the same, as enchanting as ever. I was sitting alone in meditation by the lake when I suddenly noticed on the surface of the water the reflected image of my former sweetheart. The beautiful glow of her face had not faded in the slightest and her dress was as elegant as ever. The pearl necklace around her neck and a string of agate beads worn about her forehead added a halo of glory to her face that had not been there previously. But as I turned around, I found to my great chagrin that she was with a handsome gentleman, who was standing behind her, caressing her.[33]

The curious metaphorical narrative about romantic love is intended by the "author-narrator" to recapture his nostalgia for the city of Hangzhou after many years abroad. The city is compared here to a beautiful maiden and the narrator himself to her forsaken lover. Admittedly, the fiction (fantasy) is invented to stand in for another text, one that the narrator cannot produce. But one narrative can never quite replace another. Instead of being contained within the figure, the inserted narrative reveals an erotic imagination imbued with repressed desire and a troubled sense of selfhood that the narrator had no intention of divulging (and of which he probably has no knowledge). As the nostalgic narrative takes on the additional narrative of erotic desire, the invented fiction turns out to be more than an allegory for the narrator's nostalgia for Hangzhou. Rather than seeing the narrator's erotic imagination and fantasized passion as a mere figurative substitute for his attachment to the city of Hangzhou, one finds in it a displaced desire that reinstates itself by means of excessive signification.[34]

Inasmuch as figurative language introduces a reality that can exist only as a literary fantasy, imaginative writing does for Yu Dafu's narrator what sorcery does for Shi Zhecun's psychotic hero. Here the boundary between the real and the unreal becomes blurred, as language is found to be both inadequate and indispensable for the representation of lived experiences. Ironic self-fantasizing, therefore, does much to help sustain the narrator's perception of the self, and he even has to invent cases of suffering from time to time with the aid of a hyperactive imagination to cast himself in roles that invite narcissistic tears. Strangely, however, this kind of fantasizing is always linked to an erotic subtext in which the female body, a central signifier, plays out the meaning of desire. Take a scene from the "Sequel to Reminiscences on Returning Home." As the narrator waits to be served at a rundown restaurant, he deplores the fine weather for its indifference to his own plight. He wishes the sky to be overcast and wet with rain so as to match his dark mood. "If I might wish for a further luxury," says the narrator, "I would also have liked a black lacquer coffin placed next to me."[35] From that point on, he makes up a fantastic tale about the death of the women he loved in order to "swim for a while in the ocean of tears I had myself manufactured."

> After a moment of frantic thought, I came up with a neatly constructed play based on my wish. I saw myself burn some paper funerary offerings and say to the person inside the coffin: "Jeanne [in English]! We are heading back home and our boat is about to leave! If you are afraid of being harassed by ghosts, here, take these offerings and use them to bribe the ghosts. . . ." As I came to the last sentence, my voice choked up, so I buried my head between my hands and bent over the dining table. At this moment I felt something warm coursing down my cheeks. I began to conjure up one after another all

the women I had loved in my whole life and saw them, mouths closed, lying hard and cold in front of me. At that I could no longer hold back my tears, so I wept aloud. The woman in the kitchen, thinking that I was pressing her to get my meal, said in a soft tone as if coaxing an infant: "Coming, coming! Dinner will be ready soon. Please be patient for just one more second." (pp. 5–6)

The narrator's fantasizing about the dead bodies of lovely women is reminiscent of the necrophiliac imaginings depicted in the story by Shi Zhecun as well as in the Shen Congwen story discussed in the next chapter. His ironic narcissism takes an odd turn in the presence of a maternal figure, whose contradictory sexual identity as "mother," at once desirable and unavailable, helps locate the libidinous source of the narrator's troubled self. More important, the younger woman in his fantasy has the Western name "Jeanne" (spelled out in English). Is she a Westerner or a Chinese woman with an adopted Western name? Judging from the context, the latter seems more probable, since it was common practice for May Fourth writers to give their heroines Western names as a mark of the modern (e.g., Sophia, Mary, and Wendy in Ding Ling's fiction).[36] If the modern condition means the coming-into-being of female subjectivity for women, Ding Ling's "Diary of Miss Sophia," to be discussed in the next chapter, clearly demonstrates the contradiction inherent in it, because whereas modernity gives a voice to desire in a female subject like Sophia, it can also defeat that desire by (re)inventing the male subject in the figure of Ling Jishi, who embodies the male-centered, modern bourgeois ideology. Focusing on male subjectivity, Yu Dafu's story brings out the interesting relationship between modernity and gender from a different perspective. The fantasizing of the female/Western name "Jeanne" points to the gendered and translingual condition of the Chinese modern.

The purpose of the narrator's trip is to visit his wife, a traditional woman, whose innocence is proportional to his sense of guilt. This guilt represents, as much as it brings into question, a May Fourth discourse that inscribes women as the opposing signifiers of modernity and tradition. Between modern women and traditional housewives, the desiring male intellectual travels, fantasizes, makes free choices, and hopes to work out his own identity crisis. Needless to say, this act of choice presupposes a male authorial position. May Fourth youths tended to imagine modernity and to invent the modern self through the mediation of desire for a modern woman of their own choice. Yu Dafu's earlier story "Sinking" embodied this desire in a most inflated form, in which male protagonist experiences the crisis of modernity as a crisis of manhood and nationhood. Weakness, impotence, and the loss of national dignity all boil down to the same frustration, as the confused protagonist projects his desire onto the body of Japanese women. Yet, as my analysis of a story by Lu Xun in Chapter 6 will demonstrate, the male subject cannot forever postpone facing himself or foreclose the crisis of identity by replacing it with a sexual economy. The mischievous urchin of guilt and doubt seems determined to catch him at all cost.

"Reminiscences on a Homebound Trip" comes to grips with the crisis of the modern (male) intellectual by emphasizing the specularity of the narrator's desire. As the narrative foregrounds the tropological construction of woman as modernity or tradition, it exposes the fictionality of the narrator's own subject-position. The following passage vividly portrays the process by which the female body is incorporated into the plot of male fantasies.

> I turned around and saw that the street was deserted. All of a sudden, I was tempted by a hideous desire: "Break the window and get some money!"
> At that, the hand in my imagination reached out and pushed open that half-closed window with the utmost care. After removing a couple of iron bars from the outside of the window, I jumped over the wall and found my feet inside the room. My mind's eye saw a woman's shoes made of white satin lying underneath the white bed curtain. Together with a black silk skirt was an elegant white silk blouse hanging from the dress stand. As I carefully pulled out the drawer of the dressing table, I discovered a woman's handbag with glittering diamonds around its opening, lying next to a small powder container and an ivory folding fan. Having glanced at the bed a few times, I finally snatched up the handbag. However, as I was making for the window, I felt somewhat ashamed. So I turned around and put the handbag back in the drawer. For the next few moments I lingered on in the room, examining the slim shoes on the floor. All of a sudden, I was seized with a strange desire. So I bent down, picked up one of the shoes, fondled it and inhaled its scent, until I finally made a firm decision to walk away with both the handbag and the shoe. At this moment, my imagination came to a sudden stop. As my consciousness slowly returned to me, I felt my cheeks burning hot and red and my forehead dripping with sweat. I waited till my blurred eyes were completely cleared before hurrying back to my inn near the railway station. (p. 31)

The fiction of burglary staged in the narrator's mind takes an odd turn when the burglar becomes absorbed in fondling the woman's shoe. Does this fetishizing of the woman's shoes mark him as a traditional literatus after all? Perhaps. That would explain why the self-conscious narrator, who aspires to the modern condition, is driven to suppress the inner monster and experiences a profound sense of shame. More important, the intrusion of sexual fantasy in this strange moment calls for a specific expression of desire: voyeurism, as the narrator imagines an urban woman's boudoir as the setting for his burglary. The whole fiction of breaking in and stealing a woman's purse and shoe takes place as the narrator positions himself as a voyeur gazing up at a hotel window. Distanced from the scene, the voyeur avoids the dangers and disappointments of action while indulging his imagination in the pleasure of transgression. It is transgression that links the imaginary acts of burglary with eroticism in the scene and produces the accompanying feelings of sin and guilt. What is particularly interesting about this voyeuristic narrator is that he fantasizes a fictional self to fill the role of a transgressor, thus allowing himself to play the role of an *imaginary* voyeur.

Voyeurism in this story is more than a matter of protest against sexual taboos or a mere display of moral decadence and sexual perversion, as is often charged.[37] In the context of Yu Dafu's works, it also symbolizes the anxiety of the modern intellectual who desires action but feels excluded from it. The consciousness of his own inadequacy paralyzes the will to act. The image of the voyeur epitomizes this state of loneliness and frustration. By the same token, imaginative literature, with which the author engages, embodies the irony of his voyeuristic deferral of action just as the *fiction* of transgression reflects the irony of his situation. In another revealing moment, the narrator apostrophizes the peasantry from a distance: "Oh, upright peasants! You feed the world and deserve to be its masters. I wish to serve you as a beast of burden and toil for you. Would you then let me share your meals?" (pp. 12–13). The passage appears to eulogize the laboring class, but since the narrator speaks from a certain vantage point—he is taking a distant view of the rural landscape from the train—the apostrophe comes across as an empty tribute paid by an intellectual whose desire to integrate with the working class is restricted to a simile ("as a beast of burden").

What does the narrator's figurative language tell us about the condition of his consciousness except that he fantasizes profusely? In Shi Zhecun's story, the recuperation of the fantastic motif transforms a psychological narrative into a modern *zhiguai* tale. Yu Dafu's narrator, as I suggested earlier, turns the very condition of being modern and real into a tale of fantasy. The object of that fantasy is desired yet somehow placed beyond reach, and it takes writing to establish a meaningful contact between what is real and what is unreal. In that sense, the psychological narrative in this story can be viewed as yet another kind of fantastic tale, one that ventures forth into the unknown of the mind and returns with the miraculous message of having made some sort of contact. As Leo Lee has noted in a different context, the "modern" quality of Yu's works often lies in their emphasis on journeys that are "incomplete, aimless, and marked with uncertainties."[38] These uncertainties reside at the heart of what Michael Egan identifies as Yu's tendency to undercut his hero's sentimental view and to show "the basic absurdity of his self-image."[39] Between woman and man, East and West, tradition and modernity, intellectual and peasant, Yu Dafu's traveler cannot find a secure foothold for himself. This condition of exile from the homeland of meaning is best captured by the figure of nocturnal wanderer near the end of the story: "Walking toward the city, I stumbled a couple of times on the rugged pavement. A nameless fear began to assail my heart. I began to compare this fear with my earlier attempt at suicide in the daytime and couldn't help laughing at myself. Ah, presumptuous man, calling yourself the noblest of all bipeds, what rationality, what philosophy? What are the human mind and feelings but a bunch of contradictions?" (p. 22).

It takes a first-person narrative to capture a self-reflexive moment like that and to testify to the reality of the self by speaking and fantasizing about it. To borrow the words of Paul de Man, this narrative mode "demonstrates in a striking way the impossibility of closure and of totalization (that is the impossibility of coming into being) of all textual systems made up of tropological substitutions."[40] In the next chapter, I treat first-person narrative as a deictic mode of writing, a kind of writing that distances and connects at the same time by positing a temporal, spatial, and social relation between the speaking subject, the object of address, the addressee, and the act of writing itself.

CHAPTER 6

The Deixis of Writing in the First Person

It is in and through language that man constitutes himself as a *subject*.

—Emile Benveniste

The grammatical category of person, especially the first person, has recently evolved into a major theoretical category in contemporary linguistics, semiotics, psychoanalysis, and poststructuralism. Foucault, Althusser, Derrida, and Lacan hold different views about what constitutes a subject, but they would not dispute that the formation of the subject has much to do with language and discourse. As French linguist Emile Benveniste aptly puts it, "It is in and through language that man constitutes himself as a *subject*, because language alone establishes the concept of 'ego' in reality, in *its* reality which is that of being." [1] If language occupies a central place in the contemporary critique of subjectivity, it is worth pursuing exactly what kind of language is being posited here. I am reminded of an illuminating commentary Kaja Silverman has made about a typical passage from Part IV of Descartes's *Discourse on Method*. Silverman points out that the first-person pronoun is ubiquitous in Descartes's writing, and yet the philosopher imagines that "he speaks without simultaneously being spoken" and "believes himself to exist outside of discourse." [2] Poststructuralism succeeds in overturning the Cartesian notion of the autonomous self by calling attention to the role of cultural overdetermination in the making of the subject and, in particular, the primary role of language and discourse. Nevertheless, in the very act of exposing Descartes's dependency on the first-person pronoun, contemporary critics fail to take stock of the grammatical ground on which their own notion of language seems to stand. Does the act of making the linguistic "I" coincide with the poststructuralist understanding of the subject have something to do with the inflected grammar of certain languages? Is not the contemporary critique of Descartes just as much indebted to the situation of the first-person pronoun in inflected languages as the philosopher's earlier reliance on the "I" when he posited a fantasy of the self? A satisfactory answer to those questions would require another book. For the moment, let me concentrate on what is immediately relevant to the subject of this chapter: the deixis of writing in the first person.

Below, I explore the possibility of rethinking first-person narrative in modern Chinese literature as a translingual mode of representation in which the deictic trope of person is played out in modern Chinese as well as between Chinese and inflected languages. By emphasizing the deixis of person, I intend to take the question of the first person beyond some such familiar concerns as whether first-person narrative in modern Chinese fiction gave rise to a new sense of the self under the influence of Western notions of self-consciousness or whether it simply evolved out of the time-honored tradition of Chinese autobiographical writing.[3] My approach will raise a different set of questions regarding the meaning of first-person narrative in modern Chinese literature, questions that relate to borrowed narrative forms and the theory of person in a noninflected language and writing. In order to situate my problem in the contemporary theoretical context, I begin with a discussion of the deixis of person in inflected languages.

Deixis of Person in Inflected Languages

Benveniste's concept of the subject as a deictic category merits special attention here, because it reveals, wittingly or unwittingly, the linguistic ground on which some of the key notions of subjectivity are formulated in contemporary theory. In *Problems in General Linguistics*, Benveniste devotes several chapters to the personal pronoun and other deictic categories in inflected languages, mainly French. The linguistic category of person is crucial to the linguist because it introduces the primary characteristic of *la deixis* to ordinary discursive situations. Pronouns like *je* or *tu* are always self-referential and mutually implicated in the sense that they never refer to anything or anybody outside language itself, for *je* is not synonymous with the person who speaks but marks the deictic position of the speaker from which s/he addresses the interlocutor identified simultaneously as *tu*. In other words, "language is so organized that it permits each speaker to *appropriate to himself* an entire language by designating himself as I" (p. 226). Moreover, each of these appropriations is accompanied by deictic correlatives of here, there, now, then, today, yesterday, and other such adverbs, adjectives, and demonstratives that help organize temporal and spatial relations of speech around the "speaking subject."

To me, Benveniste's theory has the obvious advantage of recasting the stylistic study of discourse, especially first-person narrative, in terms of deictic relations rather than posing the nebulous question of the self in some kind of uncontested relationship to language. That is to say, he is concerned not with the *adequatio* of language to reality, but with how individual speakers occupy the subject positions provided by language itself with the help of a few empty place markers, namely, the personal pronoun. These in turn conjugate with verbs and other syntactical elements to constitute a meaningful speech in specific discursive situations. As far as inflected languages are concerned, such formulations present no problem; however, not all languages privilege the personal pronoun as a primary deictic category. For instance, what about those noninflected languages that do not resort to conjugation and do not always emphasize the importance of the personal pronoun? Benveniste is not unaware of this problem and tries to solve it by appealing to the knowledge of foreign language experts and native informants, as in his use of G. J. Ramstedt's study of Korean and Li-Long-Tseu's information (p. 226). In a typical passage that reminds me of George Steiner's statement about the Chinese language discussed in Chapter 1, he says:

> A language without the expression of person cannot be imagined. It can only happen that in certain languages, under certain circumstances, these "pronouns" are deliberately omitted; this is the case in most of the Far Eastern societies, in which a convention of politeness imposes the use of periphrases or of special forms between certain groups of individuals in order to replace the direct personal references. But these usages only serve to underline the value of the avoided forms; it is the implicit existence of these pronouns that gives social and cultural value to the substitutes imposed by class relationships. (pp. 225–26)

If European languages are taken as the norm for a universal theory of language, any deviation from the norm, such as the ones Benveniste supposedly identifies in non-inflected languages, must be explained as instances of omission or suppression. What, however, if these are not instances of omission or suppression but something else? Is there a more viable way to explain differences in deictic constructions in these languages than polite forms of speech among people of different class background? Is Benveniste confusing the linguistic with the stylistic? In point of style, the argument about the omission of certain forms of address makes sense when the original verbal sign to be substituted is supposed to be there in the first place. But that situation is by no means limited to Far Eastern languages, for we find numerous polite forms of address among French and English speakers that may not be the exact replacements of certain "original" forms of expression but arise in response to socio-stylistic needs.

As a linguistic problem, however, we are dealing with a totally different situation. If the deictic categories in non-inflected languages differ radically from those to be found in Indo-European languages, how are we to conceptualize that difference without using the latter as the explanatory norm for proper linguistic behavior? Between languages that conjugate on the basis of pronouns and ones that do not take inflected grammar as a principle of syntactic combination in speech or writing, there seems little common ground to talk about similarities or difference in that regard. For instance, it is perfectly common to construct Chinese sentences, especially written ones, without personal pronouns to convey a deictic situation, so much so that one often has to "supply" those redundancies when rendering them into inflected languages. Personal pronouns are absent in those sentences—"absent" retroactively from a translator's point of view—not because, as Benveniste has inferred, other verbal signs are substituted for them out of a regard for social etiquette, but because the subject-verb construct, among other things, is not the norm of the Chinese language, but one of many syntactical options. We are looking at a language that enjoys the freedom to have or not have a grammatical subject, be it in the form of pronouns or nouns, in order to constitute a statement.[4] Of course, to those unfamiliar with these features of a non-inflected language, the possibility of not having a grammatical subject and still making sense may be difficult to grasp or even seem crazy.[5]

Differences between the Chinese language and Indo-European languages should not, however, be emphasized at the expense of ignoring many of the important changes in written and spoken Chinese since the recent contact with inflected languages. As I mentioned in Chapter 3, the very notion of inflection has found its way into the discourse of the New Culturalists in the form of a trope. As far as May Fourth literature is concerned, the speaking subject and the narrative modes in which s/he speaks are almost always placed in a direct or indirect dialogue with European literature. Reading Lu Xun, Yu Dafu, Ding Ling, and other May Fourth writers often means crossing linguistic boundaries in one and the same text and being exposed to translingual modes of representation. But if the concern with person, or *la personne* in Benveniste's understanding of the term, becomes increasingly pronounced in the works of these writers, how should we interpret its ramifications for the modern Chinese literary language?

As I argued above, Benveniste's emphasis on *la personne* has the limitation of universalizing a linguistic phenomenon on the ground of inflected grammar. How can one overcome this limitation without, however, relinquishing the need to talk about these issues in theoretical terms? Is there an alternative that would allow us to identify deictic patterns and uses of personal pronouns in modern Chinese narratives that might bear meaningful relation to inflected languages but are not otherwise derivative of their grammar? In Chapter 1, I argue that the splitting of a formerly ungendered Chinese *ta* into feminine, masculine, and other gendered forms around the early 1920's introduced a new level of symbolic reality into the written Chinese language. I am not suggesting that women and men were not previously spoken of as sexual beings or as *yin-yang* categories, but that the *deictic relationship*—man speaking to and about woman, and woman speaking to and about man, or addressing each other—caused by such a split at formal levels of the written vernacular allowed gender to shape social relations of power in a language unimaginable at an earlier time.

Can we detect a similar process taking place in the deixis of first-person writing? Literature written in an autobiographical vein existed long before the arrival of modern first-person narratives, and one could argue endlessly over the similarities and differences between classical and modern vernacular first-person narratives. One possible approach would be, for example, to historicize the different etymologies of the pronouns for the first person in each case: such as the classical pronoun *yu* versus *wo* (I) favored by the modern vernacular. For the purpose of this chapter, however, I will limit myself to the kinds of *deictic relations* constructed around *wo* in modern vernacular first-person narrative. What is the deictic status of the first-person pronoun in modern vernacular Chinese fiction? Without risking too much generalization, let us briefly recall that, in the texts of Guo Moruo, Shi Zhicun, and Yu Dafu discussed in the preceding chapter, the first-person narrator always finds himself embedded in an interlocking set of symbolic correlatives: I/she (gender), the real/the fantastic (psychological), now/then (temporal), here/there (spatial), the living/the dead (metaphysical), Chinese/foreign (national/linguistic), the modern/the traditional (historical), and the like, each being organized around the desire of the male narrator *wo*. It is important to bear in mind that these deictic constructions no longer reflect a purely linguistic reality that Benveniste identifies in inflected languages, but offer themselves up as *literary tropes* that cut across linguistic boundaries. They are deictic tropes, so to speak, of gender, subjectivity, time, and space that are constructed as such to represent the Chinese experience of the modern while never ceasing to make reference to non-Chinese languages and literatures. *Wo* in modern vernacular texts signifies at least two things: it acts as a first-person singular in the language, and it carries the signified of translated deixis. It is, therefore, a perfectly translatable pronoun.

From this perspective, I propose to take on three first-person narratives written by Shen Congwen, Lu Xun, and Ding Ling and explore the ways in which these texts deploy the trope of person and other deictic categories to articulate certain types of historical experience. Specifically, I address the following: What do we mean when we talk about subjectivity and self-consciousness in May Fourth fiction? How does writing represent desire in a deictic moment? Does gender matter in the voice of the first-person narrator? Was it self-contradictory that May Fourth writers tried to negotiate a subject position for themselves even as they spoke in a "borrowed" voice? Does the Chinese experience of the modern testify to its own deictic impasse—I being non-I—even as it tries to capture some genuine forms of historical experience in the flux of translingual practice?

Male Desire and the Deictic Narrative of Class

In my analysis in Chapter 4 of Xiangzi's conversation with Mr. Cao, I reflect on the question of narrative voice, self-representation, and the power of speech in Lao She's novel. The fact that Xiangzi is crippled by an inability to tell his own story is contrasted with the omniscience of the third-person narrator who speaks for him and about him throughout the novel. The reader might wonder what the novel would have been like if it had been told in Xiangzi's own voice. Or, could it have been told in his voice without contradicting itself at the same time? One is reminded of Spivak's famous question, "Can the subaltern speak?"[6]

Shen Congwen's "Sange nanren he yige nüren" (Three men and a woman; 1930) provides an interesting case in this regard, because it attempts to tell the story of a lower-class man in his own voice, albeit a highly stylized one.[7] A macabre tale of sexual desire, violence, suicide, and necrophilia, the story delves into the repressive conditions under which desire is engendered and denied fulfillment.[8] The narrator opens by addressing his audience directly in the manner of an oral storyteller, though not a professional storyteller as in premodern vernacular fiction but a melancholy figure cast in the likeness of Conrad's Marlow who reminisces about an unforgettable event he witnessed in the past. The rainy weather, which serves as a backdrop for this story just as evening does for Conrad's narrator, introduces a moment of suspension that detaches "the storyteller and his ideal audience from their routine activities."[9] Having prepared the reader for a fictional mode of storytelling, the narrator *wo* (I) proceeds to the story proper, which is about a psychological tug-of-war among three men: the narrator himself, his friend the bugler, and a mysterious bean-curd shop owner. These three lower-class men fall in love with a young gentrywoman, but all they can do is admire her from a respectful distance while watching pompous, well-dressed young men walking up to her door and being admitted to the family compound. The story reaches its climax when the young woman commits suicide for some mysterious reason, thus relieving the three men of their tremendous anxiety. A few days after her funeral, however, the woman's dead body is reported missing from the tomb. Apparently, someone has dug it out, carried it to a cave on a nearby hillside, slept with it, and strewn it with wild flowers. But the narrator is not sure which of his two friends did it, the bugler or the beancurd shop owner. The story ends with the narrator's account of his painful journey into the underworld of his own necrophiliac imagination.

This description does little more than scratch the surface of this enigmatic tale. At one level, the story presents a psychological drama about desire, repression, and necrophilia; at another level, it eroticizes the tension between the upper and lower classes, turning the pathological narrative into a powerful social drama. To the narrator, the desirability of the woman, who is the daughter of a gentry family, says as much about her exalted status as about his own exclusion from social entitlement. Sexual desire thus serves as a trope of lack and fulfillment to illuminate the social conditions under which the narrator and his fellow soldiers struggle for survival. The narrator rejects the "undesirability" of his social status and deplores the situation as a form of castration, impotence, and repression, as he and his friend the bugler fantasize about the body of the gentry-woman as if it promised the entrance to self-fulfillment. If Shi Zhecun's fantastic story converts Freudianism into a figure of representation that relegitimizes the classical topos of the fantastic associated with the *zhiguai* tradition, the Freudian allegory of sexual repression in "Three Men and a Woman" speaks the unspeakable about class, which, in a way, carries its own profound taboo and challenges our familiar notions about social oppression. At the same time, the tropological status of the psychoana-lytical language stands exposed as no more and no less than a story— a trope of literary representation, so to speak, that seeks to allegorize a class narrative in erotic terms. This allegorical representation successfully turns a psychotic tale of necrophilia into a narrative of homosocial desire between classes.

"Three Men and a Woman" is a deictic narrative of desire that organizes itself around a skillful manipulation of the terms of I/we, she; here, there; this, that; now, then. Stylistically speaking, the prominence of the personal and deictic pronouns in comparison to proper names immediately declares the translingual status of the text. It is not so much because some of these forms of address, such as the occasional use of the feminine third-person singular *ta* and its genitive *tade*, are neologisms invented at the time of the New Culture and the May Fourth movements for the express purpose of establishing an equivalence between Chinese and Indo-European languages in translation, as because the slippage between the first-person singular and plural pronouns (*wo, women*) constructs a narrative voice that marks it own deictic identity as male.[10] The curious thing is that, although none of the characters in the story is given a proper name, their professional attributes (through metonymical associations) are stressed to the point of becoming individual identities. The narrator speaks of himself as a squad leader and addresses his two friends as "bugler" and "beancurd shop owner," respectively. The we and the I, which include and exclude in terms of gender and class, structure the deictic relationship in such a way that makes the stylistics of male desire and class narrative possible.

The absence of proper names has the obvious function of drawing attention to the palpable presence of deictic relationships that motivate much of the drama in this story, one that has a great deal to do with inclusion and exclusion. For instance, the narrator and his bugler friend use the feminine *ta* and the deictic reference *na nüren* (that woman) to refer exclusively to the anonymous gentrywoman. These expressions almost acquire the status of a proper noun that excludes all other women from this deictic form of address. The narrator and his friends look down on women who occupy the same social status as the soldiers themselves, such as the military officers' concubines who prostitute themselves, and despise female students who are "neither graceful nor dainty" and resemble earthy "water buffaloes" (pp. 229, 256). Against the feminine *ta* or *na nüren*, the first-person singular and plural pronouns also become "gendered" as male in the course of the story, and this gendering lays the stylistic ground for the dynamic interplay of desire across class boundaries.

The first-person plural *women*, signifying a shared class background among the narrator and his comrades, undergoes subtle changes in the course of the narrative. In the beginning, it refers broadly to the military troops to which the narrator belongs; as the story progresses, the pronoun acquires the specific designation of a two-man team: the narrator and his buddy, the crippled bugler; by and by, the beancurd shop owner is also included in this form of address when the narrator discovers that he, too, is in love with the woman. Despite the extreme fluidity of the first-person plural, the pronoun is marked by a constant: namely, the underprivileged status shared by the narrator, crippled bugler, and the beancurd shop proprietor, as well as the rest of the soldiers. Take the narrator, for example. He is a squad leader in the troops, a low military rank slightly above private. "Once outside the camp," says the narrator, "what status could he retain? There were 12 squad leaders in a company, 36 in a battalion, over 100 in a regiment." [11] When he falls in love with the daughter of the gentry family, he describes the situation in terms of "a toad with scabies wishing to eat the meat of the heavenly goose" (pp. 229; 256). The idiom sums up the narrator's awareness of the huge chasm between the two classes.

If the squad leader occupies a position of no consequence, his friend the bugler fares even worse. After the company settles down in the village, an accident cripples the young bugler permanently. The narrator recounts the young man's misfortune in a language that invites allegorical reading.

> There was no way out for this young man of twenty, cursed by a misfortune that condemned him forever to his station of bugler. The company commander, being his fellow townsman, did not dismiss him, but he could no longer seize an opportunity to enroll in a cadre training school to prepare for promotion, like every other normal bugler. He no longer qualified for combat against the bandits and things of that sort. He could no longer, like every other young soldier, climb over an adobe wall at night to keep an appointment with a local girl. All in all, in this accidental fall *he had smashed beyond repair all his human rights and privileges.*   (pp. 226; 254–55; italics added)

The accidental fall disqualifies the young man for promotion, sexual relationships, and the future. Symbolically, he is castrated from normal life. The narrator's language is unambiguous about the implication of this fall and thus prepares the reader for the macabre tale of sexual transgression that unfolds later. Indeed, the infatuation of the three men with the daughter of the gentry family must be grasped in light of this symbolic event, for their "accidental fall" into an underprivileged social station deprives them of their "human rights and privileges" and renders them impotent. As the subsequent development of the story shows, the narrator himself, though physically normal, is just as impotent as the crippled bugler whom he pities.

A third member of this underprivileged group "we" is the beancurd shop owner, whom the narrator and his crippled friend later join in their daily ritual of admiring the object of their desire from a safe distance. The beancurd shop owner is a young rural man of brute strength, who seldom speaks but always smiles a "feminine" and mystifying smile when pressured to talk (pp. 232; *258*). He is virtually mute as a character and his manner of courting the beautiful woman is to "lift the millstone to inspect the axle, showing his handsome, muscular forearms" (pp. 236; *260*). Not unlike the crippled foot of the bugler, his lack of words and feminine smile symbolize his castration from normal social intercourse.

It is the misfortune of these symbolically "impotent" and "castrated" lower-class men, addressed repeatedly by the narrator as "we," to fall in love with this beautiful woman, whose family runs the local postal service, a profession that identifies it as the only gentry family in the small town. Her father chairs the chamber of commerce, and his store functions as the cashier's office for all the garrison troops stationed there. The narrator and his friends watch people of status, such as the regimental commander and the battalion commander, going in and out of the family courtyard while they are barred from the door.

The boundaries of class that separate these men from the young woman find a perfect embodiment in the street that separates the beancurd shop from the building owned by her family. Day after day, the narrator and the crippled bugler go to visit the beancurd shop owner and sit there waiting for hours to catch a glimpse of the woman from across the street: "Often we caught sight of a corner of her white dress next to the goldfish tank in the courtyard by the inner door of the house across the street. *Our hearts* would skip a beat and *our pulse* would quicken a pace" (pp. 230; *256–57*; italics added). The positioning of the three men stages a topographic scenario of desire. The woman on the other side of the street rarely makes an appearance, whereas the three men, whose hearts and pulses beat in a shared rhythm (a stylistic transgression of common sense), wait with great patience. The street dividing them separates two whole worlds. To the men, she is so nearby that they can hear the familiar voice summoning her dogs, and yet she is so hopelessly placed beyond their reach that even a single glimpse is difficult to come by. In this agonizing situation the men start to make friends with the two white dogs of the woman and imagine illusory contacts with her through the mediation of those animals. Their comradeship with the dogs and the language with which the narrator describes it bring to light the debased condition of their social status. During a drunken fight with his crippled friend, the narrator says:

"You're crippled, friend; old pal, you're crippled! A girl from that kind of family'll only marry a battalion commander. Go look at our reflections in the water, you'd know we haven't got a chance. Who are we anyway? Four dollars a month; the troops pull out, we march in mud. . . . We are young, yes, but what good's that? We're dogs and we're pigs, just all lined up in formation. Why do we get such wild ideas about this girl? Why don't we face up to our limitations?"   (pp. 234; *259*)

This outburst touches on the core of desire as a class narrative. Beginning with "you," the narrator switches back to "we" and "our," moving from physical lack to social lack and finally to his own symbolic castration. At stake is the symbolic crippling, as it reduces lower-class people to less than human animals: dogs and pigs. After all, the only access the narrator and his friends have to members of the gentry family is through their dogs. Sitting in the beancurd shop, they watch young officers in well-pressed woolen uniforms and long black-leather boots march in and out of the house, as their hearts fill with envy. If the young woman is upper-class privilege personified, these men's passion for her represents a desire to transgress the class boundary in order to be one of Them. Not surprisingly, their language fills with terms of class hierarchy, ambition, and upward mobility whenever the topic of the woman is brought up. The following conversation between the narrator and his crippled friend sheds illuminating light on the close link between the woman and the personal ambitions and disappointments of these men.

"We have our ambitions, with them we can do anything. Every skyscraper starts from the level ground. Some day we'll be presidents or generals. What's so precious about a woman?"

He said, "I don't reckon on becoming a president; that's too hard. Only this foot of mine, his mother's! Only this foot of mine..."

"Who's stopping you from having your life? Your foot can be taken care of some day. You can still look forward to the company commander's recommending you for cadre school. Then like all those students you can earn your position in the world on your own strength."

"I'm worse than a dog. Right now I'm thinking, if my foot gets fixed up I'll ask the company commander to reenlist me as a regular soldier. Then I would work hard on the drill ground all day and every day..."

"Bit by bit you'll get there," I said.   (pp. 236–37; *260*)

The desire to "get there" is indistinguishable from the men's desire for the woman. The irony of the situation is that this desire arises from hierarchical circumstances that *a priori* forbid its realization. The metaphors bestowed on this woman by the narrator, such as "divine creature," "beautiful flower," and "angel on earth" (pp. 229; 256), capture this huge gulf between the men and the object of their desire. In fact, seldom is she mentioned as a living, breathing human being; rather, references to her are always uplifting metaphors and symbols of displacement. She is divine, and they are earthly; she is a beautiful flower, and they are toads with ugly scabies; and she is an angel on earth, and they are worthless dogs. The inscription of desire is preconditioned by the enormous social gap separating the men from the woman. Her exalted class status, from which the narrator and his buddies are hopelessly excluded, makes her at once desirable and inaccessible. The true confrontation, however, takes place between the men and their upper-class counterparts. The woman is simply the "sign and object of men's social exchange." [12]

Sexual desire in this story, therefore, is more than a signified; it is also a signifier that represents the masochistic loathing of the narrator for his own social condition and serves as an erotic displacement of his desire for transcendence and social transgression. The woman is a symbol promising an imaginary transcendence of subjugation and class oppression. And yet just as the crippled bugler will never recover and, no matter how hard he strives, will remain a bugler for the rest of his life, so neither the narrator nor the beancurd shop owner, being symbolic cripples, can ever rise from their "fallen" positions.

The unexpected suicide of the young woman, for vaguely hinted reasons (a clandestine romance), brings relief to this unbearable situation, since it opens the hopeless desire of the three men to new possibilities. Upon hearing the news of her death, the men respond with mixed feelings of joy and sorrow. Thus the narrator confesses:

> It was difficult to tell why we were so cheerful. Perhaps each of us knew that the girl was like a pot of flowers that belonged to none of us. At first the breaking of the flower pot brought us a measure of unavoidable grief. Then we talked about how the numerous flower pots were long kept in the possession of many rascals, and how all flower pots sooner or later fell into the possession of someone powerful and rich; yet this one broke and fell to the ground. At that we naturally seemed to feel a measure of comfort. (pp. 238–39; 261)

The metaphor of the flower pot once again adds to the symbolic function of the young woman. Not only does death seem to make the rich losers in this case, but its "fallen" status promises to seal the unbridgeable chasm between these men and the once unattainable woman. It is precisely at this point that a change in the relation among the three men takes place and that the first-person plural "we" begins to give way to the predominantly individualized "I" (the narrator) and "he." The story now turns on the shocking manner in which each man pursues the "consummation" of his formerly repressed desire on his own terms.

According to the narrator, the woman's body is dug out and carried off by someone several days after the funeral. Rumor has it that she lies completely naked on a stone ledge in a cave with wild blue chrysanthemums scattered all over her body and on the ground. The narrator and his crippled friend voice the suspicion that their friend, the beancurd shop owner, is the likely culprit. Judging from the circumstance of the latter's mysterious disappearance that immediately follows the event, it is not entirely impossible that he is the one who did it.[13] However, the significance of the story does not hinge on discovering whodunit. After all, the crippled bugler would have committed the crime if the other had not. In fact, he discovers the scandal and confesses to the narrator that he had gone to the grave with the intention of digging it up, although he denies any dishonorable motive. His explains that he was simply following the folk belief that a dead girl who swallowed gold can be revived within seven days of her death and that he visited her grave in the innocent hope of rescuing her. The scenario is further complicated by the strange reaction of the narrator, who, upon learning the location of the girl's grave, begins to find his friend bugler hateful: "I didn't know why every time I saw the long face of the bugler, I felt like scolding him and hitting him. The cheerless look of this man seemed to insult my secret devotion to that young girl" (pp. 240; *262*).

Having gone through the common ordeal of desiring the same woman, the crippled bugler has grown to be more than a friend to the narrator. Evidently he now becomes a mirror and an alter ego to the narrator, who sees in him what he hates to confront in himself. The same desire to dig up the grave of the young girl is hidden in the dark recess of the narrator's mind, even though he never confesses to it. The revealing moment comes when the narrator conjures up the bugler in a feverish nightmare and wakes up to find the man sitting next to him. "In my hallucination I had just seen him fall off the stone lion and break his ankles. Now I didn't know for sure whether I was in a dream" (pp. 241; *263*). Waking up in the middle of the night and facing the ghostly figure of the bugler, the narrator faces his alter ego from the underworld. The bugler is covered with mud and looks dirty and haggard. He recounts the horrible story of the stolen corpse in broken and confused phrases and frightens the narrator with his mad ravings. "In my mind I figured that both of us were living in a dream," says the narrator. "After all, it was true that his kind of desire was humanly uncontrollable, but when translated into real action it would still be inadmissible in this world. And if he regretted his confession to me, he could very well kill me to erase what he had just said" (pp. 244; *264*). This highly Freudian confrontation between the narrator and his alter ego brings to light what the narrator has always feared: the horror of repressed desire and its dehumanizing power in his own heart. Having undergone the harrowing experience and knowing what he knows on that ghostly night, the narrator confesses that, even if he and the bugler are both innocent, they will be haunted by the nightmare for the rest of their lives: "He himself is guiltless, but what another young man did left him melancholic all his life. What do I think of the whole incident? With my melancholy I don't make good company for young people" (pp. 245; *265*). The narrator knows the cost of his nightmarish adventure into the horror of the underworld.

Indeed, if the alleged act of transgression is performed by the beancurd shop owner and attempted by the crippled bugler, it is also staged in full in the mind of the narrator. The symbolic effect is no less real than if the latter had literally done the deed. But what do death, transgression, a breach of taboo, and guilt all add up to in this symbolic drama of desire? There could be no transgression without boundaries. The class boundary, as mentioned earlier, is of the first order in this story, for neither the gender boundary alone nor that which divides the living from the dead is capable of engendering and prohibiting the kind of desire the three men experience for the gentrywoman. The violation of her dead body, therefore, symbolizes the transgression of class boundaries, although it means more wish-fulfillment than anything else. If the men are prohibited from approaching the woman of their desire by the social taboos imposed by the class system, they are unlikely to succeed in removing the taboos simply by breaching them. The loathing of the narrator and his friend for their own class and their yearning for transcendence through the symbol of the young woman can only end in a nightmare. Neither he nor his friend succeeds in joining the ranks of the upper class. Through a narrative manipulation of the deixis of the now and then, the narrator tells us that the bugler remains a cripple and a bugler in the same troops, whereas he himself has long abandoned his unsuccessful military career and drifted to the city, where he finds urban life equally disappointing. In the midst of his profound disappointment, the narrator is haunted by the knowledge of a deictic past (then) and tries to overcome it in the deictic present (now) by telling a story. Addressing his audience to that effect, the narrator concludes: "I am forever restless because the past returns to haunt me often. To each his own destiny; this I know. Some things of the past perpetually gnaw the inside of me. When I talk about them, you would think they are only stories. Nobody can understand how a person feels who lives day after day under the weight of hundreds of stories like this one" (pp. 245; 265).

It is not uncommon for Shen Congwen's narrators to discourse on the fictionality of the story they are telling.[14] In his opening remarks to this one, the narrator warns his audience that "beautiful things are often unreal; we find examples in the rainbow in the sky, and in our dreams at night" (pp. 223; 253). But rather than taking this discourse on fictionality as a disclaimer, we must look into the deictic relationship the narrator establishes between himself and his audience, for it is here that a realistic interpretation is foreclosed, as the narrator calls for a symbolic reading of his story. In other words, one is asked not to take the tale of necrophilia literally, as if whether or not it really took place should matter. What matters in the end is what takes place between the storyteller and his anonymous audience—the latter mirroring the implied reader, who in turn is a mirror image of the actual reader like you and me—as the narrator challenges his audience's ability to understand. However, the deictic act of storytelling always already presupposes the miraculous possibility of understanding, just as much as the narrator's statement of skepticism proceeds from an implied trust in the comprehensibility of his language. Perhaps what redeems the audience and the reader from this impossible hermeneutic is precisely the storyteller's trust, an invitation to understand, which replays and updates itself in the eternal present of reading and interpretation.

That brings us to Lu Xun's story "Regret for the Past" in which the deictic tropes of memory, gender, time, and writing, as well as hermeneutic understanding, play themselves out in a totally different setting. The scene is now the urban and modern city of Beijing—which also happens to be the setting of "Diary of Miss Sophia" to be discussed later—where one's wildest dream of romance is supposed to be fulfilled.

The Confessional Voice

My love gave me a bunch of roses red
What did I give her in return?
—a red-spotted snake for a pet.

Since then she has put on a long face
and heeded me no more;
But why?—better let her go and forget!
—from Lu Xun, "My Lost Love," 1924[15]

Lu Xun wrote this poem to parody "Sichou shi" (Four sorrows) by the ancient Chinese poet Zhang Heng, but his avowed intention was not to attack traditional literature but to "satirize a large number of poems on unrequited love that were in vogue at the time."[16] The lover in the poem speaks modern vernacular Chinese, and as a mark of modern courtship, he and his beloved exchange such gifts as roses, aspirin, and a gold watch chain. If Lu Xun pokes fun at modern sexual relationships in this lighthearted parody, "Regret for the Past," written a year later, begins to take such relationships seriously and to test them.[17] The story is about the disillusioning romantic relationship between the narrator, Juansheng, and his love, Zijun. Their experiment with romantic love begins as a literal translingual experience as they read translated literature together. Inspired by the works of Shelley, Ibsen, and other Romantic writers, they fall in love and decide to live together as common-law husband and wife. But things begin to deteriorate when Juansheng loses his job, and after a few months of hardship and bitterness, they drift apart. In the end, Zijun dies a lonely death.

Juansheng's narrative is revealed to be a series of *shouji* (handwritten notes) in the subtitle of the story. His act of recollection is a deictic performance that mourns Zijun's death and, at the same time, institutes a desire for forgetfulness that writing is supposed to fulfill. Lu Xun represents the narrator's recollection as profoundly gendered; it is, moreover, devoted to erasing and exorcising Zijun and casting her into the empty space between words. That does not mean, of course, that Zijun never appears in Juansheng's recollections. Precisely because her presence is disturbing, the narrator feels the need to overcome her memory in order to restore his confidence of self-knowledge, which has been shattered by the news of her death. Self-narration, therefore, comes across as an attempted deictic anchoring of the self in the here and now as the narrator guiltily rejects the then and there of his past memories. It is above all a therapeutic device for reconstituting a coherent self: "Since I am a living person, I must make a fresh start. The first step is just to write down my remorse and grief, for Zijun's sake as well as for my own. . . . I want to forget. For my own sake I don't want to remember the oblivion I gave Zijun for her burial."[18]

The strange mix of testimony and denial reveals the problematic status of the text. Juansheng's forgetfulness and his desire to forget disrupts the assumed coherence of his retrospective narrative. This tension comes out most strongly in his digressions on the act of recollection that frequently punctuate the narrative about the past: "I can't recall clearly how I expressed my most sincere and passionate love for her. Not only now—even soon after it happened, my impression grew blurred. At night when I tried to recall the scene, I could only remember snatches of what I had said. During the month or two after we started living together even those fragments vanished like a dream without a trace" (pp. 112, *199*). The confession throws into question the reliability of the retrospective narrative. How can the narrator expect the reader to trust him if he has lapses of memory? Interestingly, the event he does remember turns out to be one that he is ashamed to recall, and so he cuts short the narration to prevent further embarrassment. He remembers that, in proposing to Zijun, he ludicrously imitated a hero courting a heroine in a Hollywood film. "I clasped her hand with tears in my eyes and went down on one knee..." (pp. 113, *199*). The suspension points are supposed to suppress a portion of the unpleasant memory, but one begins to wonder how much more the narrator has suppressed.

The retrospective narrative in this story takes place on three levels of temporality, but the act of reminiscence occurs on only the first and second levels. The first temporal level is the process of writing, which places the second and third levels in the deictic past. The second level consists of the couple's life together as husband and wife up till the time of Zijun's death and Juansheng's writing. During this period, the two frequently reminiscence about the days before they came to live together. Zijun indulges in memories of the happy days of their first dates, whereas Juansheng increasingly longs for his life as a bachelor. The third temporal level goes further back to the period before the couple started living together and is marked by an absence of reminiscence.

If the title "Shang shi" (Regret for the past) refers to the time of writing (the first level), it is not difficult to see that it evokes the second level, as the narrator regrets his involvement with Zijun and mourns for his lost freedom with intense nostalgia: "I had a sudden vision of a peaceful life—the quiet of my shabby room in the hostel flashed before my eyes, and I was just going to take a good look at it when I found myself back in the dusky lamplight again" (pp. 115–16, *204*). It would accord with Lu Xun's position on the question of gender to contend that this tragic story was written to debunk the grand illusion of romantic love and female independence prevalent in his own time. The future of a Nora who leaves her comfortable home for freedom is unthinkable in Lu Xun's view if the woman has no means to support herself in a male-dominated society.[19] But the story would lose its complexity if interpreted in those terms only, for its critique of the patriarchy also involves a rethinking of the notion of modern love, whose male-centered discourse ironically reproduces the patriarchy it aims to overthrow. It is the narrator who "liberates" Zijun from tradition by feeding her with new ideas from Western literature and who entices Zijun into his project of modern love (known as *ziyou lian'ai* [romantic love] in the May Fourth period), by using imported rituals of courtship, including the cinematic scene. The two very different occasions on which the narrator brings up the names of Western Romantic poets and Ibsen suggest that he exploits the gender-biased discourse on romantic love as well as women's liberation in his own interest. If in encouraging Zijun to live with him he himself is no less taken in than she by those discourses, his words ring false when he uses the same argument to talk Zijun out of their relationship one year later:

> I deliberately brought up the past. I spoke of literature, then of foreign authors and their works, of Ibsen's *A Doll's House* and *The Lady from the Sea*. I praised Nora for being strong-minded. . . . All this had been said the previous year in the shabby room in the hostel, but now it rang hollow. As the words left my mouth I could not free myself from the suspicion that there was an unseen urchin behind me maliciously parroting all I said. (pp. 123, 209)

The project of modern love in the name of foreign literature is aborted in an absurd moment of self-parody. Who is that unseen urchin? Is it the figure of guilt, conscience, or modernity itself? The desire for a modern sexual relationship in this story is ruthlessly undercut by the narrator's own parodic treatment of foreign literature.

Juansheng's "regret" eventually leads to Zijun's death, which in turn engenders the further "regret" that his writing attempts to overcome. The desire to tamper with the past and undo it before and after Zijun's death results in the banishment of Zijun from his life and the subsequent writing of his "regret" to banish her ghost from his memory. Because of his convoluted motivations, the narrator fails to clarify whether he is writing of his "regret" for his past "regret" or trying to justify it. In any case, the ambiguity works to the advantage of the narrator: in mourning Zijun's death, he defends himself against the charge of responsibility by trying to project his past "regret" in a sympathetic light. His writing turns on the deictic projection of her as the undesirable past and takes advantage of the silence of the dead. When he suggests that Zijun did not truly understand that "love must be constantly renewed" (pp. 115, *202*), he is making an accusation Zijun cannot defend herself against. By suppressing Zijun's side of the story while passing judgments on her, he manipulates the narrative in his own favor. The episode of the pet dog Asui, which prefigures Juansheng's abandonment of Zijun, serves to highlight the point. Because they can no longer afford to keep the dog, Juansheng takes it out and abandons it in the wilderness. On returning home, he is surprised by the tragic expression on Zijun's face. Unable and unwilling to empathize with her feelings, he blames her for what has happened.

> At long last I realized she must consider me a cruel man. Actually, when I was on my own I had got along very well, although I was too proud to mix much with family acquaintances. But since my move I had become estranged from all my old friends. Still, if I could only get away from all this, there were plenty of ways open to me. Now I had to put up with all these hardships mainly because of her—getting rid of Asui was a case in point. But Zijun's understanding has become so obtuse that she did not even see that. (pp. 120, *207*)

Given that the narrator soon abandons Zijun in a similar manner, his self-defense appears singularly ironic. Zijun shares the fate of her dog at his hands.

Self-contradiction is the crux of a narrative that seeks to establish meaning out of the confused experience of a split self. On the one hand, the narrator describes his past life as if it had been a peaceful haven and only turned into hell because of Zijun's intrusion. On the other hand, in the opening paragraph the narrator makes a contrary claim: "A whole year has passed since I fell in love with Zijun and, thanks to her, escaped from this dead quiet and emptiness" (pp. 130, *197*). The discrepancy might well be attributed to a gap in perception between the narrating self and the experiencing self, as the former seemingly discredits the latter. But has the narrating self outgrown his former self?

Time, experience, and retrospection might provide the narrator with a unique perspective for self-criticism previously unavailable to him, but it does not necessarily follow that such self-criticism is unproblematic. In fact, the contradictory statements and carefully wrought images throughout the text point toward an important linkage between the narrating self and the experiencing self. That linkage is established by the escape motif that characterizes the narrating self as well as the experiencing self. Both try to flee from self-knowledge, the writing of the confession being just another attempt to escape. Take, for example, the recurrent image of the caged bird:

> In the office I had lived like a wild bird in a cage, given just enough canary-seed by its captor to keep alive, but not to grow fat. As time passed it would lose the use of its wings, so that if ever it were let out of the cage it could no longer fly. Now, at any rate, I had got out of the cage, and must soar anew in the wide sky before it was too late, while I could still flap my wings. (pp. 118, *204*)

Although there is nothing remarkable about the literary cliché the narrator uses here, Zijun's conspicuous absence in this figurative projection of a future flight toward freedom is striking. (Another interesting detail is that the narrator is a regular contributor to the journal *Freedom's Friend.*) Not only is she omitted from this solipsistic picture, but the metaphor, which quickly becomes the narrator's privileged self-image, soon alienates him from Zijun even as it frees him from the routine life of a clerk. With this metaphor, freedom suddenly becomes the first priority in the narrator's life. He wages his battle for freedom with the help of a vocabulary that successfully uncouples his relationship with Zijun:

> As I sat there alone thinking over the past, I felt that during the last half year lived for love—blind love—I had neglected all the important things in life. First and foremost, livelihood. A man must make a living before there can be any place for love. There must be a way out for those who struggle, and I hadn't yet forgotten how to *flap my wings*, though I was much weaker than before. (pp. 121, *207–8*; italics added)

The narrator now explicitly condemns Zijun to the role of the cage while giving the superior image of the bird to himself. The metaphor writes off the previous relationship between the lover and beloved in order to establish a new one, that of the bird and his cage, allowing the narrator to get rid of Zijun with an easy conscience.

In connection with the caged bird, the narrator repeatedly evokes the image of the road to embody his yearning for freedom. Harping on the need to make a fresh start, he pins his hopes for the future on Zijun's departure from his life. Lacking the courage to initiate a breakup, he decides to speak to her in allusions and metaphors: "I explained to her my views and proposals: we must explore a new path and turn over a new leaf to avoid being ruined together" (pp. 123, *209*). As far as Zijun is concerned, the new path leads to a dead-end, whereas the image helps the narrator conceptualize an escape from his immediate reality. This is a far cry from Lu Xun's "Guxiang" (My old home) in which the image of the road embodies a kind of hope. As Leo Lee points out, the road for the individual in "Regret for the Past" becomes "less certain" as it eventually turns into the sinister image of a gray serpent in the eyes of the narrator.[20] Nevertheless, the narrator decides to take his dubious road to freedom, because life for him is a solitary journey, and in order to survive alone, he must rid himself of the obstacle blocking his road.[21] To the experiencing self, that obstacle was Zijun, whereas, to the narrating self, it is her ghostly memory that disturbs his peace of mind. If formerly he removed her from his life with speech, he now relies on writing to erase her memory, cast it into oblivion, and assert his authorial, deictic control over the story of the past.

The deictic attempt to undo the past unites the narrating self with the experiencing self in a dubious confessional voice. After Zijun's death the narrator moves back into the small room he occupied as a bachelor. He begins his account by describing this room to the reader.

> The broken window with the half dead locust tree and old wisteria outside and square table inside are *the same as before. The same* too are the mouldering wall and wooden bed beside it. At night I lie in bed alone just as I did before I started living with Zijun. *The past year has been blotted out as if it had never been*—as if I had never moved out of this shabby room so hopefully to set up a small home in Jizhao street.   (pp. 110, *197*; italics added)

The narrator conveys a profound sense of futility as he surveys the room and contrasts its unchanging look with the turmoil of his life in the past year. But does that feeling of mourning and regret express a sense of loss because of Zijun's death or self-reproach for becoming involved with her in the first place? Perhaps both. In any case, the unchanging look of his room mirrors the narrator's desire to blot out the past. Indeed, when we consider Zijun's transformation from a lively young girl to a woman and finally to a ghostly memory all within the space of one year, the contrast with the narrator's own condition comes into sharp focus. Since the narrator ends where he started, the time that separates the experiencing self from the narrating self becomes circular. The unchanged space contradicts and, in effect, cancels out the temporal distance installed by the retrospective discourse between the narrator and his former self, so much so that it is impossible for us to take the narrator's regretful mourning or retrospective self-critique at face value.

The complexity of the narrative situation is borne out by the narrator's bizarre explanation of his role in Zijun's death. His chief crime, the narrator says, is his single-minded allegiance to the truth: "I shouldn't have told Zijun the truth. Since we had loved each other, I should have gone on lying to her. If truth is a treasure, it shouldn't have proved such a heavy burden of emptiness to Zijun. Of course, lies are empty too, but at least they wouldn't have proved so crushing a burden in the end" (pp. 127, 212). One wonders whether the narrator is not defending himself rather than accusing himself in setting up a spurious dichotomy between "truth" and "love." The false argument is designed to trap the reader in the dilemma of choosing one or the other. However, the story resists being reduced to an abstract lesson in metaphysics, not to mention a false one, for the tragedy of Zijun's death is caused not so much by Juansheng's allegiance to the truth as by his rejection of her love and, particularly, his inability to reconcile what he perceives as the claims of love and individualism. Individual freedom is gendered just as much as romantic love and means different things to different people. If the narrator blames himself for acting like a weakling (pp. 127, 212), his cowardice apart from social pressure seems to stem from his self-centered world rather than an inability to live with falsehood. Love is hardly an exception to his escapist view of life. He escapes from boredom through love but flees love as soon as life becomes difficult. In fact, he wants so much to be freed that he even wishes secretly that she would die (pp. 124, 209).

The logical conclusion the narrator draws from his spurious discussion of truth and love finally foregrounds the problematic of the entire narrative: "I must make a fresh start in life. I must hide the truth deep in my wounded heart, and advance silently, taking oblivion and falsehood as my guide" (pp. 130, 205). One need not accept this confession literally, for it seems to reinvent the project of modernity by substituting a relatively harmless intellectual discourse—the debate over truth and falsehood—for the deep crisis of the modern subject and by suppressing the dark reality of human relationships affected by that crisis. But even if it were taken at face value, that statement would still profoundly discredit the narrator and the entire narrative at the textual level. Just as the narrator regards nostalgic writing as the first step on this new journey, so one might ask Does it hide the truth? Is it written with the guidance of the falsehood that the narrator has embraced? Perhaps Juansheng's retrospective writing is a deictic act of violence committed not so much against "truth" as against the memory of the deceased woman. It is remarkable that the inscription of male desire on a dead woman's body appears regularly in the necrophiliac fantasy world of male writers and with such extraordinary similarity, as can be seen in my analysis of Yu Dafu, Shen Congwen, and Shi Zhicun.

Saying I as a Woman

If Zijun had lived to tell her own story, what could it have been? What does it mean to live as a "liberated" woman from a woman's own point of view? Must she always choose, as Zijun does, between a modern conjugal relationship and a traditional household? Must she always suffer and die for the love of a man? Is she capable of a sense of herself? How does she relate to her body, sexuality, and writing? And how does she relate to other women?

Like "Regret for the Past," Ding Ling's story "The Diary of Miss Sophia," which appeared within three years of Lu Xun's, tries to grapple with the problems of modern sexual relationships in gendered terms. But unlike Lu Xun, Ding Ling explores the ground of female subjectivity by allowing the narrator to speak of a woman's experience from her own perspective. Unlike Zijun, Sophia refuses to choose between a modern conjugal relationship and a traditional household. In addition, this "liberated" woman analyzes herself with something akin to masochistic pleasure, is capable of desiring women as well as men, and speaks of her body and sexuality with an openness new to the works of Chinese women writers.[22]

Upon publication in *Xiaoshuo yuebao* (The short story magazine) in February 1928, the story was an immediate success. As one critic puts it, it was like "a bombshell dropped in the midst of the literary world."[23] The author was hailed as the first female writer who "speaks out about the dilemma and conflict of the newly liberated woman"[24] and whose understanding of the "Modern Girl" (for a Chinese transliteration of this term, see Appendix F) was deeper than that of any of her contemporaries.[25] Refusing to sing eulogies to fictions of romantic love, which were extremely popular in the May Fourth era, Ding Ling's portrayal of a confused modern woman who struggles to understand her identity, sexuality, and solitude stands out from the works of her contemporaries.[26] It also assigns her to what the historians of May Fourth fiction call the tradition of female writing, associated with such names as Lu Yin, Bing Xin, Feng Yuanjun, and Ling Shuhua, among others.[27]

The deictic impulse of Ding Ling's story derives from its presentation in the form of a diary that speaks to the self by the self and, sometimes, of the self as other. In 33 entries, the diary records a period of Sophia's poverty-stricken and consumptive life during a cold Beijing winter. She lives for the most part in a hotel or rented room, except for a short interval in a hospital. Bored with her life and her friends, she pours her thoughts into the diary as if writing could solve her problems. The writing of the diary provides a pretext for Ding Ling's story, but it also helps create a female writing characterized by an extraordinary sense of gendered subjectivity, resistance to conventional portrayals of courtship and woman, an anticlimactic debunking of the romantic love plot, and the eventual undermining of writing as a reliable path toward self-knowledge.

The Chinese transliteration, Shafei, of the Western name Sophia sets the narrator immediately outside the familiar context of Chinese culture. And like her name, Sophia chooses to live an unconventional urban lifestyle away from "traditional" family and social constraints. She is one of those creatures in Ding Ling's early works who, having renounced "traditional" ways of life, find themselves stranded in an economic, social, and moral crisis. Worst of all, "what they often discover in their freewheeling, anarchistic existence is that in facing the world they must also encounter themselves."[28] Sophia's confrontation with her lone self in a hotel room is introduced by the mirror scene in the first entry: "Glancing from one side you've got a face a foot long; tilt your head slightly to the side and suddenly it gets so flat you startle yourself. . . . It all infuriates me. Maybe I'm the only one affected. Still I'd prefer something new to be displeased and dissatisfied with as long as it is new enough. But novelty, for better or worse, seems miles beyond my reach"[29] (pp. 44, 51). This manner of self-scrutiny parallels the reflexive act of diary writing.[30] The mirror serves as a deictic metaphor for Sophia's female writing in which she is I (writer), she (subject), you (reader) combined in one person. Ironically, the mirror's distortion of her image, which irritates her so much, also foreshadows the inadequacy of her narcissistic approach to the self, just as the diary falls short of providing a solution to the enigma of selfhood and leaves her disappointed in the end. Sophia's attitude toward writing and selfhood reflects the female impasse of wanting to reject male writing about female desire and yet finding no alternative fully satisfying within a male-dominated literary language.

As a "self-liberated" woman, Sophia tries to insert herself into a yet-to-be-written text in which a woman is no longer portrayed as a daughter, sister, beloved, or friend, but as an autonomous I. But this is no easy task, because the so-called autonomous self has never existed in previous literature any more than woman approached in terms other than mother, daughter, wife, sister, or lover has existed. "Can I name what I really need?" (pp. 51, 56). Sophia becomes her own enigma. Self-interrogation, ambivalence, uncertainty, and narcissism become the very hallmarks of this female writing.

The diary is written in what Chinese linguists call an *ouhua* or Europeanized Chinese vernacular. The narrator makes extensive use of lengthy conjunctive phrases and subordinate sentences, especially transposed causal clauses—conditional, concessive, and temporal causes introduced by words such as *yinwei/suoyi* (because), *suiran* (although), *dan* (but), and *jinguan* (even though).[31] This style was not uncommon in May Fourth fiction, which was responsible for the invention of a range of prose styles in modern vernacular Chinese, but its presence in Sophia's diary reflects an interesting choice by the narrator about her confused desire. The narrator's excessive ponderings about the but's and although's of her situation reveal the profound ambivalence she feels about her lack of interest in Weidi and her intense desire for the Westernized Ling Jishi. In her dealings with these two men, Sophia comes face to face with the uncertainty of her own desire: "I am at a loss to know how to analyze myself. Sometimes I can feel a kind of boundless unfathomable sorrow at the sight of a white cloud being blown and scattered by the wind. But, when faced with a young man over twenty—Weidi is actually four years older than I—I find myself laughing with the satisfaction of a savage as his tears fall on the back of my hands" (pp. 47, 53–54). Weidi's tears and sentimentality serve him ill because Sophia finds him boring and unattractive. This lack of "masculinity" or sex appeal says more about Sophia's fantasizing about masculinity and male sexuality than about Weidi himself. What kind of man does she fantasize about? "It was the chivalric European medieval knight I was dreaming about. It's still not a bad comparison; anyone who looks at Ling Jishi can see it, though he also preserves his own special Eastern gentleness" (pp. 72, 73). Sophia's fantasy is not exactly about a Caucasian man but a Chinese man with a Caucasian man's sex appeal, a fantasy that instantly disqualifies Weidi's claim to masculinity.

This brings out the sexual politics of the East–West encounter in which desire, desirability, femininity, and masculinity are redistributed along the lines of culture, nation, and race in an interesting reconfiguration of power relations. The weaker nation, so to speak, is emasculated in symbolic relation to the dominating presence of the West, which simultaneously feeds back into the sexual fantasies of both the dominated and dominator.[32] However, one must be careful not to simplify Sophia's position to that of a colonized person. In her relationship with Ling Jishi, she is able to struggle with her own erotic fantasy and to redefine desire and sexuality for herself as a Chinese woman. After all, it is she, rather than her "chivalric knight," who makes the aggressive first move and shortly decides to terminate the relationship. The diary revises the chivalric romance by casting the narrator into the role of a seducer in blatantly sexual language.

> I subjected him to the most searching scrutiny. I was possessed with a desire to mark every part of his body with my lips. Has he any idea how I'm sizing him up? Later I deliberately said that I wanted him to help me with my English. When Yunlin laughed, Ling Jishi was taken aback and gave a vague, embarrassed reply. He can't be too much of a bastard, I thought to myself, otherwise—a big tall man like that—he'd never have blushed so red in the face. My passion raged with new ferocity. (pp. 52, 57–58)

Sophia's aggressiveness and Ling's bashfulness reverse the conventional roles of man and woman in courtship. But if the former's defiance of social conventions relies on a reversal of received gender roles, what would she do if the man should decide to reciprocate? Sophia soon makes a shocking discovery about the man of her dreams.

> Our most recent conversations have taught me a lot more about his really stupid ideas. All he wants is money. Money. A young wife to entertain his business associates in the living room, and several fat, fair-skinned, well-dressed little sons. What does love mean to him? Nothing more than spending money in a brothel, squandering it on a moment of carnal pleasure, or sitting on a soft sofa fondling scented flesh, a cigarette between his lips, his legs crossed casually, laughing and talking with his friends. When it's not fun anymore, never mind; he just runs home to his little wifey. He's passionate about the Debate Club, playing tennis matches, studying at Harvard, joining the foreign service, becoming an important statesman, or inheriting his father's business and becoming a rubber merchant. He wants to be a capitalist . . . that is the extent of his ambition! (pp. 65–66, 68)

Money, power, and capitalism paint such a bleak picture of the masculinity of a Westernized Chinese man that he begins to shed his particular sexual aura in Sophia's eyes. The Western bourgeois values associated with Ling's person awaken the narrator to the socioeconomic makeup of modern masculinity, whose sexual glamor cannot be separated from its oppressive ideology. Sophia ends up rejecting Ling Jishi, and in doing so, she also bids farewell to her own fantasies about the Caucasian knight.

How, then, does the diary construct its femininity against the masculinity of capitalism in deictic terms? Facing what Yi-tsi Feuerwerker calls "the limits of writing itself," the diary examines its own ground of meaning in order to open up the possibility of female writing.[33] The textual strategy Sophia adopts in that regard is to oppose the feminine world of non-meaning to the male-dominated world of meanings and values. Take, for example, her striking use of the image of milk, which is one of her favorite liquid images for the representation of femininity. Sophia writes in the entry for December 24:

> As the sunlight hit the paper window, I was boiling my milk for the third time. I did it four times yesterday. I'm never really sure that it suits my taste, no matter how often I do it, but it's the only thing that releases frustration on a windy day. Actually, though it gets me through an hour or so, I usually end up even more irritable than I was before. So all last week I didn't play with it. Then out of desperation, I did, relying on it, as though I was already old, just to pass time.   (pp. 43, 50–51)

It has been suggested that this passage is a coded reference to masturbation, which might or might not be the case, depending on how far one wishes to push a literal reading of the text.[34] Suppose our act of reading is not simply to unravel coded messages, is it still possible for us to make a meaningful connection between Sophia's writing and reading on the one hand and her milk and masturbation on the other at a figurative level? Consider the passage that immediately follows the above:

> I read the newspaper as soon as it comes. I start, systematically, with the headlines, the national news, the important foreign reports, local gossip, and then . . . when I've finished the items on education, party propaganda, economics, and the stock markets, I go back to the same announcements I read so thoroughly yesterday . . . and the day before . . . the ones recruiting new students, the notices of lawsuits over division of family property. I even read stuff like ads for "606" and "Mongolian Lark" venereal tonics, cosmetics, Zhenguang Movie Theatre listings. When I've finished everything I toss the paper away, reluctantly.   (pp. 43–44, 51)

Sophia's reading of the newspaper makes no attempt to make sense of what she reads or reveal some hidden messages. This description curiously parallels that of her repeated act of boiling the milk that precedes it. Just as she heats up the milk for the sake of doing it, so she reads for the sake of reading. These senseless little acts are repeated to relieve a sense of ennui that weighs her down as she contemplates the unpleasant surroundings of her life. Sophia cannot relate to the modern male-dominated world of national news, foreign affairs, local gossip, talks on education, party propaganda, economics, or the stock market. She reads about these things indifferently, giving equal attention to headline news and notices of lawsuits or advertisements for venereal medicines. Her act of reading is represented as a ritualistic performance, not unlike her writing of the diary. Insofar as these are intransitive acts whose significance extends only to the subject of the action, one can make a case for a *figurative* reading of masturbation in this text. In that sense, not only the boiling of the milk but Sophia's idiosyncratic reading and writing may be viewed as textual instances of masturbation.

It is a commonplace to speak of diary writing as a figure of masturbation, but how does Sophia connect it with femininity in a text filled with contradictory expressions of self-love, self-loathing, and sadomasochism? Femininity here seems to be constructed as a contradictory state of being—sadomasochism—in relation to language and writing, the contradiction being that the narrator writes compulsively about herself while exclaiming: "How useless speech and the written word seem now" (pp. 78, *78*). Switching to the third person as if she were addressing someone else, she renounces writing altogether in the final entry of the diary: "It is truer to call this diary a collection of Sophia's tears, drop by drop upon her heart, than a record of her life. But it's time to end the diary because Sophia doesn't need those tears to comfort or release her anger, since now she understands that nothing has any meaning whatsoever and that tears are the most profound expression of that lack" (pp. 79, *78*). The metaphor of tears, another liquid image of femininity in the text, is associated with writing and release of tension. This represents a self-conscious, female signature that marks its alienation from male-dominated writing and from its proprietorship of pen and ink. Tears, with their connotations of evaporation and blankness, signify the absence of meaning, and by breaking norms of discretion, social taboos, and conventions of public writing penned in "ink," a diary of tears brings the limits of writing into view. The sense of euphoria Sophia experiences toward the close of the diary reads almost like a masochistic indulgence in a crisis of self-representation. As she goes from the third-person to the first-person form of address, she proclaims: "On this last page Sophia ought fervently to toast the fact that suddenly from the depth of disappointment she emerges to feel a satisfaction that should rightly have killed her with ecstasy. But I... I... all I feel out of that satisfaction is a sense of triumph. From triumph comes a terrible sorrow and an even profounder understanding of how pathetic and ludicrous I am" (pp. 79, *78–79*).

Sophia's narcissism is profoundly marked by the inscription of gender difference in the performative acts of writing and reading. She confesses that she keeps her diary for the sake of Yun, a female friend whom she loves: "Naturally I am unwilling to show it to anybody but her, because, first, I've recorded these trivialities to share my day-to-day existence exclusively with Yun, and, secondly, I fear the pain of being shown up by people of moral pretensions, who might make me feel just as badly as if

I had been guilty of some crime simply because they worship their moral conventions" (pp. 72, 73). Writing is understood to be a form of emotional connection between two women and resistance to moral authority embedded in conventional, male narratives about desire and sexuality.

In this light, Sophia's impulsive act of showing her diary to a male reader inadvertently transgresses against the deictic pact of reading between herself and Yun. In other words, the diary is not meant to be seen by male eyes. However, she lets Weidi read portions of her diary because she wants him to know who she really is. Weidi fails to grasp the "intended" meaning of those entries, and believes that another man, Ling Jishi, has successfully become Sophia's lover. The diary cannot explain Sophia to Weidi, because his insistence on his own gendered reading of Sophia's diary leads to a stereotypical triangle in which his rival gets the better of him. Sophia deplores Weidi's "mis"reading of her:

> Who can understand me? Even if he understood this diary which merely expresses one ten-thousandth of myself, it would only pain me to feel its inadequacy, as if it isn't painful already, in my longing for another's understanding, to have to resort to showing another a diary in which every contrivance of words has been used to explain myself. And now Wei, fearing lest I do not get his point, added: "You love him! You love him! I am not good enough for you!"
>   I wanted to grab the diary and rip it into shreds. Have I not wasted it? But to him, I can only say, "I want to go to bed. Please come tomorrow." (pp. 73; 74)

Sophia constitutes writing and reading as profoundly gendered acts in this allegorical encounter between a female text and a male reader. It is ironic that the intended female reader of the diary dies before she has a chance to read it. Sophia attributes Yun's death to victimization by traditional romantic literature. In her reminiscences of their time together in Shanghai, she recalls:

> What a life I was living last year at this time! To trick Yun into babying me unreservedly, I'd pretend to be sick and refuse to get out of bed. I'd sit and whimper about the most trivial dissatisfactions to work on her tearful anxiety and get her to fondle me. Then there were the times when after spending an entire day in silent meditation, the mood of desolation I'd finally achieved made me unwilling to do anything, since by that time I could derive such utter sweetness from it. It hurts even more to think about the nights I spent lying on the grass in French Park listening to Yun sing a song from *Peony Pavilion*. If she hadn't been tricked by God into loving that pale-faced man, she would never have died so fast and I wouldn't have wandered into Beijing

alone, trying, sick as I was, to fend for myself, friendless and without family. (pp. 70, 71–72)

Yun's singing of love appears singularly ironic in light of her unhappy marriage to the man she loved. The "pale-faced lover" refers to the stereotypical image of the scholar-lover, or *xiaosheng*, popularized in traditional fiction and drama.[35] Sophia rejects traditional romantic love and protests against its victimization of her beloved friend. Pitted against classical romantic plays like *Mudan ting* (Peony pavilion), which has won the hearts of so many romantic souls, men and women alike, her diary redefines reading and writing in gendered terms by insisting on an intimate *woman-to-woman* talk. Such feminine talk would render both the scholar-lover (indigenous male beauty) and the medieval European knight (imported Western ideal) superfluous to their existence. That this is a utopian desire is brought home by Yun's untimely death before she could read what is contained in those pages. In the end, Sophia's diary becomes a true record of tears that mourns the loss of a soul-mate.

What does this failure of *feminine talk* tell us about gender constructions in modern Chinese literature? How does it connect with texts that are not so ostensibly gendered? Does it allegorize an ideological tension between male and female writers? Finally, what is the role of criticism in the authorization of gendered or ungendered(?) readings? In my next chapter, I turn to these questions with a view to rethinking the relationship between literary criticism and China's nation-building efforts because, until this relationship is brought into our discussion, the gender question cannot be posed in a manner other than pinpointing instances of the *representation* of femininity or masculinity within individual texts, as if such representations could in and of themselves generate a sufficient intellectual ground for critical thinking. In other words, the issue of gender as it emerges in the course of this chapter needs to be reframed in terms of the broader interpretive context of modern Chinese literary discourse.

PART III

*Nation Building and
Culture Building*

CHAPTER 7

Literary Criticism as
a Discourse of Legitimation

In *Belated Modernity and Aesthetic Culture*, Gregory Jusdanis examines the circumstances attending the rise of national culture in modern Greece, suggesting that what happened there in the eighteenth and nineteenth centuries had much to do with the elites' desire to see Greece integrated with more advanced European nations and to become Westernized and modernized themselves.

> For them modernity and the West were synonymous. They too generalized from the European situation in their hopes to achieve economic, social, and political union according to European paradigms. The Greek case indicates that the dichotomous thinking underlying the whole argument for Third World modernization has been present right from the beginning. The initial encounter with modernity launched Greek society on a cataract of ideological oppositions (East-West, traditional-modern, purist-demotic, classical-contemporary, ethnicity-state) which led to instability and sometimes violence. To resolve these tensions, if only in an imaginary way, another modern construct was imported, the autonomous aesthetic.[1]

By "the aesthetic," the author is referring to a domain of symbols and representations that determine the meaning of the national culture, as in the case of English-, French-, and German-speaking countries where literature is valorized as an effective means of socializing people into the symbolic and economic values of the bourgeoisie that begins to represent national values. These symbols and representations replaced the earlier ethno-religious identities in the Ottoman empire and acted as a source of legitimation for the new state by harmonizing local loyalties and linguistic variation in an imaginary realm. National unity was experienced discursively before it became a political reality.

Although Jusdanis's analysis sometimes veers toward sociological determinism in the manner of Benedict Anderson, whom he evokes in this book, it raises interesting questions as to how one might fruitfully approach the literary and cultural projects of a society that finds itself "belated" in relation to modern metropolitan Europe and feels a need to alleviate the burden of its ancient heritage in order to catch up with the rest of the world.[2] What I find particularly relevant to the subject of this chapter is his perceptive discussion of literary criticism, canon making, and other related practices that constitute modern literature as a social institution in modern Greece. If all this sounds familiar to those of us who study twentieth-century Chinese literature, does it mean that China's experience of modernity is not unique after all? Not unlike their counterparts in modern Greece, India, Africa, and the Arab nations, Chinese intellectuals struggled to survive in an age of nation building and culture building in which they had little choice but to confront the powerful reality of the West and to come to terms with it, whether the so-called West impinges on their consciousness as a colonizer, semi-colonizer, humanist, evangelist, or cultural imperialist. This level of experience generates a surprisingly common vocabulary shared by otherwise hugely diverse cultures and societies. Terms such as "nation," "culture," "tradition," "history," and "modernity" are, therefore, not just translations of metropolitan European theories but, more important, mediated forms of expression that carry the burden of these people's experience of a totalized West.[3]

Literary criticism became a discourse of legitimation in China under these circumstances. It has provided writers and critics with a theoretical language(s) whereby they can work out their troubled relationship to the West and reflect simultaneously on their own condition of existence. To be sure, this function of theory has by no means been limited to literary discourse in modern Chinese history, but institutionalized criticism evolved into such a strange establishment in twentieth-century China that it frequently becomes the center stage for the polemical unfolding of cultural politics and national politics.[4] The beginnings of this modern critical practice can be traced to the writings of Chen Duxiu, Hu Shi, Guo Moruo, Qu Qiubai, and others, with its most exploded form of expression culminating in Mao Zedong's idiosyncratic interpretations of modern and classical literary texts with which he launched many of his political campaigns, including the Cultural Revolution. Throughout this century, the question of legitimation has lain at the heart of the Chinese elites' preoccupation with issues of culture, nationality, identity, the modern vernacular language, and the status of modern literature. Chapters 7 and 8 pursue this question at institutional levels by taking a focused look at the circumstances of literary criticism and canon making in the early Republican years. I am interested in the politics of inclusion and exclusion in each of these processes and in some of the vital consequences of the suppression of alternative narratives and counterdiscourses.

But even as I am intent on asking what was the legitimizing process that enabled *Zhongguo wenxue* (Chinese/national literature) to become what it is, the purpose of my critique is not simply to point an accusing finger at the degree of complicity between modern literary practice and the politics of nation building but to probe the *contradictory conditions* that enable such a practice to emerge and take shape. So rather than follow Jusdanis's more or less deterministic portrayal of how a national literature comes into being under the pressure of "belated" modernity, I shift the emphasis to the site of contradictory conditions and contending voices, such as gendered perspectives, in the complex process of the legitimation of the Chinese modern. The flip side of the legitimation question is therefore, Are there alternative narratives and histories alongside the dominant nationalist ideology that contest the familiar mainstream discourse about the nation, culture, and literature? That concern almost inevitably leads me, in Chapter 9, to reconsider the old debate on *guocui* (national essence) both in the late Qing period and in its subsequent re-emergence as a counterdiscourse to the New Culture movement in the post–May Fourth era. I hope the changing dynamics of this debate will illuminate a broad range of competing narratives and counterdiscourses that complicate our understanding of the meaning of national culture and translated modernity in the Republican period.[5]

National Literature and 'Weltliteratur'

In order to convey a sense of the relevance of the problem I am addressing here to the larger context of contemporary theoretical discourse on national literature, I begin with a few comments on Fredric Jameson's controversial article "Third-World Literature in the Era of Multinational Capitalism." Jameson remarks on the obsession of non-Western intellectuals with their nations; in his eyes, these intellectuals represent the "Third World" to the West, and their representation is more or less transparent, as, conversely, is his own presumed representation of "us" or the First World. This unexamined assumption about representation and authority on both sides enables him to arrive at the much disputed hypothesis of the essay; that is, all "Third World" texts are necessarily to be read as *national allegories*.[6] Aijaz Ahmad takes Jameson to task for constructing this problematic theory of the cognitive aesthetics of Third World literature and questions the imputed ground of knowledge that the author claims for the First and Second worlds while denying it to the Third World.

> As we come to the substance of what Jameson "describes," I find it significant that First and Second Worlds are defined in terms of their production systems (capitalism and socialism, respectively), whereas the third category—the Third World—is defined purely in terms of an "experience" of externally inserted phenomena. That which is constitutive of human history itself is present in the first two cases, absent in the third case. Ideologically this classification divides the world between those who make history and those who are mere objects of it.[7]

For instance, what is constitutive of a literary history that Jameson elides in his reading of Lu Xun's text? Are Third World texts to be reduced to pure "experience," whereas literatures of the First and Second worlds are capable of engineering more complicated ways of cultural production? In light of those questions, Jameson's hypothesis becomes meaningful and revealing, rather than simply false, because it plays into the nation-oriented and male-centered practice of literary criticism within the First World as well as the Third. The possibility never occurs to him, for instance, that it might well be the institution of literary criticism, rather than "Third World" literature, that canonizes a certain body of texts as "authentic national experience" and translates them as such to the West. Jameson's own reading of Lu Xun is to a large extent preconditioned by such established meanings surrounding Lu Xun's works within the modern Chinese literary canon. My point is not to dispute Jameson's particular readings of individual texts, but to draw attention to his First World blindness to the mediated reality of those texts. The mediating factor I have in mind is the institution of modern literary criticism, which is responsible for producing canons and texts in the domain of national culture as well as in relation to transnational relations of power. Such transnational relations of power are palpably present in Jameson's own "translation" of Third World literature to a First World academic audience. The result is a curious transnational coauthorship of nationalist discourse by Marxian critics in both worlds.

Perhaps contemporary appropriations of Third World literatures by First World theorists have something to do with the globalizing tendencies of multinational capitalism described so pointedly by Jameson. In many respects, however, they remind me of a nineteenth-century discourse about national literature and world literature that still survives in the contemporary critical vocabulary of both the First and Third worlds. Goethe's invention of *Weltliteratur* (1827) proposes a view of intercultural and international exchanges that aims to uncover the principle of "originary Phenomenon" (*Urphänomen*) or the Eternal One-ness through its many concrete manifestations. For the German poet, as Antoine Berman has noted, the notion of *Weltliteratur* does not refer to the totality of past and present literatures accessible to the encyclopedic gaze, or to the limited totality of masterpieces that have attained universal status and become the patrimony of so-called cultivated humanity. It is "a historical concept concerning the *modern* condition of the relation among diverse national or regional literatures."[8] *Weltliteratur*, therefore, does not signify the loss of individuality of national literatures; on the contrary, it constitutes the latter by admitting them to the hierarchical relation of a global system of economic and symbolic exchange. Not surprisingly, the appearance of world literature is contemporaneous with the appearance of a *Weltmarket*. Fritz Strich offers an illuminating commentary on the symbiosis of the literary and the economic, suggesting that *Weltliteratur* "is an intellectual barter, a traffic in ideas between peoples, a literary world market to which the nations bring their spiritual treasures for exchange. To illustrate his idea, Goethe himself was particularly fond of using such images taken from the world of trade and commerce."[9] The following passage from Goethe's famous *Conversations with Eckermann* in which the concept of *Weltliteratur* makes its first appearance supports Strich's observation.

> He who understands and studies the German language finds himself on the *market* where all nations offer their *merchandise*, he plays the interpreter in proportion as he *enriches* himself. And thus every translator should be considered a mediator striving to promote this universal spiritual *exchange* and taking it upon himself to make this generalized *trade* go forward. For whatever may be said of the inadequacy of translation, it remains one of the most essential and most worthy activities in the general traffic of the world. The Koran says: God has given to each people a prophet in their own language. In this way, each translator is a prophet to his people.[10]   (Italics added)

If Goethe's immediate concern was the essential role of translation for German culture, the economic tropes he used, however, point to the historical condition of a discourse that helped him envision a global situation in which German language and literature would become the "exchange market" par excellence of *Weltliteratur*. As, for example, he observed a little later, "It is the destiny of the German to raise himself to the state of representative for all world citizens." [11]

Interestingly, the notion of *Weltliteratur*, somewhat like today's "postmodernism," rode on the wings of global capitalism and imperialism to penetrate remote marketplaces outside Europe. From the beginning, the Chinese translation of the term, *shijie wenxue* (world literature), has assumed the enormous burden of explaining and justifying China's membership in the modern international community. [12] As it happens, Chinese writers do not share the optimistic outlook that characterizes Goethe's confidence about the German language and literature. Unlike the latter, who saw himself presiding over a *world market* wherein all nations offer their *merchandise* to him while he plays the translator magnanimously as he *enriches* himself, May Fourth writers turn to European literature largely with the intention of learning how to produce a national canon worthy of being accepted by world literature and being valued by the West. Such is the main thrust of Chen Duxiu's provocative challenge in his 1917 treatise "On Literary Revolution": "Pray, where is our Chinese Hugo, Zola, Goethe, Hauptmann, Dickens, or Wilde?" [13]

Yet, it would be inaccurate, if not downright absurd, to conclude that modern Chinese writers are merely infatuated with the dream of seeking a legitimate place for themselves in world literature. The Chinese translation of the notions of national literature and world literature must be considered along with a whole set of other competing theories and discourses—many of which are also imported from the outside—about what literature is and how it should function in modern Chinese society. These competing positions include the familiar theory of "art for art's sake," *rensheng pai* (humanist theory), *pingmin wenxue* (plebeian literature), class literature, and proletarian literature, among others. As I try to demonstrate, the dynamics surrounding the uses of these translated theories takes on different meanings at different junctures of national struggle.

For example, Zheng Boqi, a noted critic from the Creation Society, was the author of the first manifesto calling for the construction of a *guomin wenxue* (national literature) in the Republican period. His article, "Guomin wenxue lun" (On national literature), was serialized in three consecutive issues of *Creation Weekly* (nos. 33–35) in December 1923 and January 1924, in which he urged those who cared about the development of Chinese literature to treat this task as a top priority. The urgency of the matter, Zheng argued, lay in the general state of confusion and depression caused by the deteriorating domestic situation in the warlord years. [14]

Zheng reviewed and criticized several theories of art and literature influential at the time, especially those favored by fellow members of the Creation Society and members of the Literary Association. He singled out and criticized the theories of "art for art's sake," "humanism," "plebeian literature," and "class literature," as well as the notion of world literature, for failing to situate art and life "in the actuality of lived experience which, in today's world, is largely constitutive of the nation's experience and of the emotional life of national subjects." He suggested that the notion of national literature should either subsume all of these or simply replace them. But does not world literature always already implicate national literatures? Zheng's reply rests on the principle of realism: he relegated world literature to the realm of the unreal and phantasmal, in sharp contrast to Goethe, and focused on national literature as that of the real and now: "Ideally, we would all like to become world citizens and *cosmopolitans* [in English in original text] but, in reality, we are but Chinese and, moreover, *Han* Chinese."[15] Although Zheng tried to dissociate himself from the brand of nationalism known as *guojia zhuyi* (state nationalism), he was unable to devise a rigorous theoretical account of his own position except to claim "a love for the homeland" and "a consciousness of shared group identity."[16] It is true that man and woman and the young and the old are different, he asserted, "but the kind of emotional bondage that ties people to their homeland prevails at all times no matter who they are."[17] It is interesting that Zheng mentioned gender and age only to erase those marks of difference to allow for his totalizing notion of national literature. I will return to the gender politics of such critical theory shortly.

Neither Zheng Boqi nor other intellectuals of the time ever drew a clear distinction between *guojia zhuyi* (state nationalism) and *minzu zhuyi* (nationalism in a popular sense). The slippage thus generated covers a vast gray area of intellectual discourse in which different people and interest groups pick and choose from among different shades of this language to energize their own politics. Those who oppose the state allow themselves to speak for the individual, the people, or the nation against the state— some of this dynamic was analyzed in Chapter 3—but the ambiguity works the other way around as well, for the state can also take advantage of the situation by claiming to represent the people and the national interest.

A good example is the Nationalist government's unsuccessful attempt to promote what it called the *minzu zhuyi wenxue* (nationalistic literature) movement in 1930 to counter the rise of revolutionary literature. Several new journals were created expressly for that purpose, such as

Qianfeng zhoubao (Avant-garde weekly) and *Qianfeng yuebao* (Avant-garde monthly), which published works depicting heroic battle scenes and stirring examples of patriotism, written mostly by obscure people such as Wang Pingling, Zhu Yingpeng, Fu Yanchang, and Huang Zhenxia. In a perceptive reading of a story by Huang about young Chinese officers fighting against the warlords in northwest China, Lu Xun associated this brand of nationalism with colonialism and imperialism. In fact, Huang inadvertently suggested the association himself when he evoked the image of French colonialists combating the native Arabs in the African desert. Lu Xun commented bitterly:

> From the viewpoint of "a young officer" or "a nationalistic writer," the battle between the Chinese warlords seems to have less to do with the fact that the warlords are driving people of the same country to kill each other than with the illusion that both sides are foreigners, as if one country or nation is engaging another to the extent that the young officer would at night fantasize himself becoming a white man with paler skin and a higher nose, a heroic soldier from a Latin nation standing on the land of barbaric Africa. That explains why he would treat the common people as his enemy and must shoot every single one of them to death. As far as the French are concerned, their nationalism does not oblige them to love those Arabs in Africa. In this larger context, the Chinese warlords who become the claws of the imperialists go about poisoning and butchering the Chinese people, because they fantasize about being "French mercenaries." In a smaller context, one might say that the Chinese "nationalistic writers" who never stop identifying with their foreign masters have picked up this talk of "nationalism" because they, too, fantasize about being part of the Latin or Teutonic nations.[18]

Lu Xun's critique of nationalistic literature wonderfully captures the uncertain area contended by the Nationalists, warlords, imperialists, and radical intellectuals over the meaning of Chinese nationalism in the Republican era.[19] At the time the majority of leftist writers perceived themselves as the enemy of state nationalism and openly criticized the government.[20] Such conflicts escalated to violent clashes from time to time and frequently resulted in the government censorship of radical literature (see Chapter 8). But if the government's legitimate representation of the nation was to be disputed—indeed, this was the main ground on which the Communists attacked the Nationalists—how did national literature, such as the kind promoted by Zheng Boqi, fit in with these polarized constructions of nationalisms? How did it relate to the project of nation building and culture building, which, at different points in time, deeply concerned the state as well?

Guo Moruo, whose translations of Goethe's work earned him the dubious title of a Chinese Goethe among some of his contemporaries—a timely answer to Chen Duxiu's earlier challenge!—may not have shared Zheng Boqi's particular views on national literature, but his views on art and literature, which he saw as part of the nation-building function of the aesthetic in the modern world, were more theoretically informed than Zheng Boqi's patriotic approach. In a lecture delivered at Shanghai University entitled "Wenyi zhi shehui de shiming"(The social tasks of literature and art), he observed:

> Art is capable of unifying people's sentiments and of mobilizing them to work for a common goal. There is ample evidence to show that this is indeed the case, although I can't possibly cite every single instance here: Take Italy before the Unification. It was owing to Dante's *Divine Comedy* that the Unification movement was able to prevail. The same can be said of the impact that the works of Voltaire and Rousseau had on France before the French Revolution. According to Treitschke, Goethe's influence was not the least bit inferior to that of Bismarck on what was to be born as the German empire. And we all know that the great Russian Revolution was also pioneered by the devoted efforts of some men of letters.[21]

Guo saw the project of culture building as a necessary precursor to the larger event of nation building and emphasized literature as a particularly effective way of realizing that goal. Remarking on the chaos in China in the early 1920's and the general deterioration of artistic culture in the lives of ordinary folk, he called on artists and writers to forge sublime sentiments among the people and mobilize them for a greater cause. In this respect, he found the Chinese state and government totally lacking in commitment to culture building, compared with the kind of centralized leadership that most European governments provided for their countries by sponsoring artistic events, offering literary prizes, founding fine arts museums and national theaters, and the like.[22] Guo's argument about the function of artists and writers derived mainly from a comparative point of view in which Chinese national literature and culture could not come into their own without simultaneously making overt or covert references to the international arena, or *Weltliteratur*. Guo's views represent a major departure from Zheng Boqi's position.[23]

But what exactly constitutes Guo's perception of the dialectic of the global and the local? Even as he seemed to embrace the self-evident logic of nationalism and internationalism, he was not unaware of the egregiously unequal participation of China and the Western powers in the world market. As far as China was concerned, warlordism and compradore capitalism effectively blurred the boundaries between the local and the global or between Chinese and non-Chinese precisely where nationalism is supposed to do its work. Using a Leninist language typical of the leftist discourse of the time, Guo addressed this situation in a 1926 piece called "Wenyi jia de juewu" (Artists' consciousness).

> The Chinese revolution means a life and death struggle as far as those foreign capitalists and indigenous capitalists are concerned, because these people cannot do without each other and their interests are bound together. For them, there is no such a thing as homeland, because their country is the invisible kingdom of capitalism. As long as they can retain their own status as capitalists, they could not care less about what is going to happen to China or its people.[24]

I cannot resist reading this as an ironic reversal of the economic tropes (merchandise, spiritual exchange, the general traffic of the world) that Goethe earlier adopted in elaborating his concept of *Weltliteratur*. Where Goethe saw a happy scenario of universal exchange among different nations, Guo found intense class struggle across national boundaries as well as between East and West. This position led to his famous call for revolutionary literature in "Geming yu wenxue" (Revolution and literature): "Our national revolution is, by definition, world revolution, and at economic levels, the meaning of this revolution is determined by the class struggle waged between nations."[25] The theory of class struggle provided Guo with a flamboyant language of proletarian cosmopolitanism that was supposed to help redefine the function of modern Chinese literature in opposition to global capitalism and imperialism. But although the theory greatly illuminated contemporary issues and the special circumstances that Guo Moruo and his fellow writers confronted when he issued the call for revolutionary literature, it also encountered the impasse that typically confronts advocates of class theory, that is, the question of representation.

Indeed, who represents the oppressed and the proletariat? Zheng Boqi's earlier critique of "class literature" raised precisely this nagging issue:

> People who advocate class literature want to make sure that the third class [the middle class] speaks for the fourth class [the proletariat] and sings those whining tunes on its behalf. This is definitely wrong. I admit that conscientious members of the third class have a right to voice their protest against the inequalities suffered by the fourth class, but the thing to do is not step into their shoes and speak for them. The hardship endured by the fourth class is something that they alone know well and can speak for themselves, whereas the most that the other classes can do in terms of representing such

experiences would be like trying to scratch one's itchy leg from outside one's boot, if not like watching a fire burn at a safe distance on the other side of the river.[26]

Toward the end of Chapter 3, I briefly touch on the Chinese intellectuals' rejection of individualism as a "bourgeois value" in the mid-1920's and the early 1930's. The whole debate on *puluo wenxue* (proletarian literature) and *geming wenxue* (revolutionary literature) in this period centered on class consciousness and the question of representation. Although critics like Cheng Fangwu and Guo Moruo called on the "revolutionary intelligentsia" to negate themselves and acquire class consciousness, others raised honest doubts about the self-delusion inherent in progressive intellectuals' wanting to represent the experience of lower-class people.[27] Yu Dafu, a noted dissident in this group, strongly objected to the complacency of his fellow radicals. In 1927 he severed his ties with the Creation Society after a series of quarrels with Guo Moruo and others; a year later, he wrote:

> I do not deny the possibility that Chinese proletarian literature might become a reality and that the future of literature belongs to the proletariat. But neither can I ignore the fact that our generation was born in the late nineteenth century and has received a petty-bourgeois education, and there is no likelihood whatsoever that we can manage this future proletarian literature. I have already expressed these views in my little book called *Qiling ji*, and if you have read the book, you should know what I am talking about and I need not trouble to repeat myself here. In short, I vehemently reject the theory that someone who is not a worker himself should utilize and organize workers or that someone who is not a proletarian himself and only claims to possess a proletarian consciousness, though he might be the owner of several dozen vehicles, mansions, buildings, and is worth ten of millions of cash, can become a proletarian himself simply because he imagines that he has gotten a proletarian heart.[28]

Lu Xun, who often saw eye to eye with Yu Dafu on this issue, tackled the problem as early as 1924 in the story "New Year's Sacrifice," roughly at the same time as Zheng Boqi's article on national literature. As one of the most uncompromising depictions of the fateful encounter between a member of the upper class and a social underdog in modern Chinese fiction, the story stages the narrative problem of how to represent an otherwise unrepresentable experience. As Rey Chow points out in a perceptive analysis, Lu Xun's story "remarkably demonstrates that the most powerful formal effect of writing—that is, the effect of representation as *distancing*—never truly alleviates suffering but only compounds guilt."[29]

The suffering "other," Sister Xianglin, is impenetrable to the remorseful gaze of the narrator, whose sympathy for the unfortunate woman cannot in the end transcend the deixis of his own class-bound narrative. And it is no accident that "the effect of representation as *distancing*" is, at the same time, profoundly gender-bound as well.

Lu Xun was probably more aware of the problems of gender and class and *gender as class* than any of his contemporaries. But the majority of modern writers and critics, who are predominantly male, have largely shared a conspicuous blind spot when discussing the nation, class, world capitalism, culture, and representations. This blind spot has to do with the unmarked condition of their own gendered investment in those discourses, for it cannot be an accident that most of these writers have found the image of lower-class women more palatable than that of lower-class men in treating oppression and exploitation. Although some of their thoughts on representation are extremely insightful and may even be useful to today's critical discourse, such as subaltern studies, the problem with the gender-blind approach is that it often hid yet another level of oppression and exploitation that characterized the masculinist-nationalist discourse of the time. It is not as if these critics ignored the woman question or were unconcerned about women writers. In fact, no self-styled progressive thinker ever let an opportunity to offer an opinion on the so-called woman question slip by. And Lu Xun, Mao Dun, and Ye Shaojun, to name just a few, often went out of their way to help promising women writers publish their works. What I mean by the unmarked condition of gendered investment in some of their discourses has little to do with these men's intentions. Rather, it is a way of thinking and speaking that enables a politics of universal representation by erasing the marks of one's own gendered specificity and that of others'.

Readers will recall that Zheng Boqi erased gender difference from his notion of national literature and claimed that there are no distinctions in the emotional ties attaching people to their homeland between men and women, or the old and the young. Interestingly, he himself used gendered language in his subsequent descriptions of men and women: "When people are forced to leave their homes, women and children will cry profusely and soak their sleeves with tears. Tough-minded men, who despise such female and infantile weaknesses and would sooner leave than starve at home, might upon occasion also find themselves moved to tears when they return home from a trip."[30] The pejorative term he used for women and children (*furu zhi liu*) and the favorable ones for men (*mang naner* and *zhangfu*) are profoundly gendered, as is his trope of tears. Despite his argument to the contrary, his gendered language contradicts the neutrality of his project of national literature. As will be shown shortly, Xiao Hong's *Shen si chang* (Field of life and death) provides a powerful counterstatement to nationalist discourse on the questions of homeland, nation, woman, class, and literature.

Gender and Criticism

Is literary criticism gendered? In a recent study of Lu Yin and Bing Xin, Wendy Larson argues that "modern literature proposed a new subject position for women that was gender specific: that of woman writer. The situation for men writers was different, because although they also took on the task of representing the new self, it was a generalized, modernized self that was not specifically male." [31] The unmarking of the male gender as a gendered position pointed out here by Larson has the function of masking the true condition of gender politics in the universalizing discourse of modern literary criticism. This is the condition that concerns me most as I continue to ponder the meaning of national literature from a gendered point of view. The thrust of my critique in the present section centers not on Zheng Boqi's particular formulation of *guomin wenxue* discussed above but on the gendered situation of institutionalized criticism and related discursive practices in the nation-building process of the Republican era.

Rey Chow's discussion in *Women and Chinese Modernity* of previous scholarship on Mandarin Ducks and Butterfly fiction offers a powerful critique of male-centered literary criticism. Her oppositional approach in reading Butterfly stories and other texts successfully unravels the gendered politics of literary representation as well as of institutionalized criticism. She takes the previous studies of Butterfly fiction to task not because those critics have generally failed to notice or talk about female characters in their works—they have, abundantly—but because "the issue of women does not become for them a point of rupture, an opening into a different type of reading. Women may be mentioned, but only under the 'larger' headings of history, society, tradition, and the like." [32] Her observation is timely and important, because it shows us that feminist gender criticism is not just about real women and sexuality—critics whose work is not theoretically informed by feminist gender criticism invariably express an interest in the so-called images of women or women writers—but rather, as Joan W. Scott, whom Chow quotes here, would put it, it is a way of reading and intervention into the dominant theoretical and critical practices. As a means of formal analysis, this interventionist criticism deals "not only with gender but also with the power-invested processes of hierarchization and marginalization that are involved in readings of culture." [33]

The tropes of gender and sexuality dominate both Butterfly fiction and the May Fourth criticism of it. In *Mandarin Ducks and Butterflies*, Perry Link mentions an eye-catching advertisement that the publisher of Butterfly fiction or the so-called *Libai liu* (Saturday) school placed in a Shanghai newspaper in 1921 that reads: "I would rather not take a concubine / Than miss out once on *Saturday*." [34] Ye Shengtao, a prominent member of the Literary Association, protested the obscene language of the ads. "This is sheer insult," he said, "a universal insult. These people not only insult themselves, but they also insult literature and the readers as well." [35] Why did Ye Shengtao react so strongly toward something he would have ignored a few years before? What is at stake here? Could it be that the advertisement's unabashed equation of reading with sexual experience had the dangerous power to subvert the agenda of the new literature? [36]

The agenda in question was the reformist program of the recently organized Literary Association (1921), which devoted itself single-mindedly to the task of transforming Shanghai's consumers of low-brow fiction to readers of serious works of national literature. Much was thus at stake in the battle between the reformed *Short Story Magazine* and *Saturday* in terms of readership, gender politics, ideology, and nation building. Interestingly, the gendered construction of Butterfly fiction as *literary prostitution* began not with its opponents, as is commonly alleged, but with its own sexual politics. The logic of entertainment consumption that enabled the equation of a concubine and a Butterfly novel signals a kind of ideological construction of femininity different from that of the Literary Association, but no less problematic. Lu Xun, for example, ridiculed this trope of femininity and prostitution in writing about Butterfly fiction.

> Novels about talented scholars and beautiful maidens prevailed for a good number of years, until recently the talented scholar made the new discovery that the beautiful maidens prostitute themselves not because they are attracted to his talent but because they love his money. Of course, since it is totally unacceptable for them to be enamored of his money, the scholar racks his brains for all kinds of tricks to outsmart these women so that he can take advantage of the situation rather than be defeated by them. As a result, novels that depict these clever tricks begin to sell well, and readers are supposed to take them as textbooks for womanizing-ology. The hero in those novels is no longer a scholar-nerd, but a scholar-lecher superstar who gets the upper hand over those prostitutes. [37]

Turning on the trope of prostitution, Lu Xun's reading of the Butterfly plot seeks to unmask the gender politics of this literature. Unlike Mao Dun and other critics who denounced Butterfly literature primarily for its vulgarity and emphasis on amusement, Lu Xun raises the objection that this literature invests masculinity in money and men's purchasing power while identifying femininity with prostitution. That leads me to reconsider Rey Chow's strategic endorsement of *femininity* as the positive hallmark of Butterfly fiction.[38] Lu Xun's reading, which one may or may not accept, demands that we examine the gender politics of Butterfly fiction not only by reading it against its opponents, but also by viewing it in terms of the possible relation of complicity between the two. The complicity resides precisely in the free circulation of the trope of *femininity as prostitution* between Butterfly texts and the language of leftist critics. In my view, our task is not to accept the femininity of Butterfly fiction as such but to dismantle its fundamental gender politics, so that it becomes possible for us to read both May Fourth criticism and Butterfly fiction as masculine constructions of femininity. As I suggested earlier, a gendered reading does not seek to reduce a text to femininity or masculinity, much less to woman or man, nor is it a matter of deciding *a priori* what femininity is or should be, be it posed as a problem of essence or a constructed identity. To me, a more fruitful approach is to delve into specific historical formations and practices that allow "femininity" or "masculinity" to enter the changing field of meaning *in relation* to other discursive constructs. In other words, it is only *with reference to the performability of such relations* that a particular construction of "femininity" or "masculinity" becomes meaningful in its context.[39]

Apart from drawing attention to the levels of complicity between Butterfly writers and their critics, Lu Xun's reading of Butterfly fiction also invites a contrastive look at the construction of masculinity and femininity by the liberal and leftist advocates of new literature. For example, in the project of nation building and culture building endorsed equally by the Literary Association and radical leftists of the time, femininity and masculinity were constructed not so much in terms of men's purchasing power and women's prostitution as in terms of a different set of values understood as masculine, namely, those of nationalist ideology. Instead of prostitution, rape, with its usual association with female sexuality and femininity, becomes one of the most commonly used tropes in national literature and anti-imperialist propaganda. But, as my analysis will show, this trope is handled differently by male and female writers, and the discrepancy along gender lines is often surprisingly consistent. At issue is not the portrayal of the real cases of Japanese atrocities and the hideous crimes committed against Chinese women, but the question of how Chinese men and women writers choose to interpret such acts of sexual violence differently in the context of nationalist struggle. The difference in their interpretation says a great deal about how gender participates in nationalist discourses.

Take the male writer Xiao Jun's novel *Village in August* (1935). One of its plot lines is a story about a peasant widow named Li Qisao. This woman suffers the horrible fate of losing her husband, lover, and child to the war and, on top of all her bereavements, is raped by a Japanese soldier. As a rape victim, she joins the ranks of many other rape victims portrayed by male writers whose tales are supposed to inspire average Chinese men and women to follow the path of revolution. As a sign of symbolic exchange, however, her female body is displaced by a nationalist agenda and denied the meaning of its specifically female experience, for the nation decides all the meanings for it: China as woman is being violated by the Japanese rapist.[40] Since the nation itself is at stake, the crime of rape does not acquire meaning until it is committed by foreign intruders. But as one of the guerrilla fighters in *Village in August* inadvertently reveals, nationalist revolution is gendered as male, although women are also asked to participate in it:

> "Revolution? It means exterminating all those parasites that have lorded it over us since our ancestor's days. It means driving away all the Japanese soldiers that are now occupying Manchuria so that we will have our own land to farm. We won't have to pay the excise tax to feed those blood-sucking parasites. You understand? Let me give you an example. Before the revolution, one rich guy alone has three, five, eight, or even ten wives, whereas you, in your thirties, cannot even afford a single one. *After the revolution, you can get a wife without having to pay a penny!*"[41]   (Italics added)

The gender politics of national revolution encountered strong resistance in the works of some women writers. Both Ding Ling and Xiao Hong protested the subjugation of women by the new forms of patriarchy brought on by national revolution.[42] Tani Barlow's brilliant analysis of Ding Ling's "Wo zai Xiacun de shihou" (When I was in Xia Village) helps illuminate the conflict between woman and nationalist discourse during the anti-Japanese resistance. The protagonist Zhenzhen, a victim of rape by Japanese soldiers, is recruited by the resistance forces to work as a spy. Her body thus becomes the symbolic battleground on which military men from the opposite camps engage with each other in their bid for sovereignty. In the eyes of her fellow villagers, she becomes a whore, whereas to the revolutionary fighters she is a heroine who sacrifices her body for the noble cause of the nation. Yet, neither reading makes sense to Zhenzhen herself, who refuses to be read as a rape victim and, in the end, decides to leave her native village in pursuit of education, knowledge, and the right to define the meaning of her own existence. In short, the story refuses to let the trope of rape signify the victimization of China.[43]

Like Ding's Ling's story, Xiao Hong's *Field of Life and Death* (1935) radically subverts the trope of the raped woman in nationalist discourse. As if in deliberate parody of Xiao Jun's novel—despite the fact that the two writers lived together as lovers—the rape that occurs in Xiao Hong's work, which is also set on the eve of the Anti-Japanese War, is committed by a Chinese man instead of a Japanese soldier. This is worth pondering. Xiao Hong's novel situates the problem of national identity at the intersection of the female body and nationalist discourse and challenges the nationalist hold over the meaning and ownership of that body. Unlike the male peasants, the peasant woman Golden Bough, for example, never succeeds in becoming a national subject, because the physical experience she is forced to undergo at the hands of her husband and the rapist contradicts the national identity that the presence of the Japanese imposes on her. Xiao Hong's refusal to sublimate or displace the female body leads to a gendered position that intervenes in a nationalist discourse the novel seemingly establishes but in actuality subverts. Nationalism comes across as a profoundly patriarchal ideology that grants subject positions to men who fight over territory, possession, and the right to dominate. The women in this novel, being themselves possessed by men, do not automatically share the male-centered sense of territory.

The Female Body and the Nationalist Discourse: *'The Field of Life and Death'*

Xiao Hong, a woman writer from Manchuria, lived and suffered in a time of national crises. She wrote several novels and numerous short stories and essays in response to those crises until her life was prematurely cut short in 1942.[44] As a novelist, she has met with more fortunate treatment at the hands of literary historians than some other women such as Ling Shuhua, Zhang Ailing, and Lu Yin, who, until recently, have been more or less marginalized in Chinese literature. This is partly due to the enduring influence of Lu Xun, who mentored Xiao Hong and spoke

highly of her work in the 1930's and also because, in the eyes of the majority of male critics, she did not confine herself to the "triviality" of
women's lives but reached out to broader themes of national survival and
anti-imperialist struggle. This salutary reading secures a canonical place
for Xiao Hong in modern Chinese literature, however low that place may
be, but at the cost of erasing the profound tensions in her thinking of
woman and nation.

My goal in discussing her is not to elevate the canonical status of
this writer but to critique the practice of a nation-oriented and male-
dominated literary criticism responsible for the appropriation of her work
for nationalist purposes. I confess that I am uncomfortable with the entitlement discourse that takes canonization as everyone's birthright. Discourses on rights and entitlement incapacitate critical thinking as often as
they enable it. It is here that my feminist approach departs from some of
the revisionary feminist criticisms that concentrate mainly on women's
absence from or marginalization in established literary canons. The importance of revisionary criticism should, of course, continue to be recognized, but the rhetoric of center and margin cannot by itself generate rigorous critical thinking. One cannot but face the fact that some people are
historically relegated to the margins whereas others can willfully choose
their marginal position, the better to launch attacks at the center.[45] The
inclusion of a previously marginalized writer in literary history, for instance, may make the canon look a little different from before and even
improve it, but does it necessarily challenge the idea of canonization itself,
or help strengthen the canon by giving it a more liberal, pluralistic appearance? Spivak may be too optimistic when she states: "We are attempting
not merely to enlarge the canon with a counter-canon but to dethrone canonical *method*," but I find the critical insight behind her statement worth
keeping in mind.[46]

Xiao Hong's struggle with nationalist discourse in her life and work
can be brought to bear fruitfully on the gendered condition of modern
Chinese criticism and its nationalist ideology. Ever since *The Field of Life
and Death* was published as part of the Slave Society Series (along with
Ye Zi's *Fengshou* [Harvest] and Xiao Jun's *Village in August*), sponsored by
Lu Xun, its reception and criticism have been dominated by a nationalist reading that seeks to erase her ambivalence about nationalism and
her subversion of the male appropriation of the female body.[47] The majority of critics celebrate the work as a national allegory, a quintessential
anti-imperialist novel imbued with patriotic spirit. Consequently one can
hardly read Xiao Hong today without an awareness of the highly devel-

oped, institutionalized, male-centered critical tradition that has tried to frame and determine the meaning of her work. Yet, such gendered politics in the practice of literary criticism has generally escaped the notice of critics and scholars.[48]

The interpretation of Xiao Hong's novel as a national allegory was initially framed by the views of Hu Feng and Lu Xun, each of whom contributed an epilogue and a preface to the first edition. As editor of the Slave Society Series, Hu Feng wrote his epilogue to praise the anti-Japanese spirit of the book and the awakening of the Chinese peasantry to nationalism. "These ant-like, ignorant men and women, sad but resolute, stood on the front line of the sacred war of nationalism," he said. "Once they were like ants, living in order to die. Now they were titans, dying in order to live."[49] Lu Xun did not force the epithet "nationalism" onto the novel in his much quoted "Preface," but he too obscured the fact that Xiao Hong's novel is more about the lives of rural women than "the tenacity of the people of northern China in their struggle for survival and resistance to death."[50] The field of *sheng* (birth, life) and *si* (death), as I demonstrate below, represents primarily the experience of the female body; specifically, two areas of experience relating to peasant women: childbearing and death from suicide, sickness, or abuse. Lu Xun's own national agenda, which emerges clearly in his allusions to the rumor of war in Shanghai's Zhabei district and to places such as Harbin, or the British and French Concessions, is responsible for the blind spot in his reading.

In my analysis of *The Field of Life and Death*, I concentrate on the body of peasant woman as an important site of contestatory meanings. Such a reading was in part suggested by the controversy over the cover design of the novel the author herself made in 1935, which consists of a black patch containing the title superimposed on a deep crimson background (see Fig. 3). Needless to say, critics have had a hard time pinning down the exact meaning of the drawing. Some say that the black shadow suggests an old fortress, and the crimson the blood of the people of Manchuria who died during the war of resistance. Others hold that the black area represents the map of Japanese-occupied Manchuria.[51] In an interesting article on Xiao Hong as an artist, Liu Fuchen points out that the black shadow is the profile of a woman's head and suggests that the diagonal line across the cover symbolizes the divided territory of China. He reads the uplifted face of the peasant woman as well as the firm lines of her neck and mouth as representing the anger and strength of the people of Manchuria in their struggle against the Japanese.[52] But Liu fails to explain why Xiao Hong uses a female head instead of a male head to represent the

FIG. 3. Xiao Hong's cover design for the 1935 edition of her *Field of Life and Death*

people of Manchuria. Having hinted at a possible reading from a gendered point of view, he immediately displaces it with nationalist interpretation. If one takes the black shadow as representing a female head coinciding with (and parodying) the map of Manchuria, the diagonal line across the page may very well be interpreted as a symbol of the split national subject as well as the divided territory of China. As for the conjecture that the crimson may signify the color of the blood shed by the people of Manchuria, there is also strong evidence within the text that it refers to women's blood specifically, because the female body in this novel is always linked with bleeding, injury, deformation, or death, be it from childbirth, beatings, sickness, or suicide. The omnipresence of the female body casts an ominous shadow over nationalist discourse and insists on assigning its idiosyncratic meanings to the life-and-death struggle in rural Manchuria. Of course, one need not accept any of these readings, but it is worth noting that the controversy surrounding the cover design calls into question the authority of a single nationalist interpretation that has heretofore prevailed in Xiao Hong scholarship and thus opens up a space for alternative readings.

What does the female body have to do with nationalism? Critics have often wondered about the fact that Xiao Hong's "anti-Japanese novel" is filled with details about village women's lives and does not begin to deal with the Japanese invasion until the last few chapters. Two Chinese women critics, Meng Yue and Dai Jinhua, suggest in *Fuchu lishi dibiao* (Emerging from the horizon of history) that the meaning of life and death in this novel should be perceived in terms of the experience of the female body, although their reading does not directly engage the legacy of nationalist critical discourse.[53] In what follows, I intend to push their reading further by showing that the female body provides the critical angle for viewing the rise and fall of the nation and not vice versa.

The boundary of the female body in this novel is chiefly defined by rural women's experience of childbirth, disease, sexuality, aging, and death. Despite the apparent allusion to the Buddhist concept of *samsara* in *sheng* (birth, life) and *si* (death), the novel does not espouse the Buddhist faith of some of its characters; on the contrary, it stresses the plight of the female body, locating the meaning of its suffering in the immediate socio-economic context of this world rather than in a world of *karma*. Death, for example, is a horrible disintegration of the body rather than the ultimate escape from the distresses of life. Poverty, ignorance, class exploitation, imperialism, and the patriarchy all conspire to reduce the rural people, especially women, to no more than an animalistic existence.

Women give birth excessively in this novel, but fertility is cast in a strikingly negative light. The excess of human lives aggravates poverty in this rural village; worse still, in the act of bringing forth new life, the female body is severely punished. As the narrator describes this uniquely female world, her language is punctuated alternately with compassion for the agonizing body of the mother and bitter mockery of the disaster inflicted by human instinct to continue the species. Her compassion shines forth in a description of a woman's labor: "The naked woman could no longer even crawl; she was unable to muster the final burst of effort in this moment of *sheng* [birth, life] and *si* [death]."[54] Besides Fifth Sister's elder sister, three more village women give birth in a single chapter. Golden Bough's labor is made more difficult because her husband demanded sex the night before. With the help of Mother Wang, she gives birth to a baby daughter, who dies after being dashed to the ground by her own father a month later. Second Aunt Li has a miscarriage that nearly costs her her own life. Even the foolish wife of Two-and-a-half Li struggles in labor. The birth of her baby is followed by a sow giving birth outside the window at the foot of the wall. The narrator's insistence on drawing the parallel between animals and humans in sexuality and childbirth some-times verges on sarcasm. "Cows and horses in their ignorance plant the seeds of their own suffering. At night as the people sat in the cool breeze, they could hear odd noises coming from the stable or cowshed. A bull that was probably battling for its mate crashed out of the shed, breaking the fence. . . . In the village, folks and beasts busied themselves at *sheng* and *si*" (pp. 74; 56).

If life and childbirth are horrible realities for women, death is hardly a desirable alternative. Innumerable deaths from infanticide, fatal diseases, war, and epidemics occur in the space of this short novel. Although men also die, the female sex seems to succumb to death more often. In most of those cases, the narrator individualizes the female victim for us. Among those victims are, for instance, Mother Wang's three-year old daughter, Xiao Zhong, and her grown-up daughter, the Feng girl; Golden Bough's little daughter, who is murdered by her own father; an old woman from North Village who hangs herself together with her granddaughter; the beautiful Yueying, who dies of paralysis and neglect; and, finally, Two-and-a-half Li's wife and her child, who die during the war. The few deaths of men are meaningful only inasmuch as they affect the lives of the women. When Golden Bough becomes a widow and is forced to make her own living, we are not told when, where, why, or how her husband died, whereas the manner of women's deaths, such as Mother Wang's suicide, receive extended treatment. Two women attempt suicide in this novel, Mother Wang before the Japanese occupation and the old woman from North Village after that. The reason is one and the same; namely, the loss of a beloved son. Instead of elaborating on Mother Wang's inner sorrow when she hears the news of her son's execution by the government, the narrator plunges directly into a description of the physical aspects of her suicide and the deformation of her body, giving such details as the froth on her black lips, her bloated stomach and chest, her terrifying howling, and the ghostly stare of her eyes. Mother Wang's attempted suicide is presented neither as a heroic act nor as social protest. It is the horrifying deformation of the body that is emphasized.

Since rural women live intensely with their bodies, the transformation of the body in sickness is no less shocking than its deformation in death. Yueying was once a beauty. After she becomes paralyzed, her husband begins to lose patience and decides to give her up completely. He refuses to give her water and, to torture her further, places a pile of bricks on her bed as a prop for her weak body. When village women come to offer their help, they discover that the poor woman has been so neglected that the lower part of her body is soaked with excrement and that the former beauty has been reduced to a horrible freak:

> The whites of her eyes had turned greenish, and so had her straight front teeth. Her frizzled hair stuck close to her scalp. She looked like a sick cat, abandoned and without hope. . . . With her legs like two white bamboo poles stretched out before her, her skeleton formed a right angle with the *kang*. It was a human shape composed of nothing but threads. Only the head was broader; it sat on the torso like a lantern atop a pole. (pp. 51–52; *40*)

Yueying's bottom is so rotten that it has turned into caves for maggots. Little white crawling creatures drop on Mother Wang's arms as she tries to wipe the sick woman's buttocks. Yueying dies in the end, but not until after witnessing the horrible decomposition of her body in the mirror.

Finally, the precariousness of the female body in this novel lies in rural women's experience of sexuality, which is always connected with pregnancy. Compared with the male body, the female body signifies a woman's lack of control over her destiny, not so much because sexual desire is an animal instinct as because patriarchy determines the meaning of desire and chastity and hence the female body serves the interest of men. Golden Bough finds herself in deep trouble when she becomes pregnant before marriage, and she begins to fear and loathe her body:

> Golden Bough was in torment. Her stomach had become a hideous monstrosity. She felt a hard object inside, which, when she pressed hard on it, became even more apparent. After she was certain that she was pregnant, her heart shuddered as though it were retching. She was seized with terror. When two butterflies wondrously alighted one on top of the other on her knees, she only stared at the two copulating insects and did not brush them off. Golden Bough seemed to have become a scarecrow in a rice field. (pp. 30; *25*)

It is common for a woman to perceive literal alterations of the boundaries of her body such as violence, disease, and maiming as extreme threats to selfhood. Pregnancy, however, occupies a rather ambiguous domain of signification in which meaning must be decided according to the social codes that govern a woman's behavior by regulating her body. In this instance, Golden Bough experiences her premarital pregnancy as a bodily deformation (monstrosity) and her illegal fetus as an alien intruder. The free copulation of the butterflies brings out, by way of contrast, the impasse a woman faces in human society: the patriarchy desires her body, demands her chastity, and punishes her for transgressive acts. Like a scarecrow, her body is emptied of its contents and reduced to a signifier of predetermined functions. This gendered knowledge is transmitted to the daughter through the mother, who forbids Golden Bough to go near the edge of the river, where men seduce women: " 'The wife of Fufa, didn't she come to ruin at the edge of the river? Even the children in the village were talking about it. Ai! . . . What kind of woman is that? Afterwards she had to marry Fufa. Her mother suffered such terrible shame that she couldn't hold her head up among the villagers any more' " (pp. 25; 21). It turns out that not only does Golden Bough tread the path of Fufa's wife, but she is seduced by none other than Fufa's nephew Chengye. Like Fufa before him, Chengye does not care much for the woman he seduces. Whenever they meet, he simply pulls her down to the ground and pounces on her body. He neither kisses her nor says words of love; rather, he is driven by a basic desire. Their marriage, arranged by Golden Bough's mother, who wants to cover up the daughter's shame, repeats the ancient story of conjugal hostility in the patriarchal Chinese family. The husband curses the wife: "You lazy wife, what were you doing during the day?" and it does not take long for the wife to learn how to curse a husband and conclude that "men are heartless human beings, a feeling shared by the rest of the village women" (pp. 73; 55).

Among the rural women treated in this novel, Mother Wang deserves special attention, for she commands the respect of the village women and, to some extent, that of her own husband for possessing unusual wisdom, verbal power, courage, and an independent mind. In her youth, she left the home of her first husband permanently in protest against his physical abuse. Her present husband, Zhao San, is her third. The village women often gather in her home and absorb her stories. Mother Wang's profound knowledge about *sheng* and *si* comes from personal experience of love, loss, poverty, and sorrow. When she tells stories, she speaks as an authority on women's "history," and her audience, all women, are awestruck by her manner and voice. Since Chinese women are denied subject positions in male-centered historiographies, storytelling or gossip becomes the only means of transmitting women's unique knowledge about life and death among themselves. One of the stories Mother Wang tells in the novel concerns the fatal fall of her three-year-old daughter. As she speaks, a streak of lightning appears in the sky, and the speaker is suddenly transformed into a disembodied voice.

> "Ah... I threw her in the haystack, with blood flowing all over the hay. Her little hand was trembling and blood was trickling from her nostrils and her mouth. It was like her throat had been cut. I could still hear a rumbling in her stomach. It was like a puppy run over by a cart. I've seen that happen with my own eyes. I've seen everything. . . .
> "My child's name was Xiao Zhong. For several nights I suffered. I couldn't sleep. What was all that wheat worth? From then on, grains of wheat didn't matter much to me. Even now, nothing matters to me. I was only twenty then." (pp. 11–12; *11–12*)

From her intimate experience of death, which is so vividly filled with bleeding nostrils, mouths, throats, hands and stomachs, Mother Wang learns about the precariousness of the human body. It is this knowledge that gives her a strong character and a compassionate heart as she goes about assisting the village women in childbirth, nursing them in sickness, or even walking an old mare to the slaughterhouse. But Mother Wang's plight as a woman in the patriarchal society is also the cause of her ultimate rejection of female identity. After her attempted suicide fails, she sets out to teach her daughter to be a woman warrior in order to avenge the death of her son. On the arrival of the Japanese in Manchuria, Mother Wang joins men in their struggle for national survival. It is no surprise that, from then to the end of the novel, her authority dwindles in proportion to the rising significance of the village males as nationalist fighters.

This brings us to Xiao Hong's position on nationalism, which Hu Feng emphasized in his epilogue. If we compare her treatment of rural life prior to the Japanese invasion with that of Xiao Jun in *Village in August*, the ambivalence of her attitude immediately comes into focus. For Xiao Jun, rural life is not at all sordid. The following description from *Village in August* is typical: "He [Little Red Face] recalled the peaceful days in his past. Would he once again feel free to enjoy his plow and his pipe as before? How soon would all this happen? When that wonderful day came about, was it true that everyone of those who had bullied him and every Japanese who had taken his land would have been shot and killed?"[55] The discrepancy between the visions of the two authors is clearly attributable to the role that gender plays in each novel. Xiao Jun's work concentrates on the soldiers' life and on their skirmishes against the Japanese enemy, whereas Xiao Hong deals primarily with the life of women whose oppression makes it difficult to idealize the patriarchal society before or after the Japanese occupation. Whatever happens to the nation, the female body always suffers the most.

The final chapters of her novel make it clear that national identity is largely a male prerogative; it allows the village men to acquire national consciousness and preach the new gospel to their women despite their own lowly status in society. Mother Wang's husband, Zhao San, for example, shows great enthusiasm for nationalist propaganda and particularly enjoys preaching to the widows.

> That night old Zhao San came home very late. He had been talking to everyone he met about the loss of the country, about saving the country, about volunteer armies and revolutionary armies... all these strange-sounding terms. . . . He roused his son from his slumber and, with pride, told him about the propaganda work he had been doing: how the widow in the east village had sent her children back to her mother's house so that she could join the volunteer army, and how the young men were gathering together. The old man was acting like an official in a magistrate's office, swaying from side to side as he spoke. His heart was also swaying, and his soul was taking giant strides. (pp. 114–15; *82–83*)

Zhao San's propaganda work elevates his worth in his own eyes, for nationalism enables the poor village males to transcend their class status by giving them a new identity. This empowered identity, however, does not seem so different from that of an "official in a magistrate's office" because it reproduces the old patriarchal relation by putting men in the subject position of a new discourse of power. Interestingly enough, women who join the army, all of whom are widows, must reject their female identity in a suicidal manner to become Chinese and fight for the nation. With men it is a different matter. Not only does nationalism give them a new sense of identity, but it enhances their manhood at the same time. Li Qingshan's speech, delivered during a solemn occasion at which the village people pledge their loyalty to the nation shortly before taking off on an expeditionary journey, indicates that nationalist discourse is unequivocally gendered: " 'Brothers, what day is today? Do you know? Today is the day we dare to die. . . . It is decided . . . even if all our heads swing from the tops of the trees throughout the village, we shall not flinch, right? Isn't that right, brothers?' " (pp. 120; *87*). When the widows respond to the call, they immediately lose their gender and join the ranks of the brothers. Ironically, they are the first to shout: "Yes, even if we are cut into a million pieces!" (ibid.). One can hardly miss the familiar tone of the tragic Qiu Jin in their vows.[56]

Chapter 13 represents the height of anti-Japanese sentiment in the novel. Instead of endorsing nationalism, it demonstrates how the national subject came into being. In the past, Zhao San was merely the head of a rural household like the rest of the rural men, and he was also a coward who dared not even defy his landlord. He "had not understood what a nation was. In prior days he could even have forgotten his own nationality" (pp. 119–20; *86*). It is through a discourse—nationalist discourse—that Zhao (re)constitutes himself as a national subject and is reborn. Speaking to the volunteer fighters, he pours out torrents of nationalist emotions.

> "The nation... the nation is lost! I... I am old, too. You are still young, you go and save the nation! My old bones are useless! I'm an old nationless slave, and I'll never see you rip up the Japanese flag with my own eyes. Wait until I'm buried... then plant the Chinese flag over my grave, for I am a Chinese!... I want a Chinese flag over my grave, for I am a Chinese!... I want a Chinese flag. I don't want to be a nationless slave. Alive I am Chinese, and when I'm dead, I'll be a Chinese ghost... not a nation... nationless slave." (pp. 121; *87*)

This is characteristic of all nationalist discourses in which the individual assumes a subject position ("I," "I am," etc.) in a homogeneous space ("Chinese," "nation") and thereby acquires a new identity and finds a new purpose in life ("save the nation"). Even Two-and-a-half Li, who cannot live without his goat, ends up joining the revolution.

Unlike other men, Two-and-a-half Li is a cripple and is symbolically castrated from his own sex; moreover, his unusual attachment to an animal marks him out as someone closer to women in identity than men. Just like Mother Wang, who caresses and talks to her mare, Two-and-a-half Li treats his goat like a family member. It is his "feminine" character that prevents him from joining the national cause at the outset. After the assembly persuades him to offer his goat for the sacrificial ritual, he manages to find a rooster somewhere in order to save his beloved goat from the blade. "He was the only person who did not take the oath. He did not seem particularly distressed about the fate of the nation as he led the goat home. Everyone's eyes, especially old Zhao San's, angrily followed his departure. 'You crippled old thing. Don't you want to go on living?' "(p. 121–22; *88*). After the death of his wife and child, however, his "masculine" character begins to assert itself, and the novel closes with

Two-and-a-half Li leaving home in search of the People's Revolutionary Army. His transformation from a self-absorbed peasant to a national subject once again demonstrates that the stakes involved in becoming a national subject are very different for men and women. The patriarchy measures a man's power in terms of his possessions: wife, children, livelihood, if not in nobler forms of property. It is the loss of those possessions that turns Two-and-a-half Li against Japanese imperialism. Nationalist discourse enables this man to gain in manhood by giving him a new subject position. Compared with him, a woman, who has lost her husband, is left without many resources. The novel offers two grim possibilities for a rural widow: she either rejects her female identity, joins the ranks of the "brothers" without the comfort of the elevated sense of manhood that real brothers enjoy, and gets herself killed like Mother Wang's daughter, or, like Golden Bough, subjects herself to rape and exploitation in order to survive.

After the death of her brutish husband, Golden Bough goes to the city of Harbin to earn money as a seamstress. Afraid of being caught by the Japanese, she smears her face with dust until she looks like an old, ugly beggar woman. On the road, she encounters a troop of Japanese soldiers who stop her but let her go unharmed after they see her appearance. Having escaped from the Japanese, Golden Bough falls into the hands of a Chinese man in the city. As a seamstress she must visit the homes of her clients, and during one of those visits she is raped. This experience gives her a new perspective on her life as a woman; when Mother Wang discourses on the atrocities committed by Japanese soldiers, such as slitting the bellies of pregnant women and killing innocent babies: "Golden Bough snorted: 'I used to hate men only; now I hate the Japanese instead.' She finally reached the nadir of personal grief: 'Perhaps I hate the Chinese as well? Then there is nothing else for me to hate.' It seemed that Mother Wang's knowledge was no longer the equal of Golden Bough's" (pp. 140; 100). Golden Bough's knowledge is earned at the expense of her body. In order to protect her body from men, she decides to become a nun. To her disappointment, the Buddhist temple in the village has long been abandoned, and she is left with no hope for the future. The ending of the novel presents a sharp contrast between a homeless Golden Bough and a revolutionary Two-and-a-half Li.

It is interesting that, in spite of all the evidence to the contrary, nationalist interpretation of this novel is the rule rather than an exception in Xiao Hong scholarship. In his preface to one of Xiao's later novels, *Tales of Hulan River*, Mao Dun, a leading critic of the time, also judged the author on a basis of her commitment to the national cause, although his opinion ran counter to that of Hu Feng. In short, he criticized Xiao Hong for *not* participating in the national struggle. Recalling the last moment of her life in Hong Kong, Mao said:

> It is hard to understand how a woman with her high ideals, who had struggled against reaction, could "hibernate" in such stirring times as the years just before and after 1940. A friend of hers, trying to explain her frustration and apathy, ascribed them to a series of emotional shocks which confined this poet richer in feeling than intellect within the small circle of her private life. (Although she condemned that circle, some inertia kept her from breaking boldly with it.) She was cut off completely from the tremendous *life* and *death* struggle being waged outside. As a result, although her high principles made her frown on the activities of the intellectuals of her class and regard them as futile talk, she would not plunge into the laboring masses of workers and peasants or change her life radically. Inevitably, then, she was frustrated and lonely.[57]   (Italics added)

It is true Xiao Hong did not show the enthusiasm for the national cause with which Hu Feng credited her. As a matter of fact, she hardly involved herself in the antiwar propaganda organized by the Chinese Writers' Anti-aggression Association.[58] As a woman, denigrated as "richer in feeling than intellect" by Mao Dun, she was engaged in a different kind of struggle, a struggle that did not oblige her to share Mao's view of private and collective experience or, for that matter, male-centered notions of society, nation, and war. If, to the author of *The Field of Life and Death* and *Tales of Hulan River*, the meaning of "life" and "death" resides in the individual body, particularly the female body, more than in the rise and fall of a nation, then her lack of commitment to nationalism can hardly be construed a failure. It is not that Xiao Hong did not wish to resist Japanese aggression or feel attracted to the national cause. Her dilemma was that she had to face two enemies, rather than one: imperialism and patriarchy. The latter tended to reinvent itself in multifarious forms, and national revolution was no exception.

"As far as I am concerned," wrote Xiao Hong at the outbreak of the Anti-Japanese War: "it always comes down to the same thing: either riding to an alien place on the back of a donkey, or staying put in other people's home. I am never keen on the idea of homeland. Whenever people talk about home, I cannot help being moved, but I am perfectly aware that I had become 'homeless' even before the Japanese set their feet on the land." Her skepticism is directed at Xiao Jun, her lover, whose nationalist fervor struck her as a very male-dominated sentiment. Speaking in a woman's voice, she questioned his glorification of the homeland. When Xiao Jun mentioned the idea of returning to his Manchurian village after the war, she pondered: "But what about me. Would your family treat an outsider such as a *xifu* [daughter-in-law] equally well?"[59]

"My home was dreary," says Xiao Hong's narrator in a refrain in *Tales of Hulan River*. There are two temples in the narrator's home village, the Temple of the Patriarch and the Temple of the Immortal Matron—even the immortals are subject to gender discrimination. The clay idols in the Temple of the Patriarch are given stern and imposing features, whereas those in the Temple of the Immortal Matron look benign and submissive. We are told that the people who cast those clay idols are all men:

> It is obvious that for a man to beat a woman is a Heaven-ordained right, which also holds true for gods and demons alike. No wonder the idols in the Temple of the Immortal Matron have such obedient looks about them—this comes from having been beaten so often. It becomes apparent that obedience is not the exceptionally fine natural trait it has been thought to be, but rather the result of being beaten, or perhaps an invitation to receive beatings.[60]

Indeed, the reason that the author herself fled home at the age of twenty was that her father, who embodied the evils of the patriarchy in her eyes, tried to force her into an arranged marriage.[61] In "Chu dong" (Early winter), published along with the author's other familiar prose in the 1936 collection *Qiao* (Bridge), Xiao Hong's narrator expresses her firm resolution of never setting foot in her father's house again: "I will never think of going back to a home like that. My father and I are adamantly opposed to each other, and I simply cannot live on his charity."[62] This father figure haunted Xiao Hong throughout her short, stormy life as an exile in Qingdao, Shanghai, Tokyo, and many other places, until she died in Hong Kong in 1942.[63]

As I argued earlier, Xiao Hong is not one of those marginalized women writers who needs to be restored to literary history. On the contrary, that history itself must be subjected to critical examination through a re-reading of her writing in conjunction with the received interpretations. Indeed, the subcategory of women writers in modern Chinese criticism has itself been invented and legitimized in the name of a "national" literature that, however, fails to name its own gendered condition as male. The subcategory allows male critics to patronize women's writing and subsume it under the larger category of the nation in much the same way as the state deploys the category of *funü* for political mobilization. Such a gendered practice of literary criticism, I wish to empha-size, has been a major site for the production of nationalist discourse. Within this framework of knowledge, the long-standing practice of read-ing literary texts, traditional or modern, within a nation-oriented and male-dominated critical tradition is easily justified and simply cannot be brought into question.[64] Therefore, besides looking toward female writ-ing as a dissenting voice, I see the feminist interpretation of women's works as an act of intervention into the hegemonic practice of modern literary criticism. It is a way of saying that national literature, nation-oriented literary criticism, discipline, and institution must be opened up, interrogated, and radically rethought.

My next chapter turns to the problem of canon making itself. By exploring the history of how an obscure young editor from a small pub-lishing house succeeded in bringing out an authoritative anthology of modern Chinese literature, I hope to highlight some crucial moments and aspects of a literary history that have not received adequate attention in the previous scholarship on May Fourth literature.

CHAPTER 8

The Making of
the 'Compendium of Modern
Chinese Literature'

Lu Xun's favorite rendezvous between the late 1920's and his death in 1936 was a Japanese-language bookstore in the city of Shanghai, the Uchiyama Shoten (Neishan shudian, in Chinese).[1] The strong tie of friendship between the Chinese writer and the Japanese owner of the bookstore, Uchiyama Kanzō, is apparent in Lu Xun's letters and diaries.[2] Lu Xun regularly attended the reading sessions known as *mantan hui* (free-conversation meetings) organized by Uchiyama, and he organized three exhibitions of German and Russian woodcuts from his own and others' collections at the bookstore.[3] During the last, eventful years of his life in Shanghai, he had most of his letters sent to Uchiyama's address, and whenever his leftist friends and business contacts wished to see him, they would invariably find him there.[4] These fascinating details of Lu Xun's activities in Shanghai notwithstanding, the protagonist of this chapter is not the writer, but a young man in his mid-twenties who also visited the Japanese bookstore on a regular basis. The main purpose of his visits was not to buy books, since he had no more knowledge of Japanese than the ability to peruse the *kanji* characters, but to see Lu Xun and discuss business with him.[5] The young man was Zhao Jiabi, a junior editor from Liangyou tushu gongsi (Good friend book company, hereafter the Liangyou Company), which was located in the same neighborhood as the Uchiyama Bookstore. Zhao's name is permanently associated with the canonical project known as *Zhongguo xin wenxue daxi* (Compendium of modern Chinese literature; hereinafter the *Compendium*), which owed its initial conception and publication almost entirely to his imagination and social talents.

Publishing and Radical Literature in the 1930's

Zhao is one of those obscure figures who pop up on a scholar's index card from time to time and serve as a reminder of the unreliability of historical narratives about big names and big events. A self-styled lover of literature, Zhao was born too late (1908) to participate in May Fourth activism, yet he learned how to use his special talents as an editor of a small publishing house to cultivate friendships with eminent writers and scholars from the May Fourth period.[6] He reminds one of James Boswell, though probably a much toned-down version of the British biographer. Like the latter, he had a tendency to emphasize his personal role in the affairs of famous people, as is attested by some of his published biographical pieces such as "Lao She and I," "Recollection of Ten Episodes Relating to Myself and Yu Dafu," and "The Years Jin Yi and I Worked Together."[7] To be sure, Zhao never attempted the kind of self-aggrandizing interviews and lengthy biographies that Boswell did, but he did manage to pull off a remarkable literary project that has made a major difference, for better or for worse, in the history of modern Chinese literature.

By Zhao's own recollection, the idea of editing, periodizing, and anthologizing May Fourth literature on a grand scale occurred to him during a visit to the Uchiyama Bookstore in 1933 when he came across a Japanese literary compendium in a publisher's catalogue.

> One day, Mr. Uchiyama gave me a few catalogues of recent publications in Japanese, one of which contained information on a set of comprehensive anthologies of Japanese creative literature arranged in chronological order. At that time, the reactionary movement in China was raging high, as the Nationalist party exhorted students to go back to the Confucian classics. Progressive intellectuals had different ideas. They insisted that the revolutionary legacy of the "May Fourth" movement should be the only path toward national salvation and must be remembered and carried forward. No more than a dozen years had passed since the "May Fourth" movement, and I couldn't help but notice that many of the representative May Fourth works had already gone out of circulation. The younger generation of writers would have to look for them in places that sold used books, as in the case of ancient books. I got inspiration from this Japanese anthology and thought of editing and publishing something similar to it, such as "A Hundred Famous Works Since the May Fourth Movement."[8]

That idea was soon to materialize into the ambitious ten-volume *Compendium*. Zhao borrowed the word for "compendium" (*daxi*) from the Japanese *kanji* word *taikei* and introduced the neologism into modern Chinese. He discussed the title with his longtime friend Shi Zhecun, then editor-in-chief of *Les Contemporains*, and with his co-worker and mentor Zheng Boqi, who had joined the Liangyou Company the year before, and received a warm endorsement from both. He later recalled Zheng saying that nobody had ever used this generic term for a book series in Chinese publishing before and that it would be an ingenious coinage. After further consultation with his manager, Zhao decided to adopt the translingual term *daxi* to accentuate the novel or foreign aspect of his idea in place of the homespun *congshu* (book series) he had used several times in editing multivolume works, such as Yijiao congshu (The ten-cent book series) or Liangyou wenxue congshu (Liangyou literary series).[9]

The compilation of the *Compendium*, which got under way in the second half of 1934, involved almost every living author and critic of note from the May Fourth period. But an interesting detail stands out in the passage quoted above: May Fourth literature was in the decline and fast receding from memory in the early 1930's. This seems to contradict the usual story told by official literary histories about its rise and growth. Does Zhao's perception accurately capture the situation of May Fourth literature in the 1930's? We cannot give a straightforward answer. Certainly, for a long period of time, this "high-brow" literature, whose audience consisted mainly of progressive students and small circles of radical intellectuals, had not been hugely popular among middle-class and lower-middle-class urbanites in Shanghai, who preferred to go to the movies or buy Mandarin Ducks and Butterfly fiction for leisurely consumption.[10] One must, however, be extremely careful about familiar theoretical terms such as "elite" and "popular" when talking about forms of cultural production in the Republican period.

As far as the 1930's are concerned, the distinction between elite literature and popular fiction is difficult to maintain—one probably needs more imaginative categories of analysis here—not only because the debates on *dazhong wenyi* (mass art and literature) and *tongsu wenxue* (popular literature) dominated the theoretical language of leftist writers and critics of the period, but, more important, because fiction writers confounded the distinction by bringing out bestsellers, such as Ba Jin's sentimental novel *Jia* (Family; 1931–32) that embodied both the legacy of May Fourth literature and the commercial success of Butterfly fiction.[11] As "serious" literature began to claim a larger share of the commercial market, Butterfly fiction underwent a visible change of status, and it no longer monopolized the reading of middle- and lower-middle-class urbanites. Perry Link observes of this changing situation:

Butterfly fiction as a whole began to lose its predominant hold on China's urban readership. May Fourth writers like Pa Chin, Mao Tun, and Ts'ao Yu by then were enjoying substantial readership among students and other "new style" readers who in the 1910's might have read Butterfly stories exclusively. (By 1935 most urban readers no doubt read both kinds of literature, though in somewhat different moods.) Of at least equal importance in the relative decline of Butterfly fiction during the 1930's were the Japanese attacks on China and the consequent feeling of acute national emergency among the urban populace. Public opinion induced some of the leading popular writers, including Chang Hen-shui, Chou Shou-chüan, and Pao T'ien-hsiao, to step unequivocally into the political arena with calls for national unity and resistance of Japan. This move drew them closer to the May Fourth writers, who all along had been saying that literature should serve the modern nation.[12]

If Link is correct, and I think he is, what then can one make of Zhao Jiabi's claim that May Fourth literature had all but disappeared in the early 1930's? Note that, in his assertion, Zhao did not address the May Fourth writers' lack of popular appeal as opposed to Butterfly fiction and would probably have dismissed such concerns as irrelevant. Echoing the ideas of the leftist intellectuals of his time, he expressed concern over what he saw as the repressive cultural policy of Chiang Kai-shek, who was about to launch his New Life movement (February 1934) to promote traditional Confucian values. In response to those changes, Zhao conceived of his project as a form of resistance to the backlash against the New Culture movement. As a shrewd editor, he was not above using the "imminent" extinction of May Fourth literature to get others involved, and the people he had in mind were without exception pioneers from the New Culture era who had the highest stake in the success of his project. This also gave Zhao a long-coveted opportunity to become personally acquainted with many whom he had admired from a distance.

It is also likely that Zhao picked up the idea of political resistance from leftist writers and critics and recast it retroactively as his personal opinion. If that is the case, his comments on May Fourth literature should be more than a ploy to rally people around his project. My speculation is borne out by an account by Zhao of an early conversation with Marxist critic A Ying, as well as by written comments by A Ying at that time. A Ying received Zhao's new idea with enthusiasm and offered generous help by making his own private library of May Fourth materials available to him, a library known for its excellence.[13] In fact, the critic himself had just finished working on a book called *Zhongguo xin wenxue yundong shi ziliao* (Research materials on the history of the modern Chinese literary movement) published under the pen name Zhang Ruoying by the Guangming Book Company in September 1934. During their conversation, he gave Zhao an autographed copy of this book and urged him to consult Liu Bannong's recently published collection of May Fourth experimental poetry entitled *Chuqi baihua shigao* (Early vernacular poetry). A Ying mentioned, in particular, the preface to this book in which Liu looked back on the heyday of May Fourth literature with a profound sense of nostalgia. In the preface to his own book, A Ying quoted Liu's words to underscore the importance of preserving the fruits of modern vernacular literature from the debilitating effects of time.

> Twenty years is not a very long time, yet one is nearly overcome by a sense of hazy memories. When Liu Bannong, one of the pioneering figures of the modern literary movement, wrote his preface to *Early Vernacular Poetry*, he recorded these thoughts: "When I collected these poems at that time, I had no clear goals in mind and was just doing it to please myself. It never occurred to me that these things could turn into antiques within a short period of time, as they now have, indeed, become so." When he told a fellow writer [Chen Hengzhe] about his desire to have this collection of poetry published, she reacted by saying: "These things happened three generations ago. Alas, we all belong to the time of the bygone generation." In fact, not only is it hard to retrieve the memories of those bygone years, but it is no easy matter to gather the related historical materials, even though we are separated from the period by only a short span of twenty years.[14]

Needless to say, the body of works perceived as *xin wenxue* (or May Fourth literature) by A Ying's and Liu Bannong's generation covers a much shorter period of time than the period the term suggests to literary historians of our own time. In A Ying's formulation, the period of May Fourth literature coincides formally with the interval between two revolutionary movements—May 4, 1919, and May 30, 1925—although he did not fail to acknowledge the pioneering role played by the New Culture movement.[15] As discussed below, Mao Dun disagreed with this periodization. My purpose in raising the issue, however, is not to engage with their strategies of periodization, which I deal with later in this chapter, but to probe the interesting coincidence of A Ying's, Liu's, and Zhao's assertion of the *absence* of May Fourth literature on the one hand and the anthologizing and canonizing of this literature in the form of Liu's poetry anthology, A Ying's collection of theoretical essays, and Zhao's *Compendium* on the other. This is not to deny that some May Fourth writers might well have been forgotten by this time, but to demand a reading that attends to the claims of these people in relation to certain forms of practice. Beyond and above assigning political motives to their work—A Ying, for instance, was a staunch Marxist and had every reason to promote May Fourth literature—what other clues do we have about these various projects and the historical circumstances that produced and were produced by them? Perhaps the canonizing efforts of the early 1930's can tell us much about the struggles between leftist writers and the Nationalist government, the legitimizing discourses that accompanied those struggles, the complex scenario of publishing in Shanghai, and some of the personal stakes invested in these various moments.

As I mentioned earlier, Ba Jin's best-selling novel *Family* burst on the commercial market of the 1930's as a commodified progressive literature and stole much of the show from Butterfly fiction. The novel was serialized in the Shanghai newspaper *Shi bao* under the title *Jiliu* (Turbulent stream) in April 1931 and ran for 246 installments through May 1932. The novel's popularity led to the subsequent publication of the first single-volume edition by the Kaiming Bookstore under its new title *Family* in 1933. By early 1937 *Family* had gone through as many as ten editions, and between 1933 and 1951, a total of 33 editions were printed.[16] Ba Jin's popularity was by no means an isolated phenomenon in Shanghai's cultural production and consumption in the 1930's and 1940's. Wen-hsin Yeh's study of Zou Taofen and his journalistic enterprise demonstrates that a popular journal like *Shenghuo zhoukan* (Life weekly), which boasted a weekly circulation of 150,000 copies (the highest ever reached by a single periodical in modern Chinese publishing before 1949), was engaged precisely "in serious commentaries on contemporary affairs and introduced its readers to a wide range of social science publications that were considered 'progressive' or sympathetic to social reforms."[17] Indeed, the changing scenario of cultural production in Shanghai made it possible for publishers and booksellers to market radical politics despite the adverse political climate. Some of these entrepreneurs knew that they were risking their business by investing in leftist literature, but common sense probably told them that radical politics would sell well and that they were getting their money's worth.

In a letter commenting on this situation, Lu Xun observed with acute insight that publishers and booksellers were motivated to sell books written by members of the League of Left-Wing Writers, despite the tremendous adverse pressure exerted by the Nationalist authorities, not so much because they sympathized with the leftist cause as because they often saw an opportunity to cash in on politics. "They know pretty well that if they removed all of the left-wing books from the shelves, the bookstore would go bankrupt. So they decide to continue the business for profit while looking out for ways to alleviate the sting of those works. Some government officials are themselves board members of the bookstores, and they are setting up a snare for us. One could imagine what's going to happen to the future of publishing, for, in my judgment, they are sure to adopt the measure."[18] The "snare" and the "measure" refer to the possible imposition of government censorship. Considering the date of this letter (November 5, 1933) and the founding of the Newspaper and Magazine Censorship Committee by the Nationalist party in the spring of 1934, one cannot help but marvel at Lu Xun's foresight.

Nineteen thirty-three was an eventful year for enterprising publishers and filmmakers in Shanghai. On November 12, a gang of armed men identifying themselves as members of the Zhongguo dianying jie changong tongzhi hui (Society of comrades for the extermination of the Communists in the Chinese film world) stormed the Yihua Film Studio in Shanghai, smashing camera equipment and distributing pamphlets calling for immediate action against Communist agitators who had taken control of the film industry and were propagandizing class struggle on the screen.[19] On November 13, the shop window of the Liangyou Company at 851 North Sichuan Road was hammered to pieces by an unidentified person. A few days later, a self-styled writer turned up with a bundle of manuscripts and insisted on selling them for a good price to the same company.[20] The window incident and the blackmail were widely believed to be warning signs sent by the Nationalist authorities to the Liangyou Company, to signal the dire consequences of continuing to print the works of Ding Ling, Lu Xun, Qian Xingcun, Zhou Yang, Xia Yan, and other leftist writers.

The immediate cause of the incident was the publication of Ding Ling's unfinished novel *Muqin* (Mother) in Zhao Jiabi's Liangyou Literary Series in June 1933. On May 14, the secret police kidnapped Ding Ling and her lover Feng Da, with whom she had been living since Hu Yepin's death, and put them under house arrest in Nanjing.[21] The Liangyou Company did not waste time cashing in on this event, because many thought Ding had been murdered by the Nationalists.[22] The event was widely publicized, and numerous articles mourning her presumed death appeared in the newspapers.[23] Zhao Jiabi happened to have Ding Ling's unfinished manuscript in his possession as well as a hundred copies of an autographed page that he had wisely obtained from the author when she signed the contract.[24] Toward the end of June, the company intensified its efforts to advertise Ding Ling's novel in newspapers, including two of Shanghai's largest-circulation papers, *Shen bao* and *Shishi xinbao*. According to Zhao's recollection, the hundred autographed copies sold out on June 28, and all 4,000 copies of the first printing were gone within a month. The company had to run two more printings in October and December, reprinting 2,000 copies each time.[25] Indeed, the novel became the number-one best-seller of all the titles heretofore published in the Liangyou Literary Series and earned a sizable profit for the business.[26] Seeing the success of Ding Ling's autobiographical novel, Zhao immediately contracted to publish Shen Congwen's *Ji Ding Ling* (A memoir on Ding Ling), which came out in September 1934.[27] The book sold so well that it had to be reprinted in June 1935.[28] In retrospect, the damage to the shop window brought increased publicity and symbolic capital to the company.

Zhao Jiabi and the Liangyou Company

The Liangyou Company was founded by a Cantonese named Wu Liande in July 1925. A former art editor for the Commercial Press, Wu began as a manager of a small printing shop specializing in single-page pictorials for other businesses, but soon turned himself into a full-fledged publisher when he launched the *Liangyou huabao* (Liangyou pictorial) in January 1926.[29] The magazine had a fast-growing circulation in cities nationwide and did particularly well in areas of popular appeal such as sports, women's issues, and film.[30] Wu Liande took an interest in Zhao Jiabi as early as 1928 when the latter was still a senior and editor of a student journal at the Affiliate High School of Guanghua University. After Zhao became a college student at Guanghua University, Wu provided him with an opportunity to work for the company on a part-time basis by appointing him editor of a pictorial monthly called *Zhongguo xuesheng* (Chinese students). Zhao's three-year stint as editor won the company's trust, and the moment he graduated from college in 1932, Wu Liande offered him a position.

When Zhao joined the company, he was a young man in his mid-twenties for whom money, politics, and the battle over ideologies were but part of the game. The main drive behind his various projects was a long-cherished ambition of becoming a major editor and publisher in China. Zhao later confessed to having a taste for handsomely made books. He was attracted to the Liangyou Company because the *Liangyou Pictorial*, which was printed on top-quality paper, illustrated with fashionable photographs, and bound with expensive materials, embodied the ideal and beauty of the profession in his eyes.[31] In his student days at Guanghua University, he had dreamed of creating nice-looking books and publishing canonical works of literature. He had studied English literature and taken courses with Xu Zhimo, Hu Shi, Pan Guangdan, Luo Longji, and other writers and scholars associated with the Crescent Moon Society, whose membership consisted mainly of returned students from England and the United States.[32] Zhao identified himself as a student of Xu Zhimo's, who had studied in the United States and England and earned an M.A. degree at Cambridge University.[33] Like his teacher, he flaunted his admiration for Western literature and, particularly, for its canonical works. In an essay describing the first book series he edited for the Liangyou Company, Zhao recalled spending countless hours in the campus library leafing through books on Western literature and falling in love with the full sets of literary works by individual writers like Shakespeare, Balzac, and Tolstoy. His professional interest also took him to Fourth Avenue in Shanghai, where the Commercial Press, World Book Company, and other major publishers were located. In his avid browsing at those places, he found himself gravitating toward collections and book series that bore titles such as Encyclopedia Library or ABC Book Series. Above all, he attributed the shaping influence on his professional outlook to several Western-language bookstores located at the intersection of Nanjing Road and Sichuan Road, such as Zhongmei tushu gongsi (Sino-American book company).

> I was in the habit of visiting those places during lunch breaks or after work, and often found myself so absorbed with what I was reading that I forgot the time. What gripped my attention was the broad array of imported books, especially the complete sets of literary works, such as the Harvard Literary Series, Everyman's Library, and the Modern Library books, all of which were made accessible to the customer by the stores' open-stack policy. I felt as if I had accidentally set foot in the treasure house of knowledge, where not only the authors, titles, and works themselves opened my eyes to the vast world of literature, but the beautifully edited book series and their overall design, including the size, title page, book cover, binding, etc., made a deep impression on my mind. I fell madly in love with these nice-looking and richly informative books, wondering whether I myself would be able to edit and publish a series like these in the future to benefit the publishing cause in Chinese literature and to satisfy the needs of the readers in my country. Of course, being who I was at that time, this kind of thought was sheer fantasy, but I knew I must do it from scratch.[34]

Zhao's youthful ambitions generally coincided with the interests of the Liangyou Company. When in 1932 he presented a budget to Wu Liande for approval of the first book series he proposed to edit, The Ten-Cent Books—estimating that 3,000 copies sold at 10 cents per volume would break even—Wu found his idea interesting and profitable and gave him permission to proceed.[35] In his first two years of formal employment with the company, Zhao had numerous opportunities to demonstrate his ability to carry out difficult tasks with skill and persistence. When he created the Liangyou Literary Series in 1933, he managed to attract manuscripts from some of the best-known authors in modern Chinese literature, such as Lao She (the novel *Lihun* [Divorce]), Lu Xun (a translation of ten Soviet stories published under the title *Shuqin* [The harp]), Ba Jin (three short story collections called *Yu* [Rain], *Wu* [Fog] and *Dian* [Lightning] known as the "Love Trilogy"), Shi Zhecun (the short story collection *Shan nüren xingpin* [The morals of good women]), Mao Dun (*Huaxia zi* [Chatterbox]), Ling Shuhua (*Xiao ge'er lia* [Two brothers]), Yu Dafu (*Xianshu* [Casual readings]), Xie Bingying (the best-selling *Yige nübing de zizhuan* [Autobiography of a female soldier]), and Ye Shaojun (*Sansi ji* [At the age of thirty-four]).[36]

At the close of 1934, Zhao was basking in the glow of his initial success, because he had by then brought out as many as ten titles in his second book series, including the best-selling works by Ding Ling and Shen Congwen mentioned above. So when he proposed the idea of the ten-volume *Compendium of Modern Chinese Literature* in 1934, he was able to obtain the manager's approval with little difficulty.[37] To Wu Liande, the multivolume project required a larger investment than he had been willing to make before, but it also meant a larger profit than could be earned from the individually contracted volumes in Zhao's first two book series. This, indeed, proved to be the case, because the clothbound edition of the *Compendium* was marketed and sold at 20 *yuan* per set, or 2 *yuan* for each volume. By comparison, the Ten-Cent Book Series had operated at a much lower scale, namely, only 10 cents apiece. Although Zhao's second series, the Liangyou Literary Series, did better financially, prices were set at 90 cents a copy for the clothbound edition and 50–70 cents for the paperback edition. For example, the paperback edition of Ding Ling's *Mother* was priced at 50 cents and Shen Congwen's memoir on her and its sequel at 60 cents each.[38]

Zhao's well-orchestrated advertising campaign for the *Compendium* in early 1935 included a 40-page *yangben* (sample) brochure consisting of each editor's description of the individual volumes in a short paragraph called *bianxuan ganxiang* (Reflections on the selection), a reproduction of the condensed general introduction written by Cai Yuanpei in his much admired calligraphy, the editors' photos, and a color reproduction of the books' cover, as well as blurbs by famous writers and critics. Thanks to

these efforts, the majority of the sets were sold by subscription well before the publishing date. Altogether, the company printed 2,000 copies
of the initial clothbound edition, 2,000 copies of reprints, and an equal
number of paperbacks. For a relatively small business, 6,000 copies of a
ten-volume book (five million words) made a big difference not only in
terms of profit but in terms of its professional image in the publishing
world.[39]

Compiling the 'Compendium'

It would be unfair to equate Wu Liande's business ambition with Zhao
Jiabi's pursuit of success. As I mentioned earlier, money and politics were
but part of the game as far as Zhao was concerned. The *Compendium* was,
above all, an opportunity for him to realize a long-cherished dream and
to establish himself as a capable editor in the publishing profession. In
the beginning, Zhao encountered numerous difficulties with copyrighted
materials and government censorship, and in simply trying to get people
to cooperate with him.[40] Lu Xun's letter to him dated December 25, 1934,
allows us to reconstruct some sense of the background.[41] In the letter Lu
Xun declined Zhao's request that he make the selections and contribute an
introductory essay to one of the three fiction volumes of the *Compendium*.[42]
Lu Xun began by mentioning an earlier article for a literary journal and
expressed his anger that three-quarters of his 6,000-word essay had been
suppressed by the government censor before its publication. His random
reflections on the late Ming dynasty and occasional allusions to the classics were considered a camouflaged attack on the Nationalist government
(they may well have been).[43] He then continued:

> That brings me to the subject of your *Compendium of Modern Chinese Litera-
> ture*. My selections would not get you in trouble as long as the censors didn't
> know who made them. But when you send in the introductory essay, it is
> bound to cause problems for you. Surely, the May Fourth period is closer
> to our own time than the Ming dynasty, isn't it, besides I am simply in-
> capable of producing a 10,000-word essay about "today's weather, ha, ha,
> ha," which is not supposed to offend anybody. If my opinion clashed with
> that of the authorities, there would be enough complexities for you to deal
> with. When that happened, you should not expect me to change my words
> or start a new article to comply with their wishes, and moreover it'd be too
> late for you to find a substitute, for the person wouldn't know what to do
> with the selections I had made and his opinion would certainly differ from
> mine. In any case, it would mean either a waste of your money or my time,
> so I have decided not to get involved in this matter. To play it safe, I suggest

you choose someone who is not on their hate list. The censors openly declare that they only check on the contents, not the identity of the author, but I tend not to believe in the existence of people whose heart and mouth are one. Even if they exist, they'd not be found among those censors who are prone to playing tricks on people. I am not going to fall into their traps and am determined to oppose them eye to eye.[44]

Three months later, Lu Xun changed his mind. In a brief note dated March 6, 1935, Lu Xun informed Zhao that the introductory essay had reached 10,000 words and was ready to go to press. Apropos of the sensitive nature of his political opinions, he said: "As the saying goes, 'It's easier to change the face of the landscape than one's own essential nature.' I have tried hard but found myself unable to resist the temptation of saying 'inappropriate' things after all." And, in contrast to his earlier message, he added: "If they cause trouble, please feel free to make whatever revisions you see fit. You need not consult me about any of your revisions, as I told you earlier in person."[45] What is it that caused Lu Xun to reverse his earlier decision so dramatically?

In an essay commemorating Zheng Boqi, Zhao reveals that Zheng interceded on his behalf and successfully talked Lu Xun into changing his mind.[46] This detail is confirmed by a letter dated January 4, 1935, addressed to both Zheng Boqi and Zhao Jiabi in which Lu Xun requests copies of *New Youth* and *Renaissance* to be sent to the Uchiyama Bookstore so he may start working on the selections.[47] How did Zheng Boqi get involved in this matter? Zheng, whose work I discussed in Chapter 7, had been an influential figure from the early days of the Creation Society and joined the Liangyou Company in 1932 under the pseudonym Zheng Junping.[48] Thanks to Zheng's broad-based connections, Zhao Jiabi was able to get acquainted with Lu Xun, A Ying, Xia Yan, Zhou Yang, Ding Ling, Zhang Tianyi, Mao Dun, He Wei, Lou Shiyi, and others, all of whom either contributed to his Ten-Cent Series, Liangyou Literary Series, or the widely circulated *Liangyou Pictorial*. With few exceptions, Zhao chose all ten editors for the *Compendium* in close consultation with Zheng Boqi. They were Zheng Zhenduo, Yu Dafu, Lu Xun, Mao Dun, A Ying, Guo Moruo (later replaced by Zhu Ziqing at the insistence of the Censorship Committee), Hu Shi, Zhou Zuoren, Hong Shen, and Zheng Boqi himself. Zhao became acquainted with Yu Dafu as early as October 1932 when he asked Yu to contribute a volume to his Liangyou Literary Series.[49] The introduction, which took place in Yu Dafu's home, was arranged by Zheng Boqi, who had to overcome a tremendous emotional barrier to do so, because the two former members of the Creation Society had had a

serious clash on the occasion of Yu's expulsion from the League of the
Left-Wing Writers.[50]

The contract with Zheng Zhenduo, on the other hand, was facilitated
by Ba Jin, who was editing *Wenxue jikan* (Literary quarterly) in Beijing
with Jin Yi and Zheng Zhenduo.[51] Zhao had a chance to talk to Zheng
Zhenduo when the latter visited Shanghai in August 1934. Zheng not only
gave him useful advice on how to structure the *Compendium* but helped
him get in touch with Hu Shi, then the president of Beijing University.
Hu had long parted company with radical politics and was regarded by
left-wing intellectuals as a pro-establishment reactionary. Zhao sought
his participation in this predominantly leftist project in face of the an-
tipathy of people like A Ying and Zheng Boqi, because, as he recalled
years later, Hu's name would serve as a smoke screen to help protect the
Compendium from excessive interference from government censors.[52] One
need not dispute the truth of Zhao's statement to note that Hu Shi's name
certainly lent a great deal of prestige to the project.[53]

Nor should one forget that the Nationalist government had executed
five members of the League of Left-Wing Writers including Rou Shi and
Hu Yepin (Ding Ling's common-law husband) in February 1931. Such
cold-blooded crackdowns led to increasingly tighter control over publication of certain kinds of leftist works, culminating in the founding of the
Censorship Committee itself in early 1934.[54] The government required
publishers to submit all manuscripts for approval by the Censorship Committee before going into production. On March 14, 1934—nine months
before Zhao received Lu Xun's note declining the post of volume editor—the newspaper *Damei wanbao* reported that the Shanghai branch of
the Nationalist party had banned 149 book titles involving as many as
25 publishers in Shanghai.[55] The censored authors included Lu Xun, Guo
Moruo, Ding Ling, Tian Han, Ba Jin, Hu Yepin, Jiang Guangci, Qian
Xingcun (A Ying), Rou Shi, Mao Dun, and Feng Xuefeng. In view of this
harsh reality, Zhao's ability to maneuver on the left as well as on the right
is truly remarkable, since he invited as many as four of the above—Lu
Xun, Guo Moruo, Mao Dun, and Qian Xingcun—to serve as guest editors. Except for Guo Moruo, for whom Zhu Ziqing had to be substituted
at the last minute, Zhao's project miraculously survived censorship without his making too many compromises.[56] Mao Dun's volume of fiction
(May 1935) was the first to roll off the press, and all other volumes except
for A Ying's work of research material were scheduled to appear within a
month or two. A Ying was the last to turn in his completed manuscript
because of an unexpected interruption, but Zhao managed to publish the

full set of the *Compendium* in February 1936. The actual compilation and printing of this book from beginning to end took less than two years.[57]

Canon, Theory, and Legitimation

Within the limited scope of this chapter, it is neither possible nor necessary for me to reiterate what each editor said about the significance of his own selections. Some of these views are so well known that they have long become clichés. One always begins with *New Youth*, the literary revolution, the formation of literary societies, the vernacular language movement, the rise of realist fiction, ... The same narrative has been told again and again in mainland China, the United States, and Europe since Hu Shi, Zheng Zhenduo, Lu Xun, and the other editors of the *Compendium* lay the foundation of the canonical view of modern Chinese literary history. For instance, Mao Dun's suggestion of taking literary societies as an organizing principle was adopted in the fiction volumes.[58] Mao Dun's own selections turn around the work of the Literary Association, Zheng Boqi's volume focuses on the Creation Society, and Lu Xun covered the publications of miscellaneous societies. Fictional works outside the publications of these particular societies and literary circles were excluded from consideration. However, the criterion that applied so well to one literary form seemed to collapse when applied to another. The two volumes on familiar prose, for example, were built on a totally different set of principles. In his original conception of the series, Zhao Jiabi saw the editorial role of Zhou Zuoren and Yu Dafu in terms of the geographic locations each occupied at the time and thought they would come up with a list of writers representative of the North and the South.[59] But the editors themselves chose not to honor such geopolitical concerns or literary organizations and preferred, instead, to follow the dictates of their own "taste," picking those authors whose "individual style" they liked.[60]

The *Compendium* consists of ten volumes whose generic criteria of selection derived from the prevailing assumption about what *wenxue* (literature) is or should be. These individual volumes further reinforced that assumption by naturalizing such criteria in an authoritative presentation of the historical materials. Thus, the division of the chosen literary works into four cardinal categories, *xiaoshuo* (fiction), *shige* (poetry), *xiju* (drama), and *sanwen* (familiar prose), relegitimized them in this canonizing effort. Three out of the ten volumes are devoted to short stories selected by Mao Dun, Lu Xun, and Zheng Boqi, respectively. As a rule, longer works and novels are left out (except as indexed by A Ying in a few cases) not only because May Fourth writers favored shorter forms, but because most of the longer works were copyrighted independently and could not be easily reproduced.[61] In addition, two volumes edited separately by Zhou Zuoren and Yu Dafu are devoted to the genre of familiar prose, one compiled by Zhu Ziqing to poetry, and one by Hong Shen to drama. More important, the "theory" aspect of May Fourth literature is highlighted by the fact that Volumes 1 and 2, edited by Hu Shi and Zheng Zhenduo, respectively, cover "Constructive Theory" and "Literary Debates." These "theory" volumes and the introductory essay that precedes each volume, along with Cai Yuanpei's general introduction and A Ying's concluding volume "Research Materials and Index," essentially define the ways in which selected works in the *Compendium*, and certainly modern Chinese literature itself, are supposed to be read and evaluated.

If the legacy of the *Compendium* needs to be reconsidered from a contemporary point of view, on what ground should one pursue such a task? The notion that a "pure" literature ought to be kept separate from politics is of little avail because it often serves to hide the political agenda of those who make this assertion. On the other hand, one could easily pinpoint certain "distortions" or omissions of this and that school or author, and take general issue with the editors' politics of selection, periodization, and ideological biases. But how do we know that we would not be producing another equally biased account? Does a counternarrative that presumes to tell a more balanced story about twentieth-century Chinese literature automatically lead to an interesting and productive critique of the legacy of the *Compendium*? My suspicion is that the desire to "complete" or "correct" the canon of modern Chinese literature is itself driven by a myth of plenitude often accompanied by the false hope that the writing of literary history will someday produce an unbiased account of the total picture and thereby do justice to history itself. In other words, a well-established canon may be called into question from time to time but the practice of canon making need not be seriously questioned. I wonder, however, if canon making can be criticized on more interesting grounds than those of "plenitude" or "fidelity." But, are such grounds available? Can we ask, for instance, how literary historiography fabricates its own terms of legitimacy in a moment of perceived need?

The circumstances surrounding the compilation of the *Compendium* reveal that the editors raised no false expectations about their desired goals in presenting the legacy of May Fourth literature in the way they did. They were not nearly as concerned with striking a balanced view of the achievements of modern Chinese writers as with laying a particular claim to legitimacy in the discursive field of tradition versus modernity. Although each editor followed his own inclinations in deciding what to include, the crux of the claim to legitimacy lay ultimately in the high-powered collective (male) image that the *Compendium* was calculated to project. And I would argue that it was the question of legitimation that made the editors' collective effort meaningful to themselves and to their readers. The following analysis tries to explore the manifold aspects of this legitimation problem, centering on the kinds of linkages the *Compendium* tried to establish between its literary enterprise and the perceived historical exigencies of the time.

Liangyou's advertisement for the *Compendium* carries a conspicuous subtitle describing the project as a "Recapitulation of the First Ten-Year Period of the Modern Literary Movement, 1917–1927." One should not dismiss this as a pretension or a marketing ruse, because periodization was precisely one of the major theoretical fronts on which the *Compendium* editors staked their claim to authoritative representation of modern Chinese literary history. Of course, the *Compendium* was not the first attempt at a formal periodization of modern Chinese literature. As early as 1922, Hu Shi had published *Wushi nian lai Zhongguo zhi wenxue* (Chinese literature in the past fifty years), which was meant to be a preliminary periodization of late Qing and modern literature.[62] In the early 1930's, historiographies devoted exclusively to modern literature began to appear, including Chen Bingkun's *Zuijin sanshi nian Zhongguo wenxue shi* (Chinese literature in the past thirty years; 1930), Lu Yongheng's *Zhongguo xin wenxue gailun* (A brief study of modern Chinese literature; 1932), Wang Zhefu's *Zhongguo xin wenxue yundong shi* (A history of the modern Chinese literary movement; 1933), Qian Jibo's *Xiandai Zhongguo wenxue shi* (A history of modern Chinese literature; 1933), and Zhou Zuoren's *Zhongguo xin wenxue zhi yuanliu* (The origins of new Chinese literature; 1934).[63] Wang Zhefu's book deserves special mention here, because it is generally regarded as the first serious scholarly work on the genesis of modern literature. In terms of periodization, the author proposes two phases: the first covers the time from Hu Shi's call for literary reform in 1917 through the anti-imperialist uprising of May 30, 1925, and the second extends from May 30, 1925, to the date of the writing and publication of his study in 1933.[64] In an April 1934 review of Wang's book, Mao Dun expressed strong dissatisfaction with the author's command of his subject and material and called for a more comprehensive research project that would include theoretical essays, information on the founding and dissolution of the various literary societies as well as their journals, synopses of literary works, and criticisms and commentaries on these works.[65] Even if Mao Dun's call was not directly responsible for the genesis of Zhao Jiabi's *Compendium*, his participation greatly shaped the orientation and structure of the book. Whenever the editors disagreed on a particular issue, Mao Dun's opinion was usually adopted.

In the matter of periodization, A Ying proposed May 4, 1919, and May 30, 1925, as the beginning and end of the first period of the modern literary movement in his preface to *Research Materials on the History of the Modern Chinese Literary Movement* (1934), but Mao Dun and Zheng Zhenduo drew the line differently.[66] Recalling a letter he wrote to Zhao Jiabi in 1934, Mao Dun says:

> It seemed to me that the periodization should begin in 1917 and close with the 1927 Northern Expedition, for the modern literary movement had germinated two years prior to the May Fourth incident. The six-year period between May 4, 1919, and May 30, 1925, saw an outburst of events in modern literary history, although the actual number of creative works published at this time was not very impressive. At around the time of the May Thirtieth movement, there was no dearth of talk about "revolutionary literature," but most of that discussion did not go beyond the stage of theory and had little impact on literary works. This situation began to change dramatically after the failure of the 1927 Revolution and has been that way up to the present time.[67]

Thereupon, he proposed the ten-year period between 1917 and 1927 as the first phase of modern Chinese literature, a proposal eventually adopted by Zhao Jiabi and the other members of the editorial collective. Mao Dun's periodization modeled literary events closely on the corresponding political events, and in that sense, there was no fundamental difference between him and A Ying, although the emphasis shifted from anti-imperialist struggles to the battle between the Nationalists and Communists.

Since publication of the *Compendium*, later works have expanded its contents and updated them to accommodate new developments in modern literary history after 1927, but the conceptual paradigm of the *Compendium*—periodization, genre, and so on—has hardly changed in subsequent literary histories written by mainland Chinese scholars, except that later histories tend to be increasingly politicized along the line of the Communist ideology.[68] When Li Helin wrote his version of modern literary history in 1939, for example, he inherited and revised the *Compendium*'s sociological approach to literary periodization and helped consolidate the leftist hold on the reality of modern Chinese literature. After the founding of the PRC, Wang Yao's *Zhongguo xin wenxue shigao* (A draft history of modern Chinese literature; 1951) sought to project a politically correct view of modern literary history by deleting some writers included in the *Compendium*, but neither Wang nor those official literary historians who came after him ceased to use the sources, periodization methods, and genre categorization provided by the *Compendium*.[69] These elements and the ways in which they were put together significantly affected these historians' choice of authors and texts, perhaps more so than they care to admit.

By comparison, C. T. Hsia's *History of Modern Chinese Fiction, 1917–1957* (1961) stands out as an early attempt to break away from the official literary histories written by mainland scholars.[70] In many ways, contemporary scholarship in the field of modern Chinese literature on both sides of the Pacific is indebted to Hsia's work for drawing attention to formerly marginalized or suppressed writers such as Zhang Ailing and Shen Congwen. His book changed our view of modern literature by reinserting those writers into Chinese literary history.[71] Of course, it is one thing to challenge the established canon by replacing it with a counternarrative of one's own and quite another to engage with the writing of literary history itself at a theoretical level. It is the latter that I find missing in Hsia's revisionary approach, as he tackles the problem of canon making consistently in terms of a Cold War ideological crusade against Communism. The high-profile debate between him and Průšek further speaks to the intensity of ideological battles at the time.[72] In retrospect, I am greatly struck by the fact that academics in Communist China and the democratic United States in those years (and even today) had an equally difficult time maintaining their independence as scholars, in spite of their various claims to the contrary.

In Taiwan in the 1970's, Yu Guangzhong and his co-editors published a countercanon of literary works written by Taiwanese Mandarin-speaking writers entitled *Zhongguo xiandai wenxue daxi* (A compendium of modern Chinese literature). The fact that this multivolume anthology calls itself a *daxi* indicates the debt of this countercanon to the *Compendium*. But a far more significant event in the perpetuation of this legacy was the publication of an ambitious twenty-volume sequel (1927–37) to the original *Compendium* by the Shanghai Wenyi Publishing House in the mid-1980's.[73] When the compilation first got under way in 1982, the head of the publishing house, Ding Jingtang, not only consulted Zhao Jiabi, then in his mid-seventies, but copied the original format of the *Compendium* almost verbatim.[74] Except for the addition of reportage literature and film, the generic categories in the sequel basically consist of theory, fiction, familiar prose, poetry, and drama. Like the original, the sequel also has a volume on research materials. The usual authoritative introduction to each volume was assigned to critics and writers of official status, including Zhou Yang, Ba Jin, Wu Zuxiang, Nie Gannu, Lu Fen (Shi Tuo), Ai Qing, Yu Ling, and Xia Yan.[75]

That brings me to another important aspect of the *Compendium* often overlooked by revisionary critics who focus primarily on the inclusion or exclusion problem. I am referring to the theoretical volumes and introductory essays that frame the editors' choice of authors and works. Indeed, one cannot help but be struck by the heavy weight of theory in the overall conceptualization of the *Compendium*. As Marston Anderson notes in *The Limits of Realism*, "The apparently inflated power accorded to theory in modern Chinese letters can only be understood in the context of the cultural emergency from which the new literature was born and in light of the particular kind of literary borrowing in which Chinese intellectuals are engaged."[76] Perhaps, the cultural emergency can be further specified in this case as a need for legitimation, for the editors were quick, from early on, to grasp the central importance of theoretical discourse as a field of contention for legitimacy. When Zhao Jiabi first mentioned this project, for example, to his friend Shi Zhecun, who was then editor of the *Les Contemporains*, Shi pointed out that the inclusion of literary texts alone could not do justice to a project of such magnitude and that it was absolutely necessary to integrate theory and research materials as well.[77] As mentioned earlier, Mao Dun had expressed a similar opinion in his review of Wang Zhefu's book. Zheng Boqi and A Ying, whom Zhao also consulted at that time, urged him to consider adopting Shi's idea. The two men even came up with an eligible candidate for the theory volume—Zheng Zhenduo, former editor of *The Short Story Magazine* and the theory guru of the Literary Association. Zheng Zhenduo not only accepted the offer but made a few suggestions of his own, all of which were subsequently implemented by the general editor. One of the things he proposed was the division of the theory part under two separate headings: Volume 1, "Constructive Theory," should deal with the important theoretical essays published since the early beginnings of the literary revolution, and Volume 2, "Literary Debates," should concentrate on the major debates on literary reform between the old and new camps as well as those between the Literary Association and the Creation Society. Zheng volunteered to edit the second volume and suggested Hu Shi for "Constructive Theory."[78]

Theory, criticism, and polemical debates are generally privileged by the *Compendium* and assigned conspicuous places in the volumes. One might go as far as to suggest that, because of their concerted efforts to promote *lilun* (theory), May Fourth writers were able to gain an edge over their rivals such as the Mandarin Ducks and Butterfly school. Theory here plays the role of legitimation in a discursive area where in the long run symbolic capital proved a better investment than hard cash. Whereas Butterfly fiction thrived solely on the entertainment market and found its returns more or less guaranteed by popular consumption, May Fourth writers were bent on producing their own terms of legitimacy by relying on theoretical discourses and institutionalized practices such as canon making, criticism, and the writing of literary history. Theory legitimizes and is in turn legitimated; and, in its ability to name, cite, invoke, and perform rhetorical acts, it reproduces, multiplies, and distributes *symbolic wealth and power*. May Fourth writers and critics relied on such symbolic authority to appoint themselves the harbingers of modern literature and, by the same token, relegated their rivals to the traditional camp, thereby reaping the benefits of naming and speaking for both sides of the game. By comparison, Butterfly writers' lack of interest in theoretical discourse served them ill.

I am not suggesting that May Fourth writers and critics have silenced the other. Self-legitimation relies on a simultaneous delegitimation of the other that often requires the invention of the other's language in one's own terms more than the actual silencing of the other's voice. To give an example, Zheng Zhenduo's volume of literary debates includes the notorious exchange between Wang Jingxuan and Liu Bannong in the March 1918 number of *New Youth*. The episode, well known to literary historians, involved two radical thinkers impatient with the general indifference of old-style literati to their call for literary revolution who wanted to provoke a reaction. To that end, Qian Xuantong fabricated a Wang Jingxuan, who attacked progressive thinkers in the voice of an old-style literatus. This fictional challenge was countered by his friend Liu Bannong, who was instantly joined by others until the debate escalated to the famous battle between the defenders of classical Chinese headed by Lin Shu and the *New Youth* advocates of the modern vernacular language. Interestingly, when Lin Shu identifies with the fictional character and speaks in his own voice, he is stepping into a discursive position already prepared for him and finds himself engaged in a losing battle on the enemy's territory. In a figurative sense, Zheng Zhenduo's volume is a further extension of this extreme example, in which all subsequent debates between the New Culturalists and the "conservatives" are arranged and framed in terms that serve to legitimize the position of the former on their own theoretical ground.[79]

What is the discursive ground on which the New Culturalists and their opponents waged the battle over terms of self-legitimation? If Lin Shu represented a lost cause when he was relegated to the "traditional camp," the *Critical Review* group raised enough noise to challenge the New Culturalists on its own ground, namely, knowledge of the West.[80] But this second debate, as I show in the next chapter, was forcibly framed by the New Culturalists, and inevitably by the *Compendium* editors, as if the National Essence critics amounted to little more than a conservative backlash in the Chinese revolution. The stakes in these battles consisted ultimately in who owned the right to speak for China and the West. Cai Yuanpei's General Introduction to the *Compendium* offers an important insight into the discursive strategy that the New Culturalists regularly deployed in their contention for intellectual authority. The opening paragraph of the Introduction states:

> It is commonly acknowledged that modern European culture has evolved from the Renaissance era in which the Greek and Roman classics were revived. Our own ancient culture from the Zhou dynasty roughly corresponds to that of the Greeks and Romans, and we have experienced a similar period of sophism and scholasticism as the Europeans did in the Middle Ages. Unless we start a renaissance movement likewise, our culture cannot hope to shake off its current state of decline. The New Literary movement during the May Fourth period is the beginning point of our renaissance.[81]

Cai went on to elaborate on the importance of science and art in modern Western culture and concluded with a call for the birth of a Raphael and Shakespeare in China. Cai's interpretation of Chinese culture and history in terms of European classical and medieval traditions and the Renaissance reflects the crisis of Chinese intellectual authority, since modern intellectuals could no longer assume a comfortable position in intellectual discourses without borrowing authority from the West, although, in saying so, one must be careful not to exaggerate the importance of the West at the expense of underestimating the meaning of the local struggle between various political groups fighting for the right to impose their own agenda on one another. Cai's language was hardly new. It echoed what Hu Shi and most New Culturalists had asserted all along about the New Culture and the May Fourth movements.[82] What it did in the immediate context of the *Compendium*, however, was to play out the legitimation issue at the concrete level of canon making and the writing of modern literary history.[83] In short, the European Renaissance is deployed here as an undisputed trope to legitimize and canonize the work of May Fourth writers, and hence the *Compendium* itself.[84]

In a sense, the *Compendium* was a self-colonizing project in which the West served as the ultimate source of authority in terms of which one had to renegotiate what was meaningful in Chinese literature. Take the four-way division of generic forms: *xiaoshuo, shige, xiju,* and *sanwen.* The *Compendium* organized all literary works around these categories, which were understood to be perfectly translatable into "fiction," "poetry," "drama," and "familiar prose," respectively, in English. The canonization of these "translated" norms of literary form crystallized something that has been desired since, perhaps, Liang Qichao's time—namely, a radical subversion of the classical canon as the legitimate source of meaning for Chinese culture and literature. I am not referring just to the now-familiar knowledge that, since Liang's promotion of the political novel, fiction has steadily risen to become a dominant literary form in the modern Chinese canon and that modern poets have by and large abandoned traditional prosody. What I have in mind is the changing view of what kind of writing counts as *wenxue* (literature) and how that view has greatly impacted the writing and study of modern literature as well as shaped the contemporary view of what is worth teaching or receiving scholarly attention in the area of classical literature.

A Ying's *Compendium* volume on research material lists ten titles in Chinese literary historiography published between 1924 and 1931, as well as over a dozen titles in foreign literary historiography. Among the ten titles, some have exerted a lasting impact on scholarship in Chinese literature, such as Lu Xun's pioneering *An Outline History of Chinese Fiction* (1924, rev. 1931), Hu Shi's *Chinese Literature in the Past Fifty Years* (1924), Zheng Zhenduo's *General Outline of Literature* (1926), and Tan Zhengbi's *General History of Chinese Literature* (1927).[85] Zheng Zhenduo's *Illustrated History of Chinese Literature*, which was meant to be a major reconceptualization of classical Chinese literature, rightfully belongs to this genealogy of modern literary historiography, although its publication was much delayed because of the war and therefore it was not included in A Ying's volume. In the preface to *The Illustrated History*, Zheng gives an illuminating account of why the rewriting of the classical tradition is necessary:

If a history of English literature forgot to include its Shakespeare and Dickens, or if an Italian literary history omitted its Dante and Boccaccio, would people take it lightly and forgive the author? This is precisely the unforgivable sin committed by most Chinese literary histories written up to date. Has any of the "Chinese literary historiographies" ever paid attention to the "vernacular Buddhist narratives" of the Tang and Five Dynasties, or the several "song-medleys" of the Jin and Yuan, or the countless number of vernacular short stories of the Song and Ming, or the important *baojuan* [precious scrolls] and *tanci* [ballads with string accompaniment] of the Ming and Qing?[86]

The promotion of vernacular literature and popular forms unleashed a tremendous amount of energy among twentieth-century scholars, in China and subsequently in sinological studies abroad, who have virtually rewritten Chinese literary history in terms of a contemporary, though profoundly mediated, understanding of modern European literary forms and genres. Although one must give full credit to the results, it is easy to forget that whatever is rediscovered on that basis can never exist independently of the history of a scholarship and a legitimizing process in which European literature is always already a participant. One can always raise the objection: Why do fiction, poetry, drama, and familiar prose have to limit one's imaginative horizon of what is possible in the Chinese written language in terms of genre and form? Why have certain forms of writing been excluded from literary history because they do not happen to fit in any of these formal categories? What is truly at stake in the simple and impossible question people often ask: What is *wenxue*? The etymology of this round-trip neologism since the turn of the century seems to suggest a tautological answer in terms of its English translation; that is, *wenxue* is "literature." But why not more or less than "literature"?

Is there a difference between colonization and self-colonization? If so, what does the difference tell us about the meaning of agency? How does it help us understand the central predicament of the Chinese who try to work out the contradiction of their existence by articulating the identity of *Zhongguo ren* (men and women of the Middle Kingdom) in terms of *the other* or *the beyond* of the Middle Kingdom? Such a contradiction endorses as well as undermines their unprecedented move of positing Chinese literature and culture as one among the diverse national literatures and cultures of the world. That brings me back to the question of world literature discussed in the preceding chapter. Once again, Zhao Jiabi's efforts can serve as an example. Shortly after publication of the *Compendium*, Zhao began work on a ten-volume companion anthology, little known to contemporary scholars, to be entitled "Shijie duanpian xiaoshuo daxi" (A compendium of short stories from throughout the world). The project, set afoot in spring 1937, one year after the complete set of the *Compendium* had come out, was aborted by the Japanese occupation of Shanghai in the fall of that year.

Cai Yuanpei suggested the idea of a sister series as early as the fall of 1935 when Zhao brought him a copy of one of the newly published volumes of the *Compendium*. Zhao recalls that Cai was greatly pleased with the book and said: "If the sale of this work is successful, you should by all means go ahead and start a sequel. But, in my personal view, it is more important to publish an anthology of translated works than the sequel, because modern creative literature could not possibly have achieved so much if Western masterpieces had not been introduced to China."[87] To launch his new project, Zhao drew up a list of ten well-established translators and writers, some of whom were members of the editorial collective of the first *Compendium*, and invited them to participate in the compilation of the new work. Reflecting the status of each national literature in the world and the degree of its influence on Chinese writers, the compendium devoted one volume each to English, American, French, German, and Japanese literatures, and the remaining volumes to the literatures of Southern Europe, Scandinavia, Russia, the Soviet Union, and newly born nations (Baltic nations).[88] Most of the texts were to be translations published during the May Fourth period. By the time of the Japanese invasion on August 13, 1937, Zhao already had in his possession several manuscripts, including Cai Yuanpei's introduction, the page proofs for the volume on Southern European literature, which was scheduled to appear in November 1937, and a portion of the proofs for the volume on Japanese literature.[89] Prior to this, *Liangyou Pictorial* had run pages of advertisements for the ill-fated book.

The war brought the project to a premature close. Even so, one still catches a glimpse of the changing perception of national literature and world literature in the mid- and late 1930's. From Zheng Boqi's early depiction of *Weltliteratur* as mere fantasy to Zhao's plans for this ambitious compendium that would put modern Chinese literature on a comparable, if not equal, footing with foreign literature, one perceives a growing confidence—which also punctuates Cai's ready acknowledgment of foreign influence—in the status of modern Chinese literature as one of many worthy national literatures. That confidence feeds back into the making of the canon, the institutionalization of literary criticism, theoretical discourse, and the writing of literary history. In fact, the *Compendium* has arrogated all these functions to itself and created a sizable legacy of its own.[90] In the making of the sister anthology, the unspoken word suggests that, taken together, these two anthologies would make a statement about modern Chinese literature and its relation to world literature. The irony is that the arrival of the Japanese did not give that statement a chance to be heard, at least, not for many years to come.

Postscript

In 1946, Zhao received a letter from a Chinese journalist living in Tokyo who wrote to forward a message from a Japanese translator, Kuraishi Takeshirō. The latter requested permission to translate the ten-volume *Compendium* into Japanese, which Zhao promptly granted.[91] A year later, Zhao received from the Tokyo publisher Kōdansha a copy of volume 3—the fiction volume edited by Mao Dun—in Japanese translation as well as an eight-page brochure advertising the *Compendium*. He did not hear from the Japanese translator again until 1954, when Kuraishi visited China and the two met in Shanghai for the first time. When asked about the translation, Kuraishi explained that he had been able to publish only the one volume and then had to quit for reasons he hesitated to talk about. In 1984, Zhao Jiabi visited Tokyo, where he met with Uchiyama Kakichi, brother of deceased Kanzō, as well as with the original publisher of the translation of Mao Dun's volume. With the help of his Japanese colleagues, he discovered the true circumstances behind the abrupt discontinuation of the translation project. It turns out that the censorship had been imposed in 1947 by the General Headquarters of the U.S. occupation forces. The project fell victim to the anti-Communist policy of U.S. authorities, much to the regret of its Chinese editor.[92]

CHAPTER 9

Rethinking Culture and
National Essence

Inasmuch as the project of nation building necessarily thrives on a certain understanding of what culture is or does in the modern context, in this concluding chapter I focus on the question of *wenhua* (culture) as a way of recapitulating my own thoughts as well as seeking a different angle on some of the problems addressed in the preceding chapters. Taking the National Essence movements as a point of departure, this discussion looks into the larger discursive formations that lay the groundwork for the construction of *wenhua* and consequently *wenxue* (literature) as principal sites of ideological struggle in the twentieth century. I am asking how "culture" came to preoccupy most Chinese intellectuals as a fundamental bearer of difference between countries and people. If the debate over national essence was predicated on cultural difference, did that difference preclude the consideration of power? If not, how did the advocates of a Chinese national essence negotiate difference and power and *difference as power* in their discourses on culture?

Despite its antiquity as a Chinese word, the classical Chinese term *wenhua* carries none of the modern ethnographic connotations of "culture" now associated with the word.[1] In its earlier usage, *wenhua* denoted the state of *wen* or artistic cultivation in contrast to *wu* or military prowess. The new ethnographic notion of *wenhua* did not enter the Chinese language until after *bunka*, the Japanese *kanji* translational equivalent of "culture," was borrowed back by the Chinese at the turn of the twentieth century.[2] What this history means is that the changing meaning of *wenhua* in twentieth-century China has to be investigated in light of its specific historical ties to other languages and discourses and cannot always be traced to its original Chinese etymology.

That culture arises as a privileged sphere of discourse in a time of colonialist and imperialist expansion is hardly surprising. The modern notion of *wenhua* or culture has resulted from the recent history of East–West encounter that forces the questions of race, evolution, civilization, and national identity upon the attention of native intellectuals. As Edward Said puts it: "What is *another* culture? Is the notion of a distinct culture (or race, or religion, or civilization) a useful one, or does it always get involved in self-congratulation (when one discusses one's own) or hostility and aggression (when one discusses the 'other')?"[3] Said's questions demand that, instead of an ethnographic object, we think of culture as a discursive notion that has historically been instrumental in the production and legitimation of the West's Orientalist/imperialist knowledge about the other, as opposed to the self.[4] I have found this discursive notion of culture generally helpful in my own rethinking of the Chinese debates on national essence, but I am more attracted to the question of what happens to a cultural discourse when non-Western intellectuals participate in the production of Orientalized knowledge about themselves and about the Western other. Are there changes in the meaning, purpose, and context of the borrowed language? What purpose does translated knowledge serve in the host-language context? Is Occidentalism the flip side of Orientalism?[5]

In a study of the National Essence movement in China, Laurence A. Schneider points out: "The idea of 'national essence' (*kuo ts'ui*) and the activities of the social groups associated with it are among the earliest manifestations of the emergence of this intelligentsia preoccupied with culture."[6] Several other historians have also remarked that the discovery of *wenhua* (culture) as an avenue toward national identity is indicative of the disintegration of the Chinese holistic world outlook under the impact of Western imperialism.[7] Indeed, *guocui* (Japanese *kokusui*; national essence), like the related terms *minzu* (*minzoku*; nation) and *guoxue* (*kokugaku*; national learning), was first imported from Japan as part of a cultural discourse, and it provided the Chinese with a theoretical language to talk about race, civilization, and national identity, and to deal with the contradiction of being Chinese in a modern world.[8] When the notion of national essence first entered Chinese discourse in the late Qing period, it immediately assumed an important role in the anti-Manchu revolution. With its emphasis on the unique national identity of the Han people embodied by their history, cultural heritage, and classical learning, this idea had an enormous appeal to late Qing rebels like Zhang Binglin who devoted themselves wholeheartedly to the anti-Manchu cause.[9] In Zhang's view, national essence consists mainly of the Han language and writing, its law and bureaucratic system, and the loyal deeds of ancient heroes, all of which are preserved in national learning.[10] The task of preserving the Han race falls to the educated elite who have the foresight and ability to restore and protect that body of knowledge. After the founding of the new Republic, the notion of national essence began to shed some of the earlier rhetoric about the racial superiority of the Han Chinese and to veer more toward connoting literary culture.

In this chapter, I analyze the different rhetorical strategies used by advocates of the two National Essence movements for the purpose of understanding the important shift in the meaning of "national essence" from racial/cultural connotations to predominantly literary/cultural ones. I trace the first of these movements through the activities of a circle of writers, scholars, and educators represented mainly by the Guoxue baocun hui (Society for the protection of national learning), whose seminal publication, *Guocui xuebao* (National essence journal), was founded in 1905. My discussion of the second movement focuses on the journal *Xueheng* (Critical review) founded in 1922 and the group of Harvard-educated scholars affiliated with it, who promoted classical Chinese literature as national essence after they returned from abroad and took up teaching posts at the Southeastern University.

Scholars have done a great amount of research on the activities of several circles of writers, scholars, and educators involved in the promotion of national essence, including the Guoxue baocun hui and the Nan she (Southern society), a poetry society founded in 1909.[11] But much of this scholarship tends to treat these groups as the "conservative" camp in the Chinese revolution. Although I find myself using the term "radical" loosely from time to time, I have doubts about the three-way division of modern Chinese intellectuals into radicals, liberals, and conservatives, for it cannot but reduce modern China's history to a localized version of a universal (European) narrative of progress.[12] In fact, both the National Essence group (conservatives?) and the New Culturalists (radicals?) were centrally preoccupied with the problem of Chinese national identity, a concern that renders their ideological boundaries exceedingly permeable. My approach, therefore, seeks to uncover some of their shared intellectual background as well as their mutual antagonisms that enabled the rival groups to engage with one another, not as radicals, liberals, or conservatives, but as competing voices and alternative narratives in the process of China's nation building and culture building.

The 'National Essence Journal'

In a public speech to a group of Chinese students in Tokyo, Zhang Binglin briefly summarized his intentions for promoting a national essence movement: "Why is it important for us to uphold national essence? It is not that one needs to worship Confucianism but that the history of the Han people must be cherished in our hearts."[13] Likewise, the editors and contributors to the *National Essence Journal*, such as Liu Shipei, Huang Jie, and Deng Shi, were without exception dedicated classical scholars, but scholars who conceived of learning less as an end in itself than as part of an ambitious project to secure and legitimate a racial identity distinct from the identities of the Manchus and other alien races.[14] On the one hand, these scholars identified with the Ming loyalist tradition and saw themselves as the true heirs to the authentic Chinese culture, which was being threatened by intruding forces. On the other hand, the derivation of their notion of *guo hun* (Japanese *kunidamashii*), or the national soul, from the Japanese translation of German nationalist discourse (*die deutsche Seele*) profoundly undercuts their claims of cultural authenticity.[15] Of these conflicting notions of national identity, the Ming loyalist discourse was blatantly subversive in the pre-1911 years as anti-Manchu propaganda. This was evident in a variety of activities organized by society members. Besides publishing biographies of Ming loyalists and compiling a detailed bibliography of literature previously banned by the Qing regime, the group went to great lengths to edit and reprint books by the loyalists themselves, some of which were clearly seditious. Political activism against the Qing regime on behalf of the Han accounts for only one side of the story, however; deeper than anything else was the feeling of crisis concerning the status of Chinese racial and cultural identity in a modern world they saw as defined by competing nation-states.

Huang Jie's "Huang shi" (Yellow history), which was serialized in *National Essence Journal*, represents the most ambitious effort of this group of scholars to claim a Chinese identity. Ironically, Huang's racial theory was taken from the French Orientalist scholar Terrien de LaCouperie, who had been adapted by Liu Shipei and Zhang Binglin for a Chinese audience.[16] This Frenchman's work, mostly written in the 1880's, was published in a journal he edited in Britain called *The Babylonian and Oriental Record*. By 1900 most of his themes had been incorporated into a Japanese work, *History of Chinese Culture*, which in turn profoundly influenced the Chinese.[17] Interestingly enough, Terrien de LaCouperie simultaneously expressed admiration for Chinese culture and contempt for its people.

This Orientalist preference for the lost civilization seems to fit nicely into the program of the National Essence group, whose mission was, after all, to restore a true national identity (from the distant past) to the Chinese. Nonetheless, there is a major difference between Terrien de LaCouperie's Orientalism and the Chinese coauthorship of such knowledge in the course of translingual practice. Whereas Terrien de LaCouperie never had to call into question his own subjectivity or his relationship with the Orient, the Chinese were compelled to reject an undesirable modern self in exchange for an ancient ideal hopelessly beyond their reach.

What exactly does this so-called national essence coauthored by Western Orientalists and Chinese scholars comprise? In an introductory essay to the first issue of the *National Essence Journal*, Huang Jie pinpoints *guoxue* (national learning) as the repository of true Chinese essence: "When national learning disappears, so does the nation. When the nation goes, so must the race."[18] He alluded to Miyake Setsurei and Shiga Shigetaka, two of the foremost Meiji advocates of Japanese national essence, in support of his own project of promoting national learning in the *National Essence Journal*. Ironically, when the Japanese first promoted the idea of national learning in the Tokugawa period, they were reacting against the sinophile intellectual atmosphere of the time. In fact, *kokugaku* began as a nativist philological study of ancient poetry and a concern with the revival of Shinto as the "ancient way" (*kodō*), which opposed itself against Confucianism and *karagokoro* (the Chinese mind).[19] Huang and his fellow Chinese scholars appropriated the idea to help energize the Han resistance movement against the Manchu regime. He even attributed the downfall of the Song dynasty in the thirteenth century to the debilitation of Chinese national learning caused by those who chose to forsake their heritage and admire the language and writing of the Mongols. Huang's patriotic stance notwithstanding, it is unclear what exactly he meant by national learning. If he had the Han race in mind in alluding to Mongol invasion, he seems to have meant something totally different when he promoted the works of the *zhuzi* (ancient noncanonical philosophers) to oppose the long-established Confucian canon. The idea of national learning thus captures the unstable constructs of ethnic identity and cultural essence. The slippage between the two reveals more about Huang's sense of crisis as a modern man than about the nature of either ethnic identity or culture essence that he sought to establish.

If all national learning is predicated on a national essence, it does not take much thought to arrive at a totalizing conclusion about the cultural difference between East and West. In "Lun guocui wu zu yu ouhua" (On national essence not being a roadblock to Europeanization), Xu Shouwei negotiated that difference in terms of Chinese spiritualism and Western materialism. National essence was said to fulfill one's spiritual needs, whereas Western culture supplies material nourishment, both of which are indispensable to the well-being of a nation. Here, one seems to catch a familiar echo of Zhang Zhidong's earlier formulation of Chinese learning and Western science. But as soon as Xu Shouwei draws on the authority of the European Renaissance to justify his own effort to revive the ancient Chinese learning, the spiritualism–materialism divide collapses. It turns out that the European Renaissance provides the justification and theoretical framework needed to construct the Chinese national essence. The note of self-contradiction in his argument reflects an unresolved tension between his desire to assert cultural identity in the face of imperialism and his profound ambiguity about the sources and authority of that identity in a world system that no longer legitimizes the voice of the dominated on its own ground.

Deng Shi, co-founder and editor of the journal, wrote several articles in an attempt to name the contents of national learning. By placing miscellaneous ancient schools of philosophy both above and against Confucianism, he and his fellow contributors foreshadowed the iconoclasm of the New Culturalists and inadvertently revealed the common discursive ground of the two groups. Although all of Deng's work revolves on the premise that there is indeed a national essence to be recovered from centuries of political censorship under Confucianism since the Han dynasty, his view about what constitutes national learning or national essence by no means supports that premise. For instance, in "Guoxue zhenlun" (On authentic national learning) and "Guoxue wuyong bian" (A rebuttal to the view that national learning is useless), he distinguished guoxue (national learning) and junxue (imperial learning). We are told that this distinction is modeled on Western political theory, which sees the nation-state and the imperial order as two incompatible systems, the former destined to triumph over the latter in the evolutionary order of things. "We all know that in political theory a line must be drawn between the nation-state and the imperial system," argued Deng Shi. "So why not make a similar distinction between national learning and imperial learning in scholarship? What happens is that people frequently collapse the two. They imagine themselves loyal servants of our nation, whereas in fact they are serving the interest of the emperor. As a result, the kind of scholarship used to advance self-interest is often regarded as true national learning."[20]

Anti-Manchu propaganda notwithstanding, what makes Deng Shi's argument so intriguing is not so much the inherent contradiction between his essentialist view of national identity and his non-Chinese framework of reference, as the explicit parallel between national learning and the modern nation-state, both inventions of the modern age. Once again, the theory of the National Essence group seems to herald the arrival of modern Chinese literature, a literature that the New Culturalists would redefine twenty years later as a national project in opposition to the "feudal" and elitist literary practice of the imperial past. The idea that every civilized nation-state must have a unique national literature represented by individual geniuses, such as Shakespeare, Goethe, and Balzac in English, German, and French literatures, respectively, was part of the modern European nationalist theory often associated with the name of Herder. When the National Essence group embraced this theory as a timeless truth and brought it to bear on the reassessment of their own classical heritage, it did not occur to them that the national essence thus extracted from the ancient past already carried the unmistakable imprint of the modern age.

The 1908 debate between Zhang Binglin and the editors of the Paris-based student journal *Xin shiji* (The new century) on the worth of the Chinese writing system illustrates some of the issues that emerged in the first National Essence movement and the political stakes of the discussion. *The New Century* condemned the Chinese pictographic/ideographic language as primitive and called for its abolition and replacement by Esperanto, a self-proclaimed international language.[21] In rebuttal, Zhang Binglin published a lengthy article in *Min bao* (People's journal), also serialized in the *National Essence Journal*, in which he contested the internationalist claims of Esperanto by emphasizing its Eurocentric origins: "Esperanto has taken European languages as its model, and in forming its grammar, it has extracted the simplest and most accessible rules from those languages. For that reason, it cannot very well apply to places outside continental Europe. Besides, the world is such a vast, variegated, multicolored place that it should not be taken as belonging to the white race alone."[22] Drawing on his profound learning as a *xiaoxue* (small learning) philologist, Zhang Binglin described the evolution of the Chinese language and rejected the ahistorical and Eurocentric view espoused by *The New Century* group.[23]

The intellectual virtuosity of Zhang's argument reflects his extraordinary achievements as a classical scholar, but I am also struck by his early insight that cultural difference cannot adequately be grasped within the Enlightenment framework of power and domination. According to his view, the inability to translate one language completely into another says nothing about the superiority of the one or the barbarity of the other;

rather, it shows the intransigence of their irreducible differences. Using the Chinese translation of Byron's poetry as an example, he argued that a poem considered beautiful by the standards of one language may be judged thoroughly insipid by those of another. The philologist drives home the central problematic of the whole debate on the racial and cultural identity of the Chinese when he asks: In whose name does Europe constitute itself as the legitimate bearer of universal values? In the presence of the overwhelming dominance of the West, Zhang was well aware that his philological work might not carry any weight with *The New Century* group. So he even quoted the words of a Western missionary at one point to defend Chinese characters.[24]

With few exceptions, the predicament of having to establish national identity in resistance to the threat of the West and yet do so with reference to a borrowed authority characterizes the enterprise of the National Essence group from beginning to end. One of the regular columns of this journal, entitled "Aiguo suibi" (Patriotic miscellany), can be taken as emblematic of this paradox. As editor of this column, Deng Shi took great pride in reporting episode after episode of foreigners' admiring the glories of ancient Chinese culture. For instance, a Danish sinologist who fell in love with a Buddhist inscription in Xi'an goes to great lengths to have a copy made; the Japanese worship Confucius and hold elaborate ceremonies in his honor; a French collector obtains a great number of ancient artworks in the Far East and displays them in the Louvre.[25] At one level, this is reverse Orientalism; and yet, at another level, this desire to become the subject of their own history and to claim the past for the present struggle inevitably contradicts the logic of Western Orientalism criticized by Said, which assigns the power of representation to the West where "the exteriority of the representation is always governed by some version of the truism that if Orient could represent itself, it would; since it cannot, the representation does the job, for the West, and *faute de mieux*, for the poor Orient. 'Sie können sich nicht vertreten, sie müssen vertreten werden' [They cannot represent themselves; they must be represented], as Marx wrote in *The Eighteenth Brumaire of Louis Bonaparte*.[26]

'Critical Review'

The national essence project continued well beyond the life span of the journal of the National Essence movement, which began to fall apart after 1911 and increasingly came under attack by the so-called radical intellectuals associated with *New Youth*.[27] In 1919, Liu Shipei started the short-lived journal *Guo gu* (National heritage) in a last-ditch attempt to counteract the New Culture movement and salvage the cause of national essence, but the journal ceased following his death that same year. It was not until the founding of *Critical Review* (hereafter *CR*) in 1922 that the issue of national essence began to attract serious attention from diverse literary and political camps. In fact, the new journal was the only publication in the post-1911 years that matched the *National Essence Journal* in its commitment to the cause of national learning and its organized efforts to implement concrete programs. The manifesto of the journal declared its intellectual affiliation with the earlier group: "Our goal is to engage in learning and scholarship, pursuing truth, promoting national essence, and integrating new knowledge."[28] But does the notion of national essence here convey the same meanings as it did in the pre-1911 years when Zhang Binglin, Liu Shipei, Huang Jie, and others first made it popular in public discourse? If not, what does that shift in meaning tell us about changes in the authority of knowledge during the May Fourth period and about the continued preoccupation with national identity among intellectuals of different ideological persuasion?

Scholars have remarked on the interesting shift in the intellectual climate around the time the discussion of national essence was resumed with the arrival of the *CR* group. Laurence Schneider captures the situation succinctly: "By the time the *CR* was established, the Manchus were gone and the monarchy as well, so that the tasks at hand for poets were more diffuse and less consonant with singular and strikingly dramatic acts. Now the images of the Tung-lin Academy, the Fu she, and the knight-errant were set aside for a more recent and Western-derived model—Matthew Arnold's poet-*critic*."[29] Indeed, what could be more emblematic of this change than the fact that the first issue of *Critical Review* was adorned with stately portraits of Confucius and Socrates printed back to back? By contrast, the earlier *National Essence Journal* had been devoted exclusively to promoting traditional literature, paintings, and calligraphy by Han artists. Subsequent numbers of the new journal continued to feature great men of the European past and, only occasionally, those of Eastern cultures. Shakespeare's portrait was paired with that of John Milton (issue no. 3), Charles Dickens's with William Thackeray's (no. 4), Sakyamuni's with Christ's (no. 6), Samuel Johnson's with Matthew Arnold's (no. 12), and so forth.

Although the word *guocui* (national essence) continues to be evoked, its meaning has undergone drastic transformation at the hands of the *CR* group. Most important, the ambivalence toward the West that had marked the National Essence movement was replaced by a system of justification firmly grounded in the Western humanist tradition. If the *National Essence Journal* relegated Confucius to a secondary priority, which brings it closer to *New Youth* in spirit than to *Critical Review*, the latter resurrects the sage in the belief that every great civilization has its own sage. The idea that Socrates and Confucius respectively represent the humanist essence of Western and Eastern civilizations was not the invention of the group. They got it from Harvard professor Irving Babbitt (1865–1933), whose neo-humanist theory was the decisive influence on their thinking.[30]

It was common for literary associations and cliques in early Republican China to form on the basis of something like an alumni association as well as on ideological grounds. For instance, the Creation Society was founded by a group of Japanese-educated students, and most members of the Crescent Moon Society had an Anglo-American educational background. In the case of the *Critical Review*, most of the founding members were educated in North America. Wu Mi and Mei Guangdi were exposed at Harvard to the teachings of Irving Babbitt, who was professor of French literature there. Hu Xiansu studied science at the University of California at Berkeley. These American-educated students developed their notion of national essence through the mediation of Irving Babbitt and his neo-humanism. Babbitt's essay "Humanistic Education in China and the West" was translated into Chinese by Hu Xiansu and appeared in the March 1922 issue of *CR*. In it, the author expressed disapproval of the popularity of Rousseau, Ibsen, Strindberg, Tolstoy, and Bernard Shaw among Chinese youth and urged them to follow what he called a humanistic internationalism that blended the essential Greek background of the West with the essential Confucian background of the East:

> You will find that the two backgrounds confirm one another especially on the humanistic side, and constitute what one may term the wisdom of the ages. It seems to me regrettable that there are less than a dozen Chinese students in America today who are making a serious study of our occidental background in art and literature and philosophy. . . . My hope is that, if such a humanistic movement gets started in the West, it will have a response in a neo-Confucian [*sic*] movement in China.[31]

It does not take much guesswork to figure out the identities of the exceptional Chinese students in America. The journal exerted itself to establish the authority of Irving Babbitt, yet the self-advertisement in this quotation reveals the manner in which that authority was exploited within the Chinese context. Evoking the name of Irving Babbitt as an alternative authority empowered the *CR* group in its battles with the rival New Culturalists, who had translated and introduced John Dewey and Bertrand Russell and designated themselves the specialists in Western knowledge. The oppositional stance of the *CR* could not but bring about a profound change in the status of Chinese knowledge about the self and the West. If one Western authority could thus be enlisted to discredit another, a homogeneous view of the West no longer obtained. However, the *CR* group was not interested in pursuing the potentials of heterogeneous knowledge about the West that their intervention opened up so expediently at this point. In lieu of the East–West divide, they introduced a new rhetoric of binary opposition or a discourse of *zhen* (authenticity) and *wei* (inauthenticity). The idols of the New Culturalists such as Rousseau, Ibsen, Tolstoy, and Nietzsche were now dubbed "inauthentic" and rejected, and the true essence of the West came to be embodied by the Greco-Roman and Judaeo-Christian traditions, which Irving Babbitt and his Chinese students chose to honor.[32] The crux of the matter, in their view, was not to oppose Western culture to the essence of Chinese culture as if the two were incompatible systems (the perception of the earlier National Essence group and the New Culturalists), but to determine who had the authority to speak on either and to integrate the essence of the two to build what Mei Guangdi called a "zhenzheng xin wenhua" (genuine new culture).[33]

Lu Xun was acutely aware of the historical contingencies of the various claims to national essence staked since the turn of the century. In commenting on the advocates of national essence in "Suigan lu 35" (Random thoughts no. 35) in 1918, he pointed out:

> From the last moments of the Qing dynasty down to our own time, people have kept bringing up the topic of "the preservation of national essence." In the earlier period, two kinds of people were particularly fond of this topic, one being nationalist patriots and the other being Qing diplomats who held office abroad. The topic had different hidden meanings depending on who happened to be using it. When the patriots talked about preserving national essence, they were trying to restore the Ming order, whereas in the mouths of state officials it meant that students should not cut off their queues. Now that we are living in the Republican era and neither Ming loyalism nor the queue is a cause for concern, I wonder what our contemporaries are really up to when they bring up the topic again.[34]

Zhou Zuoren made a poignant observation on the *CR* group in April 1922: "The national essence movements that prevail today are mobilized to resist new literature. In the future, they will probably evolve into some kind of national traditionalism." [35] True, the stakes seemed to consist less in the preservation of so-called national essence than in establishing an alternative authority in the production of new knowledge about national identity and national literature. Like Liu Shipei's *Guo gu* journal before it, the *CR* took as its mission presenting an oppositional voice to the New Culture movement and, in particular, to modern vernacular literature.[36] This exigency is behind the *CR*'s concerted effort to develop arguments for national essence or polemics against the New Culture movement rather than full-fledged scholarship on the classics. Indeed, given their apotheosis of Confucius as a national sage, there are surprisingly few detailed studies of Confucianism as national essence or national learning, a further reminder that the signifier of *guocui* has never been able to contain the meaning of national essence. The latter is defined and redefined in response to the flux of changing historical events.

The declared antagonism of the *CR* group to the New Culture movement is often perceived as the conservative strain in modern Chinese history. The danger of this reading is that one easily falls into the rhetorical trap of their opponents, the New Culturalists, who were the first to brand the group as a roadblock to social progress. To me, the circumstances seem rather complex and deserve further investigation. Wu Mi, for instance, anticipated this reading in an article entitled "Lun xin wenhua yundong" (The New Culture movement): "Those of us that disapprove of this [New Culture] movement do not necessarily oppose new learning or resist the introduction of European or American culture. It is unreasonable, therefore, to dub our position as stubborn and conservative."[37] But a number of scholars have pointed out that the similarities between the *CR* group and conservative strains in the West are such that one cannot very well take what they said in self-defense as the truth either.[38]

Do we then conclude that this group practiced cultural conservatism without knowing it? To do so, however, would be again to foreclose the issue and fail to account for the means by which the group arrived at the position it did. It seems to me that one must look into the discursive strategies that the members of the group employed to constitute themselves as a protagonist in what they saw as a global contest between humanism and radicalism. In other words, it is crucial to explain the means by which the *CR* group managed to *establish a discursive relationship with the West* rather than simply describe observable similarities or differences between conservatives in the West and their presumed counterparts in modern China. One possible explanation is that this group tried to reframe the debate on national essence in terms of a contemporary American academic discourse, whose authority they claimed alone to represent.

Thus, these American-returned students perceived Chen Duxiu and Hu Shi as the local manifestations of a global problem (the battle between neo-humanism and radicalism), which they took upon themselves to resolve. Had not Irving Babbitt inspired them with this humanistic and evangelical mission and called for a new Confucian movement? The first thing they set out to do was to expose and correct the New Culturalists' "misrepresentation" of the West and of the Chinese past. Irving Babbitt's neo-humanism was supposed to counter the rampant effects of liberalism and Romanticism.

The theory of national essence thus opened up a hermeneutic space that enables the group to reread and reconstitute Confucianism as *renwen zhuyi* or the humanistic essence of Chinese culture. Unlike Kang You-wei before them, however, they were not concerned with the need for a state religion when redefining Confucianism for the modern age; rather, they try to locate a common ground on which the Eastern and Western essences blended in an ideal fashion so that a universal humanistic future could be imagined. By now, the notion of national essence had shed its earlier connotations of race, as it came to represent a cultural hierarchy in which the spirit of belle lettres reigns. This world of cultural and literary values contains "the best of what has been thought and said in the world," as Wu Mi quoted Matthew Arnold.[39] By the same token, Confucianism is no longer a fixed body of knowledge, but a transcendental spirit capable of generating new meanings and providing new symbolic resources in a global context. Hence the neologism *xin* (new) Confucianism.[40] The word "new" is crucial here, for, on the one hand, it suggests the manner in which the disciples of Irving Babbitt appropriated Confucianism and made it relevant to modern experience and, on the other, it uncovers the discursive ground that the group shared with the New Culturalists.[41] All this is a far cry from the view expressed by the National Essence group, for whom Han identity or ancient philosophies outside the Confucian canon made up the intransigent essence of the Chinese. By eschewing the earlier East–West binary opposition, the *CR* group launched a critique of modernity on the same discursive ground as the New Culturalists, with a view to eroding their opponents' monopoly of Western knowledge.

Although *CR* drew on the modern European philosophical thinking no less than *New Youth*, its insistence on historical understanding rubbed up against the dominant "cultural" discourse of May Fourth anti-traditionalism, causing moments of rupture in the perceived inevitability of modernity. Faced with the harrowing question of the modern age, "What's wrong with China?" the New Culturalists typically looked for answers in the evils of traditional culture or flaws in national character. The CR group, by contrast, pursued a different line of thinking. For instance, Liu Yizheng argued that China's vicissitudes were caused by the contingencies of historical events rather than imputed cultural traditions such as Confucianism. "The evils of China's illness today," he said, "should by no means be imputed to the teachings of Confucius. . . . They were caused by the Manchus, the Opium War, corrupt government officials, warlords, robbers who don the cloak of the revolutionary, and evil politicians who pay lip service to democracy, as well as a whole spectrum of maggots of our society, none of whom is what you might call a Confucian." [42] The author concluded that the absence of Confucian morality rather than its entrenched presence caused the decline of the nation. In prescribing Confucianism as a cure for national illness, Liu Yizheng somehow retreated from the historical insight that his poignant diagnosis touched upon, which, if pursued further, would have led to an interesting critique of the discourse of modernity as embedded in the enlightenment ideology of the New Culture. [43]

When Hu Xiansu condemned materialism, scientism, and instrumentalism as the chief evils of modern society and, like Liu Yizheng, attributed the degeneration of public morals in China to the intrusion of capitalist values, he nonetheless assumed Chinese culture to be a fixed, homogeneous, and ahistorical site of meaning. "It pains me to think that our ancient civilization would be one day destroyed by the evils of Western culture." [44] This view is largely in tune with that expressed by Liang Qichao in his *Ouyou xinying lu* (Reflections on a European journey; 1920) written after a tour of post–World War I Europe, and to some extent by Liang Shuming in his controversial *Dong xi wenhua jiqi zhexue* (Eastern and Western cultures and their philosophies; 1921). Disenchantment with the materialist culture of the West seems to have prompted these scholars to look for alternative solutions in the symbolic resources of their own culture. Complicating the picture is the contemporary tendency of Westerners, themselves experiencing a period of crisis in the aftermath of World War I, to project this desire for the other partly onto the East. Liang Qichao's recorded experience on his tour of the West, Oswald Spengler's enormously popular *Decline of the West*, and Irving Babbitt's critique of modernity all bear witness to the rise of a postwar wave of disenchantment with modernity. [45]

Mei Guangdi's quarrel with the New Culturalists, on the other hand, presented a unique possibility for a critique of modernity without insisting on an East–West binary opposition. This is clearly seen in Mei's impassioned criticism of the evolutionist view of Chinese literature that prevailed among the New Culturalists. As can be seen below, his argument is based on something other than the incompatibility of East–West literary traditions.

> Those of us who blindly follow the evolutionist notion of literature should be advised that critics of good repute in the West, such as nineteenth-century essayist and critic Hazlitt, have already dismissed that idea as a vulgar mistake. It is not even supported by the evidence from the history of Western literature itself. The idea that Romanticism has evolved out of the classical tradition and then grown into realism which in turn becomes Impressionism, Futurism, and Neo-Romanticism, and that whatever comes after is superior to that which precedes it or that the rise of the former means the certain demise of the latter is completely false. If one had only a slight knowledge of the history of Western literature and of the views of well-established Western critics, one would not entertain an absurdity of such magnitude.[46]

Notice that his rejection of evolutionism is predicated not on cultural difference, for Mei was not arguing the incompatibility of the Western notion with Chinese literature, but on the absence of evidence within the Western tradition itself. To the extent that his critique was aimed at a dominant mode of Western knowledge of his time, it constitutes a valid intervention in that context. The fact that he was one of the few who dared go against the grain bears strong witness to the heterogeneity of the May Fourth intellectual discourses. Mei was trying to beat the New Culturalists at their own game by appealing to the authority of the West. However, the power of his critique, be it directed at evolutionism, democracy, or vernacular literature, is greatly weakened by his conspicuous lack of awareness of the dubious sources of his own authority. Since Mei Guangdi refused to deal with the thorny question of imperialism and European domination in his critique of modernity, he ended up reviving the discourse of modernity by identifying with the conservative line of the European Enlightenment. Herein lay the fundamental impasse of his politics. On the one hand, he was genuinely concerned with national essence, national literature, and the survival of Chinese culture. On the other hand, his cultural elitism prevented him from perceiving the logical link between the theory of national essence and the nationalist struggle against foreign domination, on which the earlier national essence movement had thrived. In a later essay, Mei stressed the nation's dire need for true and dedicated scholars, who must be mobilized to "ensure the survival of the nation and give their lives to the cause of truth."[47] Evidently, his passion for scholarship and cultural essence was no less fueled by nationalism than that of the earlier National Essence group. Yet, unlike his predecessors, who had established a meaningful connection between national learning and anti-Manchu movements, Mei Guangdi had difficulty grounding his theory and remained a nationalist manqué who refused to criticize imperialism or make his effort relevant to the nationalist movement of the time.

It is apparent that the project of cultural essence and global humanism envisioned by the group downplayed the historical conflict between China and the West. According to Wu Mi, because the essence of one great civilization is isomorphic to that of another, the project of Westernization need not be incompatible with that of national essence. In "Lun xin wenhua yundong," Mei explained:

> Since the turn of the century there has been a good deal of anxious debate over the conflict between *ouhua* [Europeanization] and national essence, as if the rise of the former would bring about the end of the latter. Conversely, scholars who favor new learning nowadays proclaim that national essence must be cleared away before the process of Europeanization can begin. In my view, both arguments are false. The fact is that very few of those who advocate new learning have more than a superficial knowledge of the essence of the Western civilization. If they are willing to read more and penetrate deeper, they should soon discover that the authentic culture of the West, and our own national essence may very well benefit and help reinvent each other. The blending of the two is conducive to the mutual good and makes it possible for us to preserve national essence and promote Europeanization at the same time.[48]

As Wu Mi unfolds his humanistic program, it becomes clear that the national essence he talks about is modeled on the West. For just as the Western civilization consists of a classical Greek tradition and Judaeo-Christian religion, so must China maintain its Confucian humanism and Buddhist religion. Everything outside the scope of this classical-religious humanist paradigm, whether it be Romanticism, Realism, Naturalism, or Daoism, is either false or unauthentic.[49] Humanism alone contains "the truth that is taught by the sages" or "ideal [men]," and these sages are Confucius, Plato, Aristotle, Jesus Christ, and Sakyamuni.[50]

The *CR* group had embraced Irving Babbitt's theory of humanism from the start. The theory allowed them to criticize the evils of modern society in China and the West, but it also prevented them from questioning the problematic practice of their own mentor, whose universal humanism not only sought to appropriate ancient Greek civilization for modern Europe on the basis of nineteenth-century philological scholarship but presumed to speak with authority on Confucianism as well.[51] Translating the voice of Irving Babbitt for the Chinese audience at home, they helped reinforce, rather than contest, a discourse of power that had dominated the relationship between May Fourth radicals and progressive Western thinkers.

Needless to say, the advocates of national essence met with forceful resistance from the New Culturalists. Lu Xun, Hu Shi, Zhou Zuoren, Chen Duxiu, and others wrote poignant essays criticizing what they perceived as the reactionary implications of cultural essentialism.[52] Hu Shi's review of Liang Shuming's ambitious theory about East and West, for example, criticized Liang for taking a totalizing and ahistorical view of Chinese culture.[53] Against Liang's assertion that the Chinese were lovers of peace and moderation and did not practice materialism, Hu Shi cited evidence of polygyny, prostitution, drinking, and pornography to prove the contrary.[54]

When Bertrand Russell arrived in Beijing in 1920 and delivered a public speech on the importance of preserving the Chinese national essence, Zhou Zuoren gave the following response:

> Russell has arrived in China. In his first lecture, he tried to persuade the Chinese to preserve their national essence, which no doubt pleases many of our countrymen, old and young. . . . It is by no means clear to me, however, which aspect of our national character [*guomin xing*] is worth preserving except for that same old desire to glorify the emperor and expel the barbarian or, put otherwise, to restore the past and oppose everything that comes from the outside.
>
> Of course, Russell arrived in China only recently, and one cannot expect him to know much about the situation here. But I do hope that he will soon find out that there is more bad stuff than good stuff in this country. Our fellow countrymen are simply too conceited to deserve his praise. I certainly welcome the opportunity to have Russell share with us some of his constructive thoughts on social reform. The latter alone is what we expect to learn from him.[55]

Zhou Zuoren's negative view of national character might be taken as representative of the overall position of the New Culturalists, who adamantly opposed the theory of national essence and strove to tell a different story about national identity. It is interesting to note that this passage about Russell comes close to a critique of the coauthorship of national essence between East and West, but that perspective immediately gets lost when Zhou endorsed the equally problematic notion of national character in place of national essence.

In retrospect, the notions of national character and national essence played a complementary role in the invention of the idea of *Zhongguo wenxue* (Chinese/national literature), which has been perceived as an important component of modern national culture. Whereas national essence addressed itself to the reinvention of the Chinese classics in terms of contemporary needs, the theory of national character led to a literary movement that privileged the ameliorative function of fiction, with an emphasis on realism. However, the *CR* group and the New Culturalists had several things in common: a shared vision of Chinese literature as one among other national literatures, a shared anxiety about the place of Chinese culture in a world increasingly dominated by non-Chinese values, and the contradiction of having to fashion a self-identity in terms of translated modernity. The tensions between their shared telos and declared mutual opposition often obscured the question of legitimation that lay at the heart of much of the rhetoric about Chinese culture and literature in the 1920's and 1930's.

The struggle between the two camps for recognition as the sole, legitimate voice of Chinese culture masked a vast area of undisputed knowledge, and this made the contending discourses and their mutual engagement possible in the first place. This gray area, I suggest, is where the legitimation question comes in, namely, the legitimating of Chinese literature in the name of nation and culture, be it the Confucian classics or vernacular literature. In that sense, the second National Essence movement should be viewed in light of a larger nation-building project that tried to join national politics and literary practice. As such, it shared a common telos with its radical opponents who rejected tradition. But it is precisely where the two camps did not seem to engage each other and where they seemed unaware of the very question of legitimation that the problem of legitimation becomes enormously interesting for us. What constitutes Chinese culture? Who represents it? And who has the authority to say what counts and what does not count as Chineseness? Although those earlier struggles have largely receded to the distant horizon of history, the questions themselves, however, still remain obstinately with us today, as familiar notions such as culture, nation, tradition, modernity, and East and West continue to be evoked, repeated, translated, and circulated in a transnational mode of "cultural" production where China's uniqueness cannot but be circumscribed by its profound linkages with other localities and other histories.

APPENDIXES

Appendixes

How does the positing of hypothetical equivalences between words articulate the historical condition of the mutual intelligibility or nonintelligibility of languages? How do we historicize the equating of elements of different languages in the face of often naturalized and reified translations? The historico-translingual landscape described in this book suggests that the study of modern Chinese be approached with absolute attention to the types of translatability—which we now take for granted —that have been constructed between Chinese, modern Japanese, and European languages since the nineteenth century. For better or for worse, loanwords and neologisms have penetrated Chinese and other Asian languages so deeply that to expel these "foreign" elements would be tantamount to undermining the intelligibility of the host languages themselves. The Appendixes that follow seek to trace and interpret the "routes" of traffic between Chinese, Japanese, and European languages in the recent past; they are provided here to help the reader recapture a sense of the *radical historicity* of constructed — often contingent — linguistic equivalences interrogated by this book.

As I mentioned in the introductory chapter, linguists have expended much effort in classifying modern Chinese loanwords, especially Sino-Japanese and Sino-Japanese-European neologisms. *Hanyu wailai ci cidian* 漢語外來詞詞典 (A dictionary of Chinese loanwords, 1985), which synthesizes much of this work, is probably the most comprehensive dictionary of its kind published to date. Although the dictionary provides useful historical coverage of Chinese loanwords past and present, its extremely abbreviated etymologies (many of which are clearly erroneous, as Masini has pointed out) cannot illuminate the extraordinary circumstances under which different types of loanwords entered modern Chinese. In compiling the Appendixes, I have followed and expanded the system of classification adopted by Gao Mingkai and Liu Zhengtan in *Xiandai hanyu wailai ci yanjiu* 現代漢語外來詞研究 (A study of loanwords in modern Chinese). The individual entries are divided into seven categories, each illuminating a major loanword type or etymological route whereby modern loanwords and neologisms took up residence in the Chinese language. Gao and Liu's initial findings are supplemented by the research of Wang Lida, Sanetō Keishū, Yue-him Tam, Zdenka Novotná, Guan Choi Wah, Federico Masini, and others. I have also consulted *Hanyu da cidian* 漢語大詞典 (A dictionary of Chinese), *Dai kanwa jiten* 大漢和辭典 (Morohashi's Chinese-Japanese dictionary), *Zhongwen da cidian* 中文大辭典 (A dictionary of Chinese), *Ciyuan* 辭源 (A dictionary of etymology), and Morrison's *Dictionary of the Chinese Language* (1815). This latter work, which has been overlooked by previous scholars except Masini, preceded the rise of round-trip loanwords between Chinese and Japanese and, when viewed together with missionary-Chinese translations from the early nineteenth century, sheds important light on the Japanese use of *kanji* characters in Meiji translations of European texts.

Appendix A draws mainly from Masini's recently published monograph on missionary-Chinese loanwords and neologisms from the nineteenth century, whereas the remaining lists are built upon Gao and Liu's work and that of those who followed in their footsteps. In deciding which loanword should go into a particular category, especially with regard to Appendixes B and D, I adopt the criterion of "ideographic coincidence" rather than that of "semantic equation" used by Gao, Liu, Masini, and the others. By "ideographic coincidence," I refer to the use of existing *Chinese-character* compounds in the translation process *regardless* of what happens at the level of so-called meaning. "Semantic equation," on the other hand, cannot but begin with the thorny question of whether the meaning of a classical Chinese compound has undergone changes—as if non-change was possible—after the Japanese used it to translate a word from a European language. For example, the word *jingji* 經濟 (Japanese *keizai*; economy) is generally assigned to the category of "modern Japanese loanwords" because the *meaning* of this two-character compound is found to be very different from that of its classical Chinese counterpart. The underlying assumption is that classification of loanwords as "modern Japanese loanwords" indicates change whereas those in the category of "return graphic loans" (i.e., classical Chinese-character compounds used by the Japanese to render European words and reimported by the Chinese) exhibit little or no change.

The criterion of "ideographic coincidence" implies no such arbitrary decisions about the changing or non-changing status of meaning. Instead, it focuses on the manner in which ideographic characters traveled through the various Asian languages *regardless* of how they were pronounced or used in a particular linguistic context—phonemic loans being an exceptional category that rarely, if ever, involve semantic translation. (Incidentally, such considerations could also apply to similar situations in Korea and Vietnam.) Thus, whenever I can identify classical Chinese sources for a loanword that other scholars have assigned to the category of original Japanese loanwords, I relocate that word to the category of return graphic loans and supply the relevant etymologies along with contrastive usages from classical texts. (I do not rule out the possibility that a number of such words might have eluded my attention.) Compare, for example, the current 224 entries in Appendix D with the original 68 entries listed in Gao and Liu's category of classical *kanji* terms.

The process of compilation has proved extremely laborious, and I found myself spending many hours trying to correct the technical errors of previous scholars. The classical sources provided by Gao and Liu, which I initially used to compile Appendix D, contain numerous mistakes and inaccuracies. Take the two-character compound *quanli* 權利 (App. A.). To illustrate its classical usages, Gao and Liu quote a passage from *Shiji* 史記 (Records of the grand historian) which they claim derives from a section of the narrative entitled "Guan Fu zhuan" 灌夫傳 (Biography of Guan Fu), which does not exist. (Compare "Dou, Tian, Guan, Han zhuan" 竇田灌韓傳 [Biographies of Dou, Tian, Guan, Han] in *Hanshu* 漢書.) The *Shiji* story of Guan Fu is actually contained in "Weiqi Wu'an hou liezhuan" 魏其武安侯列傳 (Biographies of Lords Weiqi and Wu'an). Another typical problem with their handling of classical sources is inadequate attention to changing and multiple etymologies. To illustrate, the term *fengjian* 封建 (App. D.) had had an interesting etymological history in classical Chinese texts before it was equated with English "feudal" by Japanese and Chinese translators and became a return graphic loan in modern Chinese. Gao and Liu give a straightforward definition of the term as it was used before the First Emperor of the Qin; however, they fail to take account of the changing usage of this term since the Han dynasty. Since 封建 ("feudal"?) happens to be one of those seminal translations in modern translingual history that have provoked much controversy surrounding Marxist interpretations of pre-capitalist Asian societies and consequently exerted a huge impact on these societies' perception of their own past, the etymology of the term deserves more than casual attention.

The difficulty in identifying and verifying the classical sources has been greatly simplified by the recent publication of *Hanyu da cidian*. I drew much of the useful etymological information from this dictionary in compiling Appendixes A and D, and in the course of doing so, I noticed that even the authoritative *Hanyu da cidian* is not entirely free of occasional errors. One of the passages from *Zuozhuan* 左傳 (Zuo commentary) quoted under "autocracy" in Appendix D illustrating the ancient usage of the term *zhuanzhi* 專治 contains the phrase "heguo zhi wei" 何國之爲 (Could it still be a country?) taken from "The Nineteenth Year of Duke Zhao" (the same usage also appears elsewhere in *Zuozhuan* such as "The Thirteenth Year of Duke Zhao"). This phrase is misquoted by *Hanyu da cidian* as "heguo weizhi" 何國爲之 (What country could do this?). I have tried my best to minimize errors and inaccurate information such as the above, although readers might still find problematic areas of which I am not aware. To do full justice to this fascinating topic, one would need to spend a great deal more time and energy than the subject of this book requires.

When deciding whether to add or drop certain entries as modern loanwords, I have tended to err on the conservative side. Like Gao and Liu, I have eschewed scientific and technical terms that do not usually circulate beyond their specialized fields, such as chemistry or medicine. Readers should be advised that these Appendixes are preliminary and by no means exhaustive. A more complete and better documented study of modern Chinese loanwords is yet to be written. Unlike the author of this book, future scholars need not be constrained by the original conceptual model proposed by Gao and Liu and can provide us with more imaginative ways of classifying and interpreting modern Chinese loanwords. (I apologize for the non-standard use of certain punctuation marks for the Chinese quotation in Appendixes A and D, for the word processor I used in preparing this manuscript does not contain the symbols adopted in the standard modern editions of classical texts. These include the "pause" comma, for which I substitute a regular comma or a period, as well as the centered dot used between quoted titles and chapter headings, for which a colon is used instead.)

Finally, the Appendixes are prepared exclusively for bilingual readers and require good knowledge of modern and classical Chinese, for I had compelling reasons to leave the original quotations from classical Chinese texts untranslated and to retain the explications in modern Chinese provided by my sources, which, being a kind of translation themselves, create a complicated situation. The decision not to render these passages into English derives from the theoretical impulse of this book as well as from a dilemma inherent in cross-cultural translation: Is it possible to translate without speaking in other words?

Neologisms Derived from Missionary-Chinese Texts and Their Routes of Diffusion

English	Chinese character	Chinese romanization	Notes on sources and round-trip diffusion
acoustics	聲學	*shengxue*	
air	空氣	*kongqi*	Round-trip diffusion via Japan? Cf. classical Chinese usage: 宋蘇軾《龍虎鉛汞論》：「方調息時，則漱而烹之，須滿口而後嚥。若未滿，且留口中，候後次，仍以空氣送至丹田，常以意養之」，道教謂元氣，清氣。
aerostat	氣毬飛車	*qiqiu feiche*	Also *feiche* 飛車
airplane	飛機	*feiji*	
algebra	代數	*daishu*	Round-trip diffusion via Japanese *daisū?*
auction	拍賣	*paimai*	
bank	銀館	*yinguan*	Cf. Japanese-derived replacement *ginkō* 銀行 in App. B.
battery	電池	*dianchi*	Round-trip diffusion via Japanese *denchi.*
bicycle	自行車	*zixingche*	Also *jiaotache* 腳踏車.
blue book	藍皮書	*lanpishu*	
botany	植物學	*zhiwuxue*	Cf. alternative Japanese translation *shokugaku* 植學 and phonemic loan *botanika* 菩多尼訶.

English	Chinese	Pinyin	Notes
botanical garden	植物場	*zhiwuchang*	Cf. Japanese-derived replacement *shokubutsuen* 植物園 in App. B.
brain	大腦	*danao*	Cf. *xiaonao*小腦 (the cerebellum) below.
bread	面包	*mianbao*	
briefcase	手箱	*shouxiang*	
calculus	代微積	*daiweiji*	Later replaced by *weijifen* 微積分 through the round-trip diffusion of Japanese *sekibun*. Compare classical Chinese usages: 一。《穀梁傳: 文公六年 》:「閏月者，附月之餘日也，積分而成於月者也」，范甯注:「積眾月之餘分，以成此月」，謂積累時差。二。《元史: 選舉志一 》:「泰定三年夏六月，更積分而為貢舉，並依世祖舊制」，謂元，明，清三代國子監考核學生成績，選拔人才之方法。
carbon content	炭性	*tanxing*	
carpet	洋毯	*yangtan*	
cerebellum	小腦	*xiaonao*	Cf. *danao* 大腦 and *quantixue* 全體學.
chemical element	原質	*yuanzhi*	Cf. Japanese-derived replacement *genso* 元素 in App. B.
chemistry	化學	*huaxue*	
cold zone	冷帶	*lengdai*	Introduced by Ricci in 1602 and used by Aleni in 1623 (Masini, p. 186). Cf. *handai* 寒帶 in App. B.
communication device	通信線機	*tongxin-xianji*	
concrete	水泥	*shuini*	Cf. the co-existing Japanese loan *konkuriito* 混凝土 in App. B.
Congress	國會	*guohui*	Or *zonghui* 總會. The term 國會 was also used to render the English "Parliament." Round-trip diffusion via Japanese *kokkai* ? Cf. *yiyuan* 議院 below.
consumption	消流	*xiaoliu*	As glossed in Morrison (1815). Cf. Japanese replacement *shōhi* 消費 in App. B.
court of law	法院	*fayuan*	Cf. *fating* 法庭 in App. D.

daily newspaper	日報	*ribao*	Cf. *baozhi* 報紙 (newspaper) below. The first paper to use the term in translating the English phrase was probably the *Huazi ribao* 華字日報 founded in Hong Kong in 1864 (Masini, p. 193). Round-trip diffusion via Japanese *nippō*. Cf. classical Chinese usages:一。《漢書: 食貨志下》:「夫事有召禍而法有起姦，今令細民人操造幣之勢，各隱屏而鑄作，因欲禁其厚利微姦，雖鯨罪日報，其勢不止」，謂每日審判定罪。二。清黃六鴻《福惠全書: 錢穀: 流水日報簿》:「日報簿與日收簿，同時印發」，謂逐日呈報。
dance	跳舞	*tiaowu*	
debt	債欠	*zhaiqian*	Cf. Japanese-derived replacement *saimu* 債務 in App. B.
democracy (formerly, republican)	民主	*minzhu*	W. A. P. Martin first adopted the compound *minzhu* 民主 to translate "republican" (form of government) in the phrase *minzhu zhi guo* 民主之國, as opposed to "monarchic" (form of govern-ment) or *junzhu zhi guo* 君主之國 in his *Wanguo gongfa* 萬國公法 in 1864, a translation of Henry Wheaton's *Elements of International Law* (see Masini, p. 189). This translation of "republican" was later replaced by the return graphic loan *kyōwa* 共和 (App. D). According to Sanetō, the term 民主 was used to render "democracy" by Wang Zhi 王芝 in his 1872 edition of *Haike ritan* 海客日潭. The widespread diffusion of this later translation in modern Chinese is attributable to Japanese *minshu*. Compare the classical Chinese usage below:《書: 多方》:「天惟時求民主，乃大降顯休命于成湯」，謂民之主宰者，多指帝王或官吏。又見《左傳: 文公十七年》:「齊君之語偷。臧文仲有言曰:「民主偷必

死」」。《文選: 班固＜典
引＞》：「肇命民主，五德初
始」，蔡邕注：「民主，天子
也。」《資治通鑒: 晉惠帝太安二
年》：「昌遂據江夏，造妖言云:
「當有聖人出為民主」。」

department store	大貨鋪	*dahuopu*	Cf. Japanese *hyakkaten* 百貨店 in App. B.
Department of Foreign Affairs	外部	*waibu*	
divorce	離婚	*lihun*	Cf. 17th-century translation (Aleni, 1623): *xiangxiuli* 相休離 (Masini, p. 186)
drain pipe (dragon mouth)	龍口	*longkou*	Also *longzui* 龍嘴. Cf. *longtou* 龍頭 (dragon head) for "tap" below.
duty, obligation	義務	*yiwu*	Round-trip diffusion via Japanese *gimu*. Cf. 漢徐幹《中論: 貴驗》：「《詩》曰：「伐木丁丁，鳥鳴嚶嚶，出自幽谷，遷於喬木」，言朋友之義務，在切直以升於善道者」，謂合乎正道的事。
dynamic mechanics	動重學	*dongzhong xue*	Later replaced by *donglixue* 動力學.
economy	富國策	*fuguoce*	Also *fuguoxue* 富國學, *zishengxue* 資生學, *pingzhunxue* 平準學, etc. Yan Fu adopted *jixue* 計學 in his translation of Western texts. Cf. *aikangnuomi (yikanglaomi)* 愛康諾米 (依康老米) in App. F and the return graphic loan *jingji* 經濟 (Japanese-derived replacement *keizai*) in App. D.
elect, election	選舉	*xuanju*	Also *gongju* 公舉; round-trip diffusion via Japanese *senkyo*. Cf.《文子: 上義》：「仁義足以懷天下之民，事業足以當天下之急，選舉足以得賢士之心，謀慮足以決輕重之權，此上義之道也」，指選拔舉用賢能。又見《後漢書: 陳蕃傳》：「自蕃為光祿勳，與五官中郎將黃琬共典選舉，不偏權富，而為執家郎所譖訴，坐免歸。」

electric bell	電線鈴	*dianxianling*	Also *dianqiling* 電氣鈴; later replaced by *dianling* 電鈴
electric cable	電纜	*dianlan*	
electric circuit	電路	*dianlu*	
electric lamp	電氣燈	*dianqideng*	Also *qideng* 氣燈? Later replaced by *diandeng* 電燈
electric light	電氣光	*dianqiguang*	
electric motor	電機	*dianji*	Also *dianqiji* 電氣機.
electric pile?	電堆	*diandui*	
electric wire	電線	*dianxian*	Also *dianqixian* 電氣線
electricity (the study of)	電學	*dianxue*	
electricity	電氣	*dianqi*	Also *dian* 電
elevator	自行屋	*zixingwu*	Later replaced by *dianti* 電梯.
empire	帝國	*diguo*	Yan Fu adopted a phonemic loan *yingbai'er* 英拜兒 in rendering "empire"(1901-1902), adding the following note of explanation: 近人譯帝國. (Masini, p. 168). It is unclear, though, whether the equating of 帝國 and "empire" first appeared in missionary-Chinese translations or entered the language via Japanese. Cf. 宋周邦彥《看花回》詞之二:「雪飛帝國,人在雲邊心暗折」,指京都。
entomology	虫學	*chongxue*	
entrance	入口	*rukou*	Used with the meaning of "import" as early as 1844; round-trip diffusion via the Japanese *iriguchi*. Cf. *jinkou* 進口 below.
equation	方程	*fangcheng*	Cf.《九章算術: 方程》:白尚恕註釋:「「方」即方形,「程」即表達相課的意思,或者是表達式……所謂「方程」即現今的增廣矩陣」,今指含未知數的等式。Also see *fangcheng shi* 方程式 in App. B.
equator	赤道	*chidao*	17th-century Jesuit neologism: Ricci; 1602; Aleni, 1623.

Esperanto	萬國新語	*wanguoxinyu*	Cf. the phonemic loan *Aisibunandu* 愛斯不難讀 in App. F and Japanese-derived replacement *sekaigo* 世界語 in App. B.
evening newspaper	晚報	*wanbao*	
exhibition	博物會	*bowuhui*	Also rendered as *xuanqihui* 炫奇會 and *saiqihui* 賽奇會. Cf. Japanese *hakurankai* 博覽會 and *tenrankai* 展覽會 in App. B.
experimental laboratory	試驗場	*shiyanchang*	Cf. Japanese *shikensho* 試驗所 in App. B. The word *shiyan* 試驗 exists in 晉干寶《搜神記》卷十六：「願重啟候，何惜不一試驗之？」
export	出口	*chukou*	Cf. Japanese *deguchi* for "exit" in App. B.
extractor?	拔機	*baji*	
foreign language	洋語	*yangyu*	Later *waiguo yu* 外國語 and *waiyu* 外語.
French communication wire	法通線	*fatongxian*	Cf. *dianbao* 電報 (telegraph).
gas lamp	煤氣燈	*meiqideng*	Also called *zilaihuo* 自來火. Cf. the Cantonese replacement *huochai* 火柴 (matches) below.
Gatling gun	藕心炮	*ouxinpao*	Cf. *gelin pao* 格林炮 in App. F.
geology	地質	*dizhi*	Round-trip diffusion via Japanese *chishitsu*. Cf.《易: 坤》：「六二，直方大」，三國魏王弼注：「居中得正，極於地質，任其自然而物自生」，孔穎達疏：「質為形質。地之形質，直方又大，此六二居中得正是盡極地之體質也。」
geology (the study of)	地質學	*dizhixue*	Also *dixue* 地學. Cf. Japanese *chishitsugaku.*
geometry	几何	*jihe*	
globe	地球	*diqiu*	17th-century Jesuit neologism: Ricci, 1602.
goggles	風鏡	*fengjing*	
governor	正統領	*zhengtong- ling*	Later replaced by *zhouzhang* 州長.

guarantee	保障	*baozhang*	Used to translate "to guarantee" as early as the 1830s; round-trip diffusion via Japanese *hoshō*. Cf. 一。《左傳: 定公十二年》:「且成,孟氏之保障也。無成,是無孟氏也」,謂特以為保護障蔽者。二。清昭槤《嘯亭雜彔: 宋金形勢》:「然建炎之初,河北尚為宋守,河南淮右堅城數十,自相保障」,謂保衛,保護。
handicrafts	手工	*shougong*	As glossed in Morrison (1815). See also Japanese-derived replacement *shukōgyō* 手工業 in App. B. Cf.《三國志: 吳書: 孫休傳》:「(孫) 謂先是科郡上手工千餘人送建業」,謂工匠。
hospital	醫院	*yiyuan*	First used to translate "hospital" in the early 19th century. Cf. the classical Chinese expression *taiyiyuan* 太醫院 or the "Imperial Academy of Medicine."
hothouse; greenhouse	暖房	*nuanfang*	Cf. Japanese *onshō* 溫床 (hotbed or breeding ground) in App. B and the return graphic loan *wenshi* 溫室 (greenhouse; Japanese *onshitsu*) in App. D.
House of Commons	鄉紳房	*xiangshen fang*	Also see the phonemic loan *ganwen haosi* 甘文好司 in App. F.
House of Lords	爵房	*juefang*	Also see *lühaosi* 律好司 in App. F.
hydrant	水龍	*shuilong*	Also *niuhou* 牛喉. Cf. the Japanese semantic loan *shōkasen* 消火栓 in App. B.
hydraulics	水學	*shuixue*	
import	進口	*jinkou*	Cf. *rukou* 入口 (entrance) above.
independence	自主	*zizhu*	
information, signal	消息	*xiaoxi*	
international	萬國	*wanguo*	Literal meaning "ten thousand countries," used to render English "international" by W.A.P. Martin in *Wanguo gongfa* in 1864. Later replaced by the Japanese loan *kokusai* 國際 as in *kokusai kōhō*

			國際公法 (App. B). See also the phonemic loan *yingtenaxiongna'er* 英特那雄那爾 in App. F.
journalist	記者	*jizhe*	Used by Morrison as early as the 1810s (Masini, p. 184). Later also *xinwenguan jizhe* 新聞館記者.
judgment, to judge	判斷	*panduan*	A derivative term *panduanchu* 判斷處 was used to render the "British law court" in 1866 (Masini, p. 191).
jurist	公師	*gongshi*	Later replaced by *falixuejia* 法理學家.
kerosene	煤油	*meiyou*	Cf. *shiyou* 石油 below.
law	法律	*falü*	Used to translate "law" by 17th-century Jesuit missionaries (Aleni, 1623); glossed in this sense by Morrison in 1815; round-trip diffusion via Japanese *hōritsu*. Cf. classical Chinese usages: 一。《莊子: 徐無鬼》:「法律之士廣治。」又見《管子》:「夫法者,所以興功懼暴也,律者,所以定分止爭也:令者,所以令人知事也。法律政令者,吏民規矩繩墨也」,指刑法,律令。二。明胡應麟《詩藪: 古體上》:「近體之攻,務先法律」,指詩文創作所依據的格式和規律。三。元吳昌齡《張天師》第四折:「豈不知張真人法律精嚴,早仗劍都驅在五雷壇內,一個個供下狀吐出真情」,指道行戒律。
law (the study of)	法學	*faxue*	Round-trip diffusion via Japanese *hōgaku*. Cf. classical Chinese usages: 一。《南史: 范曄傳》:「曄性精微,有思致,觸類多善,衣裳器服,莫不增損制度,世人皆法學之」,指傚法。二。《南齊書: 孔雉珪傳》:「尋古之名流,多有法學,故釋之,定國,聲光漢室,元常,文惠,續映魏閣」,古指刑名,法治之學。
lawyer	律師	*lüshi*	Also *lüshi* 律士. Cf. classical Chinese usages:《涅槃經: 金剛身品》:「如是能知佛法所作。善能解說,是名律師」,指佛教稱善解戒律者。Cf. Japanese *bengoshi* 辯護士 in App. B.

letter of credence	信憑	*xinping*	Used to the translate this English phrase as early as 1864.
life-belt	保險圈	*baoxianquan*	Also *jiumingquan* 救命圈
literary subjects	文科	*wenke*	According to Masini (p. 204), this usage appeared in 17th-century Jesuit texts (Aleni)and came back into use together with *like* 理科 or *shike* 實科 (sciences) in the 19th century via the round-trip diffusion of Japanese *bunka*. Cf. classical Chinese: 唐劉禹錫《蘇州謝上表》：「謬以薄伎，三登文科」，指科舉制時以經學考選文士之科。又見《舊五代史: 選舉志》：「近代設文科，選冑子，所以綱維名教，崇樹邦本也。」
literature	文學	*wenxue*	The equating of *wenxue* 文學 and "literature"(?) may be dated back to 17th-century Jesuit translations (Aleni, 1623). The compound was later used by 19th century Protestant missionaries to translate the modern English term "literature" and became widespread via the round-trip diffusion of Japanese *bungaku* (cf. Masini, p. 204). Compare: 一。《論語: 先進》：「文學：子游，子夏」，邢昺疏：「若文章博學，則有子游，子夏二人也」，謂孔門四科之一。二。《韓非子: 六反》：「學道立方，離法之民也，而世尊之曰文學之士」，指儒家學說。三。南朝梁劉勰《文心雕龍: 時序》：「自獻帝播遷，文學蓬轉」，謂儒生，亦泛指有學問的人。四。北魏酈道元《水經注: 江水一》：「南岸道東，有文學。始文翁為蜀守，立講堂作石室於南城」，謂學校，習儒之所。五。官名。漢代於州郡及王國置文學，或稱文學掾，或稱文學史，為後世教官所由來。
locomotive	汽車	*qiche*	Also *xuhuoji* 蓄火機. *Qiche* 汽車 was later used to render "motor vehicle."
Lower House	下房	*xiafang*	Also *xiatang* 下堂; later replaced by *xiayiyuan* 下議院. Cf. *yiyuan* 議院 (parliament)

lunatic asylum	養瘋院	*yangfeng yuan*	Also *fengrenyuan* 瘋人院.
magazine	雜誌	*zazhi*	Probably first used in *Zhongwai zazhi* 中外雜誌 published by John Macgowan in Shanghai in 1862, a few yearas before the 1867 Japanese magazine *Seiyō zasshi* 西洋雜誌 (Masini, p. 216). Round-trip diffusion via Japan.
manage, management	管理	*guanli*	As glossed in Morrison (1815); round-trip diffusion via Japanese *kanri*. In *Shengwu ji* 聖武記 (1842), Wei Yuan 魏源 wrote "近日西洋英吉利，自稱管理五印度" (England from the West has recently laid claims to the management of India). Cf. 明劉兌《嬌紅記》：「去年聽除回來，為見姪兒申純在家管理事務，十分停當。」
master (degree)	碩士	*shuoshi*	Round-trip diffusion via Japan? Cf.《五代史: 張居翰傳》：「前後左右者日益親，則忠臣碩士日益疏」，謂品節卓著，學問淵博之士。
matches	火柴	*huochai*	This Cantonese neologism succeeded in replacing *zilaihuo* 自來火 in Mandarin.
mechanics	力學	*lixue*	Also *zhongxue* 重學. According to Masini (p. 187), the word *lixue* 力學 probably reached Japan through W. A. P. Martin's *Gewu rumen* (Introduction to science, 1868) and, through round-trip diffusion, it eventually replaced the alternative translation 重學.
mediator	中保者	*zhongbaozhe*	Used to translate English "mediating power" in *Wanguo gongfa* (1864). Cf.《説岳全傳》第一回：「〔師父〕逼他寫賣華山文契，卻是小青龍柴世榮，餓虎星鄭子明做中保」，謂居中作保之人。
medicine	醫學	*yixue*	Used by 17th-century Jesuit missionaries to translate "the study of medicine;" round-trip

			diffusion via Japanese *igaku* Cf.《舊唐書: 太宗本紀上》:「(貞觀三年) 九月癸丑，諸州置醫學」，謂古代培養醫藥人才的機構。 Also *yike* (醫科).
meeting, assembly	會議	*huiyi*	Used as a noun as early as the 1830s; round-trip diffusion via Japanese *kaigi*? Cf.《史記: 平津侯主父列傳》:「每朝會議，開陳其端，令人主自擇，不肯面折庭爭」。宋蘇軾《東坡志林: 勃遜之》:「與勃遜之會議於穎，或言洛人善接花，歲出新枝，而菊品尤多」。又見清孔尚任《桃花扇: 辭院》:「這等又會議不成，如何是好」，謂聚會論議。
megaphone?	傳聲筒	*chuansheng tong*	Also *chuansheng zhi qi* 傳聲之器; *chuanshengqi* 傳聲器. Cf. *anxiaoxi* 暗消息 (secret informer?); *xiaoxi* 消息 (information, signal).
member, deputy	委員	*weiyuan*	Round-trip diffusion via Japanese *iin*.
meridian of longitude	經線	*jingxian*	17th-century neologism (Ricci, 1602 and Aleni, 1623). See also *weixian* 緯線 below.
microscope	顯微鏡	*xianweijing*	Also *dianqi guangshi xianweijing* 電氣光視顯微鏡.
middle school	中學	*zhongxue*	Also *zhongxueguan* 中學館 According to Masini (p. 219), the term 中學 appeared briefly in the 17th-century (Aleni, 1623) and was reintroduced by 19th-century missionary-Chinese translations. Round-trip diffusion via Japanese *chūgaku*.
montgolfier	天船	*tianchuan*	
museum	博物院	*bowuyuan*	Also *bolanyuan* 博覽院; *bowuchang* 博物場. Cf. Japanese-derived replacement *hakubutsu kan* 博物館 in App. B.
natural science	博物	*bowu*	Used to translate "natural science" as early as the 1850s. Cf. Japanese-derived replacement *shizen kagaku* 自然科學 in App. B and the return grahpic loans 自然

			(natural, and 科學 (science) in App. D. Also compare《左傳: 昭公元年》:「晉侯聞子產之言，日：博物君子也」，謂通曉眾物。漢桓寬《鹽鐵論: 雜論》:「桑大夫據當世，合時變，推道術，尚權利，辟略小辯，雖非正法，然巨儒宿學，惡然大能自解，可謂博物通士也。」又見宋歐陽修《筆説: 博物説》:「草木虫魚，「詩」家自為一學，博物尤難。」
news	新聞	*xinwen*	Used to translate "news" in *Tianxia xinwen* 天下新聞, one of the first missionary-Chinese magazines printed in Malacca in 1828. Cf. 一。唐李咸用《春日喜逢鄉人劉松》詩:「舊業久拋耕釣侶，新聞多説戰爭功」，謂近日聽來的事。二。宋蘇軾《次韻高要令劉湜峽山寺見寄》:「新聞妙無多，舊學閑可束」，指新知識。三。宋趙昇《朝野類要: 文書》:「朝報，日出事宜也。每日門下後省編定，請給事判報，方行下都進奏院報行天下。其有所謂內探，省探，衙探之類，皆衷私小報，率有漏泄之禁，故隱而號之曰新聞」，指有別於正式朝報的小報。
newspaper	報紙	*baozhi*	Also *xinwenzhi* 新聞紙. Cf.《自作孽》:「鄉裡人家看報紙，大奇！大奇」，謂邸報，朝報。
North Pole	北極	*beiji*	17th-century Jesuit neologism: Ricci, 1602; Aleni, 1623.
parallel of latitude	緯線	*weixian*	17th-century neologism (Ricci, 1602 and Aleni, 1623). See also *jingxian* 經線 above.
parliament	議院	*yiyuan*	Round-trip diffusion via Japanese *giin*. Also *yizhengyuan* 議政院, *gongyitang* 公議堂, *gongyiting* 公議庭, *yishiting* 議事廳, *huitang* 會堂, *gonghui* 公會 (later used to translate trade union). Cf. Japanese-derived replacement *gikai* 議會 in App. B and phonemic loans: *baliman/balimen* 巴厘滿／巴力門 in App. F.
parliament-ary official	紳士	*shenshi*	Replaced by the Japanese loan *giin* 議員 (App. B) and later used

			to translate "gentleman" instead (see App. F).
personal property	動物	*dongwu*	Used to translate English "personal property" in *Wanguo gongfa* (Masini, p. 170). The Japanese-derived loan *dōsan* 動產 (App. B) later replaced this translation to prevent confusion with the homonym 動物 meaning "animal."
personal right	人之權利	*ren zhi quanli*	See *quanli* 權利 or "right" below.
people's assembly	民間大會	*minjian dahui*	Also used to translate "corporation" in Martin's *Wanguo gongfa*.
petroleum	石油	*shiyou*	Also used to translate "kerosene" interchangeably with *meiyou* 煤油. Cf. 宋沈括《夢溪筆談: 雜志一》:「鄜延境內有石油，舊説高奴縣出脂水，即此也」，又見明李時珍《本草綱目: 石一: 石腦油》:「石油所出不一。國朝正德末年，嘉州開鹽井，偶得油水，可以照夜，其光加倍。近復開出數井，官司主之，此亦石油，但出於井爾。」
photography	照像法	*zhaoxiangfa*	Also *yingxiang* 影像, *riying xiang* 日影像. Cf. the return graphic loan *xiezhen* 寫真 in App. D.
photographic camera	照像鏡	*zhaoxiang-jing*	Also *zhaoxiangqi* 照相器 and *shenjing* 神鏡 (literally "magic mirror").
physics	物理	*wuli*	Used to translate "physics" early as the 1634 translation known as *Qiqi tushuo* 奇器圖説 (Description of mechanical instruments) by Johann Schreck and Wang Zheng 王徵; 19th-century round-trip diffusion via Japanese *butsuri*. Also see the Japanese loan *butsurigaku* 物理學 in App. E. Cf. classical Chinese usages: 一。《鶡冠子: 王鈇》:「龐子曰:「願聞其人情物理」」，謂事理。二。《周書: 明帝紀》:「天地有窮已，五常有推移，人安得常在，是以生而有死者，物理之必然」，謂常理，道理。

physiology; anatomy	全體	*quanti*	Later replaced by the return graphic loan *seiri* 生理 (App. D), as was the case of *quantixue* 全體學 and its Japanese loan replacement *seirigaku* 生理學 (App. E) and *kaibōgaku* 解剖學 (App. D). Cf. classical Chinese usages: 一。《釋名: 釋飲食》:「貊炙，全體炙之，各自以刀割，出於胡貊之為也」，又見清俞樾《茶香室續鈔: 天上人》:「予亦曾見三人，一人全體，二半坐云」，指整個身體。二。宋劉克莊《郊行》詩:「山晴全體出，樹老半身枯」，指事物的全部。
piano	洋琴	*yangqin*	Later replaced by *gangqin* 鋼琴.
pistol	手槍	*shouqiang*	
plenipotentiary	全權	*quanquan*	
pneumatics	氣學	*qixue*	
post office	郵局	*youju*	Abbreviation of 郵政局 from Japanese *yūsei* 郵政. Also *xinju* 信局, *gongxinju* 公信局, *diannqiju* 電氣局. Cf. Japanese *yūbinkyoku* 郵便局.
post-stamp	郵票	*youpiao*	Also *xiaopiao* 小票 and *longtou* 龍頭.
premier, prime minister	總理	*zongli*	Round-trip diffusion via Japanese *sōri* . In Japanese, the term is used to translate both "prime minister" (*Sōri daijin* 總理大臣) and "president." Cf. classical Chinese usages: 一。宋蘇軾《德威堂銘》:「其總理庶務，酬酢事物，雖精練少年有不如」，指全面管理。二。明劉若愚《酌中志: 客魏始末紀略》:「謙於嘉靖四十一年選入，歷陞內官監總理」，指總管某部門或事務的負責人。
president	統領	*tongling*	Also *shouling* 首領, *zongtonglin* 總統領, *dazongtong* 大總統 and *zongtong* 總統 (The last term is probably a return graphic loan from Japanese.) See phonemic loans: *bolicitiande* 伯力賜天德, *bolixidun* 佰理喜頓, *bolixitiande* 佰理璽天德 in App. F. Compare

classical Chinese: 一。《後漢書:
何進傳》:「中官統領禁省,自古
及今,漢家故事,不可廢也」,謂
統率。二。軍官名。宋清兩代置。
見《宋史: 設職官志七》,《清史
稿: 職官志四》。

printer	印文機	*yinwenji*	
privilege	特權	*tequan*	Used by Martin in 1864 to render "conditional or hypothetical rights" (偶有之特權) versus "primitive or absolute rights" (自有之原權) (Masini, p. 199).
propeller	蕩機	*dangji*	
railway	鐵路	*tielu*	Found in K. F. A. Gützlaff, *Maoyi tongzhi* 貿易通志 (A general account of commerce, 1840). Masini (p. 200) suggests convincingly that the Chinese compound was a loan-translation (calque) of the German *Eisenbahn*. Also see *tiezhe* 鐵轍 (now obsolete) and *tiedao* 鐵道; the latter probably reached Japan in the 1870s (cf. *tetsudō*).
real estate	植物	*zhiwu*	Used to translate English "real property" as opposed to "personal property" (*dongwu* 動物) in *Wanguo gongfa* (Masini, p. 218). The Japanese-derived loan *fudōsan* 不動產 (App. B) later replaced this translation to prevent confusion with the homonym 植物 meaning "plant."
reasoning	推論道理	*tuilun daoli*	As glossed by Morrison (1815). Cf. the Japanese-derived replacement *suiron* 推論 in App. B.
residence	住所	*zhusuo*	As glossed in Morrison (1815); round-trip diffusion via Japanese *jūsho*. Cf.《蘇舜欽詩》:「念君住所近不遠」,泛言所居之處。
rifle	火槍	*huoqiang*	Cf. *dapenpao* 大噴炮 (air rifle?).
right	權利	*quanli*	Used to translate "rights" as early as the 1860s; possible round-trip diffusion through Japanese *kenri*.

			The translation purged the classical Chinese term of its negative connotations associated with "power," "money," and "privilege." Cf.《史記: 魏其武安侯列傳》:「陂池田園，宗族賓客為權利，橫于潁川」，謂權勢貨財。
right of property	掌物之權	*zhangwu zhi quan*	Cf. Japanese-derived replacement *sanken* 產權 in App. B.
rolling mill	軋機	*zhaji*	
school	學校	*xuexiaao*	Used by Aleni to describe the European school system in 1623; 19th-century round-trip diffusion via Japanese *gakkō,* the replacement for *xuetang* 學堂, *xueshu* 學塾, and *xueshe* 學舍. Cf.《孟子: 滕文公上》:「設為庠，序，學，校以教之」。漢揚雄《官箴: 博士箴》:「國有學校，侯有泮宮」。宋歐陽修《議學狀》:「夫建學校以養賢，論材德而取士，此皆有國之本務。」
school for the mute	養啞院	*yangyayuan*	
sciences	理科	*like*	Used by Jesuit missionaries as early as the 17th century. It came back into use in the 19th century via Japanese *rika.* In 1896, Liang Qichao explained its meaning as *gezhi* 格致 (Masini, p. 186). Cf. *kexue* 科學 for "science" in App. D.
self-preservation	自護	*zihu*	
secret informer?	暗消息	*an xiaoxi*	Now obsolete. Cf. *xiaoxi* 消息 (information, signal); *chuan shengtong* 傳聲筒 (megaphone)
semi-sovereign	半主	*banzhu*	Later replaced by *ban zhimindi* 半殖民地.
sextant	量天尺	*liangtianchi*	
silvering (?)	銀性	*yinxing*	
social intercourse	交際	*jiaoji*	Originally used to translate "political relations" in the 1860s

English	Chinese	Pinyin	Notes
			(Masini, p. 180); current translation associated with Japanese *kōsai* via round-trip diffusion. Cf. classical Chinese usages: 一。《孟子: 万章下》：「敢問交際，何心也」，朱熹集注：「際，接也。交際，謂人以禮儀幣帛相交接也」。二。《魏書: 尒朱榮傳》：「陛下登祚之始，人情未安，大兵交際，難可齊一」，猶會合。三。《樂府詩集: 唐祭太社樂章: 蕭和》：「九域底平，兩儀交際」，謂融和感通。
South Pole	南極	*nanji*	17th-century Jesuit neologism: Ricci, 1602; Aleni, 1623.
sovereignty	主權	*zhuquan*	Round-trip diffusion via Japanese *shuken* . Cf. classical Chinese usages: 一。《管子: 七臣七主》：「藏竭則主權喪，法傷則姦門闖」，謂君主的權力。二。《資治通鑒: 唐穆宗長慶三年》：「上憐之，盡取弘 (韓弘) 財簿自閱視，凡中外主權，多納弘貨」，指有職權的管吏。
static mechanics	靜重學	*jingzhongxue*	Later replaced by *jinglixue* 靜力學. Cf. *dongzhongxue* 動重學 and *donglixue* 動力學.
station	站	*zhan*	Used to translate "railway station" as early as 1866. The word was originally a phonemic loan from Mongolian *jam*, meaning a military post station (Masini, p. 216).
steam boat	輪船	*lun chuan*	Also *an lunchuan* 暗火輪船, *huochuan* 火船, *huolun chuan* 火輪船; *huolunzhou* 火輪舟, *huoyanzhou* 火煙舟. Cf. Japanese-derived alternative *kisen* 汽船 in App. B.
steam engine	火輪機	*huolunji*	Also *huoji* 火機, *lunji* 輪機, *qiji* 汽機, *huolunjiqi* 火輪機器, *huolunqiju* 火輪器具.
steam pump	火輪取水具	*huolun qushuiju*	
stoker	司火食者	*sihuoshizhe*	
students studying abroad	洋學生業童	*yangxue-sheng yetong*	Also *chuyang xuesheng* 出洋學生. Cf. Japanese-derived replacement *ryūgakusei* 留學生 in App. B.

substance	實體	*shiti*	As glossed in Morrison, 1815; round-trip diffusion via Japanese *jittai*. Cf. 晉陸機《浮雲賦》:「有輕虛之艷象,無實體之真形」,指真實,具體的東西。二。南朝梁劉勰《文心雕龍: 總術》:「昔陸氏《文賦》,號為曲盡,然汎論纖悉,而實體未該」,謂要點。
tap (dragon head)	龍頭	*longtou*	Cf. *longtou* 龍頭 (post-stamp) above.
technology?	術學, 藝學	*shuxue, yixue*	
telegram office	電報局	*dianbaoju*	Cf. *dianqiju* 電氣局 (post office).
telegraph, telegram	電報	*dianbao*	Also *dianjixin* 電機信; *dianliji* 電理機; *dianqibao* 電氣報; *dianqixin* 電氣信; *tongxianxin* 通線信, *xintongxian* 信通線. Round-trip diffusion via Japanese
temperate zone	溫帶	*wendai*	Introduced by the Jesuit missionary Aleni, 1623.
textile machine	織機	*zhiji*	
thermal level(?)	火性	*huoxing*	Cf. colloquial Chinese for "hot temper."
thermo-dynamics	火學	*huoxue*	Replaced by *relixue* 熱力學.
tonnage	蠆船	*dunchuan*	Cf. *dun* 蠆 or 噸 in App. F.
tropical zone	熱帶	*redai*	Introduced by Ricci in 1602 and used by Aleni in 1623 (Masini, p. 193).
trade	交易	*jiaoyi*	Used to render "trade" in *Haiguo tuzhi* 海國圖志 (1844). Masini (p. 181) suggests that Aleni adopted this translation as early as 1623. Yan Fu explained the term as 謂相易以物者 (1901-1902). Cf. Japanese *kōeki* and classical Chinese usages: 一。《易: 繫辭下》:「日中為市,致天下之民,聚天下之貨,交易而退,各得其所」,謂物物交換,後多指做買賣,貿易。二。《公羊傳: 宣公十二年》:「君之不令臣交易為言」,猶往來。三。《後漢書: 朱浮傳》:「帝以二千石長吏多不勝任,時有 纖微之過者,必見斥

			罷，交易紛擾，百姓不寧」，指官吏的更換。
train	火車	*huoche*	Used as early as 1840s; also *huolunche* 火輪車.
train ticket	車票	*chepiao*	
underground	地內火輪車	*dinei huolunshe*	Also *dixia huolun chelu* 地下火輪車路; now replaced by *ditie* 地鐵.
university	大學	*daxue*	Also *dashuyuan* 大書院, *daxue guan* 大學館, *daxue gongtang* 大學公堂, *daxuetang* 大學堂, *wenxueguan* 文學館, etc.; round-trip diffusion via Japanese *daigaku*. According to Masini (p. 164), *daxue* 大學 was used for the first time to translate "university" by Jesuit missionaries (Aleni, 1623).
Upper House	上房	*shangfang*	Also *shanghuitang* 上會堂 and *shangtang* 上堂; later replaced by the round-trip loan-translation *shangyiyuan* 上議院. Cf. *giin* 議院 (parliament) in App. B.
zoological garden	動物院	*dongwuyuan*	Also *wanshouyuan* 萬獸園 and *wanshengyuan* 萬生園. Cf. Japanese-derived replacement *dōbutsuen* 動物園 in App. B.

Sino-Japanese-European Loanwords
in Modern Chinese *

English	Japanese romanization	Chinese character	Chinese romanization
abstract	*chūshō*	抽象	*chouxiang*
academic association	*gakkai*	學會	*xuehui*
active service, duty	*gen'eki*	現役	*xianyi*
adjust, adjustment	*chōsei*	調整	*tiaozheng*
admission ticket	*nyūjōken*	入場卷	*ruchangjuan*
advertisement	*kōkoku*	廣告	*guanggao*
affirmative	*kōtei*	肯定	*kending*
agreement, accord	*kyōtei*	協定	*xieding*
agricultural product	*nōsanbutsu*	農產物	*nongchan wu*
agriculture	*nōgaku*	農學	*nongxue*
aim, objective	*mokuteki*	目的	*mudi*
air raid alarm	*kūshū keihō*	空襲警報	*kongxi jingbao*
air raid drill	*bōkū enshū*	防空演習	*fangkong yanxi*
aircraft carrier	*kōkū bokan*	航空母艦	*hangkong mujian*
airspace	*ryōkū*	領空	*lingkong*
appear in court	*shuttei*	出庭	*chuting*
approval, adoption of a resolution	*kaketsu*	可決	*kejue*

---

*This category corresponds to what Gao, Liu, and other linguists call "loanwords from modern Japanese." It consists of *kanji* terms coined by the Japanese using Chinese characters to translate European words, especially English words.

aqueous rock	*suiseigan*	水成岩	*shuicheng yan*
arbitration	*chūsai*	仲裁	*zhongcai*
arc light, arc	*kokō*	弧光*	*huguang*
artery	*dōmyaku*	動脈	*dongmai*
asphalt	*rekisei*	瀝青	*liqing*
association	*kyōkai*	協會	*xiehui*
association, union	*kumiai*	組合	*zuhe*
assumption, supposition	*katei*	假定	*jiading*
atom	*genshi*	原子	*yuanzi*
background	*haikei*	背景	*beijing*
bank	*ginkō*	銀行	*yinhang*
basic criterion	*kijun*	基準	*jizhun*
belligerent (party, group)	*kōsen dantai*	交戰團體	*jiaozhan tuanti*
bicotyledous	*sōshiyō*	雙子葉	*shuangzi ye*
bill, measure	*gian*	議案	*yi'an*
biology	*seibutsugaku*	生物學	*shengwuxue*
blackout	*tōka kansei*	燈火管制	*denghuo guanzhi*
book series	*bunko*	文庫	*wenku*
botanical garden	*shokubutsuen*	植物園	*zhiwuyuan*
broad sense	*kōgi*	廣義	*guangyi*
broadcast	*hōsō*	放送	*fangsong*
business trip	*shutchō*	出張	*chuzhang*
cadre	*kanbu*	幹部	*ganbu*
cancer	*gan*	癌	*ai*
capitalist	*shihonka*	資本家	*ziben jia*
cartoon, comic book	*manga*	漫畫	*manhua*
case, legal case, measure	*hōan*	法案	*fa'an*
cash, specie	*genkin*	現金**	*xianjin*
category	*hanchū*	范疇	*fanchou*
cell	*saibō*	細胞	*xibao*
chamber of commerce	*shōkai*	商會	*shanghui*
characteristic	*tokuchō*	特徵	*tezheng*
circulating assets	*ryūtsū shihon*	流通資本	*liutong ziben*
civil code, civil law	*minpō*	民法	*minfa*
civil engineering	*doboku kōji*	土木工事	*tumu gongshi*
civil rights	*minken*	民權	*minquan*

---

* Cf. "arc" glossed as 弧 in Morrison (1815).

** Cf. "cash" glossed as 現銀子 in Morrison (1815)

climax, high tide	*takashio*	高潮	*gaochao*
club	*kurabu*	俱樂部	*julebu*
cold current	*kanryū*	寒流	*hanliu*
cold zone	*kantai*	寒帶*	*handai*
collaboration	*bōshō*	傍証	*bangzheng*
collection	*kaishū*	回收	*huishou*
commerce, trade	*shōgyō*	商業	*shangye*
common sense	*jōshiki*	常識	*changshi*
communize	*kyōsan*	共產	*gongchan*
company	*kaisha*	會社**	*huishe*
compendium	*taikei*	大系	*daxi*
complication (medical)	*heihatsushō*	併發症	*bingfa zheng*
component, ingredient	*seibun*	成分	*chengfen*
concentration	*shūchū*	集中	*jizhong*
concept	*gainen*	概念	*gainian*
conclusion	*ketsuron*	結論	*jielun*
concrete	*konkuriito*	混凝土	*hunning tu*
condition, control	*seiyaku*	制約	*zhiyue*
conductor	*dōtai*	導體	*daoti*
conference, deliberation	*kyōgi*	協議	*xieyi*
connection, contact	*renkei*	連係 (聯係)	*lianxi*
constitutional government	*kensei*	憲政	*xianzheng*
construct, architecture	*kenchiku*	建築	*jianzhu*
consumer	*shōhisha*	消費者	*xiaofei zhe*
consumption, spending	*shōhi*	消費	*xiaofei*
contract, exclusive arrangement	*tokuyaku*	特約	*teyue*
contrast, comparison	*taihi*	對比***	*duibi*
control	*kansei*	管制	*guanzhi*
conversation	*kaidan*	會談	*huitan*
copy right	*hanken*	板權，版權	*banquan*
corporation, association	*shadan*	社團	*shetuan*
course of lectures	*kōza*	講座	*jiangzuo*
credit	*saiken*	債權	*zhaiquan*

---

* Cf. *lengdai* 冷帶 in App. A.

** Cf. *gongsi* 公司 in App. A.

*** Cf. "contrast" glossed as 放在相對且比較 in Morrison (1815).

creditor	*kashikata*	貸方*	*daifang*
crop, plant	*nōsakubutsu*	農作物	*nongzuowu*
cryptogram	*inkashokubu-tsu*	隱花植物	*yinhua zhiwu*
cycle	*shūha*	周波	*zhoubo*
debt	*saimu*	債務	*zhaiwu*
debtor	*karikata*	借方	*jiefang*
decision, judgment	*dantei*	斷定	*duanding*
declaration of war	*sensen*	宣戰	*xuanzhan*
decorative pattern	*zuanga*	圖案畫	*tu'an hua*
defect, flaw	*ketten*	欠點	*qiandian*
definition	*teigi*	定義	*dingyi*
deflation	*tsūka shūshuku*	通貨收縮	*tonghuo shousuo*
degree (academic)	*gakui*	學位	*xuewei*
demobilization	*fukuin*	復員	*fuyuan*
denial	*hinin*	否認	*fouren*
department store	*hyakkaten*	百貨店**	*baihuo dian*
designation, number	*bangō*	番號	*fanhao*
detective, spy	*teitan*	偵探	*zhentan*
	tantei	探偵	*tanzhen*
detector	*kempaki*	檢波器	*jianbo qi*
development, progress	*shinten*	進展	*jinzhan*
dialectics	*benshō*	辯証	*bianzheng*
direct	*chokusetsu*	直接	*zhijie*
direct current (DC)	*chokuryū*	直流	*zhiliu*
disinfection, sterilization	*shōdoku*	消毒	*xiaodu*
dispatch, send	*haken*	派遣	*paiqian*
distillation	*jōryū*	蒸餾	*zhengliu*
duet	*nijūsō*	二重奏	*erchong zou*
economic panic	*keizai kyōkō*	經濟恐慌	*jingji konghuang*
efficiency	*kōritsu*	效率	*xiaolu*
electric industry	*dengyō*	電業	*dianye*
electrical conductor	*dendōtai*	電導體	*diandaoti*
electrical current	*denryū*	電流	*dianliu*
electrical switch	*haidenban*	配電盤	*peidian pan*
electromagnetic wave	*dempa*	電波	*dianbo*
electron, electronics	*denshi*	電子	*dianzi*
element	*genso*	元素	*yuansu*
employee	*koin*	僱員	*guyuan*
endocrine	*naibunpitsu*	內分泌	*nei fenmi*

---

* Cf. "creditor" glossed as 債主 in Morrison (1815).
** *dahuopu* 大貨鋪 in App. A.

engineering (the study of)	kōka	工科*	gonke
ensure, guarantee	kakuho	確保	quebao
enterprise	kigyō	企業	qiye
epidemic, infectious disease	densenbyō	傳染病	chuanran bing
equality	heiken	平權	pingquan
equation	hōteishiki	方程式**	fangchengshi
Esperanto	sekaigo	世界語	shijieyu
estimate	gaisan	概算	gaisuan
evaporation	jōhatsu	蒸發	zhengfa
evolution	shinka	進化	jinhua
exchange value	kōkan kachi	交換價值	jiaohuan jiazhi
exemplar	tenkei	典型	dianxing
exemption, remission	menjo	免除	mianchu
exercise, gymnastics	taisō	體操	ticao
exhibition	tenrankai	展覽會	zhanlanhui
exit	deguchi	出口	chukou
exocrine	gaibunpitsu	外分泌	wai fenmi
experimental laboratory	shikensho	試驗所***	shiyansuo
explanation	setsumei	説明	shuoming
externality	gaizai	外在	waizai
extra (of a newspaper)	gōgai	號外	haowai
extradite	hikiwatashi	引渡	yindu
extraterritoriality	chigaihōken	治外法權	zhiwai faquan
extreme	kyokutan	極端	jiduan
facilitate	sokusei	促成	cucheng
factory	kōshō	工廠	gongchang
fair, exposition	hakurankai	博覽會****	bolan hui
farm	nōjō	農場	nongchang
fiber, staple	sen'i	纖維	xianwei
field, domain	ryōiki	領域	lingyu
finance	zaisei	財政	caizheng
finances	zaimu	財務	caiwu
fine arts	bijutsu	美術*****	meishu

---

* Cf. *wenke* 文科 and *like* 理科 in App. A.

** Cf. *fangcheng* 方程 in App. A.

*** Cf. *shiyanchang* 試驗場 in App. A.

**** Cf. *bowuhui* 博物會, *xuanqihui* 炫奇會, *saiqihui* 賽奇會, etc. in App. A.

***** Cf. *yishu* 藝術 in App. D.

fire extinguisher	*shōkaki*	消火器	*xiaohuo qi*
fire hydrant	*shōkasen*	消火栓	*xiaohuo shuan*
firefighting	*shōbō*	消防	*xiaofang*
fixed assets	*fuhen shihon,*	不變資本,	*bubian ziben,*
	kotei shihon	固定資本	*guding ziben*
flu (influenza)	*ryūkan*	流感	*liugan*
fluid	*ryūtai*	流體	*liuti*
foot (measure)	*shaku*	呎*	*chi*
forum, criticism	*rondan*	論壇	*luntan*
fossil	*kaseki*	化石**	*huashi*
foundation (organization)	*zaidan*	財團	*caituan*
function, property	*seinō*	性能	*xingneng*
fuse	*dōkasen*	導火線	*daohuoxian*
gas	*gasu*	瓦斯***	*wasi*
	kitai	氣體	*qiti*
general mobilization	*sōdōin*	總動員	*zongdong yuan*
glossy (paper)	*katazuya*	片艶 (紙)	*pianyan*
goods, merchandise	*shōhin*	商品	*shangpin*
groundwater	*chikasui*	地下水	*dixia shui*
guarantee, assurance	*hoshō*	保證	*baozheng*
guerrilla group	*yūgekitai*	游擊隊****	*youjidui*
guerrilla warfare	*yūgekisen*	游擊戰	*youjizhan*
hand grenade	*shuryūdan* (*teryūdan*)	手榴彈	*shouliu dan*
handicrafts	*shukōgyō*	手工業*****	*shougongye*
hardening of arteries	*dōmyakukōka*	動脈硬化	*dongmai yinghua*
head, chief	*shunin*	主任	*zhuren*
heavy industry	*jūkōgyō*	重工業	*zhonggongye*
hemoglobin	*kesshikiso*	血色素	*xuese su*
high pressure/ voltage	*kōatsu*	高壓	*gaoya*
high temperature	*kōon*	高溫	*gaowen*
high-frequency	*kōshūha*	高周波	*gaozhou bo*

---

* Cf. *futuo* 幅脱 in App. F.

** Zhang Deyi 張德彝 used the phrase *hua wei shi* 化為石 in *Hanghai shuqi* 航海述奇 (1866) to refer to the fossils he had seen in a Swedish museum (Masini, p. 177).

*** In Japanese, 瓦斯 is a phonemic loan from Dutch since 1822 (Masini, p. 201). See also the Chinese phonemic loan *jiasi* 加斯 in App. F.

**** Cf. *youji* 游擊 in App. D.

***** Cf. *shougong* 手工 in App. A.

hotbed, breeding ground	*onshō*	溫床	*wenchuang*
huge sum	*kyogaku*	巨額	*ju'e*
hygiene, sanitation	*eisei*	衞生	*weisheng*
hypnotism	*saiminjutsu*	催眠術	*cuimian shu*
idea, doctrine	*rinen*	理念	*linian*
ideal	*risō*	理想	*lixiang*
ideology	*ishiki keitai*	意識形態	*yishi xingtai*
igneous	*kaseigan*	火成岩	*huocheng yan*
imaginary, hypothetical	*kasō*	假想	*jiaxiang*
immanence, inherence	*naizai*	內在	*neizai*
immediate decision	*sokketsu*	即決	*jijue*
imported goods	*hakuraihin*	舶來品	*bolaipin*
improvement	*kaishin*	改進	*gaijin*
inch	*sun*	吋	*cun*
income tax	*shotokuzei*	所得稅	*suode shui*
incorporated foundation	*zaidan hōjin*	財團法人	*caituan faren*
index number	*shisū*	指數	*zhishu*
indirect	*kansetsu*	間接	*jianjie*
individual	*kotai*	個體*	*geti*
induction	*kinō*	歸納	*guina*
industry	*kōgyō*	工業	*gongye*
inferiority	*ressei*	劣勢	*lieshi*
inflation	*tsūka bōchō*	通貨膨脹	*tonghuo pengzhang*
information, intelligence	*jōhō*	情報	*qingbao*
initiative, leadership	*shudō*	主動	*zhudong*
inorganic	*muki*	無機	*wuji*
inspect, inspection	*kensa*	檢查	*jiancha*
instructor	*kyōin*	教員	*jiaoyuan*
intellectual trend	*shichō*	思潮	*sichao*
international	*kokusai*	國際	*guoji*
international law	*kokusai kōhō*	國際公法**	*guoji gongfa*
intuition	*chokkaku*	直覺	*zhijue*
investment	*tōshi*	投資	*touzi*
journalist, reporter	*shimbun kisha*	新聞記者***	*xinwen jizhe*

---

* Cf. *geren* 個人 in App. D and *gebie* 個別 in App. C.

** Cf. *wenguo gongfa* 萬國公法 in App. A.

*** Cf. *jizhe* 記者 and *xinwenguan jizhe* 新聞館記者 in App. A.

judgment, expert opinion	*kantei*	鑑定	*jianding*
judicial officer	*hōjin*	法人	*faren*
key point	*yōshō*	要衝	*yaochong*
kindergarten	*yōchien*	幼稚園	*youzhiyuan*
labor organization	*rōdō kumiai*	勞動組合	*laodong zuhe*
law department	*hōka*	法科	*fake*
lawyer	*bengoshi*	辯護士*	*bianhu shi*
lecture, address	*kōen*	講演	*jiangyan*
left wing	*sayoku*	左翼	*zuoyi*
legal, statutory	*hōtei*	法定	*fading*
library	*toshokan*	圖書館**	*tushuguan*
license, permit	*menkyo*	免許	*mianxu*
light industry	*keikōgyō*	輕工業	*qing gongye*
limitation	*kyokugen*	局限	*juxian*
liquid	*ekitai*	液體	*yeti*
liquid assets	*kahen shihon*	可變資本	*kebian ziben*
long-wave	*chōha*	長波	*changbo*
look forward, long	*akogare*	憧憬	*chongjing*
low frequency	*teishūha*	低周波	*dizhou bo*
low pressure/ voltage	*teiatsu*	低壓	*diya*
low temperature	*teion*	低溫	*diwen*
low tide, nadir	*teichō*	低潮	*dichao*
lymph	*rinpa*	淋巴	*linba*
magnate, tycoon	*kyotō*	巨頭	*jutou*
maritime affairs	*kaiji*	海事	*haishi*
match	*taiō*	對應	*duiying*
means of production	*seisan shudan*	生產手段	*shengchan- shouduan*
means, material, data	*shiryō*	資料	*ziliao*
meeting, gathering	*shūgō*	集合	*jihe*
member, membership	*kaiin*	會員	*huiyuan*
meter	*metoru*	米	*mi*
microbe	*biseibutsu*	微生物	*weishengwu*
military affairs	*heiji*	兵事***	*bingshi*
military alliance	*kōshu dōmei*	攻守同盟	*gongshou tongmeng*
military supplies	*gunjuhin*	軍需品	*junxu pin*
miniature	*kogata*	小型	*xiaoxing*

---

* Cf. *lüshi* 律師 and *lüshi* 律士 in App. A.

** According to Masini (p. 201), the missionary T. Richard used *tushuguan* 圖書館 in his article *Xinxue bazhang* 新學八章 (1889) published after a trip from Japan.

*** Cf. *junshi* 軍事 (Japanese: *gunji*) in App. D.

mobilization	*dōin*	動員	*dongyuan*
modern	*gendai*	現代*	*xiandai*
molecule	*bunshi*	分子	*fenzi*
monocotyledous	*tanshiyō*	單子葉	*danzi ye*
monopoly	*senbai*	專賣	*zhuanmai*
monosodium glutamate	*aji no moto*	味之素	*wei zhi su*
most-favored nation	*saikeikoku*	最惠國	*zuihui guo*
motion	*dōgi*	動議	*dongyi*
motive	*dōki*	動機	*dongji*
movement	*dōtai*	動態	*dongtai*
moving body	*dōtai*	動體	*dongti*
museum	*hakubutsukan*	博物館**	*bowuguan*
narrow sense	*kyōgi*	狹義	*xiayi*
nation, race	*minzoku*	民族	*minzu*
national character	*kokuminsei*	國民性	*guomin xing*
national essence	*kokusui*	國粹	*guocui*
national soul	*kunidamashii*	國魂	*guohun*
natural science	*shizen kagaku*	自然科學	*ziran kexue*
natural selection	*shizen tōta*	自然淘汰	*ziran taotai*
naval cruiser	*jun'yōkan*	巡洋艦	*xunyangjian*
naval destroyer	*kuchikukan*	驅逐艦	*quzhujian*
negate, negation	*hitei*	否定	*fouding*
negative pole, cathode	*inkyoku*	陰極	*yinji*
negative, negativity	*shōkyoku*	消極	*xiaoji*
negotiation	*danpan*	談判	*tanpan*
nervous	*kinchō*	緊張	*jinzhang*
neurasthenia	*shinkei suijaku*	神經衰弱	*shenjing shuairuo*
neuroticism	*shinkei kabin*	神經過敏	*shenjing guomin*
noncombatant	*hisendōin*	非戰動員	*feizhan dong yuan*
nonmetallic	*hikinzoku*	非金屬	*fei jinshu*
notary	*kōshōnin*	公證人	*gongzheng ren*
nutrition	*eiyō*	營養	*yingyang*
object	*kakutai*	客體	*keti*
object	*mokutekibutsu*	目的物	*mudi wu*
object	*taishō*	對象	*duixiang*
objectivity	*kyakkan*	客觀	*keguan*
offer, proffer	*teikyō*	提供	*tigong*

---

* Cf. the phonemic loan *modeng* 摩登 in App. F.

** Cf. *bowuyuan* 博物院, *bowuchang* 博物場, and *bolanyuan* 博覽院 in App. A.

oligarchy	katōseiji	寡頭政治	guatou zhengzhi
ordinary	futsū	普通	putong
organic	yūki	有機	youji
organization	dantai	團體	tuanti
outline	gairon	概論	gailun
ownership	shoyūken	所有權	suoyou quan
parliament	gikai	議會*	yihui
parliamentary official	giin	議員	yiyuan
parole	karishaku	假釋	jiashi
passenger	jōkyaku	乘客	chengke
passive	hidō	被動	beidong
peasant-worker government	rōnō seifu	勞農政府	laonong zhengfu
pedagogy	kyōikugaku	教育學	jiaoyuxue
period, periodic time	shūki	周期	zhouqi
period of effect(iveness)	jikō	時效	shixiao
persecution	hakugai	迫害	pohai
personal property	dōsan	動產**	dongchan
personality	jinkaku	人格	renge
petition	seigan	請願	qingyuan
phanerogam (flowering plant)	kenka-shokubutsu	顯花植物	xianhua zhiwu
philosophy	tetsugaku	哲學	zhexue
plan, program	hōan	方案	fang'an
plant diseases and insect pests	byōchūgai	病虫害	bingchong hai
play an instrument	ensō	演奏	yanzou
playing fields	undōjō	運動場	yundong chang
plutocracy, industrial conglomerate	zaibatsu	財閥	caifa
polemic	ronsen	論戰	lunzhan
policy	seisaku	政策	zhengce
political party	seitō	政黨	zhengdang
politics (the study of)	seijigaku	政治學***	zhengzhixue
positive	sekkyoku	積極	jiji
positive pole, anode	yōkyoku	陽極	yangji
potato	bareisho	馬鈴薯	malingshu
premise	zentei	前提	qianti

---

* Cf. *yiyuan* 議院 in App. A and *baliman* 巴厘滿, etc. in App. F.
** Cf. *dongwu* 動物 in App. A.
*** Cf. *zhengzhi* 政治 in App. D.

preparatory school	*yobikō*	預備校	*yubei xiao*
principle	*gensoku*	原則	*yuanze*
principle, theory	*genri*	原理	*yuanli*
printed matter	*insatsuhin*	印刷品	*yinshua pin*
	insatsubutsu	印刷物	*yinshua wu*
proletarian	*rōdōsha*	勞動者	*laodongzhe*
promotion	*sokushin*	促進	*cujin*
proposal, proposition	*teian*	提案	*ti'an*
prostate gland	*setsugosen*	攝護腺	*shehu mai*
psychology	*shinreigaku*	心靈學	*xinlingxue*
	shinrigaku	心理學*	*xinlixue*
public debt	*kōsai*	公債	*gongzhai*
public, open	*kōkai*	公開	*gongkai*
publish, issue	*shuppan*	出版	*chuban*
published material	*shuppanbutsu*	出版物	*chuban wu*
quality, mass (physics)	*shitsuryō*	質量	*zhiliang*
quantity	*suryō*	數量	*shuliang*
quantum	*ryōshi*	量子	*liangzi*
quota	*teigaku*	定額	*ding'e*
race	*shuzoku*	種族	*zhongzu*
radiation	*hōsha*	放射	*fangshe*
rambling chat	*mandan*	漫談	*mantan*
random notes	*manpitsu*	漫筆	*manbi*
rate of progress	*shindo*	進度	*jindu*
rationing, distribution	*haikyū*	配給	*peiji*
real estate	*fudōsan*	不動產**	*budong chan*
reality	*genjitsu*	現實	*xianshi*
reasoning	*suiron*	推論***	*tuilun*
reciprocity	*gokei*	互惠	*huhui*
recognition, admission	*shōnin*	承認	*chengren*
reconnaissance,	*teisatsu*	偵察	*zhencha*
reconnoiter, scouting			
reduce, retrench	*kinshuku*	緊縮	*jinsuo*
reference book	*sankōsho*	參考書	*cankao shu*
reflection	*hansha*	反射	*fanshe*
reflection	*han'ei*	反映****	*fanying*
reform	*kairyō*	改良	*gailiang*

---

* Cf. *xinli* 心理 in App. D.

** Cf. *zhiwu* 植物 in App. A.

*** Cf. the missionary-Chinese semantic translation: *tuilun daoli* 推論道理 in App. A.

****Cf. "reflection" glossed as *fanzhao* 反照 in Morrison (1815).

refrigeration	*reizōko*	冷藏庫	*lengcang ku*
regular army	*jobi-hei*	常備兵	*changbeibing*
regulate, regulation	*chōsetsu*	調節	*tiaojie*
rejection	*hiketsu*	否決	*foujue*
relations of production	*seisan kankei*	生產關係	*shengchan guanxi*
report	*hōkoku*	報告	*baogao*
representative	*daigenjin*	代言人	*daiyan ren*
retarded child	*teinōji*	低能兒	*dineng'er*
right wing	*uyoku*	右翼	*youyi*
rupture	*dankō*	斷交	*duanjiao*
safe, depository	*kinko*	金庫	*jinku*
school age	*gakurei*	學齡	*xueling*
school master	*kōchō*	校長	*xiaozhang*
script	*kyakuhon*	腳本	*jiaoben*
secession	*dattō*	脱黨	*tuodang*
second supporting troops	*kōbi-hei*	後備兵	*houbeibing*
securities (financial), fixed assets	*kotei shihon*	固定資本	*guding ziben*
securities, negotiable instruments	*yūkashōken*	有价証卷	*youjia zhengjuan*
see off	*kansō*	歡送	*huansong*
semester	*gakki*	學期	*xueqi*
sewer	*gesuidō*	下水道	*xia shuidao*
shortwave	*tanpa*	短波	*duanbo*
signal	*shingō*	信號	*xinhao*
silencer, muffler	*shōonki*	消音器	*xiaoyin qi*
slide	*gentō*	幻燈	*huandeng*
soda	*sōda*	曹達*	*caoda*
solid	*kotai*	固體	*guti*
solution (to a mathematical problem), quotient	*tokusū*	得數	*deshu*
space, room	*kūkan*	空間	*kongjian*
special agent	*tokumu*	特務	*tewu*
special permission	*tokkyo*	特許	*texu*
sports, physical education	*tai'iku*	體育	*tiyu*
spy	*kanchō*	間諜	*jiandie*
staff, personnel	*shokuin*	職員	*zhiyuan*

---

* Cf. *suda* 蔬打 and 蘇達 in App. F. *Sōda* 曹達 is a Japanese phonemic loan from Dutch (Masini, p. 162).

standard, criterion	*kihan*	規範	*guifan*
standard-bearer	*kishu*	旗手	*qishou*
standing army	*jōbihei*	常備兵	*changbei bing*
standpoint	*tachiba*	立場	*lichang*
static, stationary	*seitai*	靜態	*jingtai*
steamboat	*kisen*	汽船	*qichuan*
stencil, mimeograph	*tōshaban*	騰寫版	*tengxie ban*
storage battery	*chikudenchi*	蓄電池	*xu dianchi*
store	*shōten*	商店	*shangdian*
storm troops	*totsugekitai*	突擊隊	*tujidui*
strike, walkout	*dōmei hikō*	同盟罷工	*tongmeng bagong*
struggle	*tōsō*	鬥爭	*douzheng*
students studying abroad	*ryūgakusei*	留學生*	*liuxuesheng*
subjectivity	*shukan*	主觀	*zhuguan*
sublation (aufheben)	*yōki*	揚棄**	*yangqi*
sue, bring a case to court	*shusso*	出訴	*chusu*
sum, amount	*kingaku*	金額	*jin'e*
summary	*gaikatsu*	概括	*gaikuo*
summons, voucher	*denpyō*	傳票	*chuanpiao*
sunlamp	*taiyō tō*	太陽燈	*taiyang deng*
superiority	*yūsei*	優勢	*youshi*
supporting troops	*yobieki*	預備役	*yubeiyi*
surface water	*chijōsui*	地上水	*dishang shui*
symbol	*shōchō*	象徵	*xiangzheng*
symmetry	*taishō*	對稱	*duicheng*
sympathetic nerve	*kōkan shinkei*	交感神經	*jiaogan shenjing*
symphony	*kōkyōgaku*	交響樂	*jiaoxiang yue*
syncope, suspended animation	*kashi*	假死	*jiasi*
synthesis	*sōgō*	綜合	*zonghe*
system	*keitō*	系統	*xitong*
tear gas shell	*sairuidan*	催淚彈	*cuilei dan*
technician	*gishi*	技師	*jishi*
telegraph, cable	*denshin*	電信***	*dianxin*
telegraph machine	*denshinki*	電信機	*dianxinji*

---

* Cf. *yangxueye shengtong* 洋學業生童 and *chuyang xuesheng* 出洋學生 in App. A.

** Cf. the phonemic loan *aofuhebian* 奧伏赫變 in App. F.

*** Cf. *dianbo* 電報; *dianjixin* 電機信; *dianqixin* 電氣信; *tongxianxin* 通線信, *xintongxian* 信通線, etc. in App. A.

telephone	*denwa*	電話*	*dianhua*
telephone set	*denwaki*	電話機	*dianhuaji*
temperature	*ondo*	溫度	*wendu*
territorial water	*ryōkai*	領海	*linghai*
territory	*ryōdo*	領土	*lingtu*
theater	*gekijō*	劇場	*juchang*
thermometer	*kanshohari*	寒暑針**	*hanshuzhen*
thyroid gland	*kōjōsen*	甲狀腺	*jiazhuang xian*
tractor, tractor truck	*ken'insha*	牽引車	*qianyin che*
trade deficit	*nyūchō*	入超	*ruchao*
trade law	*shōhō*	商法	*shangfa*
trade surplus	*shutchō*	出超	*chuchao*
train	*ressha*	列車***	*lieche*
tram	*densha*	電車	*dianche*
transformer	*hen'atsuki*	變壓器	*bianya qi*
treatise, dissertation	*ronbun*	論文	*lunwen*
trench mortar	*hakugekihō*	迫擊砲	*pojipao*
trend, tendency	*dōkō*	動向	*dongxiang*
truce, armistice	*kyūsen*	休戰	*xiuzhan*
trust	*shintaku*	信詫****	*xintuo*
tuberculosis	*kekkaku*	結核	*jiehe*
tutor, teacher	*dōshi*	導師	*daoshi*
type	*ruikei*	類型	*leixing*
ulcer	*kaiyō*	潰瘍	*kuiyang*
ultimatum	*saigotsūchō*	最後通牒	*zuihou tongdie*
ultrashortwave	*chōtanpa*	超短波	*chao duanbo*
unknown quantity	*michisū*	未知數	*weizhi shu*
Ursa major	*ōkumaza*	大熊座	*daxiong zuo*
Ursa minor	*kogumaza*	小熊座	*xiaoxiong zuo*
use value	*shiyō kachi*	使用价值	*shiyong jiazhi*
usury	*kōrigashi*	高利貸	*gaoli dai*
uvula	*ken'yōsui*	懸雍垂	*xuanyongchui*
vacuum	*shinkū*	真空	*zhenkong*
vacuum tube	*shinkūkan*	真空管	*zhenkong guan*
vapor, steam	*jōki*	蒸氣	*zhengqi*
vein	*jōmyaku*	靜脈	*jingmai*

---

* Cf. *delifeng* 得利風 and *delüfeng* 得律風 in App. F.
** Cf. *hanshubiao* 寒暑表 in App. A.
*** Cf. *huoche* 火車 in App. A.
**** Cf. *xinyong* 信用 in App. D.

ventilator, fan	*senpūki*	扇風機	*shanfengji*
view, prospect	*tenbō*	展望	*zhanwang*
viewpoint	*kanten*	觀點	*guandian*
vocation	*gyōmu*	業務	*yewu*
volume	*taiseki*	體積	*tiji*
vote, decision	*hyōketsu*	表決	*biaojue*
voting, polling	*tōhyō*	投票	*toupiao*
vow, oath	*sensei*	宣誓	*xuanshi*
warm current	*danryū*	暖流	*nuanliu*
water-supply line	*jōsuidō*	上水道	*shang shuidao*
whole	*sōtai*	總體	*zongti*
woodcut	*hanga*	版畫	*banhua*
workers, staff	*shokkō*	職工	*zhigong*
works (writings, artwork)	*sakuhin*	作品	*zuopin*
workshop	*kōjō*	工場	*gongchang*
year, annual	*nendo*	年度	*niandu*
zoological garden	*dōbutsujō*	動物場[*]	*dongwuchang*
	dōbutsuen	動物園	*dongwuyuan*
zoology	*dōbutsugaku*	動物學	*dongwuxue*

---

[*] Cf. *dongwuyuan* 動物院 in App. A.

Sino-Japanese Loanwords
in Modern Chinese *

Japanese romanization	Chinese character	Chinese romanization	English
baai	場合	changhe	case, occasion
bamen	場面	changmian	scene
basho	場所	changsuo	place, scene, setting
benjo	便所	biansuo	toilet, lavatory
bihin	備品	beipin	equipment, parts, fixtures
bushidō	武士道	wushi dao	bushido
chōsei	調製	tiaozhi	preparation, modulation
daihon'ei	大本營	dabenying	headquarters
fukeiki	不景氣**	bu jingqi	recession, slump, gloom
fukumu	服務	fuwu	service
fukushoku- butsu	副食物	fushi wu	supplementary food, groceries
fukushū	復習	fuxi	review, practice
geta	吉地	jidi	wooden clogs
hamon	破門	pomen	expulsion, excommunication

---

* With the exception of the entries identified as return graphic loans and relocated to App. D, this list strictly follows Gao's and Liu's findings (pp. 82-83) in the category of what they call "loanwords of premodern Japanese coinage," namely, *kanji* loan terms that arrived in modern Chinese without necessarily involving European languages.
** Cf. *jingqi* 景氣 in App. D. See also Sanetō's discussion of this word in *Zhongguoren liuxue Riben shi*, p. 222.

hashutsujo	派出所	*paichusuo*	police station, branch office
hoken	保健	*baojian*	health, hygiene
hōshin	方針	*fangzhen*	policy, direction, guiding principle
hyōgen	表現	*biaoxian*	expression, manifestation
ichiranhyō	一覽表	*yilanbiao*	table, list
jinrikisha	人力車*	*renliche*	rickshaw
keshō	化妝	*huazhuang*	makeup
keshōhin	化妝品	*huazhuangpin*	cosmetics
kobetsu	個別**	*gebie*	individual, singular
kokufuku	克服	*kefu*	overcome
koshō	故障	*guzhang*	obstacle, hitch
kyori	距離	*juli*	distance, interval
minarai	見習	*jianxi*	apprenticeship, probation
minogami	美濃紙	*meinongzhi*	*Gifu* paper (decorative)
mokuhyō	目標	*mubiao*	goal
monoga-tari	物語	*wuyu*	story, tale
naifuku	內服	*neifu*	oral ingestion (of medicine)
naiyō	內容	*neirong*	content
naiyō	內用	*neiyong*	internal use, private, classified
ninka	認可	*renke*	recognition, approval
rōnin	浪人	*langren*	masterless samurai, wanderer
rensō	聯想	*lianxiang*	association (of ideas)
sanrinsha	三輪車	*sanlunche*	three-wheeled cart, trishaw
shibu	支部	*zhibu*	branch office, local chapter, party branch
shiten	支店	*zhidian*	branch store
shoho	初步	*chubu*	beginning, rudimentary
shōjō	癥狀	*zhengzhuang*	symptoms
shojosaku	處女作	*chunü zuo*	literary debut
shokei	處刑	*chuxing*	execute, punishment
shūdan	集團	*jituan*	group, corporation

---

* Cf. *dongyangche* 東洋車 or *yangche* 洋車 in App. A. The latter is discussed in Chapter 4 in connection with Lao She's novel *Camel Xiangzi*.

** Cf. *kotai* 個體 in App. B. and *kojin* 個人 in App. D.

shūkyō	宗教	*zongjiao*	religion
tadashi- gaki	但書	*danshu*	proviso
tetsuzuki	手續	*shouxu*	procedures
torishimari	取締	*qudi*	outlaw
uchikeshi	打消	*daxiao*	cancel
yōso	要素	*yaosu*	element, factor
yōten	要點	*yaodian*	point, gist

Return Graphic Loans: 'Kanji' Terms
Derived from Classical Chinese *

English	Japanese roman-ization	Chinese character	Chinese roman-ization	Contrastive usage from classical Chinese texts
absolute	*zettai*	絕對	*juedui*	一。《鏡花緣》第七七回：「春輝道，長春對半夏，字字工穩，竟是絕對」，謂絕妙的對仗。 二。清李漁《奈何天: 鬧對》：「天生絕對，佳人才子」，謂最佳配偶。三。唐張鷟《游仙窟》：「比目絕對，雙鳧失伴，日日衣寬，朝朝帶緩」，謂不能成雙。
accounting, accountant	*kaikei*	會計*	*kuaiji*	一。《周禮: 地官: 舍人》：「歲終則會計其政」，謂核計，計算。 二。《孟子: 萬章下》：「孔子嘗為委吏矣，曰會計當而已矣」，謂管理財物及出

---

* The term "return graphic loan" refers to classical Chinese-character compounds that were used by the Japanese to translate modern European words and were reintroduced into modern Chinese. By the principle of "ideographic coincidence" as explained in the headnote and in light of the new sources I used in identifying the loan items, the total number of entries turns out to quadruple the original list provided by Gao and Liu (marked by asterisks).

納等事。　三。《史記: 夏本記》：「自虞夏時，貢賦備矣。或言禹會諸侯江南，計功而崩，因葬焉，命曰會稽。會稽者，會計也」，謂古天子大會諸侯，計功行賞。

English	Japanese		Chinese		Gloss
activity	*katsudō*	活動	*huodong*		一。宋文祥《和蕭秋屋韻》：「星辰活動驚歌笑，風露輕寒敵拍浮」，指物體運動。　二。《京本通俗小說: 錯斬崔寧》：「那人見劉官人手腳活動，便拔步出房」，謂靈活，不固定。三。《紅樓夢》第九五回：「見妙玉略有活動，便起身拜了幾拜」，謂動搖。四。元劉壎《隱居通議: 駢儷三》：「所病者，層砌堆疊而乏疏暢活動之工」，指言語生動活潑。五。《醒世恆言: 一文錢隙造奇冤》：「那楊氏三十六歲，貌頗不醜，也肯與人活動，只為老公利害，只好背地裡偶一為之，卻不敢明當做事」，謂與人偷情。
administration	*gyōsei*	行政	*xing zheng*		《孟子: 梁惠王上》：「為民父母行政，不免於率獸而食人，惡在其為民父母也」，謂執掌國家政權，管理國家事務。(The noun form of 行政 as used in modern Chinese probably derives from Japanese *gyōsei*)
agency	*dairi*	代理	*daili*		漢董仲舒《春秋繁露: 天道無二》：「陰與陽，相反之物也，故或出或入，或左或右。春俱南，秋俱北，夏交於前，冬交於後，并行而不同路，交會而各代理，此其文與天之道有一出一入一休一伏，其度一也，然而不同意」，指日月更替為治。(Cf. "agent" glossed as 代理事的 in Morrison, 1815)
alliance	*dōmei*	同盟	*tong meng*		《左傳: 僖公九年》：「秋，齊候盟諸候於葵丘，曰：「凡我同盟之人，既盟之後，言歸於好」」，指古代候國歃血為誓，締結盟約。後泛指國與國共締盟約，亦指人與人成密友，結伴。

allotment	*bunpai*	分配	*fenpei*	一。《左傳: 昭公二十年 》:「聲亦如味,一氣,二體,三類,四物,五聲 」,唐孔穎達疏:「聲之清濁,凡有五品,自然之理也。聖人配於五方,官居其中,商,角,徵,羽,分配四方 」,謂分別相配,配合。二。《後漢書: 光武帝紀上 》:「悉將降人分配諸將,眾遂數十萬 」,謂按一定標準分給。(Cf. "allot" glossed as 分派 in Morrison, 1815)
analysis	*bunseki*	分析*	*fenxi*	一。《漢書: 孔安國傳 》:「世所傳《百兩篇 》者,出東萊張霸,分析合二十九篇以為數十,又采《左氏傳 》,《書敘 》為作首尾,凡百二篇 」,謂分開,區分。二。《後漢書: 馬援傳 》:「又於帝前聚米為山谷,指畫形勢,開示眾軍所從道徑往來,分悉曲折,昭然可曉 」,謂分解辨析。三。《舊唐書: 劉君良傳 》:「大業末,天下饑饉,君良妻勸其分析 」,謂分家。四。宋王安石《上仁宗皇帝言事書 》:「於是諸侯王之子弟,各有分土,而勢強地大者,卒以分析弱小 」,謂分割,離析。五。《宋書: 謝靈運傳 》:「於時內慢神器,外侮戎狄。君子橫流,庶萌分析 」,謂離別,分離。六。《古今小説: 沈小霞相會出師表 》:「張千,李萬被這婦人一哭一訴,就要分析几句,沒處插嘴 」,謂申辨,辨白。
apply, application	*shinsei*	申請	*shenqing*	《晉書: 劉毅傳 》:「前已口白,謹復申請 」,指向上司或有關部門説明理由,提出請求。又見《新唐書: 張濬傳 》:「朝廷震動,即日下詔罷濬為武昌軍節度使,三貶繡州司戶參軍。全忠為申請,詔聽使便。」
appointment	*yoyaku*	預約	*yuyue*	唐李商隱《憶雪 》詩:「預約延枚酒,虛乘訪戴船 」,謂事先約定。又見,宋侯寘《風入松 》詞:「錦箋預約西湖上,共幽深,竹院松莊。」

approach	*sekkin*	接近	*jiejin*	一。《呂氏春秋: 知接 》:「智者其所能接遠也，愚者其所能接近也」，謂所見不遠。二。《後漢書: 西域傳車師 》:「帝以車師六國接近北虜，為西域蔽捍」，謂關係親近。
arithmetic	*sanjutsu*	算術	*suanshu*	《三國志: 蜀書: 李譔傳 》:「（譔）五經，諸子，無不該覽，加博好技藝，算術，卜數，醫藥，弓弩，機械之巧，皆致思焉」，謂數學的一個分科，論數的性質，關係及其計算方法。
army	*rikugun*	陸軍	*lujun*	《晉書: 宣帝紀 》:「若為陸軍以向皖城，引權東下，為水戰軍向夏口，乘其虛而擊之，此神兵從天而墮，破之必矣」，謂陸地作戰的軍隊。
art	*geijutsu*	藝術*	*yishu*	《後漢書: 孝安帝記 》:「詔謁者劉珍及五經博士，校定東觀五經，諸子，傳記，百家藝術」，注:「藝謂書，數，射，御，術謂醫，方，卜，筮」，泛指各種技術技能。
artistic conception	*ishō*	意匠	*yijiang*	唐楊炯《 ＜王勃集＞序 》:「六合殊材，並推心於意匠。八方好事，咸受氣於文樞」，又見宋陸游《 題嚴州王秀才山水枕屏 》詩:「壯君落筆寫岷嶓，意匠自到非身過。偉哉千仞天相摩，谷裏人家藏綠蘿」，謂作文，繪畫的精心構思。
aspect	*hōmen*	方面*	*fangmian*	一。《後漢書: 馮異傳 》:「（異）受任方面，以立微功。」李賢注:「謂西方一面專以委之」，指一個地方的軍政要職或其長官。二。《後漢書: 逢萌傳 》:「詔書征萌，託以老耄，迷路東西，語使者曰，尚不知方面所在安能濟時乎？」，謂方向。
authority	*ken'i*	權威	*quanwei*	《呂氏春秋: 審分 》:「萬邪並起，權威分移」，指權力，威勢。又見《 北史: 周紀上論 》:「昔者水運將終，群凶放命，或權威震主，或釁逆滔天。」

autocracy	*sensei*	專制	*zhuanzhi*	一。《左傳: 昭公十九年》:「若寡君之二三臣,其即世者,晉大夫而專制其位,是晉之縣鄙也,何國之為」,指控制,掌管。二。《漢書: 西域傳下: 烏孫國》:「昆莫年老國分,不能專制,乃發使送騫,因獻馬數十匹報謝」,又見《韓非子: 亡徵》:「嬰兒為君,大臣專制,樹羈旅以為黨,數割地以待交者,可亡也」,謂獨斷專行。
autonomy	*jichi*	自治	*zizhi*	一。《史記: 陳涉世家》:「諸將徇地,至,令之不是者,繫而罪之,以苛察為忠,其所不善者,弗下吏,輒自治之」,謂自行管理或處理。二。《淮南子: 詮言訓》:「德可以自修,而不可以使人暴。道可以自治,而不可以使人亂」,謂修養自身的德性。三。《尹文子: 大道上》:「法用則反道,道用則無為而自治」,謂自然安治。四。《漢書: 張禹傳》:「禹年老,自治冢塋,起祠室」,猶自營。(Used to translate English "self-government" in W. A. P. Martin's 1864 *Wanguo gongfa* [Masini, p. 222].)
bachelor	*gakushi*	學士*	*xueshi*	一。《周禮: 春官: 樂師》:「詔及徹,帥學士而歌徹」,鄭玄注「學士,國子也」,謂在學的貴族子弟。二。《莊子: 盜跖》:「搖唇鼓舌,擅生是非,以迷天下之主,使天下學士,不反其本,妄做孝弟,而徼倖於封侯富貴者也」,指文士。三。官名,始于魏晉六朝,主掌典禮,編鑽,撰述諸事。其後各朝代皆置有學士之官。
bail, bond	*hoshaku*	保釋	*baoshi*	清東軒主人《述異記》卷下:「天成見盜婦色美,力為保釋」,謂請求釋放被拘押者,並擔保其隨時接受傳訓或不再犯罪。
bankruptcy	*hasan*	破產	*pochan*	《史記: 孔子世家》:「夫儒者滑稽而不可軌法,倨傲自順,不

				可以為下，崇喪遂哀，破產厚葬，不可以為俗」，謂喪失全部財產。
base	*kichi*	基地	*jidi*	《北史: 魏臨淮王譚傳》:「（端）位大行臺尚書，華州刺吏。性疏很，頗以基地驕物，時論鄙之」，猶門第、地位。
battle, make war	*sakusen*	作戰	*zuozhan*	《孫子》有《作戰》篇。指軍隊之間的敵對行動。
budget	*yosan*	預算*	*yusuan*	宋葉適《上寧宗皇帝札子》:「今陛下申令大臣，先慮預算，思報積恥，規恢祖業，蓋欲改弱已就強矣」，謂預先計算，事先估計。
business	*eigyō*	營業	*yingye*	一。《三國志: 吳志: 駱統傳》:「百姓虛竭，嗷然愁擾，愁擾則不營業，不營業則致窮困」，謂營謀生計。二。《儒林外史》第二四回:「他家本是几代的戲行，如今仍舊做這戲行營業」，謂職業。
capital	*shihon*	資本	*ziben*	宋何薳《春渚紀聞: 蘇劉互謔》:「吾之鄰人，有一子稍長，因使之代掌小解。不逾歲，偶誤質盜物，資本耗折殆盡」，謂經營工商業的本錢。(Cf. 母財 used by Yan Fu 嚴復 to render "capital" in *Yuanfu* 原富, a 1901-1902 translation of Adam Smith's *Inquiry into the Nature and Causes of the Wealth of Nations*)
cease-fire	*teisen*	停戰	*tingzhan*	清平步青《霞外攟屑: 時事: 彭尚書奏摺》:「三月十一日停戰，華兵拔隊齊回」，指交戰雙方停止作戰。
century	*seiki*	世紀	*shiji*	記錄帝王世系之書，如晉皇甫謐《帝王世紀》。
chairman	*shuseki*	主席*	*zhuxi*	一。《史記: 絳侯周勃世家》:「景帝居禁中，召條候，賜食，獨置大胾，無切肉，又不置櫡。條候心不平，顧謂尚席取櫡」，

				應劭注：「尚席，主席者」，謂主持宴席者。二。《警世通言：俞伯牙摔琴謝知音》：「伯牙推子期坐於客位，自己主席相陪」，指宴席中的主人座位。三。《金史：食貨志一》：「寺觀主席亦量其貲而鬻之」，指寺觀的主持。
chance	*gūzen*	偶然	*ouran*	一。《後漢書：儒林傳劉昆》：「詔問昆曰，「前在江陵，反風滅火，後守弘農，虎北度河，行何德政而致是事？」昆對曰：「偶然耳」」，謂事理上不一定要發生而發生的。二。唐元稹《劉氏館集隱客》詩：「偶然沽市酒，不越四五升」，謂間或有時侯。(Glossed as 偶然的 in Morrison, 1815)
China	*shina*	支那	*zhina*	唐義淨《南海寄歸內法傳：師資道》：「且如西國名大唐為支那者，直是其名，更無別義」，又見：《宋史：外國傳六：天竺》：「太平興國七年，益州僧光遠至自天竺，以其王沒徙曩表來上。上令天竺僧施護譯云：「近聞支那國內有大明王，至聖至明，威力自在……伏願支那皇帝福慧圓滿，壽命延長」。」
circulation	*ryūtsū*	流通	*liutong*	一。《尸子》卷上：「水有四德，沐浴群生，流通萬物，仁也」，又見《資治通鑒：漢光武帝建武二年》：「三郡清靜，邊路流通」，謂流傳通行，不停滯。二。漢桓寬《鹽鐵論：通有》：「山居澤處，蓬蒿墝埆，財物流通，有以均之」，特指商品，貨幣流傳。
citizen	*kokumin*	國民	*guomin*	《左傳：昭公十三年》：「先神命之，國民信之」，謂一國或藩封所轄百姓。
civilization	*bunmei*	文明*	*wenming*	一。《易：乾》：「見龍在田，天下文明」，孔穎達疏：「天下文明者，陽氣在田，始生萬物，故天下有文章而光明也」，指文采光明。二。《書：舜典》：「濬哲文明，溫恭允塞」，孔穎

達疏：「經天緯地曰文，照臨四方曰明」，謂文德輝耀。三。前蜀杜光庭《賀黃雲表》：「柔遠俗以文明，懾凶奴以武略」，謂文治教化。四。漢焦贛《易林:節之頤》：「文明之世，銷鋒鑄鏑」，謂文教昌明。五。《易:明夷》：「內文明而外柔順，以蒙大難，文王以之」，猶明察。

class (social)	*kaikyū*	階級*	*jieji*	一。唐陸龜蒙《野廟碑》：「升階級，坐堂筵，耳弦匏，口粱肉，載車馬，擁徒隸者，皆是也」，指臺階。二。漢王符《潛夫論: 班祿》：「上下大小，貴賤親疏，皆有等威，階級衰殺」，指尊卑上下的等級。三。《舊唐書: 高宗紀上》：「佐命功臣子孫及大將軍府僚佐已下今見存者，賜階級有差，量才處分」，指官的品位，等級。四。《朱子語類》卷一〇三：「然為學自有許多階級，不可不知也」，謂階段，段落。
classics, classical	*koten*	古典	*gudian*	一。《漢書: 王莽傳》：「漢氏諸候或稱王，至于四夷亦如之，違於古典，繆於一統」，又見《隋書: 地理志上》：「（漢高祖）掃清禍亂，矯秦皇之失策，封建王候，並跨州連邑，有踰古典，而郡縣之制，無改於秦」，謂古代典章制度。二。《後漢書: 樊準傳》：「（孝明皇帝）庶政萬機，無不簡心，而垂情於古典，游意經藝」，謂典籍。
common, together	*kyōdō*	共同	*gongtong*	一。《孟子: 梁惠王上》：「古之人，與民偕樂，故樂也」，漢趙岐注：「古言之賢君，與民共同其所樂，故能樂之」，猶言一同。二。《前漢書平話》卷上：「劉武受詔牌金帛了，即請宋公達，李德，程彥雄共同商議」，指大家一起（做）。
comprehension	*ryōkai*	領會*	*linghui*	一。晉向秀《思舊賦》：「託運遇於領會兮，寄餘命於寸陰」，李善注引司馬彪曰：「領會，言人運命，如衣領之相交會，或合或開」，謂遭遇。

二。《廣弘明集二十: 南朝梁簡
文帝莊嚴旻法師成實論義疏
序》:「於是標撮領會,商榷異
端,刪夷浮詭,搜聚貞實,造百
有二品,以為斯論」,謂體會。

concrete	*gutai*	具體*	*juti*	《孟子: 公孫丑》:「冉牛,閔子,顏淵,則具體而微」,謂大體具備。
condition	*jōken*	條件	*tiaojian*	一。《北史: 郎基傳》:「遂條件申臺省,仍以情量事科處,自非極刑,一皆決放」,謂逐條逐件。二。唐陸贄《奉天改元大赦制》:「內外官有冗員及百司有不急之費,委中書門下即商量條件,停減聞奏」,謂為某事而提出的要求或標準。
confession	*jihaku*	自白	*zibai*	《史記: 吳王濞列傳》:「吳王身有內病,不能朝請二十餘年,嘗患見疑,無以自白」,指自我表白。
conscious-ness	*ishiki*	意識	*yishi*	一。漢王充《論衡: 實知》:「眾人闊略,寡所意識,見賢聖之名物,則謂之神」,又見《北齊書: 文宣帝紀》:「高祖嘗試觀諸子意識,各使治亂絲,帝獨抽刀斬之,曰:「亂者須斬。」高祖是之」,謂見識。二。宋王明清《揮麈後錄》卷二:「子之所陳,心存意識,或欲周知,何從皆得」,指先入之見。
constitution	*kenpō*	憲法	*xianfa*	一。《集韻: 去願》:「《周禮》:縣法示人曰憲法。後人因謂憲為法」,謂公布法令。二。《國語: 晉語九》:「賞善罰姦,國之憲法也」,謂法典,法度。
construct, construct-ion	*kōzō*	構造*	*gouzao*	一。《後漢書: 徐璆傳》:「張忠怨璆,與諸閹官構造無端,璆遂以罪徵」,又見《宋書: 恩倖傳序》:「構造同異,興樹禍隙」,猶捏造。二。《三國志: 魏書: 陳留王奐傳》:「癸巳,詔曰:「前逆臣鐘會構造反亂,聚集征行將士,劫以兵威,始吐姦謀,發言桀逆,逼脅眾人,皆

使下議，倉卒之際，莫不驚
懼」，謂人為地造成某種氣氛或
局面。三。明何景明《略陽縣遷
建廟學記》：「今茲之建是宅，
阜隆以降湍悍，構造維新，地復
其舊」，謂結構。

contact	*renraku*	連絡	*lianluo*	《舊唐書: 朱敬則傳》：「分山裂河，設磐石之固，內守外禦，有維城之基。連絡遍於域中，膠葛盡於封內」，猶組織聯系。又見《紅樓夢》第四回：「四家皆連絡有親，一損俱損，一榮俱榮。」
conversat-ion	*kaiwa*	會話	*huihua*	唐無名氏《玉泉子》：「乾符末，有客寓止廣陵開元寺，因文會話云：「頃在京寄青龍寺日，有客嘗訪知寺僧，屬其匆遽不暇留連」」，又見宋歐陽修《與吳正肅公書》：「前約臨行少留會話，終不克遂，至今為恨」，謂聚談。
copy, duplicate	*fukusha*	複寫	*fuxie*	清葉廷琯《吹网錄: 石林家訓》：「跋語論士大夫作小説云云，與《避暑錄話》中一條全文無異……是《錄話》複寫此書跋語，非此書跋語勦取《錄話》之文也」，謂重複抄錄。
countless	*musū*	無數	*wushu*	一。《東觀漢記: 張堪》：「珍寶珠玉委積無數」，言無法計算。二。《周禮: 春官: 宗伯》：「男巫無數，女巫無數」，又見《禮記: 禮器》：「天子一食，諸侯再，大夫，士三，食力無數」，指沒有限定的數量或規定的次數。
course, curriculum	*katei*	課程*	*kecheng*	一。《詩經: 小雅: 巧言》：「奕奕寢廟，君子作之」，唐孔穎達疏：「以教護課程，必君子監之，乃得依法制也」，謂做事，學習須遵循的規定進程。二。《舊唐書: 職官志二》：「（刑部比部）郎中，員外郎之職，掌勾諸司百僚俸料，公廨，贓贖，調斂，徒役，課程，逋懸數物，周知內外之經費，而總勾之」，指交納稅物的限期。三。

《金史: 孫鐸傳》:「鐸上言:
「民間鈔多,宜收斂。院務課程
及諸窠名錢須要全收交鈔」」,
指按稅率交納的賦稅。四。宋劉
昌詩《蘆浦筆記: 白玉樓賦》:
「唯五城一睹之珍,三獻不逢之
寶,蓋於此山積而雲駢。然後大
匠課程,群工謹度,琢瑗礱瑛,
門珪疊璐」,指規劃工程。五。
清曹寅《真州述懷奉答徐道積編
修龀月見寄原韻》:「課吏不課
程,百里半九十。讀書不讀律,
知一二乃失」,指攷核工作進
程。

court of law	*hōtei*	法庭	*fating*	唐柳宗元《柳州文宣王新修廟碑》:「十月乙丑,王宮正室成。乃安神樓,乃正法庭」,指孔廟正殿。(Cf. *fayuan* 法院 in App. A)
criminal law	*keihō*	刑法	*xingfa*	《國語: 魯語上》:「堯能單均刑法以儀民」,對刑罰規範的總稱。又見《左傳: 昭公二十六年》:「貫瀆鬼神,慢棄刑法。」
criticism	*hihan*	批判	*pipan*	一。宋司馬光《進呈上官均奏乞尚書省扎子》:「所有都省常程文字,並只委左右丞一面批判,指揮施行」,謂批示判斷。二。《朱子語類》卷一:「而今説天有箇人在那裡批判罪惡,固不可,説道全無主之者,又不可」,謂評論,評斷。
critique	*hihyō*	批評	*piping*	明李贄《寄答留都書》:「前與楊太史書亦有批評,倘一一寄去,乃足見兄與彼相處之厚也」,謂評論,評判。("Critics of books" glossed as 善批評書士 in Morrison, 1815)
crop	*saku motsu*	作物	*zuowu*	南朝梁任昉《到大司馬記室箋》:「明公道冠二儀,勳超邃古,將使伊周奉轡,桓文扶轂,神功無紀,作物何稱」,指造物,主宰萬物之神。
culture	*bunka*	文化*	*wenhua*	漢劉向《説苑: 指武》:「凡武之興,為不服也,文化不改,然

				後加誅」，又見晉束皙《補亡詩：由儀》：「文化內輯，武功外悠」，謂文治教化。
deduction	en'eki	演繹	yanyi	宋朱熹《中庸章句序》：「於是推本堯舜以來相傳之意，質以平日所聞父師之言，更互演繹，作為此書」，謂推演鋪陳。
delusion	mōsō	妄想	wang-xiang	一。《楞嚴經》：「一切眾生，從無始來，生死相續，皆由不知常住真心性淨明體，用諸妄想，此想不真 ，故有輪轉」，佛家指幻念。二。唐白居易《飲後夜醒》詩：「直至曉來猶妄想，耳中如有管弦聲」，謂胡思亂想。三。宋陸游《山園草木四絕句》之一：「少年妄想今除盡，但愛清樽浸晚霞」，謂不切實際或非分的想法。
detention	kōryū	拘留	juliu	《漢書：匈奴傳贊》：「匈奴人民每來降漢，單于亦輒拘留漢使，以相報復」，謂扣留。
dictatorship	dokusai	獨裁	ducai	《晉書：李續載記》：「慕容恪欲以續為尚書右僕射，暐憾續往言，不許。恪屢請，乃謂恪曰，「萬機之事委之叔父，伯陽（李續）一人，暐請獨裁。」續遂憂死」，謂獨自裁斷，獨自決定。
digest	shōka	消化	xiaohua	一。《釋名：釋天》：「火，化也，消化物也」，謂熔化。二。晉王羲之《雜帖》：「前卻食小差，數數便得疾，政由不消化故」，謂消化食物。(Cf. "Digest food in the stomach" glossed as 胃中消化 in Morrison , 1815.)
director	riji	理事	lishi	一。《管子：問》：「官承吏之無田餼而徒理事者幾何人」，謂治事，處理事務。二。官名。清宗人府設有理事官，掌宗室事。
disappear	shissō	失蹤	shizong	唐裴鉶《傳奇：崔煒》：「煒因迷道失足，墮於大枯井中。追者失蹤而返」，謂尋不到蹤跡。
dissection	kaibō	解剖	jiepou	《靈樞經：經水》：「若夫八尺之士，皮肉在此，外可度量切循

而得之，其死可解剖而視之」，
謂把人或動植物體剖開。In the
19th century, the term was reintroduced from Japan along
with *jiepouxue* 解剖學 or
kaibōgaku.

doctor, Ph.D.	*hakase* *hakushi*	博士*	*boshi*	一。《戰國策: 趙策三》：「鄭同北見趙王，趙王曰：「子南方之博士也」，指博通古今的人。二。《史記: 循吏列傳》：「公儀休者，魯博士也，以高第為魯相」，古代學官名。六國時有博士，秦因之。兩漢太常屬官，皆有博士。漢武帝置五經博士，掌以五經教子第。晉又置國子博士，歷代因之。唐有太學國子諸博士，和律學博士及算學博士等，并為教授之官。明清有國子博士，太常博士，而以五經博士為聖賢後裔的世襲官。三。《敦煌變文集: 父母恩重經講經文》：「學音樂，屈博士，弄坡調絃渾舍喜」，猶師傅。四。自唐以來，江南俗稱賣茶者曰博士，見《封氏見聞記》。
doctrine	*shugi*	主義	*zhuyi*	一。《逸周書: 諡法解》：「主義行德曰元」，謂謹守仁義。二。《史記: 太史公自序》：「敢犯顏色，以達主義，不顧其身，為國家樹長畫」，謂對事情的主張。(See suffix "-ism" in App. E)
dominate	*shihai*	支配	*zhipei*	《北齊書: 唐邕傳》：「及世宗崩，事出倉卒，顯祖部分將士，鎮壓四方，夜中召邕支配，造次便了。顯祖甚重之」，謂調派，安排。
dormitory	*shuku sha*	宿舍	*sushe*	《史記: 張儀列傳》：「（蘇秦）乃言趙王，發金幣車馬，使人微隨張儀，與同宿舍，稍稍近就之」，謂住宿停留。
duty (military service)	*kinmu*	勤務	*qinwu*	《廣韻: 去御》：「劇，勤務也」，謂勤於事務，對事務用力多。

economy	*keizai*	經濟*	*jingji*	一。《晉書: 殷浩傳》:「足下沈識淹長，思綜通練，起而明之，足以經濟」，又見唐李白《贈別舍人弟臺卿之江南》詩:「令弟經濟士，謫居我何傷」，謂經世濟民。二。清孔尚任《桃花扇: 修札》:「寫的激切婉轉，有情有理，叫他不好不依，又不敢不依，足見世兄經濟」，指治國的才幹。(Cf. 富國策 in App. A and 愛康諾米 in App. F)
editor-in-chief	*shuhitsu*	主筆	*zhubi*	明沈德符《野獲編史部大計糾內閣》:「每年初冬，朝審罪犯，俱太宰主筆，相仍已久」，謂主持判案。
education	*kyōiku*	教育*	*jiaoyu*	《孟子: 盡心》:「得天下英才而教育之」，謂教誨培育。
effect	*sayō*	作用	*zuoyong*	一。《魏書: 孫紹傳》:「治乖人理，雖合必難，作用失機，雖成必敗」，謂作為，行為。二。唐白居易《贈楊使君》:「時命到來須作用，功名未立莫思量」，謂努力。三。唐皎然《詩式: 李少卿并古詩十九首》:「《十九首》辭精義炳，婉而成章，始見作用之功」，謂著意加工刻畫。四。《水滸傳》第五四回:「便把劍在馬上望空作用，口中也念念有詞」，謂施行法術。
encroach-ment, infringe-ment	*shingai*	侵害	*qinhai*	《韓非子: 難三》:「物之所謂難者，必借人成勢而勿使侵害己，可謂一難也」，謂侵犯損害。又見《後漢書: 李固傳》:「自頃選舉牧守，多非其人，至行無道，侵害百姓。」
environ-ment	*kankyō*	環境*	*huanjing*	一。《新唐書: 王凝傳》:「時江南環境為盜區，凝以彊弩據采石，張疑幟，遣別將馬穎，解和州之圍」，指周圍的地方。二。《元史: 余闕傳》:「環境築堡塞，選精甲外扞，而耕稼其中」，指環繞所管轄之區域。

erosion	*shin-shoku*	侵蝕	*qinshi*	宋陸游《玉局觀拜東坡先生海外畫像》:「至寶不侵蝕,終亦老侍從」,謂逐漸侵害使之毀壞。又見明王鏊《震澤長語: 國猷》:「魏本都安邑,為秦侵蝕,不得已東徙大梁。」
ethics	*rinri*	倫理	*lunli*	一。《禮記: 樂記》:「凡音者,生於人心者也,樂者,通倫理者也」,鄭玄注:「倫,猶類也。理,分也」,謂事物的條理。二。漢賈誼《新書: 時變》:「商君違禮義,棄倫理」,謂人倫道德之理,指人與人相處的各種道德准則。
examin-ation, self-criticism	*kentō*	檢討*	*jiantao*	一。唐白居易《與元九書》:「僕數月來,檢討囊帙中,得新舊詩,各以類分,分為卷目」,謂查核,整理。二。官名。宋有史館檢討。明時始屬翰林院,位次於編修,與修撰編修同謂之史官。
exception (to a rule)	*reigai*	例外	*liwai*	宋沈作喆《寓簡》卷五:「大臣例外受賜不辭,若人主例外作事,何以止之?」,指在規定,常規之外。
exchange, communi-cate	*kōryū*	交流	*jiaoliu*	漢班昭《東征賦》:「望河路之交流兮,看成皋之旋門」,謂江河之水匯合而流。
exchange, trade	*kōkan*	交換	*jiaohuan*	《通典: 兵十》:「其虞候軍職掌準初發交換」,指各自把己有之物交給對方。
experience	*keiken*	經驗	*jingyan*	一。晉陶潛《搜神後記》卷二:「高平郗超……得重病。盧江杜愆少就外祖郭璞學《易》卜,頗有經驗。超令試占之,卦成,不愆」,謂效驗,驗証。二。《紅樓夢》第四二回:「雖然住了兩三天,日子卻不多,把古往今來沒見過的,沒吃過的,沒聽見的,都經驗過了」,指親身經歷過。
experience	*taiken*	體驗	*tiyan*	一。《朱子語類》卷一一九:「講論自是講論,須是將來自體驗。說一段過又一段,何補!……體驗是自心里暗自講量一

次」，謂親身領會。二。宋司馬
光《涑水記聞》卷十二：「或斫
倒人頭，或傷中重，係第一等功
勞者，凡一百一十五人，伏乞體
驗」，謂查核，考察。

English	Japanese	Chinese	Pinyin	Source
expression (of emotion)	*hyōjō*	表情*	*biaoqing*	漢班固《白虎通: 性名》：「人所以相拜者何？所以表情見意，屈節卑體尊事之者也」，謂表達感情，情意。
feudal	*hōken*	封建*	*fengjian*	一。《詩: 商頌: 殷武》：「命于下國，封建厥福」，謂大立。二。《禮記: 王制》：「王者之制祿爵，公，侯，伯，子，男凡五等……天子之田方千里，公，侯田方百里，伯七十里，子，男五十里」，謂封邦建國。又見《左傳: 僖公二十四年》：「昔周公吊二叔之不咸，故封建親戚，以蕃屏周」，孔穎達疏：「故封立親戚為諸侯之君，以為蕃籬，屏立周室。」三。《史記: 三王世家》：「昔五帝異制，周爵五等，春秋三等，皆因時而序尊卑。高皇帝撥亂世反諸正，昭至德，定海內，封建諸侯，爵位二等」，按秦統一中國，廢封建而立郡縣。但漢自景帝平七國之亂後，雖行封王侯建邦國之制，實集權於中央。
freedom	*jiyū*	自由*	*ziyou*	一。《玉台新詠: 古詩「為焦仲卿妻作」》：「吾意久懷忿，汝豈得自由」，謂由自己作主，不受限制和拘束。(Used to translate "freedom" as early as 1868 [Masini, p. 221]. The term became widespread in China via round-trip diffusion from Japan.)
frugal, frugality	*setsu yaku*	節約	*jieyue*	一。《漢書: 辛慶忌傳》：「慶忌居處恭儉，食欲被服尤節約」，謂節省，儉約。二。《墨子: 節葬下》：「金玉珠璣比乎身，綸組節約，車馬藏乎壙」，孫詒讓間詁：「《淮南子: 齊俗訓》云：「古者非不能竭國麋民，虛府殫財，含珠麟施，綸組

竭束追送死也。」許注云：
「綸，絮也。束，縛也」，案，
「節約」與《淮南》書「節束」
義同。」三。《朱子語類》卷五
二：「今學者要須事事節約，莫
教過當，此便是養氣之道也」，
謂節制約束。四。明王世貞
《藝苑卮言》卷二：「傅武仲有
《舞賦》，所少十分之七…
…豈武仲衍玉賦以為己作耶？抑
後人節約武仲之賦，因序語而誤
以為玉作也」，猶節錄。

government	*seifu*	政府	*zhengfu*	《資治通鑒: 唐宣宗大中二年》：「前鳳翔節度使石雄詣政府自陳黑山，烏嶺之功，求一鎮以終老」，胡三省注：「政府，即謂政事堂」，唐宋時稱宰相治理政務的處所為政府。
grammar	*bunpō*	文法*	*wenfa*	一。《史記: 李將軍列傳》：「程不識孝景時以數直諫為太中大夫，為人廉，謹于文法」，原意為法律規則之屬。二。元劉壎《隱居通議：文章四》：「公為文斬截峻刻，得左氏文法」，指文章的作法。(The equating of 文法 and "grammar" [?] may be traced back to the 17th century when the Portuguese Jesuit missionary Francisco Furtado and Li Zhizao 李之藻 collaborated on a translation entitled *Mingli tan* 名理探. It was via the Japanese *bunpō* -- documented in Huang Zunxiang's writing in 1878 (Masini, p. 203) --that the modern meaning of "grammar" began to replace the classical Chinese connotions. Cf. *gelangma* 葛郎瑪 in App. F.)
guerrilla warfare	*yūgeki*	遊擊* (游擊)	*youji*	一。官名，漢置游擊將軍，歷代皆有之，為武散官，元廢，明復置，為軍之將官，后省稱游擊，清因之，位次參軍，與今之中校相等。二。唐沈亞之《萬勝岡新

				城記》:「是時李時亮為先鋒將,使百騎游擊左右」,謂或東或西,流動襲擊。
guidance	*shidō*	指導	*zhidao*	漢荀悦《漢紀: 宣帝記》:「囚人不勝痛,則飾妄辭以示之,吏治者利其然,則指導以明之」,謂指示教導,指點引導。
history	*rekishi*	歷史		《三國志: 吳書: 吳主傳第二》:「納魯肅於凡品,是其聰也……屈身於陛下,是其略也」,宋裴松之注:「(吳王)志存經略,雖有餘閒,博覽書傳歷史,藉採奇異,不效諸生尋章摘句而已」,指對過去事實的記載。
hope	*kibō*	希望	*xiwang*	一。《周髀算經》:「立八尺表,以繩繫表顛,希望北極中大星」,謂仰望、瞻望。二。《後漢書: 李固傳》:「初,順帝時所除官,多不以次。及固在事,奏免百餘人。此等既怨,又希望冀旨,遂共作飛章虛誣固罪」,謂揣測別人的意圖而加以迎合。三。《後漢書: 班固傳》:「(匈奴)徒以畏漢威靈,逼憚南虜,故希望報命,以安其離叛」,謂盼著出現某種情況或達到某種目地。四。《宋書: 殷孝祖傳》:「國亂朝危,宜立長主…而群小相煽,構造無端,貪利幼弱,競懷希望」,謂欲望。
hothouse	*onshitsu*	溫室	*wenshi*	《漢書: 孔光傳》:「或問光溫室省中樹,皆何木也。光嘿不應,更答以它語」,謂暖和的房舍。(Cf. the missionary-Chinese translation 暖房 in App. A and the modern Japanese coinage *onshō* 溫床 [hotbed or breeding ground] in App. B)
humanity	*jindō*	人道	*rendao*	一。《易經: 繫辭下》:「有天道焉,有人道焉。」,謂為人之道。二。《禮記: 喪服小記》:「親親,尊尊,長長,男女之有別,人道之大者也」,謂人倫。三。《詩經: 大雅: 生民》:

「以弗無子，履帝武敏歆」，漢鄭玄箋：「心體歆歆然，其左右所止住，如有人道感己者也」，謂男女交合。四。明馮夢龍《智囊補: 明智: 唐六如》：「唐六如知其必反，遂佯狂以處。宸濠遣人饋物，則裸形箕踞，以手弄其人道，讒呵使者」，謂男性生殖器。五。佛教用語，猶言人界。

hypothesis	*kasetsu*	假説	*jiashuo*	唐劉知幾《史通: 雜説下》：「夫以園吏之寓言，騷人之假説，而定為實錄，斯已謬矣」，謂虛構的事。
idealism	*yuishin*	唯心	*weixin*	《楞伽經》：「由自心執著，心似外境傳，彼見所非有，是故説唯心」，佛教語，謂一切諸法（指萬事萬物），唯有內心，無心外之法。
image (portrait)	*shashin*	寫真	*xiezhen*	一。北齊嚴之推《嚴氏家訓: 雜藝》：「武烈太子偏能寫真，坐上賓客，隨宜點染，即成數人，以問童孺，皆知姓名也」，謂畫人的真容。二。宋王安石《胡笳十八拍》之八：「死生難有卻回身，不忍重看舊寫真」，指肖像畫。三。南朝梁劉勰《文心雕龍: 情采》：「為情者要約而寫真，為文者淫麗而煩濫」，指如實描繪事物。(Used by Wang Tao 王韜 to translate "photography" in 1879: 寫真即西法影像 [Masini, p. 208]. Other related Japanese *kanji* terms derived from this return graphic loan include 鏡寫真, 寫真鏡, 寫真器. Cf. 日影像, 照像法, 神鏡, etc. for "photography" in App. A.)
imagine	*sōzō*	想像	*xiang xiang*	一。《楚辭: 遠遊》：「思舊故以想像兮，長太息而掩涕」，謂緬懷，回憶。二。《列子: 湯問》：「伯牙乃舍琴而嘆曰：「善哉，善哉，子之聽夫，志想像猶吾心也」」，猶設想。

implement, carry out	*shikkō*	執行	*zhixing*	一。漢劉向《列女傳: 黎莊夫人》:「黎莊夫人,執行不衰,莊公不遇,行節反乖」,謂堅守情操。二。唐元稹《彈奏劍南東川節度使狀》:「追得所沒莊宅,奴婢文案,及執行案典耿琚,馬元亮等檢勘得實」,謂承辦,經辦。
improvement	*kaizen*	改善	*gaishan*	《後漢書: 獨行列傳: 王烈》:「盜懼吾聞其過,是有恥惡之心。既懷恥惡,必能改善」,謂改正過失或錯誤,回心向善。
incident	*jihen*	事變	*shibian*	《荀子: 富國》:「萬物得宜,事變得應」,泛指事物的變化。又見《詩序》:「吟詠情性,以風其上,達於事變而懷其舊俗者也。」
index	*sakuin*	索引	*suoyin*	宋曾鞏《移滄州過闕上殿札子》:「航浮索引之國,非有發召,而贏糧橐負,以致其贄者,惟恐不及」,指用繩索牽引。
individual	*kojin*	個人	*geren*	宋陳亮《念奴嬌: 至金陵》詞:「因念舊日山城,個人如畫,已作中州想」,謂彼人,那人,多指所愛的人。又見清曹垂璨《憶秦娥: 蟋蟀》詞「個人今夜秋腸千結」(Cf. *kotai* 個體 in App. B and *kobetsu* 個別 in App. C)
inheritance	*iden*	遺傳	*yichuan*	一。《史記: 扁鵲倉公列傳》:「慶有古先道遺傳黃帝,扁鵲之脈書」,猶留傳。二。北魏酈道元《水經注: 易水》:「余按遺傳,舊跡多在武陽,似不餞此也」,指遺留下來的傳聞。
injection	*chūsha*	注射	*zhushe*	《新唐書: 陸贄傳》:「工屬辭,敏速若注射然」,謂傾瀉,流射。
intentional, purposeful	*koi*	故意*	*guyi*	《杜甫詩》:「千觴亦不醉,感子故意長」,謂故人之情意。(Cf. "intentional" glossed as 固意做的 in Morrison, 1815)
intention, purpose	*ito*	意圖	*yitu*	《元典章: 刑部三: 不義》:「(劉世英)意圖陞遷,強將李丑驢執縛,親手用力割去囊腎,

欲作行求之物。以人為貨，重爵
輕生」，謂希望達到某種目的的
打算。

invasion, invade	*shin ryaku*	侵略	*qinlüe*	《史記: 五帝記》：「舜耕歷山，歷山之人皆讓畔」，張守節正義：「韓非子「歷山之農相侵略，舜往耕，期年，耕者讓畔」也」，謂侵犯掠取。
judgment, judge	*hanketsu*	判決	*panjue*	一。《南史: 孔覬傳》：「醒時判決，未嘗有壅」，謂裁斷，確定。二。《元典章: 臺綱一: 內臺》：「諸官府見問未決之事，監察御史不得輒憑告人餙詞取人追卷，候判決了畢，果有違錯，依例糾彈其罪」，指官府斷案。
judiciary	*shihō*	司法	*sifa*	一。官名。兩漢有決曹，賊曹掾，主刑法。歷代皆有。如唐制在府曰法曹參軍，在州曰司法參軍。二。星官名。清惲敬《文昌宮碑陰錄》：「《晉書: 天文志》「文昌六星在北斗魁前，天之六府也。四曰司祿，司中，司隸賞功進。」與《天官書》「四曰司命，五曰司中，六曰司祿」不同。《星經》又曰「六曰司法」。」
knowledge	*chishiki*	知識	*zhishi*	一。《墨子: 號令》：「其有知識兄弟欲見之，為召，勿令入里巷中」，謂相識之人。二。《南史: 虞悰傳》：「悰性敦實，與人知識，必相存訪，親疏皆有終始，世以此稱之」，謂結識，交游。三。漢劉向《列女傳: 齊管妾婧》：「人已語君矣，君不知識邪」，謂了解，辨識。四。《壇經》：「能大師言：「善知識！淨心念摩訶般若波羅蜜法」，佛教文獻中常把道德學問素養高的僧人或居士稱為善知識，有時泛稱聽講佛經的聽眾。
labor	*rōdō*	勞動*	*laodong*	一。《莊子: 讓王》：「春耕種，形足以勞動」，謂操作，活動。二。《三國志: 魏書: 鍾會傳》：「諸葛孔明仍規秦川，姜伯約屢出隴右，勞動我邊境，侵擾我氐羌」，謂使之不安寧。三。三國魏曹植《陳審舉表》：

「陛下可得雍容都城，何事勞動
鑾駕暴露於邊境哉」，謂煩勞。
四。《紅樓夢》第四二回：「賈
母笑道：「勞動了。珍兒讓出去
好生看茶」」，猶言勞駕，多
謝。

landlord	*jinushi*	地主	*dizhu*	一。唐郎士元《春宴王補闕城東別業》詩：「山下古松當綺席，簷前片雨滴春苔，地主同聲復同舍，留歡不畏夕陽催」，謂當地的主人，對客而言。二。《國語: 越語下》：「皇天后土，四鄉地主正之」，神名。三。《元典章: 刑部十八: 宿藏》：「王拜驢等於賀二地內掘得埋藏之物，於所得物內，一半沒官，一半付告人，於地內得者，依上令，得物之人與地主停分」，謂田地的主人。
law, rule	*hōsoku*	法則	*faze*	一。《周禮: 天官: 大宰》：「二曰法則，以馭其官」，鄭玄注：「法則，其官之制度」，謂制度，法度。二。《荀子: 勸學》：「君子之學也，入乎耳，箸乎心，布乎四體，形乎動靜，端而言，蝡而動，一可以為法則」，謂准則，規則 (Cf. *guize* 規則 in App. A)。三。《尉繚子: 治本》：「帝王之君，誰為法則」，謂榜樣，表率。四。《史記: 周本記》：「及為成人，遂好耕農，相地之宜，宜穀者稼穡焉，民皆法則之」，謂效法。五。《西游記》第十回：「蓋因猴原是弼馬溫，在天上看養龍馬的，有些法則，故此凡馬見他害怕」，謂法術。
lecture	*kōgi*	講義*	*jiangyi*	一。宋梅堯臣《聞臨淄公薨》詩：「官為喉舌動爵一品兮，經筵講義尊蕭匡」，謂講説經義。二。 講説經義之書，為經筵進講而作，亦有師儒講學，匯錄其説以成書者。如宋湯義《周義講義》。
liberation	*kaihō*	解放	*jiefang*	一。北魏賈思勰《齊民要術: 安石榴》：「十月中，以蒲　裹而纏之，二月初乃解放」，謂解

開，放松。二。《三國志：魏書：
趙儼傳》：「儼既囚之，乃表府
解放，自是威恩並著」，謂除罪
釋放。三。元貫云石《青江引：
惜別》曲：「閑來唱會「青江
引」，解放愁和悶」，謂消釋，
融化。

machinery	*kikai*	機械*	*jixie*	一。《庄子：天地》：「吾聞之吾師，有機械者必有機事，有機事者必有機心」，器之巧者曰機械。二。《淮南子：原道訓》：「故機械之心，藏於胸中，則純白不粹，神德不全」，高誘注：「機械，巧詐也」。三。金蔡松年《庚申閏月從師還自潁上對新月獨酌》：「自要塵網中，低眉受機械」，謂桎梏，束縛。
manager	*keiri*	經理*	*jingli*	一。《史記：秦始皇本紀》：「皇帝明德，經理宇內」，謂治理。二。《荀子：正名》：「心也者，道之工宰，道也者，治之經理也」，謂常理。
maneuver, drill	*enshū*	演習	*yanxi*	一。《新唐書：南詔傳》：「大府主將曰演習，副曰演覽」，官名。二。元汪元亨《沈醉東風：歸田》曲之二：「薰陶成野叟情，剗削去時官樣，演習會牧歌樵唱」，謂練習，溫習使熟悉。
market	*shijō*	市場	*shichang*	南唐尉遲偓《中朝故事》：「每閱市場，登酒肆，逢人即與相喜」，商品買賣的場所。
material	*shiryō*	材料	*cailiao*	一。宋蘇軾《乞降度牒修定州禁軍營房狀》：「一面置場和買材料燒造磚瓦」，謂用來造成品之物。二。元張可久《慶東原：次馬致遠先輩韻》曲：「山容瘦，木葉彫。對西窗盡是詩材料」，謂寫作素材。
matter	*busshi-tsu*	物質	*wuzhi*	金刁白《物質》詩：「物質方圓定，營營止自疲」，謂物的形體。
meaning, signify	*imi*	意味*	*yiwei*	《敦煌變文集：歡喜國王緣》：「無限難思意味長，速須覺悟禮空王」，謂意境，趣味。又見宋張戒《歲寒堂詩話》：「大抵句

<table>
<tr><td></td><td></td><td></td><td></td><td>子中若無意味，譬之山無煙雲，
春無草樹，豈復可觀？」</td></tr>
<tr><td>means</td><td>*shudan*</td><td>手段*</td><td>*shouduan*</td><td>宋蘇軾《與循守周文之書》之
二：「鄭君知其俊敏，篤問學，
觀所為詩文，非止科場手段
也」，謂本領，技巧。</td></tr>
<tr><td>memory</td><td>*kioku*</td><td>記憶</td><td>*jiyi*</td><td>《隋書: 儒林傳何妥》：「臣少
好音律，留意管絃，年雖耆老，
頗皆記憶」，謂記得，不忘。</td></tr>
<tr><td>meta-
  physical</td><td>*keijijō*</td><td>形而上</td><td>*xing'er
shang*</td><td>《易經: 系辭》：「形而上者謂
之道，形而下者謂之器」，謂無
形，抽象。</td></tr>
<tr><td>method</td><td>*hōhō*</td><td>方法</td><td>*fangfa*</td><td>一。《墨子: 天志中》：「中吾
矩者謂之方，不中吾矩者謂之不
方，是以方與不方，皆可得而知
之。此其故何？則方法明也」，
謂測定方形之法。二。《朱子語
類》卷一一七：「伯豐有才氣，
為學精苦，守官治事，皆有方
法」，謂辦法，門徑。三。唐張
籍《書懷》詩：「別從仙客求方
法，時到僧家問苦空」，謂方
術，法術。</td></tr>
<tr><td>military
affairs</td><td>*gunji*</td><td>軍事</td><td>*junshi*</td><td>《史記: 律書》：「會高祖厭苦
軍事，亦有蕭張之謀，故偃武一
休息，羈縻不備」，謂有關軍旅
或戰爭之事。(Cf. the Japanese
loan *heiji* 兵事 in App. B)</td></tr>
<tr><td>military
official</td><td>*shikan*</td><td>士官</td><td>*shiguan*</td><td>《書: 立政》：「準人」，孔
傳：「準人，平法，謂士官」，
即士師，掌刑獄之官。</td></tr>
<tr><td>monograph</td><td>*tankō
hon*</td><td>單行本</td><td>*danxing
ben*</td><td>清葉廷琯《吹網錄: 胡注失收考
異》：「散入時實有遺漏數條，
幸有單行本在，尚可勘對而
知」，謂單獨印行之書籍，以別
於叢書或散附它書而流行者。</td></tr>
<tr><td>monopoly</td><td>*dokusen*</td><td>獨占</td><td>*duzhan*</td><td>唐方干《贈鄭仁規》詩：「一石
雄才獨占難，應分二斗借人
寰」，謂單獨占有。</td></tr>
<tr><td>move,
movement</td><td>*undō*</td><td>運動*</td><td>*yundong*</td><td>一。漢董仲舒《雨雹對》：「運
動抑揚，更相動薄」，謂運行移
動。二。漢陸賈《新語: 慎
微》：「若湯武之君，伊呂之</td></tr>
</table>

臣，因天時而行罰，順陰陽而運動」，猶行動。三。《隋書: 天文志上》：「梁華林重雲殿前所置銅儀……其運動得東西轉，以象天行」，謂轉動。四。《太平廣記》卷二二六引唐顏師古《大業拾遺記: 水飾圖經》：「木人長二尺許，衣以綺羅，裝以金碧，及作雜禽獸魚鳥，皆能運動如生，隨曲水而行」，謂人或動物在空間的移動。五。《朱子語類》卷一一五：「又如人作商，亦須先安排許多財本，方可運動。若財本不贍，則運動未得」，指為達到目地而奔走活動。六。《英烈傳》第三十回：「劉基便登將臺，把五方旗號，按方運動，發出了三聲號炮，擊了三聲鼓，諸將都臺下聽令」，謂揮動，舞動。七。《西游記》第三二回：「只看你騰那乖巧，運動神機，仔細保你師父。假若怠慢了些兒，西天路莫想去得》，謂施展。

national learning	*koku gaku*	國學	*guoxue*	《周禮: 春官: 樂師》：「樂師掌國學之政，以教國子小舞」，古代指國家設立學校。
nationwide	*zengoku*	全國	*quanguo*	一。《孫子: 謀攻》：「凡用兵之法，全國為上，破國次之」，謂使敵國不戰而降。二。三國魏曹植《又贈丁儀王粲》：「權家雖愛勝，全國為令名」，謂保全國家。
nature, natural	*shizen*	自然*	*ziran*	《老子》：「人法地，地法天，天法道，道法自然」，又見《淮南子》：「因天地之自然」，謂宇宙萬物之存在。二。《陳繹會詩譜》：「謝靈運以險為主，以自然為工」，謂渾成，詩不加雕琢。三。《晉書: 裴秀傳》：「生而岐嶷，長蹈自然」，謂無所勉強。(The term 自然 was used as an adjective by W. A. P. Martin in his rendering of English "natural right" 自然之權 in *Wanguo gongfa* 萬國公法 [Masini, p. 221].)

navy	*kaigun*	海軍	haijun	《資治通鑑: 後梁均王龍德二年》：「大封王躬乂，性殘忍，海軍統帥王建殺之。自立，復稱高麗王」，指在海上作戰的軍隊。
necessity	*hitsuyō*	必要	biyao	《二刻拍案惊奇》卷二一：「即差快手李彪隨著王爵跟捕賊人，必要擒獲，方準銷牌」，謂非此不行，不可缺少的。
negotiate, negotiation	*kōshō*	交涉*	jiaoshe	一。前蜀貫休《聞無相道人順世》詩之五：「百千萬億偈，共他勿交涉」，又見宋范成大《病中聞西園新花已茂及竹徑皆成而海棠亦未過》詩：「春雖與病無交涉，雨莫將花便破除」，謂關係，牽涉。二。宋朱彧《萍洲可談》卷三：「熙嘏但言平生不喜與福建子交涉」，謂接觸。
nerve	*shinkei*	神經	shenjing	《後漢書: 方術列傳》：「然神經怪牒，玉策金繩，關扃於明靈之府，封滕於瑤壇之上者，靡得而闚也」，謂神秘奧妙之典籍。
normal (school)	*shihan*	師範	shifan	一。《北史: 楊播傳》：「恭德慎行，為世師範」，謂模範。二。南朝梁劉勰《文心雕龍: 通變》：「今才穎之士，刻意學文，多略漢篇，師範宋集」，謂傚法。三。元喬吉《金錢記》第二折：「著宋玉為師範，巫娥做生員」，指師傅，老師。
obey	*fukujū*	服從	fucong	《禮記: 內則》：「四十始仕，方物出謀發慮，道合則服從，不可則去」，孫希旦集解：「服從，謂服其事而從君也」，後以順服，遵從為服從。
office, organ	*kikan*	機關*	jiguan	一。《漢書: 藝文志》：「技巧者，習手足，便器械，積機關，以立攻守之勝者也」，謂機所以發，關所以閉，凡設有機件而能制動的機械。二。元戴善夫《風光好》第三折：「不想陶學士被某識破十二字隱語，用些機關，果中其計」，謂計謀。三。《素問: 厥論》：「少陽厥逆，機關不利。機關不利者，腰不可以行，項不可以顧」，指人體的關節。

only, sole	*yuiitsu*	惟一* （唯一）	*weiyi*	《書: 大禹謨》：「唯精唯一，允執厥中」，又見李邕《春賦》：「邁惟一之德」，專一之意。
opinion	*iken*	意見	*yijian*	一。《後漢書: 王充王府仲長統列傳》：「夫遭運無恆，意見偏雜，故是非之論，紛然相乖」，謂見解。二。明李贄《與焦漪園太史書》：「蓋意見太多，窠臼遂定，雖真師真友將如之何哉」，指不滿的想法。三。元張光祖《＜言行龜鑒＞序》：「雖然人之氣質意見終有限，惟學問義理為無窮」，謂識見。
opportunity	*kikai*	機會*	*jihui*	唐韓愈《與柳中丞書》：「動皆中于機會」，又見《蘇軾詩》：「東鄰小兒識機會，半年外舍無不知」，謂可借以行事之時機。(Glossed as 機會 in Morrison, 1815)
oppose	*hantai*	反對	*fandui*	一。南朝梁劉勰《文心雕龍: 麗辭》：「故麗辭之體，凡有四對，言對為易，事對為難，反對為優，正對為劣」，謂對偶一法。二。《明史: 天文志一》：「東方見日早，西方見日遲……相距一百八十度則晝夜時刻俱反對矣」，謂相反，對立。
optimistic	*rakkan*	樂觀	*leguan*	一。《史記: 貨殖列傳》：「當魏文侯時，李克務盡地力，而白圭樂觀時變，故人棄我取，人取我與」，謂善於觀察。二。唐韓愈《送王秀才序》：「自孔子沒，群弟子莫不有書，獨孟軻氏之傳得其宗，故吾少而樂觀焉」，謂喜歡觀看。
order	*meirei*	命令	*mingling*	一。《後漢書: 皇后紀上》：「時后前母姊女賈氏亦以選入，生肅宗。帝以后無子，命令養之」，謂發令以使之。二。《楚辭: 天問》：「何親揆發足，周之命以咨嗟」。漢王逸注：「當此之時，周之命令已行天下，百姓咨嗟歡而美之也」，指帝王的詔命，朝廷的文書。

organize, organization	*soshiki*	組織	*zuzhi*	一。《呂氏春秋: 先己》:「《詩》曰:「執轡如組」」, 漢高誘注:「組讀組織之組。夫組織之匠,成文於手,猶良御執轡於手而調馬口,以致萬里也」,謂經緯相交,織作布帛。二。南朝梁劉勰《文心雕龍:詮賦》:「麗詞雅義,符采相勝,如組織之品朱紫,畫繪之著玄黃」,謂織成的織物。三。劉勰《文心雕龍: 原道》:「雕琢情性,組織辭令」,指詩文的造句構辭。四。元姜個翁《霓裳中序第一: 春晚旅寓》:「園林罷組織,樹樹東風翠雲滴」,謂安排,整頓。五。唐李白《敍舊贈江陽宰陸調》詩:「邀遮相組織,呵嚇來煎熬」,謂構陷,猶羅織。
park	*kōen*	公園	*gong yuan*	《魏書: 任城王傳》:「(元澄)又明黜陟賞罰之法,表減公園之地以給無業貧口」,謂古代官家的園林。
peasant, farmer	*nōmin*	農民	*nongmin*	《穀梁傳: 成公元年》:「古者有四民。有士民,有商民,有農民,有工民」,范甯注:「農民,播殖耕稼者」,指務農的人。又見北齊顏之推《顏氏家訓: 勉學》:「人生在世,會當有業,農民則計量耕稼,商賈則討論貨賄。」
pencil	*enpitsu*	鉛筆*	*qianbi*	《東觀漢記: 曹褒傳》:「寢則懷鉛筆,行則誦文書」,指蘸鉛粉涂改錯字之筆。
perform	*enshutsu*	演出	*yanchu*	一。唐黃滔《誤筆牛賦》:「於是逐手摛成,隨宜演出,斯須亡墮落之所,頃刻見下來之質」,謂演變而出,演變而來。二。《好逑傳》第二回:「(鐵公子)騎了一匹白馬,只叫一人跟隨,竟暗暗演出齊化門來,並不使一人知覺」,偷偷地出行。
period, era	*jidai*	時代	*shidai*	一。《宋書: 禮志一》:「況三國鼎峙,歷晉至宋,時代移改,各隨事立」,指改朝易代中的某個時期。二。唐高適《酬馬八效

古見贈》詩:「時代種桃李,無
人顧此君」,猶世代。

pessimism	*hikan*	悲觀	*beiguan*	《法華經: 八普門品》:「悲觀及慈觀,常願常膽仰」,佛教語,五觀之一。謂以慈悲之心觀察眾生,救人苦難。
phenomena	*genshō*	現象	*xian xiang*	《寶行經》:「觀世音現象三十有九,文殊現象七十一」,謂神,佛,菩薩等現身於人間。
physiology	*seiri*	生理	*shengli*	一。《百喻經: 種熬胡麻子喻》:「昔有愚人,生食胡麻子,以為不美,熬而食之為美。便生念言,不如熬而種之,後得美者。便熬而種之。永無生理」,謂生長繁殖之理。二。宋蘇軾《問養生》:「安則物之感我者輕,和則我之應物者順。外輕內順,而生理備矣」,謂養生之理。三。唐杜甫《自京赴奉先縣詠懷五百字》:「以茲悟生理,獨恥事干謁」,謂為人之道。(Cf. *seirigaku* 生理學 in App. E.)
plan, project	*keikaku*	計劃*	*jihua*	元無名氏《符金錠》第二折:「我忙回住宅,自有個計劃,便著你花燭筵會賓客」,謂計策,打算。
poetry	*shika*	詩歌	*shige*	《漢書: 禮樂志》:「和親之說難形,則發之於詩歌詠言,鐘石筦弦」,古代不合樂的為詩,合樂的為歌,現代一般統稱為詩歌。
police	*keisatsu*	警察	*jingcha*	一。唐玄奘《大唐西域記: 籃摩國》:「野象群行,採花以散,冥力警察,初無間替」,謂警戒,監察。二。《金史: 百官志》:「諸京警巡院使,掌平理獄訟警察別部」,謂監督,檢察。三。明陳敬宗《題晦庵先生書簡墨跡卷後》:「乃知先生雖已造大賢之域,亦有資於警察涵養之功也」,謂警惕,省察。
politics	*seiji*	政治*	*zhengzhi*	一。《書: 畢命》:「道洽政治,澤潤生民」,謂政事得以治理,政事清明。二。《周禮: 地

				官: 遂人》:「掌其政治禁令」,指治理國家所施行的一切措施。三。《宋書: 沈攸之傳》:「至荊州,政治如在夏口,營造舟甲,常如敵至」,謂政事的治理。
popular	*ryūkō*	流行*	*liuxing*	《孟子》:「孔子曰德之流行,速于置郵而傳命」,謂如水之流行,所及者遠之意。
preach	*sekkyō*	説教	*shuojiao*	《漢書: 儒林傳: 梁丘賀》:「待詔黃門數入説教侍中,以召賀」,謂講解和教授。
prejudice	*henken*	偏見	*pianjian*	一。《漢書: 杜鄴傳》:「疏賤獨偏見,疑內亦有此類」,顏師古注:「鄴自謂傍觀而見之也」,謂從側面看到。二。《庄子: 齊物論》:「與物相刃相靡……不亦悲乎」,晉郭象注:「各信其偏見,而恣其所行,莫能自反」,謂片面的見解。(Cf. "prejudice" glossed as 偏私之見 in Morrison, 1815)
present, attend (a meeting)	*shusseki*	出席	*chuxi*	《金瓶梅詞話》第四九回:「蔡御史便説:「深擾一日,酒告止了罷。」因起身出席」,謂離開席位。
present-ation, symbol	*hyōshō*	表象*	*biao-xiang*	一。《史記: 龜策列傳》:「會上欲擊匈奴,西攘大宛,南收百越,卜筮至預見表象,先圖其利」,謂顯露在外的徵象。二。《後漢書: 天文志》:「言其事星辰之變,表象之應,以顯天戒,明王事焉」,謂徵兆。
production	*seisan*	生產	*sheng-chan*	一。《史記: 貨殖列傳》:「吾治生產,猶伊尹,呂尚之謀,孫吳用兵,商鞅行法是也」,謂生計。二。明陶宗儀《輟耕錄: 傳國璽》:「大師國王之孫曰拾得者,嘗官同知通政院事,今既歿矣,生產散失,家計窘極」,謂財產,產業。三。《三國志: 吳書: 駱統傳》:「又聞民間,非居處小能自供,生產兒子,多不起養,屯田貧民,亦多棄子」,謂生育。

professor	*kyōju*	教授*	*jiaoshou*	一。《史記: 仲尼弟子列傳》：「子夏居西河教授，為魏文候師」，謂以道藝傳授生徒。二。學官名，宋代除宗學，律學，醫學，武學等置教授傳授學業外，各路的州，縣學均置教授，掌管學校課試等事，位居提督學事司之下。三。《京本通俗小說: 西山一窟鬼》：「吳教授看那入來的人，不是別人，卻是十年前搬去的鄰舍王婆」，對私塾先生的尊稱。
progress	*shinpo*	進步*	*jinbu*	《傳燈錄》：「百尺竿頭須進步，十方世界是全身」，謂逐次前進，如行步之不已。
propagation	*denpa*	傳播	*chuanbo*	《北史: 突厥傳》：「宜傳播天下，咸使知聞」，又見元辛文房《唐才子傳: 高適》：「每一篇已，好事者輒為傳播吟玩」。清袁枚《隨園詩話》卷十四：「一硯一銚，主人俱繪形作冊，傳播藝林」，謂廣泛散布。(Masini [p. 162] attributes the use of the noun 傳播 in modern Chinese to round-trip diffusion via Japan.)
proposition	*meidai*	命題	*mingti*	宋王禹偁《贈別鮑秀才序》：「公出文數十章，即進士鮑生之作也。命題立意，殆非常人」，指所確定的詩文等的主旨。
props	*dōgu*	道具	*daoju*	唐嚴維《送桃岩成上人歸本寺》詩：「道具門人捧，齋糧谷鳥銜」，佛教語。指修行者用的衣物器具。又見宋惠洪《冷齋夜話: 石崖僧》：「師寄此山如今几年矣，道具何在？伴侶為誰？」
prosperity, economic boom	*keiki*	景氣	*jingqi*	晉殷仲文《南州桓公九井作》詩：「景氣多明遠，風物自淒緊」，景色，景象之意。(Cf. Japanese *fukeiki* 不景氣 in App. C.)
protest	*kōgi*	抗議*	*kangyi*	一。《後漢書: 盧植傳》：「（董卓）大會百官於朝堂，議

欲廢立，群僚無敢言，植獨抗議
不同」，謂持論正直。二。《舊
唐書: 裴耀卿傳》：「李懷光以
河中叛，朝廷欲以含垢為意，佶
抗議請討。上深器之，前席慰
勉」，指進言，獻議。

psyche, psychology	*shinri*	心理	*xinli*	一。南朝梁劉勰《文心雕龍: 情采》：「是以聯辭結采，將欲明理，采濫辭詭，則心理愈翳」，謂心中包含的情理。二。明王守仁《傳習祿》卷中：「此區區心理合一之體，知行並進之功，所以異於後世者, 正在於是」，理學名詞，謂情與理。
reaction, reactionary	*handō*	反動	*fandong*	《北齊書: 楊愔傳》：「高歸彥初雖同德，後尋反動，以疏忌之跡盡告兩王」，謂與原來的行動相反。
reaction, response	*hannō*	反應	*fanying*	《後漢書: 劉焉傳》：「（趙趲）還共繫璋（劉璋），蜀郡，廣漢，犍為皆反應」，謂響應反叛。
record	*kiroku*	記錄	*jilu*	一。《後漢書: 班彪傳》：「太中大夫陸賈記錄時功，作《楚漢春秋》一篇」，謂載錄，記載。二。宋曾鞏《太子賓客致仕陳公神道碑銘》：「惟陳氏，其先虞舜之後，封於陳。春秋時，陳滅入楚，其子孫以國為氏，世為顯姓，見於記錄」，謂史冊，記載的材料。三。唐崔致遠《謝生料啟》：「豈料司空相公俯念海人久為廛吏，特垂記錄，繼賜沾濡」，指記名在冊，以備錄用或治罪。
reform	*kaizō*	改造*	*gaizao*	一。《通鑑: 秦昭襄王五十二年》：「改造則不易同也」，謂更選擇也。二。《宋史: 律歷志》：「請改造新歷」，謂重行制造。
registration	*tōki*	登記	*dengji*	明李頤《條陳海防疏》：「兵部量發馬價，於密，薊，永三道，每道二萬兩，聽專備前項買馬造器及海防雜辦一應必需之物，詳為登記」，指記載在冊籍上。

relation, connection	*kankei*	關係	*guanxi*	《宣和遺事》前集：「這箇陰陽，都關係著皇帝一人心術之邪正是也」，謂關聯，牽涉。又見《金瓶梅詞話》第五六回：「哥教唱此詞，關係心間之事，莫非想起過世的嫂子來。」
relativity	*sōtai*	相對	*xiangdui*	一。《儀禮: 士昏禮》：「婦乘以几，從者二人，坐持几相對」，謂面對面，相向。二。唐韓愈《朝歸》詩：「服章豈不好？不與德相對」，謂相符，相稱。三。宋張載《正蒙: 太和》：「反者，屈伸聚散相對之謂」，指兩相對應。四。宋沈括《夢溪筆談: 雜志一》：「以變化相對言之，既能變而為大毒，豈不能變而為大善？既能變而殺人，則宜有能生人之理」，指依條件而存在或變化。
represent, delegate	*daihyō*	代表	*daibiao*	明吳承恩《壽蘇山陳公章詞》：「郢中寡和，風高《白雪》之篇，日下無雙，代表青雲之業」，謂顯耀於一代。
republic	*kyōwa*	共和*	*gonghe*	一。《史記: 周本紀第四》：「召公，周公二相行政，號曰共和」韋昭注：「公卿相與和而脩政事，號曰共和也。」二。《竹書紀年》：「厲王十二年出奔彘，十三年共伯和攝行天子事，號曰共和」。三。《漢書: 古今人表》注：「師古曰「共，國名也。伯，爵也。和，共伯之名也。共音恭。而《遷史》以為周召二公行政，號曰共和，無所據也。」
request	*seikyū*	請求	*qingqiu*	一。《史記: 游俠列傳》：「解（郭解）執恭敬，不敢乘車入其縣廷。之旁郡國，為人請求事，事可出，出之」，以私事相求。二。《漢書: 宣帝記》：「虛閭權渠單于請求和親」，說明要求，希望得到滿足。
resolution	*giketsu*	議決*	*yijue*	《漢書: 酷吏傳》：「延年按劍廷叱群臣，即日議決」，謂議論并作出決定。

retreat	*taikyaku*	退卻	*tuique*	《後漢書: 皇甫規傳》:「郡將知規有兵略,乃命為功曹,使率甲士八百,與羌交戰,斬首數級,賊遂退卻」,謂倒退,多用於軍隊在作戰中向後撤退。
revolution	*kakumei*	革命*	*geming*	《易: 革》:「天地革而四時成,湯武革命,順乎天而應乎人」,孔穎達疏:「夏桀,殷紂,凶狂無度,天既震怒,人亦叛主,殷湯,周武,聰明睿智,上順天命,下應人心,放桀鳴條,誅紂牧野,革其王命,改其惡俗,故曰湯武革命,順乎天而應乎人」,謂天子受命於天,王者易姓。
romantic	*rōman*	浪漫	*langman*	宋蘇軾《與孟震同游常州僧舍》詩之一:「年來轉覺此生浮,又作三吳浪漫游。」,謂縱情,任意。 (Cf. the phonemic loan 浪漫蒂克 in App. F)
rule, method	*hōshiki*	法式*	*fashi*	《史記: 秦始皇本紀》:「治道運行,諸產得宜,皆有法式」,又見《管子: 明法解》:「案法式而驗得失,非法度不留意焉。」
rule, regulation	*kisoku*	規則*	*guize*	一。唐李群玉《湘中別成威闍黎》詩:「至哉彼上人,冰雪凜規則」,指儀範。二。明徐光啟《農政全書》卷九:「在京各衙門,仍照軍民糧運見行規則,刊刷易知單冊,給與納戶,以便交納扣除」,謂規章,法則。
sanction	*seisai*	制裁	*zhicai*	《資治通鑒: 後唐明宗天成三年》:「及安重誨用事,稍以法制裁之」,謂懲處,管束。
satire	*fūshi*	諷刺*	*fengci*	南朝梁劉勰《文心雕龍: 書記》:「刺者,達也,詩人諷刺」,謂以婉言隱語相譏刺。
savings	*chochiku*	貯蓄	*zhuxu*	唐白居易《唐故湖州長城縣令贈戶部侍郎博陵崔府君神道碑銘》:「大丈夫貯蓄材術,樹置功利,鎡基富貴,焯燿家邦」,謂儲存,積聚。

science	*kagaku*	科學	*kexue*	宋陳亮《送叔祖主筠州高要簿序》：「自科學之興，世之為士者往往困於一日之程文，甚至於老死而或不遇」，謂科舉之學。
secretary	*kanji*	幹事	*ganshi*	《易: 乾》：「貞固足以幹事」，謂辦事。又見宋朱熹《答黃子耕書》：「今且造一小書院，以為往來幹事休息之處。」(The noun form and the unstressed *shi* 事 in modern Chinese usage set the return graphic loan 幹事 apart from its verb form. In fact, the two compounds should be treated as homo-ideographs rather than homophones.)
self	*jiga*	自我	*ziwo*	一。《文選: 陸機<豪士賦>序》：「夫我之自我，智士猶嬰其累。物之相物，昆蟲皆有此情」，指自己肯定自己。二。宋蘇軾《戲書樂天身心問答後》詩：「淵明形神自我，樂天身心相物」，猶相，謂相偶。
society	*shakai*	社會*	*shehui*	《東京夢華錄》：「八月秋舍，市學先生，預斂諸生錢作社會，春社重午重九，亦是如是」，又見《夢梁錄》：「安排社會，結縛台閣，迎列于道」。《二程全書》亦有「鄉民為社會」之語，謂里社之民，逢節日舉行集會行賽之活動。(Cf. *shehuixue* 社會學 in App. E)
solve, solution	*kaiketsu*	解決	*jiejue*	一。漢王充《論衡: 案書》：「至於論，不務全疑，兩傳並紀，不宜明處。執與剖破渾沌，解決亂絲，言無不可知，文無不可曉哉」，謂梳理清楚，作出決斷。二。唐杜牧《李府君墓志銘》：「年三十，盡明六經書，解決微隱，蘇融雪釋，鄭玄至於孔穎達輩凡所為疏注，皆能短長其得失」，謂解釋，疏通。
special	*toku betsu*	特別	*tebie*	《三國志平話》卷上：「呂布東北而進。數日，見桑麻地土特別」，謂不一般，與眾不同。

speculation	*tōki*	投機*	*touji*	一。唐司空圖《復安南碑》:「投機扼險,委勁待時」,謂設置有機件而能制動的器械。二。《新唐書: 屈突通張公謹等傳贊》:「投機之會,間不容髮」,謂切中時機。三。《宋陳師道《和黃預病起》:「似聞藥病已投機,牛鬥蛇妖頓覺非」,指兩相契合。四。清徐大椿《洄溪道情: 行醫嘆》:「要入世投機,只打聽近日時醫,貫用的是何方何味,試一試偶然得效,倒覺得希奇」,指乘機牟利。五。《續傳燈錄: 法光禪師》:「使言言相副,句句投機」,佛家語。謂契合佛祖心機,喻徹底大悟。
speech	*enzetsu*	演説*	*yanshuo*	一。《書: 洪范》:「初一曰五行……威用六極」,(疏):「自初一曰已下,至此六極已上,皆是禹所次第而紋之,下文更將此九類而演説之」,謂引申其説。二。《蓮社高賢傳: 慧遠法師》:「又見水流光明,分十四支流注上下,演説空苦無常無我之音」,謂闡述。三。清李漁《蜃中樓: 獻壽》:「待兄弟手舞足蹈,演説一番,只當作一齣戲文」,謂表演紋説。
square, plaza	*hiroba*	廣場	*guang-chang*	一。漢張衡《西京賦》:「臨迴望之廣場,程角觝之妙戲」,謂廣闊的場地。二。宋王禹偁《贈別鮑秀才序》:「其為學也,依道而據德,其為才也,通古而達變,其為識也,利物而務成。求之廣場,未易多得」,謂人多的場合。
stage	*butai*	舞臺	*wutai*	唐顏師古《隋遺錄》:「舟前為舞臺,臺上垂蔽日簾」,指供演出的臺。又見宋趙令時《侯鯖錄》卷二:「淚臉補痕勞獺髓,舞臺收影費鸞腸。」
staple food	*shu-shoku*	主食*	*zhushi*	《資治通鑑: 梁武帝普通元年》:「使主食中黃門胡定自列」,胡三省注:「主食,主御食者也」,指主管君主膳食的官。

statistics	*tōkei*	統計	*tongji*	明胡應麟《少室山房筆叢: 經籍會通一》:「古今書籍,統計一代,前後之藏,往往無過十萬。統計一朝,公私之蓄,往往不能十萬」,謂總括的計算。
status, personal background	*minbun*	身分	*shenfen*	一。《宋書: 王僧達傳》:「固宜退省身分,識恩之厚,不知報答,當在何期」,指出身,地位。二。明陶宗儀《輟耕錄: 寫山水訣》:「樹要有身分,畫家謂之紐子,要折搭得中,樹身各要有發生」,指模樣,姿態。三。《儒林外史》第十二回:「張鐵臂一上一下,一左一右,舞出許多身分來」,指手段,本領。四。《初刻拍案惊奇》卷二十:「(那婆子)所以閒常也與人做些不伶俐的身分」,指行為,勾當。五。《金瓶梅詞話》第二五回:「比杭州織來的花樣身分更強十倍」,謂質地,質量。
stop, cease	*teishi*	停止	*tingzhi*	一。《梁書: 武帝紀中》:「屬車之間,見讖前世,便可自今停止」,指不再進行,不再實行。二。《周書: 柳慶傳》:「有賈人持金二十斤,詣京師交易,寄人停止」,謂住宿。三。元吳昌齡《張天師》第一折:「仙子,您直恁般慌速,便再停止一會兒也好」,指停留。
subject	*shutai*	主體	*zhuti*	《漢書: 東方朔傳》:「上以安主體,下以便萬民,則五帝三王之道可幾而見也」,指君主的統治地位。
sum total	*sōkei*	總計	*zongji*	一。《三國志: 魏書: 劉廙傳》:「可以死效,難用筆陳」,裴松之注引《劉廙別傳》:「歲課之能,三年總計,乃加黜陟」,謂總共計算。二。《宋史: 外國傳五: 闍婆》:「有文吏三百餘員,目為秀才,掌文本,總計貨財」,猶統計。
supply	*kyōkyū*	供給	*gongji*	一。《管子: 地圖》:「論功勞,行賞罰,不敢蔽賢有私,供給軍之求索」,謂以物資,錢財

				等給人而供其所需。二。唐杜甫《有客》詩:「不嫌野外無供給,乘興還來看藥欄」,謂生活所需之錢物。
support	*shiji*	支持*	*zhichi*	一。《淮南子: 本經訓》:「標林欀櫨,以相支持」,謂支撐。二。《元典章: 聖政二: 均賦役》:「中書省官人每奏國家應辦,支持浩大」,謂開支,供應。三。元蕭德祥《殺狗勸夫》第二折:「他覺來我自支持他,包你無事」,謂對付,應付。四。《英烈傳》第六五回:「徐達傳令水陸三軍一齊進戰,以防賊眾彼此支持」,指支援。五。元孟漢卿《魔合羅》:「不要你狂言詐語,花唇巧舌,信口支持」,謂説話不老實。六。元鄭廷玉《後庭花》第四折:「好教我不解其中之意,起初道眼迷奚。他如今則把手支持,真個是啞子做夢説不的」,謂做出姿勢。
teaching assistant	*jokyō*	助教	*zhujiao*	古代學官名。晉咸寧時設置,協助國子祭酒,博士教授生徒。其後除個別朝代外,國學中都設經學助教,稱國子助教,太學助教,四門助教,廣文助教等。
theory	*riron*	理論	*lilun*	一。晉常琢《華陽國志: 後賢志李宓》:「著述理論,論中和仁義儒學道化之事凡十篇」,謂説理立論。二。《水滸傳》二十四回:「如若有人欺負你,不要和他爭執,待我回來,自和他理論」,謂據理辯論。
thought	*shisō*	思想*	*sixiang*	一。《公羊傳: 桓公二年》:「納於大廟」,漢何休注:「廟之言貌也,思想儀貌而事之」,謂想念,懷念。二。《素問: 上古天真論》:「外不勞形於事,內無思想之患」,謂思忖,攷慮。
time	*jikan*	時間	*shijian*	金董解元《西廂記諸宮調》卷一:「時間尚在白衣,目下風雲未遂」,猶眼下,一時。二。《西游記》第四回:「如若不

				依，時間就打上靈霄寶殿，教他龍床定坐不成 」，猶立即，馬上。
topic (of conversation)	*wadai*	話題	*huati*	明無名氏《白兔記: 團圓》：「貧者休要相輕棄，否極終有泰時，留與人間作話題 」，談話的題目。
toy	*omocha*	玩具	*wanju*	明唐順之《重修涇縣儒學記》：「周衰，王道廢缺……《易》象，《春秋》，十六國之樂，徒以誇於諸侯賓客，為古物玩具，而未嘗以教諸弟子 」，指供玩耍游戲的器物。
tradition	*dentō*	傳統	*chuan-tong*	《後漢書: 東夷傳》：「自武帝滅朝鮮，使驛通於漢者三十許國，國皆稱王，世世傳統 」，又見南朝梁沈約《立太子恩詔》：「守器傳統，於斯為重。」明胡應麟《少室山房筆叢: 九流序論上》：「儒主傳統翼教，而碩士名賢之訓附之 」，謂帝業，學說等世代相傳。
traffic	*kōtsū*	交通	*jiaotong*	一。《管子: 度地》：「山川涸落，天氣下，地氣上，萬物交通 」，謂交相通達。二。《莊子: 田子方》：「至陰肅肅，至陽赫赫。肅肅出乎天，赫赫發乎地。兩者交通成和而物生焉 」，謂感通，感應。三。《韓詩外傳》卷十：「淵願貧如富，賤如貴，無勇而威，與士交通終身無患難 」，謂交往，往來。四。《漢書: 江充傳》：「（充）詣闕告太子丹與同產姊及王後宮姦亂，交通郡國豪猾，攻剽為姦，吏不能禁 」，指勾結，串通。五。《百喻經: 摩尼水寶喻》：「昔有一人與他婦通，交通未竟，夫從外來，即便覺之 」，指交媾。
transition, interim	*kato*	過渡	*guodu*	宋蘇軾《荊州十首》：「野市分獐鬧，官帆過渡遲 」，謂橫越江河。
trust, credit	*shin'yō*	信用*	*xinyong*	一。《左傳: 宣公十二年》：「王曰：「其君能下人，必能

信用其民矣，庸可幾乎？」，謂
以誠信使用人。二。《三國志:
魏書:董卓傳》:「悉發掘陵
墓，取寶物」，裴松之注引晉
司馬彪《續漢書》:「《石苞室
讖》，妖邪之書，豈可信用？」
謂相信，采用。

truth	*shinri*	真理	*zhenli*	南朝梁蕭統《令旨解二諦義》:「真理虛寂，惑心不解，雖不解真，何防解俗」，謂最純真的道理，亦指佛法。
understand-ing (the power of)	*gosei*	悟性	*wuxing*	宋趙師秀《送湯干》詩:「能文兼悟性，前是惠休身」，明謝榛《四溟詩話》卷四:「詩固有定體，人各有悟性」，謂領會事物的能力。
unfold	*tenkai*	展開	*zhankai*	《朱子語類》卷十八:「欲致其知者，須先存得此心。此心既存，卻看這箇道理是如何，又推之於身，又推之於物，只管一層展開一層，又見得許多道理」，謂鋪開，張開。
unique, special	*tokushu*	特殊	*teshu*	晉夏侯湛《芙蓉賦》:「固陂池之麗觀，尊終世之特殊」，謂不同一般。又見宋蘇轍《謝改著作佐郎啟》:「固天地付予之特殊，宜朝廷進退之亦異。」
unit	*tan'i*	單位	*danwei*	《敕修清規日用規范》:「昏鍾鳴，須先歸單位坐禪」，謂禪位。
view, outlook	*kannen*	觀念	*guannian*	唐魏靜《禪宗永嘉集序》:「物物斯安，觀念相續，心心靡間，始終抗節」，佛教用語，對特定對象或義理的思維和記憶。
violate, violation	*shinpan*	侵犯	*qinfan*	一。《史記:律書》:「大至君辱失守，小乃侵犯削弱」，謂侵凌觸犯。二。《朱子語類》卷九四:「只是那一箇定理在此中截然不相侵犯」，謂抵觸。
warehouse	*sōko*	倉庫	*cangku*	《國語:晉語九》:「從者曰:「邯鄲之倉庫實」」，貯藏糧食之處為倉，貯藏兵車之處為庫。後即以倉庫泛指貯存保管大宗物

品的建筑物或場所。又見《 史記: 萬石張叔列傳 》:「城郭倉庫空虛。」

| will | *ishi* | 意志 | *yizhi* | 《商君書: 定分 》:「夫微妙意志之言，上知之所難也 」，指決定達到某種目的而產生的內心狀態，常以語言或行動表現出來。 |

| world | *sekai* | 世界 | *shijie* | 《楞嚴經 》卷四:「何名為眾生世界？世為遷流，界為方位。汝今當知，東，西，南，北，東南，西南，東北，西北，上，下為界，過去，未來，現在為世 」，佛教語。世猶指時間，界指空間。二。唐孟浩然《 臘月八日於剡縣石城寺禮拜 》詩:「竹柏禪庭古 ，樓台世界稀 」，謂人間。三 。宋陸游《 老學庵筆記 》卷一：「 金腰帶，銀腰帶，趙家世界朱家坏 」，謂天下，江山。(Note that the equating of 世界 and the English term "world" was mediated through Japanese *sekai* and, significantly, this worlding of *shijie* 世界 successfully replaced the earlier Chinese conceptual naming of temporal and spacial boundaries such as *tianxia* 天下. Cf. the missionary-Chinese rendering of "international" as *wanguo* 萬國 in App. A and the subsequent Japanese loan replacement *kokusei* 國際 in App. B.) |

A Sampling of Suffixed and Prefixed Compounds from Modern Japanese

English	Japanese romanization	Chinese characters	Chinese romanization
1. "anti-"	*han-*	反	*fan-*
anti-party	*hantō*	反党	*fandang*
counter-revolution	*hankakumei*	反革命	*fan geming*
oppose, counter	*hantai*	反對	*fandui*
reaction	*handō*	反動	*fandong*
2. "as"	*to-*	為	*-wei*
become	*to naru*	成為	*chengwei*
believe, consider as	*to mitomeru*	認為	*renwei*
view as	*to minasu*	視為	*shiwei*
3. "class"	*kaikyū*	階級	*jieji*
bourgeoisie	*shisan kaikyū*	資產階級	*zichan jieji*
landlord class	*jinushi kaikyū*	地主階級	*dizhu jieji*
peasant class	*nōmin kaikyū*	農民階級	*nongmin jieji*
proletariat	*musan kaikyū*	無產階級	*wuchan jieji*
propertied class	*yūsan kaikyū*	有產階級	*youchan jieji*

4. **"effect,"** **"function"**	*-sayō*	作用	*-zuoyong*
alienation	*ika sayō*	異化作用	*yihua zuoyong*
assimilation	*dōka sayō*	同化作用	*tonghua zuoyong*
psychological function	*shinri sayō*	心理作用	*xinli zuoyong*
spiritual effect	*seishin sayō*	精神作用	*jingshen zuoyong*

5. **"era," "age"**	*-jidai*	時代	*-shidai*
Atomic Age	*genshi jidai*	原子時代	*yuanzi shidai*
Bronze Age	*dōki jidai*	銅器時代	*tongqi shidai*
Iron Age	*tekki jidai*	鐵器時代	*tieqi shidai*
Neolithic	*shin sekki jidai*	新石器時代	*xinshiqi shidai*
Paleolithic	*kyū sekki jidai*	舊石器時代	*jiushiqi shidai*

6. **"-feeling"**	*-kan*	感	*-gan*
aesthetic feeling	*bikan*	美感	*meigan*
anxiety	*kinchōkan*	緊張感	*jinzhang gan*
bad impression	*akkan*	惡感	*egan*
favorable impression	*kōkan*	好感	*haogan*
feeling, emotion	*jōkan*	情感	*qinggan*
impression of a literary work	*dokugokan*	讀後感	*duhou gan*
sensitivity	*binkan*	敏感	*mingan*
sex appeal	*seikan*	性感	*xinggan*
superiority complex	*yūetsukan*	優越感	*youyue gan*

7. **"-ism"**	*-shugi*	主義	*-zhuyi*
anarchism	*museifu shugi*	無政府主義	*wuzhengfu zhuyi*
capitalism	*shihon shugi*	資本主義	*ziben zhuyi*
communism	*kyōsan shugi*	共產主義	*gongchan zhuyi*
feudalism	*hōken shugi*	封建主義	*fengjian zhuyi*
humanism	*jinbun shugi*	人文主義	*renwen zhuyi*
imperialism	*teikoku shugi*	帝國主義	*diguo zhuyi*
individualism	*kojin shugi*	個人主義	*geren zhuyi*
militarism	*gunkoku shugi*	軍國主義	*junguo zhuyi*

nationalism	*minzoku shugi*	民族主義	*minzoku zhuyi*
naturalism	*shizen shugi*	自然主義	*ziran zhuyi*
realism	*genjitsu shugi*	現實主義	*xianshi zhuyi*
romanticism	*rōman shugi*	浪漫主義	*langman zhuyi*
socialism	*shakai shugi*	社會主義	*shehui zhuyi*
state socialism	*kokka shakai-hugi*	國家社會主義	*guojia shehui zhuyi*
national essentialism	*kokusui shugi*	國粹主義	*guocui zhuyi*

8. "-itis" | **-en** | 炎 | **-yan**

arthritis	*kansetsuen*	關節炎	*guanjie yan*
coronary inflammation	*shinzō-naimaku'en*	心藏內膜炎	*xinzang neimo yan*
encephalitis	*nōen*	腦炎	*nao yan*
enteritis	*chōen*	腸炎	*chang yan*
gastritis	*ien*	胃炎	*wei yan*
pleurisy	*rokumakuen*	肋膜炎	*lemo yan*
pneumonia	*haien*	肺炎	*fei yan*
tracheitis	*kikan'en*	氣管炎	*qiguan yan*

9. "-ization" | **-ka** | 化 | **-hua**

arterial-sclerosis	*dōmyaku kōka*	動脈硬化	*dongmai yinghua*
automation	*jidōka*	自動化	*zidong hua*
beautification	*bika*	美化	*meihua*
centralization	*ichigenka*	一元化	*yiyuan hua*
colloquialization	*kōgoka*	口語化	*kouyu hua*
degeneration	*taika*	退化	*tuihua*
electrification	*denki ka*	電氣化	*dianqi hua*
formulism, formulaic	*kōshiki ka*	公式化	*gongshi hua*
generalization	*ippanka*	一般化	*yiban hua*
idealization	*risō ka*	理想化	*lixiang hua*
industrialization	*kōgyō ka*	工業化	*gongye hua*
modernization	*gendai ka*	現代化	*xiandai hua*
nationalized	*minzoku ka*	民族化	*minzu hua*
pluralization	*tagenka*	多元化	*duoyuan hua*
popularization	*taishūka*	大眾化	*dazhong hua*
protracted	*chōki ka*	長期化	*changqi hua*

scientific, scientized	*kagakuka*	科學化	*kexue hua*
softening	*nanka*	軟化	*ruanhua*
specialization	*tokushuka*	特殊化	*teshu hua*
strengthening	*kyōka*	強化	*qianghua*
tree planting, greening	*ryokka*	綠化	*luhua*
weakening	*jakuka*	弱化	*ruohua*

10. "-line," "ray"   *-sen*   線   **-xian**

battleline	*sensen*	戰線	*zhanxian*
branch line, feeder line	*shisen*	支線	*zhixian*
high-voltage power lines	*kō'atsusen*	高壓線	*gaoya xian*
hunger line	*kigasen*	饑餓線	*ji'e xian*
lifeline, lifeblood	*seimeisen*	生命線	*shengming xian*
radiation rays	*hōshasen*	放射線	*fangshe xian*
traffic corridor	*kōtsūsen*	交通線	*jiaotong xian*
trunk line, main line, artery	*kansen*	幹線	*ganxian*
ultraviolet ray	*shigaisen*	紫外線	*ziwai xian*

11. "method," "law"   *-hō*   法   **-fa**

analytic method	*bunsekihō*	分析法	*fenxi fa*
deductive method	*enekihō*	演繹法	*yanyi fa*
dialectics	*benshōhō*	辯証法	*bianzheng fa*
expressive mode	*hyōgenhō*	表現法	*biaoxian fa*
inductive method	*kinōhō*	歸納法	*guina fa*
synthesis	*sōgōhō*	總合法	*zonghe fa*
trigonometry	*sankakuhō*	三角法	*sanjiao fa*

12. "of"   *-teki*   的*   **-de**

| artificial | *jin'iteki* | 人為的 | *renwei de* |

* For a recent discussion of this particle, see Gunn, *Rewriting Chinese*, p. 89, p. 305n24; and Fogel, "Recent Translation Theory and Linguistic Borrowing," pp. 30-31.

fundamental	*konponteki*	根本的	*genben de*
historical	*rekishiteki*	歷史的	*lishi de*
national	*minzokuteki*	民族的	*minzu de*
natural	*shizenteki*	自然的	*ziran de*
necessary	*hitsuzenteki*	必然的	*biran de*
of social intercourse	*shakōteki*	社交的	*shejiao de*
of the masses	*taishūteki*	大眾的	*dazhong de*
open, overt	*kōkaiteki*	公開的	*gongkai de*
scientific	*kagakuteki*	科學的	*kexue de*
secretive, covert	*himitsuteki*	秘密的	*mimi de*
spontaneous	*jihatsuteki*	自發的	*zifa de*

13. "-on"	*ni-shite*	于*	***-yu***
about, relating to	*ni kanshite*	關于	*guanyu*
as for, about	*ni taishite*	對于	*duiyu*
based on	*ni motoshite*	基于	*jiyu*
owing to	*ni yotte*	由于	*youyu*

14. "-point"	*-ten*	點	***-dian***
focal point	*shōten*	焦點	*jiaodian*
important point, emphasis	*jūten*	重點	*zhongdian*
main point, gist	*yōten*	要點	*yaodian*
main point, purpose	*chūiten*	注意點	*zhuyi dian*
point of departure	*shuppatsuten*	出發點	*chufa dian*
viewpoint	*kanten*	觀點	*guandian*

15. "power"	*-ryoku*	力	***-li***
consumer buying power	*shōhiryoku*	消費力	*xiaofei li*
electric power	*denryoku*	電力	*dianli*
imagination, imaginative power	*sōzōryoku*	想像力	*xiangxiang li*
impetus	*dōryoku*	動力	*dongli*

---

* For a discussion of this suffix, see Edward Gunn, *Rewriting Chinese*, pp. 217–18.

labor, manpower, workforce	*rōdōryoku*	勞動力	*laodong li*
memory	*kiokuryoku*	記憶力	*jiyi li*
power, control	*shihai ryoku*	支配力	*zhipei li*
powers of expression	*hyōgenryoku*	表現力	*biaoxian li*
productivity	*seisan ryoku*	生產力	*shengchan li*
static	*seiriki*	靜力	*jingli*
16. "problem," "question"	***-mondai***	問題	***-wenti***
international problem	*kokusai mondai*	國際問題	*guoji wenti*
land problem	*tochi mondai*	土地問題	*tudi wenti*
nationality problem	*minzoku-mondai*	民族問題	*minzu wenti*
population problem	*jinkō mondai*	人口問題	*renkou wenti*
social problem	*shakai mondai*	社會問題	*shehui wenti*
17. "quality"	***-sei***	性	***-xing***
actuality	*genjitsusei*	現實性	*xianshi xing*
class character	*kaikyūsei*	階級性	*jieji xing*
contingency, chance	*gūzensei*	偶然性	*ouran xing*
creativity, creativeness	*kōzōsei*	創造性	*chuangzao xing*
distinctive quality	*tokusei*	特性	*texing*
extensiveness, wide-ranging	*kōhansei*	廣泛性	*guangfan xing*
habituality	*shūkansei*	習慣性	*xiguan xing*
impenetrability	*fuka'nyūsei*	不可入性	*bukeru xing*
importance	*jūyōsei*	重要性	*zhongyao xing*
inevitability	*hitsuzensei*	必然性	*biran xing*
in principle	*gensoku sei*	原則性	*yuanze xing*
necessity	*hitsuyōsei*	必要性	*biyao xing*
periodicity	*shūkisei*	週期性	*zhouqi xing*
possibility	*kanōsei*	可能性	*keneng xing*
radioactivity	*hōshasei*	放射性	*fangshe xing*
reason	*risei*	理性	*lixing*

revolutionary character	*kakumeisei*	革命性	*geming xing*
seductiveness	*yūwakusei*	誘惑性	*youhuo xing*
sensibility, sensitivity	*kanjusei*	感受性	*ganshou xing*
sensitivity	*kansei*	感性	*ganxing*
social nature	*shakaisei*	社會性	*shehui xing*
traditional character	*dentōsei*	傳統性	*chuantong xing*
truth, authenticity, credibility	*shinjitsusei*	真實性	*zhenshi xing*
18. "rate"	*-ritsu*	率	**-lü**
efficiency	*kōritsu*	效率	*xiaolü*
	nōritsu	能率	*nenglü*
rate of production	*seisanritsu*	生產率	*shengchan lü*
utilization ratio	*shiyōritsu*	使用率	*shiyong lü*
19. "-scale," "type"	*-kei, -kata, -gata*	型	**-xing**
large-scale	*ōgata*	大型	*daxing*
medium-scale	*chūgata*	中型	*zhongxing*
model, typical example	*tenkei*	典型	*dianxing*
new type	*shingata*	新型	*xinxing*
small-scale	*kogata*	小型	*xiaoxing*
standard type	*hyōjungata*	標準型	*biaozhun xing*
streamlined	*ryūsenkei*	流線型	*liuxian xing*
type	*ruikei*	類型	*leixing*
20. "society"	*-shakai*	社會	**-shehui**
capitalist society	*shihon shakai*	資本社會	*ziben shehui*
communist society	*kyōsan shakai*	共產社會	*gongchan shehui*
feudal society	*hōken shakai*	封建社會	*fengjian shehui*
primitive communist society	*genshi kyōsan-shakai*	原始共產社會	*yuanshi gongchan-shehui*
slave society	*dorei shakai*	奴隸社會	*nuli shehui*

21. "studies," "-ology"	-gaku	學*	-xue
accounting	bokigaku	簿記學	buji xue
aesthetics	bigaku	美學	meixue
anatomy	kaibōgaku	解剖學	jiepou xue
applied fine arts	kōgei-bijutsugaku	工藝美術學	gongyi meishu xue
architecture	kenchikugaku	建筑學	jianzhu xue
biology	seibutsugaku	生物學	shengwu xue
chemistry	kagaku	化學	huaxue
civil engineering	doboku kōtei-gaku	土木工程學	tumu gongcheng xue
economics	keizai gaku	經濟學	jingji xue
ethics	rinrigaku	倫理學	lunli xue
ethnology	minzokugaku	民族學	minzu xue
geography	chirigaku	地理學	dilixue
harmonics	waseigaku	和聲學	hesheng xue
horticulture, garden design	engeigaku	園藝學	yuanyi xue
hydraulic engineering	suiryoku-kōgaku	水力工學	shuili gongxue
hygienics	eiseigaku	衛生學	weisheng xue
law, jurisprudence	hōgaku	法學	faxue
logic	ronrigaku	論理學	lunli xue
mathematics	sūgaku	數學	shuxue
mechanical engineering	kikai kōgaku	機械工學	jixie gongxue
medical jurisprudence	hōigaku	法醫學	fayi xue
medicine	igaku	醫學	yixue
metallurgy	yakingaku	冶金學	yejin xue
metaphysics	keijijōgaku	形而上學	xing'er shang xue
natural science	shizen kagaku	自然科學	ziran kexue
pathology	byōrigaku	病理學	bingli xue
philosophy	tetsugaku	哲學	zhexue
physics	butsurigaku	物理學	wuli xue
physiology	seirigaku	生理學	shenglixue

*The use of *xue* 學 as a suffix can be found in earlier missionary-Chinese texts (Cf. App. A) and, therefore, should be regarded as a Chinese neologistic usage rather than a Japanese import. I include it in this category in order to underscore its widely acknowledged path of diffusion via modern Japanese.

psychology	*shinrigaku*	心理學	*xinli xue*
sociology	*shakaigaku*	社會學	*shehui xue*
statics	*seirikigaku*	靜力學	*jingli xue*
study of finance	*zaiseigaku*	財政學	*caizheng xue*
study of plant diseases and insect pests	*byōchūgaku*	病蟲學	*bingchong xue*
telecommunications	*denki tsūshin-gaku*	電氣通信學	*dianqi tongxin xue*
trigonometry	*sankakugaku*	三角學	*sanjiao xue*

22. "-style", "form"
	-shiki	式	*-shi*
accelerated	*sokuseishiki*	速成式	*sucheng shi*
equation	*hōteishiki*	方程式	*fangcheng shi*
identical equation	*kōtōshiki*	恆等式	*hengdeng shi*
Japanese-style	*nihonshiki*	日本式	*riben shi*
mobile form	*ryūdōshiki*	流動式	*liudong shi*
rhetorical form	*mondōshiki*	問答式	*wenda shi*
simple form	*kan'ishiki*	簡易式	*jianyi shi*
Western-style	*yōshiki*	洋式	*yang shi*

23. "super-," "sur-"
	chō-	超	**chao-**
superman	*chōnin*	超人	*chaoren*
supernatural	*chō shizen*	超自然	*chao ziran*
surreal	*chōgenjitsu*	超現實	*chao xianshi*
ultra shortwave	*chōtanha*	超短波	*chao duanbo*

24. "theory," "-ism"
	-ron	論	**-lun**
atheism	*mushinron*	無神論	*wushen lun*
conclusion (of a syllogism), verdict	*ketsuron*	結論	*jielun*
dualism	*nigenron*	二元論	*eryuan lun*
epistemology	*ninshikiron*	認識論	*renshi lun*
fatalism	*shukumeiron*	宿命論	*suming lun*
idealism	*yuishinron*	唯心論	*weixin lun*
inference	*suiron*	推論	*tuilun*
materialism	*yuibutsuron*	唯物論	*weiwu lun*
methodology	*hōhōron*	方法論	*fangfa lun*

monism	*ichigenron*	一元論	*yiyuan lun*
pantheism	*hanshinron*	泛神論	*fanshen lun*
pluralism	*tagenron*	多元論	*duoyuan lun*
rationalism	*yuiriron*	唯理論	*weili lun*
solipsism	*yuigaron*	唯我論	*weiwo lun*
spiritualism	*yuishinron*	唯神論	*weishen lun*
theory of evolution	*shinkaron*	進化論	*jinhua lun*

25. "view"	**-kan**	**觀**	**-guan**
historical materialism	*yuibutsushikan*	唯物史觀	*weiwu shiguan*
life outlook	*jinseikan*	人生觀	*rensheng guan*
objective	*kyakkan*	客觀	*keguan*
scientific outlook	*kagakukan*	科學觀	*kexue guan*
subjective	*shukan*	主觀	*zhuguan*
universal view	*uchūkan*	宇宙觀	*yuzhou guan*
world view	*sekaikan*	世界觀	*shijie guan*

26. "world," "circles"	**-kai**	**界**	**-jie**
artistic circles	*geijutsukai*	藝術界	*yishu jie*
educational circles	*kyō'ikukai*	教育界	*jiaoyu jie*
financial world	*kin'yūkai*	金融界	*jinrong jie*
intellectual world	*shisōkai*	思想界	*sixiang jie*
journalistic circles	*shinbunkai*	新聞界	*xinwen jie*
judicial world	*shihōkai*	司法界	*sifa jie*
literary circles	*bungakukai*	文學界	*wenxue jie*
publishing circles	*shuppankai*	出版界	*chuban jie*

Transliterations from English, French, and German

Source language	Chinese character	Chinese romanization	Notes
academy	阿加的米	*ajiademi*	Japanese-derived replacement 學院
acetylene	阿西台林	*axitailin*	
acre	愛克	*aike*	
adieu	亞丟	*yadiu*	
albite	阿勒倍得	*alebeide*	
alcohol	阿爾科爾	*a'erke'er*	
alizarine	阿里殺林	*alishalin*	
alkali	阿爾加里	*a'erjiali*	
Allah	阿拉	*Ala*	
alpha waves	阿爾法射線	*a'erfa shexian*	
alto	耳朵	*erduo*	
amateur	愛美的	*aimeide*	
amen	阿們	*amen*	
ammonia	阿摩尼亞	*amoniya*	
amoeba	阿米巴	*amiba*	
ampère	安培	*anpei*	
ampère mètre	安培表	*anpei biao*	
ampoule	安浦耳	*anpu'er*	
anabaptist	安那巴達派	*anabada pai*	
anarchism	安那其主義	*anaqi zhuyi*	Japanese-derived replacement 無政府主義
angel	安琪兒	*anqi'er*	

angora	安格拉	*angela*	
aniline	阿尼林	*anilin*	
anonym	阿囊	*anang*	
anthracene	安特拉生	*antelasheng*	
Anti-dumping Party	反屯併党	*fan tunbing dang*	
antimony	安的摩尼	*andimoni*	
antipyrine	安提比林	*antibilin*	
apomorphine	阿朴嗎啡	*apumafei*	
apple pie	苹果排	*pingguo pai*	
are	阿爾	*a'er*	
armored troops	坦克兵	*tanke bing*	
arnica	亞尼架	*yanijia*	
Arrow shirt	鴉佬恤	*yalao xu*	Exclusive to Cantonese: *alou seut*
aspirin	阿士匹林	*ashipilin*	alternative: asipiling 阿司匹靈
Atlas	亞脫拉斯	*yatuolasi*	
atropine	阿託品	*atuopin*	
aufheben	奧伏赫變	*aofuhebian*	Japanese-derived replacement 揚棄
autarkie	亞太基	*yataiji*	Japanese-derived replacement 自治運動
baby	啤仔	*pizai*	Cantonese origin: *bijai*.
	啤啤	*pipi*	Exclusive to Cantonese: *bihbi*
bacon	培根	*peigen*	
bacteria	撥克替里亞	*boketiliya*	
ball	波	*bo*	Min dialect origin
ballet	芭蕾舞	*balei wu*	
band	扮	*ban*	Cantonese origin: *baan*
bandage	繃帶	*bengdai*	
bank	版克	*banke*	Japanese-derived replacement 銀行
bar	酒巴	*jiuba*	alternative: jiuba jian 酒巴間
Barbary ape	巴巴利	*babali*	
barbitol	巴比妥	*babituo*	
baritone	巴利東	*balidong*	
baroque	巴洛哥	*baluoge*	
	巴羅克	*boluoke*	
barrel	把列而	*balie'er*	
barricade	巴列卡台	*baliekatai*	
barroom	酒排間	*jiupaijian*	
bass	巴斯	*basi*	
bass guitar	貝司	*beisi*	

bassoon	巴松	*basong*	
Bastille	巴士的獄	*Bashidi yu*	
beer	啤酒	*pijiu*	Cantonese origin: *bejau*
	必耳酒	*bi'erjiu*	
benzene	遍西尼	*bianxini*	
benzol	遍蔬爾	*biansu'er*	
bergamot	巴機密油	*bajimi you*	
bloc	布洛克	*buluoke*	
boron	硼	*peng*	
boss	波士	*boshi*	Exclusive to Cantonese: *bosi*
bourgeois	布爾喬亞	*bu'erqiaoya*	Japanese-derived replacements 資產階級, 中產階級
bourgeoisie	布爾喬亞汜	*bu'erqiaoyasi*	Japanese-derived replacement 資產階級
bowling	保齡球	*baoling qiu*	Cantonese origin: *boulihng kauh*
boxing	扑克胜	*bukesheng*	Cantonese: 卜成 *boksing*
boy (servant)	僕歐	*pu'ou*	
boycott	杯葛	*beige*	Cantonese origin: *buigot*
boycotters	杯葛派	*beige pai*	
Brahman	婆羅門	*poluomen*	
brandy	白蘭地	*bailandi*	
Browning	李郎寧	*Bolangning*	
bund	崩得	*bengde*	
Bunsen burner	本生燈	*besheng deng*	
bus	巴士	*bashi*	Cantonese origin: *basi*
bushel	蒲式耳	*pushi'er*	
bust	半身	*banshen*	
butter	白脱	*baituo*	
bye-bye	拜拜	*baibai*	Cantonese: *baaibaai*
cable	開勃兒	*kaibo'er*	
cacao	卡高	*kagao*	
café (coffee)	架菲，架非	*jiafei*	Glossed as *kafei* 咖啡 in Morrison (1815)
	咖啡	*kafei*	
café (coffeehouse)	咖啡館	*kafeiguan*	
caffeine	咖啡因	*kafeiyin*	
cake	極仔	*jizai*	Min dialect origin
caliph	哈利發	*halifa*	
calorie	卡路里	*kaluli*	
Calvinism	加爾文教	*jia'erwen jiao*	
Cambrian Period	寒武記	*Hanwu ji*	
Cambrian system	寒武系	*Hanwu xi*	

camera	開麥拉	*kaimaila*	
cancer	n/a	*n/a*	Exclusive to Cantonese: *kensa.* Cf. 癌.
cannon	加農砲	*jianongpao*	
caoutchouc (Indian rubber)	羔求	*gaoqiu*	
captain	甲必丹	*jiabidan*	
car	卡車	*kache*	
carat	卡刺特	*kalate*	
carbine	卡賓槍	*kabin qiang*	
carbolic acid	加波力克酸	*jiabolike suan*	
carborandum	卡波蘭登	*kabolandeng*	
card	卡片	*kapian*	Cantonese: *kaat* 卡
carpet-bag	急必袋	*jibidai*	Cantonese origin: *gapbit doi*
carré	街害	*jiehai*	Cantonese: *gaaihoih*
car tire	車胎	*chetai*	alternative forms: *luntai* 輪胎, *lundai* 輪帶 Cantonese origin *chetaai*
cartoon	卡通	*katong*	Japanese-derived replacement 漫畫
cash	n/a	*n/a*	Exclusive to Cantonese: *kesyuh.* Cf. *xianjin* 現金 in App. B.
cashmere	開四米	*kaisimi*	Cantonese equivalent: *kesihme* 茄士米
caste	喀士德	*keshide*	
catarrh	加答兒	*jiada'er*	
Catholic mass	瑪斯	*masi*	alternate form: *misa* 彌撒
catsup	茄汁	*jiazhi*	Exclusive to Cantonese: *kejap*
cavatina	卡弗鐵茄	*kafutieqie*	
cello	塞洛	*sailuo*	
cellophane	塞璐玢	*sailufen*	
celluloid	寫留路以德	*xieliuluyide*	
cellulose	寫留路斯	*xieliulusi*	
Celtic Revival	克勒特復興運動	*Kelete fuxing yundong*	
cement	士敏士	*shiminshi*	
cent (Dutch and Swedish currency)	生式	*shengshi*	
cent (U.S. penny)	生脫	*shengtuo*	Cantonese equivalent: 仙 *sin*
cental	生脫爾	*shengtuo'er*	

centiare	生的阿爾	*shengdia'er*	
centigramme	生的克蘭姆	*shengdike lanmu*	
centiliter	生的立脫爾	*shengdilituo'er*	
centime	生丁	*shengding*	
centimètre	生的米突	*shengdimitu*	
certificate	沙紙	*shazhi*	Exclusive to Cantonese: *saji*
chain	奢因	*sheyin*	
chaldron	巧特侖	*qiaotelun*	
champagne	三鞭	*sanbian*	
	香檳酒	*xiangbinjiu*	
champion	香賓	*xiangbin*	
Charlie Chaplin	差利	*Chali*	Exclusive to Cantonese: *chalei*
chauvinism	沙文主義	*shawen zhuyi*	See also App. G
check	乞克	*qike*	Cantonese equivalent: *chek* 仄
cheese	吉士	*jishi*	Cantonese: 芝士 *jisi*, replaced in Mandarin by 奶酪
chef d'oeuvre	賽的物兒	*saidewu'er*	
chloroform	哥羅仿	*geluofang*	
chocolate	炒扣來	*chaokoulai*	Cantonese equivalent: 朱古力 *jyugulik*
	巧克力	*qiaokeli*	
cholera	虎列拉	*huliela*	
Christianity	基督教	*Jidu jiao*	
chrome	克羅米	*keluomi*	
cigar	雪茄	*xuejia*	
clarinet	克拉管	*kela guan*	
clarinetti	卡拉理納提	*kalalinati*	
coal tar	可爾脫	*ke'er tuo*	
coca	可加	*kejia*	
Coca-cola	可口可樂	*kekou kele*	
cocaine	可加因	*kejiayin*	Cantonese equivalent: 高加因 *gougayan*
cocktail	雞尾酒	*jiwei jiu*	Cantonese origin: *gaimeihjau*
cocoa	可可	*keke*	Cantonese equivalent: 谷咕 *gukgu*
codeine	可提因	*ketiyin*	alternative: *kedaiyin* 可待因
collotype	珂羅版	*keluoban*	
combination	康拜因維雄	*kangbaiyinwei-xiong*	
commendam	康門達	*kangmenda*	
commission	孔米兄	*kongmixiong*	

English	Chinese	Pinyin	Notes
communism	康門尼斯姆	*kangmen nisimu*	Japanese-derived replacement: 共產主義
communist	康門尼斯特	*kangmennisite*	Japanese-derived replacements: 共產主義者, 共產党員
compania	康班尼亞	*kangbanniya*	
comprador	康白度	*kangbaidu*	
condor	公度兒	*gongdu'er*	
conga	康茄	*kangjia*	
consul	公修爾	*gongxiu'er*	
cookie	曲奇	*quqi*	Cantonese origin: *kukkeih*
coolie	咕喱 / 苦力	*guli* / *kuli*	Exclusive to Cantonese: *guleih*
copal	古派爾	*gupai'er*	
copy	拷貝	*kaobei*	
cornet (musical instrument)	柯爾納提	*ke'ernati*	
corset	哥塞脱	*gesaituo*	
cortisone	可的松	*kedesong*	
coulomb	庫侖	*kulun*	
coup d'etat	苦迭達	*kudieda*	Japanese-derived replacement 政變
coupling	靠背輪	*kaobeilun*	
crayon	古麗容	*gulirong*	
cray-pas	古麗巴斯	*gulibasi*	
cream soda	忌廉梳打	*jilian shuda*	Exclusive to Cantonese: *geihlimsoda*
creosote	几阿蔬油	*jiasu you*	
Crookes glasses	克羅克眼鏡	*Keluoke yanjing*	
crown	克倫	*kelun*	
cruzeiro (currency)	克魯塞羅	*kelusailuo*	
cube	朱勃	*zhubo*	
curry	加/咖喱	*jiali/kali*	Cantonese origin: *galei*
cushion	箍臣	*guchen*	Cantonese origin: *guchahn*
cut	卡脱	*katuo*	
cyanide	山埃	*shan'ai*	Cantonese origin: *saanngaai*
cymbal	省擺爾	*shengbai'er*	
cynicism	昔匿克學派	*xinike xuepai*	
dadaism	達達主義	*dada zhuyi*	
daddy	爹地	*diedi*	Exclusive to Cantonese: *dedih*

dahlia	大理花	*dalihua*	
dancing girl	彈性女郎	*tanxing nülang*	
darling	達爾玲	*da'erling*	Cantonese: 打玲
Darwinism	達爾文主義	*da'erwen zhuyi*	
Davis cup	台微斯盃	*Taiweisi bei*	
DDT	涕涕涕	*diditi*	
décadent	頹加湯	*tuijiatang*	
décagramme	特卡克蘭姆	*tekakelanmu*	
décalitre	特卡立脫爾	*tekalituo'er*	
décamètre	特卡米突	*tekamitu*	
décigramme	特西克蘭姆	*texikelanmu*	
décilitre	特西立脫爾	*texilituo'er*	
décimètre	特西米突	*teximitu*	
democracy	德謨克拉西	*demokelaxi*	Japanese-derived replacement 民主主義
dermitol	代馬妥兒	*daimatuo'er*	
deutschmark	馬克	*make*	
dialectic	第亞納蒂克	*diyanadike*	Japanese-derived replacement 辯証法
diastase	對阿斯打斯	*duiasidasi*	
dictator	狄克推多	*diketuiduo*	Japanese-derived alternatives 獨裁，專政
dictatorship	狄克推多制	*diketuiduo zhi*	
diesel engine	狄塞爾機	*disai'er ji*	
diptheria	實扶的里亞	*shifudiliya*	
doctor, Ph.D.	多看透	*duokantou*	Round-trip loan replacement 博士
dollar	他拉	*tala*	
Don Quixote type	唐吉詞德型	*Tang Jicide xing*	
Dowling paper	道林紙	*Daolin zhi*	
Downing Street	唐寧街	*Tangning jie*	
dozen	打	*da*	Cantonese equivalent: 打臣 *dachahn*
drachma	德拉馬	*delama*	
dram	打蘭	*dalan*	
duce	刁時	*diaoshi*	Exclusive to Cantonese: *diusih*
dumdum bullet	達姆達姆彈	*damu damu dan*	
dumping	屯併	*tunbing*	
duralumin	杜拉鋁	*dulalu*	
dynamism	代納密斯	*dainamisi*	
dynamite	代那美脫	*dainameituo*	
dynamo	代那模	*dainamo*	
dyne	達因	*dayin*	

economy	愛康諾米 （依康老米）	*aikangnuomi* *(yikanglaomi)*	Cf. *fuguoce* 富國策 in App. A and the return graphic loan *jingji* 經濟 in App. D.
Eden	伊甸	*Yidian*	
Eleatic School	埃理亞學派	*Ailiya xuepai*	
emir	阿米爾	*ami'er*	
empire	英拜兒	*yingbai'er*	Yan Fu's transliteration. Cf. *diguo* 帝國 in App. A.
energy	愛納爾基	*aina'erji*	
engine	引擊	*yinji*	
English horn	英國杭	*Yingguo hang*	
entelechy	隱德來希	*yindelaixi*	
erg	厄格	*ege*	
Esperanto	愛斯不難讀	*Aisibunandu*	Cf. *wangguo xinyu* 萬國新語 in App. A and Japanese-derived replacement 世界語 in App. B.
essay	愛說	*aishuo*	
Essene	曷生派	*hesheng pai*	
ester	愛斯他	*aisita*	
Etagone	愛泰岡	*Aitaigang*	
ether	以太（伊太）	*yitai*	
ethyl	以脱	*yituo*	
ethylene	以脱林	*yituolin*	
exarch	埃塞克	*aisaike*	
Fabian Society	費邊社	*Feibian she*	
fail	肥佬	*feilao*	Exclusive to Cantonese: *feihlou*
fair play	費厄潑賴	*fei'e polai*	
farad	法拉特	*falate*	
farthing	法新	*faxin*	
fascism	法西斯主義	*faxisi zhuyi*	
fascists	法西斯分子	*faxisi fenzi*	
fashion	花臣	*huachen*	Cantonese origin: *fachahn*
fathom	花當	*huadang*	Cantonese origin: *faadang*
feminism	弗彌涅士姆	*feiminieshimu*	Japanese-derived replacement: 女權主義
feuilleton	阜利通	*fulitong*	
file, holder	快勞	*kuailao*	Exclusive to Cantonese: *faailou*
film	非林	*feilin*	Cantonese origin: *feilam*
flannel	法蘭絨	*falan rong*	
florin	福祿林	*fululin*	
flute	弗柳特	*fuliute*	
foot (measure)	幅脱	*futuo*	

formalin	福爾馬林	*fu'ermalin*	
franc	法郎	*falang*	
Franciscans	法蘭西斯党	*Falanxisi dang*	
fugue	賦格曲	*fuge qu*	
funt	風脱	*fengtuo*	
furlong	富呵浪	*fu'a lang*	
gabardine	戈別丁	*gebieding*	
gallon	加侖	*jialun*	Cantonese origin: *galeun*
gallop	加羅普	*jialuopu*	
gas	加斯	*jiasi*	Japanese-derived replacement *gasu* 瓦斯 (App. B)
gasoline	格士林	*geshilin*	
Gatling gun	格林炮	*gelin pao*	Cf. *ouxin pao* 藕心炮 in App. A.
Gauss	高斯	*Gaosi*	
gene	基因	*jiyin*	
gentleman	竟得爾曼	*jingde'erman*	Round-trip loan replacement 紳士
geometry	几合學	*jihe xue*	
Gestapo	蓋世太保	*Gaishitaibao*	
gill	及耳	*ji'er*	
gin	氈酒	*zhanjiu*	Cantonese origin: *jinjau*
giraffe	其拉夫	*qilafu*	
	支列胡	*zhiliehu*	
gluten	格路登	*geludeng*	
glycerin	各里司林	*gelisilin*	
golf	高爾夫	*gaoerfu*	
gothic	峨特式	*gete shi*	alternative: 哥特，哥德
grain (measure)	克泠	*keling*	
grammar	葛郎瑪	*gelangma*	Round-trip loan replacement 文法 (App. D)
gramme	克蘭姆	*kelanmu*	
Groschen	克羅欽	*Keluoqin*	
gross	哥羅	*geluo*	
grotesque	格洛特斯克	*geluotesike*	
Grub Street	格剌布街	*Gelabu jie*	
guild	基爾德	*ji'erde*	
guilder	克爾達	*ke'erda*	
guillotine	吉羅丁	*jiluoding*	
guitar	吉他	*jita*	
gulash	古拉士	*gulashi*	
gypsy	吉普賽	*jipusai*	

haemoglobin	希瑪格洛賓	*ximageluobin*	Cf. Japanese-derived replacement 血色素 in App. B.
hallelujah	哈利路亞	*haliluya*	
Halley's Comet	哈雷雪星	*haleixue xing*	
Hamlet type	哈蒙雷特型	*Hamengleite xing*	
handsome maid	鹹水妹	*xianshuimei*	Cantonese origin: *haahmseui muih*
hectare	海克脱阿爾	*haiketuo'a'er*	
hectogramme	海克脱克蘭姆	*haiketuokelan-mu*	
hectolitre	海克脱立脱爾	*haiketuolituo'er*	
hectomètre	海克脱米突	*haiketuomitu*	
Helicon	海利空	*Hailikong*	
Hellenism	希臘主義	*Xila zhuyi*	Cantonese origin: *heilaah*
Hellenistic period	希臘時代	*Xila shidai*	
Heller	海來	*Hailai*	
hello	哈囉	*haluo*	
henry (physics)	享利	*hengli*	
hernia	赫尼亞	*heniya*	
heroin	海洛因	*hailuoyin*	
hertz	赫芝	*hezhi*	
homespun	霍姆斯本	*huomusiben*	
hormone	荷爾蒙	*he'ermeng*	
hops	忽布	*hubu*	
horse power	馬力	*mali*	
hot dog	熱狗	*regou*	
House of Commons	甘文好司	*ganwen haosi*	Cantonese origin: *gemmen housi.* Cf. *juefang* 鄉紳房 (App. A)
House of Lords	律好司	*lü haosi*	Cf. *juefang* 爵房 (App. A)
(l')humanité	虞芒尼德	*lumangnide*	Japanese-derived alternatives: 人類，人道，人性
humor	幽默	*youmo*	
humorist	幽默家	*youmo jia*	
hundred-weight	漢厥懷特	*hanjue huaite*	
husband	黑漆板凳	*heiqibandeng*	
hyena	海乙那	*haiyina*	
hypo	海波	*haibo*	
hystérie	歇斯的里	*xiesidili*	
ice cream	冰積凌	*bingjiling*	
	冰琪林	*bingqilin*	

idea	依提亞	*yitiya*	Japanese-derived replacements 意見, 概念, 觀念
idéologie	意德沃羅基	*yidewoluoji*	Cf. Japanese-derived replacement 意識形態 in App. B.
inch	因制	*yinzhi*	
indanthrene	隱丹士林	*yindanshilin*	
index	引得	*yinde*	
inflation	因發熱凶	*yinfarexiong*	Cf. Japanese-derived replacement 通貨膨脹 in App. B.
ink	因克	*yinke*	
inspiration	煙士披和純	*yanshipihechun*	
insulin	因素林	*yinsulin*	
insure	燕梳	*yanshu*	Cantonese origin: *yinso*
international	英特那雄那爾	*yingtenaxiong-na'er*	Cf. *wanguo* 萬國 in App.A and Japanese-derived replacement 國際 in App. B.
iodine	碘	*dian*	
iodine tincture	碘酒	*dianjiu*	
ion	伊洪	*yihong*	
jacket	甲克	*jiake*	alternative: 夾克
jam	占	*zhan*	Cantonese origin: *jim*
James Bond	占士邦	*Zhanshi Bang*	Cantonese origin: *jimsihbong*
Janissary	惹尼恰利	*reniqiali*	
jasmine	耶悉茗	*yeximing*	
jazz	爵士樂	*jueshi yue*	
jeep	吉普車	*jipu che*	
Jehovah	耶和華	*Yehehua*	
jelly	這喱凍	*zheli dong*	Cantonese origin: *jelei dung*
jelly	者哩	*zheli*	Cantonese origin: *jelei*
John Bull	約翰勃爾	*Yuehan Bo'er*	
joule	朱爾	*zhu'er*	
journal	集納	*jina*	
journalism	集納主義	*jina zhuyi*	Japanese-derived replacement 新聞事業
Judaism	猶太教	*youtai jiao*	
Junker	兜哥兒	*xiongge'er*	
Jurassic period	侏羅紀	*Zhuluo ji*	
Jurassic system	侏羅系	*Zhuluo xi*	
kaiser	愷撒	*kaisa*	
kangaroo	更格盧	*genggelu*	

English	Chinese	Pinyin	Notes
kapron	卡布龍	*kabulong*	
Kartell	卡忒爾	*katei'er*	
katarrh	卡他	*kata*	
kettle drum	克脫鼓	*ketuo gu*	
khaki	卡嘰	*kaji*	
kilo	基羅	*jiluo*	
kilogramme	基羅克蘭姆	*jiluokelanmu*	
kilolitre	基羅立脫爾	*jiluolituo'er*	
kilomètre	基羅米突	*jiluomitu*	alternative: *qiankemi* 千克米
kilowatt	基羅瓦特	*jiluowate*	alternative: *qianwa* 千瓦
kiss	開司	*kaisi*	
knot (nautical)	諾脫	*nuote*	
Kodak	柯達	*keda*	
konzern	康采恩	*kangcai'en*	
Koran	可蘭經	*Kelan jing*	
Kremlin	克里姆林宮	*Kelimulin gong*	
krona	克羅納	*keluona*	
Krupp	克盧砲	*Kelupao*	
kvass	可瓦士	*kewasi*	
L'école de l'ermitage	歐爾密太西學校	*ou'ermitaixi xuexiao*	
laine	冷	*leng*	Cantonese origin: *laahng*
Lamarckism	拉馬克學説	*lamake xueshuo*	
lamp	濫斧	*lanfu*	Min dialect origin
last	拉司	*lasi*	
last car	拉斯卡	*lasi ka*	Shanghainese origin
lemon	檸檬	*ningmeng*	Cantonese origin: *lihngmung*
lemonade	檸檬水	*ningmeng shui*	
lemon time	檸檬時間	*ningmeng shijian*	
lepton	雷波頓	*leibodun*	
Leveler (political party)	尼微拉党	*niweila dang*	
liaison	連詠	*lianyong*	
libido	來比多	*laibiduo*	
lift (elevator)	n/a	*n/a*	Exclusive to Cantonese: *lip.* Cf. 自行屋 in App. A and its later replacements *sheng-jiangji* 升降機 and *dianti* 電梯
linen	連仁	*lianren*	Cantonese origin: *lihnyahn*
link	令克	*lingke*	
lira	里拉	*lila*	
litmus	立低莫斯	*lidimosi*	
litre	立脫爾	*lituo'er*	

logic	邏輯	*luoji*	Japanese-derived equivalent 論理
logic (the study of)	邏輯學	*luoji xue*	
logos	邏格司	*luogesi*	
lorry	羅釐	*luoli*	Cantonese origin: *lohleih*
lumen	流明	*liuming*	
luminol	魯米那	*lumina*	
lux	勒克斯	*lekesi*	
Lysol	來沙而	*laisha'er*	
malina	馬林	*malin*	
Malthusianism	馬爾薩斯主義	*Ma'ersasi zhuyi*	
mandolin	曼獨林	*mandulin*	
manganese	曼淹	*manyan*	
mango	芒果	*mangguo*	
manorial system	馬納制度	*mana zhidu*	
mantle	幔袉	*mantuo*	
marathon	瑪拉忪賽	*malasong sai*	
mark	嚜，麥	*mo, mai*	Cantonese origin: *mok, maak*
Marseillaise	馬賽曲	*Masai qu*	
martini	馬天尼	*matianni*	Exclusive to Cantonese: *mahtinneih*
Marx-boy	馬克斯少年	*makesi shaonian*	
Marx-girl	馬克斯少女	*makesi shaonü*	
Marxism	馬克斯主義	*makesi zhuyi*	See also App. G
Marxism-Leninism	馬克斯列寧主義	*makesi liening zhuyi*	See also App. G
mauser	毛瑟槍	*maose qiang*	
maxwell	馬克斯維爾	*makesiwei'er*	
meat pie	肉批	*roupi*	Cantonese origin: *yuhkpai*
Mendelism	孟德爾主義	*mengde'er zhuyi*	
mentholatum	面速力達姆	*miansulidamu*	
merchant	孖氈，馬占	*mazhan*	Cantonese origin: *majin*
messiah	彌賽亞	*misaiya*	
meter	咪表	*mibiao*	Exclusive to Cantonese: *maibiu*
methane	滅坦	*mietan*	
mètre	米突	*mitu*	
micron	密侖	*milun*	
microphone	麥克風	*maikefeng*	Cantonese alternative: *mai* 咪. Cf. *chuansheng qi* 傳聲器 in App. A.

mile	邁爾	*mai'er*	Cantonese equivalent: 咪 *mai*
	咪	*mi*	Exclusive to Cantonese: *mai*
milkshake	奶昔	*naixi*	Exclusive to Cantonese: *naaih sik*
milliampere	毫安	*hao'an*	
milligramme	密理克蘭姆	*milikelanmu*	
millilitre	密理立脫爾	*mililituo'er*	
millimètre	密理米突	*milimitu*	alternative: haomi 毫米
milreis (currency)	密而斯	*mi'ersi*	
mince	免治	*mianzhi*	Exclusive to Cantonese: *mihnjih*
miniskirt	迷你	*mini*	
ministerialism	米勒蘭主義	*milelan zhuyi*	
minotaur	梅拿爾	*meina'er*	
misanthrope	蜜桑素羅普	*misangsuluopu*	
miss	密斯	*misi*	
missal	彌撒書	*misashu*	
mister	密斯特	*misite*	
mistress	密昔司	*mixisi*	
mocha	磨加咖啡	*mojia kafei*	
model	模特兒	*mote'er*	
modern	摩登	*modeng*	Japanese-derived alternative 現代 (App. B)
modern girl	磨登鉤兒	*modeng gou'er*	
molecule	磨勒	*mole*	
mommy	媽咪	*mami*	Exclusive to Cantonese: *mamih*
montage	蒙太奇	*mengtaiqi*	
Moorish	摩爾式	*Mo'er shi*	
morphine	嗎啡	*mafei*	
mosaic	馬塞克	*masaike*	
motor	摩托	*motuo*	Cantonese equivalent: *moda* 摩打
motorboat	摩托船	*motuo chuan*	
motorcar	摩托卡	*motuo ka*	
motorcycle	摩托車	*motuo che*	
mummy	木乃伊	*munaiyi*	
muslim	穆士林	*mushilin*	
muslin	毛絲綸	*maosilun*	
myriagramme	邁里格蘭姆	*mailigelanmu*	
naphthalene	納他連	*natalian*	
narcissism	臘西雪茲姆	*laxixuezimu*	
nautical mile	諾脫埋爾	*nuotuo mai'er*	

Nazi party	納粹党	*Nacui dang*	
Nazism	納粹主義	*nacui zhuyi*	
neck tie	呔	*dai*	·Cantonese origin: *taai*; Mandarin equivalent 領帶
neon light	霓虹燈	*nihong deng*	
neuter	菇脫	*nütuo*	
nicotine	尼古丁	*niguding*	
nip	夾鑷	*jianie*	
novocaine	奴佛卡因	*nufokayin*	
number	林巴	*linba*	Cantonese origin: *lahmba*
number one	那麼溫	*name wen*	Shanghainese origin
nylon	尼龍	*nilong*	Cantonese origin: *naihluhng*
oboe	歐勃	*oubo*	
Oedipus Complex	耶的卜斯錯綜	*Yedibusi cuozong*	
office	奧非斯	*aofeisi*	
ohm	歐姆	*oumu*	
oil pump	油砵	*youbeng*	
old man	阿爾邁	*a'er mai*	
oleic acid	哇勒因酸	*waleyin suan*	
olive oil	俄列夫油	*eliefu you*	
Olympic Games	奧林匹克運動會	*Aolinpike yundong hui*	
opium	鴉片	*yapian*	
orcin	俄爾幸	*e'erxing*	
ounce	盎斯	*angsi*	Cantonese equivalent: *onsi* 安士
Ovaltine	阿華田	*Ahuatian*	Exclusive to Cantonese: *owahtihn*
oxygen	沃克順更氣	*wokeshungeng qi*	
ozone	阿巽	*axun*	
pair	啤（派）	*pi (pai)*	Cantonese origin: *pe*
palmitic acid	拍爾味忝酸	*pai'erweitian suan*	
pan-European	泛歐	*fan'ou*	
pan-Germanism	泛日耳曼主義	*fan ri'erman zhuyi*	
pancake	班戟	*banji*	Exclusive to Cantonese: *baankik*
paradoxical	怕拉多客思的	*paladuokeside*	
paraffin	巴拉芬	*balafen*	
pariah	巴利亞	*baliya*	
Parker pen	派克筆	*paike bi*	

parliament	巴厘滿	*baliman*	Cf. *gongyitang* 公議堂,
	巴厘滿衙門	*baliman yamen*	*gongyiting* 公議庭, *huitang*
	巴力門	*balimen*	會堂, *guohui* 國會 etc. in
	巴力門會	*balimen hui*	App. A; and Japanese-derived replacements *yihui* 議會 and *yiyuan* 議院 in App. B
partner	n/a	*n/a*	Exclusive to Cantonese: *paatnah*
pass	派司	*paisi*	
pass	n/a	*n/a*	Exclusive to Cantonese: *pasih*
passport	n/a	*n/a*	Exclusive to Cantonese: *pasihpot*
pastel	巴斯推爾	*basitui'er*	
pastorale	派斯禿萊爾	*paisitulaier*	
pear	啤梨	*pili*	Exclusive to Cantonese: *belei*
peck	配克	*peike*	
pence	辨士	*bianshi*	
penicillin	盤尼西林	*pannixilin*	
pennyweight	本尼懷脫	*benni huaituo*	
pepsin	百布聖	*baibusheng*	
peptone	百布頓	*baibudun*	
percent	配生	*peisheng*	
pest	百斯篤	*baisidu*	
petite bourgeoisie	小布爾喬亞階級	*xiao buerqiaoya jieji*	Japanese-derived replacement 小資產階級
pfennig	分尼	*fenni*	
phalanx	法郎其	*falangqi*	
phenazone	非納宗	*feinazong*	
phenobarbital	苯巴比妥	*benbabituo*	
philosophy	菲洛素菲 （非羅沙非）	*feiluosufei* *(feiluoshafei)*	Japanese-derived replacement 哲學
piano	披亞諾	*piyanuo*	
piastre	披亞斯特	*piyasite*	
piccolo	皮可羅	*pikeluo*	
pickles	必克爾	*bike'er*	
picnic	辟克涅克	*bikenieke*	
pin	邊扣	*biankou*	Cantonese origin: *binkau*
ping-pong	乒乓球	*pingpang qiu*	
pint	品脫	*pintuo*	
platije	布拉及	*bulaji*	
platonic (love)	柏拉圖式 (戀愛)	*bolatu shi lian'ai*	

plug	扑落	*puluo*	
point	磅音	*pangyin*	
poker	扑克	*puke*	
pole	布爾	*bu'er*	
polka	坡爾卡	*po'erka*	
porter	波打	*boda*	
port wine	菩提萬酒	*putiwan jiu*	Cantonese equivalent: 砵 *but*
postcard	甫士咭	*pushiji*	Exclusive to Cantonese: *pouhsikaat*
pound	磅	*bang*	Cantonese origin: *bong*
pound sterling	鎊	*bang*	
powder	泡打粉	*paoda fen*	Cantonese origin: *paauda fan*
president	伯力賜天德	*bolicitiande*	Cf. *tongling* 統領, *shouling*
	佰理天德	*bolitiande*	首領, and *zongtongling*
	佰理喜頓	*bolixidun*	總統領, in App. A and the
	佰理璽天德	*bolixitiande*	round-trip loan (?) replacement: 總統
procaine	普魯卡因	*pulukayin*	
proletarian	普羅列太林	*puluolitailin*	Japanese-derived replacements: 無產者, 無產階級
proletarian literature	普羅文學	*puluo wenxue*	Japanese-derived replacement: 無產階級文學
prolétariat	普羅列塔利亞	*puluolietalieya*	Japanese-derived replacement: 無產階級
property	伯勞伯的	*bolaobodi*	
ptyalin	普起阿林	*puqi'alin*	
pud	普特	*pute*	
pudding	布丁	*buding*	Cantonese equivalent: 布甸 *boudin*
pump	幫浦	*bangpu*	
pyramidon	匹拉米洞	*pilamidong*	
quart	夸爾	*kua'er*	
quarter	塊雅特爾	*kuaiyate'er*	Cantonese equivalent: 骨 *gwat*
Quartier Latin	拉丁區	*Lading qu*	
quinine	奎寧	*kuining*	
quinquina	貴林那	*guilinna*	
quintal	貴里特	*guilite*	
quixotism	吉詞德主義	*jicide zhuyi*	
radar	雷達	*leida*	
ramifon	雷米封	*leimifeng*	
resorcin	利鎖耳金	*lisuoerjin*	

rhetoric	勒托列克	*letuolieke*	
rheumatism	僂麻質斯	*loumazhisi*	
rial	里爾	*li'er*	
ribbon	禮鳳	*lifeng* .	
rifle	來福	*laifu*	Cf. *huoqiang* 火槍
	來復槍	*laifu qiang*	
romanesque	羅馬式	*luoma shi*	
romantic	浪漫蒂克	*langmandike*	Round-trip loan replacement 浪漫
rood	路得	*lude*	
rugby football	辣古皮式足球	*lagupishi zuqiu*	
rum	林酒	*linjiu*	Cantonese origin: *lahmjau*
rumba	倫巴舞	*lunba wu*	
rupee (currency)	盧比	*lubi*	
rye	拉愛	*la'ai*	
safety valve	安全閥	*anquan fa*	
salad	沙辣	*shala*	Cantonese equivalent: 沙律 *saleut*
salmon	薩門魚	*samen yu*	Cantonese equivalent: 三文 *saammahn*
salon	沙龍	*shalong*	
salpa	薩爾帕	*sa'erpa*	
Salvarsan	沙爾法爾散	*Sha'erfa'ersan*	
sandwich	三明治	*sanmingzhi*	
santonin	珊篤寧	*shanduning*	
Sapphism	沙弗式戀愛	*shafushi lian'ai*	
sardine	沙汀魚	*shating yu*	
Satan	撒但	*Sadan*	
saxhorn	薩克斯喇叭	*sakesi laba*	
saxophone	沙士風	*shashifeng*	Cantonese alternate: 色士風 *siksifung*
schilling (currency)	先令	*xianling*	
science	塞因斯	*saiyinsi*	Japanese-derived replacement 科學
screen	斯庫林	*sikulin*	
scruple	斯克路步	*sikelubu*	
sentimental	生的悶特	*shengdemente*	
sequin	西袞	*xigun*	
serge	嗶嘰	*biji*	
servant	沙文	*shawen*	Cantonese origin: *samen*
	西崽	*xizai*	
shaft	車溼	*cheshi*	Cantonese origin: *chesap*

shellac	舍來克	*shelaike*	
sherry	舍利	*sheli*	
sherry cobbler	沙士水	*shashi shui*	
shilling	先令	*xianling*	
shirt	恤衫	*xushan*	Cantonese origin: *seutsam*
shock	休克	*xiuke*	
sidewalk	街(該)娃克	*jiewake*	Cantonese origin: *gaai mahthaak*
silon	西龍	*xilong*	
sir	阿蛇	*a she*	Exclusive to Cantonese: *aseuh*
siren	塞連	*sailian*	
sister	雪絲黛	*xuesidai*	
size	西士	*shaishi*	Exclusive to Cantonese: *saaisi*
Slavic studies	斯拉夫學	*silafu xue*	
snuff	士拿	*shina*	
Social Darwinism	社會達爾文主義	*shehui da'erwen zhuyi*	
soda	蔬打，蘇達	*suda*	Cf. *sōda* 曹達 in App. B.
sofa	沙發	*shafa*	Cantonese equivalent: *sofa* 梳化
sofabed	沙發床	*shafa chuang*	
solo	n/a	*n/a*	Exclusive to Cantonese: *soulouh*
sonata	朔拿大	*shuonada*	
sonnet	商籟式	*shanglai shi*	
sophist	蔬斐斯特	*sufeisite*	
sovereign (currency)	索佛令	*sufoling*	
sovereignty	薩威稜帖（梭威稜帖）	*saweilingtie (suoweilingtie)*	Round-trip loan replacement 主權
soviet	蘇維埃	*suwei'ai*	See also App. G
spanner	士巴拿	*shibana*	Cantonese origin: *sibanah*
spare	士啤	*shipi*	Exclusive to Cantonese: *sihbe*
Spartakus Grupe	斯巴特卡斯團	*Sibatekasi tuan*	
spermine	賜保命	*cibaoming*	
sphinx	斯芬克士	*sifenkeshi*	
sportax	司泡汀	*sipaoting*	
spring	司必令	*sibiling*	
stamp	士担	*shidan*	Cantonese origin: *sidaam*

steam	水汀	*shuiting*	Shanghainese origin; Cantonese *sidihn* 士店; Japanese-derived replacement in Mandarin: 蒸氣
stearin	司替阿林	*siti'alin*	
stick	士的克	*sidike*	
store	士多	*shiduo*	Cantonese origin: *sihdo*
strawberry	士多啤梨	*shiduopili*	Exclusive to Cantonese: *sihdobelei*
streptomycin	史他杜邁仙	*shitadumaixian*	Cantonese origin: *sitadomaisin*
strychnine	士的寧	*shidening*	
sultan	蔬丹	*sudan*	
Sunkist	新奇士	*Xinqishi*	Exclusive to Cantonese: *sankeisih*
sweater	司衛脱	*siweituo*	Shanghainese origin
symphony	生風尼	*shengfengni*	Japanese-derived replacement 交響樂
syndicalism	幸狄開主義	*xingdikai zhuyi*	Japanese-derived replacement 工團主義
syndicate	幸狄開	*xingdikai*	
syrup	舍利別	*shelibie*	
taboo	達波	*dabo*	
talkie (movie)	託劇	*tuoju*	
tambourine	湯簿鈴	*tangboling*	
tango	探戈舞	*tange wu*	
tank	坦克車	*tanke che*	
tannic acid	單寧酸	*danning suan*	
tarantella	塔蘭台拉舞曲	*talantaila wuqu*	
tart	蛋噠	*danda*	Cantonese origin: *daan daaht*
taxi	的士	*dishi*	Cantonese origin: *diksi*
tcheka	切卡	*qieka*	
technocracy	推克諾克拉西	*tuikenuokelaxi*	Japanese-derived replacement: 技術統治
telephone	得利風 德律風	*delifeng* *delufeng*	Japanese-derived replacement 電話 (App. B)
television	德律維雄	*delüweixiong*	
tempo	停破	*tingpo*	
tenant	佃農	*diannong*	
terylene	特麗令	*teliling*	
Thames River	泰晤士河	*taiwushi he*	Cantonese origin: *taimhsi*
Thermidor	齊密圖	*qimitu*	

thymol	替摩耳	*timo'er*	
Times (newspaper)	泰晤士	*taiwushi*	Cantonese origin: *taimhsi*
tin	廳	*ting*	
tincture	丁几	*dingji*	
tip (gratuity)	貼士	*tieshi*	Cantonese origin: *tipsi*
tissue	體素	*tisu*	
title	抬頭	*taitou*	
tittup	踢踏舞	*titawu*	
toast	吐斯	*tusi*	Cantonese equivalent: 多士 *dosi*
tobacco	旦把孤 淡巴菰	*danbagu* *danbagu*	
toffee	太妃糖	*taifei tang*	Cantonese equivalent: 拖肥糖 *tofeitong*
tommy gun	湯姆式槍	*tangmu shi qiang*	
ton	吨, 噸	*dun*	Cantonese origin: *den*
tonne	脱因	*tuoyin*	
topology	拓扑學	*tuopu xue*	
Tory party	托利党	*Tuoli dang*	
total	拓都	*tadu*	Japanese-derived replacement 總體
totem	圖騰	*tuteng*	
trachoma	托拉火姆	*tuolahuomu*	
tractor	拖拉机	*tuolaji*	
troubadour	特魯巴多爾	*telubaduo'er*	
trumpet	屈郎拍	*qulangpai*	
trust	托辣斯	*tuolasi*	See also *shin'yō* 信用 in App. D.
tsar	沙爾	*sha'er*	See also App. G
tuba	提優把	*tiyouba*	
turbine	透平機	*toupingji*	
Turkic studies	突厥學	*tujue xue*	
typhus	窒扶斯	*zhifusi*	
tyrant	代蘭得	*dailande*	
ultimatum	愛的美頓	*aidimeidun*	Japanese-derived replacement 最後通牒
Uncle Sam	山姆叔叔	*Shanmu shushu*	
union	由任	*youren*	Shanghainese origin
unit	么匿	*yaoni*	Round-trip loan replacement 單位
United Harvester combine	聯合收割机	*lianhe shouge ji*	

utopia	烏托邦	*wutuobang*	
	烏有幫	*wuyoubang*	
varnish	凡立司	*fanlisi*	
Vaseline	凡士林	*Fanshilin*	
vermouth	維爾木	*wei'ermu*	
vernier	佛逆	*foni*	
Veronal	肥羅那	*Feiluona*	
vicar	維克爾	*weike'er*	
viedro	浮駝羅	*futuoluo*	
viersta	阜斯特	*fusite*	
violin	梵啞鈴	*fanyaling*	
violoncello	費屋龍	*feiwulong*	
vitamin	維他命	*weitaming*	
volt	伏特	*fute*	
voltmeter	伏特機	*fute ji*	
waffle	威化	*weihua*	Cantonese origin: *waifa*
Wall Street	華爾街	*Hua'er jie*	
waltz	華爾茲舞	*hua'erzi wu*	
waste	威士	*weishi*	Cantonese origin: *waisi*
water pump	水砵	*shuibeng*	
watt	瓦特	*wate*	
Werthersfieber	維特熱	*Weite re*	
Whig party	輝格党	*Huige dang*	
whiskey	威士忌	*weishiji*	Cantonese origin: *waisihgei*
wire	威也	*weiye*	Cantonese origin: *waiyeh*
x-ray	愛克司光	*aikesi guang*	Cantonese equivalent: *iksihgwong* X光
Yankeeism	洋鬼風	*yanggui feng*	
yard (measure)	依亞	*yiya*	
yelling	夜冷	*yeleng*	Cantonese origin: *yehlaahng*
yes	也司	*yesi*	
zinc	鋅	*xin*	
Zionism	西雄主義	*xixiong zhuyi*	Cantonese: *Saihuhng*

Transliterations from Russian

Russian	Chinese character	Chinese romanization	Explanatory notes
Большевик	布爾什維克 （鮑爾扎維克）	*bu'ershiweike (bao'er- zhaweike)*	Bolshevik
Буза	布乍	*buzha*	a fermented Russian beverage
Бунд	崩得	*bengde*	Bund (Jewish federation for social democracy)
ведро	浮駝羅	*futuoluo*	bucket, dustbin, a measure word
верста	阜斯得	*fuside*	verst (Russian mile)
вершок	胃索	*weisuo*	Russian inch
водка	伏特加	*futejia*	vodka
госплан	高士潑林	*gaoshipolin*	gosplan (Government Planning Commission)
Г.П.У.	戒白伍（葛杯 吳，葛柏烏）	*jiebaiwu (gebeiwu, gebaiwu)*	GPU (Government Political Bureau)
дума	杜馬	*duma*	duma (tsarist period parliament)
Иванович	伊凡諾維基	*Yifannuoweiji*	Ivanovich

интелли-генция	印貼列根追亞	*yintieliegen zhuiya*	intelligentsia
катюша	喀秋沙（卡秋霞）	*kaqiusha (kaqiuxia)*	katiusha (rocket launcher)
квас	可瓦斯（葛瓦斯，喀瓦士，喀瓦斯）	*kewasi (gewasi, kawashi, kawasi)*	kvas (drink made from fermented bread)
колхоз	科爾火支	*ke'erhuozhi*	collectivized farm
комбайн	康拜因	*kangbaiyin*	combine
Коминтерн	康民團	*Kangmintuan*	Comintern
комиссар	康密沙	*kangmisha*	commissar
комсомол	康沙模爾（共莎莫勒）	*kangsha mo'er (gong shamole)*	Komsomol (Communist Youth League)
комсомолка	康沙模爾卡	*kangshamo'erka*	Komsomolka (a female member of the Communist Youth League)
копейка	戈比（哥比）	*gebi (gebi)*	kopek
Крестинтерн	克雷斯丁團	*Keleisiding tuan*	Krestintern (Red Peasants International)
Лапп	拉普	*Lapu*	LAPP (Leningrad Association of Proletarian Writers)
ленинец	列寧主義者	*Liening zhuyizhe*	Leninist
ленинизм	列寧主義	*Liening zhuyi*	Leninism
ленинист	列寧主義者	*Liening zhuyizhe*	Leninist
Ленинский уголок	列寧紀念室	*Liening jinianshi*	Lenin memorial
малина	馬林果	*malinguo*	raspberry
марксизм	馬克思主義	*Makesi zhuyi*	Marxism
марксизм-ленинизм	馬克思列寧主義	*Makesi-Liening zhuyi*	Marxism-Leninism
марксист	馬克思主義者	*Makesi zhuyizhe*	Marxist

машина	馬神（中國東北方言）	*mashen*	machine, mechanized plow (Dongbei dialect)
меньшевик	孟什維克（門塞維克）	*Mengshi weike (Men saiweike)*	Menshevik
мир	米爾	*mi'er*	peasant collective, village group
Московское общество художников станковистов	莫斯科勞動者藝術家協會	*Mosike laodongzhe yishujia xiehui*	Moscow Society of Worker-Artists
нзп	納普	*Napu*	NEP (New Economic Policy)
нзпман	耐普曼（耐潑曼）	*Naipuman (Naipoman)*	Nepman (used to describe supporters of the New Economic Policy)
паёк	排雅克	*paiyake*	ration
печь	壁里砌（壁里氣一東北方言）	*biliqi (biliqi)*	wall stove (Dongbei dialect)
платье	布拉吉（不拉及）	*bulaji (bulaji)*	dress
пуд	普特（波特，鋪德）	*pute (bote, pude)*	pood—a Russian measure equal to 16.38 kilograms
рубль	盧布	*lubu*	ruble
самовар	沙莫瓦	*shamowa*	samovar
семинар	習明納爾	*ximingna'er*	seminar
совет	蘇維埃	*Suwei'ai*	Soviet
союз	沙油子（東北方言）	*shayouzi*	union (Dongbei dialect)
стахановец	斯達漢諾夫工作者	*Sidahannuofu gongzuozhe*	Stakhanovite
товарищ	杜瓦里希	*duwalixi*	comrade
трактор	拖拉機	*tuolaji*	tractor
троцкизм	托洛斯基主義（托洛茨基主義）	*Tuoluosiji zhuyi (Tuo luociji zhuyi)*	Trotskyism

троцкист	托派	*Tuopai*	Trotskyite
ура	烏拉	*wula*	hurrah, viva
фунт	諷脱	*fengtuo*	Russian pound (weight)
халат	哈喇呢	*halani*	"oriental" robe
хлеба	裂粑（東北方言）	*lieba*	black bread (Dongbei dialect)
царь	沙皇（沙爾）	*shahuang (sha'er)*	Tsar
Чека	切卡（乞卡，傑克）	*qieka (qika, jieke)*	Cheka (Secret Police)
червонец	丘峰尼支（次爾伏尼雀）	*qiufengnizhi (ci'erfunique)*	chervonets (Soviet currency equal to ten rubles)
шовенизм	沙文主義	*Shawen zhuyi*	Chauvinism
шовенист	沙文主義者	*Shawen zhuyizhe*	Chauvinist

REFERENCE MATTER

Notes

For complete author names, titles, and publication data for the works cited here in short form, see the Selected Bibliography, pp. 433–58. The abbreviation *LXQJ* is used for *Lu Xun quanji* (Complete works of Lu Xun). Unless otherwise noted, all English translations are mine.

Chapter 1

1. These traditional concepts of translation theory will be replaced by "guest language" and "host language" in my formulation of translingual practice.

2. Anthropologists, sociologists, and poststructuralist critics have discussed the politics of culture along this line and raised numerous questions about knowledge, power, scholarship, and academic disciplines. See, e.g., Bourdieu, *Distinction*; and idem, *Homo Academicus*.

3. A word about my own positioning in this book. Since I work simultaneously with two languages, Chinese and English, I find myself occupying a shifting position: moving back and forth between these languages and learning to negotiate the irreducible differences. The concept of translingual practice, therefore, applies to my personal situation as an analyst just as much as to the earlier historical encounter between China and the West that I explore here. Of course, this book would have a different look if I were to write it in Chinese. But writing for a Chinese-speaking audience, as I do from time to time, does not automatically solve the problem of intellectual authority and one's positioning in a given situation. It simply raises different questions in a different context and must be dealt with in terms of that context.

4. Edmund R. Leach, "Ourselves and Others"; as quoted in Talal Asad, "The Concept of Cultural Translation in British Social Anthropology," in Clifford and Marcus, p. 142.

5. Asad, in Clifford and Marcus, pp. 157–58.

6. The main target of Asad's critique is Ernest Gellner, but the essay also mentions other anthropologists in the field including Godfrey Lienhardt, John Beattie, Edmund Leach, Max Gluckman, and Rodney Needham.

7. Nietzsche, "On Truth and Falsity in Their Ultramoral Sense" (1873), in *The Complete Works of Nietzsche*, 2: 180.

8. Spivak, "Translator's Preface," in Derrida, *Of Grammatology*, p. xxii.

9. Borges, p. 51.

10. Heidegger, *Unterwegs zur Sprache*, pp. 141–43; idem, *On the Way to Language*, p. 45.

11. Ibid., p. 153; trans., p. 53.

12. For a discussion of Heidegger's interest in the philosophies of Asia, see Park.

13. Eoyang, p. 238.

14. For the concept of the "trope of equivalence," see Robinson, who uses this notion to criticize the idea of substantial equivalence that prevails in the traditional theories of translation and language.

15. To give a few examples, in *Expressions of Self in Chinese Literature*, co-edited by Robert E. Hegel and Richard C. Hessney, the concept of the self appears as a general rubric under which essays that focus on a number of different issues are supposed to fall: author's psyche, identity, individual, female image, literary characterization, and so forth. It is interesting that no two essays in this collection seem to share a homogeneous view of the self, and some of the views differ vastly from one another. This suggests that not only is the concept of self extremely elusive—a situation that can hardly be remedied by a better definition, since meaning defies fixing—but one may be treading precarious ground when using the notion as a transhistorical category. *Culture and Self*, edited by Anthony J. Marsella et al., seeks to critique logical positivism by introducing the concept of the self into social science theory and using it as a comparative basis for cultural studies. While all the essays in this volume exhibit a genuine desire to understand cultural differences (Western, Chinese, Japanese, Hindu, etc.), the deployment of the self as a universal category is taken for granted, as the editors put it: "All of the chapters proceed from the premise that the self is a necessary construct for explaining those emergent qualities of human behaviour that proceed from person-context relationships" (p. ix). However, the category of the self we often find used in comparative studies has evolved only recently in the scholarly practices of the West.

16. Tu Wei-ming, the foremost Confucian theorist in the U.S. to expound on the differences between Neo-Confucian *ji* and the Western notion of the self, assumes the mutual translatability of the two words. In fact, his humanist notion of *ji* is predicated on the idea that the former can be readily translated into the English word "self" without the mediation of the modern history of translation. In a number of his works, such as *Humanity and Self-Cultivation: Essays in Confucian Thought* and *Confucian Thought: Selfhood as Creative Transformation*, his argument appears tautological: the Neo-Confucian *ji* differs from (by which he means is superior to) the Western notion of the self, but it remains a notion of the "self."

For a discussion of the relegitimation of Neo-Confucianism in the international context, see the section on the *Critical Review* in Chapter 9 of this book

17. Saussy, p. 185.

18. In an earlier essay entitled "The Person," Taylor defines the agent as a human being who encompasses purposes and to whom things matter (i.e., human significance), whereas the notion of the public space of disclosure is associated with his view of language as social intercourse.

19. Taylor, *Sources of the Self*, esp. "The Self in Moral Space," chap. 2, pt. I, pp. 2–5, and "A Digression on Historical Explanation," chap. 12, pt. II, pp. 199–207. In the latter, Taylor anticipates criticism of his philosophical/religious approach, explaining that the advantage of such an approach lies in its emphasis on the question of *idées-forces*, of which reductive Marxism has not given an adequate account. But it is by no means clear why he refuses to engage post-Althusserian Marxism, which has already moved beyond the base-structure/superstructure paradigm. Although Taylor seems to have a well-developed notion of "practice" (pp. 204–5), there is little evidence that this notion is integrated with his study of philosophical ideas.

20. Taylor's totalistic impulse sometimes leads to a slippage between the notion of the person and that of the human species, which stands out strikingly in his tendency to stress the distinction between the person and non-human (rather than non-person) categories such as animal and machine, as if the stakes remain the same as those of Enlightenment philosophy, which was obsessed with the human-beast distinction and their hierarchical order. This is also true of his earlier essay, "The Person," where he re-introduces a universal, albeit modern, concept of the person capable of explaining all human conditions.

21. Collins, "Categories, Concepts or Predicaments? Remarks on Mauss's Use of Philosophical Terminology," in Carrithers et al., pp. 68–69.

22. See Marcel Mauss, "A Category of the Human Mind: The Notion of Person; the Notion of Self" (pp. 1–25); J. S. La Fontaine, "Person and Individual: Some Anthropological Reflections" (pp. 123–40); Mark Elvin, "Between the Earth and the Heaven: Conceptions of the Self in China" (pp. 156–89); Martin Hollis, "Of Masks and Men" (pp. 217–33); and Michael Carrithers, "An Alternative Social History of the Self" (pp. 234–56); all in Carrithers et al.

23. See Martin Hollis, "Of Masks and Men," in Carrithers et al., p. 217.

24. Roman Jakobson, "On Linguistic Aspects of Translation," in idem, p. 435. Jakobson (p. 423) defines "paronomasia" as "a semantic confrontation of phonemically similar words irrespective of any etymological connection."

25. Derrida, *Of Grammatology*; see also Barbara Johnson, pp. 142–48; and Niranjana, pp. 57–58. In a study of the modern theory of translation and German romanticism, Antoine Berman (p. 35) points out that *Treue* (fidelity) was given distinct marital overtones by Breitinger, Voss, and Herder in the second half of the eighteenth century, whereas, at about the same time, French translators continued their tradition of embellishing and poeticizing in a more or less free vein. Also, the idea of double fidelity can be traced back to Rosenzweig, who held the view that to translate is "to serve two masters": the foreign work and the foreign language

on the one hand, and one's own public and one's own language on the other. It stands to reason that a double fidelity is incessantly threatened by the specter of a double treason.

26. Following Jakobson, comparative linguists have done much work on the kind of formal analysis of the translation process we observe in his essay, including the technical problem of translatability. See Catford; Popoviōc; and Mounin.

27. For the prehistory of the Babel story and its implication for the theory of translation, see Barnstone, pp. 135–52.

28. Steiner, p. 58.

29. Barnstone, p. 43. And, indeed, there is a great deal more at stake politically surrounding the translation of the Scriptures. As we know, Martin Luther's revolutionary *Verdeutschung* of the Bible into common German became the cornerstone of the Protestant Reformation in Germany. He was also celebrated as a great writer, a creator of literary German by Herder and Klopstock.

30. See Steiner, pp. 236–38.

31. For a critique of Steiner's periodization, see Berman, p. 2.

32. Whorf, p. 60; as quoted in Steiner, pp. 90–91.

33. Steiner, p. 94

34. Benjamin, p. 70.

35. Ibid., p. 80.

36. See Derrida, "Des Tours de Babel," discussed below. See also de Man, *Resistance to Theory*, pp. 73–105.

37. Martin Jay (esp. chap. 12, "Politics of Translation: Siegfried Kracauer and Walter Benjamin on the Buber-Rosenzweig Bible," pp. 198–216) situates Benjamin's language in the context of the so-called Jewish Renaissance in Germany, particularly the important twentieth-century translation of the Old Testament (1926–61) by Martin Buber and Franz Rosenzweig.

38. See Benjamin, pp. 70, 82.

39. Ibid. He has Luther and others in mind who "have extended the boundaries of the German language" through translation (p. 80).

40. Derrida, "Des Tours de Babel," p. 171.

41. Derrida, *Positions*, p. 20.

42. Derrida, "Des Tours de Babel," p. 201.

43. Steiner, p. 357.

44. Fang, p. 130.

45. I am referring to the numbers 3.1 through 4.12 in Gunn's appendix, pp. 217–70.

46. See Gao Mingkai and Liu Zhengtan. Portions of their work are mentioned and cited in Liu Yu-ning and Zdneka Novotná. The percentage of direct borrowings from the Indo-European languages in the period Gao and Liu have documented (ca. 1900's–1950's) is much lower than borrowing of loanwords of Japanese *kanji* origin. See the Appendixes.

47. See Wang Lida, pp. 90–94.

48. See Sanetō, *Kindai Nitchū kōshō shiwa*, pp. 311–27.

49. See Tam, *Jindai Zhong-Ri wenhua guanxi yanjiu*, pp. 317–49; and idem, "Meiji

Japan and the Educational and Language Reforms in Late Ch'ing China," p. 71. If we include loanwords from sources other than Japanese *kanji*, the total figure reached by these scholars should be around 1,600. The Appendixes to this book contain slightly over 1,800 loanwords and neologisms, mainly because I have included a sampling of neologistic affixes.

50. See Masini, pp. 157–223.

51. For studies and dictionaries of loanwords in Japanese, see Arakawa's *Japanized English* and his dictionaries of loanwords. See also Shi Qun; and Chen Shanlong. In an earlier comparison of Japanese and Chinese, Miller (pp. 235–68) makes a curious suggestion that "Chinese, in all of its historical forms and modern Chinese as well, has generally reacted to outside linguistic stimulus in this extremely conservative fashion, preferring to translate new lexical items made necessary by its contacts with the outside world, rather than to take them over as loanwords" (p. 236). As far as modern Chinese is concerned, Miller's conclusion is easily contradicted by the research of linguists and other scholars, such as Gao Mingkai, Liu Zhengtan, Sanetō Keishū, Edward Gunn, Tam Yue-him, and Federico Masini.

52. See Gao Mingkai and Liu Zhengtan, esp. chap. 2 on a description and list of earlier Chinese loanwords from Persian, Sogdian, Sanskrit, Mongolian, Manchu, and other Asian languages. For further discussions, see Luo; Chmielewski; and Mair, "Buddhism."

53. Bakhtin, *Rabelais and His World*, p. 465.

54. Although Ezra Pound's translation and introduction of Chinese poetry marks a major turning point in modernist literature, it has not shaken the fundamentals of the English language as the latter has done to Chinese.

55. For a critique of the notion of "critical consciousness," see Dhareshwar.

56. Said, *The World, the Text, and the Critic*, pp. 226–27.

57. Clifford, p. 185.

58. See Said's recent *Culture and Imperialism*.

59. The journal *Inscriptions* published a special issue entitled "Traveling Theories and Traveling Theorists" in 1989. This, I believe, is a major collective effort to apply and revise Said's theory. Nearly all the eight fine essays and three commentaries contained in this volume center on the question of location. Lata Mani's essay, "Multiple Mediations: Feminist Scholarship in the Age of Multinational Reception," illustrates the politics of location by comparing the differing receptions of her own history of *sati* in the United States, Great Britain, and India. Following Chandra Mohanty's definition of the politics of location as "the historical, geographic, cultural, psychic and imaginative boundaries which provide the ground for political definition and self definition," Mani emphasizes that "location" is not a fixed point but a "temporality of struggle" and that its politics is characterized by processes of movement "between cultures, languages, and complex configurations of meaning and power" (p. 5). By focusing on the complexity of the self-positioning of the theorist in the postcolonial context, this move helps revise Said's original conception of traveling theory. At the same time, however, traveling theory is replaced by the postcolonial traveling theorist as the privileged

Notes to Pages 22–23

subject in the multiple mediations of different locations. To the extent that the fuzzy notion of location helps cut a discursive space for postcolonial theory and the Third World "diaspora" in the First World, it might work very well, but it is not clear to me exactly how the postcolonial theorist relates to the "Third World" except that s/he travels in and out of it and points out its difference from that of the "First World."

David Scott's analysis of the postcolonial situation in "Locating the Anthropological Subject: Postcolonial Anthropologists in Other Places" in the same issue suggests that the direction in which the postcolonial travels matters just as much as the difference of locations as s/he leaves one place for another:

> The postcolonial is now, in Derek Walcott's felicitously ironic phrase, a "fortunate traveller." However, even as we recognize this irreversible redistribution of the postcolonial map (one which Louise Bennett has so inimitably satirized in such poems as "Colonization in Reverse"), we should not lose sight of the fact that these movements are rather *one* way than the other. Colonial and postcolonial peoples were/are going *west*. (p. 75)

Ironically, as immigrants arrive in large numbers in the *West*, theory is simultaneously penetrating the *East*. In her essay "Postcolonial Feminists in the Western Intellectual Field: Anthropologists *and* Native Informants?" Mary E. John points out that "the choice of the term itself is telling—not emigrant, but immigrant" (p. 57).

The linkages between the two phenomena can hardly escape one's notice. In this respect it is doubtful that the postcolonial condition differs that much from that of the colonial era. But I will defer the subject of immigrant culture to the scholars of diaspora, whose excellent work has attracted increased attention in the United States, and concentrate instead on the subject of traveling theory between East and West. My question is this: What happens when theory produced in one language gets translated into another?

60. See Niranjana, p. 37. For the concepts of *wirkliche Historie* and *Wirkungsgeschichte*, see Nietzsche's *The Use and Abuse of History*; and Hans-Georg Gadamer, *Truth and Method*.

61. Niranjana, p. 35.

62. Pratt, p. 5.

63. Fabian, *Language and Colonial Power*, p. 79.

64. Ibid., p. 137. For more on colonialism in Africa, see Chinweizu et al., vol. 1; and JanMohamed.

65. For the development of languages in relation to the formation of modern nation-states and the history of colonialism and imperialism, see Certeau et al.; Mazrui; B. Anderson; Cooper; Burke and Porter; Bourdieu, *Language and Symbolic Power*; and Pratt.

66. Fabian, *Language and Colonial Power*, p. 73. See also Fabian's other influential book, *Time and Other: How Anthropology Makes Its Object*.

67. See Fabian, *Language and Colonial Power*, pp. 1–2.

68. Fodor; as cited in Fabian, *Language and Colonial Power*, p. 1.

69. Niranjana, pp. 11, 7, 172. The convergence of poststructualism and post-colonial theory in the study of colonial India has produced some exciting research in the past decade. For an informed study of the ideological uses of English literature in the colonial period, see Viswanathan.

70. Eric Cheyfitz's *Poetics of Imperialism*, which offers a strong critique of the colonialist and imperialist impulses of modern European literature, also exemplifies some of the problems I mention here.

71. Rafael, p. 21.

72. See also Homi Bhabha's essay on this issue as it pertains to British India, "Signs Taken for Wonders: Questions of Ambivalence and Authority Under a Tree Outside Delhi, May 1817," in Gates, *"Race," Writing, and Difference*, pp. 163–84.

73. Among scholars of postcolonial history, Partha Chatterjee is aware of this problem and tries to negotiate it in his *Nationalist Thought and the Colonial World: A Derivative Discourse*.

74. Lowe, p. 7.

75. See Schwartz, *In Search of Wealth and Power*.

76. See Lee, *Romantic Generation*, p. 44.

77. Qian Xingcun (A Ying), *Wanqing xiaoshuo shi*, p. 1. Perry Link (p. 135*n*27) has compared two editions of A Ying's study—the Taiwanese Renren wenku edition (1968) and the Hong Kong edition (1973)—and discovered a discrepancy in the estimated figure. The former gives about 1,500 titles, whereas the latter mentions 1,000. He argues convincingly that the Taiwan edition makes better sense: "Ch'ien [Qian] states that 'almost 400' titles of translated novels and 'about 120' original novels appear in *Han-fen-lou hsin-shu fen-lei mu-lu*. He then states that his own estimate is 'about three times' what appears in this index." In a recent study, Chen Pingyuan (p. 20) has come up with a figure of 1,145 fiction titles published between 1898 and 1911. Of these, 647 were translated novels, and 498 indigenous creations. The ratio of translated fiction to original compositions in this case is roughly three to two.

78. On the rise of modern publishing institutions in the late Qing and Republican periods, see Link, esp. chap. 3; Lee and Nathan; Barnett, "Silent Evangelism"; Qian Xingcun (A Ying), *Wanqing wenyi baokan shulüe*; Zhang Jinglu, *Zhongguo jindai chuban shiliao*; idem, *Zhongguo xiandai chuban shiliao*, vols. 1–4; idem, *Zhongguo chuban shiliao bubian*; and Lin Yutang.

79. Literary historians tend to emphasize the importance of the journal *Xiaoshuo yuebao* (The short story magazine, 1910–32) in terms of its contribution to the rise of modern fiction—which is part of an official narrative about the beginnings of modern literature—and often mention in passing the journal's commitment to the translation of foreign literatures. In fact, the evidence calls for a different interpretation. Between its conversion from a Butterfly magazine to a "serious" modern literary journal by the Literary Association in 1921 (vol. 12, no. 1) and its demise in January 1932, this monthly set up sections and numerous programs aimed at introducing foreign literature, theory, and criticism. By comparison, the original works of fiction and poetry we now call "modern" literature occupy only a fraction of the total space. Among the regular sections featured by the journal were

a "translation series," a "literature abroad" feature, and a "criticism" section. Well over half of the essays in the last section were devoted to the discussion of foreign literature. In addition, there were serialized studies on foreign literature, including Russian literature (supplementary issue, 1921) and French literature (supplementary issue, 1924); and a special number "Literature of the Abused Nations" (1921), which contained translations of the literature of marginal European nations such as Poland, Finland, Greece, and others, to mention a few. For a full-length study of Russian influence on early modern Chinese writers, see Ng.

80. Although it is common knowledge, I emphasize that modern Japan played a central role during this period as Chinese students who had studied there brought back numerous translations and a massive infusion of loanwords and neologisms into the Chinese language. See Sanetō, *Zhongguoren liuxue Riben shi*.

81. For a study of Chinese translations of foreign literature and related publications in this period, see Ma Zuyi, *Zhongguo fanyi jianshi*.

82. Lee, "In Search of Modernity," p. 110.

83. Cohen, *Discovering History in China*, pp. 3, 4.

84. Rey Chow, p. xv.

85. Bourdieu, *Language and Symbolic Power*, p. 221.

86. For a salient critique of Cold War social science and regional studies in the China field, see Barlow, "Postwar China Studies."

87. It is important to keep in mind that what has happened to modern Chinese is not restricted to the elite Chinese alone. Although they were the ones who introduced or invented the neologisms and for whom the problematic of East and West has been a preoccupation (the very reason we must take this problematic seriously in any critique of the East-West binary opposition), words do not stay with those who invent them but travel and circulate in other areas of social discourses as well. Like other verbal signs, neologisms in modern Chinese have long penetrated the popular and lower levels of Chinese society.

88. Huters, "Ideologies of Realism in Modern China," p. 149.

89. Spivak, *In Other Worlds*, p. 197. See also Guha and Spivak. Guha's preface to this volume summarizes the genesis of this historiography.

90. This is not to downplay some of the problematic areas in the historical writings of this group, such as their treatment of various class formations criticized in O'Hanlon; Hershatter; and Chen Xiaomei.

91. A recent example is the debate on the notions of the public sphere and civil society in *Modern China* 19 (1993).

92. *LXQJ*, 1: 196. Jon Kowallis's translation. I am grateful to Kowallis for allowing me to use his unpublished translations of Lu Xun's early essays (p. 7).

93. *LXQJ*, 1: 516n18. The original lyrics are "Bolan mie, Yindu wang, / Youtai yimin san si fang"; "Qing kan Yindu guotu bing fei xiao, / wei nu wei ma bude tuo long lao." The English translation is by William A. Lyell, as quoted in Kowallis (p. 4).

94. In a recent article, Wang Liwei argues that the Japanese had borrowed modern Chinese character translations of English terms from nineteenth-century missionary dictionaries, in particular, Robert Morrison's *Dictionary of the Chinese*

Language (1815), long before the reverse process began. He (p. 281) suggests 1875(?) as the date when this one-way traffic in lexical borrowing gave way to the predominantly Chinese importation of Japanese *kanji* compounds; Japanese translators had ordered bilingual dictionaries compiled by Protestant missionaries (Morrison, Williams, and Medhurst) from China and relied heavily on them in their translations until the first English-Japanese dictionary appeared in 1862. Wang's study complicates our view of the flow of neologisms between Chinese and Japanese, but it tends to exaggerate the situation by attributing a greater role to these early missionary dictionaries in the rise of modern Japanese *kanji* compounds than can be fully substantiated by textual evidence. I have not been able to verify more than a limited number of such earlier compounds in Morrison's dictionary that coincide exactly with the Sino-Japanese-European loanwords that Gao, Liu, and others have pointed out. For these particular compounds, see the footnotes to the Appendixes. A more reliable source of Japanese borrowing from missionary works would be in their translations of Wei Yuan's *Haiguo tuzhi*. See the discussion below.

95. Gao and Liu (pp. 82–83) list of total of 91 items in this category. A native speaker of Chinese cannot usually tell that some of these words did not exist in Chinese before the twentieth century. Further examples are *bu jingji* (recession; *fukeiki*), *changsuo* (site; *basho*), *paichusuo* (police station; *hashutsujo*), *fuwu* (service; *fukumu*), *gebie* (individual; *kobetsu*), *juli* (distance; *kyori*), *neirong* (contents; *naiyō*), *zhibu* (party branch; *shibu*). In Appendix C, I modify and correct this list with my findings and those of other scholars.

96. The pre-loanword meaning of *geming* (now revolution) was "to follow the Mandate of Heaven"; *wenxue* (now literature) meant "the state of being learned or erudite"; *jingji* (now economy) used to mean "governing and assisting" (the people). *Kexue* (now science), which is not considered a return-graphic loan by Gao, Liu, and Masini but which I reassigned to the present category (see Appendix D), originally meant "study programs for the civil service examination." For a fascinating account of the Chinese translation of the word "science" in the Ming dynasty as *gezhi* and its later replacement by the Japanese *kanji* term *kagaku* or *kexue* in modern Chinese, see Wang Hui. Gao and Liu (pp. 83–88) list 67 lexical items in this category. Further examples are *wenxue* (literature; *bungaku*), *wenming* (civilization; *bunmei*), *fenxi* (analysis; *bunseki*), *fengjian* (feudal; *hōken*), *falü* (law; *hōritsu*), *ziyou* (freedom; *jiyū*), *jieji* (class; *kaikyū*), *laodong* (labor; *rōdō*), *zhengzhi* (politics; *seiji*), *sixiang* (thought; *shisō*), *yundong* (movement; *undō*), *weiyi* (only/sole; *yuiitsu*). Masini has contested some of these terms, such as *wenxue*. See the discussion below as well the Appendixes, especially A and D.

97. This is by far the largest of the three groups of loanwords. Gao and Liu (pp. 88–98) list 100 compounds in this category; with few exceptions, all are *kanji* translations of English terms. Other examples are *yihui* (parliament; *gikai*), *wuzhi* (matter/substance; *busshitsu*), *fandui* (oppose/opposition; *hantai*), *xianshi* (reality; *genjitsu*), *zhexue* (philosophy; *tetsugaku*). See Appendix B.

98. De Man, *Resistance to Theory*, p. 104.

99. The term is Masini's. An alternative label, "round-trip words," was coined

by Victor Mair ("Anthologizing and Anthropologizing," p. 3). Either term should be helpful in specifying the second of the three categories of Sino-Japanese-European neologisms that Gao Mingkai and Liu Zhengtan classify.

100. I am not implying that the meaning of classical Chinese *wenhua* or the English "culture" did not go through mutations in its separate existence. It certainly did (see Williams, *Keywords*, pp. 76–82). What I am trying to do here is to call attention to a unique historical situation within a limited period of time between the nineteenth and early twentieth centuries. During this time—neither before nor after—a large number of Chinese compounds were reinvented, radically, via the mediation of Japanese *kanji* translations of European terms.

101. It is well known that Yan Fu had to defend the Chinese lexicon against the influx of Japanese loanwords when he started translating John Mill, Thomas Huxley, Herbert Spencer, Adam Smith, and other Westerners at the turn of the century. He preferred to use ancient terms or coin his own, refusing to adopt those existing in contemporary works. For example, he uses *mucai* to translate "capital" instead of the return-graphic loanword *ziben* (*shihon*) and renders "bank" as *chaodian, chaoshang,* or *banke* (a transliteration) in place of the already known Japanese loan *yinhang* (*ginkō*). Interestingly, despite the great impact of Yan Fu's translations on his generation, his neologisms were quickly rendered obsolete by the growing popularity of Japanese loanword translations (Schwartz, *In Search of Wealth and Power,* pp. 95–96). Joshua Fogel ("Recent Translation Theory") has tried to reopen the question of exactly how Yan Fu's idiosyncratic neologism should be viewed in relation to Japanese loanwords in this time. Speculating on why *tianyanlun,* Yan Fu's famous coinage for the "theory of evolution," was soon replaced in the new Chinese lexicon by the Japanese term *shinkaron* (Chinese *jinhualun*), Fogel (p. 28) says

> Why such terms did not "take" in China cannot simply be sluffed off on the fact that they were too literary or assumed too profound a knowledge of classical Chinese lore. When Yan Fu was writing, there was no widespread vernacular Chinese language in use, and most of those who were able to read his translations undoubtedly understood his allusions (even if the Western ideas behind them remained partially obscured). Was Yan Fu aware of the Japanese translations by Nakamura Keiu of the same texts he labored over? Has anyone ever compared the vocabularies devised by Nakamura and Yan to render Western philosophical, political, and economic concepts?

Masini's recent study of late Qing neologisms and loanwords in the Chinese lexicon sheds oblique light on these questions—oblique in the sense that he does not tackle directly the comparative question along the lines suggested by Fogel. He (p. 115) shows that even Yan Fu himself had trouble keeping all Japanese-associated neologisms out of his own translations. The examples he gives are *yiyuan* (parliament; *giin*), *ziyou* (freedom; *jiyū*), *wenxue* (literature; *bungaku*), etc. (Note that the modern term *wenxue,* unlike *ziyou,* is not exactly a return-graphic loan; however, its round-trip dissemination through the mediation of Japanese *bungaku* has much to do with the establishment of the new translingual meaning of *wenxue* in the modern Chinese lexicon. See the discussion below.) Also worth mentioning is the important point Masini makes about Yan Fu's translation of the English terms "economy" and "sociology," which would substantiate Fogel's point. Yan Fu's renderings *jixue* and *qunxue* were soon replaced by the Japanese *jingji* and *shehuixue*, which later became standard. Did Yan Fu oppose the Japanese loans or was he unaware of their existence? As far as Yan Fu is concerned, it would probably have come to the same result; a more interesting question has to do with the complex circumstances under which Yan Fu made the choices he did. Masini's study claims that no evidence of the Japanese loanwords *jingji* and *shehuixue* could be found in the earlier Chinese translations of Western texts he examined—that is, before Yan Fu's invention of *jixue* and *qunxue* in 1898. If true, this would establish Yan Fu as "first and foremost an innovator and not only an opponent of Japanese loans" (Masini, p. 115).

102. See also Mair, "Anthologizing and Anthropologizing," p. 3.

103. Masini, pp. 24–25. For a fascinating account of the changing meaning of *gongsi*, see ibid., p. 174.

104. Ibid., 25.

105. The original meaning of *wenxue* goes back to the Confucian *Analects* (11.2), where it denotes "the state of being learned or erudite." Masini (p. 204) proposes that the term with this modern meaning of "literature" should be dated further back to Jesuit missionary Giulio Aleni's work *Zhifang waiji* (Record of the places outside the jurisdiction of the Office of Geography; 1623). He cites as evidence the phrase *ouluoba zhuguo shang wenxue*, which he renders as "all Western countries highly esteem literature." This translation strikes me as anachronistic, since "literature" or whatever its Italian counterpart happened to be covered a different and much broader semantic field in the seventeenth century than what we mean by "literature" in the post-Enlightenment era.

106. There remain, however, a number of transliterations that have not been replaced by loanword translations. See Appendixes F and G.

107. Before *minzhu* became a standard translation for "democracy," it had been used in this modern sense of "people rule" by missionary W.A.P Martin to render the word "republic" (now *gonghe*) in his 1864 *Wanguo gongfa*, a translation of Henry Wheaton's *Elements of International Law*. This earlier transvaluation of *minzhu* via the translation of "republic" contributed indirectly to the reversal of its classical meaning. Masini (pp. 189–90) speculates that the Japanese probably picked up this two-character compound through their secondhand translation of *Wanguo gongfa* in 1865 and later used it to translate "democracy" (*minshu*).

108. This is probably because deictic words are more closely tied to the logic of indigenous word formation than other parts of speech, such as nouns and verbs.

109. For the fascinating debate on the invention of the feminine third-person singular in 1920, see the following articles published in *Xue deng* (Scholarly lamp), a supplement to the Shanghai newspaper *Shishi xinbao* (Current affairs), plus one published in the journal *Xin ren* (New humans): Sun Zuji, "'Ta' zi de yanjiu"; Han Bing, "Bo 'ta zi de yanjiu'"; Sun Zuji, "Fei 'Bo ta zi de yanjiu'"; Meng Shen; Han Bing, "Zhe shi Liu Bannong de cuo"; and Liu Fu (Liu Bannong), "Ta zi wenti."

For a comparative study of the personal pronoun in modern and classical Chinese, see Wang Li, 2: 1–60; Gao Mingkai; Lu Shuxiang and Huang Shengzhang.

110. The invention of the feminine *pronoun* should not be confused here with the existence of the same character written with the *nü* radical, which used to be a noun and bore no etymological relationship with the original Chinese pronoun *ta* written with a *ren* radical. According to Morohashi (*Dai Kanwa jiten*, 3: 626), the premodern character *ta* is pronounced /ch'i/ or /jie/ (the same as in *jie*, sister), signifying "mother" in the Sichuan dialect.

111. See Shan Shi. At the same time the feminine pronoun was invented, the neuter form of *ta* was also considered; see Liu Fu, "Ta zi wenti."

112. Edward Gunn mentions Zhou Zuoren as one of the sources of information on the circumstances surrounding Liu Fu's invention of the feminine pronoun *ta* (p. 305n24). In addition, Lu Xun also refers to this fact in his "Yi Liu Bannong" (Remembering Liu Bannong), in *LXQJ*, 6: 55. Chinese linguist Wang Li (2: 351n22) cites two more sources: Hu Shi's memorial speech at the funeral service for Liu Fu (Liu Bannong) in which he describes Liu as the engineer of the neologism and Lin Yutang's book *Kaiming Yingwen wenfa* (An illuminating English grammar) in which the author pinpoints the year 1917 as the exact date of the birth of the character.

113. See Liu Fu, "Ta zi wenti."

114. Interestingly, during Liu's term as the president of Women's College in Beijing, he issued an order forbidding female students to use the fashionable transliteration *misi* of the English word "miss" as a form of address and insisting on the adoption of indigenous Chinese terms, such as *guniang* (girl or unmarried woman), *xiaojie* (young lady), and *nüshi* (lady). See his interview with a journalist from *Shijie ribao*, Apr. 1, 1931.

115. The pluralizing suffix *men*, which is tagged on to nouns and pronouns, was another hot subject of debate during the language reform; see Gunn, pp. 266–68.

116. For a discussion of the modern statist construction of gender from a post-structuralist and feminist point of view, see Barlow, "Theorizing Women."

117. Adorno, 2: 190.

118. For a discussion of the invention of tradition in modern national histories, see Hobsbawm and Ranger.

119. Levenson, p. 157.

120. Thomas Metzger's continuity model, which is meant to criticize Levenson's impact theory, operates, nevertheless, on the same reified binaries (tradition/modernity; China/West) as Levenson used. Metzger argues (p. 17) that "to a large extent, it was the indigenous, intense, centuries-old desire to escape from a metaphysical, psychological, political, and economic predicament which led many Chinese enthusiastically to devote their lives to the overthrow of traditionally revered institutions and the adoption of strange and foreign ways." This attempt to minimize the presence of a mediated West in favor of a self-explanatory indigenous past cannot, however, explain the process by which the "modern" and the "West" get legitimized in twentieth-century Chinese intellectual discourse.

121. There are two translations for anarchism: the Chinese transliteration as

anaqi zhuyi and the Japanese *kanji* translation as *museifu shugi*. The *kanji* translation, pronounced *wuzhengfu zhuyi* in Mandarin, eventually replaced the transliteration. See Appendix F.

122. Dirlik, *Anarchism*, pp. 50, 55.

123. I am concerned with an order of reality that might sometimes coincide with, but should by no means be leveled down to, the state's brute regulation and manipulation of the written and spoken word. For a discussion of the latter in China, see Schoenhals.

124. For a discussion of this debate, see Liu Kang, "Subjectivity, Marxism, and Cultural Theory in China," in Liu Kang and Xiaobing Tang, pp. 23–55.

125. See Liu Zaifu. Initially published in *Wenxue pinglun* (Literary criticism) (1985, no. 6, and 1986, no. 1), Liu's essay was attacked by an official critic named Chen Yong.

Chapter 2

1. Russell, *Problem of China*, pp. 220–21.

2. Ibid., p. 210.

3. Russell, "Zhongguo guomin xing de jige tedian." The original essay appeared in *Atlantic Monthly* 128, no. 6 (Dec. 1921).

4. For a critical response to Russell's portrayal of Chinese character, see my discussion of Lu Xun below.

5. In an earlier critique of May Fourth radicalism, Yu-sheng Lin raises a number of issues that coincide with the question of national character and literary modernity that I am discussing here. In *The Crisis of Chinese Consciousness*, Lin diagnoses a number of problematic areas in the intellectual discourse of the May Fourth period, especially as it concerns the dubious practice of totalistic iconoclasm. I agree with the author on the need to rethink the May Fourth legacy but will take a different approach. For example, Lin (pp. 104–51) argues that in the eyes of Lu Xun the Chinese people are "worse than stupid, weak, hypocritical, and self-deceiving" and yet the existence of good persons such as Xiang Lin sao in "New Year's Sacrifice," Runtu in "My Old Home," and Shan si saozi in "Tomorrow" seems to reveal a self-contradiction in the writer's mind. From this he concludes that Lu Xun's problem derives from a holistic mode of thinking that cannot resolve his crisis of consciousness. But when Lin thus attributes Lu Xun's holistic mode of thinking to the predominant influence of Confucian philosophical tradition, he merely reverses the May Fourth rhetoric of tradition versus modernity by turning it against those radicals who had first invented it, rather than probe into the heart of their assumptions and tease out the implications of the rhetoric of modernity as it bears upon the immediate historical experience of those intellectuals. To my mind, an approach that chooses to dwell on so-called individual consciousness and its philosophical origins precisely empties out the discursive context that would help illuminate the self-contradiction perceived in Lu Xun's thinking. I find it impossible in the absence of a preliminary understanding of the May Fourth discourse about national character to imagine the difficult situation

of intellectuals such as Lu Xun torn between an Orientalized knowledge about Chinese identity and an intense desire to overcome that knowledge. In my view, the radical anti-traditionalism of Lu Xun's generation "originates" in something more than traditional Chinese holism. It comes, above all, from the violence of early modern history that Chinese intellectuals had to endure, whether as radical, traditionalist, or other, in the hope that they would eventually come to terms with modernity. The latter is every bit a rival of traditional Chinese holism in its totalistic claim upon the teleology of human history. In *Chuantong yu Zhongguo ren* (Tradition and the Chinese), a more recent effort to rethink the May Fourth legacy, coauthors Liu Zaifu and Lin Gang (chaps. 4 and 5) point out that the question of national character is indispensable to an understanding of major historical figures such as Liang Qichao and Lu Xun. However, Liu and Lin's faith in modernity prevents them from questioning the discourse of national character.

Partha Chatterjee's *Nationalist Thought and the Colonial World* and Abdullah Laroui's *Crisis of the Arab Intellectuals* are very illuminating in this respect. What they see in Indian nationalism and the circumstances of the Arab intellectual presents a striking parallel to the Chinese situation as described by Yu-sheng Lin, but these authors reach radically different conclusions. Based on an analysis of the reaction of Indian and Arab intellectuals to European domination and hegemony, they suggest that the violence of colonial and imperialist history thrust the totalistic ideologies of progress, nation-state, and modernity into the thinking of the native intellectuals in each case. The comparable nature of such disparate histories should alert us to the fact that it is relatively easy to criticize the iconoclastic intellectual in non-Western nations, but far less so to dismantle the rhetoric of modernity that has named tradition as its opposite in the first place. The tyranny of that binary opposition may sometimes return in the guise of criticism. In a more recent article, Yu-sheng Lin ("Lu Xun geren zhuyi") begins to see Lu Xun's concept of national character as a problem in his early thought.

6. Herder's decisive work was *Outlines of a Philosophy of the History of Man.* For historical studies of Herder and his influence on German nationalism, see Anthony D. Smith; Berlin; Barnard; and Iggers.

7. For discussion of the contemporary discourse of *Nihonjinron* in Japan, see, e.g., Yoshino; Befu, "Nationalism and *Nihonjinron*"; and Dale.

8. For an illuminating critique of the complicity between this theory and imperialism, see Goody.

9. See Chapter 9 for a discussion of Zhang's critique of the New Century group.

10. "Xinmin yi," in Liang, *wenji*, 3: 105–6.

11. Ibid., 5: 14.1–5.

12. Respectively in Liang, *wenji*, 2: 5.12–42, 5.42–51, 3.48–54, and 3.61–65; and *zhuanji*, 3: 4.1–162.

13. See "Jianguo fanglüe" (A blueprint for nation building; 1917) and "Minzu zhuyi" (Nationalism; 1924), in Sun Zhongshan, pp. 170–77, 615–91.

14. Nearly all major journals published before and after 1911, progressive or conservative, were drawn into the debate on national character at one time or

another. Between the years 1906 and 1919, *Dongfang zazhi* (The eastern miscellany) published a good number of articles discussing Chinese character. Some of these offered positive or mixed descriptions; others were negative. Among these seminal essays are, e.g., "Lun Zhongguo renmin zhi yilai xing zhi qiyuan" (appeared previously in *Jinzhong bao* [Alarm post], July 8, 1904); "Lun Zhongguo zhi guomin xing" (also published in *Yulun ribao* [Public opinion daily], May 13, 1908); Du Yaquan, "Jing de wenming yu dong de wenming"; Qian Zhixiu; and Zhang Xichen. For the most part, these essays echoed Liang Qichao's view criticizing Chinese character for failing to live up to the demands of historical progress. Although the authors contradicted one another as to the exact nature of national character or disagreed on the detail of its relative strengths or weaknesses, none raised doubts concerning the premise of the argument. This testifies to the success of the discourse of national character in converting the nebulous question "What's wrong with China?" into a shared assumption that the Chinese character more or less was responsible for what had happened to the country since the Opium War. The debate continued unabated through the New Culture movement and the May Fourth period.

15. Guang Sheng, p. 505.

16. For a discussion of China's response to Darwinism, see Pusey.

17. See Chen Duxiu, "Dong xi minzu genben sixiang zhi chayi" and "Wo zhi aiguo zhuyi"; Li Dazhao, "Dong xi wenming genben zhi yidian" (1918), in *Li Dazhao wenji*, pp. 557–71; and Meng Zhen. Kang Baiqing's article "Lun Zhongguo zhi minzu qizhi," which appeared in the same issue of *Xin chao* as Meng's, is a notable exception. Kang rejected the totalistic view of national character and proposed serious ethnographic studies of the Chinese in different areas. But as his own effort shows, ethnography is not particularly objective. It, too, is informed by a desire to improve the Chinese character according to a Eurocentric criterion.

18. As further testimony to the success of May Fourth radicalism, Mei Guangdi and Hu Xiansu of the *Xueheng* (Critical review) group accepted the negative sense of the word when they used it to criticize the evils of modern society, although they attributed the flaws in the national character to the corrupting influence of the modern world rather than to traditional values. The transvaluation helped support their argument for the revival of national essence that the group promoted. See, e.g., Mei Guangdi, "Ping jin ren tichang xueshu zhi fangfa"; and Hu Xiansu. For an analysis of the *Critical Review* group, see Chapter 9.

19. For a Marxist critique of national character, see Sun Yushi.

20. Lee, *Voices from the Iron House*, p. 19.

21. Lu Xun's first used the term *guomin xing* in "Moluo shili shuo" (The power of Mara poetry), *LXQJ*, 1: 213, 221. This essay was written in 1907 and appeared in nos. 2 and 3 of the journal *He'nan* (Feb. and Mar. 1908) published by Chinese intellectuals living in Japan.

22. See, e.g., Sha Lianxiang, which contains useful historical and bibliographical sources for the study of this problem. In Taiwan and Hong Kong, national character seems to be an ongoing concern; see Li Yiyuan and Yang Guoshu.

23. For discussions of Smith and his work, see Li Jinghan's introduction to Pan

Guangdan, *Minzu texing he minzu weisheng*, pp. 1–25, as well as Pan's preface, pp. 1–9. See also Hayford; and Mackerras. For a discussion of Arthur Smith's ministry at the En County Pangzhuang base, see Esherick.

24. Hayford, p. 153.

25. Ibid., p. 165.

26. For studies of the work of Christian missionaries in late Qing China in addition to those mentioned in the previous notes, see Cohen, *China and Christianity*; Forsythe; Fairbank; Albert Feuerwerker; Hevia; and Cooley.

27. For detailed information on the circumstances of Lu Xun's exposure to the Japanese source, see Zhang Mengyang. See also Kamei Shunsuke's study of Meiji nationalism, national essence, and literary discourse in early modern Japan.

28. This playful diary was first serialized in the journal *Yu si* (Thread of talk).

29. Yasuoka Hideo's book was published in Tokyo in 1926 and was filled with hostile, racist remarks about the Chinese.

30. Lu Xun, "Ma shang zhi riji" (July 2, 1926, entry) in "Huagai ji xubian" (Supplement to the flower-canopy collection), *LXQJ*, 3: 240. This literary diary was published in 1926. All translations in this chapter are mine unless otherwise indicated.

31. Ibid., p. 245.

32. Lu Xun, *Lu Xun shuxin ji*, 1: 425.

33. Lu Xun, "Li ci cunzhao, no. 3," *LXQJ*, 6: 509.

34. Zhang Mengyang, pp. 216–17. In his essay, Zhang Mengyang approves of Arthur Smith's view of Chinese national character but underlines its usefulness for the state agenda of the Four Modernizations in the 1980's. We have come full circle in less than a century.

35. It was purely by accident that I found this 1903 version in the Treasure Room of the Harvard-Yenching Library. The publisher, Zuoxin she, claims to be the translator of the Japanese version but gives no information on the specific individual(s) responsible for the translation.

36. As further evidence of Smith's continuing influence through Pan Guangdan, excerpts from Pan's translation are included in Sha Lianxiang's 1989 collection *Zhongguo minzu xing* (The Chinese national character).

37. Hayford, p. 173.

38. Recent theoretical work among anthropologists has thrown much light on the ethnocentrism of modern practices of ethnography; see Clifford and Marcus. Late twentieth-century disciplines of social science (sociology, political science, anthropology, area studies, etc.) have long replaced crude missionary narratives, but the knowledge claims made by some of these fields and disciplines often closely resemble those of their less sophisticated predecessors. For a critique, see Hevia, p. 328n12.

39. This categorical method goes back to the classificatory taxonomy of natural history in mid-eighteenth-century Europe, as exemplified by Linnaeus' hugely influential *Systema naturae* (1735). For a critique of the knowledge/power relationship in the development of scientific discourse, see Pratt, pp. 15–85.

40. Some of these categories were adopted by Bertrand Russell in *The Problem of*

China and continue to circulate in the works of contemporary scholars. See, e.g., two recent titles (Allinson; Bond) from Oxford University Press, which claim to study the "Chinese mind" and its national "psychology."

41. Arthur Smith, pp. 93–94.

42. Ibid., p. 322.

43. Ibid., p. 329.

44. Lao She, *Er Ma*, in *Lao She wenji*, p. 407. The English translation used here is by Julie Jimmerson, *Mr. Ma and Son*, p. 12.

45. Albert Feuerwerker (p. 57) warns that Christian missionaries should not be simply collapsed with the foreign powers who imposed unequal treaties by force on China. However, it is equally untenable to make light of the complicity between the two as "the Achilles heel of the missionary effort." After all, the treaties of 1842, 1844, and 1858 spelled out the rights and privileges of missionaries and, as Feuerwerker himself points out, "Extraterritoriality—even the tiniest chapel flew a national flag—residence in the interior, intervention in lawsuits and justification of the use of force, a demeaning attitude of moral superiority which took away with one hand the virtues it ascribed to the Chinese with the other—all these antagonized not only the anti-Christian nationalist but also a growing number of Chinese Christians" (ibid.).

46. Hevia, p. 305.

47. In the past two or three decades, Michel Foucault, Richard Rorty, Jacques Derrida, and Paul de Man have made tremendous contributions, each in his own way, to our understanding of the problem of representation and epistemology. See Foucault, *The Archaeology of Knowledge and the Discourse on Language*, and *The Order of Things*; Rorty; Derrida, *Of Grammatology*, *Writing and Difference*, and *Dissemination*; and de Man, *Allegories of Reading* and *Blindness and Insight*. See also Paul Rabinow's essay, "Representations Are Social Facts: Modernity and Post-Modernity in Anthropology," in Clifford and Marcus, pp. 234–61.

48. Lao She's adult recollection of his early loss of his father and fear of the "foreign devils" is vividly captured in these words: "I was sleeping soundly when they entered our house. If I had awakened, they would have sliced me up with their swords, since they were angry not to find anything valuable in our home"; see "*Shenquan* houji" (Afterword to *Magical Boxers*), in Hu Jieqing, p. 175; as cited and translated by David Wang, p. 112.

49. Cooke, p. vii. Compare Arthur Smith's quotation of this passage in *Chinese Characteristics*, p. 10.

50. Arthur Smith, p. 11.

51. In 1935, a Japanese named Ōtani Kotarō translated and compiled a wide-ranging selection of writings about Chinese character including selections by the aforementioned missionaries and journalists, as well as Japanese scholars from the nineteenth century. The timing of this volume to coincide with World War II and the eve of the Japanese invasion is hardly surprising. This book was subsequently adapted and translated into Chinese by Yuan Fang under the title *Zhongguo ren jing-shen jiegou yanjiu* (Studies in the psychological structure of the Chinese). As further testimony to its influence, it became one of the key sources for a recent collection

of essays on Chinese national character published in the 1980's; see Sha Lianxiang. It is interesting to note that the editors of this collection collapse the notion of *guomin xing* with *minzu xing* in an attempt to eliminate the pejorative connotation of the former. The slippage is indicative of the changing political climate in post-Mao China where the dominant discourse now emphasizes the uniqueness of Chinese characteristics in face of the threat posed by transnational capitalism, which is a far cry from the earlier uses of national character in Lu Xun's time.

52. Xu Shoushang, *Wang you Lu Xun yinxiang ji*, p. 19.

53. Lu Xun, "Zi xu" (Author's preface), in *LXQJ*, 1: 5 (idem, *Selected Stories*, p. 2).

54. See Lee, *Voices from the Iron House*, p. 203n61.

55. See Ōta Susumu.

56. For a critical discussion of the use of free indirect style in scholarly writing, see Sperber, pp. 13–48.

57. David Wang (p. 215) has given an interesting reading of Lu Xun's fascination with the cinematic scene. He calls it the decapitation complex, pointing out that "Lu Xun's anxiety over decapitation and headlessness serves as the secret fountainhead of his literary inspiration." Marston Anderson's (*Limits of Realism*, pp. 76–85) analysis focuses more on violence as a problem of representation involving the observer's alienation and complicity.

58. Lu Xun, "Tengye xiansheng," in *LXQJ*, 2: 275–76.

59. See Feng Xuefeng; Wang Xiyan; and Li Helin, "Cong 'guomin xing' wenti." Among the critics who share their view are Tang Tao, Shao Bozhou, Liu Panxi, Zhu Tong, and Hua Gang; see Bao Jing, pp. 415–39.

60. See Bao Chang, "Lun Lu Xun de 'gaige guomin xing' sixiang" (A study of Lu Xun's concept of "the transformation of national character"), in Bao Jing, pp. 124–45.

61. For a notable exception, see Sun Yushi.

62. Li Tuo, p. 5.

63. See Yanbing (Shen Yanbing), "Du *Nahan*" (Reading *Call to Arms*), and Xidi (Zheng Zhenduo) "*Nahan*" (*Call to Arms*), in Li Helin, pp. 182–89, 197–99, respectively; Wang Xiyan; and articles by Li Helin, Yang Zhansheng, Ding Ergang, Qiu Wenzhi, Zhang Xuezhi, and Su Zhenlu in Bao Jing, pp. 337–414; Xu Shoushang, *Wo suo renshi de Lu Xun*; Zheng Xinmiao; and Liu Zaifu and Lin Gang.

64. The most frequently used texts are Lu Xun's preface to *Call to Arms*, quoted above, and the following essays from *LXQJ*: "Lun zheng le yan kan" (On looking with open eyes; 1: 328–32), "Suigan lu" (Random thoughts, no. 38; 1: 387–90), "Letter no. 8" in *Liang di shu* (Correspondence with Xu Guangping; 9: 25–28), "Huran xiangdao" (Thoughts that suddenly occurred to me, nos. 1–4; 3: 10–15), "Zhege yu nage" (This and that; 3: 102–9), "Xuanchuan yu zuoxi" (Propaganda and acting; 4: 266–67), "Zaitan baoliu" (My further reservation; 5: 114–15), and "E wen ben 'Ah Q zhengzhuan' xu ji zhuzhe zixu zhuanlüe" (Preface to the Russian edition of "The True Story of Ah Q" and a brief self-description of the author; 7: 77–82).

65. "The True Story of Ah Q," *LXQJ*, 1: 111; Yang and Yang's translation in *Selected Stories*, p. 109.

66. For a similar discussion of the Chinese obsession with face, written in 1904, see Arthur Brown.

67. Arthur Smith, *Chinese Characteristics*, p. 18.

68. Hevia, p. 316.

69. *LXQJ*, 1: 113.

70. "Mashang zhi riji" (The sub-chapter of instant diary), *LXQJ*, 3: 240. *Shina* and *Shinajin* were the most commonly used terms for "China" and "the Chinese" in Japan from the Meiji period through 1945. For a fascinating account of the etymological origins of *Shina* and its loan transformations in Sanskrit, French, German, Dutch, English, Spanish, and other languages, see Fogel, *Cultural Dimension*, pp. 66–76.

71. Hanan, p. 71.

72. See ibid., p. 70. Dostoyevsky's novel *Brothers Karamazov* has a similar prologue.

73. The famous attack on Lu Xun led by the Sun Society in 1928 represents the earliest moment of this Marxist legacy in the criticism of "The True Story of Ah Q." See Qian Xingcun's "Si qu le de A Q shidai" (The age of Ah Q is dead) and other essays in Qian Xingcun (A Ying), *Xiandai Zhongguo wenxue zuojia*, pp. 1–53.

74. Marxist critics are particularly fond of quoting the following essays from *LXQJ*: "Chunmo xian tan" (Idle talk in late spring; 1: 304–8), "Deng xia manbi" (Writing under the lamplight; 1: 309–16), "Xuejie de sanhun" (Three souls in academia; 3: 150–52), "Ying yiben *Duanpian xiaoshuo xuanji* ziqu" (Author's preface to the English translation of *The Short Stories of Lu Xun;* 7: 632–33), "Da Xi zhoukan bianzhe xin" (Letter to the editor of *Theatre* weekly; 6: 112–16), "Shuo mianzi" (On face; 6: 98–100), and "Nanren yu beiren" (The southerner and the northerner; 5: 354–55).

75. Interestingly, Lu Xun's notions of *shangdeng ren* and *xiadeng ren* are not exactly predicated on a Marxian theory of class. Their meanings are by and large determined by economic and educational hierarchies of Chinese society, as will be seen in my analysis of "Ah Q."

76. Russell, p. 212.

77. *LXQJ*, 1: 316. Previous Chinese writers had written on chair-bearers in terms that Lu Xun, though not Russell, could grasp fairly easily. An example is a poem entitled "On His Chair-Bearers: A Case of Misplaced Sympathy," which substantiates the irony of the contrast between Russell's essentialist view of Chinese culture and Lu Xun's profound understanding of the Chinese system of social hierarchy. The poem, written by the famous eighteenth-century literatus named Yuan Mei and given here in Arthur Waley's paraphrase, reflects on the huge chasm that separates the speaker from his chair-bearers.

> Today my carriers have had a double task;
> We have gone up a mountain and then down into a valley.

For the moment they are through with all their hardships and dangers;
Night is falling, and at last they can rest their feet.
I was quite certain that directly they put down their burden
Tired out, they would sink into a heavy sleep.
To my great surprise they re-trimmed the lamp
And all night long played at games of chance.
A quarrel began; feeling ran high.
One of them absconded; another went in chase.
All the fuss was about a handful of pence;
Hardly enough to pay for a cup of gruel.
Yet they throw down those pence with as high and mighty an air
As if they were flinging a shower of golden stars.
Next day when they shouldered their burdens again
Their strength was greater than that of Pen and Yu.
The same thing happened five nights on end;
It was almost as if some demon had possessed them.
Can it be, I wonder, that when the dice are thrown
The Owl and the Black have the power to cure fatigue?
But different creatures have their different natures;
What suits the fish will not please the bear.
The simplest folk and the most learned men
Cannot possibly be measured by the same rules.
Rather than sorrow over other people's sorrows
It is better, when one can, to enjoy one's own pleasure.

—Quoted from Birch, pp. 194–95

As a liberal thinker, Russell would not have adopted a blatant tone of condescension toward the lower class. It is interesting, though, he used the language of national character in his account.

78. There are a vast number of studies in this area. To sample a few, see Bao; Jin Hongda; and Li Zehou. It is worth mentioning that Mao Zedong also spoke of Ah Q in this fashion in his April 1956 speech "Lun shi da guanxi" (On ten major relations); see Ge, p. 371.

79. For a neo-Marxist criticism of the teleological view of history, see Althusser.

80. See "E wen ben 'Ah Q zhengzhuan' xu ji zhuzhe zixu zhuanlüe," *LXQJ*, 7: 77.

81. "Zaitan baoliu," *LXQJ*, 5: 114.

82. "Xie zai *Fen* houmian," *LXQJ*, 1: 362.

83. See Hanan, p. 81. Hanan makes a distinction between what he calls "situational irony," "presentational irony," and a third type called "juxtapositional irony." To summarize his definitions briefly, situational irony is one in which both object and factor of irony lie in the dramatized part of a fictional work, whereas in presentational irony the voice of the narrator who stands outside the action being recounted becomes the chief factor of irony. According to the degree that the narrator is given an explicit persona, the kinds of presentational irony vary.

By contrast, juxtapositional irony, which is used most frequently in graphic arts, produces a "lowering" or "raising" effect by having one section or element of the structure act ironically upon another (see ibid., p. 77).

84. Bakhtin, *Dialogic Imagination*, pp. 304, 305n18.

85. André Gide's novel, *Les Faux monnayeurs* is a classic example of such self-reflexive narration, a device that French critics term "mise en abyme"; see Dallenbach.

86. "Ah Q zhengzhuan," in *LXQJ*, p. 74; Yang and Yang, p. 68. The English translation is by Yang Hsien-yi and Gladys Yang. I have substituted *pinyin* for the Yangs' Wade-Giles transliterations of Chinese names. Hereinafter cited in the text, with page number of the Chinese original given first, followed by the page number in the translation in italics.

87. In an earlier story, "Kong Yiji," Lu Xun explored the tensions between the upper and lower classes in a somewhat different vein. The poor scholar Kong Yiji, who aspires to academic honors and writes archaic Chinese, is described with irony by a narrator who writes in modern vernacular Chinese retrospectively about his childhood memories of Kong. In other words, the hierarchy of archaic and vernacular Chinese, rather than that of the illiterate and the literate, structures the narrative of class in that story. See *LXQJ*, 1: 20–24,

Chapter 3

1. Průšek, p. 3.

2. Ibid., p. 4.

3. *Midnight* was published in 1933. Mao Dun intended it to be a macroscopic portrait of modern capitalist society in urban Shanghai. By this time, he had long since distanced himself from the May Fourth legacy, apropos of which he observed in an 1931 essay: "The discovery of *ren*, that is, the promotion of individuality or individualism, was one of the main goals of the modern literary movement in the 'May Fourth' period" (see "Guanyu 'chuangzuo,' " in *Mao Dun quanji*, p. 19, 266). As discussed below, Hu Shi and Zhou Zuoren, as well as many of those who began to reject individualism as early as the late 1920's, shared this mainstream view of May Fourth literature.

4. For an earlier study of the significance of the individual in May Fourth literature, see also Lee, *Romantic Generation*.

5. Like some of the other concepts analyzed in this book, the notion of *geren zhuyi* is treated here strictly as a translingual idea. Its English equivalent "individualism" will not be used as an essential category of analysis, but as part of the Chinese etymology through translation. In combing through many of the studies on individualism in the China field across disciplines, I found that the etymology of the word has been consistently ignored, with the result that "individualism," however defined, becomes an arbitrary category of analysis applicable to all times and all places. For example, in *Individualism and Holism: Studies in Confucian and Taoist Values*, edited by Donald Munro, the concept of individualism is used as a technical (universal) term and a given value, despite its avowed origin in the West,

to provide a common basis of comparison between East and West. The trouble is that the traces of history cannot be erased so easily by the presence of an essential category. The contending views of "individualism" in this collection testify to the tremendous difficulties encountered in applying Western "technical" terms to the study of Chinese philosophy. For instance, whereas the majority of the essays seem to take the dialectic of individualism and holism for granted, Chad Hansen's "Individualism in Chinese Thought" and "Punishment and Dignity in China" argue strongly against the possibility of individualism in Chinese culture. Interestingly, though, both argument and counterargument regarding the existence of individualism in China collaborate in privileging a Eurocentric mode of thinking. Indeed, it is extraordinary to me that such a question was raised in the first place.

6. See Chapter 8 for a discussion of the importance of the *Compendium*.

7. Hu Shi, "Dao yan," 1: 28. For a critique of the ungendered "individual," see p. 171.

8. Zhou Zuoren, "Ren de wenxue," pp. 29–30.

9. Thomas Metzger's analysis (p. 197) of what he calls the ethos of traditional Chinese interdependence exemplifies the ways in which "evidence" can be constructed and deployed to prove contrary points. "Absorbed by the spectacle of the Chinese failure, we could easily accept the interpretation of her traditional orientations as stagnative, particularistic, authoritarian, and pathological. Any indigenous ideas not fitting in with this pattern could be dismissed as epiphenomenal rhetoric. Trying now to explain her success, however, we are beginning to see how this very rhetoric functioned as part of the behavioral situation, articulating and molding the sentiments of solidarity."

10. In a sense, the old meaning of the word *ji* continues to exist in connection with Neo-Confucianism and related scholarship, although it is increasingly mediated through the newly established equivalence between *ji* and the English word "self," or other foreign words, in the process of translingual practice. The complexity of this situation has huge implications for those of us engaged in comparative scholarship. To give an example, Gao Yihan used *xiaoji* and *daji* respectively to translate Bernard Bosanquet's notion of "self" and "greater self" (from *Philosophical Theory of the State*, chap. 6) in an early essay entitled "Zizhi yu ziyou" (Autonomy and freedom) published by *New Youth* in 1916. In this essay he followed the common practice of his time: namely, he placed the foreign original in parentheses following the Chinese word (p. 1).

11. Chen Jia'ai, p. 36. All English translations in this chapter are mine unless otherwise indicated.

12. Lee, "In Search of Modernity," p. 111.

13. Blumenberg, p. 33*n*6.

14. I wish to stress this historical difference, because to measure the Chinese experience of modernity with the yardstick of the Western Enlightenment is to downplay the history of imperialism.

15. In Meiji Japan, *kanji* terms such as *jiga* (Chinese *ziwo*) and *kojin* (*geren*) were used to translate "self" and "individual," respectively. According to Yu Liming (pp. 87–88), *ziwo* first appeared in classical Chinese as a result of Buddhist transla-

tions in the Six Dynasties, but *wo* was used as a verb in the two-character phrase. In another quote Yu provides, *ziwo* comes close in meaning to *ziji* and *zishen*. However, the equivalence of *ziwo* and "self" should not be assumed until we begin to investigate what modern translations have done to these words in Chinese and Japanese.

16. Jia Yi, p. 9.

17. Russell, *Problem of China*, p. 215.

18. See Li Zehou, *Zhongguo xiandai sixiang shi lun*, pp. 7–49; and Schwarcz.

19. The intellectual tradition of the European Enlightenment is itself fraught with heterogeneous elements and counterdiscourses. For instance, the critique of modernity has always been part of the Enlightenment legacy from the Romantics to Nietzsche, Marx, Heidegger, Horkheimer, Adorno, Foucault, Derrida, and even Habermas.

20. Gan, p. 70.

21. Cascardi, p. 179; see esp. his chapter "The Subject and the State."

22. Lu Xun, "Wenhua pianzhi lun" (Concerning imbalanced cultural development), in *LXQJ*, 1: 186–87; trans. Jon Kowallis.

23. Ibid., p. 185. Lu Xun's deviation from the mainstream discourse on "wealth and power" in the late Qing period should help correct Marston Anderson's earlier description of modern Chinese intellectuals (*Limits of Change*, p. 3): "Increasingly challenged by the West, they [Chinese writers] scanned Europe's diverse cultural weave for the strand that held the secret of its 'wealth and power'; in their haste they eagerly seized on the isms by which Westerners categorized their own tradition." Anderson's observation is largely accurate when it comes to the ethos of the dominant group of intellectuals, but many others such as Lu Xun were concerned more with the moral well-being of the Chinese when they seized on certain isms than with the state's "wealth and power." In *Chinese Intellectuals in Crisis*, Hao Chang (Introduction) argues against seeing the problems of Chinese intellectuals as exclusively political and social and urges us to take their ethical concerns seriously. That does not mean, of course, that these concerns can always be returned to Confucianism. Take the case of Chinese anarchism studied by Dirlik (*Anarchism*, p. 48), who observes a multidimensional relationship between nationalism and anarchist movements. The anarchist presence "suggests that this discourse [nationalism] is not reducible to a one-dimensional defensive or parochial search for 'wealth' and 'power.'" As he points out, the term *wuzhengfu zhuyi*, first used in 1903 in Chinese, derives from the Japanese *kanji* translation of "anarchism" (p. 83).

24. See Barshay, pp. 55–56.

25. Fujii, p. 10.

26. For a study of earlier discussions of individualism, see Schwartz, *In Search of Wealth and Power*; Chang, *Liang Ch'i-chao*; and Zheng.

27. For a survey of the political events (warlordism, government corruption, imperialist invasion, etc.) between 1911 and 1919 that underlie Du's attitude toward the Republican Revolution of 1911, see Tse-tsung Chow, *May Fourth Movement*. See also Schwartz, *Reflections on the May Fourth Movement*.

28. Du Yaquan (writing as Cang Fu), "Geren zhi gaige," p. 2.

29. Ibid., p. 3.

30. See *Xinmin shuo* in Liang Qichao, *zhuanji* (topics), 3: 4.1–162; and *Ziyou shu*, ibid., 2: 2.1–123. See also Chang, *Liang Ch'i-chao*.

31. Said, *The World, the Text, and the Critic*, p. 237.

32. Min Zhi, p. 16. The influence of Yan Fu's translation of Huxley's *Evolution and Ethics* is clearly discernible in Min Zhi's argument.

33. Jia Yi, pp. 7–8. Individualism is translated in this article as *gewei zhuyi* rather than the usual *geren zhuyi* probably because it evokes a corresponding sociological (scientific?) term, *geren benwei zhuyi* (doctrine of the individual unit).

34. Max Stirner expounded a theory of extreme individualism in *Die Einzige und sein Eigentum* (The ego and his own); this work was introduced into China at the turn of the century and became widely popular among the Chinese anarchists. For the role of Chinese anarchism in the propagation of individualism, socialism, and other revolutionary ideas in this period, see Dirlik, *Anarchism*, esp. chap. 4. An allusion to Stirner's theory of individualism in the essay "Wenhua pianzhi lun" (*LXQJ*, 1: 186), quoted earlier, reveals Lu Xun's indebtedness to early anarchist thinking.

35. Du Yaquan (writing under the pseudonym Gao Lao), "Geren yu guojia zhi jieshuo," p. 2. Du Yuquan frequently wrote under the names Gao Lao and Cang Fu.

36. Humboldt's formulations about the limits of the state are contained in his classic work *Ideen zu einem Versuch die Grenzen der Wirksamkeit des Staats zu bestimmen* (Ideas on an attempt to define the limits of the state's sphere of action).

37. Tse-tsung Chow, "Anti-Confucian Movement in Early Republican China," p. 312.

38. Gao Yihan, "Guojia fei rensheng," p. 7. In this particular article, the author uses the word *xiaoji* alone but with the implication that *daji* is its antithetical counterpart. In another essay, "Zizhi yu ziyou" (Autonomy and freedom), Gao used both terms as translations of Bosanquet's notions of "self" and "greater self" (see note 10 to this chapter).

39. Hu Shi later took up this dialectic in an essay entitled "Bu xiu" (Immortality) but, for him, the greater self stands for *shehui* (society) rather than the state.

40. Li Yishi, p. 5.

41. Chen Duxiu, "Dong xi minzu genben sixiang zhi chayi," p. 284.

42. Li Dazhao (writing under the pseudonym Shou Chang), "Qingchun Zhonghua zhi chuangzao."

43. See Hu Shi, "Wenxue gailiang chuyi," and "Jianshe de wenxue geming lun."

44. Zhou Zuoren, "Ren de wenxue," p. 195.

45. See Chapter 6 for a detailed discussion of this literature. See also my Ph.D. dissertation, "Politics of First-Person Narrative."

46. The "autobiographical subject" is a narratological term and refers to the autodiegetic narrator *within* the text rather than the author. For the distinction between homodiegetic and autodiegetic narratives in the first-person, see Genette, chap. 5.

47. For a study of the relationship between Russian and modern Chinese writers, see Ng.

48. Hu Shi, "Bu xiu," p. 101.

49. Fu, p. 15.

50. Wang Xinggong, pp. 2–3.

51. Chen Duxiu, "Xuwu de geren zhuyi ji ren ziran zhuyi," p. 4.

52. Deng Feihuang.

53. See Dirlik, *Origins of Chinese Communism.*

54. The word *puluo* is the Chinese transliteration of the English "proletariat." As with most such Chinese transliterations, for example, "democracy" (*demokelaxi*; Japanese: *minshu*; Chinese loanword: *minzhu*) and "bourgeoisie" (*bu'erqiaoyasi*; Japanese: *shisan kaikyū*; Chinese loanword: *zichan jieji*), this transliteration coexisted with the Japanese loanword translation *wuchan jieji* (*musan kaikyū*) and was soon replaced by it. See Appendix F.

55. For an interesting exchange on this issue in 1928, see Huang Yaomian; and Shi Heng.

56. Cheng Fangwu, p. 169. This essay was written in 1923 and first published in the Feb. 1928 issue of *Chuangzao yuekan* (Creation monthly). Of course, it was not uncommon for traditional Chinese fiction to incorporate some elements of class awareness. In fact, the best classical fiction always explores the problem of social hierarchy, such as *Jin Ping Mei, Water Margin,* and particularly, *The Dream of the Red Chamber.* But it was not until the rise of Marxian criticism that classical works began to be interpreted in terms of class. Li Xifan and Lan Ling, for example, were among the first to apply Marxian criticism to the study of *The Dream of the Red Chamber* and other classical texts.

57. Lu Xun, "Geming shidai de wenxue," *LXQJ,* 3: 422. See Chapter 7 for a more detailed discussion of this body of literary criticism.

58. See "Si qu le de A Q shidai" (The age of Ah Q is dead), in Qian Xingcun (A Ying), *Xiandai Zhongguo wenxue zuojia,* pp. 1–53.

59. For a discussion of Jiang Guangci and his involvement with the Sun Society, see C. T. Hsia, p. 259. See also my dissertation, "Politics of First-Person Narrative," pp. 189–98. *Shaonian piaobo zhe* was first published by Yadong tushu guan in 1926 and is now included in *Jiang Guangci wenji.* A prolific writer and an active member of the Sun Society, Jiang contracted pneumonia and died in 1931 at age 30.

60. Huters, "Ideologies of Realism in Modern China," esp. pp. 159–62.

Chapter 4

1. For a discussion of narrative conventions in premodern Chinese fiction, see Plaks.

2. Cao, *Story of the Stone,* 1: 101. The Chinese original (Cao, *Honglou meng,* 1: 30) reads:

黛玉一見，便大吃一驚，心下想到："好生奇怪，倒象在那里見過一般，何等眼熟到如此！

3. For discussions of free indirect style, see Ullman; Lips; Lethcoe; Spitzer; McHale; and Cohn.

4. Cao, *Traum der Roten Kammer*, p. 45.

5. The adoption of the modern punctuation system in various twentieth-century editions of *Honglou meng* seeks to accentuate this stylistic feature by putting direct quotation within quotation marks.

6. Perhaps a somewhat closer analogy would be Ezra Pound's free translation of Li Po, which helped revolutionize the language of poetry in modern English.

7. Lao She, *Luotuo xiangzi* (Camel Xiangzi), p. 31, James trans., p. 25. The original text reads:

他放了心，緩緩的走着，自要老天保佑他，什麼也不怕。走到什麼地方了？ 不想問了，雖然田間已有男女來作工。走吧，就是一時賣不出駱駝去，似乎也沒大關係了；先到城里再説，他渴想看見城市，．．．

This novel was originally serialized in the periodical *Yuzhou feng* (Celestial winds) from September 1936 to May 1937. The edition I use here is the eighth edition published in 1949 by the Culture and Life Publishing House in Shanghai. I adopt Jean M. James's English translation *Rickshaw*, substituting the *pinyin* forms for her Wade-Giles romanizations. Hereinafter cited in the text, with page number of the Chinese original given first, followed by the page number in the translation in italics.

8. Ding Ling's story "A Mao guniang" (A girl named Ah Mao) is an earlier example of such narrative of desire in which the protagonist finds herself caught up between urban culture and rural ways of life (Ding Ling, *Ding Ling xiaoshuo xuan*, 1: 83–123). Mao Dun, Shen Congwen, and other writers have consistently explored the ambivalent meanings of Chinese modernity by dramatizing the irreconcilable difference between these two modes of life in their fiction. But it seems to me that none of their works takes the problem of individualism to such great lengths as does Lao She's novel.

9. See Joseph Lau, "Naturalism in Chinese Fiction," *Literature East and West* 2 (1970): 150; as quoted in David Wang, p. 144.

10. See David Wang, pp. 144–56.

11. Incidentally, there are twelve attributive clauses in the original introduced by recurrent *de* particles, or what Edward Gunn (p. 89) would call "Euro-Japanese syntax" in modern Chinese literary language.

12. Strand, p. 38.

13. To mention a few, the novel in Lukács's early study (1920) is understood as a genre that seeks to give form to the modern age "in which the extensive totality of life is no longer directly given," as compared with the epic, and "in which the immanence of meaning in life has become a problem, yet which still thinks in terms of totality" (p. 56). Later theoretical works—Auerbach's *Mimesis*, Ian Watt's *The Rise of the Novel*, Wayne Booth's *Rhetoric of Fiction*, Genette's *Narrative Discourse*, Cohn's *Transparent Minds*, and Barthes's *S/Z*, and Bakhtin's *Dialogic Imagination*, to cite a few familiar titles—have vastly transformed our understanding of the problem of literary representation in the novel. Bakhtin's study of the stylistics of

the genre of the novel has taught us that it is not "the image of a man in his own right, but a man who is precisely the *image of a language* that the novel represents" (*Dialogic Imagination*, p. 336).

14. Rosenberg, p. 30.

15. Marston Anderson, *Limits of Realism*, p. 7. In a recent study of modern fiction, Peng Xiaoyan (p. 4) chooses to reconsider the problem of realism in relation to the Chinese pursuit of utopia throughout the twentieth century.

16. After the publication of *Camel Xiangzi*, the manuscript remained in the possession of Tao Kangde, former editor of *Yuzhou feng*, where the novel was first serialized, until it was confiscated by Red Guards during the Cultural Revolution. In 1982 it was rediscovered among the "confiscated goods" in the Shanghai Library by Ding Jingtang. For an account of this manuscript and a study of the novel's editions and revisions, see Ding's "Lao She *Luotuo Xiangzi* yuangao."

17. See Lao She, "*Lao She xuanji zixu*" (Author's preface to *Selected Works of Lao She*), in Zeng Guangcan and Wu Huaibin, 2: 630–31.

18. See Shi Chengjun; and also Xu Lin.

19. Shi Chengjun believes the new editions are improvements on the old ones.

20. Jean M. James's English translation restores the missing chapters by using a Hong Kong reprint of one of the pre-1955 editions. Both James and Strand misread "Ruan" as "Yuan."

21. David Wang, p. 156.

22. Not everybody is concerned about the realism of Lao She's novel. Evan King's 1945 English version of the novel, called *Rickshaw Boy*, for example, does something rather drastic. More daring than the Chinese revisions of the 1950's, this translation invents characters, cuts and rewrites the novel, and even provides a happy ending that allows Xiangzi and Xiao Fuzi to escape from the grim reality and achieve freedom. For a critique of this ending, see Fan Jun.

23. For example, Strand (p. 282) criticizes Lao She's harsh treatment of politicians, such as the Nationalist labor organizer Ruan Ming. Out of a desire to correct the novel's supposedly biased view, he says:

> To the degree that Lao She's deft portrayals of politicians like Yuan [*sic*] Ming and Siye resemble the images polemicists created for their adversaries in the 1920s, one can appreciate both the opportunism rampant in city politics and the underlying quest for a moral center present among activists and ordinary citizens. However, Lao She's loathing for modern politics, a sentiment shared by many of its contemporaries who saw politicians as "bureaucratic gangsters" or worse, obscures the points at which popular aspirations, traditional political motifs, and modern ideology fit together in urban China in the 1920s.

Anticipating Strand's critique, the *xinban* editions also eliminate the passages that portray Ruan Ming's revolutionary activity in a negative light and significantly change the original wording whenever Ruan Ming's name is mentioned. For a detailed discussion of these passages and the cuts in the *xinban* editions, see Shi Chengjun.

24. The second mention of "rickshaw" still belongs to the narrator's own vo-

cabulary, because it would not be characteristic of a rickshaw puller to use abstract political terms like *ziyou* (free) and *duli* (independent).

25. For the distinction between a narrative voice and a narrative point of view, see Genette.

26. Erich Kahler's *Inward Turn of Narrative* gives a good historical overview of how European fiction underwent this internalizing process in the past centuries. Although the same process "spilled over" to modern Chinese fiction at the turn of the twentieth century, it remains yet to be seen what it means for a novelist like Lao She to write about the inner experience of a laborer.

27. After Xiangzi's arrival at Mr. Cao's home, for example, the narrator describes the ways in which he *figures out* his situation there: "When food and living quarters are agreeable and the work is not exhausting, you don't lose anything by getting yourself well taken care of. He certainly would not have eaten that well if he had spent his own money on food. Well, then, since the food was provided and it wasn't the sort that gagged you, why not eat your fill for free? Food cost money; now there was an account he knew how to add up" (pp. 65, 59). Passages like this abound in the novel.

28. James's rendering of the last sentence is a mistranslation. *You yiben zhang* does not mean "to have a bill due" but "to have an account balance."

29. See Bakhtin, *Dialogic Imagination*, p. 247.

30. Watt, p. 63.

31. For the author's account of his life at the University of London between the fall of 1924 and the summer of 1929, see Lao She, "Dongfang xueyuan" (Oriental institute), in Zeng Guangcan and Wu Huaibin, 1: 135–40; "Wo de jige fangdong" (My landlords), ibid., pp. 129–34; "Du yu xie" (Reading and writing), in Hu Jieqing, pp. 377–86; "Wo zenyang xie *Lao Zhang de zhexue*" (How I came to write *The Philosophy of Lao Zhang*), ibid., pp. 3–9; "Wo zenyang xie *Er Ma*" (How I came to write *Mr. Ma and Son*), ibid., pp. 15–21; "Wo zenyang xie *Xiaopo de shengri*" (How I came to write *Xiaopo's Birthday*), ibid., pp. 22–30.

32. Lao She, "Wo de 'hua'" (My "words"), in Wu Huaibin and Zeng Guangcan, p. 583.

33. See David Wang, pp. 126–27, 189–90. In fact, during the same period that Lao She was working on *Camel Xiangzi*, he wrote a short story called "Xin Hamuliete" (New Hamlet; 1936). In 1942, he wrote a play called *Guiqulaixi* (Homecoming), originally titled *Xin Hamuliete* (New Hamlet). He decided to change the title because he did not want his audience to mistake the Chinese transliteration of Hamlet's name for some fancy Western medicine, such as *asipilin* or aspirin (which does not have a Chinese calque). See Lao She, "Xianhua wode qige huaju" (Idle words on seven of my plays), in Hu Jieqing, pp. 118–19.

34. The Chinese original is more colloquial than the English translation and, therefore, closer to Xiangzi's own language.

35. Lao She discusses his use of the Beijing dialect in "Wo zenyang xie *Luotuo Xiangzi*" (How I came to write *Camel Xiangzi*), in Hu Jieqing, p. 70. For more detailed discussion of his use of this dialect, see "Wo zenyang xuexi yuyan" (How I learned my language), ibid., pp. 139–47.

36. Lao She, "Wo zenyang xie *Luotuo Xiangzi*" (How I came to write *Camel Xiangzi*), in Hu Jieqing, pp. 68–69.

37. For a discussion of Li Jinghan's work, see Strand, pp. 21, 30.

38. Strand, p. 36.

39. "Peking in the Eighties," in Werner, p. 167, as cited in Strand, p. 24.

40. In *Er Ma* (Mr. Ma and son), an early novel set in London, Lao She's narrator makes a curious allusion to Robinson and Friday when he describes the first encounter between Li Zirong, a student entrepreneur who has lived in London for some years, and Ma Wei, the protagonist who just arrives from China; see Lao She, *Lao She wenji*, 1: 466.

41. Earlier in the novel, Mr. Cao is described as a self-styled socialist and aesthetician, someone who has come under the influence of William Morris. According to the narrator, this university professor "had no deep opinions about government and art but he did have one good point: what he believed in could actually be acted upon in the small affairs of everyday life. He seemed to have realized that he had no talent that would astonish mankind and enable him to perform some earthshaking deed, and so he arranged his work and household according to his own ideals. Even though his ideals added nothing to society, at least he spoke and acted toward the same end and didn't go around passing off bravado as ability. He paid close attention to small matters as if to say that he needed only to regulate this little household; society could do as it liked. Still, sometimes he was ashamed of himself and sometimes he was pleased. He apparently saw his household as a small oasis of green in a desert. It could offer a little water and a little food only to those who came there; it had no greater significance" (pp. 66–67, 60–61). Could the narrator's mixed tone of admiration and mockery for Mr. Cao be Lao She's own self-portrait as a novelist and university lecturer in the 1930's? Much in the same way as Mr. Cao sympathizes with Xiangzi in the condescending manner of a left-leaning intellectual, so Lao She provides an ambivalent space for a lower-class laborer to establish his own claim on the reader's attention.

42. Bakhtin, *Dialogic Imagination*, pp. 262–63.

43. I was not sure whether this particular driver had read Lao She's novel or seen the film version of it. Although the difference between reading and viewing should be properly registered in an age of mass media, I want to emphasize that the notions of elite literature, mass culture, and popular culture should be carefully rethought before being applied to the Chinese situation. *Camel Xiangzi*, for example, is widely read by elite intellectuals, professionals, and workers, as well as the urban lower classes in mainland China.

Chapter 5

1. Yu Dafu, "Riji wenxue" (Diary literature), in *Yu Dafu quanji*, 4: 115.

2. Kahler, p. 21.

3. Lu Xun, "Kuangren riji," in *LXQJ*, 1: 9. Trans. from *Selected Stories of Lu Hsun*, p. 7.

4. For a detailed analysis of Lu Xun's contrastive use of the classical and literary languages in this story, see Yi-tsi Mei Feuerwerker, "Text, Intertext, and the

Representation of the Writing Self," pp. 167–77; and Lee, *Voices from the Iron House*, p. 54. See also my Ph.D. dissertation, "Politics of First-Person Narrative," pp. 42–46.

5. For a detailed study, see Jingyuan Zhang, *Psychoanalysis in China*. See also idem, "The First Chinese Translation of Sigmund Freud"; and Lin Jicheng.

6. For a discussion of Lu Xun's widely known translation of Kuriyagawa Hakuson's *Kumon no shōchō* (The symbols of repression), see Jingyuan Zhang, *Psychoanalysis in China*, pp. 59–68. See also Lee, *Voices from the Iron House*, pp. 33, 92; and Marston Anderson, "Lu Xun's Facetious Muse."

7. For a discussion of Freudian dream imagery in Lu Xun, see Carolyn T. Brown, "Lu Xun's Interpretation of Dreams," in Brown, pp. 67–79; and Marston Anderson, "Lu Xun's Facetious Muse," esp. pp. 260–68. For Pan Guangdan's psychoanalytical reading of Feng Xiaoqing, see his *Feng Xiaoqing: yijian yinglian zhi yanjiu*. Recently, Pan's study has been re-edited and reprinted under the sensational title *Feng Xiaoqing xing xinli biantai jie mi*. For a study of the life and work of the Ming woman poet Feng Xiaoqing in English, see Widmer; for a full-length study of Zhang Jingsheng, see Leary.

8. Guo Moruo, 5: 13–28.

9. These include an essay by Cheng Fangwu that appeared in the same journal (*Chuangzao jikan*, 1.4: 6–11) as well as a piece of criticism by a person named She Sheng (pen name) in *Xue deng*, published on Oct. 2, 1922.

10. "Piping yu meng," in Guo Moruo, 10: 116.

11. See Yan Jiayan's Introduction to *Xin ganjue pai xiaoshuo xuan*, pp. 33–36; and idem, *Zhongguo xiandai xiaoshuo liupai shi*, p. 134.

12. Lee, "In Search of Modernity," pp. 130, 131.

13. Zhou Zuoren, "Ren de wenxue," 1: 197.

14. A word of explanation is in order for the term "fantastic" as I use it here. Todorov's distinction between the uncanny, the fantastic, and the marvelous is interesting, but not very useful for my discussion of the relationship between Freudianism and fantastic literature, because his definition of these terms hinges on the narrator's manipulation of the readers' expectation in plot construction. My use of the term "fantastic" is a rough translation of the Chinese term *zhiguai*. For a discussion of this and related genres in English, see Plaks.

15. Shi Zhecun's fame as a writer of fiction has recently been revived by Yan Jiayan, who discusses his work mainly in association with a group of modernist writers known as the *xin ganjue pai* (Neo-perceptionists) in Shanghai, including Liu Na'ou, Mu Shiying, Du Heng, Dai Wangshu, and others. See Yan's Introduction to *Xin ganjue pai xiaoshuo xuan*, pp. 1–38. According to Yan, the term "Neo-perceptionists" applies to a group of Japanese writers of the 1920's who espoused German expressionism, dadaism, French surrealism, and Anglo-American modernism and decided to create a comparable modernist tradition in their own literature with emphasis on interiority and the unconscious. For a more recent discussion of Shi's work in English, see Lee, "In Search of Modernity," esp. pp. 129–31.

16. See Shi Zhecun, "Modao" (Sorcery), in *Meiyü zhi xi* (An evening in the plum rain), p. 49; hereinafter cited in the text.

17. Breton, p. 5.

18. Suleiman, *Subversive Intent*, p. 107.

19. For a discussion of this story, see Jones.

20. For a psychoanalytical notion of the uncanny, see Freud, "The Uncanny."

21. Freud, *Interpretation of Dreams*, p. 277.

22. Freud, *Dora*, p. 32.

23. Marcus, p. 278; as quoted in Suleiman, p. 128.

24. There is a vast body of scholarship and critical studies on Freud and psychoanalysis. See, e.g., Marcuse; Deleuze and Guattari; Certeau, *Heterologies*; and Derrida, *Postcard*.

25. The Tang classical *chuanqi* tale brought the *zhiguai* tradition to a new pinnacle of artistic achievement. One thinks of such well-known stories as "Ren Shi zhuan" (The story of Mrs. Ren) and "You xianku" (Visit to the cave of the immortals), although not all *chuanqi* tales have a supernatural component. "Li Wa zhuan" (The story of Courtesan Li Wa) is a case in point. To understand the Chinese concepts of *qi* and *guai*, one must stretch the notion of the fantastic to include a full range of meanings from the marvelous to the types of unfamiliar experience that one may loosely call strange or unusual. As Andrew Plaks (p. 351) points out, "In the Chinese context the term *ch'i* [*qi*] covers a semantic range that, in addition to the patently marvelous, may also refer to that which is 'odd.'"

26. For a discussion of the early beginnings of the *zhiguai* tale, see Kenneth J. DeWoskin, "The Six Dynasties *Chih-kuai* and the Birth of Fiction," in Plaks, pp. 21–52. For its later development, see Judith Zeitlin's study of Pu Songling.

27. In an earlier discussion of this story, Leo Lee (*Xin ganjue pai xiaoshuo xuan*, p. 5) also stresses the symbolic presence of these literary texts.

28. See Freud, chap. 6, "The Dream-Work," in *Interpretation of Dreams*.

29. I am stretching Genette's term as defined in *Narrative Discourse* to describe an interpretive situation here. "Heterodiegesis" refers to the relative position of the narrator who speaks from outside the fictional world which s/he recounts. A homodiegetic narrator would speak from within that world and be considered part of it.

30. The tension between love and friendship is one of the author's favorite subjects. "Shi Xiu," a Freudian rewriting of an episode from *Water Margin*, which Shi Zhicun wrote shortly before this, depicts the torment of love that the protagonist feels for the wife of his sworn brother.

31. For a more recent discussion of the influence of Freud and the Japanese "I-novel" on Yu's writing, see Xu Zidong. For a discussion of the Japanese I-novel in English, see Miyoshi.

32. In his preface to a collection that includes "Huanxiang ji" (Reminiscences on a homebound trip), Yu Dafu described his writing as a blend of *sanwen* (familiar prose) and *xiaoshuo* (fiction). However, the *Compendium of Modern Chinese Literature* arbitrarily classifies "Reminiscences on a Homebound Trip" and its sequel as *sanwen* while assigning Yu's other works from the same story collection to the category of *xiaoshuo*.

33. Yu Dafu, "Huanxiang ji" in *Yu Dafu quanji*, 2: 19. All translations are mine; hereinafter cited in the text.

34. Incidently, this erotic imagination is also reflected in the patriotic fervor of the protagonist in "Sinking," whose troubled love for women and the motherland reveals a Freudian displacement. For a discussion of this tale, see Rey Chow, pp. 138–45.

35. Yu Dafu, "Huanxiang houji" (A sequel to "Reminiscences on Returning Home"), in *Yu Dafu quanji*, 2: 5; hereinafter cited in the text.

36. See Barlow, Introduction, in Ding Ling, *I Myself Am a Woman*, p. 26.

37. The main cause of this charge is his earlier story "Sinking," in which the protagonist peeps at his landlord's daughter while she is bathing and later overhears a couple making love in an open field.

38. Lee, "The Solitary Traveler: Images of the Self in Modern Chinese Literature," in Hegel and Hessney, p. 290.

39. Egan, p. 212.

40. De Man, *Rhetoric of Romanticism*, p. 71.

Chapter 6

1. Benveniste, p. 224; hereinafter cited in the text.

2. Silverman, p. 128.

3. A typical question raised in that regard is whether an autobiographical tradition comparable to that in the West existed in classical Chinese literature. To me, this kind of question reveals more about the Eurocentric impasse of comparative literature than the presence of a genuinely interesting problem. It is similar to such questions as Does China have an epic tradition? Does tragedy exist in Chinese literature? Regardless of the answer, the questions themselves are meaningful only if something called Western literature is taken as a norm for all literatures. Wu Peiyi's *Confucian's Progress* is a recent example of how the old question of have or have-not continues to be debated in sinological studies. This chapter is also a major rethinking of my earlier position on modern Chinese narrative in my Ph.D. dissertation "Politics of First-Person Narrative."

4. Of all literatures written in inflected languages, the French writer Alain Robbe-Grillet's *nouveau roman La Jalousie* probably comes closest to overcoming the formal constraints imposed by his native tongue. One often-celebrated innovation in his novel is the attempt to avoid any marks of self-referential address by the narrator. The result, of course, is a perfect formalistic parody of the I-centered psychological novel, but the author can do only so much against the limits of his language. He cannot, for example, go out of his way to eliminate the grammatical subject of his sentences without committing a capital crime against the French language, whereas this is precisely what someone writing in Chinese language can do easily within the wide range of stylistic possibilities opened by the nonexistence of verb conjugations.

5. To help those who have difficulty imagining the linguistic situation, let me risk a less than perfect analogy with imperative mood in English. Take, for example, imperative sentences such as "Let's go for a walk" and "Come and stay with us." The subject in each case is implied but not stated, and the verb retains its infinitive form. In fact, it would be impossible to restore the formal subject to

the first sentence, because it was never there to begin with. As far as the second example is concerned, one could add the pronoun "you" to obtain an effect of emphasis but, under ordinary circumstances, the presence of the second-person pronoun is redundant. By a slight stretch of the imagination, one can infer roughly how a non-inflected language works in that regard. In Chinese languages, an ordinary statement makes perfect sense without a grammatical subject, and in certain situations, the adding of a subject would create redundancy or absurdity, such as in the analogous examples of "You come and stay with us" or "(We, you?) let's go for a walk."

6. See Spivak, "Can the Subaltern Speak."

7. For a discussion of Shen Congwen's interest in marginal people, such as rustic women, the lower class, and ethnic minorities, see Kinkley.

8. For a biographical study of Shen Congwen, see Kinkley. For the circumstances of this particular story, see David Wang, pp. 284–86.

9. David Wang, p. 222.

10. See my discussion of the feminine *ta* in Chapter 1.

11. Shen Congwen, "Sange nanren he yige nüren" (Three men and a woman), in *Shen Congwen xiaoshuo xuan*, p. 229; Kai-yu Hsü's translation in Lau et al., p. 256. Hereinafter cited in the text, with page number of the Chinese original given first, followed by the page number in the translation in italics.

12. I find Teresa de Lauretis's (p. 5) expression useful in illuminating this situation.

13. The beancurd shop owner's possible involvement in the macabre event is foreshadowed in an earlier scene. When watching a public execution, the crippled bugler asks the young man whether he is scared by the sight of the dead bodies. "The young man's response was the same smile," recalls the narrator, "so kind and at the same time so mystifying. It made us feel happy about our friendship, just like hearing the voice of that young girl, which made us feel that our lives had been fulfilled" (pp. 233; *258*). Death, sexual desire, and the fulfillment of their lives all converge at this point.

14. For example, in another story called "Deng" (The lamp; *Shen Congwen xiaoshuo xuan*, pp. 154–74), Shen's narrator also plays with the convention of storytelling. For a translation of this story by Kai-yu Hsü, see Lau et al., pp. 237–46.

15. *Yecao* (Wild grass), in *LXQJ*, 2: 170;. trans. from Lu Xun, *Complete Poems*, p. 171.

16. "*Yecao* yingwen yiben xu" (Preface to the English translation of *Wild Grass*), in *LXQJ*, 4: 356; as quoted in Lu Xun, *Complete Poems*, p. 256. Lu Xun repeated this idea in an essay entitled "Wo he *Yu si* de shizhong" (My involvement with *Yu si* from the beginning to end), in *LXQJ*, 4: 166.

17. In "Xingfu de jiating" (A happy family; 1924), a story also included in the *Pang huang* collection, Lu Xun ridiculed the notion of the bourgeois nuclear family with good humor by depicting a fiction writer who dreams of a modern family that would consist of a happy couple. Not only would they marry for love, but "their marriage contract would contain over forty clauses going into great detail, so that they would have extraordinary equality and absolute freedom.

Moreover they would both have had a higher education and belonged to the cultured élite. . . . Since Japanese-returned students were no longer the fashion, so let them be Western-returned students" (*LXQJ*, 2: 36; trans. from *Selected Stories of Lu Hsun*, pp. 157–58, with minor modifications).

18. Lu Xun, "Shang shi," in *LXQJ*; 2: 130; trans. from *Selected Stories of Lu Hsun*, p. 215, with slight changes in wording. The romanization of Chinese names has been converted from Wade-Giles to pinyin. Hereinafter cited in the text, with page number of the Chinese original given first, followed by the page number in the translation in italics.

19. See, e.g., Lu Xun's essay "Nala zouhou zenyang" (After Nora leaves home), *LXQJ*, 1: 268–74, which was originally a speech delivered to students at Beijing Women's Normal College on December 26, 1923. See also Hanan, p. 71.

20. Lee, *Voices from the Iron House*, p. 88.

21. As Leo Lee has pointed out, the solitary journey or "the solitary traveler" is a prominent image in modern Chinese fiction; see his "The Solitary Traveler: Images of the Self in Modern Chinese Literature," in Hegel and Hessney.

22. For studies of Ding Ling's life and work in English, see Yi-tsi Mei Feuerwerker, *Ding Ling's Fiction*; and Tani E. Barlow's Introduction to Ding Ling, *I Myself Am a Woman*.

23. Yi Zhen, "Ding Ling nüshi" (Miss Ding Ling) in Yuan Liangjun, *Ding Ling yanjiu ziliao*, p. 223.

24. Mao Dun, "Nü zuojia Ding Ling" (Woman writer Ding Ling), in Yuan Liangjun, *Ding Ling yanjiu ziliao*, p. 253.

25. Qian Qianwu, "Ding Ling," in Huang Ying, pp. 185–206.

26. For a discussion of the legacy of romantic love and its related background, see Lee, *Romantic Generation*, esp. chap. 13, "The Journey of Sentiment," and chap. 14, "The Romantic Heritage."

27. For recent discussions of this female tradition, see Larson, "The End of *Funü Wenxue*"; and idem, "Female Subjectivity and Gender Relations"; Lydia Liu, "Invention and Intervention"; Rey Chow; and Meng Yue and Dai Jinhua.

28. See Yi-tsi Mei Feuerwerker, *Ding Ling's Fiction*, p. 28.

29. "Shafei nüshi de riji," in *Ding Ling xiaoshuo xuan*, p. 44; trans. follows version by Tani E. Barlow in Ding Ling, *I Myself Am a Woman*, pp. 49–81. Phrases and words are occasionally recast from the original and in comparison with A. L. Chin's earlier version in Isaacs, pp. 129–69. Hereinafter cited in the text, with page number of the Chinese original given first, followed by page number in the translation in italics.

Ding Ling published a sequel in *Wenxue* (Literature, 1.4 [1933]) five years later. Entitled "The Diary of Miss Sophia, Part II," this work cannot compare with the earlier work. None of the earlier psychological insights and richness is to be seen. The diary writer admits that she can no longer produce the kind of writing she did before. The author's adherence to the cause of proletarian literature may have taken a toll on her creative talent.

30. Incidently, Colette's *La Vagabonde*, a French feminist novel narrated in the first person, also begins with a narcissistic mirror scene and ends with the nar-

rator's diary-like letters to the lover whom she rejects in pursuing freedom and integrity of female selfhood. The two texts have a lot in common, revealing a number of striking features characterizing female writing.

31. For a discussion of this aspect of the Europeanized style in modern Chinese writing, see Gunn, pp. 239–40.

32. See Fanon.

33. Yi-tsi Mei Feuerwerker, *Ding Ling's Fiction*, p. 48.

34. See Ding Ling, *I Myself Am a Woman*, p. 355n1.

35. It would be interesting to speculate whether Sophia is not twisting the meaning of *Peony Pavilion* to suit her own needs. If gender in "The Diary of Miss Sophia" is explicitly linked with the act of reading and writing, what is the status of reading as represented in the classical play possibly overlooked by Sophia? In Scene 7 of *Peony Pavilion* ("the schoolroom scene") preceding the heroine's fatal visit to the garden, a series of comic exchanges between the schoolteacher Chen Zuiliang on the one hand and his young student Liniang and Chunxiang the maid on the other centers on the interpretation of the *Book of Songs*. This scene of female education begins when the teacher explicates the meaning of a poem from the classic to his young female student. He starts out by quoting the famous poem: "Guan-guan cries the ospreys / On the islet in the river. / So delicate the virtuous maiden / A fit mate for our Prince," and then offers a canonical interpretation of the poem as follows: "Of all Six Classics, / the *Book of Songs* is the flower / with 'Airs' and 'Refinements' most apt for lady's chamber: for practical instruction" and "in every verse an edifying homily / to 'fit a maid for husband and family.' " He concludes by invoking Confucius: " 'The *Songs* are three hundred, but their meaning may be expressed in a single phrase': no more than this: 'to set aside evil thoughts,' / and this I pass to you" (Tang Xianzu, *Peony Pavilion*, p. 26; Birch's translation). However, Liniang and Chunxiang take no interest whatsoever in his allegorical commentary and insist on a literal interpretation of the poem; that is, they read it as a lyric about love and mating. When Chunxiang asks, "What sort of cry is that?" or "What is he seeking from her?" Chunxiang offers a reading that effectively subverts an established exegetical tradition that dominated the interpretation of that particular poem for centuries. It is worth recalling that the incidents that subsequently happen to Liniang (her romantic encounter with Liu Mengmei in the dream after the visit in the garden as well as her lovesickness) are directly attributable to this initial moment of subversive reading of the classics.

It does not follow, however, that the gendered reading we find in the play exists to establish a woman's point of view, although the latter can be inferred from the text. The situation is greatly complicated by the fact that the subversive act of interpretation voiced through the female characters was not new to the Ming literati. It was part of a much larger philosophical discourse on *qing* and *li* that was raging in the Ming dynasty. Moreover, given the inferior status of the popular form of drama in the overall hierarchy of classical literature, the gendered reading of the poem from the *Book of Songs* within the play is particularly significant in that it embodies the voice of popular forms of literature and, in so doing, ridicules the time-honored tradition of allegoresis represented by the figure of the schoolteacher. That being the case, our reading of *Peony Pavilion*, or of any traditional text for that matter, must be carefully reconditioned by and account for the evidence of reading to be found in the text itself. Understood this way, gendered reading is no longer a matter of identifying positive or negative portrayals of women by male or female writers in a literary text, but rather a way of unraveling complex forms of staged or camouflaged opposition—often coded as feminine in traditional literati culture—to the dominant literary and intellectual practices of the time.

Chapter 7

1. Jusdanis, p. xiv.
2. See Benedict Anderson.
3. For a discussion of this problem, see Chatterjee.
4. For a historical account of different schools of modern Chinese criticism in English, see Gálik; and McDougall.
5. For a discussion of Chinese nationalism as a problem in the larger historical contexts, see Duara, *Rescuing History from the Nation*.
6. See Jameson.
7. Ahmad, *In Theory*, pp. 99–100. This criticism was published earlier as an article called "Jameson's Rhetoric of Otherness and the 'National Allegory.' " Elsewhere in his book, Ahmad also criticizes the notion of "Third World" (chaps. 1, 2, 7, 8). He dealt with the same issue in an earlier article entitled " 'Third World Literature' and the Nationalist Ideology."
8. Berman, p. 55.
9. Strich, p. 17; as quoted in Berman, p. 55.
10. Goethe, p. 18.
11. Ibid., p. 30.
12. For a study of Goethe's reception in China, see Debon and Hsia. Gálik (p. 171) dates the first appearance of the neologism *shijie wenxue* to Hu Shi's article, "Wenxue jinhua guannian yu xiju gailiang," written in 1918. But I doublechecked the original text and found that the phrase Hu Shi uses in that article is *shijie de xiju wenxue* (dramatic literature of the world). Also the page numbers cited by Gálik are wrong; they should be pp. 382–85. For Hu's article, see Zhao Jiabi, 1: 376–86.
13. Chen Duxiu, "Wenxue geming lun," in Zhao Jiabi, *Zhongguo xin wenxue daxi*, 1: 47.
14. In a later piece (1942), Zheng recalled that the article was written before the Northern Expedition when nationalist sentiment against warlordism and imperialism was raging. He hurriedly finished it, he confessed, without taking the time to think through some of the issues. See Zheng Boqi, "Ershi niandai de yimian" (One aspect of the 1920's), in Rao et al., 2: 761–62.
15. Zheng Boqi, pp. 76–77.
16. For an account of Zheng's disclaimer, see Zhang Yingjin, "Building a National Literature in Modern China," p. 15.
17. Zheng Boqi, p. 80.
18. Lu Xun, " 'Minzu zhuyi wenxue' de renwu he yunming" (The tasks and missions of 'nationalistic literature'), in *LXQJ*, 4: 246–47.

19. Duara's article "Provincial Narratives of the Nation" provides an interesting new look at the relationship between provincial and national identities in this period. The situation he describes is not only analogous but related to that in literary discourse.

20. Yu Dafu's article, "Yishu yu guojia" (Art and the state; in Rao et al., pp. 55–59), published in *Creation Weekly* seven months before Zheng's treatise, should probably be grasped in this light.

21. Guo Moruo, "Wenyi zhi shehui de shiming" (1925), in Rao et al., p. 103. My translation. In the Chinese original, the names of Dante, Treitschke, and Bismarck are given in the original language within parentheses.

22. Ibid., pp. 104–5. If one detects a dangerous move here, which would materialize in the Chinese state's unprecedented supervision of artistic and literary production in the years to come, it should not surprise us at this point. A quarter of a century later, Guo himself would become a high-ranking official in charge of deciding what should and should not be written.

23. For a discussion of nationalism and internationalism in the earlier context of Chinese anarchism, see Dirlik, *Anarchism*, chaps. 1 and 2.

24. Guo Morou, "Wenyi jia de juewu," in Rao et al., p. 121.

25. Guo Morou, "Geming yu wenxue," in Rao et al., 1: 133.

26. Zheng Boqi, p. 79.

27. See Lu Xun, "Shanghai wenyi zhi yipie" (A glimpse at Shanghai's art and literature), in *LXQJ*, 4: 228–41 (also in Rao et al., 2: 954–64).

28. Yu Dafu, "Duiyu shehui de taidu" (Attitudes toward society), in Rao et al., 2: 1071. See also his "Wuchan jieji zhuanzheng he wuchan jieji wenxue" (Proletarian dictatorship and proletarian literature), in Rao et al., 1: 146–48. Yu Dafu's split with the Creation Society was formally announced in *Shenbao* on Aug. 15, 1927; see Rao et al., 2: 1065.

29. Rey Chow, p. 111. Both Theodore Huters ("Blossoms in the Snow") and Marston Anderson (*Limits of Realism*, pp. 76–92) have remarked on the mediatory role of the ironic narrator in this story.

30. Zheng Boqi, p. 80.

31. Larson, "Female Subjectivity and Gender Relations," p. 127. See also Larson, "The End of *Funü Wenxue*."

32. Rey Chow, p. 50.

33. Ibid., p. 52.

34. Link, p. 171.

35. Ye Shengtao, "Wuru renmen de ren" (People who insult other people), in Wei Shaochang, p. 47.

36. See Zhang Yingjin, "Building a National Literature," p. 8.

37. Lu Xun, "Shanghai wenyi zhi yipie" (A glance at Shanghai's literature), *LXQJ*, 4: 229.

38. See Rey Chow, p. 55.

39. For a discussion of gender and performativity, see Butler, *Gender Trouble*.

40. This is not to deny the atrocities committed by Japanese troops against Chinese women during the war. What I am trying to do here is suggest the com-

plexities in women's experience of nationalism as borne out by the discursive practices of that period.

41. Xiao Jun, p. 129. My translation.

42. See her essay "Thoughts on March 8," in Ding Ling, *I Myself Am a Woman.*

43. Tani Barlow, Introduction, in Ding Ling, *I Myself Am a Woman*, p. 38.

44. For a study of her life and work in English, see Goldblatt.

45. Suleiman's analysis in *Subversive Intent* (pp. 11–32) of the gendered politics of marginality in French avant-garde movements illustrates this point very well.

46. Spivak, *Outside in the Teaching Machine*, p. 276.

47. See *Xiao Hong yanjiu.*

48. A notable exception is Howard Goldblatt, who refuses to treat the novel as an anti-imperialist work. For a more radical break with the nationalist reading of Xiao Hong, see the work of two women critics from mainland China, Meng Yue and Dai Jinhua, pp. 174–99.

49. Hu Feng, "Du houji" (Epilogue), p. 3 (Goldblatt's translation, p. 280), in *Sheng si chang.* Unless otherwise noted, the English translation used is that by Howard Goldblatt.

50. Lu Xun, Preface to *Sheng si chang* , p. 1. My translation.

51. Liu Fuchen, "Xiao Hong huihua suotan" (Xiao Hong as an artist), in *Xiao Hong yanjiu*, pp. 209–10.

52. Ibid., p. 210.

53. See Meng Yue and Dai Jinhua, esp. pp. 174–99.

54. Xiao Hong, *Sheng si chang*, pp. 70, 53. Unless otherwise noted, the English translation used is that by Howard Goldblatt and Ellen Yeung in *The Field of Life and Death and Tales of Hulan River.* In this quote, I leave *sheng* and *si* untranslated to retain the ambiguity of these words. Hereinafter cited in the text, with the page number of the Chinese original cited first, followed by the page number in the translation in italics.

55. Xiao Jun, p. 4.

56. Qiu Jin (1875–1907) was a young female martyr who died for the Republican revolution. For studies of her life and work in English, see Rankin, "Emergence of Women at the End of the Ch'ing"; Spence, pp. 83–93; and Ono, pp. 59–65. For Qiu Jin's own works, see *Qiu Jin ji.*

57. Mao Dun, Preface to Xiao Hong, *Hulan he zhuan*, p. 10; Goldblatt's translation, pp. 289–90.

58. Goldblatt, p. 78.

59. Xiao Hong, "Shimian zhi ye" (Night of insomnia), in Xiao Hong, *Daibiao zuo*, p. 59.

60. Xiao Hong, *Hulan he zhuan*, p. 174; Goldblatt's translation, p. 174. The novel was finished in Hong Kong on December 20, 1940, and published posthumously.

61. In an autobiographical piece, "Yongyuan de chongjing he zhuiqiu" (Perpetual dream and pursuit; see Xiao Hong, *Daibiao zuo*, pp. 3–4), the author describes her father as a man totally devoid of human compassion and decency. He was an influential scholar and powerful landlord in Hulan, who despised his daughter and often beat her. Xiao Hong's mother was also cruel to her. The only

family member that loved her was her grandfather, but he was powerless and virtually an outcast in the family.

62. Xiao Hong, "Chu dong" (Early winter), in Xiao Hong, *Daibiao zuo*, p. 7.

63. Indeed, it was not only in her writing that Xiao Hong engaged with the contending discourses fought out on the symbolic terrain of the female body. Her own life consisted of a long series of desperate attempts to sort out the meaning of being a woman and Chinese. She had fled from her tyrannical father long before she and Xiao Jun escaped from Japanese-occupied Manchuria. In the subsequent years she spent with Xiao Jun in Shanghai and elsewhere, she had the misfortune of being repeatedly abused and physically assaulted by him. When she could no longer bear his violence, she often ran away. Once, she went so far as to leave China for Japan in order to avoid Xiao Jun for a period of time. Given the deteriorating relationship between the two countries in 1936, the choice of Japan as her country of sojourn invites a symptomatic reading. Whatever reasons might lie behind it, her choice indicates a strong desire to protect her body and mind from male domination even if it means exile from her homeland and loneliness in the enemy country.

64. As I note in my article "Invention and Intervention," women critics in mainland China have recently begun to use words like "female literature" and "female tradition" to reclaim women's works from male-centered criticism.

Chapter 8

1. The bookshop was founded in 1917 and was one of the oldest Japanese bookstores in Shanghai. For a study of Uchiyama Kanzō, see Ozawa; P. Scott; and Fogel, "Japanese in Shanghai." See also Uchiyama, *Ro Jin no omoide*; Koizumi; Zhao Jiabi, "Neishan shudian liangxiongdi," in his *Shu bi ren changshou*, pp. 292–98; and Xue Suizhi, "Lu Xun yu Neishan Wanzao" (Lu Xun and Uchiyama Kanzō), and Wang Baoliang, "Lu Xun xiansheng yu Neishan shudian" (Mr. Lu Xun and the Uchiyama Bookstore), both in Liu Xianbiao and Lin Zhiguang, pp. 227–41, 242–46, respectively.

2. Lu Xun first met Uchiyama in December 1927 at the bookstore after he relocated to Shanghai and moved to a nearby neighborhood. Lu Xun was an incurable bibliophile and avid reader. According to the monetary transactions recorded in his diary, between the years 1928 and 1935 his average annual spending on books in this bookstore alone ranged from 600 to 2,400 *yuan* (see Xue Suizhi, "Lu Xun yu Neishan Wanzao," in *Liu Xianbiao and Lin Zhiguang*, p. 231). The friendship between Lu Xun and Uchiyama grew to the extent that Lu Xun visited the place almost daily. If he failed to show up because of illness, Uchiyama would send an inquiry or pay a visit to him. Uchiyama also helped Lu Xun and his family escape to the British concession when the Japanese attacked Shanghai on Jan. 28, 1932. On numerous occasions when the secret police threatened Lu Xun, Uchiyama found hiding places for him and his family or let them stay in his own house. For one such occasion, see Lu Xun, "Hou ji" (Afterword), in *LXQJ*, 6: 360. In 1935 when Uchiyama published a book on contemporary China, Lu Xun wrote a

preface for it. This book was rendered into Chinese by You Bingqi as *Yige Riben ren de Zhongguo guan* (A Japanese perspective on China); see "Neishan Wanzao zuo *Huo Zhongguo de zitai* xu" (Preface to Uchiyama Kanzō's *Image of a Living China*), in *LXQJ*, 6: 209–11.

3. Uchiyama's book (see previous note) grew out of those conversations.

4. For the sake of personal safety and convenience, Lu Xun asked his correspondents to send their mail to "Zhou Yucai, c/o Uchiyama Bookstore." Prior to this, he had used the Beixin Book Company on Fourth Avenue as his mailing address. The letters he wrote after April 1932 contain numerous references to the Uchiyama Bookstore as his new address; see, e.g., letters no. 330, 337, 396, 399, and 406, in Lu Xun, *Shuxin ji*, 1: 302–61. Also, in his essay "Kan Xiao he 'kan Xiao de renmen' ji" (On meeting Shaw and those who met him) written in February 1933, Lu Xun mentioned a telegram received at the Uchiyama Bookstore from the Reform Society inviting him to a reception in honor of George Bernard Shaw's visit to Shanghai (Lu Xun, *LXQJ*, 4: 379).

5. See Zhao Jiabi, "Bianji yijiu," p. 172.

6. In a reminiscence commemorating his late friend Jin Yi, Zhao mentioned that he was one year older than Jin, who died at age 50 in 1959. If this information is reliable, then Zhao himself must have been born in 1908. I have not been able to verify this date. See Zhao Jiabi, "He Jin Yi zai yiqi de rizi," p. 120.

7. See Zhao Jiabi, "Lao She he wo" and "Huiyi Yu Dafu." See also his "Huiyi Zheng Zhenduo" and "Huiyi Zheng Boqi."

8. Zhao Jiabi, "Bianji yijiu," p. 172. All translations are mine unless otherwise noted.

9. Zhao Jiabi, "Hua shuo *Zhongguo xin wenxue daxi*," p. 167. Next to serialized works in journals, the generic category of *congshu*, or book series in a mass mode of production, is one of the most important aspects of literary publishing and other humanities publishing in twentieth-century China. Zhao's book series had to compete with some of the most popular *congshu* of the time by major publishers as well as obscure presses. For instance, Wang Yunwu, who became director of the Commercial Press in the early 1930's, was publishing his well-known Renwen shengwuxue luncong (Humanities and biology series) at the time.

10. See Link; and Rey Chow, esp. chap. 2.

11. The circumstances of the publication of Ding Ling's unfinished autobiographical novel *Mother*, to be described below, also speak eloquently of how "serious" literature got marketed and sold, and made a profit for the publisher.

12. Link, pp. 14–15.

13. Zhao Jiabi, "Hua shuo *Zhongguo xin wenxue daxi*," pp. 166–67.

14. Qian Xingcun (A Ying) [Zhang Ruoying], *Zhongguo xin wenxue yundong shi ziliao*, pp. 1–2. See also Liu Fu [Liu Bannong], *Chuqi baihua shigao* (Early Vernacular Poetry), in *Bannong zawen erji*, p. 353.

15. Qian Xingcun (A Ying), *Zhongguo xin wenxue yundong shi ziliao*, p. 1.

16. See Gong Mingde, "Ba Jin *Jia* de xiugai" (Ba Jin's revisions of *Family*), in idem, pp. 246–63.

17. Wen-hsin Yeh, "Progressive Journalism and Shanghai's Petty Urbanites:

Zou Taofen and the *Shenghuo Weekly, 1926–1945*," in Wakeman and Yeh, p. 191. For a study of the readership for fiction and journalism in modern China, also see Lee and Nathan.

18. The quote comes from a letter addressed to Yao Ke on Nov. 5, 1933; see letter no. 504, in Lu Xun, *Shuxin ji*, 1: 431.

19. The society issued a ban on films made by Tian Han, Xia Yan (Shen Rui-xian), Jin Yan, Hu Ping, and a few others, and forbade theaters in Shanghai to show them; see Lu Xun, "Houji" (Afterword) to *Zhun fengyue tan* (Wind and moon talks permitted), in *LXQJ*, 5: 321–23.

20. Lu Xun gave a detailed description of these related acts of violence perpe-trated against the Liangyou Company in ibid., as well as in his "Zhongguo wentan shang de guimei" (Devils in the Chinese literary field), in *LXQJ*, 6: 123–24. Mao Dun also mentioned these memorable events in 1933 in his "Yijiusansi nian de wenhua 'weijiao' he 'fan weijiao,'" p. 1. See also Zhao Jiabi, "Hua shuo *Zhongguo xin wenxue daxi*," p. 163; and idem, *Bianji shengya yi Lu Xun*, pp. 11–12.

21. On the circumstances of her arrest and imprisonment, see Ding Ling, "Wangliang shijie"; Zhang Weifu; Yuan Liangjun, *Ding Ling yanjiu wushi nian*; and idem, *Ding Ling yanjiu ziliao*.

22. In *Shu bi ren changshou*, Zhao claimed that Lu Xun was the one who urged him to advertise and publish Ding Ling's unfinished novel (p. 6). There is no doubt that Lu Xun was gravely concerned about Ding Ling's life and even risked his own life to show support for the rescue action. But I take Zhao's claim with a grain of salt because, as my analysis shows below, this is clearly a case of commercial interests and politics coinciding in the perceived contingency of the moment.

23. Lu Xun also wrote an elegiac poem mourning her presumed death; see Chen Shuyu, "Lu Xun he Ding Ling" (Lu Xun and Ding Ling), in Yuan Liangjun, *Ding Ling yanjiu ziliao*, pp. 86–89; and Zhao Jiabi, *Shu bi ren changshou*, pp. 66–67.

24. Ding Ling had started the novel with the intention of having it serialized in *Dalu xinwen* (Continental news) in 1932, but the newspaper was closed down within twenty days of the date the first installment was to appear. Zhao Jiabi inter-vened at this point and offered Ding Ling a contract with the Liangyou Company. Upon finishing each new chapter, she sent it to Zhao, which explains the location of the manuscript at the time of her arrest. Prior to this, Ding Ling had already published a short story, "Fawang" (The net of law), in Zhao's Ten-Cent Book Series; see Zhao Jiabi, *Shu bi ren changshou*, pp. 61–62.

25. See Zhao Jiabi, *Shu bi ren changshou*, p. 67.

26. My rough estimate of the gross income brought in by the 8,000 copies sold within the first six-month period would be around 7,200 *yuan* based on the fixed rate of 90 cents per copy for the clothbound editions of Zhao's series. One can also get a sense of the financial success of this enterprise through Zhao's transactions with Ding Ling's relatives in Hunan, who flooded his office with letters request-ing a share of the royalties upon hearing the news. In a letter to Zhao Jiabi on Jan. 22, 1934, Lu Xun advised Zhao not to send money to all that had requested it, but only an initial installment of 100 *yuan* to Ding Ling's mother, with subsequent payments to be made only after receiving a letter in her own handwriting. Lu Xun

also enclosed the mailing address of Ding Ling's mother; see letter no. 561, in Lu Xun, *Shuxin ji*, 1: 482.

27. Before he published this book with the Liangyou Company, Shen had published several reminiscent pieces in newspapers, some of which eventually went into the book, such as his "Ding Ling shizong" (The disappearance of Ding Ling), published in *Dagong bao*, June 12, 1933; and "Ji Ding Ling nüshi" (Memoir on Ms. Ding Ling) in *Guowen zhoubao* a month later. Shen Congwen had been close friends with Ding Ling and Hu Yepin, but they began to drift apart as Ding and Hu became more and more radical. The memoir further and permanently ruptured the relationship between the two; see Yuan Liangjun, *Ding Ling yanjiu wushi nian*, pp. 45–50.

28. The information is published on the reverse side of the title page; see Shen Congwen, *Ji Ding Ling*. On the same page, the process of government censorship is revealed in the fine print at the bottom: "Duly approved by the Newspaper and Magazine Censorship Committee of the Central Propaganda Bureau, file no. 97." Also on the last page, there is a notice by the editor: "Mr. Shen Congwen's original manuscript on Ding Ling contains 30,000 more words than we could possibly print here, and they cover up to the year of 1932. For special reasons, we were unable to publish the whole manuscript and would like to notify our readers of the circumstances" (ibid., p. 188). In a letter to Zhao Jiabi, Lu Xun also mentions the censorship of Shen's book by the Nationalist government; see letter no. 736, in Lu Xun, *Shuxin ji*, 1: 621.

29. See Zhao Jiabi, "Huiyi wo biande diyibu chengtao shu," pp. 227–28.

30. The company suffered huge losses during the Japanese attack in 1937. For the reorganization of the company during the war, see Zhao Jiabi, "Huiyi Zheng Zhenduo," pp. 184–85; and "Lao She he wo," p. 118.

31. See Zhao Jiabi, "Huiyi wo biande diyibu chengtao shu," p. 227.

32. On the founding of Guanghua University, see Yeh, p. 84.

33. This is mentioned by Yu Dafu in one of his letters to Cai Yuanpei in the late 1920's; see Zhao Jiabi's appendix to "Huiyi Yu Dafu," p. 43.

34. Zhao Jiabi, "Huiyi wo biande diyibu chengtao shu," pp. 227–37.

35. On the Ten-Cent Book Series and the other publications by the Liangyou Company, see ibid., p. 227. The word *yijiao* puns on the monetary unit of ten cents and a corner.

36. Zhao himself wrote a critical study of contemporary American writers, including Hemingway, Faulkner, and Pearl Buck, and published it in the series; see Zhao Jiabi, *Xin chuantong*.

37. See Zhao, "Hua shuo *Zhongguo xin wenxue daxi*," p. 175.

38. This sort of information is always printed on the reverse side of the title page and occasionally appears on the advertisement page on the last page of the book.

39. See Zhao, *Bianji shengya yi Lu Xun*, pp. 63–66.

40. For example, one of Lu Xun's selections was Xiang Peiliang's "Wo likai shizi jietou" (When I left the crossroads), which could not be included because it

had been copyrighted by Guanghua (Glorious China) Book Company; see Zhao, *Bianji shengya yi Lu Xun*, pp. 69–70.

41. The two started correspondence in early 1933. Of a total of 49 letters Lu Xun wrote to Zhao, 46 survive. Zhao donated the originals to the Lu Xun Memorial Hall in Shanghai, and they were subsequently published in *Lu Xun shuxin ji*.

42. On Lu Xun's earlier involvement with Zhao's Liangyou Literary Series, see Zhao, "Huiyi Lu Xun."

43. The essay in question is "Binghou zatan" (Miscellaneous thoughts after illness), which was due to appear in issue 4.2 of *Wenxue* (Literature). For the complete essay, see *LXQJ*, 6: 128–39.

44. Letter no. 838, in Lu Xun, *Shuxin ji*, 2: 704. In fact, Zhao received two letters from Lu Xun regarding the *Compendium* bearing the date December 25. In the first one, Lu Xun agreed to write the introductory essay but requested a possible extension of time for health reasons. In the second letter, he reversed the earlier decision for reasons stated in the quote. Compare letters no. 836 and no. 838, in Lu Xun, *Shuxin ji*, 2: 702–4. Zhao believed that Lu Xun got his dates mixed up and that letter no. 838 should properly be dated December 26 instead of 25, for Huang Yuan (Huang Heqing), who brought the news to Lu Xun about the censorship of his essay in *Literature*, visited the writer on the evening of December 26, which is recorded in Lu Xun's diary and subsequently confirmed by Huang himself in a conversation with Zhao. Lu Xun could have written his follow-up letter to Zhao only after Huang's visit. I am convinced that Zhao's reconstruction of events is correct; see Zhao, *Bianji shengya yi Lu Xun*, p. 60.

45. Letter no. 906 in Lu Xun, *Shuxin ji*, 2: 766–67. The actual date of completion was March 2, 1935. The essay is also included in Lu Xun's *Qiejie ting zawen erji* (Random essays from the Midway House, vol. 2); see *LXQJ*, 6: 189–208. Critics treat it, not without good reason, as an authoritative document on May Fourth fiction.

46. According to Zhao, the meeting took place on January 2 in the reception room at the Uchiyama Bookstore; see his *Bianji shengya yi Lu Xun*, p. 62. For a similar account, see Zhao, "Huiyi Zheng Boqi," p. 231.

47. Letter no. 852, in Lu Xun, *Shuxin ji*, 2: 718.

48. It was later revealed that Zheng was sent there by the League of Left-Wing Writers to infiltrate the publishing and entertainment business of Shanghai; see Zhao, "Huiyi Zheng Boqi," p. 227. Zhao Jiabi thought that Zheng was a member of the Chinese Communist party, since he was so deeply involved with the party's underground artists and writers who penetrated Shanghai's film and literary circles in the 1930's, such as A Ying and Xia Yan. He found out from Xia Yan in 1978 that Zheng had not been a CCP member at the time.

49. See Zhao, "Huiyi Yu Dafu," pp. 33–34.

50. The event took place at the fourth convention of the League of Left-Wing Writers on Jan. 16, 1930, presided over by Zheng Boqi himself, then a member of the Standing Committee. The reason for Yu Dafu's expulsion was that he reportedly remarked to Xu Zhimo in English: "I am a writer, not a fighter." The

decision is contained in Resolution No. 6, which reads: "We must purge all oppor-
tunists and reactionaries, and it is hereby announced that Yu Dafu is expelled from
the League as of today." See "Zuoyi zuojia lianmeng disici quanti dahui buzhi"
(Supplement to the minutes of the fourth convention of the League of Left-Wing
Writers), *Hongqi ribao* (Red-flag daily), Nov. 22, 1930. In a later essay called "Wo
dui nimen que meiyou shiwang" (I am not disappointed in you), published in
Xingzhou ribao on Jan. 23, 1939, Yu himself recalled having said similar words to
Agnes Smedley. (For a study of Smedley, her publications, and her dealings with
the CCP and Chinese leftist intellectuals, see McKinnon.)

51. The quarterly folded in the winter of 1935 and was revived for a brief period
of time by Zhao at the Liangyou Company in Shanghai. Zhao and Jin Yi, the
former executive editor of *Literary Quarterly*, reshaped the original journal into a
monthly called the *Literary Monthly* in June 1936. Before the government shut it
down at the end of the year, they had published some of the best-known works in
modern Chinese literature, such as Cao Yu's *Sunrise* and Ba Jin's *Spring*, a sequel
to *Family*. Today, the legacy of this journal survives in the prestigious mainland
journal *Shouhuo* (Harvest), created by Jin Yi in 1957 and co-edited by Jin Yi and Ba
Jin. Jin Yi died of a heart attack in 1959, and Ba Jin resumed the post of editor-in-
chief of the journal after the Cultural Revolution and still remains in that capacity
at the time of my writing on Sept. 26, 1994. On the seminal role Jin Yi and Ba Jin
played in Chinese literary editing and publishing, see Zhao Jiabi, "He Jin Yi zai
yiqi de shihou."

52. Zhao, "Hua shuo *Zhongguo xin wenxue daxi*," p. 169.

53. Later, Zhao was to be annoyed by Hu Shi's open show of contempt for the
Liangyou Company. Zhao had prepared Xu Zhimo's posthumous manuscripts
for publication in collaboration with Xu's widow, Lu Xiaoman, soon after the
poet died in a plane crash. But Hu Shi persuaded Lu Xiaoman to surrender the
manuscripts to the Commercial Press and left Zhao in the lurch; see "Huiyi Xu
Zhimo he Lu Xiaoman" (Reminiscing about Xu Zhimo and Lu Xiaoman), in
Zhao, *Shu bi ren changshou*, pp. 44–58.

54. On the political persecution and martyrdom of leftist writers, see Tsi-an
Hsia.

55. Lu Xun records this and other related news item in his appendix to *Qiejie
ting zawen erji*; see *LXQJ*, 6: 361–73. For detailed documentation, see Zhang Jinglu,
Zhongguo xiandai chuban shiliao, 2: 190–254, 510–52.

56. As to how Zhao managed to overcome the hurdle of censorship, the following description should suffice. In his student days at Guanghua University,
Zhao had made friends with Mu Shiying, then a promising writer and soon to
become known as an experimental writer of metropolitan fiction commonly associated with Shi Zhicun, Liu Na'ou, and the so-called Neo-perceptionist camp (see
the discussion of Shi Zhicun in Chapter 6). Mu led a flamboyant life as a man
and writer in Shanghai and Hong Kong and offered his services to the Nationalist
party at various times. When Zhao Jiabi tried to contact the head of the Censorship Committee, Xiang Deyan, about getting prior approval for the *Compendium*,

he discovered that one of the committee members was Mu Shiying. (Mu was as-
sassinated in June 1940 when serving as the director of *Guomin xinwen* [Citizen
news], a newspaper published by the much-hated Wang Jingwei collaborationist
government in the occupied areas.) Thereupon followed a succession of deals that
involved bribery and string-pulling.

Zhao took his proposal and a list of the editors' names in person to the Censorship Committee in December 1934 and asked the clerk to forward the packet
to the head of the committee himself. Within a few days, he was visited by Mu
Shiying, who relayed Xiang Deyan's message and invited him to Xiang's house
for a chat. Xiang had a manuscript to sell and tried to negotiate a good price for it.
This was not the first time that the Liangyou Company had been blackmailed for
taking the risk of publishing leftist literature, especially since the company was
known for its greater flexibility in financial arrangements than some other publishers toward writers in dire need of cash. According to Zhao, most publishers
in those days adopted one or the other way of paying their authors and sometimes
both. Either the company would buy the rights in a manuscript from the author
by paying a fixed sum of money at the going rate for each thousand words. Or the
author would retain copyright and receive royalties figured at 10–20 percent of the
earnings on sales of the book. For example, Lu Xun was one of those outstanding
cases whose royalties were usually set at the rate of 20 percent (see Zhao, *Bianji
shengya yi Lu Xun*, p. 10).

Since Xiang Deyan was well versed in these aspects of publishing, he told Zhao
pointblank at their first meeting that he needed cash and wanted to sell the manuscript and his copyright for a lump sum. The process of negotiation was not very
smooth because, in addition to wanting the money, Xiang also harbored literary ambitions and insisted that Zhao include his collection of short stories in the
respectable Liangyou Literary Series. Zhao and his manager agreed to buy the
manuscript but refused to include it in the series. After much negotiating, Mu
Shiying suggested the next best option of printing Xiang's book in an elegant,
clothbound edition. His suggestion was adopted and helped settle the disagree-
ment. In the end, the book was published independently of the Liangyou Literary Series, under the author's pseudonym, Jiao Ren, and the title *Sanbai bashi ge*
(Three-hundred eighty songs; see Zhao, "Hua shuo *Zhongguo xin wenxue daxi*,"
pp. 175–77).

As for Zhao's proposal, Xiang started by striking out the names of Lu Xun
and Guo Moruo from the list of editors and pointed out that these names would
seriously jeopardize the chances of getting approval from the Censorship Committee for the project. After extorting 500 *yuan* from the Liangyou Company for
his manuscript, Xiang allowed Lu Xun's name to remain on the list, although
he refused to concede further on the question of Guo Moruo, because Guo "has
written articles attacking Generalissimo Chiang's person and writing. He is condemned in those documents from above, and there is nothing I can do about it"
(ibid., p. 176). There is no knowing whether Xiang would have found it possible
to do something if Zhao had agreed to publish his book in the Liangyou Liter-

ary Series. At least, under these circumstances, Zhao obtained, or more exactly bought, Xiang's promise not to tamper with the manuscripts to be submitted for censorship (ibid., p. 177).

The process of negotiation caused some delay, since Zhao had to find a substitute editor to compile the poetry volume. At the suggestion of Zheng Zhenduo and Mao Dun, he contacted Zhu Ziqing (ibid., pp. 177–78). Zhu, who was teaching at Qinghua University in Beijing, agreed to do the job at the insistence of his old friend Zheng Zhenduo, although he did not seem to know the real circumstances behind the extremely short notice he received. "That the poetry volume of the *Compendium of Modern Chinese Literature* should fall on my shoulders came as a genuine surprise," recalled Zhu Ziqing in his reflections on the poetry selection: "My friend Zheng Zhenduo recommended me, probably because I have taught some literature classes. He insisted that Mr. Zhao Jiabi lay this matter in my hands and even suggested that it'd be all right for me to get additional help if necessary. Since I was concerned that other people's involvement might complicate the matter, I decided to brace myself for the task" (Zhu Ziqing, p. 16). Zhu started his selection process in July 1935 and was able to submit the entire manuscript to the publisher on August 13.

57. According to Zhao Jiabi, the delay on A Ying's part was caused by the secret police, who had taken his father hostage in order to capture him. To avoid arrest, A Ying had to stay away from home for a period of time and was thus unable to retrieve his library materials; see Zhao Jiabi, "Hua shuo *Zhongguo xin wenxue daxi*," p. 184.

58. See Mao Dun, "Yijiusanwu nian jishi," p. 9.

59. See Zhao Jiabi, "Hua shuo *Zhongguo xin wenxue daxi*," p. 173.

60. See Zhou Zuoren, "Xiandai sanwen daolun (shang)" (Introduction to modern familiar prose, part I), and Yu Dafu, "Xiandai sanwen daolun (xia)" (Introduction to modern familiar prose, part II), in Cai et al., pp. 179–97, 199–222.

61. I mentioned in an earlier quote that Zhao Jiabi's initial plan was to publish a library of 100 canonical titles in modern Chinese literature, but he soon realized the impracticability of that idea: "To publish a hundred titles means that one must deal with a dozen publishers. Who would be so kind to grant you the permission to publish copyrighted materials? Most writers had sold their works and copyrights to the publishers for a lump-sum price under economic pressure. But even if the author retained his or her copyright and gave permission to republish, the original publisher would still not let the work be part of the Liangyou library" (Zhao, "Bianji yijiu," pp. 172–73).

62. Included in Hu Shi, *Wencun.*

63. For a discussion of these works, see Zhang Yingjin, "Institutionalization of Modern Literary History in China," pp. 351–53.

64. See Wang Zhefu, p. 95.

65. For Mao Dun's review, see "*Zhongguo xin wenxue yundong shi*," in *Mao Dun quanji*, 20: 241–48.

66. See Qian Xingcun (A Ying), *Zhongguo xin wenxue yundong shi ziliao*, p. 1. See also Zhao, "Hua shuo *Zhongguo xin wenxue daxi*," p. 171.

67. See Mao Dun, "Yijiusanwu nian jishi," p. 9. Parts of this letter are confirmed by a quote in Zhao Jiabi's essay "Bianji yijiu" (An editor's recollections), first published in *People's Daily*, Mar. 19, 1957.

68. It is worth mentioning that Mao's 1940 periodization of the Chinese revolution in *Xin minzhu zhuyi lun* (On new democratism) coincides with that found in literary histories written in the 1930's. See Mao, *Mao Zedong xuanji* (Selected writings of Mao Zedong), pp. 623–70. There are other areas outside literature where the influence of the *Compendium* can be observed. For instance, Zhang Jinglu's early writings on publishing and, to a certain degree, his authoritative research on the history of publishing in modern China were inspired directly by Zhao's work. In the opening passage of *Zai chuban jie ershi nian* (My twenty years in the publishing world, pp. 1–2), Zhang recalls:

> In the fall of 1935, "my friend" A Ying had been asked by the Liangyou Company to compile a volume of research materials for the *Compendium of Modern Chinese Literature*. At the same time, he was also in the process of editing a book series called Rare Books in Chinese Literature for the Shanghai Magazine Company. One day, I was chatting with some of my friends from the Translation Institute about the past, present, and future of the New Culture movement, in the middle of which A Ying said to me: "If one ever writes a complete history of the New Culture movement, it is important that you should not be left out of it." I was quite struck by his words and felt unworthy of his compliment. Chewing it over, I figured that what he meant was not that I had contributed much to the enlightenment project of the New Culture movement in the capacity of a writer so much as that of a publisher or practitioner who assisted in the movement. So, even though his remark was meant to flatter, I saw some truth in it. I have the self-confidence to claim that I devoted my time and energy to the development of new directions in Shanghai's publishing world from the May Fourth movement of 1919 down to the present time. That this is an ineluctable fact is something to which my progressive colleagues in the profession all bear witness, which explains why A Ying and my other friends urged me to write an autobiography to tell about the evolution and transformation of modern publishing in Shanghai, so I would leave behind some "more or less useful" materials to those who study the New Culture movement.

69. For a discussion of Li, Wang, and other PRC literary historians, see Zhang Yingjin, "Institutionalization of Modern Literary History in China," pp. 356–64. However, Zhang fails to mention the *Compendium* and the seminal role it has played in the ongoing institutionalization of modern literary history.

70. Recent writings in modern literary history continue to confront the official canon in variety of ways. They range from feminist readings of canonical texts (Meng Yue and Dai Jinhua) to the restoration of Butterfly fiction (Link, Rey Chow) as well as the rediscovery of modernist writers in Shanghai (Yan Jiayan, Leo Lee) and other previously neglected schools. I should also mention a group of critics and scholars associated with *Shanghai wenlun* (Shanghai literary theory) who

started a project called "the rewriting of literary history" in 1988, but soon had to drop the matter because of the changing political situation after the June 4 incident in 1989. That project, however, was revived in 1991 by *Jintian* (Today), a Chinese overseas journal. Thanks to the initiative of editors Li Tuo and Huang Ziping, the journal has devoted columns and special issues to the "rewriting" project on a continuing basis for over three years as of the time of this writing.

71. For example, Jeffrey C. Kinkley's *Odyssey of Shen Congwen* and David Wang's *Fictional Realism* are important contributions to this ongoing process of remapping the landscape of modern Chinese literary history initiated by Hsia in the 1960's.

72. For a critique of the Hsia-Průšek debate, see Liu Kang.

73. In fact, Zhao had plans to compile a sequel to the *Compendium* as early as 1936, but the Japanese invasion and the trouble within the Liangyou Company prevented him from carrying them out; see Zhao, *Shu bi ren changshou*, pp. 34–35.

74. Ibid., p. 35.

75. See Ding Jingtang, *Zhongguo xin wenxue daxi*. In 1989, a new multivolume compendium was brought out by Zhongguo wenlian publishing company in Beijing. Edited by Ge Luo and Liu Jianqing, this ambitious anthology is called *Zhongguo xin wenyi daxi* (A compendium of modern Chinese art and literature) and claims to cover the entire modern time divided into five periods: 1917–27, 1927–37, 1937–49, 1949–66, and 1976–82.

76. Marston Anderson, *Limits of Realism*, p. 2.

77. Shi also suggested A Ying's name for the compilation of the research volume; see Zhao Jiabi, "Hua shuo *Zhongguo xin wenxue daxi*," p. 167. On his relationship with Shi, see Zhao, "Huiyi wo biande diyibu chengtao shu," p. 232.

78. Zhao, "Huiyu wo biande diyibu chengtao shu," pp. 168–69.

79. Zheng's introduction to the volume makes no secret of this intent. See "Wusi yilai wenxue shang de lunzheng" (Debates on literature since the May Fourth), in Cai et al., pp. 53–80.

80. It is interesting that Wang Zhefu, whose work was rejected by Mao Dun, refused to see Lin Shu as a representative of the traditional camp on the exclusive basis of the classical language. "How can we treat Lin Shu's translation of *La Dame aux Camélias* as old or dead literature?" asked Wang (p. 1).

81. Cai Yuanpei, "Zhongguo de xin wenxue yundong—zongxu" (The new literary movement in China: a general introduction), in Cai et al, p. 3.

82. The journal *Xin chao*, for example, used "The Renaissance" as the English translation of its title.

83. The modern genre of literary historical writing flourished in the 1920's and 1930's. A Ying's research index, which covers the period between 1917 and 1927, gives eleven titles in Chinese literary history and thirteen in the writing of foreign literary histories. In particular, the publication of Lu Xun's *Zhongguo xiaoshuo shilüe* (An outline history of Chinese fiction; 1924, 1931), Tan Zhengbi's *Zhongguo wenxue shi dagang* (A general history of Chinese literature; 1927), and Hu Shi's *Wushi nian lai zhi Zhongguo wenxue* (Chinese literature in the past fifty years; 1924) has had a lasting impact on the twentieth-century interpretation of traditional as well as modern Chinese literature, especially vernacular works.

84. The incommensurability between the two is borne out instantly by the fact May Fourth writers depicted themselves more as crusaders against tradition than its heirs.

85. See Zhao Jiabi, *Zhongguo xin wenxue daxi*, 10: 267.

86. Zheng Zhenduo, *Chatu ben Zhongguo wenxue shi*, p. 1.

87. Zhao, "Bianji yijiu," p. 62.

88. The editors assigned for each volume are Fu Donghua (English), Zhao Jiabi (American), Li Liewen (French), Zheng Boqi (Japanese), Guo Moruo (German), Yu Dafu (Scandinavian), Dai Wangshu (Southern Europe, mainly Italian and Spanish literature), Lu Yan (Baltic nations), Geng Jizhi (Russian), and Cao Jinghua (Soviet). See Zhao Jiabi, "Bianji yijiu," pp. 63, 173–75. The censorship against Guo Moruo was no longer effective by this time, because the Censorship Committee had been shut down in 1936 following the so-called *Xinsheng* incident. The May 1935 issue of the Nationalist journal *Xinsheng* (New life) had published an article entitled "Xianhua huangdi" (Speaking of emperors), which led to a Japanese protest against the alleged insinuations against the Japanese emperor. See Si Mazu, "Xinsheng shijian gaishu" (A brief account of the *New* Life incident), in Zhang Jinglu, *Zhongguo xiandai chuban shiliao*, 2: 146–54.

89. Zhao, "Bianji yijiu," pp. 174–75.

90. But Lu Xun expressed dissatisfaction with the outcome. In a letter to Wang Yeqiu on December 4, 1935, he observed: "There are ten editors for this book, and each of us has received 300 *yuan* and additional compensation for the introductory essay calculated at the rate of 10 *yuan* per 1,000 words. Although the thing cost the publisher a fortune, some of the volumes are quite mediocre; nor do I think much of the introductory essays either" (Letter no. 1102, in Lu Xun, *Shuxin ji*, p. 917).

91. See "*Zhongguo xin wenxue daxi* Riyi ben de ku'nan jingli" (The odyssey of the Japanese translation of the *Compendium of Modern Chinese Literature*), in Zhao, *Shu bi ren changshou*, p. 265.

92. Zhao published a Chinese translation of the file that records the circumstances of the censorship (ibid., pp. 280–81).

Chapter 9

1. I am not suggesting that the English word "culture" does not have multiple or unstable meanings; of course, it does (see Raymond Williams, *Keywords*, pp. 76–82). My point is that translation is capable of *selectively* introducing meanings and equivalents that heretofore did not exist between and within the two languages.

2. See my discussion of Sino-Japanese-English neologisms in Chapter 1 and Appendix D on Japanese *kanji* terms originally derived from classical Chinese.

3. Said, *Orientalism*, p. 325.

4. Arif Dirlik's critique of culturalism from a Marxian dialectic point of view shows that, when culture is used as an autonomous notion, it "mystifies the priority of the socio-political relationships that go into its production" ("Culturalism as Hegemonic Ideology and Liberating Practice," p. 15). See also his earlier article "Culture, Society and Revolution."

5. For a discussion of Chinese Occidentalism, see Chen Xiaomei.

6. Schneider, p. 58.

7. See Furth, *Limits of Change.*

8. On Japanese ideas on national essence, see Kamei; and Hiraoka, esp. chap. 1. See also White et al.

9. We are dealing with a level of historical experience that cannot and should not be trivialized into something like xenophobia, which is said to be a universal condition, so universal that it stops being interesting as a historical problem. The idea of the "yellow peril" prevalent in the nineteenth century, for instance, had much to do with the history of colonialism and Western imperialist expansion in Asian countries, and it would be ahistorical, if not absurd, to view the Chinese protest against the imperialist presence in their country as simply an expression of Chinese xenophobia or a counterpart of the "yellow peril." Frank Dikötter argues in his recent *Discourse of Race in Modern China* that the Chinese have their own history of racial prejudices which should not be blamed on the West and that " 'the white peril' was indeed a remarkable Chinese counterpart of the 'yellow peril' fear then prevailing in the West" (p. 71). Quoting Harold Isaacs's 1967 article in *Daedalus,* he adds: "Racial prejudice among non-Europeans existed long before their exposure to the ideas of the conquering white Europeans, and . . . the charge of Western responsibility for the racial attitude of ex-colonies was only partly valid" (p. 1). My problem with this argument is that, methodologically, it confuses xenophobia with the theory of race as a historical discourse. The implied parallelism in the view that the Chinese are just as prejudiced as Westerners obscures some of the most violent moments of interaction between China and the West. For instance, how can one explain the fact that some Chinese continued to write about the dangers of themselves as *huang huo* (the yellow peril) well into the late 1980's?

10. Zhang Binglin [writing as Zhang Taiyan], "Dongjing liuxue sheng huanying hui yanshuo ci" (A speech delivered at a meeting with Chinese students in Tokyo) on July 15, 1906, in idem, *Zhang Taiyan zhenglun xuanji,* 1: 276.

11. See Rankin, *Early Chinese Revolutionaries*; Schneider; and Bernal, "Liu Shihp'ei and National Essence"; and Furth, "The Sage as Rebel." See also Rosen; Shen Songqiao; and Yue Daiyun.

12. For a critique of the Mannheim model that calls attention to the limited explanatory power of the concept of conservatism, see Schwartz, "Notes on Conservatism in General and in China in Particular," in Furth, *Limits of Change,* pp. 3–21.

13. Zhang Binglin, *Zhang Taiyan zhenglun xuanji,* 1: 276.

14. For a discussion of Liu Shipei's life and work, see Bernal, "Liu Shih-p'ei and National Essence."

15. Both neologisms were imported from Meiji Japan, where they had been translations of Western terms. For an early discussion of *guohun* in this context, see Xu Zhiheng, p. 4.

16. Schneider, p. 66.

17. See Bernal, "Liu Shih-p'ei and National Essence," pp. 96–97.

18. Huang Jie, p. 2.

19. See Harootunian; and Najita and Scheiner.

20. Deng Shi, "Guoxue zhenlun," p. 1.

21. In the early years of Meiji Japan, it was proposed that the Chinese characters be banished from Japanese in favor of a Latinized language corresponding to colloquial speech. For Japanese influence on the late Qing vernacular movement, see Shen Dizhong.

22. Zhang Binglin, "Bo Zhongguo yong wanguo xinyu shuo," p. 6.

23. For a discussion of Zhang Binglin's *xiaoxue* philological approach in English, see Furth, "The Sage as Rebel."

24. Ibid., p. 9.

25. Deng Shi, "Aiguo suibi."

26. Said, *Orientalism*, p. 21.

27. For an account of the changing circumstances at this time, see Schneider; and Bernal, "Liu Shih-pei and National Essence."

28. "*Xueheng zazhi* jianzhang" (The *Critical Review*: a statement of purpose). *Xueheng* 1, no. 1 (1922).

29. Schneider, p. 79.

30. Irving Babbitt was best known as the author of *Rousseau and Romanticism* (1919), *Literature and the American College: Essays in Defense of the Humanities* (1908), *The New Laokoön* (1910), and *The Masters of Modern French Criticism* (1912).

31. Babbitt, "Humanistic Education in China and the West," p. 91. Hu Xiansu published the translation, "Bai Bide zhongxi renwen jiaoyu tan," in *Xueheng* in March 1922. Unless otherwise indicated, all page numbers in *CR* are from the "Tong lun" (general discussion) section.

32. Mei Guangdi consistently criticized the New Culturalists for being advocates of a *wei ouhua* (fake Europeanization). See his articles "Ping tichang xin wenhua zhe"; "Lun jinri wuguo xueshu jie zhi xuyao"; and "Xianjin xiyang renwen zhuyi." See also Hu Xiansu.

33. The quote is from his phrase "zhenzheng xin wenhua zhi jianshe" (the construction of a genuine new culture; Mei Guangdi, "Ping tichang xin wenhua zhe," p. 8).

34. Lu Xun, "Suigan lu 35" (Random thoughts no. 35), in *LXQJ*, 1: 382.

35. Zhou Zuoren (writing as Zhong Mi), "Sixiang jie de qingxiang" (Intellectual trends today), in *Zhou Zuoren daibiao zuo*, p. 60. The essay first appeared in *Chenbao fukan* (Supplement to *Morning Post*), Apr. 23, 1922.

36. For a detailed discussion of the confrontation between the *National Heritage* and the *Renaissance* at Beijing University, see Shen Songqiao, esp. chap. 1.

37. Wu Mi, pp. 2–3.

38. See Shen Songqiao; and Yue Daiyun.

39. Wu Mi, pp. 13–14. Raymond Williams (*Marxism and Literature*) observes that this notion of culture, which stresses an achieved state of development, goes back to the Enlightenment itself.

40. The tremendous impact of this concept can be gauged in subsequent "xin

rujia" (new Confucianism) movements. See Tu Weiming's "Hsiung Shi-li's Quest for Authentic Experience" and Hao Chang's "New Confucianism and the Intellectual Crisis of Contemporary China," in Furth, *Limits of Change*, pp. 242–302.

41. For all its essentialist claims, the idea of new Confucianism was first imported from the West. See Hu Xiansu's 1922 translation of Irving Babbitt's essay, "Humanistic Education in China and the West," p. 12.

42. Liu Yizheng, pp. 1–2.

43. Ironically, the critique of imperialism was taken up by the New Culturalists themselves when Marxism was introduced.

44. Hu Xiansu, p. 9.

45. Liang Qichao left a vivid description of an encounter with an American reporter in his travels: "I remember chatting with a renowned American journalist by the name of Simon (he is the author of one of the most authoritative books on the subject of the War). He asked me: 'What is your plan when you return? Are you thinking of bringing some of our Western civilization back to China?' I said: 'Well, of course,' upon which he sighed and added: 'What a pity. Western civilization is gone.' I asked: 'What are you going to do with yourself back in the U.S.?' 'I am going to lock myself in and expect Chinese civilization to come and save me'" (*Ouyou xinying lu*, chap. 9, as quoted in Chen Song, pp. 365–66). These chapters first appeared in *Chenbao fukan* (Supplement to *Morning Post*), Mar. 6–Aug. 17, 1920. Oswald Spengler's book is also mentioned by Irving Babbitt ("Bai Bide zhongxi renwen jiaoyu tan," p. 4).

46. Mei Guangdi, "Ping tichang xin wenhua zhe," p. 2.

47. Mei Guangdi, "Lun jinri wuguo xueshu jie zhi xuyao," p. 7.

48. Wu Mi, p. 6.

49. Ibid., p. 14.

50. Ibid., p. 23. The material within the quotation marks is in English in the original.

51. For a critique of European philological practice and its racist exploitation of Greek civilization between 1785 and 1985, see Bernal, *Black Athena*; and Paliakov.

52. See Lu Xun, "Suigan lu 35" (Random thoughts no. 35) discussed in Chapter 2; Zhou Zuoren, "Luo Su yu guocui" (Russell and national essence), in idem, *Zhou Zuoren daibiao zuo*; and Chen Duxiu, "Xueshu yu guocui" (Scholarship and national essence), in *Duxiu wencun*, pp. 545–46.

53. For a study of Liang Shuming, see Alitto.

54. Hu Shi, "Du Liang Shuming xiansheng de *Dong xi wenhua jiqi zhexue*" (On reading Mr. Liang Shuming's *Eastern and Western Cultures and Their Philosophies*), in idem, *Wencun*, 2: 72.

55. Zhou Zuoren, "Luo Su yu guocui" (Russell and national essence), in idem, *Zhou Zuoren daibiao zuo*, pp. 9–10. The essay first appeared under the pen name Zhong Mi in *Chenbao fukan* (Supplement to *Morning Post*), Oct. 19, 1920.

Selected Bibliography

Adorno, Theodor W. *Notes to Literature.* Trans. Shierry Weber Nicholsen. 2 vols. New York: Columbia University Press, 1991.

Ahmad, Aijaz. *In Theory: Classes, Nations, Literatures.* London: Verso, 1992.

———. "Jameson's Rhetoric of Otherness and the 'National Allegory.'" *Social Text* 17 (Spring 1987): 3–25.

———. "'Third-World Literature' and the Nationalist Ideology." *Journal of Arts & Ideas* 17–18 (June 1989): 117–35.

Alitto, Guy S. *The Last Confucian: Liang Shu-ming and the Chinese Dilemma of Modernity.* Berkeley: University of California Press, 1979.

Allinson, Robert E., ed. *Understanding the Chinese Mind: The Philosophical Roots.* Hong Kong: Oxford University Press, 1989.

Althusser, Louis. *For Marx.* London: New Left Books, 1977.

Anderson, Benedict. *Imagined Communities: Reflections on the Origin and Spread of Nationalism.* Rev. ed. London: Verso, 1991.

Anderson, Marston. *The Limits of Realism: Chinese Fiction in the Revolutionary Period.* Berkeley: University of California Press, 1990.

———. "Lu Xun's Facetious Muse: The Creative Imperative in Modern Chinese Fiction." In Ellen Widmer and David Der-wei Wang, eds., *From May Fourth to June Fourth: Fiction and Film in Twentieth-Century China.* Cambridge, Mass.: Harvard University Press, 1993: 249–68.

Arakawa Sōbe 荒川惣兵衛. *Gairaigo jiten* 外来語辞典 (Dictionary of loanwords). Tokyo: Fukuyamabō, 1941.

———. *Gairaigo ni manabu* 外来語に学ぶ (Learning from loanwords). Tokyo: Shinsensha, 1980.

———. *Japanized English.* Rev. 4th ed. Tokyo: Kenkyūsha, 1931.

Auerbach, Erich. *Mimesis: The Representation of Reality in Western Literature.* Trans. W. R. Trask. Princeton: Princeton University Press, 1953.

Babbitt, Irving. "Bai Bide zhongxi renwen jiaoyu tan" 白璧德中西人文教育談 (Irving

Babbitt's discussion of humanistic education in China and the West). Trans. Hu Xiansu 胡先驌. *Xueheng* 3 (Mar. 1922): 1–12.

———. "Humanistic Education in China and the West." *Chinese Students' Monthly* 17.2 (1921): 85–91.

Bakhtin, Mikhail. *The Dialogic Imagination*. Trans. Michael Holquist and Caryl Emerson. Austin: University of Texas Press, 1981.

———. *Rabelais and His World*. Trans. H. Iswolsky. Cambridge, Mass.: MIT Press, 1968.

Bao Jing 鮑晶, ed. *Lu Xun 'guomin xing sixiang' taolun ji* 魯迅「國民性思想」討論集 (Collected discussions of Lu Xun's 'concept of national character'). Tianjin: Tianjin renmin chubanshe, 1982.

Barlow, Tani E. "Colonialism's Career in Postwar China Studies." *Positions* 1 (Spring 1993): 224–67.

———. "Theorizing Woman: *Funü, Guojia, Jiating* [Chinese women, Chinese state, Chinese family]." *Genders* 10 (Spring 1991): 132–60.

Barnard, F. M., ed. *J. G. Herder on Social and Political Culture*. Cambridge, Eng.: Cambridge University Press, 1969.

Barnett, Suzanne W. "Silent Evangelism: Presbyterians and the Mission Press in China, 1807–1860." *Journal of Presbyterian History* 49 (Winter 1971): 287–302.

Barnett, Suzanne W., and John King Fairbank, eds. *Christianity in China: Early Protestant Missionary Writings*. Cambridge, Mass.: The Committee on American-East Asian Relations of the Department of History in collaboration with the Council on East Asian Studies, Harvard University, 1985.

Barnstone, Willis. *The Poetics of Translation: History, Theory, Practice*. New Haven: Yale University Press, 1993.

Barshay, Andrew E. *State and Intellectual in Imperial Japan: The Public Man in Crisis*. Berkeley: University of California Press, 1988.

Barthes, Roland. *S/Z*. Paris: Seuil, 1970.

Befu, Harumi. "Nationalism and *Nihonjinron*." In idem, ed., *Cultural Nationalism in East Asia: Representation and Identity*. Berkeley: Institute of East Asian Studies, University of California, 1993, 107–35.

Befu, Harumi, ed. *Cultural Nationalism in East Asia: Representation and Identity*. Berkeley: Institute of East Asian Studies, University of California, 1993.

Benjamin, Walter. *Illuminations*. Trans. Harry Zohn. New York: Schocken Books, 1968.

Benveniste, Emile. *Problems in General Linguistics*. Trans. Mary Elizabeth Meek. Coral Gables, Fla.: University of Miami Press, 1971.

Berlin, Isaiah. *Vico and Herder*. London: Hogarth, 1976.

Berman, Antoine. *The Experience of the Foreign: Culture and Translation in Romantic Germany*. Trans. S. Heyvaert. Albany, N.Y.: SUNY Press, 1992.

Bernal, Martin. *Black Athena: The Afroasiatic Roots of Classical Civilization*. Vol. 1. New Brunswick, N.J.: Rutgers University Press, 1987.

———. "Liu Shih-p'ei and National Essence." In Charlotte Furth, ed., *The Limits of Change: Essays on Conservative Alternatives in Republican China*. Cambridge, Mass.: Harvard University Press, 1976: 90–112.

Bhabha, Homi K. *The Location of Culture*. London and New York: Routledge, 1994.

Bhabha, Homi K., ed. *Nation and Narration*. London: Routledge and Kegan Paul, 1990.

Birch, Cyril, ed. *Anthology of Chinese Literature*. 2 vols. New York: Grove Press, 1972.

Blumenberg, Hans. "The Concept of Reality and the Possibility of the Novel." In Richard E. Amacher and Victor Lange, eds., *New Perspectives in German Literary Criticism*. Princeton: Princeton University Press, 1979, 29–48.

Bond, Michael Harris, ed. *The Psychology of the Chinese People*. Hong Kong: Oxford University Press, 1986.

Booth, Wayne. *The Rhetoria of Fiction*. Chicago: University of Chicago Press, 1961.

Borges, Jorge Luis. *Twenty-four Conversations with Borges, Including a Selection of Poems: Interviews by Roberto Alifano, 1981–1983*. Trans. Nicomedes Suárez Araúz, Willis Barnstone, and Noemí Escandell. Housatonic, Mass.: Lascaux Publishers, 1984.

Bourdieu, Pierre. *Distinction: A Social Critique of the Judgement of Taste*. Trans. Richard Nice. Cambridge, Mass.: Harvard University Press, 1984.

———. *Homo Academicus*. Paris: Minuit, 1984.

———. *Language and Symbolic Power*. Ed. John B. Thompson; trans. Gino Raymond and Matthew Adamson. Cambridge, Mass.: Harvard University Press, 1991.

———. *Outline of a Theory of Practice*. Trans. Richard Nice. Cambridge, Eng.: Cambridge University Press, 1990.

Breton, André. *Manifestoes of Surrealism*. Trans. Richard Seaver and Helen R. Lane. Ann Arbor: University of Michigan Press, 1969.

Brower, Reuben, ed. *On Translation*. Cambridge, Mass.: Harvard University Press, 1959.

Brown, Arthur. *New Forces in Old China: An Unwelcome but Inevitable Awakening*. New York: Fleming H. Revell, 1904.

Brown, Carolyn T., ed. *Psycho-Sinology: The Universe of Dreams in Chinese Culture*. A conference report. Asian Program, Woodrow Wilson International Center for Scholars, 1987.

Burke, Peter, and Roy Porter, eds. *The Social History of Language*. Cambridge, Eng.: Cambridge University Press, 1987.

Butler, Judith. *Bodies That Matter: On the Discursive Limits of "Sex."* New York: Routledge, 1993.

———. *Gender Trouble: Feminism and Subversion of Identity*. New York: Routledge, 1990.

Cai Yuanpei 蔡元培 et al. *Zhongguo xin wenxue daxi daolun ji* 中國新文學大系導論集 (Collected introductions to the *Compendium of Modern Chinese Literature*). Shanghai: Liangyou fuxing tushu yinshua gongsi, 1940.

Cao Xueqin 曹雪芹. *Honglou meng* 紅樓夢 (The dream of the red chamber, or The story of the stone). 3 vols. Beijing: Renmin wenxue chubanshe, 1957.

———. *The Story of the Stone*. Trans. David Hawkes. 5 vols. London: Penguin Books, 1973.

———. *Der Traum der Roten Kammer: Ein Roman aus der Frühen*. Trans. Franz Kuhn. Wiesbaden: Insel-Verlag, 1959.

Carrithers, Michael, Steven Collins, and Steven Lukes, eds. *The Category of the Person: Anthropology, Philosophy, History*. Cambridge, Eng.: Cambridge University Press, 1985.

Cascardi, Anthony J. *The Subject of Modernity*. Cambridge, Eng.: Cambridge University Press, 1992.

Catford, J. C. *A Linguistic Theory of Translation: An Essay in Applied Linguistics*. London: Oxford University Press, 1965.

Certeau, Michel de. *Heterologies: Discourse on the Other*. Trans. Brian Massumi. Minneapolis: University of Minnesota Press, 1986.

Certeau, Michel de, D. Julia, and J. Revel. *Une Politique de la langue: la révolution française et les patois*. Paris: Gallimard, 1975.

Chang, Hao. *Chinese Intellectuals in Crisis: Search for Order and Meaning (1890–1911)*. Berkeley: University of California Press, 1987.

———. *Liang Ch'i-ch'ao and Intellectual Transition in China, 1890–1907*. Cambridge, Mass.: Harvard University Press, 1971.

Chatterjee, Partha. *Nationalist Thought and the Colonial World: A Derivative Discourse*. Tokyo and London: Zed Books, 1986.

Chen Bingkun 陳炳坤. *Zuijin sanshi nian Zhongguo wenxue shi* 最近三十年中國文學史 (Chinese literature in the past thirty years). Shanghai: Taiping yang shudian, 1930.

Chen Duxiu 陳獨秀. "Dong xi minzu genben sixiang zhi chayi" 東西民族根本思想之差異 (The fundamental difference between the intellectual traditions of Eastern and Western peoples). *Xin qingnian* 1.4 (1915): 283–87.

———. *Duxiu wencun* 獨秀文存 (Collected works of Duxiu). Hefei: Anhui renmin chubanshe, 1987.

———. "Wo zhi aiguo zhuyi" 我之愛國主義 (My kind of patriotism). *Xin qingnian* 2.2 (1916): 107–12.

———. "Xuwu de geren zhuyi ji ren ziran zhuyi" 虛無的個人主義及任自然主義 (Nihilistic individualism and laissez-faire theory). *Xin chao* 8.4 (1920): 637–38.

Chen Huangmei 陳荒煤, ed. *Zhongguo xin wenyi daxi* 中國新文藝大系 (A compendium of new Chinese art and literature). 20 vols. Beijing: Zhongguo wenlian chubanshe, 1989.

Chen Jia'ai 陳家藹. "Xin" 新 (The new). *Xin chao* 1.1 (1919): 35–44.

Chen Pingyuan 陳平原. *Zhongguo xiaoshuo xushi moshi de zhuanbian* 中國小説敍事模式的轉變 (The transformation of Chinese narrative modes). Shanghai: Shanghai renmin chubanshe, 1988.

Chen Shanlong 陳山龍. *Ri-Hua wailaiyu cidian* 日華外來語辭典 (Dictionary of Chinese-Japanese loanwords). Taipei: Hongrutang chubanshe, 1989.

Chen Song 陳崧, ed. *Wusi qianhou dongxi wenhua wenti lunzhan wenxuan* 五四前後東西文化問題論戰文選 (Debates on Eastern and Western cultures around the May Fourth period). Beijing: Zhongguo shehui kexue chubanshe, 1989.

Chen Xiaomei 陳小眉. *Occidentalism: A Theory of Counter-Discourse in Post-Mao China*. Oxford: Oxford University Press, 1994.

Cheng Fangwu 成仿吾. "Cong wenxue geming dao geming wenxue" 從文學革命到革命文學 (From literary revolution to revolutionary literature). In Rao Hongjing 饒鴻競 et al., eds., *Chuangzao she ziliao* 創造社資料 (Research materials on the Creation Society), vol. 1. Fuzhou: Fujian renmin chubanshe, 1985, 164–70.

Cheyfitz, Eric. *The Poetics of Imperialism: Translation and Colonization from "The Tempest" to "Tarzan."* New York: Oxford University Press, 1991.

Chinweizu, Onwuchekwa Jemie, and Ihechukwu Madubuike. *Toward the Decolonization of African Literature.* Washington, D.C.: Howard University Press, 1983.

Chmielewski, J. "Yi putao yici weili lun gudai hanyu de jieci wenti" 以葡萄一詞為例論古代漢語的借詞問題 (A study of loanwords in classical Chinese: the case of the word "grape"). *Beijing daxue xuebao: renwen kexue* 1 (1957): 71–81.

Chow, Rey. *Woman and Chinese Modernity: The Politics of Reading Between West and East.* Minneapolis: University of Minnesota Press, 1991.

Chow, Tse-tsung. "The Anti-Confucian Movement in Early Republican China." In Arthur F. Wright, ed., *The Confucian Persuasion.* Stanford: Stanford University Press, 1960, 288–312.

———. *The May Fourth Movement: Intellectual Revolution in China.* Cambridge, Mass.: Harvard University Press, 1960.

Ciyuan 辭源 (A dictionary of etymology). Rev. ed. 4 vols. Beijing: Shangwu yinshuguan, 1988.

Clifford, James. "Notes on Travel and Theory." *Inscriptions* 5 (1989): 177–88.

Clifford, James, and George E. Marcus, eds. *Writing Culture: The Poetics and Politics of Ethnography.* Berkeley: University of California Press, 1986.

Cohen, Paul A. *China and Christianity: The Missionary Movement and the Growth of Chinese Antiforeignism, 1860–1870.* Cambridge, Mass.: Harvard University Press, 1963.

———. *Discovering History in China: American Historical Writing on the Recent Chinese Past.* New York: Columbia University Press, 1984.

Cohen, Paul A., and Merle Goldman, eds. *Ideas Across Cultures: Essays on Chinese Thought in Honor of Benjamin I. Schwartz.* Cambridge, Mass.: Council on East Asian Studies, Harvard University, 1990.

Cohn, Dorrit. *Transparent Minds: Narrative Modes for Presenting Consciousness in Fiction.* Princeton: Princeton University Press, 1978.

Cooke, George Wingrove. *China: Being "The Times" Special Correspondence from China in the Years 1857–58.* London: G. Routledge & Co., 1858.

Cooley, James. "British Quaker Missionary Enterprise in West China: Its Devolution Problem." *Chinese Studies in History* 25.4 (Summer 1992): 65–82.

Cooper, R. L., ed. *Language Spread: Studies in Diffusion and Social Change.* Bloomington: Indiana University Press, 1982.

Dale, Peter. *The Myth of Japanese Uniqueness.* London: Croom Helm, 1986.

Dallenbach, Lucien. *Le Récit speculaire: essai sur la mise en abyme.* Paris: Seuil, 1977.

Debon, Günther, and Adrian Hsia, eds. *Goethe und China—China und Goethe.* Bern: Peter Lang, 1985.

de Lauretis, Teresa. *Alice Doesn't: Feminism, Semiotics, Cinema.* Bloomington: Indiana University Press, 1984.

Deleuze, Gilles, and Félix Guattari. *Anti-Oedipus: Capitalism and Schizophrenia.* Trans. Robert Hurley et al. Minneapolis: University of Minnesota Press, 1983.

de Man, Paul. *Allegories of Reading: Figural Language in Rousseau, Nietzsche, Rilke, and Proust.* New Haven: Yale University Press, 1979.

———. *Blindness and Insight: Essays in the Rhetoric of Contemporary Criticism.* Minneapolis: University of Minnesota Press, 1983.

———. *The Resistance to Theory.* Minneapolis: University of Minnesota Press, 1986.

———. *The Rhetoric of Romanticism.* New York: Columbia University Press, 1984.

Deng Feihuang 鄧飛黃. "Geren zhuyi de youlai jiqi yingxiang" 個人主義的由來及其影響 (The origin and impact of individualism). *Dongfang zazhi* 19.7 (1922): 35–46.

Deng Shi 鄧實. "Aiguo suibi" 愛國隨筆 (Patriotic miscellany). *Guocui xuebao* 33 (1909): 3–4.

———. "Aiguo suibi" 愛國隨筆 (Patriotic miscellany). *Guocui xuebao* 38 (1909): 6.

———. "Guoxue wuyong bian" 國學無用辯 (A rebuttal to the view that national learning is useless). *Guocui xuebao* 30 (1908): 1–3.

———. "Guoxue zhenlun" 國學真論 (On authentic national learning). *Guocui xuebao* 27 (1908): 1–4.

Derrida, Jacques. "Des Tours de Babel." Trans. Joseph F. Graham. In J. F. Graham, ed., *Difference in Translation.* Ithaca: Cornell University Press, 1985, 165–208.

———. *Dissemination.* Trans. Barbara Johnson. Chicago: University of Chicago Press, 1981.

———. *Of Grammatology.* Trans. Gayatri Chakravorty Spivak. Baltimore: Johns Hopkins University Press, 1976.

———. *Positions.* Trans. Alan Bass. Chicago: Chicago University Press, 1981.

———. *The Postcard: From Socrates to Freud and Beyond.* Trans. Alan Bass. Chicago: University of Chicago Press, 1987.

———. *Writing and Difference.* Trans. Alan Bass. Chicago: University of Chicago Press, 1978.

Dhareshwar, Vivek. "Toward a Narrative Epistemology of the Postcolonial Predicament." *Inscriptions* 5 (1989): 135–57.

Dikötter, Frank. *The Discourse of Race in Modern China.* Stanford: Stanford University Press, 1992.

Ding Jingtang 丁景唐. "Cong Lao She *Luotuo xiangzi* yuangao de chongxin faxian tanqi" 從老舍《駱駝祥子》原稿的重新發現談起 (The rediscovery of Lao She's *Camel Xiangzi* and related matters). *Xin wenxue shiliao* 4 (Nov. 1983): 120–28.

Ding Jintang, ed. *Zhongguo xin wenxue daxi 1927–1937* 中國新文學大系 1927–1937 (Compendium of modern Chinese literature, 1927–37). 20 vols. Shanghai: Shanghai wenyi chubanshe, 1984.

Ding Ling 丁玲. *Ding Ling xiaoshuo xuan* 丁玲小説選 (Selected short stories of Ding Ling). 2 vols. Beijing: 1981.

———. *I Myself Am a Woman: Selected Writings of Ding Ling.* Ed. Tani E. Barlow and Gary J. Bjorge. Boston: Beacon Press, 1989.

———. "Wangliang shijie: Nanjing qiuju huiyi" 魍魎世界：南京囚居回憶 (A world of demons and devils: recollections of my confinement in Nanjing). *Xin wenxue shiliao* 1 (Feb. 1987): 4–75.

Dirlik, Arif. *Anarchism in the Chinese Revolution.* Berkeley: University of California Press, 1991.

———. "Culturalism as Hegemonic Ideology and Liberating Practice." *Cultural Critique* 6 (Winter 1987): 13–50.

————. "Culture, Society, and Revolution: A Critical Discussion of American Studies of Chinese Thought." Working Papers in Asian/Pacific Studies, 1. Durham, N.C.: Asian/Pacific Studies Institute, Duke University, 1985.

————. *The Origins of Chinese Communism*. Oxford: Oxford University Press, 1989.

Du Yaquan 杜亞泉 [Cang Fu 傖父, Gao Lao 高勞]. "Geren yu guojia zhi jieshuo" 個人與國家之界說 (The boundary between the individual and the state). *Dongfang zazhi* 14.3 (1917): 1–5.

————. "Geren zhi gaige" 個人之改革 (Reforming the individual). *Dongfang zazhi* 10.12 (1914): 1–4.

————. "Jing de wenming yu dong de wenming" 靜的文明與動的文明 (Lethargic versus dynamic civilization). *Dongfang zazhi* 13.10 (1916): 1–8.

Duara, Prasenjit. *Rescuing History from the Nation: Questioning Narratives of Modern China*. Chicago: University of Chicago Press, 1995.

————. "Provincial Narratives of the Nation: Centralism and Federalism in Republican China." In Harumi Befu, ed., *Cultural Nationalism in East Asia: Representation and Identity*. Berkeley: Institute of East Asian Studies, University of California, 1993, 9–35.

Eagleton, Terry. *The Ideology of the Aesthetic*. Oxford: Basil Blackwell, 1990.

Editors of *Xueheng* (Critical Review). "*Xueheng* zazhi jianzhang" 學衡雜志簡章 (The *Critical Review*: a statement of purpose). *Xueheng* 1 (Jan. 1922): i.

Egan, Michael. "Yu Dafu and the Transition to Modern Chinese Literature." In Merle Goldman, ed., *Modern Chinese Literature in the May Fourth Era*. Cambridge, Mass.: Harvard University Press, 1977, 209–38.

Eoyang, Eugene. *The Transparent Eye: Reflections on Translation, Chinese Literature, and Comparative Poetics*. Honolulu: University of Hawaii Press, 1993.

Esherick, Joseph W. *The Origins of the Boxer Uprising*. Berkeley: University of California Press, 1987.

Fabian, Johannes. *Language and Colonial Power: The Appropriation of Swahili in the Former Belgian Congo, 1880–1938*. Cambridge, Eng.: Cambridge University Press, 1986.

————. *Time and the Other: How Anthropology Makes Its Object*. New York: Columbia University Press, 1983.

Fairbank, John, ed. *The Missionary Enterprise in China and America*. Cambridge, Mass.: Harvard University Press, 1974.

Fan Jun 樊駿. "Lun *Luotuo xiangzi* de xianshi zhuyi: jinian Lao She xiansheng bashi danchen" 論《駱駝祥子》的現實主義：紀念老舍先生八十誕辰 (On realism in *Camel Xiangzi*: commemorating Lao She's eightieth birthday). *Wenxue pinglun* 1 (1979): 26–39.

Fang, Achilles. "Some Reflections on the Difficulty of Translation." In Reuben Brower, ed., *On Translation*. Cambridge, Mass.: Harvard University Press, 1959, 111–33.

Fanon, Franz. *Black Skin, White Masks*. New York: Grove Press, 1967.

Feng Xuefeng 馮雪峰. "Lu Xun shengping jiqi sixiang fazhan de genggai" 魯迅生平及其思想發展的梗概 (An outline of Lu Xun's life and the development of his thought). *Wenyi bao* 4 (Oct. 1951): 11–12.

Feuerwerker, Albert. *The Foreign Establishment in China in the Early Twentieth-Century.* Ann Arbor: University of Michigan, Center for Chinese Studies, 1976.

Feuerwerker, Yi-tsi Mei. *Ding Ling's Fiction: Ideology and Narrative in Modern Chinese Literature.* Cambridge, Mass.: Harvard University Press, 1982.

————. "Text, Intertext, and the Representation of the Writing Self in Lu Xun, Yu Dafu, and Wang Meng." In Ellen Widmer and David Der-wei Wang, eds., *From May Fourth to June Fourth: Fiction and Film in Twentieth-Century China.* Cambridge, Mass.: Harvard University Press, 1993, 167–93.

Fodor, István. *Pallas und andere afrikanische Vokabularien vor dem 19. Jahrhundert.* Hamburg: H. Buske, 1975.

Fogel, Joshua. *The Cultural Dimension of Sino-Japanese Relations.* Armonk, N.Y.: M.E. Sharpe, 1994.

————. "The Japanese in Shanghai and the Sino-Japanese War." Paper presented at the Luce Seminar "Wartime Shanghai," University of California, Berkeley, 1994.

————. "Recent Translation Theory and Linguistic Borrowing in the Modern Sino-Chinese Cultural Context." Working Paper Series on Language and Politics in Modern China. Indiana University, East Asian Studies Center, Bloomington, Ind., 1993.

Forsythe, Samuel. *An American Missionary Community in China, 1895–1905.* Harvard East Asian Monograph 43. Cambridge, Mass.: Council on East Asian Studies, Harvard University, 1971.

Foucault, Michel. *The Archaeology of Knowledge and the Discourse on Language.* Trans. A. M. Sheridan Smith. New York: Pantheon Books, 1972.

————. *The Order of Things: An Archaeology of the Human Sciences.* New York: Random House, 1973.

Freud, Sigmund. *Dora: An Analysis of a Case of Hysteria.* New York: Collier Books, 1963.

————. *The Interpretation of Dreams.* The Standard Edition of the Complete Psychological Works of Sigmund Freud, Vols. 4–5. London: Hogarth Press, 1953.

————. "The Uncanny." Standard Edition, Vol. 17. London: Hogarth Press, 1955, 218–53.

Fu Sinian 傅斯年. "Rensheng wenti faduan" 人生問題發端 (Introduction to the problem of human life). *Xin chao* 1.1 (1919): 5–17.

Fujii, James. *Complicit Fictions: The Subject in the Modern Japanese Prose Narrative.* Berkeley: University of California Press, 1992.

Furth, Charlotte. "The Sage as Rebel: The Inner World of Chang Ping-lin." In idem, ed., *The Limits of Change: Essays on Conservative Alternatives in Republican China.* Cambridge, Mass.: Harvard University Press, 1976, 113–50.

Furth, Charlotte, ed. *The Limits of Change: Essays on Conservative Alternatives in Republican China.* Cambridge, Mass.: Harvard University Press, 1976.

Gadamer, Hans-Georg. *Truth and Method.* Trans. Garrett Barden and John Cumming. New York: Crossroad, 1982.

Gálik, Marián. *The Genesis of Modern Chinese Literary Criticism (1917–1930).* London: Curzon Press, 1980.

Gan Yang 甘陽. "Ziyou de linian: wusi chuantong zhi queshi mian" 自由的理念：五四傳統之闕失面 (The ideal of freedom: negative aspects of the May Fourth tradition). In Liu Qingfeng 劉青峰, ed., *Lishi de fanxiang* 歷史的反響 (Reverberations of history). Hong Kong: Joint Publishing, 1990, 62–81.

Gao Mingkai 高名凱. *Hanyu yufa lun* 漢語語法論 (On Chinese grammar). Shanghai: Kaiming shudian, 1948.

Gao Mingkai 高名凱 and Liu Zhengtan 劉正埮. *Xiandai hanyu wailai ci yanjiu* 現代漢語外來詞研究 (Studies of loanwords in modern Chinese). Beijing: Wenzi gaige chubanshe, 1958.

Gao Yihan 高一涵. "Guojia fei rensheng zhi guisu lun" 國家非人生之歸宿論 (The state is not the ultimate goal of human life). *Xin qingnian* 1.4 (1915): 287–94.

———. "Zizhi yu ziyou" 自治與自由 (Autonomy and freedom). *Xin qingnian* 1.5 (1916): 381–84.

Gates, Henry Louis, Jr. "Critical Fanonism." *Critical Inquiry* 17.3 (Spring 1991): 457–70.

Gates, Henry Louis, Jr., ed. *"Race," Writing, and Difference.* Chicago: University of Chicago Press, 1986.

Ge Baoquan 戈寶權. "Lu Xun shengqian 'Ah Q zhengzhuan' de waiwen yiben" 魯迅生前《阿Q正傳》的外文譯本 (Translations of Lu Xun's "True Story of Ah Q" in foreign languages published before his death). In *Lu Xun yanjiu jikan* 魯迅研究集刊 (Collected studies of Lu Xun), vol. 1. Shanghai: Shanghai wenyi chubanshe, 1979: 371–98.

Genette, Gerard. *Narrative Discourse.* Trans. Jane E. Lewin. Ithaca: Cornell University Press, 1980.

Goethe, Johann Wolfgang von. *Conversations with Eckermann.* Trans. John Oxenford. San Francisco: North Point Press, 1984.

Goldblatt, Howard. *Hsiao Hong.* Boston: Twayne Publishers, 1976.

Goldman, Merle, ed. *Modern Chinese Literature in the May Fourth Era.* Cambridge, Mass.: Harvard University Press, 1977.

Gong Mingde 龔明德. *Ba Jin yanjiu lunji* 巴金研究論集 (Studies of Ba Jin). Chongqing: Chongqing chubanshe, 1988.

Goody, Jack. *The Domestication of the Savage Mind.* Cambridge, Eng.: Cambridge University Press, 1977.

Graham, Joseph F., ed. *Difference in Translation.* Ithaca: Cornell University Press, 1985.

Grewal, Inderpal, and Caren Kaplan, eds. *Scattered Hegemonies: Postmodernity and Transnational Feminist Practices.* Minneapolis: University of Minnesota Press, 1994.

Guan, Choi Wah. *The Right Word in Cantonese.* Hong Kong: Commercial Press, 1989.

Guang Sheng 光升. "Zhongguo guomin xing jiqi ruodian" 中國國民性及其弱點 (The national character of the Chinese and its weaknesses). *Xin qingnian* 2.6 (1917): 495–505.

Guha, Ranajit, and Gayatri Chakravorty Spivak, eds. *Selected Subaltern Studies.* London: Oxford University Press, 1988.

Gunn, Edward. *Rewriting Chinese: Style and Innovation in Twentieth-Century Chinese Prose.* Stanford: Stanford University Press, 1991.

Guo Moruo 郭沫若. *Moruo wenji* 沫若文集 (Collected works of Moruo). 17 vols. Beijing: Renmin wenxue chubanshe, 1957.

Hammami, Reza, and Martina Rieker. "Feminist Orientalism and Orientalist Marxism." *New Left Review* 70 (July/Aug. 1988): 93–106.

Han Bing 寒冰. "Bo 'Ta zi de yanjiu'" 駁她字的研究 (A rebuttal to "On feminine ta"). *Xue deng*, Apr. 20, 1920.

Hanan, Patrick. "The Technique of Lu Hsün's Fiction." *Harvard Journal of Asiatic Studies* 34 (1974): 53–96.

Harootunian, H. D. *Things Seen and Unseen: Discourse and Ideology in Tokugawa Nativism*. Chicago: University of Chicago Press, 1988.

Hayford, Charles. "Chinese and American Characteristics: Arthur Smith and His China Book." In Susan Barnett and John Fairbank, eds., *Christianity in China*. Cambridge, Mass.: Harvard University Press, 1985, 153–74.

He Yubo 賀玉波. *Zhongguo xiandai nüzuojia* 中國現代女作家 (Modern Chinese women writers). Shanghai: Fuxing shuju, 1936.

Hegel, Robert, and Richard C. Hessney, eds. *Expressions of the Self in Chinese Literature*. New York: Columbia University Press, 1985.

Heidegger, Martin. *Unterwegs zur Sprache*. Verlag Günther Neskar, 1959. Trans. Peter D. Hertz. *On the Way to Language*. San Francisco: Harper & Row, 1971.

Herder, Johann Gottfried von. *Outlines of a Philosophy of the History of Man*. Trans. T. Churchill. New York: Bergman, 1966.

Hershatter, Gail. "The Subaltern Talks Back: Reflections on Subaltern Theory and Chinese History." *Positions: East Asia Cultures Critique* 1.1 (1993): 103–30.

Hevia, James. "Leaving a Brand in China: Missionary Discourse in the Wake of the Boxer Movement." *Modern China* 18.3 (July 1992): 304–32.

Hiraoka Toshio 平岡敏夫. *Meiji bungakushi shūhen* 明治文学史週辺 (The background of Meiji literary history). Tokyo: Yuseido, 1976.

Hobsbawn, Eric, and Terence Ranger, eds. *The Invention of Tradition*. Cambridge, Eng.: Cambridge University Press, 1983.

Hsia, C. T. *A History of Modern Chinese Fiction, 1917–1957*. New Haven: Yale University Press, 1961.

Hsia Tsi-an. *The Gate of Darkness: Studies in the Leftist Literary Movement in China*. Seattle: University of Washington Press, 1968.

Hu Jieqing 胡絜青, ed. *Lao She shenghuo yu chuangzuo zishu* 老舍生活與創作自述 (An account of Lao She's life and creative work in his own words). Hong Kong: Sanlian shudian, 1980.

Hu Shi 胡適. "Bu xiu" 不朽 (Immortality). *Xin qingnian* 6.2 (1919): 113–22.

———. "Dao yan" 導言 (General introduction). In Zhao Jiabi 趙家璧, ed., *Zhongguo xin wenxue daxi* 中國新文學大系 (Compendium of modern Chinese literature), vol. 1. Shanghai: Liangyou tushu gongsi, 1935, 1–32.

———. *Hu Shi wencun* 胡適文存 (Collected works of Hu Shi). 4 vols. Shanghai: Yadong tushuguan, 1924.

———. "Jianshe de wenxue geming lun" 建設的文學革命論 (Toward a constructive theory of literary revolution). In Zhao Jiabi 趙家璧, ed., *Zhongguo xin wenxue daxi* 中國新文學大系 (Compendium of modern Chinese literature), vol. 1. Shanghai: Liangyou tushu gongsi, 1935, 127–40.

———. "Wenxue gailiang chuyi" 文學改良芻議 (Suggestions for literary reform). In Zhao Jiabi 趙家璧, ed., *Zhongguo xin wenxue daxi* 中國新文學大系 (Compendium of modern Chinese literature), vol. 1. Shanghai: Liangyou tushu gongsi, 1935, 34–43.

———. "Wenxue jinhua guannian yu xiju gailiang" 文學進化觀念與戲劇改良 (The concept of literary evolution and theater reform). In Zhao Jiabi, ed., *Zhongguo xin wenxue daxi* 中國新文學大系 (Compendium of modern Chinese literature), vol. 1. Shanghai: Liangyou tushu gongsi, 1935, 376–86.

Hu Xiansu 胡先驌. "Shuo jinri jiaoyu zhi weiji" 説今日教育之危機 (The crisis of today's education). *Xueheng* 4 (1922): 1–10.

Huang Jie 黃節. "*Guocui xuebao* xu" 國粹學報序 (Preface to *National Essence Journal*). *Guocui xuebao* 1 (1905): 1–5.

Huang Shengzhang 黃盛璋. "Gu hanyu de renshen daici yanjiu" 古漢語的人身代詞研究 (A study of pronouns in classical Chinese). *Zhongguo yuwen* 127 (June 1963): 443–72.

Huang Yaomian 黃藥眠. "Fei geren zhuyi de wenxue" 非個人主義的文學 (A non-individualistic literature). In Li Helin 李何林, ed., *Zhongguo wenyi lunzhan* 中國文藝論戰 (Debates on Chinese literature and art). Shanghai: Zhongguo wenyi she, 1932, 298–302.

Huang Ying 黃英, ed. *Xiandai Zhongguo nü zuojia* 現代中國女作家 (Modern women writers in China). Shanghai: Beixin shuju, 1931.

Huters, Theodore. "Blossoms in the Snow: Lu Xun and the Dilemma of Modern Chinese Literature." *Modern China* 10.1 (Jan. 1984): 49–77.

———. "Ideologies of Realism in Modern China: The Hard Imperatives of Imported Theory." In Liu Kang and Xiaobing Tang, eds., *Politics, Ideology, and Literary Discourse in Modern China*. Durham, N.C.: Duke University Press, 1993, 147–73.

Iggers, Georg G. *The German Conception of History: The National Tradition of Thought from Herder to the Present*. Middletown, Conn.: Wesleyan University Press, 1968.

Isaacs, Harold R., ed. *Straw Sandals: Chinese Short Stories, 1918–1933*. Cambridge, Mass.: MIT Press, 1974.

Jakobson, Roman. *Language in Literature*. Ed. Krystyna Pomorska and Stephen Rudy. Cambridge, Mass.: Harvard University Press, 1987.

Jameson, Fredric. "Third-World Literature in the Era of Multinational Capitalism." *Social Text* 15 (Fall 1986): 65–88.

JanMohamed, Abdul R. *Manichean Aesthetics: The Politics of Literature in Colonial Africa*. Amherst: University of Massachusetts Press, 1983.

Jay, Martin. *Permanent Exiles: Essays on the Intellectual Migration from Germany to America*. New York: Columbia University Press, 1985.

Jia Yi 家義. "Gewei zhuyi" 個位主義 (Individualism). *Dongfang zazhi* 13.2 (1916): 6–10.

Jia Zhifang 賈植芳 et al., eds. *Wenxue yanjiu hui ziliao* 文學研究會資料 (Research materials on the Association for Literary Research). 3 vols. Zhengzhou: Henan renmin chubanshe, 1985.

Jiang Guangci 蔣光慈. *Jiang Guangci wenji* 蔣光慈文集 (Collected works of Jiang Guangci). Shanghai: Shanghai wenyi chubanshe, 1982.

Jin Hongda 金宏達. *Lu Xun wenhua sixiang tansuo* 魯迅文化思想探索 (An inquiry into Lu Xun's thoughts on culture). Beijing: Beijing shifan daxue chubanshe, 1986.

John, Mary E. "Postcolonial Feminists in the Western Intellectual Field: Anthropologists *and* Native Informants?" *Inscriptions* 5 (1989): 49–53.

Johnson, Barbara. "Taking Fidelity Philosophically." In Joseph F. Graham, ed., *Difference in Translation*. Ithaca: Cornell University Press, 1985, 142–48.

Johnson, David, Andrew Nathan, and Evelyn S. Rawski, eds. *Popular Culture in Late Imperial China*. Berkeley: University of California Press, 1985.

Jones, Andrew F. "The Violence of the Text: Reading Yu Hua and Shi Zhicun." *Positions: East Asia Cultures Critique* 2.3 (Winter 1994): 570–602.

Jusdanis, Gregory. *Belated Modernity and Aesthetic Culture: Inventing National Literature*. Minneapolis: University of Minnesota Press, 1991.

Kahler, Erich. *The Inward Turn of Narrative*. Trans. Richard and Clara Winston. Princeton: Princeton University Press, 1973.

Kamei, Shunsuke 亀井俊介. *Nihon nashonarizumu no bungaku: Meiji no seishin no tankyū* 日本ナショナリズムの文学：明治の精神の探求 (The literature of nationalism: an inquiry into the Meiji spirit). Tokyo: Kenkyūsha, 1971.

Kang Baiqing 康白情. "Lun Zhongguo zhi minzu qizhi" 論中國之民族氣質 (On the national mentality of China). *Xin chao* 1.2 (1919): 197–244.

Kang Youwei 康有為. *Wuxu bianfa* 戊戌變法 (The 1898 reform movement), vol. 2. Ed. Chinese Historical Association. Shanghai, 1953.

Kinkley, Jeffrey C. *The Odyssey of Shen Congwen*. Stanford: Stanford Universiry Press, 1987.

Koizumi, Yuzuru 小泉譲. *Ro Jin to Uchiyama Kanzō* 魯迅と内山完造 (Lu Xun and Uchiyama Kanzō). Tokyo: Tosho shuppan, 1989.

Kowallis, Jon. "*On the Power of Mara Poetry* and Other Early Wenyan Essays by Lu Xun." Unpublished manuscript, 1994.

Lao She 老舍. *Lao She wenji* 老舍文集 (Collected works of Lao She). 16 vols. Beijing: Renmin wenxue chubanshe, 1980.

―――. *Luotuo Xiangzi* 駱駝祥子 (Camel Xiangzi). Shanghai: Wenhua shenghuo chubanshe, 1949.

―――. *Mr. Ma and Son: A Sojourn in London*. Trans. Julie Jimmerson. Beijing: Phoenix Books, 1991.

―――. *Rickshaw*. Trans. Jean M. James. Honolulu: University of Hawaii Press, 1979.

Laroui, Abdullah. *The Crisis of the Arab Intellectuals: Traditionalism or Historicism?* Trans. Diarmid Cammel. Berkeley: University of California Press, 1976.

Larson, Wendy. "The End of '*Funü wenxue*': Women's Literature from 1925 to 1935." In Tani E. Barlow, ed., *Gender Politics in Modern China: Writing and Feminism*. Durham, N.C.: Duke University Press, 1993, 58–73.

―――. "Female Subjectivity and Gender Relations: The Early Stories of Lu Yin and Bing Xin." In Liu Kang and Xiaobing Tang, eds., *Politics, Ideology, and Literary Discourse in Modern China*. Durham, N.C.: Duke University Press, 1993, 124–43.

Lau, Joseph, C. T. Hsia, and Leo Ou-fan Lee, eds. *Modern Chinese Stories and Novellas, 1919–1949*. New York: Columbia University Press, 1981.

Leach, Edmund R. "Ourselves and Others." *Times Literary Supplement*, July 6, 1973, 772.

Leary, Charles. "Sexual Modernism in China: Zhang Jingsheng and 1920's Urban Culture." Ph.D. diss., Cornell University, 1993.

Lee, Leo Ou-fan 李歐梵. "In Search of Modernity: Some Reflections on a New Mode of Consciousness in Twentieth-Century Chinese History and Literature." In Paul A. Cohen and Merle Goldman, eds., *Ideas Across Cultures: Essays on Chinese Thought in Honor of Benjamin I. Schwartz.* Cambridge, Mass.: Council on East Asian Studies, Harvard University, 1990, 109–35.

———. *The Romantic Generation of Modern Chinese Writers.* Cambridge, Mass.: Harvard University Press, 1973.

———. *Voices from the Iron House: A Study of Lu Xun.* Bloomington: Indiana University Press, 1987.

Lee, Leo Ou-fan, ed. *Xin ganjue pai xiaoshuo xuan* 新感覺派小說選 (A selection of Neo-perceptionist fiction). Taipei: Yongchen wenhua shiye, 1988.

Lee, Leo Ou-fan, and Andrew Nathan. "The Beginnings of Mass Culture: Journalism and Fiction in the Late Ch'ing and Beyond." In David Johnson, Andrew Nathan, and Evelyn S. Rawski, eds., *Popular Culture in Late Imperial China.* Berkeley: University of California Press, 1985, 360–95.

Lethcoe, R. J. "Narrated Speech and Consciousness." Ph.D. diss., University of Wisconsin, 1969.

Levenson, Joseph. *Confucian China and Its Modern Fate: A Trilogy.* Berkeley: University of California Press, 1968.

Li Dazhao 李大釗 [Shou Chang 守常]. *Li Dazhao wenji* 李大釗文集 (Collected essays of Li Dazhao). Beijing: Renmin chubanshe, 1984.

———. "Qingchun Zhongguo zhi chuangzao" 青春中國之創造 (Creating a youthful China). *Chenzhong bao*, Aug. 15, 1916.

Li Helin 李何林. *Lu Xun lun* 魯迅論 (On Lu Xun). Shanghai: Beixin shuju, 1930.

Li Helin, ed. *Zhongguo wenyi lunzhan* 中國文藝論戰 (Debates on Chinese literature and art). Shanghai: Zhongguo wenyi she, 1932.

Li Tuo 李陀. "Xuebeng hechu?" 雪崩何處 (Where does the avalanche fall?). Preface to Yu Hua 余華, *Shiba sui chumen yuanxing* 十八歲出門遠行 (Leaving home at the age of eighteen). Taipei: Yuanliu, 1990, 5–14.

Li Xifan 李希凡. *"Honglou meng" pinglun ji* 紅樓夢評論集 (Critical essays on the *Dream of the Red Chamber*). Beijing: Zuojia chubanshe, 1957.

Li Yishi 李亦氏. "Rensheng weiyi zhi mudi" 人生唯一之目的 (The sole purpose of life). *Xin qingnian* 1.2 (1915): 125–32.

Li Yiyuan 李亦園 and Yang Guoshu 楊國樞, eds. *Zhongguo ren de xingge* 中國人的性格 (The character of the Chinese). Taipei: Institute of Ethnology, Academia Sinica, 1972.

Li Zehou 李澤厚. "Lüelun Lu Xun sixiang de fazhan" 略論魯迅思想的發展 (An outline study of the evolution of Lu Xun's thought). In *Lu Xun yanjiu jikan* 魯迅研究集刊 (Collected studies of Lu Xun), vol. 1. Shanghai: Shanghai wenyi chubanshe, 1979, 31–61.

———. *Zhongguo xiandai sixiang shi lun* 中國現代思想史論 (A study of modern Chinese intellectual history). Beijing: Dongfang chubanshe, 1987.

Liang Qichao 梁啓超. *Yinbing shi heji* 飲冰室合集 (Collected works from the ice drinker's studio). Shanghai: Zhonghua shuju, 1936.

Lin Jicheng 林基成. "Fuluoyide de xueshuo zai Zhongguo de chuanbo, 1914–1925" 弗洛易德的學説在中國的傳播 (The dissemination of Freudian theory in China, 1914–25). *Ershiyi shiji* 4 (Apr. 1991): 20–31.

Lin, Yu-sheng 林毓生. *The Crisis of Chinese Consciousness: Radical Anti-traditionalism in the May Fourth Era*. Madison: University of Wisconsin Press, 1979.

———. "Lu Xun geren zhuyi de xingzhi yu hanyi: jianlun 'guomin xing' wenti." 魯迅個人主義的性質與涵義一兼論「國民性」問題 (The nature and meaning of Lu Xun's individualism: also on the question of "National Character"). *Ershiyi shiji* 12 (Aug. 1992): 83–91.

Lin, Yutang. *A History of the Press and Public Opinion in China*. Chicago: University of Chicago Press, 1936.

Link, Perry. *Mandarin Ducks and Butterflies: Popular Fiction in Early Twentieth-Century Chinese Cities*. Berkeley: University of California Press, 1981.

Lips, Marguerite. *Le Style indirect libre*. Paris: Payot, 1926.

Liu Fu 劉復 (Liu Bannong 劉半農). *Bannong zawen erji* 半農雜文二集 (Random essays by Bannong), vol. 2. Shanghai: Liangyou tushu gongsi, 1935.

———. "Fang Liu Bannong" 訪劉半農 (Interview with Liu Bannong). *Shijie ribao*, Apr. 1, 1931.

———. "Ta zi wenti" 她字問題 (The problem of feminine *ta*). *Xue deng*, Aug. 9, 1920.

Liu Kang 劉康. "Politics and Critical Paradigm: Reflections on the Study of Modern Chinese Literature." *Modern China* 19.1 (Jan. 1993): 13–40.

Liu Kang and Xiaobing Tang 唐小兵, eds. *Politics, Ideology, and Literary Discourse in Modern China: Theoretical Interventions and Cultural Critique*. Durham, N.C.: Duke University Press, 1993.

Liu, Lydia H. 劉禾. "Bu touming de neixin xushi: youguan fanyiti he xiandai hanyu xushi moshi de ruogan wenti" 不透明的內心敘事：有關翻譯體和現代漢語敘事模式的若干問題 (Narrating the inner world: problems in translational and modern Chinese narrative modes). *Jintian* 3 (Fall 1994): 174–92.

———. "The Female Body and Nationalist Discourse." In Inderpal Grewal and Caren Kaplan, eds., *Scattered Hegemonies: Postmodernity and Transnational Feminist Practices*. Minneapolis: University of Minnesota Press, 1994, 37–62.

———. "Invention and Intervention: The Making of a Female Tradition in Modern Chinese Literature." In Ellen Widmer and David Der-wei Wang, eds., *From May Fourth to June Fourth: Fiction and Film in Twentieth-Century China*. Cambridge, Mass.: Harvard University Press, 1993, 194–220.

———. "The Politics of First-Person Narrative in Modern Chinese Fiction." Ph.D. diss., Harvard University, 1990.

Liu Qingfeng 劉青峰. *Lishi de fanxiang* 歷史的反響 (Reverberations of history). Hong Kong: Joint Publishing, 1990.

Liu Xianbiao 劉獻彪 and Lin Zhiguang 林治廣, eds. *Lu Xun yu Zhong Ri wenhua jiaoliu* 魯迅與中日文化交流 (Lu Xun in Sino-Japanese cultural exchanges). Changsha: Hunan renmin chubanshe, 1981.

Liu Yizheng 柳詒徵. "Lun Zhongguo jinshi zhi bingyuan" 論中國近世之病源 (On the root of China's illness today). *Xueheng* 3 (Mar. 1922): 1–11.

Liu, Yu-ning. *The Introduction of Socialism into China*. New York: Columbia University Press, 1971.

Liu Zaifu 劉再復. "Lun wenxue de zhuti xing" 論文學的主體性 (On subjectivity in literature). In *Liu Zaifu ji* 劉再復集 (Works of Liu Zaifu). Harbin: Heilongjiang jiaoyu chubanshe, 1988, 72–125.

Liu Zaifu and Lin Gang 林崗. *Chuantong yu Zhongguo ren* 傳統與中國人 (Tradition and the Chinese). Hong Kong: Joint Publishing, 1988.

Liu Zhengtan 劉正埮 et al., eds. *Hanyu wailai ci cidian* 漢語外來詞詞典 (A dictionary of loanwords in Chinese). Shanghai: Shangwu yinshuguan, 1985.

Lowe, Lisa. *Critical Terrains: French and British Orientalisms*. Ithaca: Cornell University Press, 1991.

Lu Shuxiang 呂叔湘. *Zhongguo wenfa yaolüe* 中國文法要略 (An outline of Chinese grammar). Shanghai: Shangwu yinshuguan, 1942.

Lu Xun 魯迅. *Lu Hsün: Complete Poems*. Trans. David Y. Ch'en. Tempe: University of Arizona Press, 1988.

———. *Lu Xun quanji* 魯迅全集 (Complete works of Lu Xun). 16 vols. Beijing: Renmin chubanshe, 1981.

———. *Lu Xun shuxin ji* 魯迅書信集 (Collected letters of Lu Xun). 2 vols. Beijing: Renmin wenxue chubanshe, 1976.

———. *Selected Stories of Lu Hsün*. Trans. Yang Hsien-yi and Gladys Yang. New York: Norton, 1977.

Lu Xun yanjiu jikan 魯迅研究集刊 (Collected studies of Lu Xun), vol. 1. Shanghai: Shanghai wenyi chubanshe, 1979.

Lu Yongheng 陸永恆. *Zhongguo xin wenxue gailun* 中國新文學概論 (A brief study of modern Chinese literature). Guangzhou: Kewen yinshuju, 1932.

Lukács, Georg. *The Theory of the Novel*. Trans. Anna Bostock. Cambridge, Mass.: MIT Press, 1973.

"Lun Zhongguo renmin zhi yilai xing zhi qiyuan" 論中國人民之依賴性之起源 (The origins of the dependent character of the Chinese people). *Dongfang zazhi* 1.5 (1905): 91–94.

"Lun Zhongguo zhi guomin xing" 論中國之國民性 (On the national character of the Chinese). *Dongfang zazhi* 5.6 (1908): 93–99.

Luo Changpei 羅常培. *Yuyan yu wenhua* 語言與文化 (Language and culture). Beijing: Guoli Beijing daxue, 1950.

Luo Zhufeng 羅竹風, ed. *Hanyu da cidian* 漢語大詞典 (A dictionary of Chinese). 12 vols. Shanghai: Hanyu da cidian chubanshe, 1986–94.

Ma Zuyi 馬祖義. *Zhongguo fanyi jianshi: wusi yiqian bufen* 中國翻譯簡史五四以前部分 (A brief history of translation in China prior to the May Fourth period). Beijing: Zhongguo duiwai fanyi chuban gongsi, 1984.

Mackerras, Colin. *Western Images of China*. Hong Kong: Oxford University Press, 1989.

Mair, Victor H. "Anthologizing and Anthropologizing: The Place of Non-Elite and Non-Standard Culture in the Chinese Literary Tradition." Duke University Working Papers in Asian Pacific Studies, 2. Durham, N.C.: Asian Pacific Studies Institute, 1992.

————. "Buddhism and the Rise of the Written Vernacular in East Asia: The Making of National Languages." *Journal of Asian Studies* 53.3 (1994): 707–51.

————. "East Asian Round-Trip Words." Sino-Platonic Papers, 34. Department of Oriental Studies, University of Pennsylvania, 1992, 5–13.

Mani, Lata. "Multiple Mediations: Feminist Scholarship in the Age of Multinational Reception." *Inscriptions* 5 (1989): 1–23.

Mao Dun 茅盾 [Shen Yanbing 沈雁冰]. "Du *Nahan*" 讀《吶喊》(Reading *Call to Arms*). In Le Helin, ed., *Lu Xun lun* 魯迅論 (On Lu Xun). Shanghai: Beixin shuju, 1930, 182–89.

————. *Mao Dun quanji* 茅盾全集 (Complete works of Mao Dun). 22 vols. Beijing: Renmin wenxue chubanshe, 1991.

————. "Yijiusansi nian de wenhua 'weijiao' he 'fan weijiao'" 一九三四年的文化 "圍剿"和"反圍剿" (The cultural 'siege' and the 'anti-siege' in 1934). *Xin wenxue shiliao* 4 (Nov. 1982): 1–26.

————. "Yijiusanwu nian jishi: huiyilu shiba" 一九三五年記事：回憶錄十八 (Remembered events in 1935: memoir no. 18). *Xin wenxue shiliao* 1 (Feb. 1983): 1–23.

Mao Zedong 毛澤東. *Mao Zedong xuanji* 毛澤東選集 (Selected works of Mao Zedong). Beijing: Renmin chubanshe, 1964.

Marcus, Steven. *Representations: Essays on Literature and Society.* New York: Random House, 1975.

Marcuse, Herbert. *Eros and Civilization: A Philosophical Inquiry into Freud.* Boston: Beacon Press, 1966.

Marsella, Anthony J., George DeVos, and Francis L. K. Hsu, eds. *Culture and Self: Asian and Western Perspectives.* New York: Tavistock Publications, 1985.

Masini, Federico. *The Formation of Modern Chinese Lexicon and Its Evolution Toward a National Language: The Period from 1840 to 1898.* Berkeley: University of California, Berkeley, Project on Linguistic Analysis, 1993.

Mazrui, Ali. *The Political Sociology of the English Language: An African Perspective.* The Hague: Mouton, 1975.

McDougall, Bonnie. *The Introduction of Western Literary Theory into Modern China, 1919–1925.* Tokyo: Centre for East Asian Cultural Studies, 1971.

McHale, Brian. "Free Indirect Discourse: A Survey of Recent Accounts." *Poetics and Theory of Literature* 3.2 (Apr. 1978): 249–76.

McKinnon, Janice R. *Agnes Smedley: The Life and Times of an American Radical.* Berkeley: University of California Press, 1988.

Mei Guangdi 梅光迪. "Lun jinri wuguo xueshu jie zhi xuyao" 論今日吾國學術界之需要 (On what is needed in today's national scholarship). *Xueheng* 4 (Apr. 1922): 1–7.

————. "Ping jin ren tichang xueshu zhi fangfa" 評今人提倡學術之方法 (On the methodology promoted in today's scholarship). *Xueheng* 2 (Feb. 1922): 1–9.

————. "Ping tichang xin wenhua zhe" 評提倡新文化者 (A critique of the advocates of new culture). *Xueheng* 1 (Jan. 1922): 1–8.

————. "Xianjin xiyang renwen zhuyi" 現今西洋人文主義 (Humanism in the contemporary West). *Xueheng* 8 (Aug. 1922): 1–7.

Meng Shen 夢沈. "Bo '*Ta* zi de yanjiu'" 駁《她字的研究》(A rebuttal to "On Feminine *ta*"). *Xue deng*, Apr. 25, 1920.

Meng Yue 孟悦 and Dai Jinhua 戴錦華. *Fuchu lishi dibiao* 浮出歷史地表 (Emerging from the horizon of history). Zhengzhou: Henan renmin chubanshe, 1989.

Meng Zhen 孟真. "Xinqi boruo de guoren" 心氣薄弱的國人 (The demoralized Chinese). *Xin chao* 1.2 (1919): 342–43.

Metzger, Thomas. *Escape from Predicament: Neo-Confucianism and China's Evolving Political Culture.* New York: Columbia University Press, 1977.

Miller, Andrew. *The Japanese Language.* Chicago: University of Chicago Press, 1967.

Min Zhi 民質. "Wo" 我 (I). *Dongfang zazhi* 13.1 (1916): 13–16.

Miyoshi, Masao. *Accomplices of Silence: The Modern Japanese Novel.* Berkeley: University of California Press, 1974.

Morohashi Tetsuji 諸橋轍次. *Dai Kan-Wa jiten* 大漢和辭典 (Morohashi's Chinese-Japanese dictionary). 13 vols. Tokyo: Taishukan shoten, 1955–60.

Morrison, Robert. *A Dictionary of the Chinese Language in Three Parts.* Macau: East India Company Press, 1815.

Mounin, Georges. *Les Problèmes théorique de la traduction.* Paris: Gallimard, 1963.

Munro, Donald, ed. *Individualism and Holism: Studies in Confucianism and Taoist Values.* Ann Arbor: University of Michigan Center for Chinese Studies, 1985.

Nader, Laura. "Orientalism, Occidentalism, and the Control of Women." *Cultural Dynamics* 2.3 (1989): 323–55.

Najita, Tetsuo, and Irwin Scheiner, eds. *Japanese Thought in the Tokugawa Period, 1600–1868: Methods and Metaphors.* Chicago: University of Chicago Press, 1978.

Ng, Mau-sang. *The Russian Hero in Modern Chinese Fiction.* Hong Kong: Chinese University Press, 1988.

Nietzsche, Friedrich. *The Complete Works of Friedrich Nietzsche.* Ed. Oscar Levy. 18 vols. New York: Macmillan, 1911.

————. *The Use and Abuse of History.* Trans. Adrian Collins. Indianapolis: Bobbs-Merrill, 1957.

Niranjana, Tejaswini. *Siting Translation: History, Post-Structuralism, and the Colonial Context.* Berkeley: University of California Press, 1992.

Novotná, Zdenka. "Contributions to the Study of Loan Words and Hybrid Words in Modern Chinese." 3 pts. *Archiv Orientalni* 35.3 (1967): 613–48; 36.1 (1968): 295–325; 37.1 (1969): 48–75.

O'Hanlon, Rosalind. "Recovering the Subject: *Subaltern Studies* and Histories of Resistance in Colonial South Asia." *Modern Asian Studies* 22.1 (1988): 189–224.

Ono Kazuko. *Chinese Women in a Century of Revolution, 1850–1950.* Ed. and trans. Joshua A. Fogel. Stanford: Stanford University Press, 1989.

Ōta Susumu 太田進. "Shiryō issoku" 資料一束 (A piece of historical data). *Yasō* 31 (June 1983): 61–62.

Otani Kōtarō 大谷孝太郎. *Zhongguo ren jingshen jiegou yanjiu* 中國人精神結構研究 (A study of the psychological structure of the Chinese). Trans. Yuan Fang 袁方. Shanghai: Dongya tongwen shuyuan, 1935.

Ozawa Masamoto 小沢正元. *Uchiyama Kanzō den: Nitchū yūkō ni tsukushita idai na shomin* 内山完造伝：日中友好につくした偉大な庶民 (Biography of Uchiyama Kanzō: A great commoner in the establishment of Sino-Japanese friendship). Tokyo: Banchō shobō, 1972.

Paliakov, Léon. *The Aryan Myth: A History of Racist and Nationalist Ideas in Europe.* Trans. Edmund Howard. London: Sussex University Press, 1974.

Pan Guangdan 潘光旦. *Feng Xiaoqing xing xinli biantai jie mi* 馮小青性心理變態揭秘 (The secret of the abnormal sexual psychology of Feng Xiaoqing). Ed. Zhen Xiang 禎祥 and Bo Shi 柏石. Beijing: Wenhua yishu chubanshe, 1990.

———. *Feng Xiaoqing: yijian yinglian zhi yanjiu* 馮小青：一件影戀之研究 (Feng Xiaoqing: studies of a case of narcissism). Shanghai: Xinyue shudian, 1929.

———. *Minzu texing yu minzu weisheng* 民族特性與民族衛生 (National character and national hygiene). Shanghai: Shangwu yinshuguan, 1937.

Park, Graham, ed. *Heidegger and Asian Thought.* Honolulu: University of Hawaii Press, 1987.

Parry, Benita. "Problems in Current Theories of Colonial Discourse." *Oxford Literary Review* 9 (1987): 27–58.

Peng Xiaoyan 彭小妍. *Chaoyue xieshi* 超越寫實 (Beyond realism). Taipei: Lianjing chuban, 1993.

Plaks, Andrew, ed. *Chinese Narrative: Critical and Theoretical Essays.* Princeton: Princeton University Press, 1977.

Popoviōc, Anton. *A Dictionary for the Analysis of Literary Translation.* Edmonton: Department of Comparative Literature, University of Alberta, 1976.

Prakash, Gyan. "Writing Post-Orientalist Histories of the Third World: Perspectives from Indian Historiography." *Comparative Studies in Society and History* 32.2 (1990): 383–408.

Pratt, Mary Louise. *Imperial Eyes: Travel Writing and Transculturation.* New York: Routledge, 1992.

Průšek, Jaroslav. *The Lyrical and the Epic: Studies of Modern Chinese Literature.* Ed. Leo Ou-fan Lee. Bloomington: Indiana University Press, 1980.

Pusey, James Reeve. *China and Charles Darwin.* Cambridge, Mass.: Harvard University Press, 1983.

Qian Jibo 錢基博. *Xiandai Zhongguo wenxue shi* 現代中國文學史 (A history of modern Chinese literature). Shanghai: Shijie shuju, 1933.

Qian Xingcun 錢杏邨 [A Ying 阿英, Zhang Ruoying 張若英]. *Wanqing wenyi baokan shulüe* 晚清文藝報刊述略 (An account of late Qing literary periodicals). Shanghai: Gudian wenxue chubanshe, 1959.

———. *Wanqing xiaoshuo shi* 晚清小説史 (A history of late Qing fiction). Taipei: Renren wenku, 1968.

———. *Xiandai Zhongguo wenxue zuojia* 現代中國文學作家 (Modern Chinese writers of literature). Shanghai: Taidong shuju, 1929.

———. *Zhongguo xin wenxue yundong shi ziliao* 中國新文學運動史資料 (Research materials on the history of the modern Chinese literary movement). Shanghai: Guangming shuju, 1934.

Qian Zhixiu 錢智修. "Duoxing zhi guomin" 墮性之國民 (The lethargic character of the Chinese). *Dongfang zazhi* 13.11 (1916): 1–6.

Qiu Jin 秋謹. *Qiu Jin ji* 秋謹集 (Collected works of Qiu Jin). Beijing: Zhonghua shuju, 1960.

Rafael, Vicente L. *Contracting Colonialism: Translation and Christian Conversion in Tagalog Society Under Early Spanish Rule.* Ithaca: Cornell Universiry Press, 1988.

Rankin, Mary Backus. *Early Chinese Revolutionaries*. Cambridge, Mass.: Harvard University Press, 1971.

———. "The Emergence of Women at the End of the Ch'ing: The Case of Ch'iu Chin." In Margery Wolf and Roxane Witke, eds., *Women in Chinese Society*. Stanford: Stanford University Press, 1975, 39–66.

Rao Hongjing 饒鴻競 et al., eds. *Chuangzao she ziliao* 創造社資料 (Research materials on the Creation Society). 2 vols. Fuzhou: Fujian renmin chubanshe, 1985.

Robinson, Douglas. *The Translator's Turn*. Baltimore: Johns Hopkins University Press, 1991.

Rorty, Richard. *Philosophy and the Mirror of Nature*. Princeton: Princeton University Press, 1979.

Rosen, Richard Barry. "The National Heritage Opposition to the New Culture and Literary Movements in China in the 1920's." Ph.D. diss., University of California, Berkeley, 1969.

Rosenberg, Justine. *The Empire of Civil Society: A Critique of the Realist Theory of International Relations*. London: Verso, 1994.

Rushdie, Salman. *The Satanic Verses*. New York: Viking, 1988.

Russell, Bertrand. *The Problem of China*. New York: Century, 1922.

———. "Some Traits in the Chinese Character." *Atlantic Monthly* 128.6 (Dec. 1921): 771–77.

———. "Zhongguo guomin xing de jige tedian" 中國國民性的几個特點 (Some traits in the Chinese character). Trans. Yuzhi 愈之. *Dongfang zazhi* 19.1 (1922): 21–33.

Said, Edward W. *Culture and Imperialism*. New York: Alfred A. Knopf, 1993.

———. *Orientalism*. New York: Vintage Books, 1979.

———. *The World, the Text, and the Critic*. Cambridge, Mass.: Harvard University Press, 1983.

Saneto Keishū 実藤恵秀. *Kindai Nitchū kōshō shiwa* 近代日中交渉史話 (A history of modern Chinese-Japanese contact). Tokyo: Shunjusha, 1973.

———. *Zhongguoren liuxue Riben shi* 中國人留學日本史 (History of Chinese students in Japan). Trans. Tan Ruqian (Tam Yue-him) 譚汝謙 and Lin Qiyan 林啟彥. Hong Kong: Zhongwen daxue chubanshe, 1982.

Saussy, Haun. *The Problem of a Chinese Aesthetic*. Stanford: Stanford University Press, 1993.

Schneider, Laurence A. "National Essence and the New Intelligentsia." In Charlotte Furth, ed., *The Limits of Change: Essays on Conservative Alternatives in Republican China*. Cambridge, Mass.: Harvard University Press, 1976, 57–89.

Schoenhals, Michael. *Doing Things with Words in Chinese Politics: Five Studies*. Berkeley: University of California, Institute of East Asian Studies, 1992.

Schwarcz, Vera. *The Chinese Enlightenment: Intellectuals and the Legacy of the May Fourth Movement of 1919*. Berkeley: University of California Press, 1986.

Schwartz, Benjamin. *In Search of Wealth and Power: Yen Fu and the West*. Cambridge, Mass.: Harvard University Press, 1964.

Schwartz, Benjamin, ed. *Reflections on the May Fourth Movement: A Symposium*. Cambridge, Mass.: Harvard University Press, 1972.

Scott, David. "Locating the Anthropological Subject: Postcolonial Anthropologists in Other Places." *Inscriptions* 5 (1989): 75–84.

Scott, Paul. "Uchiyama Kanzō: A Case Study in Sino-Japanese Interaction." *Sino-Japanese Studies* 2.1 (May 1990): 47–56.

Sha Lianxiang 沙蓮香, ed. *Zhongguo minzu xing* 中國民族性 (The Chinese national character). 2 vols. Beijing: Zhongguo renmin daxue chubanshe, 1989.

Shan Shi 山石. "*Ta, ta, ta* bushi hanyu xingtai" 他, 她, 它, 不是漢語形態 (Masculine *ta*, feminine *ta*, and neuter *ta* are not Chinese forms). *Zhongguo yuwen* 31 (Jan. 1955): 40.

Shen Congwen 沈從文. *Ji Ding Ling* 記丁玲 (A memoir of Ding Ling). Shanghai: Liangyou, 1934.

———. *Shen Congwen xiaoshuo xuan* 沈從文小説選 (Selected stories of Shen Congwen). Ed. Ling Yu 凌宇. Beijing: Renmin wenxue chubanshe, 1982.

Shen Dizhong 沈迪中. "Qiaohe shi zenyang chansheng de: Zhongguo baihua wen yundong he Riben yanwen yizhi yundong" 巧合是怎樣產生的：中國白話文運動和日本言文一致運動 (How the coincidence occurred: the Chinese vernacular movement and the Japanese colloquial language movement). *Liaoning daxue xuebao* 5 (1985): 68–70.

Shen Songqiao 沈松僑. *Xueheng pai yu wusi shiqi de fan xin wenhua yundong* 學衡派與五四時期的反新文化運動 (The *Critical Review* group: a conservative alternative to the New Culture movement in the May Fourth era). Taipei: Guoli Taiwan daxue chubanshe, 1984.

Shi Chengjun 史承均. "Shilun jiefang hou Lao She dui *Luotuo xiangzi* de xiugai" 試論解放後老舍對《駱駝祥子》的修改 (Lao She's revisions of *Camel Xiangzi* since Liberation). *Zhongguo xiandai wenxue yanjiu congkan* 4 (1980): 278–88.

Shi Heng 待桁. "Geren zhuyi de wenxue ji qita" 個人主義的文學及其他 (Individualistic literature and other concerns). In Li Helin 李何林, ed., *Zhongguo wenyi lunzhan* 中國文藝論戰 (Debates on Chinese literature and art). Shanghai: Zhongguo wenyi she, 1932, 118–24.

Shi Qun 史群. *Xinbian Riyu wailaiyu cidian* 新編日語外來語詞典 (A new dictionary of loanwords in Japanese). Beijing: Shangwu yinshuguan, 1984.

Shi Zhicun 施蟄存. *Meiyu zhi xi* 梅雨之夕 (An evening in the plum rain). Shanghai: Xin Zhongguo shuju, 1933.

Silverman, Kaja. *The Subject of Semiotics.* Oxford: Oxford University Press, 1983.

Smith, Anthony D. *Theories of Nationalism.* New York: Holmes & Meier, 1983.

Smith, Arthur H. *Chinese Characteristics.* New York: Revell, 1894.

Spence, Jonathan D. *The Gate of Heavenly Peace: The Chinese and Their Revolution, 1895–1980.* New York: Viking, 1981.

Sperber, Dan. *On Anthropological Knowledge.* Cambridge, Eng.: Cambridge University Press, 1985.

Spitzer, Leo. *Stilstudien II.* Munich: M. Hueber, 1922.

Spivak, Gayatri Chakravorty. "Can the Subaltern Speak?" In Cary Nelson and Lawrence Grossberg, eds., *Marxism and the Interpretation of Culture.* Urbana and Chicago: University of Illinois Press, 1988, 217–313.

———. *In Other Worlds: Essays in Cultural Politics.* New York: Routledge, 1988.

———. *Outside in the Teaching Machine.* New York: Routledge, 1993.

Steiner, George. *After Babel: Aspects of Language and Translation.* London: Oxford University Press, 1973.

Stirner, Max. *The Ego and His Own.* Trans. Steven T. Byington. London: A. C. Fifield, 1912.

Strand, David. *Rickshaw Beijing.* Berkeley: University of California Press, 1988.

Strich, Fritz. *Goethe and World Literature.* Trans. C. A. M. Sym. London: Routledge & Kegan Paul, 1949.

Suleiman, Susan Robin. "Nadja, Dora, Lol V. Stein: Women, Madness, Narrative." In Shlomith Rimmon-Kenan, ed., *Discourse in Psychoanalysis and Literature.* London: Methuen, 1987, 124–51.

———. *Subversive Intent: Gender, Politics, and the Avant-Garde.* Cambridge, Mass.: Harvard University Press, 1990.

Sun Yushi 孫玉石. "Lu Xun gaizao guomin xing sixiang wenti de kaocha" 魯迅改造國民性思想問題的考查 (A study of Lu Xun's thinking on the question of national character). In *Lu Xun yanjiu jikan* 魯迅研究集刊 (Collected studies of Lu Xun). Shanghai: Shanghai wenyi chubanshe, 1979, 86–117.

Sun Zhongshan 孫中山. *Sun Zhongshan xuanji* 孫中山選集 (Selected works of Sun Yat-sen). Beijing: Renmin chubanshe, 1956.

Sun Zuji 孫祖基. "*Ta zi* de yanjiu" 她字的研究 (On feminine *ta*). *Xue deng,* Apr. 18, 1920.

———. "Fei bo '*Ta zi* de yanjiu'" 非駁《她字的研究》 (Not a rebuttal to 'On Feminine *ta*'). *Xue deng,* Apr. 24, 1920.

Tam, Yue-him (Tan Ruqian) 譚汝謙. *Jindai Zhong-Ri wenhua guanxi yanjiu* 近代中日文化關係研究 (Studies in modern Sino-Japanese cultural relations). Hong Kong: Xianggang Riben yanjiuso, 1986.

———. "Meiji Japan and the Educational and Language Reforms in Late Ch'ing China." In James W. White, Michio Umegaki, and Thomas R. H. Havens, eds., *The Ambivalence of Nationalism: Modern Japan Between East and West.* Lanham, Md.: University Press of America, 1990, 61–78.

Tang Xianzu 湯顯祖. *Mudan ting* 牡丹亭 (Peony pavilion). Beijing: Renmin wenxue chubanshe, 1963.

———. *Peony Pavilion.* Trans. Cyril Birch. Bloomington: Indiana University Press, 1980.

Taylor, Charles. "The Person." In Michael Carrithers, Steven Collins, and Steven Lukes, eds., *The Category of the Person: Anthropology, Philosophy, History.* Cambridge, Eng.: Cambridge University Press, 1985, 257–81.

———. *Sources of the Self: The Making of the Modern Identity.* Cambridge, Mass.: Harvard University Press, 1989.

Thibaudet, Albert. *Gustave Flaubert.* Paris: Gallimard, 1982.

Todorov, Tzvetan. *The Fantastic: A Structural Approach to a Literary Genre.* Trans. Richard Howard. Cleveland: Press of Case Western University, 1973.

Tu, Wei-ming. *Confucian Thought: Selfhood as Creative Transformation.* Albany: State University of New York Press, 1985.

———. *Humanity and Self-Cultivation: Essays in Confucian Thought.* Berkeley, Calif.: Asian Humanities Press, 1979.

Uchiyama Kanzō 內山完造. *Ro Jin no omoide* 魯迅の思い出 (Memories of Lu Xun). Tokyo: Shakai shisōsha, 1979.

―――. *Yige Riben ren de Zhongguo guan* 一個日本人的中國觀 (A Japanese perspective on China). Trans. You Bingqi 尤炳圻. Shanghai: Kaiming shudian, 1936.

Ullman, Stephen. *Style in the French Novel*. Cambridge, Eng.: Cambridge University Press, 1957.

Viswanathan, Gauri. *Masks of Conquest*. New York: Columbia University Press, 1989.

Wakeman, Frederic, Jr., and Wen-hsin Yeh, eds. *Shanghai Sojourners*. Berkeley: University of California Press, 1992.

Wang, David Der-wei 王德威 *Fictional Realism in Twentieth-Century China: Mao . Dun, Lao She, Shen Congwen*. New York: Columbia University Press, 1992.

Wang Hui 汪暉 "'Sai xiansheng' zai Zhongguo de mingyun: Zhongguo jinxiandai sixiang zhong de 'kexue' gainian jiqi shiyong" "賽先生" 在中國的命運一中國近現代思想中的 "科學" 概念及其使用 (The fate of "Mr. Science" in China: The concept of *kexue* and its use in modern Chinese thought). *Xueren* 1 (1991): 49–123.

Wang Li 王力. *Zhongguo yufa lilun* 中國語法理論 (A theory of Chinese grammar). Shanghai: Shangwu yinshuguan, 1947.

Wang Lida 王立達. *Xiandai hanyu zhong cong Riyu jielai de cihui* 現代漢語中從日語借來的詞彙 (Loanwords from Japanese in modern Chinese). *Zhongguo yuwen* 2 (1958): 90–94.

Wang Liwei 王力衛. "Zaoqi de Ying Hua cidian yu Riben de yangxue" 早期的英華詞典與日本的洋學 (Early English-Chinese dictionaries and foreign studies in Japan). *Yuanxue* 1 (Feb. 1994): 277–94.

Wang Xinggong 王星拱. "Wu he wo" 物和我 (Matter and self). *Xin chao* 3.1 (1921): 1–11.

Wang Xiyan 王西彥. *Lun Ah Q he tade beiju* 論阿Q和他的悲劇 (On Ah Q and his tragedy). Shanghai: Xin wenyi chubanshe, 1957.

Wang Yao 王瑤. *Zhongguo xin wenxue shigao* 中國新文學史稿 (A draft history of modern Chinese literature). Shanghai: Kaiming shudian, 1951.

Wang Zhefu 王哲甫. *Zhongguo xin wenxue yundong shi* 中國新文學運動史 (A history of the modern Chinese literary movement). Hong Kong: Yuandong, 1965.

Watt, Ian. *The Rise of the Novel: Studies in Defoe, Richardson, and Fielding*. Berkeley: University of California Press, 1957.

Wei Shaochang 魏紹昌. *Yuanyang hudie pai yanjiu ziliao* 鴛鴦蝴蝶派研究資料 (Research materials on Mandarin ducks and butterfly fiction). Hong Kong: Joint Publishing, 1980.

Werner, Edward T. C. *Autumn Leaves: An Autobiography with a Sheaf of Papers, Sociological, Philosophical, and Metaphysical*. Shanghai: Kelly & Walsh, 1928.

White, James W., Michio Umegaki, and Thomas R. H. Havens, eds. *The Ambivalence of Nationalism: Modern Japan Between East and West*. Lanham, Md.: University Press of America, 1990.

Whorf, Benjamin Lee. *Language, Thought, and Reality: Selected Writings of Benjamin Lee Whorf*. Ed. John B. Carroll. Cambridge, Mass.: Harvard University Press, 1956.

Widmer, Ellen. "Xiao Qing's Literary Legacy and the Place of the Woman Writer in Late Imperial China." *Late Imperial China* 13.1 (June 1992): 111–55.

Widmer, Ellen, and David Der-wei Wang, eds. *From May Fourth to June Fourth: Fiction and Film in Twentieth-Century China.* Cambridge, Mass.: Harvard University Press, 1993.

Williams, Raymond. *Keywords.* New York: Harper & Row, 1976.

———. *Marxism and Literature.* Oxford: Oxford University Press, 1977.

Witke, Roxane. "Woman as Politician in China of the 1920's." In Marilyn B. Young, ed., *Women in China: Studies in Social Change and Feminism.* Ann Arbor: University of Michigan Center for Chinese Studies, University of Michigan, 1973, 33–45.

Wolf, Margery, and Roxane Witke, eds. *Women in Chinese Society.* Stanford: Stanford University Press, 1975.

Wright, Arthur F., ed. *The Confucian Persuasion.* Stanford: Stanford University Press, 1960.

Wu Huaibin 吳懷斌 and Zeng Guangcan 曾廣燦, eds. *Lao She yanjiu ziliao* 老舍研究資料 (Research material on Lao She). 2 vols. Beijing: Shiyue wenyi chubanshe, 1983.

Wu Mi 吳宓. "Lun xin wenhua yundong" 論新文化運動 (The New Culture movement). *Xueheng* 4 (Apr. 1922): 1–23.

Wu, Pei-yi. *The Confucian's Progress: Autobiographical Writings in Traditional China.* Princeton: Princeton University Press, 1990.

Xiao Hong 蕭紅. *The Field of Life and Death and Tales of Hulan River.* Trans. Howard Goldblatt and Ellen Yeung. Bloomington: Indiana University Press, 1979.

———. *Hulan he zhuan* 呼蘭河傳 (Tales of Hulan river). Harbin: Heilongjiang renmin chubanshe, 1979.

———. *Sheng si chang* 生死場 (The field of life and death). Shanghai: Xinwenyi chubanshe, 1935.

———. *Xiao Hong daibiao zuo* 蕭紅代表作 (Major works of Xiao Hong). Ed. Xing Fujun 邢富君. Zhengzhou: Henan renmin chubanshe, 1987.

Xiao Hong yanjiu 蕭紅研究 (Studies of Xiao Hong). Harbin: Beifang luncong, 1983.

Xiao Jun 蕭軍. *Bayue de xiangcun* 八月的鄉村 (Village in August). Beijing: Renmin wenxue chubanshe, 1980.

Xu Lin 徐麟. "*Luotuo Xiangzi* de jiewei ji qita" 《駱駝祥子》的結尾及其他 (Reflections on the endings of *Camel Xiangzi* and other matters). *Zhongguo xiandai wenxue yanjiu congkan* 1 (1984): 255–69.

Xu Shoushang 許壽裳. *Wang you Lu Xun yinxiang ji* 亡友魯迅印象記 (Reminiscences of my late friend Lu Xun). Beijing: Renmin wenxue chubanshe, 1947; reprinted 1977.

———. *Wo suo renshi de Lu Xun* 我所認識的魯迅 (Lu Xun as I knew him). Beijing: Renmin wenxue chubanshe, 1978.

Xu Shouwei 許守微. "Lun guocui wu zu yu ouhua" 論國粹無阻於歐化 (On national essence not being a roadblock to Europeanization). *Guocui xuebao* 7 (1905): 1–5.

Xu Zhiheng 許之衡. "Du *Guocui xuebao* ganyan" 讀國粹學報感言 (Thoughts on reading *National Essence* journal). *Guocui xuebao* 6 (1905): 1–6.

Xu Zidong 許子東. *Yu Dafu xinlun* 郁達夫新論 (A new study of Yu Dafu). Hangzhou: Zhejiang renmin wenxue chubanshe, 1984.

Yan Jiayan 嚴家炎. *Xin ganjue pai xiaoshuo xuan* 新感覺派小說選 (Selected Neoperceptionist fiction). Beijing: Renmin wenxue chubanshe, 1985.

————. *Zhongguo xiandai xiaoshuo liupai shi* 中國現代小說流派史 (Diverse strands in modern Chinese fiction). Beijing: Renmin wenxue chubanshe, 1989.

Yeh, Wen-hsin. *The Alienated Academy*. Cambridge, Mass.: Council on East Asian Studies, Harvard University, 1990.

Yoshino, Kosaku. *Cultural Nationalism in Contemporary Japan*. London and New York: Routledge, 1992.

Young, Marilyn B., ed. *Women in China: Studies in Social Change and Feminism*. Ann Arbor: Center for Chinese Studies, University of Michigan, 1973.

Yu Dafu 郁達夫. "Wo dui nimen que meiyou shiwang" 我對你們卻沒有失望 (I am not disappointed with you). *Xingzhou ribao*, Jan. 23, 1939.

————. "Yishu yu guojia" 藝術與國家 (Art and the state). In Rao Hongjing 饒鴻競 et al., eds., *Chuangzao she ziliao* 創造社資料 (Research materials on the Creation Society). Fuzhou: Fujian renmin chubanshe, 1985, 1: 55–59.

————. *Yu Dafu quanji* 郁達夫全集 (The complete works of Yu Dafu). 4 vols. Shanghai: Beixin shuju, 1930.

Yu Guangzhong 余光中, ed. *Zhongguo xiandai wenxue daxi* 中國現代文學大系. Taipei: Juren chubanshe, 1972.

Yu Liming 俞理明. *Fojing wenxian yuyan* 佛經文獻語言 (The language of Buddhist texts). Chengdu: Bashu Shushe, 1993.

Yue Daiyun 樂黛雲. "Shijie wenhua duihua zhong de Zhongguo xiandai baoshou zhuyi" 世界文化對話中的中國現代保守主義 (Modern Chinese conservativism in the international cultural dialogue). *Zhongguo wenhua* 1 (Dec. 1989): 132–36.

Yuan Liangjun 袁良駿. *Ding Ling yanjiu wushi nian* 丁玲研究五十年 (Studies of Ding Ling in the past fifty years). Tianjin: Tianjin jiaoyu chubanshe, 1982.

Yuan Liangjun, ed. *Ding Ling yanjiu ziliao* 丁玲研究資料 (Research materials on Ding Ling). Tianjin: Tianjin renmin chubanshe, 1982.

Zeitlin, Judith. *Historian of the Strange: Pu Songling and the Chinese Classical Tale*. Stanford: Stanford University Press, 1993.

Zhang Binglin 章炳麟 [Zhang Taiyan 章太炎]. "Bo Zhongguo yong wanguo xinyu shuo" 駁中國用萬國新語說 (A rebuttal to the proposal for the adoption of Esperanto in China). 2 pts. *Guocui xuebao* 41 (1909): 6–10; 42 (1909): 1–10.

————. *Zhang Taiyan zhenglun xuanji* 章太炎政論選集 (The political views of Zhang Taiyan). Ed. Tang Zhijun 湯志鈞. Beijing: Zhonghua shuju, 1977.

Zhang Jinglu 張靜廬. *Zai chubanjie ershinian* 在出版界二十年 (My twenty years in the publishing world). Shanghai: Shanghai zazhi gongsi, 1938.

Zhang Jinglu, ed. *Zhongguo chuban shiliao bubian* 中國出版史料補編 (Supplement to historical materials on publishing in China). Beijing: Zhonghua shuju, 1957.

————. *Zhongguo jindai chuban shiliao* 中國近代出版史料 (Historical materials on publishing in the recent history of China). 2 vols. Beijing: Zhonghua shuju, 1957.

————. *Zhongguo xiandai chuban shiliao* 中國現代出版史料 (Historical materials on publishing in modern China). 4 vols. Beijing: Zhonghua shuju, 1957.

Zhang, Jingyuan. "The First Chinese Translation of Sigmund Freud." *Chinese Comparatist* 3.1 (July 1989): 33–35.

————. *Psychoanalysis in China: Literary Transformations, 1919–1949*. Ithaca: Cornell East Asian Series, 1992.

Zhang Mengyang 張夢陽. "Lu Xun yu Shi Misi de *Zhongguo ren qizhi*" 魯迅與史密斯的中國人氣質 (Lu Xun and Smith's *Chinese Characteristics*). *Lu Xun yanjiu niankan* 2 (1980): 208–17.

Zhang Weifu 張維夫, ed. *Guanyu Ding Ling nüshi* 關於丁玲女士 (On Ding Ling). Shanghai: Lida shuju, 1933.

Zhang Xichen 章錫琛. "Zhongguo minzu xing lun" 中國民族性論 (On the Chinese national character). Trans. from the Japanese. *Dongfang zazhi* 14.1 (1917): 1–2.

Zhang Yingjin 張英進. "Building a National Literature in Modern China: Literary Criticism, Gender Ideology, and the Public Sphere." Unpublished paper, 1994.

————. "The Institutionalization of Modern Literary History in China, 1922–1980." *Modern China* 20.3 (July 1994): 347–77.

Zhao Jiabi 趙家璧. *Bianji shengya yi Lu Xun* 編輯生涯憶魯迅 (An editor's reminiscences of Lu Xun). Beijing: Renmin wenxue chubanshe, 1981.

————. "Bianji yijiu" 編輯憶舊 (An editor's recollections). 2 pts. *Xin wenxue shiliao* 1 (Mar. 1978): 61–63; 3 (May 1979): 172–75.

————. "He Jin Yi zai yiqi de rizi" 和靳以在一起的日子 (The days Jin Yi and I worked together). *Xin wenxue shiliao* 2 (May 1988): 110–33, 151.

————. "Hua shuo *Zhongguo xin wenxue daxi*" 話說《中國新文學大系》(Speaking of the *Compendium of Modern Chinese Literature*). *Xin wenxue shiliao* 1 (Feb. 1984): 162–88.

————. "Huiyi Lu Xun gei 'Liangyou' chuban de diyibu shu'" 回憶魯迅給 "良友" 出版的第一部書 (Recollecting Lu Xun's first book for "Liangyou"). *Xin wenxue shiliao* 2 (May 1981): 172–79.

————. "Huiyi wo biande diyibu chengtao shu: yijiao congshu" 回憶我編的第一部成套書:《一角叢書》(Recollecting the first series of books I edited: the "ten-cent book series"). *Xin wenxue shiliao* 3 (Aug. 1983): 227–37.

————. "Huiyi Yu Dafu yu wo youguan de shi jianshi" 回憶郁達夫與我有關的十件事 (Recollections of ten incidents relating to myself and Yu Dafu). *Xin wenxue shiliao* 3 (Aug. 1985): 32–44.

————. "Huiyi Zheng Boqi tongzhi zai Liangyou" 回憶鄭伯奇同志在良友 (Recollections of comrade Zheng Boqi at Liangyou). *Xin wenxue shiliao* 5 (Nov. 1979): 224–32.

————. "Huiyi Zheng Zhenduo he tade Zhongguo banhua shi" 回憶鄭振鐸和他的《中國版畫史》(Recollection of Zheng Zhenduo and his *History of Chinese Woodcuts*). *Xin wenxue shiliao* 2 (May 1983): 183–94.

————. "Lao She he wo" 老舍和我 (Lao She and I). 2 pts. *Xin wenxue shiliao* 2 (May 1986): 116–37; 3 (Aug. 1986): 93–112.

————. *Shu bi ren changshou* 書比人長壽 (Books last longer than people). Hong Kong: Joint Publishing, 1988.

————. *Xin chuantong* 新傳統 (New tradition). Shanghai: Liangyou, 1936.

Zhao Jiabi, ed. *Zhongguo xin wenxue daxi* 中國新文學大系 (Compendium of modern Chinese literature). 10 vols. Shanghai: Liangyou, 1935–36.

Zheng Boqi 鄭伯奇. "Guomin wenxue lun" 國民文學論 (On national literature). In Rao Hongjing 饒鴻競 et al., eds., *Chuangzao she ziliao* 創造社資料 (Research materials on the Creation Society). Fuzhou: Fujian renmin chubanshe, 1985, 1: 72–95.

Zheng Hailin 鄭海麟. *Huang Zunxian yu jindai Zhongguo* 黃遵憲與近代中國 (Huang Zunxian and modern China). Beijing: Sanlian shudian, 1988.

Zheng Xinmiao 鄭新苗. *Wenhua pipan yu guomin xing gaizao* 文化批判與國民性改造 (Cultural criticism and the reform of national character). Xi'an: Shaanxi renmin chubanshe, 1988.

Zheng Zhenduo 鄭振鐸. *Chatuben Zhongguo wenxue shi* 插圖本中國文學史 (An illustrated history of Chinese literature). Hong Kong: Shangwu yinshuguan, 1961.

Zhongwen da cidian 中文大辭典 (A dictionary of Chinese). 40 vols. Taipei: Zhongguo wenhua yanjiu suo, 1962–68.

Zhou Zuoren 周作人. "Ren de wenxue" 人的文學 (A humane literature). In Zhao Jiabi 趙家璧, ed., *Zhongguo xin wenxue daxi* 中國新文學大系 (Compendium of modern Chinese literature). Shanghai: Liangyou, 1935, 1: 193–99.

———. *Zhou Zuoren daibiao zuo* 周作人代表作 (Representative works of Zhou Zuoren). Ed. Zhang Juxiang 張菊香. Zhengzhou: Huanghe wenyi chubanshe, 1987.

Zhu Ziqing 朱自清. "Xuanshi zaji" 選詩雜記 (Miscellaneous notes on the poetry selection). In Zhao Jiabi 趙家璧, ed., *Zhongguo xin wenxue daxi* 中國新文學大系 (Compendium of modern Chinese literature). Shanghai: Liangyou, 1935, 8: 5–19.

"Zuoyi zuojia lianmeng disi ci quanti dahui buzhi" 左翼作家聯盟第四次全體大會補志 (Supplement to the minutes of the 4th convention of the League of Left-Wing Writers). *Hongqi ribao*, Nov. 22, 1930.

Character List

"Ah Q zhengzhuan"　阿Q正傳
Aimo　愛牟
Ai Qing　艾青
"A Mao guniang"　阿毛姑娘

Ba Jin 巴金
Bai Yang　白羊
banke　版克
Bao Tianxiao (Pao T'ien-hsiao)
　包天笑
Baojuan　寶卷
Baoyü　寶玉
Ba yue de xiangcun　八月的鄉村
Bei Dao　北島
Beijing (Beiping)　北京 (北平)
bianxuan ganxiang　編選感想
Bing Xin　冰心
Bolan mie, Yindu wang, Youtai yimin
　san sifang　波蘭滅, 印度亡, 猶太遺民
　散四方
bunka (Chinese: wenhua)　文化
"Bu tian"　補天

Cai Yuanpei　蔡元培
"Can chun"　殘春
Cao Jinghua　曹靖華

Cao xiansheng　曹先生
Cao Xueqin　曹雪芹
Cao Yu (Ts'ao Yu)　曹禺
chaodian　鈔店
chaoshang　鈔商
Chen Duxiu　陳獨秀
Chen Hengzhe　陳衡哲
Chen Jia'ai　陳家藹
Chen Shuyu　陳漱渝
Chen Yong　陳涌
Chen Zuiliang　陳最良
Cheng Fangwu　成仿吾
Chengye　成業
"Chenlun"　沉淪
Chenzhong bao　晨鍾報
Chuangzao jikan　創造季刊
Chuangzao she　創造社
Chuangzao yuekan　創造月刊
chuanqi　傳奇
"Chu dong"　初冬
Chunxiang　春香
Chuqi baihua shigao　初期白話詩稿
ci　詞
congshu　叢書
"Cong xiaoshuo kanlai de Zhina minzu
　xing"　從小説看來的支那民族性

459

Dai Wangshu　戴望舒
Daiyu　黛玉
daji　大己
Damei wanbao　大美晚報
dan　但
danshu　單數
daxi (Japanese: taikei)　大系
dazhong wenyi　大眾文藝
de　的
"Deng"　燈
Deng Feihuang　鄧飛黃
Deng Shi　鄧實
"Dengxia manbi"　燈下漫筆
Dian　電
Ding Ling　丁玲
Dongfang zazhi　東方雜誌
Dong xi wenhua jiqi zhexue　東西文化
　及其哲學
Du Heng　杜衡
Du Yaquan　杜亞泉
duli　獨立

Er Ma　二馬
"Ershi niandai yimian"　二十年代一面

falü　法律
fen　分
Feng Da　馮達
Feng Yuanjun　馮沅君
Feng Xiaoqing　馮小青
Feng Xuefeng　馮雪峰
Fengshou　豐收
fenkai suan　分開算
Fu Donghua　傅東華
Fu Sinian　傅斯年
Fu Xi　伏羲
Fu Yanchang　傅彥長
Fufa　福發
Fujino Gonkyūrō　藤野嚴九郎
funü　婦女
furu zhi liu　婦孺之流
Fu she　復社

gaizao guomin xing　改造國民性
Gao Ma　高媽
Gao Mingkai　高名凱
Gao Yihan　高一涵
geming lun　革命論
geming wenxue　革命文學
"Geming yu wenxue"　革命與文學
Geng Jizhi　耿濟之
geren　個人
geren zhuyi (Japanese: kojin shugi)
　個人主義
geti　個體
gewei　個位
gezhi　格致
gonghe　共和
gongsi　公司
gongwo　公我
Guang Sheng　光升
Guanghua daxue　光華大學
Guanghua shudian　光華書店
Guangming shudian　光明書店
Guiqulaixi　歸去來兮
guniang　姑娘
Guo Moruo　郭沫若
guocui (Japanese: kokusui)　國粹
Guocui xuebao　國粹學報
Guo gu　國故
guo hun (Japanese: kunidamashii)
　國魂
guojia　國家
guojia zhuyi　國家主義
guomin　國民
guomin de pinge　國民的品格
guomin liegen xing　國民劣根性
"Guomin shida yuanqi lun"　國民十大
　元氣論
"guomin wenxue lun"　國民文學論
guomin xing　國民性
guo xing　國性
guoxue (Japanese: kokugaku)　國學
Guoxue baocun hui　國學保存會
guoyu　國語

"Gushi xinbian" 故事新編
"Guxiang" 故鄉

Haidian 海淀
han 漢
He Wei 何為
Hong Shen 洪深
Hu Feng 胡風
Hu Niu 虎妞
Hu Ping 胡平
Hu Shi 胡適
Hu Xiansu 胡先驌
Hu Yepin 胡也頻
Huang Jie 黃節
Huang Yuan (Huang Heqing)
  黃源 (黃河清)
Huang Zhenxia 黃震遐
Huang Ziping 黃子平
Huang Zunxian 黃遵憲
huang huo 黃禍
"Huang shi" 黃史
"Huanxiang houji" 還鄉後記
"Huanxiang ji" 還鄉記
hua ren 華人
Huaxia zi 華夏子
Hulan he zhuan 呼蘭河傳
huoche 火車
huolunche 火輪車
huolunchuan 火輪船

iki (Chinese: xi) 息

ji 己
Jia 家
Jia Yi 家義
Jiang Guangci 蔣光慈
Jiang Jieshi (Chiang Kai-shek) 蔣介石
"Jiangjun di tou" 將軍底頭
jiating 家庭
jiepou 解剖
jiga (Chinese: ziwo) 自我
Ji liu 激流

Jin Yi 靳以
jingjixue (Japanese: keizaigaku)
  經濟學
jingshen fenxi 精神分析
jinguan 盡管
jingzheng 競爭
Jin Ping Mei 金瓶梅
Jintian 今天
jiuban 舊版
jixue 計學
Juansheng 涓生
Jun ge 軍歌
jun xue 君學

Kaiming shudian 開明書店
Kaiming yingwen wenfa 開明英文文法
Kang Youwei 康有為
kanji (Chinese: hanzi) 漢字
karagokoro (Chinese: tang xin) 唐心
kefang yuyan 客方語言
kindai shōsetsu (Chinese: jindai
  xiaoshuo) 近代小説
kōdo (Chinese: gudao) 古道
kojin (Chinese: geren) 個人
kotoba 言葉
"Kuangren riji" 狂人日記
Kuraishi Takeshirō 倉石武四郎

Lan Ling 藍翎
Lao She 老舍
Lao Zhang de zhexue 老張的哲學
Laozi 老子
laowai 老外
Li Dazhao 李大釗
Li Jia 李嘉
Li Jinghan 李景漢
Li Liewen 黎烈文
Li Qingshan 李青山
"Li Wa zhuan" 李娃傳
Li Yiming 李一鳴
Li Zehou 李澤厚
Li Zirong 李子榮

Liang Qichao   梁啟超
Liang Shuming   梁漱溟
Liangyou huabao   良友畫報
Liangyou tushu gongsi   良友圖書公司
Liangyou wenxue congshu   良友文學叢書
Libai liu   禮拜六
Lihun   離婚
lilun   理論
Lin Shu   林紓
Lin Yutang   林語堂
Ling Jishi   凌吉士
Ling Shuhua   凌淑華
Liniang   麗娘
lishi   歷史
Liu Fu (Liu Bannong)   劉復 (劉半農)
Liu Fuchen   劉福臣
Liu Mengmei   柳夢梅
Liu Na'ou   劉吶鷗
Liu Shipei   劉師培
Liu Yizheng   柳詒徵
Liu Zaifu   劉再復
Liu Zhengtan   劉正埮
longtong   籠統
Lou Shiyi   樓適夷
Lu Xiaoman   陸小曼
Lu Xun   魯迅
Lu Yan   魯彥
Lu Yin   廬隱
"Lun Zhongguo guomin zhi pinge"
    論中國國民之品格
"Lun Zhongguo renmin zhi yilai xing
    zhi qiyuan"   論中國人民之依賴性之
    起源
"Lun Zhongguo renzhong zhi jianglai"
    論中國人種之將來
Luo Jialun   羅家倫
Luo Longji   羅隆基
lüshi   律師

Ma Wei   馬威
mang nan'er   莽男兒
mantan hui   漫談會

Mao Dun (Mao Tun)   茅盾
maoyi   貿易
"Mashang zhi riji"   馬上支日記
Mei Guangdi   梅光迪
Meiji   明治
Meiyu zhi xi   梅雨之夕
Meng Zhen   孟真
miandi   面的
mianzi   面子
Min Zhi   民質
Minbao   民報
Ming Enpu   明恩溥
minzhu (Japanese: minshu)   民主
minzu xing   民族性
minzu zhuyi   民族主義
minzu zhuyi wenxue   民族主義文學
misi   密司
Miyake Setsurei   三宅雪嶺
Miyake Yūjirō   三宅雄次郎
"Modao"   魔道
Mt. Fudetate   筆立山
Mu Shiying   穆時英
mucai   母財
Mudan ting   牡丹亭
Muqin   母親

Nahan   吶喊
Nakamura Keiu   中村敬宇
Nan she   南社
na nüren   那女人
Nie Gannu   聶紺弩
nüshi   女士

Ōtani Kotarō   大谷孝太郎
ouhua   歐化
Oulouba zhuguo shang wenxue   歐邏
    巴諸國尚文學
Ouyou xinying lu   歐游心影錄

Pan Guangdan   潘光旦
Pan Qiaoyun   潘巧雲
Panghuang   彷徨

"Panni zhe" 叛逆者
pingmin wenxue 平民文學
"Piping yu meng" 批評與夢
puluo wenxue 普羅文學
putongyu 普通語

qi 奇
Qian Qianwu 錢謙吾
Qian Xingcun [A Ying, Zhang
  Ruoying] 錢杏村〔阿英, 張若英〕
Qian Xuantong [Wang Jingxuan]
  錢玄同 [王敬軒]
Qianfeng yuebao 前鋒月報
Qianfeng zhoubao 前鋒周報
qianzai yishi 潛在意識
"Qiao" 橋
Qiling ji 奇零集
qing 情
qing kan Yindu guotu bing fei xiao,
  wei nu wei ma bude tuo long lao
  請看印度國土并非小, 為奴為馬不得
  脫籠牢
Qiu Jin 秋瑾
Qu Qiubai 瞿秋白
quanli 權利
qunxue 群學

ren 人
renliche 人力車
renmin 人民
Renmin wenxue chubanshe 人民文學
  出版社
rensheng pai 人生派
"Renshi zhuan" 任氏傳
Renwen shengwuxue luncong 人文生物學
  論叢
renwen zhuyi 人文主義
Rou Shi 柔石
Ruan Ming 阮明
Runtu 閏土

Sanbai bashige 三百八十個

Sanetō Keishū 實藤惠秀
"Sange nanren he yige nüren" 三個男
  人和一個女人
Sansi ji 三四集
sanwen 散文
"Shafei nüshi de riji" 莎菲女士的日記
shangdeng ren 上等人
Shanghai wenlun 上海文論
"Shangshi" 傷逝
Shan nüren xingpin 善女人行品
Shan si saozi 單四嫂子
Shaonian piaobo zhe 少年漂泊者
Shaonian Weite zhi fannao 少年維特之
  煩惱
shehui 社會
shehuixue (Japanese: shakaigaku)
  社會學
Shen bao 申報
Shen Congwen 沈從文
Shenghuo zhoukan 生活周刊
Sheng si chang 生死場
"Shenquan houji" 神拳後記
She Sheng 攝生
shi 詩
Shi Tuo [Lu Fen] 師陀 〔盧焚〕
Shi Zhecun 施蟄存
Shi bao 時報
Shibue Tamotsu 澀江保
Shiga Shigetake 志賀重昂
shige 詩歌
Shijing 詩經
"Shimian zhi ye" 失眠之夜
Shinajin (Chinese: Zhina ren) 支那人
Shinajin kishitsu (Chinese: Zhina ren
  qizhi) 支那人氣質
Shinatō (Chinese: Zhina tong) 支那通
shinkaron (Chinese: jinhualun) 進化論
shintō (Chinese: shendao) 神道
Shishi xinbao 時事新報
"Shi Xiu" 石秀
"Shi zhong dexing xiangfan xiangcheng
  yi" 十種德性相反相成義

shouji 手記
Shuihu zhuan 水滸傳
Shuqin 豎琴
"Sichou shi" 四愁詩
siwo 私我
"Suigan lu" 隨感錄
suiran 雖然
Sun Yat-sen 孫中山

ta (animal/non-human) 牠
ta (feminine) 她
ta (masculine) 他
ta (neuter) 它
Taiyang she 太陽社
Tan Zhengbi 譚正璧
tan ci 彈詞
Tao Kangde 陶亢德
Tian Han 田漢
Tianyanlun 天演論
ti mian 體面
tongsu wenxue 通俗文學

Uchiyama Kaikichi 內山嘉吉
Uchiyama Kanzō 內山完造

waiguoren 外國人
Wang Baoliang 王寶良
Wang Jingwei 汪精衛
Wang Jingxuan 王敬軒
Wang Lida 王立達
Wang Pingling 王平陵
Wang Xinggong 王星拱
Wang Yunwu 王雲五
Wang Zhefu 王哲甫
Wanguo gongfa 萬國公法
wei ouhua 偽歐化
Weidi 葦弟
weiwo 唯我
Weizhuang 未庄
wen 文
wenhua 文化
"Wenhua pianzhi lun" 文化偏至論

wenxue 文學
"Wenyi jia de juewu" 文藝家的覺悟
"Wenyi zhi shehui de shiming" 文藝
之社會的使命
wo 我
"Wo likai shizi jietou" 我離開十字街
頭
women 我們
"Wo zai Xiacun de shihou" 我在霞村
的時候
Wu 霧
Wu Liande 伍聯德
Wu Mi 吳宓
Wu Zuxiang 吳組緗
wuzhengfu zhuyi (Japanese: museifu
shugi) 無政府主義

Xia Yan 夏衍
xiadeng ren 下等人
Xiandai 現代
xiandai xing 現代性
Xiang Deyan [Jiao Ren] 項德言
（鮫人）
Xianglin sao 祥林嫂
Xiangzi 祥子
Xian shu 閑書
Xiao Fuzi 小福子
Xiao Hong 蕭紅
"Xiao Hong huihua suotan" 蕭紅繪
畫瑣談
Xiao Jun 蕭軍
Xiao Ma 小馬
Xiao ge'er lia 小哥兒倆
xiaoji 小己
xiaojie 小姐
xiaosheng 小生
xiaoshuo 小說
Xiaoshuo yuebao 小說月報
xiaozhong 小鍾
xiaoxue 小學
Xie Bingying 謝冰瑩
xifu 媳婦

xiju 戲劇

xin 新

xinban 新版

Xin chao 新潮

xin ganjue pai 新感覺派

"Xingfu de jiating" 幸福的家庭

Xin Hamuliete 新哈姆列特

xinli 心理

xinmin 新民

Xinmin shuo 新民説

Xinmin yi 新民議

Xin qingnian 新青年

xin rujia 新儒家

Xin shiji 新世紀

xin wenxue 新文學

xinxia xiangdao 心下想道

Xinyue she 新月社

Xixiang ji 西廂記

Xu Shoushang 許壽裳

Xu Shouwei 許守微

Xu Zhimo 徐志摩

Xue Suizhi 薛綏之

Xueheng 學衡

Xuetang ge 學堂歌

Yan Fu 嚴復

yang 洋

yangben 樣本

yangbu 洋布

yangche 洋車

yangpao 洋炮

yangqiang 洋槍

yangren 洋人

Yasuoka Hideo 安岡秀夫

Ye Shaojun 葉紹鈞

Yecao 野草

yi 伊

Yi Zhen 毅真

yibusheng zhuyi 易卜生主義

Yige nübing de zizhuan 一個女兵的自傳

Yihua dianying zhipian chang 藝華電
影制片廠

Yijiao congshu 一角叢書

yinhang 銀行

yinwei/suoyi 因為/所以

yin/yang 陰/陽

yishu chu 譯書處

"Yishu yu guojia" 藝術與國家

You Bingqi 尤炳圻

"You xianku" 遊仙窟

you yiben zhang 有一本帳

Yu 雨

yu 欲

Yu Dafu 郁達夫

Yu Guangzhong 余光中

Yu Ling 于伶

yuan 元

Yuan Fang 袁方

Yuan Shikai 袁世凱

yuanyang hudie pai 鴛鴦蝴蝶派

Yueying 月英

Yun 蘊

Yunlin 雲霖

Yu si 語絲

Yuwai xiaoshuo ji 域外小説集

yuwang 欲望

Yuzhou feng 宇宙風

"Zaitan baoliu" 再談保留

zawen 雜文

Zhang Ailing 張愛玲

Zhang Binglin 章炳麟

Zhang Heng 張衡

Zhang Henshui (Chang Hen-shui)
張恨水

Zhang Jingsheng 張競生

Zhang Mengyang 張夢陽

Zhang Tianyi 張天翼

Zhang Zhidong 張之洞

zhangfu 丈夫

Zhao Jiabi 趙家璧

zhen/wei 真/偽

Zheng Boqi [Junping] 鄭伯奇 (君平)

Zheng Zhenduo 鄭振鐸

Zhenzhen 貞貞

zhenzheng xin wenhua 真正新文化

Zhifang waiji 職方外記

zhiguai 志怪

Zhinaren zhi qizhi 支那人之氣質

Zhongguo dianying jie changong
tongzhi hui 中國電影界劃共同志會

"Zhongguo jiruo suyuan lun" 中國積
弱溯源論

Zhongguo ren jingshen jiegou yanjiu 中國
人精神結構研究

zhongguo wenxue 中國文學

Zhongguo xiandai wenxue daxi 中國現代
文學大系

Zhongguo xinwenxue daxi 中國新文學
大系

Zhongguo xuesheng 中國學生

Zhongmei tushu gongsi 中美圖書公司

zhongshu 眾數

zhong xing 種性

Zhou Shoujuan (Chou Shou-chüan)
周瘦鵑

Zhou Yang 周揚

Zhou Zuoren 周作人

Zhu Ziqing 朱自清

Zhu Yingpeng 朱應鵬

Zhuangzi 莊子

zhufang yuyan 主方語言

zhuzi 諸子

ziben 資本

ziji 自己

Zijun 子君

zishen 自身

ziwo 自我

Ziye 子夜

ziyou 自由

ziyou lian'ai 自由戀愛

zongjiao 宗教

zongjiao xing 宗教性

Zou Taofen 鄒韜奮

Index

In this index an "f" after a number indicates a separate reference on the next page, and an "ff" indicates separate references on the next two pages. A continuous discussion over two or more pages is indicated by a span of page numbers, e.g., 57–59." *Passim* is used for a cluster of references in close but not consecutive sequence.

Adorno, Theodor, 39
After Babel (Steiner), 11
Ahmad, Aijaz, 186
Ah Q (character), 65f, 68, 70–76 *passim*
"Ah Q, The True Story of," *see* "True Story of Ah Q, The"
Ah Q-ism, 65
"Aiguo suibi" (Patriotic miscellany), 246
Allies, 58, 66
Anarchism, Chinese, 39
Anderson, Benedict, 184
Anderson, Marston, 110, 232
Année Sociologique school, 9
Anti-Japanese War, 199, 221
Anti-Manchu activities, 240–44 *passim*, 254
Asad, Talal, 2f, 17
Atlantic Monthly, 46
"Aufgabe des Übersetzers, Die," *see* "Task of the Translator, The"
"Aus einen Gespräch von der Sprache" (Dialogue on language), 4f. *See also* Heidegger, Martin
Autobiography, 94, 124, 128, 151

A Ying (Qian Xingcun), 25, 68, 98, 217f, 226–35 *passim*

Babbitt, Irving, 248f, 251f, 254f
Babel, Tower of, 11, 15
Ba Jin, 216, 219, 223
Bakhtin, M. M., 18f, 71, 116, 126
Barlow, Tani E., 198, 388*n*86
Barnstone, Willis, 11
Barshay, Andrew, 86
Benjamin, Walter, 12, 14f, 33
Benveniste, Emile, 150–54 *passim*
Berman, Antoine, 187
Bible translation, 11, 15, 33
Bing Xin, 195
Blumenberg, Hans, 81
Bourdieu, Pierre, 29
Boxer Rebellion, 58, 66
Breton, André, 134f
Bridgman, Elijah C., 34
Buddhism, 96, 203
Butterfly fiction, 195ff, 216f, 219, 233
"Bu xiu" (Immortality), 95

467

letarian literature, 193; and class, 194; on Butterfly fiction, 196f; and Xiao Hong, 199–201; and censorship, 219, 224, 226
Lu Yin, 195
"Lun Zhongguo guomin zhi pingge" (On the character of the Chinese citizen; Liang Qichao), 48
Luotuo Xiangzi, *see Camel Xiangzi*

Male subject, 147
Mandarin Ducks and Butterfly fiction, *see* Butterfly fiction
Mao Dun, 77, 194, 197, 211, 218, 223, 226f, 229f, 232
Mao Zedong, 184
Marcus, Steven, 136
Marxist criticism, 50, 68f, 97, 119, 186, 415*n*56
"Mashang zhi riji" (Subchapter of the instant journal; Lu Xun), 52
Masini, Federico, 18, 34
Mauss, Marcel, 9
May Fourth Period, 27, 49f, 73, 82, 90, 94, 215f, 237, 247; writers, 47, 76, 80, 94, 132, 146, 153, 155, 188, 217f, 228, 233, 235; discourse, 47, 82, 146; movement, 49, 77, 87f, 93, 95f, 157, 234; literature, 50, 76, 79, 132, 153, 172, 174, 213–19 *passim*, 228; criticism, 81, 196f; intellectuals, 95; radicals, 255
Meadows, Thomas Taylor, 58
Medhurst, Sir Walter Henry, 59
"Medicine" (Lu Xun), 64
Mei Guangdi, 252–54
Meiligeguo zhilüe (A short history of America; Bridgman), 34
Meng Yue, 203
Meng Zhen, 49
Middle Kingdom, The (Williams), 58
Min Zhi, 89
Ming Enpu, *see* Smith, Arthur
Minzu texing yu minzu weisheng (National character and national hygiene; Pan Guangdan), 53
Minzu zhuyi (popular nationalism), 189
Missionaries, 18, 34f, 45ff, 51, 57f, 60, 65, 76, 246

"Modao," see "Sorcery"
Modernity, 27–31 *passim*, 47, 73–84 *passim*, 91, 95, 99, 146–49 *passim*, 183f, 256; Chinese, 39, 80, 86, 103; "belated," 185; "translated," 185
"Moluo shili shuo" (On the power of Mara poetry; Lu Xun), 31, 85
Muqin (Mother; Ding Ling), 220, 223

Nahan (Call to arms; Lu Xun), 61, 71
Nan she (Southern Society), 241
National character, 33, 47f, 50ff, 252; Chinese, 45ff, 49ff, 58–61, 64f, 67f, 70, 74, 76; debate on, 47; in "The True Story of Ah Q," 72
National essence, 239–44, 247–56 *passim*. *See also guocui*
National Essence critics, 234
National Essence group, 243–54 *passim*
National Essence Journal, 242–48 *passim*
National Essence movement, 239ff, 245f, 248, 256
Nationalism, 40, 189f, 199, 203, 207, 211
Nationalists, 190, 215, 219f, 224, 226, 230
National learning, 243f
Nation building, 239, 241, 256
Natsume Sōseki, 67, 86
Necrophilia, 142f, 146, 155ff, 164
Neologisms, 32–41 *passim*
Neo-perceptionists, Japanese, 133f
New Century, The, 246
New Culturalists, 233f, 241, 244f, 249–56 *passim*
New Culture movement, 49, 73, 78–95 *passim*, 157, 185, 217f, 250
Newspaper and Magazine Censorship Committee, 20. *See also* Censorship
"New Year's Sacrifice" (Lu Xun), 37f, 193
New Youth, 73, 78f, 87, 92f, 227, 233, 246, 248, 251
Nietzsche, Friedrich, 3f, 22, 93, 249
Niranjana, Tejaswini, 23f
North-China Daily News, 51

Objectification, 128
Occidentalism, 25, 56, 66, 240
"On Linguistic Aspects of Translation," *see* Jakobson, Roman

Library of Congress Cataloging-in-Publication Data

Liu, Lydia He.
   Translingual practice : literature, national culture, and translated modernity—
China, 1900–1937 / Lydia H. Liu.
      p.   cm.
   Includes bibliographical references and index.
   ISBN 0-8047-2534-9 (cl.) — ISBN 0-8047-2535-7 (pbk.)
   1. Chinese literature — 20th century.   2. Chinese literature — Foreign influences.
3. China—Civilization—20th century.   4. China—Civilization—Foreign
influences.   I. Title.
   PL2302.L534   1995
   895.1′090051—dc20
                                                               94-45961
                                                                  CIP
                                                                  Rev.